John Willis
Theatre World
1981–1982 SEASON

VOLUME 38

PN
2277
N5
A17
1981-82

CROWN PUBLISHERS, INC.

ONE PARK AVENUE • NEW YORK, NEW YORK 10016

TO
LUCILLE LORTEL

whose vibrant spirit and untiring efforts have made immeasurable contributions to all components of the theatre by discovering and encouraging new talent, and whose devotion to Off Broadway provided the impetus for its proliferation.

CONTENTS

EDITOR: JOHN WILLIS
Assistant Editor: Stanley Reeves
Staff Photographers: Joseph Abeles, Bert Andrews, J. M. Viade, Van Williams

DENZEL WASHINGTON, ADOLPH CAESAR, SAMUEL L. JACKSON, LARRY RILEY
in "A SOLDIER'S PLAY"
1982 winner of Pulitzer Prize, New York Drama Critics Circle Citation

Bert Andrews Photo

THE SEASON IN REVIEW
June 1, 1981 - May 31, 1982

For the first time in eight years attendance at Broadway theatres decreased. There were several contributing factors responsible for this decline: fewer productions (48), a shortage of musical hits, inflation, recession, a decline in tourism (New York's second largest industry), and rising ticket prices. The latter, however, was responsible for an increase in boxoffice receipts. Several hold-overs from past seasons raised admission fees to $35 and $40. The road also experienced a decrease in attendance, but not in boxofice, because of the higher priced tickets.

The Royal Shakespeare Company's epic production of "The Life and Adventures of Nicholas Nickleby" charged $100 for eight and a half hours of sheer delight, but it was performed in two parts with an hour dinner break. Such magnificent ensemble work was a theatrical experience to be cherished for a lifetime. It was cited as Best Play by the New York Drama Critics Circle and received "Tonys" for Best Play and for Best Actor in a Play (Roger Rees). Other "Tonys" went to Zoe Caldwell for the title role in 'Medea," Best Supporting "Tonys" to Amanda Plummer of "Agnes of God," Zakes Mokae for "Master Harold . . . and the boys," Liliane Montevecchi for "Nine," and Cleavant Derricks for "Dreamgirls." In the latter production, "Tonys" for Best Actress and Actor in a Musical went to Jennifer Holliday and Ben Harney. "Nine" was voted Best Musical, and "Othello" the Best Reproduction with Christopher Plummer winning rave reviews for his Iago. The Drama Critics Circle voted Off-Broadway's Pulitzer-Prize-winning "A Soldier's Play" the Best American Play, but refused to cite any musical as outstanding.

Among the better Broadway presentations this season, in addition to productions mentioned above and last year's hold-overs, there were "A Taste of Honey," "Crimes of the Heart," "The Dresser," "Mass Appeal," "Hothouse," and the musicals "Joseph and the Amazing Technicolor Dreamcoat," "Pump Boys and Dinettes." Shakespeare was represented by five productions during the year, but only "Othello" was critically applauded. There were several irreverent productions that jested about religious beliefs, Catholicism in particular. It was also a year with an abundance of wheelchairs on stage; a trend toward non-traditional, non-book musicals; and continued transplants from Off Broadway to the "Great White Way." Once again stars failed to make a hit of an unworthy vehicle. Outstanding performances were given by Karen Akers, Judith Anderson, Elizabeth Ashley, Anne Bancroft, Laurie Beechman, Claudette Colbert, Tom Courtenay, Mia Dillon, Faye Dunaway, Valerie French, Danny Glover, Carlin Glynn, David Alan Grier, Harry Groener, Rex Harrison, Katharine Hepburn, Mary Beth Hurt, Bill Hutton, James Earl Jones, Dorothy Loudon, Lizbeth Mackay, Peter MacNicol, George Martin, Lonette McKee, John McMartin, Anita Morris, Ann Morrison, Michael O'Keefe, Milo O'Shea, Geraldine Page, Paul Rogers, David Threlfall, Max von Sydow, and James Widdoes.

The theatre community rallied to save the Morosco, Helen Hayes and Bijou Theatres from being destroyed, but efforts failed. Demolition began March 22, 1982 to make way for the Portman Hotel, and part of our theatrical heritage was lost forever. The sixty-year old Ritz Theatre was being restored with special air rights of thirty stories, and plans were announced for the restoration and revitalization of several historical theatres on 42nd Street. The new owner of the ANTA changed its name to the Virginia Theatre to honor his wife.

After nine years on Broadway, the TKTS booth for half-priced tickets continued its success, but several producers complained that it is contributing to the rise in boxoffice prices. "Twofers" (two tickets for the price of one) were again helpful in keeping some shows from closing. However, at the end of the season there were fewer hold-overs than in several years, but there were also fewer openings: only 29 plays and 18 musicals. The necessity for government subsidized theatres becomes more apparent, but the prospects of its materializing are not likely in the near future.

It was an unsatisfactory season for the majority of Off-Broadway organizations. However, the Roundabout Theatre and Playwrights Horizons both enjoyed well-received productions. For financial help, many Off-Broadway groups agreed to sublet their theatres for six months of each year to other producers. The Douglas Fairbanks Theatre, an attractive and comfortable new building, was added to the group of theatres on West 42nd Street's Theatre Row. The Theatre deLys in the West Village was re-chrisened the Lucille Lortel Theatre in honor of the "Queen of Off Broadway." Happily, Off-Off-Broadway producers and Actors Equity Association resolved their differences over actors rights after appearing in a showcase production.

Among Off Broadway's better productions this year were "American Buffalo," "Sister Mary Ignatius Explains It All," "Key Exchange," "Entertaining Mr. Sloane," "The Dining Room," "Torch Song Trilogy," "Whistler," "Geniuses," "The Unseen Hand," "Potsdam Quartet," "How I Got That Story," "The Freak," "Misalliance," "The Chalk Garden," "The Browning Version," "6 O'Clock Boys," and the musical presentations "Cotton Patch Gospel," "March of the Falsettos," "Tomfoolery," "Forbidden Broadway," "Poor Little Lambs," and "Charlotte Sweet." Outstanding performers include Kevin Bacon, Lisa Banes, Scotty Bloch, Matthew Broderick, Charles Brown, Barbara Bryne, Leo Burmester, Adolph Caesar, Beeson Carroll, Maxwell Caulfield, Miles Chapin, Glenn Close, Michael Cristofer, John Cullum, Constance Cummings, Lois de Banzie, Giancarlo Esposito, Harvey Fierstein, Dann Florek, Elizabeth McGovern, Bill Moor, Mustafa Noor, Gene O'Neill, Al Pacino, Bernadette Peters, Remak Ramsay, Lee Richardson, Larry Riley, Jane Seaman, Edward Seamon, John Shea, Carole Shelley, Jimmie Ray Weeks, James Woods, Irene Worth.

The most impressive, dazzling, and memorable event of the season was February 14 when Producer Alexander H. Cohen presented "Night of 100 Stars" to mark the one hundredth year of the Actors Fund of America and to benefit its Actors Home. It will never be forgotten by the over 6000 fortunate ones who packed Radio City Music Hall, paid $250 to $1000 per seat and sat for almost six hours. It was advertised as featuring 100 stars, but over 200 appeared for the worthy cause. Many were screen and television celebrities, but all donated their time and talents to raise funds for a hospital wing at the retirement home for actors. The evening was taped for television and millions around the world were able later to enjoy this truly once-in-a-lifetime spectacular. Thank you, Mr. and Mrs. Cohen, for an unforgettable experience.

Roger Rees in "Nicholas Nickleby" *(Chris Davies Photo)*

Zoe Caldwell as Medea *(Jack Buxbaum Photo)*

Elizabeth Taylor, Alexander Cohen, Princess Grace "Night of 100 Stars" *(Sam Siegel Photo)*

BROADWAY PRODUCTIONS

JUNE 1, 1981 THROUGH MAY 31, 1982

WALLY'S CAFE

By Sam Bobrick and Ron Clark; Director, Fritz Holt; Scenery, Stuart Wurtzel; Lighting, Ken Billington; Costumes, Albert Wolsky; Hairstylist, John Quaglia; Makeup, Robert Philippe; Casting Director, Amos Abrams; Wardrobe, Sydney Smith; Production Assistant, Charles Suisman; Presented by Barry M. Brown, Lita Starr, Steven Leber, David Krebs. Opened at the Brooks Atkinson Theatre on Friday, June 12, 1981.*

CAST

Louise............................	Rita Moreno	Janet...............................	Sally Struthers
Wally.............................	James Coco	STANDBYS	Joan Welles, Jack Betts

A comedy in two acts and three scenes. The action takes place in a roadside cafe in the California desert during the summer of 1940, the summer of 1958, and the summer of 1981.

General Management: Marvin A. Krauss Associates; *Press:* Shirley Herz, Sam Rudy, Peter Cromarty; *Stage Manager:* James Pentecost

* Closed June 20, 1981 after 11 performances and 32 previews.

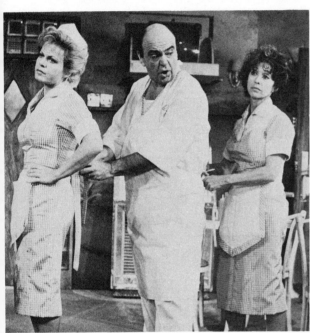 

THIS WAS BURLESQUE

Based on Ann Corio's recollections; Entire production supervised and directed by Ann Corio; Choreographer, Fred Albee; Musical Conductor, Richard DeMone; Costumes, Rex Huntington; Co-produced with Jeff Satkin Inc.; Technical Director, Frank Chorman; Presented by MPI Productions Ltd. Opened at the Princess Theatre on Tuesday, June 23, 1981.*

CAST

Ann Corio

Claude Mathis, Tami Roche, Dexter Maitland, Phil Ford, Jerry Kurland, Charlie Naples, Lili Chanel, Frank Vohs, Marilyn Simon, Patrick

The Burley Cuties: Marilyn Simon, Diane Gallagher, Bonnie Wintz, Sharon Longo, Kathleen DeFrees, Rusty Riegelman, Treva Hill, Christine Chulick, Erin Lareau

ACT I: The Queen of Burlesque, Hello Everybody, Fun in One, Persian Nights, Chaplin Reminiscences, An American Beauty, Exotic, Two Eggs, Les Girls, The Music Teacher, Feature Attraction, Finale, Candy Butcher

ACT II: Powder My Back, Lucky Pierre, The All-American Male Stripper, Charleston, Hall of Fame, Crazy House, Memories, Grand Finale

General Management: Michael P. Iannucci; *Press:* Lenny Traube; *Stage Managers:* Peter H. Russell, Cathy Lynn Sonneborn

* Closed July 17, 1981 after 28 performances and 8 previews.

Above: (L) Sally Struthers, James Coco, Rita Moreno in "Wally's Cafe" *(Martha Swope Photo)* **(R) Ann Corio,**
Charlie Naples in "This Was Burlesque"

SCENES AND REVELATIONS

By Elan Garonzik; Director, Sheldon Epps; Scenery, Jane Thurn; Costumes, Oleksa; Lighting, William Armstrong; Wardrobe, Millicent Hacker; Casting Director, Lynn Kressel; Produced Off Broadway by The Production Company; Presented by Circle in the Square (Theodore Mann, Artistic Director; Paul Libin, Managing Director). Opened at Circle in the Square/Uptown on Thursday, June 25, 1981.*

CAST

Samuel/Mr. Martin/Dr. Zeigler/Dennis Houser.......	Norman Snow	Uncle Jacob.................................	Joseph Warren
Helena.....................................	Christine Lahti	Charlotte.................................	Mary-Joan Negro
Rebecca....................................	Valerie Mahaffey	Mr. Karonk................................	Nicholas Saunders
Millie.....................................	Marilyn McIntyre		

A drama in two acts. The action takes place in the early 1890's on the Longnecker farm in Lancaster, Pa., and various other locations, including Nebraska and Manchester, England.

Company Manager: William Conn; *Press:* Merle Debuskey, David Roggensack; *Stage Managers:* Rick Ralston, Tracy B. Cohen

* Closed July 19, 1981 after 29 performances and 15 previews.

A TASTE OF HONEY

By Shelagh Delaney; Director, Tony Tanner; Set, Roger Mooney; Costumes, A. Christina Giannini; Lighting, Robert W. Mogel, Marshall S. Spiller; Sound, Philip Campanella; Presented by Roundabout Theatre (Gene Feist/Michael Fried, Producing Directors). Opened Friday, June 19, 1981.*

CAST

Helen...................................	Valerie French	The Boy.......................................	Tom Wright
Jo....................................	Amanda Plummer	Geoffrey.................................	Keith Reddin
Peter..	John Carroll		

A drama in two acts. The action takes place in Salford, Lancashire, England, in Helen and Jo's apartment.

General Managers: Paul B. Berkowsky, Sheala N. Berkowsky; *Company Manager:* Mark Johnson; *Press:* Susan Bloch, Adrian Bryan-Brown; *Stage Managers:* Howard Kolins, Chester A. Sims II

* Closed Nov. 8, 1981 after 152 performances and 5 previews. Original production opened at the Lyceum Theatre Oct. 4, 1960 with Angela Lansbury, Joan Plowright and Billy Dee Williams, and played 391 performances. See THEATRE WORLD Vol. 17.

Above: (L) Marilyn McIntyre, Christine Lahti, Mary-Joan Negro, Valerie Mahaffey in "Scenes and Revelations" (R) Amanda Plummer, Valerie French in "A Taste of Honey" *(Donna Svennevik Photo)*

FIDDLER ON THE ROOF

Book, Joseph Stein; Based on Sholom Aleichem Stories; Music, Jerry Bock; Lyrics, Sheldon Harnick; Directed and Choreographed by Jerome Robbins; Associate Director, Ruth Mitchell; Scenery, Boris Aronson; Costumes, Patricia Zipprodt; Lighting, Ken Billington; Music Supervisor, Kevin Farrell; Choreography reproduced by Tom Abbott; Musical Director, Richard Vitzhum; Associate Producer, Stella Saltonstall; Orchestrations, Don Walker; Vocal Arrangements, Milton Greene; Dance Music Arrangements, Betty Walberg; Hairstylist, Patrik D. Moreton; Assistant to Directors, Stephen Helper; Casting Director, Mary Jo Slater; Associate Producer, Cheryl Raab; Wardrobe, Nancy Schaefer; Production Assistants, Bo Metzler, Mathew Hightower; Presented by Eugene V. Wolsk and James M. Nederlander at the New York State Theater. Opened Thursday, July 9, 1981.*

CAST

Tevye	Herschel Bernardi	Rabbi	Alvin Myerovich
Golde	Maria Karnilova	Mendel	Ken Leroy
Tzeitel	Lori Ada Jaroslow	Avram	Tog Richards
Hodel	Donalyn Petrucci	Nachum	Ralph Vucci
Chava	Liz Larsen	Grandma Tzeitel	Susan Sheppard
Shprintze	Susan Sheppard	Fruma-Sarah	Joyce Martin
Bielke	Eydie Alyson†1	Constable	Paul E. Hart
Yente	Ruth Jaroslow	Fyedka	Joel Robertson
Motel	Michelan Sisti	Shandel	Bess Meisler
Perchik	James Werner	The Fiddler	Jay Fox
Lazar Wolf	Paul Lipson	Yussel	Stephen Wright†2
Mordcha	Fyvush Finkel		

VILLAGERS: Bradford Dunaway, Jimmy Ferraro, Michael Fogarty, Margo F. Gruber, Michael Lane, Mark Manley, Elaine Manzel, Joyce Martin, Bess Meisler, Robert Parola, Thomas Scalise, Charles Spoerri, Marsha Tamaroff, Susan Tilson, Timothy Tobin, Stephen Wright, Robert Yacko

STANDBYS AND UNDERSTUDIES: Paul Lipson (Tevye), Beth Meisler (Golda/Yente), Fyvush Finkel (Lazar), Susan Tilson (Hodel), Robert Yacko (Fyedka/Perchik), Timothy Tobin/Stephen Minning (Fyedka), Tog Richards (Avram/Mordcha), Vito Durante (Nachum), Charles Spoerri (Constable), Margo F. Gruber (Fruma-Sarah), Stephen Wright/Lawrence B. Leritz (Motel), Swing Dancers: Frank Colardo, Debra Timmons

MUSICAL NUMBERS: Tradition, Matchmaker, If I Were a Rich Man, Sabbath Prayer, To Life, Miracle of Miracles, The Tailor Motel Kamzoil, Sunrise Sunset, Bottle Dance, Wedding Dance, Now I Have Everything, Do You Love Me, I Just Heard, Far From the Home I Love, Chavaleh, Anatevka, Epilogue

A musical in two acts.

General Manager: Charles A. Eisler; *Press:* Alpert/LeVine, Mark Goldstaub, Alan Hale; *Stage Managers:* Ed Preston, Sally Hassenfelt, Vito Durante

* Closed Aug. 23, 1981 after a limited engagement of 53 performances and 3 previews. Original production with Zero Mostel and Maria Karnilova opened Sept. 22, 1964 at the Imperial and played 3242 performances. See THEATRE WORLD Vol. 21.
† Succeeded by 1. Kathy St. George, 2. Lawrence R. Leritz

THE SUPPORTING CAST

By George Furth; Director, Gene Saks; Scenery, William Ritman; Costumes, Jane Greenwood; Lighting, Richard Nelson; Technical Supervisor, Arthur Siccardi; Wardrobe, Penny Davis; Production Assistant, Jane E. Cooper; Presented by Terry Allen Kramer, James M. Nederlander and Twentieth Century-Fox at the Biltmore Theatre. Opened Thursday, Aug. 6, 1981.*

CAST

Ellen	Hope Lange	Arnold	Jack Gilford
Mae	Betty Garrett	Florrie	Joyce Van Patten
Sally	Sandy Dennis		

STANDBYS: Chevi Colton (Mae/Florrie), Claiborne Cary (Ellen/Sally)

A comedy in two acts. The action takes place at the present time in a beach house in Malibu, California.

General Manager: Max Allentuck; *Press:* Bill Evans, Sandra Manley, Howard Atlee, Leslie Anderson, Jim Baldassare; *Stage Managers:* Martin Herzer, Wayne Carson

* Closed Sept. 5, 1981 after 36 performances and 8 previews.

Above: (L) Maria Karnilova, Joyce Martin, Herschel Bernardi in "Fiddler on the Roof" (R) Sandy Dennis, Betty Garrett, Jack Gilford, Joyce Van Patten, Hope Lange in "The Supporting Cast" *(Martha Swope Photo)*

MY FAIR LADY

Book and Lyrics, Alan Jay Lerner; Music, Frederick Loewe; Based on "Pygmalion" by George Bernard Shaw; Director, Patrick Garland; Scenery, Oliver Smith; Costumes, Cecil Beaton; Lighting, Ken Billington; Co-Costume Designer, John David Ridge; Sound, John McClure; Conductor, Robert Kreis; Musical Arrangement, Robert Russell Bennett, Phil Lang; Casting, Julie Hughes; Barry Moss; Wigs and Hairstyles, Paul Huntley; Musical Director, Franz Allers; Musical Staging and Choreography based on Hanya Holm's original, Crandall Diehl; A Dome/Cutler Production; Associate Producers, Steve Herman, Jon Cutler; Producers Assistant, Ruthann M. Barshop; Technical Supervisor, Arthur Siccardi; Wardrobe, Carla Lawrence, Dianne Hylton; Hairstylists, Angela Gari, Dale Brownell; Presented by Don Gregory and Mike Merrick at the Uris Theatre. Opened Tuesday, August 18, 1981.*

CAST

Buskers	Eric Alderfer, Alan Gilbert, Lisa Guignard	Alfred P. Doolittle	Milo O'Shea†
Mrs. Eynsford-Hill	Harriet Medin	Mrs. Pearce	Marian Baer
Eliza Doolittle	Nancy Ringham	Mrs. Hopkins/Lady Boxington	Mary O'Brien
Freddy Eynsford-Hill	Nicholas Wyman	Butler	Frank Bouley
Colonel Pickering	Jack Gwillim	Servants	Jeralyn Glass, David Miles, Ellen McLain, Judith Thiergaard
Henry Higgins	Rex Harrison	Mrs. Higgins	Cathleen Nesbitt
Selsey Man/Harry/Ambassador	Ben Wrigley	Chauffeur/Constable	Alan Gilbert
Hoxton Man/Jamie	Clifford Fearl	Lord Boxington	Richard Ammon
Bystander/Cockney	Ned Coulter	Flower Girl	Karen Toto
1st Cockney	John Caleb	Zoltan Karpathy	Jack Sevier
Cockney/Footman/Bartender	Ned Peterson	Queen of Transylvania	Svetlana McLee Grody
Cockney	Jeffrey Calder	Mrs. Higgins' Maid	Elizabeth Worthington
Bartender/Major-Domo	David Cale Johnson		

SINGING ENSEMBLE: Frank Bouley, Jeffrey Calder, John Caleb, Ned Coulter, Diana Lynne Drew, Julie Ann Fogt, Terri Gervais, Jeralyn Glass, David Cale Johnson, Michael McGifford, Ellen McLain, David Miles, Mary O'Brien, Ned Peterson, Judith Thiergaard

DANCING ENSEMBLE: Eric Alderfer, Richard Ammon, Joseph Billone, Arlene Columbo, Ron Crofoot, Raul Gallyot, Alan Gilbert, Svetlana McLee Grody, Lisa Guignard, Scott Harris (Captain), Lynn Keeton, Gail Lohla, James Boyd Parker, Karen Paskow, Karen Toto, Elizabeth Worthington

STANDBYS AND UNDERSTUDIES: Michael Allinson (Higgins), Kitty Sullivan (Eliza), Clifford Fearl (Pickering), Ben Wrigley (Doolittle), Mary O'Brien (Mrs. Pearce), Jeffrey Calder (Freddy), Jack Sevier (Harry), Frank Bouley (Karpathy/Jamie), Harriet Medin (Mrs. Higgins/Mrs. Hopkins), Ensemble Alternates: Scott Harris, Karen Paskow

MUSICAL NUMBERS: Street Entertainers, Why Can't the English?, Wouldn't It Be Loverly?, With a Little Bit of Luck, I'm an Ordinary Man, Just You Wait, The Rain in Spain, I Could Have Danced All Night, Ascot Gavotte, On the Street Where you Live, The Embassy Waltz, You Did It, Show Me, Get Me to the Church on Time, A Hymn to Him, Without You, I've Grown Accustomed to Her Face

A musical in 2 acts and 18 scenes. The action takes place in London.

General Manager: Arthur Anagnostou; *Company Managers:* Martin Cohen, Kathryn Frawley; *Press:* Seymour Krawitz, Patricia McLean Krawitz; *Stage Managers:* Jack Welles, William Weaver, Paul Schneeberger, Scott Harris

* Closed Nov. 29, 1981 after 124 performances to resume tour. Original production with Rex Harrison, Julie Andrews and Cathleen Nesbitt opened at the Hellinger Theatre Thursday, March 15, 1956 and ran for 2715 performances.
† Succeeded by Ben Wrigley

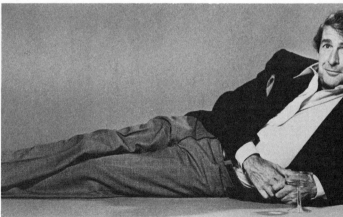

AN EVENING WITH DAVE ALLEN

Lighting, John Gleason; Production Supervisor, Jeremiah J. Harris; Presented by Chartwell Communications Inc. in association with Theatre Now Inc. at the Booth Theatre. Opened Sunday September 20, 1981.*
   A one-man performance presented in two acts.

General Managers: Theatre Now Inc.; *Press:* Les Schechter, Barbara Schwei, Timothy Fisher; *Stage Manager:* Lynne Guerra

*Closed Oct. 17, 1981 after limited engagement of 29 performances and 5 previews.

Above: (L) Rex Harrison, Nicholas Wyman, Nancy Ringham, Cathleen Nesbitt in "My Fair Lady"
(Anita Feldman Photo) (R) Dave Allen

A TALENT FOR MURDER

By Jerome Chodorov and Norman Panama; Director, Paul Aaron; Scenery, Oliver Smith; Costumes, David Murin, Bill Blass for Miss Colbert; Lighting, Ken Billington; Casting, Meg Simon, Fran Kumin; Production Assistant, John Petz; Special Effects, Chic Silber; Wardrobe, Midge Marmo; Wigs, Paul Huntley, Michael Wasula; Presented by Edwin S. Lowe at the Biltmore Theatre. Opened Thursday, October 1, 1981.*

CAST

Rashi	Shelly Desai	Lawrence McClain	Barton Heyman
Dr. Paul Marchand	Jean-Pierre Aumont	Sheila McClain	Nancy Addison Altman
Anne Royce McClain	Claudette Colbert	Mark Harrison	Stephen Schnetzer†
Pamela Harrison	Liane Longland		

STANDBYS AND UNDERSTUDIES: Betty Low (Anne), Ann Convery (Sheila/Pamela), Leon Russom (Mark/Lawrence), Maury Cooper (Paul)

A suspense-comedy in 2 acts and 7 scenes. The action takes place over a weekend at the present time in the library-study of "Twelve Oaks," the estate of Anne Royce McClain in the foothills of the Berkshires not far from Tanglewood, N.Y.

General Manager: Victor Samrock; *Company Manager:* David Hedges; *Press:* Jeffrey Richards, C. George Willard, Robert Ganshaw, Ben Morse, Helen Stern, Ted Kilmer, Stanley Evans, Richard Humleker; *Stage Managers:* Robert Townsend, Charles Kindl

* Closed Dec. 6, 1981 after 77 performances and 11 previews.
† Succeeded by Stephen Burleigh

MARLOWE

Book and Lyrics, Leo Rost; Music and Lyrics, Jimmy Horowitz; Directed and Staged by Don Price; Set, Cary Chalmers; Lighting, Mitch Acker, Rick Belzer; Costumes, Natalie Walker; Sound, Peter Fitzgerald; Orchestrations, Jimmy Horowitz; Musical Supervision, Larry Fallon; Musical Direction, Kinny Landrum; Vocal Arrangements, Jimmy Horowitz, Patrick Jude; Choral Direction, Billy Cunningham; Hairstylist, Phyllis Della; Fight Choreography, Peter Moore; Production Associate, Leon Gast; Associate Producer, Raymond Serra; Technical Consultant, Mitch Acker; Wardrobe, Cheryl Woronoff; Assistant to Producers, Ellen Feldman; Production Associate, Paul D'Angelo; Production Assistants, Tony Berk, Tony San Giovanni, Michael Stvall; A John Annunziato Production; Co-produced by Robert R. Blume in association with Billy Gaff and Howard P. Effron; Presented by Tony Conforti at the Rialto Theatre. Opened Monday, October 12, 1981.*

CAST

Queen Elizabeth I	Margaret Warncke	William Shakespeare	Lennie Del Duca, Jr.
Audrey Walsingham	Debra Greenfield	Emelia Bossano	Lisa Mordente
Captain Townsend	Steve Hall	Christopher Marlowe	Patrick Jude
Archbishop Parker	Raymond Serra	Ingram Frizer	Robert Rosen
Richard Burbage	John Henry Kurtz		

CHORUS: Kenneth D. Ard, Marlene Danielle, Robert Hoshour, Renee Dulaney, Timothy Tobin, Teri Gibson, Diane Pennington, Caryn Richmond

UNDERSTUDIES: James Sbano (Marlowe/Frizer/Parker), Diane Pennington (Emelia/Audrey), Robert Hoshour (Shakespeare), Teri Gibson (Queen Elizabeth), Steve Hall (Burbage), Timothy Tobin (Townsend), Swings: Kathy Jennings, Willie Rosario

MUSICAL NUMBERS: Prologue, Rocking the Boat, Because I'm a Woman, Live for the Moment, Emelia, I'm Coming 'Round to Your Point of View, The Ends Justify the Means, Higher Than High, Christopher, So Do I (Ode to Virginity), Two Lovers, Funeral Dirge, Can't Leave Now, Madrigal Blues
A rock musical in 2 acts and 8 scenes. The action takes place in England during 1593 A.D.

Company Manager: Barbara Carrellas, Weiler/Miller; *Press:* Max Eisen, Alan Eichler, Maria Somma; *Stage Managers:* Alisa Adler, Bo Metzler

* Closed Nov. 22, 1981 after 48 performances and 8 previews.

Above: (L) Jean-Pierre Aumont, Claudette Colbert in "A Talent for Murder" *(Peter Cunningham Photo)* **(R) John Henry Kurtz, Patrick Jude, Lisa Mordente, Lennie Del Duca, Jr in "Marlow"** *(Reed Jenkins Photo)*

THE LIFE AND ADVENTURES OF NICHOLAS NICKLEBY

By Charles Dickens; Adapted by David Edgar; Directors, Trevor Nunn, John Caird; Assisted by Leon Rubin; Design, John Napier, Dermot Hayes; Costumes, John Napier; Lighting, David Hersey; New York production designed in association with Neil Peter Jampolis (Sets and Costumes), Beverly Emmons (Lighting), Richard Fitzgerald (Sound); Music and Lyrics, Stephen Oliver; Musical Directors, Alan Gout, Donald Johnston; By arrangement with The Royal Shakespeare Theatre, Stratford-Upon-Avon, England; Production Coordinator, Brent Peek; Properties, Terry Diamond, Mel Saltzman, Karen M. Canton; Wardrobe, Susan Honey, Rosalie Lahm, Kinney Moore; Wig Master, Leon Gagliardi; Hair Dressers, Val Stubbs, Stephen Campenella, Richard Orton; Special Effects, Chic Silber, Bill McComb; Technician, Alistair Minnigin; The Royal Shakespeare Company production presented by James M. Nederlander, The Shubert Organization (Gerald Schoenfeld, Chairman; Bernard B. Jacobs, President), Elizabeth I. McCann, Nelle Nugent at the Plymouth Theatre. Opened Sunday, October 4, 1981.*

CAST

The Nickleby Family: Nicholas Nickleby (Roger Rees), Kate (Emily Richard), Ralph (John Woodvine), Mrs. Nickleby (Priscilla Morgan)

London: Newman Noggs (Edward Petherbridge), Hanna (Hilary Townley), Miss LaCreevy (Rose Hill), Sir Matthew Pupker (David Lloyd Meredith), Mr. Bonney (Andrew Hawkins), Irate Gentleman (Patrick Godfrey), Flunkey (Timothy Kightley), Mr. Snawley (William Maxwell), Snawley Major (Janet Dale), Snawley Minor (Hilary Townley), Belling (Stephen Rashbrook), William (John McEnery), Waitresses (Sharon Bower, Sally Nesbitt), Coachman (Clyde Pollitt), Mr. Mantalini (John McEnery), Mme. Mantalini (Thelma Whiteley), Flunkey (Richard Simpson), Miss Knag (Janet Dale), Rich Ladies (Sharon Bower, Shirley King), Milliners (Suzanne Bertish, Sharon Bower, Lucy Gutteridge, Cathryn Harrison, Ian East, William Maxwell, Sally Nesbitt, Stephen Rashbrook, Hilary Townley)

Yorkshire: Mr. Squeers (Alun Armstrong), Mrs. Squeers (Lila Kaye), Smike (David Threlfall), Phib (Sally Nesbitt), Fanny Squeers (Suzanne Bertish), Young Wackford Squeers (Ian McNeice), John Browdie (Bob Peck), Tilda Price (Cathryn Harrison), Boys: Tomkins (William Maxwell), Coates (Andrew Hawkins), Graymarsh (Alan Gill), Jennings (Patrick Godfrey), Mobbs (Christopher Ravenscroft), Bolder (Mark Tandy), Pitcher (Sharon Bower), Jackson (Nicholas Gecks), Cobbey (John McEnery), Peters (Teddy Kempner), Sprouter (Lucy Gutteridge), Roberts (Ian East)

London Again: Kenwigs (Patrick Godfrey), Mrs. Kenwigs (Shirley King), Morleena Kenwigs (Hilary Townley), Lillyvick (Timothy Knightley), Miss Petowker (Cathryn Harrison), Mr. Crowl (Ian East), George (Alan Gill), Cutler (Jeffery Dench), Mrs. Cutler (Janet Dale), Mrs. Kenwigs' Sister (Sharon Bower), Lady Downstairs (Rose Hill), Miss Green (Priscilla Morgan), Benjamin (Teddy Kempner), Pugstyles (Roderick Horn), Old Lord (Richard Simpson), Young Fiancee (Lucy Gutteridge), Landlord (Jeffery Dench)

Portsmouth: Vincent Crummles (Christopher Benjamin), Mrs. Crummles (Lila Kaye), Infant Phenomenon (Hilary Townley), Master Percy Crummles (Teddy Kempner), Master Crummles (Mark Tandy), Mrs. Grudden (Rose Hill), Miss Snevelicci (Suzanne Bertish), Folair (Clyde Pollitt), Lenville (Christopher Ravenscroft), Miss Ledrock (Lucy Gutteridge), Miss Bravassa (Sharon Bower), Wagstaff (Alun Armstrong), Blightey (Jeffery Dench), Miss Belvawney (Janet Dale), Miss Gazingi (Sally Nesbitt), Pailey (William Maxwell), Hetherington (Andrew Hawkins), Bane (Stephen Rashbrook), Fluggers (Richard Simpson), Mrs. Lenville (Shirley King), Curdle (Hubert Rees), Mrs. Curdle (Emily Richard), Snevellicci (John McEnery), Mrs. Snevellicci (Thelma Whiteley)

London Again: Scaley (Ian McNeice), Tix (Teddy Kempner), Sir Mulberry Hawk (Bob Peck), Lord Frederick Verisopht (Nicholas Gecks), Pluck (Teddy Kempner), Pyke (Mark Tandy), Snobb (Christopher Ravenscroft), Col. Chowser (Timothy Kightley), Brooker (Clyde Pollitt), Wititterley (Roderick Horn), Mrs. Wititterley (Janet Dale), Alphonse (Stephen Rashbrook), Opera Singers (Sharon Bower, Andrew Hawkins, John Woodvine), Charles Cheeryble (David Lloyd Meredith), Ned Cheeryble (Hubert Rees), Tim Linkinwater (Richard Simpson), Man Next Door (Patrick Godfrey), Keeper (Alan Gill), Frank Cheeryble (Christopher Ravenscroft), Nurse, (Thelma Whiteley), Arthur Gride (Jeffery Dench), Madeline Bray (Lucy Gutteridge), Walter Bray (Christopher Benjamin), Peg Sliderskew (Suzanne Bertish), Hawk's Rival (Edward Petherbridge), Capt. Adams (Andrew Hawkins), Westwood (Alan Gill), Croupier (Ian McNeice), Casino Proprietor (Patrick Godfrey), Surgeon (Timothy Kightley), Umpire (Roderick Horn), Policemen (Andrew Hawkins, Mark Tandy), Mrs. Snawley (Janet Dale), Young Woman (Hilary Townley)

Understudies: Catherine Brandon, Wilfred Grove, Katherine Levy

The action is set in England in the first half of the 19th Century. Part One (4 hours) performed with one intermission. Part two (4½ hours) performed with two intermissions.

General Management: McCann & Nugent; *Company Managers:* Harold Rogers, Robert H. Wallner; *Press:* Solters/Roskin/Friedman, Joshua Ellis, Louise Weiner Ment, Becky Flora, David LeShay, Cindy Valk; *Stage Managers:* Robert Bennett, Sally Greenhut, Michael Townsend, David Proctor, Simon Hooper, Hilary Groves

* Closed Jan. 3, 1982 after limited engagement of 102 performances and 7 previews. Recipient of 1982 "Tonys" for Best Play, Best Actor (Roger Rees), Best Direction, Best Scenic Design. It was also cited as Best Play by NY Drama Critics Circle.

Photos by George Whitear © Prime Time Television

The Crummles Company

Roger Rees as Nicholas, David Threlfall as Smike

1

CANDIDA

By George Bernard Shaw; Director, Michael Cristofer; Scenery, Kenneth Foy; Costumes, Richard Hornung; Lighting, Paul Gallo; Presented by Special Arrangement with Kenyon Festival Theater; Wardrobe, Millicent Hacker; Presented by Circle in the Square (Theodore Mann, Artistic Director; Paul Libin, Managing Director) in the Circle in the Square/Uptown. Opened Thursday, October 15, 1981.*

CAST

Prosperine Garnett	Jane Curtin†	Mr. Burgess	Ronald Bishop
Rev. James Mavor Morell	Ron Parady	Candida	Joanne Woodward
Maria	Mary Jay	Eugene Marchbanks	Tait Ruppert
Rev. Alexander Mill	John Gilliss		

STANDBYS AND UNDERSTUDIES: Mary Jay (Candida), C. B. Anderson (Morell/Burgess), Allison Mackie (Prosperine/Maria), Courtney Burr (Marchbanks/Mill)

A drama in three acts. The action takes place on a day in the spring of 1905 at the home of the Rev. James Mavor Morrell.

Company Manager: William Conn; *Press:* Merle Debuskey, David Roggensack; *Stage Managers:* Michael F. Ritchie, Allison Mackie

* Closed Jan. 3, 1982 after 91 performances and 23 previews.
† Succeeded by Ann Willis

EINSTEIN AND THE POLAR BEAR

By Tom Griffin; Director, J Ranelli; Scenery, Fred Voelpel; Costumes, Nancy Potts; Lighting, Arden Fingerhut; Technical Supervisor, Arthur Siccardi; Properties, Jan Marasek; Wardrobe, Frank Green; Casting, Marilyn Szatmary; Production Assistant, Michael O'Gara; Presented by Max Allentuck, Wayne M. Rogers, Warner Theatre Productions, Ron Dante, Tommy Valando and Emanuel Azenberg at the Cort Theatre. Opened Thursday, October 29, 1981.*

CAST

Andrew Allenson	John Wardwell	Bill Allenson	Peter Strauss
Charlie Milton	Robert Nichols	Helen Bullins	Marjorie Lovett
Diane Ashe	Maureen Anderman	Bobby Bullins	David Strathairn

STANDBYS: Ron Frazier (Bill/Bobby), Marsha Skaggs (Diane), James Cahill (Andrew/Charlie), Le Clanche du Rand (Helen)

A drama in two acts. The action takes place in Spider Lake, a small New England town during a raging February blizzard.

General Manager: Max Allentuck; *Press:* Bill Evans, Sandra Manley, Howard Atlee, Leslie Anderson, Jim Baldassare; *Stage Managers:* Frank Marino, Bill McIntyre

* Closed Oct. 31, 1981 after 4 performances and 20 previews.

Above: (L) Ron Parady, Joanne Woodward in "Candida" *(Stephanie Saia Photo)* **(R) Peter Strauss, Maureen Anderman in "Einstein and the Polar Bear"** *(Martha Swope Photo)*

CRIMES OF THE HEART

By Beth Henley; Director, Melvin Bernhardt; Sets, John Lee Beatty; Costumes, Patricia McGourty; Lighting, Dennis Parichy; Associate Producer, Ethel Watt; Production Coordinator, Brent Peek; Managerial Associate/Producer Circle, Sam Crothers; Assistant to Director, Gregory Johnson; Props, Mel Saltzman; Wardrobe, Cindy Steffens; Music, Art Bressler; Sound, Lou Shapiro; Special Effects, Chic Silber, Rob Taylor; Management Associates, Claire Calkins, David Domedion, Ann Dorszynski, Elizabeth Hermann; Production Associate, Donald M. Sunshine; Casting, Shirley Rich; Presented by Warner Theatre Productions, Claire Nichtern, Mary Lea Johnson, Martin Richards, Francine LeFrak at the John Golden Theatre. Opened Wednesday, November 4, 1981.*

CAST

Lenny MaGrath	Lizbeth Mackay	Meg MaGrath	Mary Beth Hurt †2
Chick Boyle	Sharon Ullrick	Babe Botrelle	Mia Dillon
Doc Porter	Raymond Baker†1	Barnette Lloyd	Peter MacNicol†3

UNDERSTUDIES: Susan Greenhill (Babe/Chick), Caryn West (Meg/Lenny), Harley Venton (Doc/Barnette)
   A comedy-drama in three acts. The action takes place in Hazelhurst, Mississippi, in 1974, five years after Hurricane Camille.

General Management: Elizabeth I. McCann, Nelle Nugent; *Company Managers:* Sam Pagliaro, Mary Kelley; *Press:* Betty Lee Hunt, Maria Cristina Pucci, James Sapp; *Stage Managers:* James Pentecost, David Caine

* Still playing May 31, 1982. Winner of 1981 Pulitzer Prize, New York Drama Critics Circle citation for Best New American Play. Original NY production by Manhattan Theatre Club, Sunday, Dec. 21, 1980
† Succeeded by: 1. Tom Stechschulte, 2. Holly Hunter, 3. Tom Choate for four months

NED AND JACK

By Sheldon Rosen; Director, Colleen Dewhurst; Scenery, James Leonard Joy; Costumes, David Murin; Lighting, Robby Monk; Technical Supervisor, Jeremiah H. Harris; Props, Merlyn Davis; Sound, Tony Meola; Wardrobe, Tony Karniewich; Production Assistant, Tom Bundrick; Casting, Bonnie G. Timmermann; Presented by Ken Marsolais, Martin Markinson, All Starr Productions, Axbell Productions at the Little Theatre. Opened Sunday, November 8, 1981.*

CAST

Edward (Ned) Sheldon	John Vickery	John (Jack) Barrymore	Peter Michael Goetz
Danny	Sean Griffin	Charlie	Barton
Ethel Barrymore	Barbara Sohmers		

STANDBYS AND UNDERSTUDIES: Sean Griffin (Ned), Munson Hicks (Jack/Danny)
   A drama in two acts. The action takes place in Edward Sheldon's New York penthouse apartment after midnight, November 17, 1922, John Barrymore's opening night in "Hamlet."

General Management: Joseph P. Harris, Peter T. Kulok, Steven E. Goldstein, Nancy Simmons; *Press:* Shirley Herz, Sam Rudy, Peter Cromarty; *Stage Managers:* Richard Elkow, Buzz Cohen;

* Closed Nov. 8, 1981 after one performance and ten previews. Original NY Production by the Hudson Guild Theatre, Wednesday, May 13, 1981.

Above: (L) back: Sharon Ullrick, Raymond Baker, Peter MacNicol, front: Mary Beth Hurt, Mia Dillon, Lizbeth Mackay
(Martha Swope Photo) **(R) John Vickery, Peter Michael Goetz in "Ned and Jack"** *(Martha Swope Photo)*

THE DRESSER

By Ronald Harwood; Director, Michael Elliott; Scenery, Laurie Bennett, supervised by Karen Schulz; Costumes, Stephen Doncaster, supervised by Jeanne Button; Sound, Ian Gibson, supervised by T. Richard Fitzgerald; Lighting, Beverly Emmons; Production Coordinator, Brent Peek; Props, Mel Saltzman, Jerry Kaliner; Special Effects, Chic Silber, Rob Taylor; Wardrobe, Veneda Truesdale; Wigs and Hairstylists, Leon Gagliardi, Eileen Tersago, Paul Huntley; Casting, Johnson-Liff Associates; Management Associates, Claire Calkins, Ann Dorsynski, David Domedion, Elizabeth Hermann; Production Assistant, Amy Hurlow; Presented by James M. Nederlander, Elizabeth I. McCann, Nelle Nugent, Warner Theatre Productions, Michael Codron at the Brooks Atkinson Theatre. Opened Monday, November 9, 1981.*

CAST

Norman	Tom Courtenay	Oxenby	Don McAllen Leslie
Her Ladyship	Rachel Gurney	Electrician	Geoff Garland
Madge	Marge Redmond	Kent	Jeffrey Alan Chandler
Sir	Paul Rogers	Gloucester	Leslie Barrett
Irene	Lisabeth Bartlett	Gentleman/Knight 2	Richard Frank
Geoffrey	Douglas Seale	Knight1/Albany	Jerome Collamore

STANDBYS AND UNDERSTUDIES: Richard Frank (Norman), Michael Egan (Sir), Leslie Barrett (Geoffrey), Jeffrey Alan Chandler (Oxenby), Michele Seyler (Irene), Geoff Garland (Kent/Gloucester/Albany)
   A drama in two acts. the action takes place in January 1942 in a theatre in the English provinces before curtain up and after curtain up.

General Management: McCann & Nugent; *Company Manager;* Carolyne A. Jones; *Press:* Solters/Roskin/Friedman, Joshua Ellis, Becky Flora, Cindy Valk; *Stage Managers:* Steve Beckler, Arlene Grayson

*Closed May 1, 1982 after 200 performances and 20 previews.

OH, BROTHER!

Book and Lyrics, Donald Driver; Based on Shakespeare's "The Comedy of Errors"; Music, Michael Valenti; Directed and Staged by Donald Driver; Scenery, Michael J. Hotopp, Paul DePass; Lighting, Richard Nelson; Costumes, Ann Emonts; Musical Director, Vocal and Dance Arrangements, Marvin Laird; Sound, Richard Fitzgerald; Orchestrations, Jim Tyler; Assistant Choreographer, Ahmed Hussien; Casting, Julie Hughes, Barry Moss; General Managers, William Court Cohen, Edward H. Davis, Norman E. Rothstein, Ralph Roseman, Charlotte W. Wilcox; Associate Musical Director, Dennis Buck; Assistant to Mr. Driver, David Michael Lang; Technical Supervisor, Jeremiah J. Harris; Props, Liam Herbert, Michael Gallagher; Wardrobe, Mary Coleman-Gierczak; Wigs and Hairstylists, Charles LoPresto, Peggy Scheerholz; Production Assistant, Dendrie Allyn Taylor; Presented by Zev Bufman, Kennedy Center with the Fisher Theatre Foundation, Joan Cullman, Sidney Shlenker at the ANTA Theatre. Opened Tuesday, November 10, 1981.*

CAST

Revolutionary Leader	Larry Marshall	Western Habim	Alan Weeks
Bugler	Sal Provenza	Fatatatatatima	Alyson Reed
Revolutionaries	Mark Martino, Thomas LoMonaco, Steve	Eastern Habim	Joe Morton
Bourneuf, Michael-Pierre Dean, Steve Sterner, Eric Scheps		Eastern Mousada	David-James Carroll
Revolutionary Women	Alyson Reed, Pamela Khoury, Kathy	Saroyana	Judy Kaye
Mahony-Bennett, Geraldine Hanning, Suzanne Walker, Karen Teti		Musica	Mary Mastrantonio
Lew	Richard B. Shull	Balthazar	Bruce Adler
A Camel	Steve Sterner, Eric Scheps	Ayatollah	Thomas LoMonaco
Western Mousada	Harry Groener	Lillian	Geraldine Hanning

UNDERSTUDIES: Sal Provenza (Balthazar), Steve Bourneuf (Bugler), Michael- Pierre Dean (Habim), Mark Martino (Mousada/Revolutionary Leader), Kathy Mahoney-Bennett (Saroyana), Pamela Khoury (Musica), Suzanne Walker (Fatatatatatima), Karen Teti (Lillian), Eric Scheps (Ayatollah), Swings: Nancy Meadows, David Michael Lang

MUSICAL NUMBERS: We Love an Old Story, I to the World, How Do You Want Me?, That's Him, Everybody Calls Me by My Name, O.P.E.C. Maiden, A Man, Tell Sweet Saroyana, What Do I Tell People This Time?, A Loud and Funny Song, The Chase, Oh Brother!
   A musical performed without intermission. The action takes place at the present time on the Persian Gulf.

General Management: Theatre Now Inc.; *Company Manager:* Robb Lady; *Press:* Fred Nathan, Patt Dale, Eileen McMahon, Anne S. Abrams; *Stage Managers:* Nicholas Russiyan, Robert O'Rourke, Eric Scheps

* Closed Nov. 11, 1981 after 3 performances and 13 previews.

Above: (L) Tom Courtenay, Douglas Seale, Paul Rogers, Marge Redmond, Lisabeth Bartlett in "The Dresser"
(Martha Swope Photo) **(R) Mary Mastrantonio, Judy Kaye, Harry Groener in "Oh, Brother!"** *(Martha Swope Photo)*

MASS APPEAL

By Bill C. Davis; Director, Geraldine Fitzgerald; Setting, David Gropman; Costumes, William Ivey Long; Lighting, F. Mitchell Dana; Associate Producer, Peter Jedlin; By special arrangement with Ken Berman and Pearl Tisman Minsky; Production Coordinator, Brent Peek; Props, Mel Saltzman, Joseph Feikls; Assistant to Director, Elizabeth Diamond; Sound, Richard Fitzgerald; Wardrobe, Lillian Norel; Organist, Gerard Caron; Manhattan Theatre Club Production presented by Elizabeth I. McCann, Nelle Nugent, Ray Larsen in association with Lynne Meadow, Barry Grove, Warner Theatre Productions at the Booth Theatre. Opened Thursday, November 12, 1981.*

CAST

Father Tim Farley .... Milo O'Shea
Mark Dolson .... Michael O'Keefe

STANDBYS: Malachy McCourt (Father), Charley Lang (Mark)
  A comedy in two acts. The action takes place during the autumn at the present time in the Church of St. Francis and in Father Farley's adjacent office.

General Management: McCann & Nugent; *Company Manager:* Veronica Claypool; *Press:* Solters/Roskin/Friedman, Joshua Ellis, David LeShay, Cindy Valk; *Stage Managers:* William Dodds, William Chance

* Closed May 16, 1982 after 212 performances and 16 previews. First NY production presented at Circle Repertory Theatre Oct. 21, 1979; opened at Manhattan Theatre Club Apr. 22, 1980.

CAMELOT

Book and Lyrics, Alan Jay Lerner; Based on "The Once and Future King" by T. H. White; Music, Frederick Loewe; Sets and Costumes, Desmond Heeley; Lighting, Thomas Skelton; Director, Frank Dunlop; Musical Director, Franz Allers; Conductor, Terry James; Sound, John McClure; Orchestrations, Robert Russell Bennett, Phil Lang; Musical Coordinator, Robert Kreis; Artistic Consultant, Stone Widney; Choreography, Buddy Schwab; A Dome/Cutler-Herman Production; Associate Producers, Steve Herman, Jon Cutler; Vice President Business Affairs, Jay L. Levy; Assistant to Producers, Ruthann M. Barshop; Special Effects, Robert Joyce; Props, Glenn Lloyd, David Dorr, James Edward Lee; Wardrobe, Josephine Zampedri, Peta Ullmann; Assistant Conductor, Philip Parnes; Hairstylist, Vincenzo Prestia; Assistant Choreographer, Dee Erickson; Presented by Mike Merrick and Don Gregory at the Winter Garden Theatre. Opened Sunday, November 15, 1981.*

CAST

King Arthur	Richard Harris	Lady Anne	Sally Williams
Sir Sagramore	Andy McAvin	Lady Sybil	Patrice Pickering
Merlyn	James Valentine	Sir Lionel	William James
Guenevere	Meg Bussert	King Pellinore	Barrie Ingham
Sir Dinidan	William Parry	Horrid	Daisy
Nimue	Jeanne Caryl	Sir Lionel's Squire	Steve Osborn
Lancelot DuLac	Richard Muenz	Sir Sagramore's Squire	Randy Morgan
Mordred	Richard Backus	Sir Dinidan's Squire	Richard Maxon
Dap	Robert Molnar	Tom	Thor Fields
Friar	Vincenzo Prestia	Knights of the Investiture	Bruce Sherman,
			Jack Starkey, Ken Henley, Ronald Bennett Stratton

KNIGHTS, LORDS AND LADIES: Elaine Barnes, Marie Berry, Bjarne Buchtrup, Jeanne Caryl, Melanie Clements, John Deyle, Norb Joerder, Kelby Kirk, Debra Dickinson, Kathy Flynn-McGrath, Ken Henley, William James, Dale Kristien, Lorraine Lazarus, Lauren Lipson, Craig Mason, Richard Maxon, Andy McAvin, Robert Molnar, Randy Morgan, Ann Neville, Steve Osborn, Patrice Pickering, Joel Sager, Mariellen Sereduke, D. Paul Shannon, Bruce Sherman, Jack Starkey, Ronald Bennett Stratton, Nicki Wood, Alternates: Ellyn Arons, Gary Wales

UNDERSTUDIES: William Parry (Arthur), Debra Dickinson (Guenevere), Bruce Sherman (Lancelot), James Valentine (Pellinore), Andy McAvin (Mordred), Robert Molnar (Merlyn), Sally Williams (Nemue), D. Paul Shannon/Craig Mason (Dinidan), John Deyle (Lionel), Craig Mason (Sagramore), Steve Osborn (Dap), Joel Sager (Tom)

MUSICAL NUMBERS: Guenevere, I Wonder What the King Is Doing Tonight?, The Simple Joys of Maidenhood, Camelot, Follow Me, C'Est Moi, The Lusty Month of May, How to Handle a Woman, The Jousts, Before I Gaze at You Again, If Ever I Could Leave You, The Seven Deadly Virtues, What Do Simple Folk Do?, Fie on Goodness, I Loved You Once in Silence
  A musical in 2 acts and 14 scenes.

General Manager: Arthur Anagostou; *Company Managers:* Carl Sawyer, Kathleen Turner; *Press:* Seymour Krawitz, Patricia M. Krawitz, Janet Tom; *Stage Managers:* Alan Hall, Steven Adler, Sally Ann Swarm

* Closed Jan. 2, 1982 after limited engagement of 57 performances and 15 previews to tour. Original production with Julie Andrews, Richard Burton and Robert Goulet opened at the Majestic Theatre Dec. 3, 1960 and played 873 performances. See THEATRE WORLD Vol. 17.

Above: (L) Milo O'Shea, Michael O'Keefe in "Mass Appeal" *(Martha Swope Photo)* **(R) Meg Bussert, Richard Harris, Richard Muenz in "Camelot"** *(Greg Gilbert Photo)*

17

HEY, LOOK ME OVER!

Director, Donald Saddler; Musical Director, Peter Howard; Lighting, David F. Segal; Sound, Otts Munderloh, Tony Meola; Costume Coordinator, Karen Eifert; Assistants to Producers, Richard Beck-Meyer, David Sinkler, Liz Hollis; David and Jan Marin present an all-star tribute to the work of Cy Coleman for the benefit of the American Musical and Dramatic Academy and the George Junior Republic at Avery Fisher Hall for one performance on Sunday evening, November 15, 1981.*

CAST

Beatrice Arthur, Michael Burstyn, Maria Burton, Imogene Coca, John Cullum, Mercedes Ellington, Joanna Gleason, Judy Kaye, Terri Klausner, Adriane Lenox, Michael Mark, John Miller, Monteith and Rand, Tony Orlando, Juliet Prowse, Lee Roy Reams, Wanda Richert, Nancy Ringham, Chita Rivera, George Rose, Virginia Sandifur, Joseph Saulter, Dick Shawn, Neil Simon, Jane Summerhays, Swen Swenson, Sylvia Syms, Marianne Tatum, Mel Torme, Candace Tovar, Tom Wopat, Don York, the cast of "Barnum," and the Cy Coleman Trio.

ACT I: Overture, Hey Look Me Over!, Someone Wonderful I Missed, I Love My Wife, Hey There Good Times, I've Got Your Number, Real Live Girl, Witchcraft, The Best Is Yet to Come, If My Friends Could See Me Now, There's Gotta Be Something Better Than This, Big Spender

ACT II: Overture from On the 20th Century, I Rise Again, Never, Repent, Our Private World, Seems Like Old Times, Oh Castanetta, The Riviera, Mustang, They Call Me Annie Laurie, Gulf Crest Gasoline Commercial, It's Not Where You Start, The Way I See It, French, The Colors of My Life, There's a Sucker Born Ev'ry Minute, Prince of Humbug, Why Try to Change Me Now?, You Fascinate Me So, When in Rome, Firefly, By Threes, It Amazes Me, Where Am I Going?, Pass Me By, My Personal Property, Come Follow the Band, Join the Circus

Stage Manager: Mary Porter Hall; *Press* Donald Smith

MERRILY WE ROLL ALONG

Music and Lyrics, Stephen Sondheim; Book, George Furth; From play by George S. Kaufman and Moss Hart; Director, Harold Prince; Choreography, Larry Fuller; Scenery, Eugene Lee; Costumes, Judith Dolan; Lighting, David Hersey; Orchestrations, Jonathan Tunick; Musical Director, Paul Gemignani; Makeup and Hairstyles, Richard Allen; Sound, Jack Mann; Casting, Joanna Merlin; Associate Producers, Ruth Mitchell, Howard Haines; Original Cast Album, RCA Records; Dance Arrangements, Tom Fay, Arnold Gross; Assistant Choreographer, Janie Gleason; Assistant Conductors, Tom Fay, Les Scott; Props, George Green; Wardrobe, Stephanie Edwards; Production Coordinator, Arthur Masella; Presented by Lord Grade, Martin Starger, Robert Fryer, Harold Prince at the Alvin Theatre. Opened Monday, November 16, 1981.*

CAST

Franklin Shephard	Jim Walton	Mr. Spencer	Paul Hyams
Mary Flynn	Ann Morrison	Mrs. Spencer	Mary Johansen
Charley Kringas	Lonny Price	Meg	Daisy Prince
Gussie	Terry Finn	Ru	Forest D. Ray
Joe	Jason Alexander	Bartender	Tom Shea
Beth	Sally Klein	Evelyn	Abby Pogrebin
Franklin Shepard (at age 43)	Geoffrey Horne	Valedictorian	Giancarlo Esposito
Jerome	David Cady	George, the Headwaiter	James Bonkovsky
Terry	Donna Marie Elio	Girl auditioning	Marianna Allen
Ms. Gordon	Maryrose Wood	Nightclub Waitress	Liz Callaway
Alex, Talk Show Host	Marc Moritz	Photographer	Steven Jacob
Gwen Wilson	Tonya Pinkins	Soundman	Clark Sayre
Ted	David Loud	Waiter	Gary Stevens
Les	David Shine		

UNDERSTUDIES: David Cady (Frank), Liz Callaway (Mary), David Loud (Charley), James Bonkovsky (Joe), Daisy Prince (Beth), Marianna Allen (Gussie), Janie Gleason (Swing)

MUSICAL NUMBERS: Merrily We Roll Along, Rich and Happy, Like It Was, Franklin Shepard Inc., Old Friends, Not a Day Goes By, Now You Know, It's a Hit!, Good Thing Going, Bobby and Jackie and Jack, Opening Doors, Our Time, The Hills of Tomorrow
    A musical in two acts. The action moves backward from 1980 to 1955.

General Manager: Howard Haines; *Company Manager:* David Musselman; *Press:* Mary Bryant, Francine L. Trevens, Philip Rinaldi; *Stage Managers:* Beverley Randolph, Richard Evans, Steve Knox

* Closed Nov. 28, 1982 after 16 performances and 52 previews.

Above: (L) Adriane Lenox, Nancy Ringham, Marianne Tatum, Wanda Richert, Jane Summerhays, Candace Tovar in "Hey, Look Me Over!" (R) Clark Sayre, Lonny Price, Jim Walton, Ann Morrison, David Loud, Maryrose Wood in "Merrily We Roll Along" *(Martha Swope Photos)*

THE FIRST

Book, Joel Siegel with Martin Charnin; Music, Bob Brush; Lyrics, Martin Charnin; Staged and Directed by Martin Charnin; Choreography, Alan Johnson; Scenery, David Chapman; Costumes, Carrie Robbins; Lighting, Marc B. Weiss; Sound, Louis Shapiro; Consultant, Rachel Robinson; Musical Supervision, Orchestrations, Dance Arrangements, Luther Henderson; Musical Conductor, Mark Hummel; Vocal Arranger, Joyce Brown; Associate Producer, Roger Luby; Casting, Meg Simon/Fran Kumin; Production Assistants, Heather Hewitt, Pamela Roy; Technical Coordinator, Arthur Siccardi; Props, George Green, Abe Einhorn; Wardrobe, Adelaide Laurino; Hairstylists, Gloria Rivera, Brent Dillon; Assistant Choreographer, Edward Love; Presented by Zev Bufman, Neil Bogart, Michael Harvey, Peter A. Bobley at the Martin Beck Theatre. Opened Tuesday, November 17, 1981.*

CAST

Patsy, the bartender/Dodger Coach/Brian Waterhouse . . . . . . Bill Buell	3rd Baseman/Equipment Manager/Cuban
Leo Durocher . . . . Trey Wilson	Reporter/Fan . . . . Steven Bland
Clyde Sukeforth . . . . Ray Gill	Junkyard Jones . . . . Luther Fontaine
Powers . . . . Sam Stoneburner	Catcher/Bucky/Redcap . . . . Michael Edward-Stevens
Thurman/Dodger Rookie/Pittsburgh Pirate . . . . Thomas Griffith	JoJo/Cuban Reporter/Fan . . . . Rodney Saulsberry
Branch Rickey . . . . David Huddleston	Cool Minnie . . . . Clent Bowers
Cannon/Sheriff/Huey . . . . Jack Hallett	Softball . . . . Paul Cook Tartt
Holmes/Eddie Stanky/Pittsburgh Pirate . . . . Stephen Crain	Rachel Isum . . . . Lonette McKee
Sorrentino/Umpire/Trainer/Reporter . . . . Paul Forrest	Swanee Rivers . . . . Steven Boockvor
Bartender/Hatrack Harris . . . . D. Peter Samuel	Casey Higgins . . . . Court Miller
Soldier/Pee Wee Reese . . . . Bob Morrisey	Opal/Fan . . . . Janet Hubert
Girl at bar/Dodger Wife/Hilda Chester . . . . Kim Criswell	Ruby/Fan . . . . Boncellia Lewis
Jackie Robinson . . . . David Alan Grier	Dodger Wife . . . . Margaret Lamee
	Red Barber . . . . Himself

PASSENGERS: Margaret Lamee, Sam Stoneburner, Rodney Saulsberry, Janet Hubert, Thomas Griffith, Kim Criswell, Steven Bland, Bob Morrisey, Stephen Crain, Boncellia Lewis

STANDBYS AND UNDERSTUDIES: George D. Wallace (Branch Rickey), Rodney Saulsberry (Jackie), Jackie Lowe (Rachel/Cool Minnie's Girl/Swing), Paul Cook Tartt (Cool Minnie), Michael Edward-Stevens (Junkyard), Margaret Lamee (Eunice/Hilda/Swing), Bill Buell (Clyde), Steven Boockvor (Casey), Stephen Crain (Reese), Neal Klein, Edward Love (Swings)

MUSICAL NUMBERS: Jack Roosevelt Robinson, Dancin' Off Third, The National Pastime, Will We Ever Know Each Other, The First, It Ain't Gonna Work!, The Brooklyn Dodger Strike, You Do-Do-It Good!, Is This Year Next Year?, There Are Days and There Are Days, It's a Beginning, The Opera Ain't Over

A musical in two acts. It dramatizes actual events in the life of Jackie Robinson that occurred between August of 1945 and September of 1947. Some characters have been created and some chronology and situations have been altered.

General Management: Gatchell & Neufeld Ltd.; *Company Manager:* James G. Mennen; *Press:* Fred Nathan, Eileen McMahon, Patt Dale, Anne S. Abrams; *Stage Managers:* Peter Lawrence, Jim Woolley, David Blackwell, Sarah Whitham

* Closed Dec. 12, 1981 after 37 performances and 33 previews.

THE WEST SIDE WALTZ

By Ernest Thompson; Director, Noel Willman; Set, Ben Edwards; Costumes, Jane Greenwood; Lighting, Thomas Skelton; Music supervised and arranged by David Krane; Casting, Terry Fay; Props, Robert Saltzman; Sound, James Cliney; Wardrobe, James McGaha; Hairstylist, Charles La France; Presented by Robert Whitehead and Roger L. Stevens in association with Center Theatre Group/Ahmanson at the Ethel Barrymore Theatre. Opened Thursday, November 19, 1981.*

CAST

Cara Varnum . . . . Dorothy Loudon	Robin Bird . . . . Regina Baff
Serge Barrescu . . . . David Margulies	Glen Dabrinsky . . . . Don Howard
Margaret Mary Elderdice . . . . Katharine Hepburn	

STANDBYS AND UNDERSTUDIES: Ludi Claire (Cara), Pat Santino (Serge/Glen), Corinne Neuchateau (Robin)

A comedy in 2 acts and 6 scenes. The action takes place in the living-room of Margaret Mary Elderdice's West Side New York apartment.

General Manager: Oscar E. Olesen; *Company Manager:* David Hedges; *Press:* Seymour Krawitz, Patricia Krawitz; *Stage Managers:* Ben Strobach, Valentine Mayer, Sally Lapiduss

* Closed March 13, 1982 to resume tour after limited engagement of 126 performances and 3 previews.

Above: (L) David Alan Grier (L) in "The First" *(Martha Swope Photo)* **(R) Katharine Hepburn, Dorothy Loudon in "The West Side Waltz"**

THE NEW MOON IN CONCERT

By Sigmund Romberg and Oscar Hammerstein II: Adaptation and Staging by Stuart Ross; Conductor, Evans Haile; Orchestra Manager, Ephraim Rubin; Pianists, Glen Kelly, Jim Frederick; A benefit concert performance presented by the New Amsterdam Theatre Company (Bill Tynes, Artistic Director) at Town Hall on Monday, November 23, 1981.*

CAST

Host and Hostess: Estelle Parsons, Allan Jones
Julie . . . . Debbie Shapiro
Capt. Georges Duval . . . . David Eric
Vicomte Ribaud . . . . Allan Jones
Robert . . . . John Reardon
Alexander. . . . . Russ Thacker

Besac . . . . Herndon Lackey
Marianne . . . . Meg Bussert
Phillippe . . . . Miguel Cortez
Clotilde Lombaste. . . . . Connie Coit
with the New York Choral Society (Robert De Cormier, Conductor), and the Riverside Symphony Orchestra

MUSICAL NUMBERS: Overture, Marianne, The Girl on the Prow, Gorgeous Alexander, When I Am Here with You, Tavern Scene, Softly as in a Morning Sunrise, Stouthearted Men, Rosita Tango, One Kiss, The Trial, Wanting You, Funny Little Sailor Men, Neath the New Moon, Lover Come Back to Me, Battle Scene, Love Is Quite a Simple Thing, Try Her Out at Dances, I'm Just a Sentimental Fool, Never for You, Finale
    An operetta in two acts.

Press: Sam Rudy; *Stage Manager:* Laurie F. Stone

* One performance only. (no photos)

GROWNUPS

By Jules Feiffer; Director, John Madden; Set, Andrew Jackness; Costumes, Dunya Ramicova; Lighting, Paul Gallo; Produced in association with Wayne Rogers; Originally produced by the American Repertory Theatre in Cambridge, Ma.; Technical Supervision, Theatrical Services Inc.; Props, Jan Marasek; Wardrobe, Karen Lloyd; Casting, Marilyn Szatmary; Production Assistant, Trish Suchy; Presented by Mike Nichols, Emanuel Azenberg with the Shubert Organization at the Lyceum Theatre. Opened Thursday, December 10, 1981.*

CAST

Helen . . . . Frances Sternhagen
Jack . . . . Harold Gould
Marilyn . . . . Kate McGregor-Stewart

Jake. . . . . Bob Dishy
Louise. . . . . Cheryl Giannini
Edie . . . . Jennifer Dundas

STANDBYS: Stephen D. Newman (Jake), Georgine Hall (Helen), Barbara eda-Young (Louise/Marilyn), Shelly Inglis (Edie)
    A comedy in three acts. The action takes place at the present time in Marilyn's kitchen in New Rochelle, N.Y., and in Jake and Louise's apartment in New York City.

General Manager: Jose Vega; *Company Manager:* Linda Cohen; *Press:* Bill Evans, Sandra Manley, Howard Atlee, Leslie Anderson; *Stage Managers:* Craig Jacobs, Wayne Carson

* Closed Feb. 20, 1982 after 83 performances and 15 previews.

Above: Frances Sternhagen, Cheryl Giannini, Harold Gould, Kate McGregor-Stewart, Bob Dishy in "Grownups"
(Martha Swope Photo)

KINGDOMS

By Edward Sheehan; Director, Paul Giovanni; Set, David Hays; Costumes, Patricia Zipprodt; Lighting, Paul Gallo; Sound, Chuck London; Associate Producer, Dana Matthow; Casting, Marjorie Martin; Wigs and Makeup, Joe Blitz; Props, Paul Biega; Wardrobe, Nancy Schaefer; Assistant to Director, Marc Beckerman; Consultant, Father Tex Violet; Presented by Elliot Martin at the Cort Theatre. Opened Sunday, December 13, 1981.*

CAST

Domestics	Joe Zaloom, Ralph Drischell	Emperor Napoleon I	Armand Assante
Cardinal Consalvi	Thomas Barbour	Empress Josephine	Maria Tucci
Cardinal Fesch	George Morfogen	Monks	Stephen Stout, Arthur Burns, Joe Zaloom
Papal Chamberlain	Donald Linahan	Dr. Porta	Charles White
Pope Pius VII	Roy Dotrice	Maurice	Alex Hyde-White
Soldiers	John Martinuzzi, Alex Hyde-White	Javel	Ralph Drischell
Tailor	Arthur Burns	DuBois	Stephen Stout
Radet	Michael Tolaydo		

STANDBYS AND UNDERSTUDIES: George Morfogen (Pope), Arthur Burns (Napoleon), Michael Tolaydo (Napoleon), Etain O'Malley (Josephine), Donald Linahan (Consalvi), Ralph Drischell (Fesch), Joe Zaloom (Porta), Stephen Stout (Radet)

A drama in two acts. The action takes place in France and Italy from 1804 to 1814.

General Management: Joseph P. Harris Associates, Nancy Simmons, Bruce Klinger; *Press:* Jeffrey Richards, C. George Willard, Robert Ganshaw, Ben Morse, Helen Stern, Ted Killmer, Stanley Evans, Richard Humleker; *Stage Managers:* Tom Aberger, Johnna Murray

* Closed Dec. 27, 1981 after 17 performances and 12 previews.

DUET FOR ONE

By Tom Kempinski; Director, William Friedkin; Scenery, John Lee Beatty; Costumes, Jane Greenwood; Lighting, Dennis Parichy; Technical Coordinator, Arthur Siccardi; Props, Jan Marasek; Wardrobe, Penny Davis; Sound, Thomas Morse; Casting, Marilyn Szatmary; Production Assistant, Jane E. Cooper; Assistant to Director, Toni St. Clair Lilly; Hairstylist, John D. Quaglia; Presented by Emanuel Azenberg, Ray Cooney, Wayne M. Rogers, Ron Dante, Tommy Valando and Warner Theatre Productions at the Royale Theatre. Opened Thursday, December 17, 1981.*

CAST

Stephanie Abrahams	Anne Bancroft
Dr. Alfred Feldmann	Max von Sydow

STANDBYS: Cristine Rose, Ron Randell

A play in two acts and six scenes. The action takes place at the present time in Dr. Feldmann's office on the first floor of his townhouse in the East 80's in Manhattan.

General Manager: Jose Vega; *Press:* Bill Evans, Sandra Manley, Howard Atlee, Leslie Anderson; *Stage Managers:* Charles Blackwell, Cathy B. Blaser

* Closed Jan. 2, 1982 after 20 performances and 12 previews.

Above: (L) Armand Assante, Roy Dotrice in "Kingdoms" *(Peter Cunningham Photo)* **(R) Max von Sydow, Anne Bancroft in "Duet for One"** *(Martha Swope Photo)*

DREAMGIRLS

Book and Lyrics, Tom Eyen; Music, Henry Krieger; Direction and Choreography, Michael Bennett; Co-Choreographer, Michael Peters; Scenery, Robin Wagner; Costumes, Theoni V. Aldredge; Lighting, Tharon Musser; Sound, Otts Munderloh; Musical Supervision and Orchestrations, Harold Wheeler; Musical Director, Yolanda Segovia; Vocal Arrangements, Cleavant Derricks; Hairstylist, Ted Azar; Technical Coordinator, Arthur Siccardi; Props, Michael Smanko, Alan Steiner; Wardrobe, Alyce Gilbert; Assistant Choreographer, Geneva Burke; Production Assistant, Charles Suisman; Assistant Conductor, Nick Cerrato; Casting, Olaiya, Johnson/Liff Associates; Original Cast Album on Geffen Records; Presented by Michael Bennett, Bob Avian, Geffen Records and the Shubert Organization at the Imperial Theatre. Opened Sunday, December 20, 1981.*

CAST

The Stepp Sisters	Deborah Burrell, Vanessa Bell, Tenita Jordan, Brenda Pressley
Charlene	Cheryl Alexander
Joanne	Linda Lloyd
Marty	Vondie Curtis-Hall
Curtis Taylor, Jr	Ben Harney
Deena Jones	Sheryl Lee Ralph
The M.C.	Larry Stewart
Tiny Joe Dixon	Joe Lynn
	Charles Randolph-Wright, Larry Stewart, Weyman Thompson
Lorrell Robinson	Loretta Devine †1
C. C. White	Obba Babatunde
Effie Melody White	Jennifer Holliday †2
Little Albert and the Tru-Tones/The James Early Band	
Wellington Perkins, Charles Bernard, Jamie Patterson, Charles Randolph-Wright, Weyman Thompson, Scott Plank	
James Thunder Early	Cleavant Derricks
Edna Burke	Sheila Ellis
Wayne	Tony Franklin
Dave and the Sweethearts	Paul Binotto, Candy Darling, Stephanie Eley
Frank, press agent	David Thome †3
Michelle Morris	Deborah Burrell
Jerry, nightclub owner	Joe Lynn
Five Tuxedos	Charles Bernard, Jamie Patterson, Charles Randolph-Wright, Larry Stewart, Weyman Thompson
Les Style	Cheryl Alexander, Tenita Jordan, Linda Lloyd, Brenda Pressley
Film Executives	Paul Binotto, Scott Plan, Weyman Thompson
Mr. Morgan	Larry Stewart

FANS, REPORTERS, STAGEHANDS, GUESTS, PHOTOGRAPHERS: Cheryl Alexander, Phylicia Ayers-Allen, Vanessa Bell, Charles Bernard, Paul Binotto, Candy Darling, Ronald Dunham, Stephanie Eley, Sheila Ellis, Tenita Jordan, Linda Lloyd, Joe Lynn, Frank Mastrocola, Jamie Patterson, Wellington Perkins, Scott Plank, Brenda Pressley, David Thome, Charles Randolph-Wright, Larry Stewart, Weyman Thompson

UNDERSTUDIES: Phylicia Ayers-Allen (Deena), Sheila Ellis (Effie), Cheryl Alexander (Lorrell), Linda Lloyd (Michelle), Vondie Curtis-Hall (Curtis), Larry Stewart (James), Tony Franklin (C.C.), Milton Craig Nealy (Marty/Jerry), Weyman Thompson (Wayne), Scott Plank (Frank), Swings: Brenda Braxton, Milton Craig Nealy

MUSICAL NUMBERS: I'm Looking for Something, Goin' Downtown, Takin' the Long Way Home, Move, Fake Your Way to the Top, Cadillac Car, Steppin' to the Bad Side, Party Party, I Want You Baby, Family, Dreamgirls, Press Conference, Only the Beginning, Heavy, It's All Over, And I Am Telling You I'm Not Going, Love Love You Baby, Dreams Medley, I Am Changing, One More Picture Please, When I First Saw You, Got to Be Good Times, Ain't No Party, I Meant You No Harm, Quintette, The Rap, I Miss You Old Friend, One Night Only, I'm Somebody, Faith in Myself, Hard to Say Goodbye My Love

A musical in 2 acts and 20 scenes. The action takes place in the early 1960's and early 1970's.

General Management: Marvin A. Krauss Associates; *Press:* Merle Debuskey, Diane Judge; *Stage Managers:* Jeff Hamlin, Zane Weiner, Jacqueline Yancey

* Still playing May 31, 1982. Winner of 1982 Tonys for Best Book, Lighting, Choreography, Supporting Actor (Cleavant Derricks), Actor and Actress (Ben Harney, Jennifer Holliday)
† Succeeded by: 1. Cheryl Alexander for 1 week, 2. Sheila Ellis during illness, 3. Buddy Vest

Sheryl Lee Ralph, Cleavant Derricks, Jennifer Holliday, Loretta Devine

Sheryl Lee Ralph, Cleavant Derricks, Loretta Devine, Deborah Burrell, Ben Harney, Obba Babatunde, Jennifer Holliday (*Martha Swope Photos*)

WALTZ OF THE STORK

Book, Music, Lyrics and Direction by Melvin Van Peebles; Scenery, Kurt Lundell; Lighting, Shirley Prendergast; Costumes, Bernard Johnson; Sound, Lou Gonzales; Additional Music and Lyrics, Ted Hayes, Mark Burkan; Musical Director, Bob Carten; Assistant to Mr. Van Peebles, Nate Barnett; Movement Coordinator, Andy Torres; Wardrobe, Frank Echols; Special Effects, David S. Rapkin; Presented by Melvin Van Peebles at the Century Theatre. Opened Tuesday, January 5, 1982.*

CAST

Melvin Van Peebles, Bob Carten, C. J. Critt, Mario Van Peebles

MUSICAL NUMBERS: And I Love You, The Apple Stretching, Tender Understanding , There, Mother's Prayer, My Love Belongs to You, Weddings and Funerals, One Hundred and Fifteen, Play It As It Lays, Shoulders to Lean On
 A comedy with music in two acts. The action takes place "Now and Before, Wherever and Midtown Manhattan."

General Management: Theatre Now Inc.; *Company Manager:* Robb Lady; *Press:* Susan L. Schulman, Bruce Lynn; *Stage Managers:* Nate Barnett, John N. Concannon

* Closed May 23, 1982 after 146 performances and 21 previews.

LITTLE ME

Book, Neil Simon; Based on novel by Patrick Dennis; Music, Cy Coleman; Lyrics, Carolyn Leigh; Director, Robert Drivas; Sets and Costumes, Tony Walton; Lighting, Beverly Emmons; Choreography, Peter Gennaro; Vocal and Dance Arrangements, Cy Coleman; Orchestrations, Harold Wheeler; Music Director, Donald York; Sound, Tom Morse; Technical Supervision, Theatre Services Inc.; Props, Jan Marasek, Arthur Hoagland; Casting, Marilyn Szatmary; Wardrobe, Stephanie Edwards, Benjamin Wilson; Assistant Choreographer, Wisa D'Orso; Assistant to Director, Nancy Simon; Production Assistant, John Elkins; Hairstylists, John D. Quaglia, David Brown, Burt Pitcher; Production Manager, Martin Herzer; Presented by Ron Dante, Wayne Rogers, Steven Leber, David Krebs, McLaughlin Piven Inc., Warner Theatre Productions, Emanuel Azenberg at the Eugene O'Neill Theatre. Opened Thursday, January 21, 1982.*

CAST

Announcer/Attorney/Bandleader/Preacher/German Soldier/General/Yulnick .... Gibby Brand	Flo Eggleston/Amos Pinchley/Mr. Worst/Otto Schnitzler/ Prince Cherney .... James Coco
Belle (Today) .... Jessica James	Ms. Kepplewhite .... Maris Clement
Charlie Drake/Greensleeves/Town Spokesman/Assistant	Nurse .... Sean Murphy
Director/Croupier .... Henry Sutton	Court Clerk/Henchman/Sergeant/Doctor .... Stephen Berger
Belle/Baby Belle .... Mary Gordon Murray	Pinchley Junior .... James Brennan
Momma .... Mary Small	Henchman/Captain .... Bob Freschi
Ramona .... Mary C. Holton	Frankie Polo .... Don Correia
Cerine/Boom Boom Girl .... Gail Pennington	Boom Boom Girl .... Bebe Neuwirth
Bruce/Sailor I .... Brian Quinn	Bert/Sailor II .... Mark McGrath
Noble Eggleston/Val duVal/Fred Poitrine/	Red Cross Nurse .... Andrea Green
Noble Junior .... Victor Garber	Pharoah I .... Kevin Winkler

TOWNSPEOPLE, SOLDIERS, NURSES, ETC: Stephen Berger, Michael Blevins, David Cahn, Maris Clement, Bob Freschi, Andrea Green, Mary C. Holton, Mark McGrath, Gary Mendelson, Sean Murphy, Bebe Neuwirth, Gail Pennington, Susan Powers, Brian Quinn, Kevin Brooks Winkler

UNDERSTUDIES: Gibby Brand (Mr. Coco), Gibby Brand and John Hillner (Mr. Garber), Susan Powers (Ms. Murray), Mary Small (Ms. James), James Brennan (Mr. Correia), Bob Freschi (Mr. Sutton), Maris Clement (Ms. Small), Stephen Berger (Mr. Brand), John Hillner (Mr. Brennan)

MUSICAL NUMBERS: Don't Ask a Lady, The Other Side of the Tracks, The Rich Kids Rag, I Love You, Deep Down Inside, Boom-Boom, I've Got Your Number, Real Live Girl, I Wanna Be Yours, Little Me, Goodbye, Here's to Us
 A Musical in two acts.

General Manager: Jose Vega; *Company Manager:* Bruce Birkenhead; *Press:* Bill Evans, Sandra Manley, Howard Atlee, Leslie Anderson; *Stage Managers:* Robert LoBianco, Lani Sundsten, John Hillner

* Closed Feb. 21, 1982 after 36 performances and 30 previews. Original production with Sid Caesar, Virginia Martin, Swen Swenson, Nancy Andrews and Mickey Deems opened at the Lunt-Fontanne Theatre Nov. 17, 1962 and played 257 performances. See THEATRE WORLD Vol. 19.

Above: (L) Mario Van Peebles, Bob Carten, Melvin Van Peebles, C. J. Critt in "Waltz of the Stork" *(Gerry Goodstein Photo)*
(R) Victor Garber, James Coco in "Little Me" *(Martha Swope Photo)*

THE CURSE OF AN ACHING HEART

By William Alfred; Music, Claibe Richardson; Director, Gerald Gutierrez; Set, John Lee Beatty; Costumes, Nancy Potts; Lighting, Dennis Parichy; Sound, David Rapkin; Orchestrations, Bruce Pomahac; Casting, Johnson/Liff; Associate Producers, David Jiranek, Frederick C. Venturelli; Assistant to Director, Jennifer McCray; Wardrobe, Deborah Lowman; Wigs, Paul Huntley, Suga; Presented by Margot Harley, John Houseman, Everett King, David Weil, Sidney Shlenker at the Little Theatre. Opened Monday, January 25, 1982.*

CAST

Frances Anna Duffy Walsh	Faye Dunaway	Martin "Lugs" Walsh	Terrance O'Quinn
Gertrude "Lulu" Fitter Malardino	Audrie Neenan	Minnie Crump	Francine Beers
John Joseph "Jo Jo" Finn	Bernie McInerney	J. Stanislaus McGahey	Colin Stinton
Pasquale "Packy" Malardino	Jon Polito	Aloysius "Wishy" Burke	Paul McCrane
Man with newspaper	Dale Helward	Gertrude Graham Finn	Beverly May
Herman Crump	Kurt Knudson	Martin Thomas Walsh	Raphael Sbarge

STANDBYS UNDERSTUDIES: Joan MacIntosh (Ms. Dunaway/Ms. May), Mary E. Baird (Lulu/Minnie), Rand (Wishy/Tommy), Thomas A. Stewart (Lugs/Packy/McGahey), Dale Helward (JoJo/Herman)
   A drama in five scenes with a prologue performed without intermission. The action takes place from 1923 to 1942.

General Management: Dorothy Olim Associates; *Assistant Company Manager:* George Elmer; *Press:* Fred Nathan, Eileen McMahon, Francine Trevens, Anne S. Abrams; *Stage Managers:* Franklin Keysar, Mary E. Baird

* Closed Feb. 21, 1982 after limited engagement of 32 performances and 12 previews.

JOSEPH AND THE AMAZING TECHNICOLOR DREAMCOAT

Music, Andrew Lloyd Webber; Lyrics, Tim Rice; Direction and Choreography, Tony Tanner; Scenery, Karl Eigsti; Lighting, Barry Arnold; Costumes, Judith Dolan; Sound, Tom Morse; Musical Supervision, arrangements and orchestrations, Martin Silvestri, Jeremy Stone; Musical Director, David Friedman; Associate Producers, Thomas Pennini, Jean Luskin; Casting, Meg Simon/Fran Kumin; Props, Michael Gallagher, Liam Herbert; Wardrobe, Karen Eifert; Assistant Choreographer, Joni Masella; Production Assistant, George Barlow; Assistant Conductor, Allen Cohen; Wigs, Charles LoPresto; Headpieces, Paige Southard; Presented by Zev Bufman, Susan R. Rose, Melvyn J. Estrin, Sidney Shlenker, Gail Berman by arrangement with Robert Stigwood Organization Ltd. and David Land at the Royale Theatre. Opened Wednesday, January 27, 1982.*

CAST

Narrator	Laurie Beechman	Gad	Barry Tarallo
Jacob	Gordon Stanley	Benjamin	Philip Carrubba
Reuben	Robert Hyman	Judah	Stephen Hope
Simeon	Kenneth Bryan	Joseph	Bill Hutton †2
Levi	Steve McNaughton	Ismaelites	Tom Carder, David Ardao
Napthali	Charlie Serrano	Potiphar	David Ardao
Issachar	Peter Kapetan	Mrs. Potiphar	Randon Lo
Asher	David Asher	Butler	Kenneth Bryan
Dan	James Rich †1	Baker	Barry Tarallo
Zebulon	Doug Voet	Pharaoh	Tom Carder

WOMEN'S CHORUS: Lorraine Barrett, Karen Bogan, Katharine Buffaloe, Lauren Goler, Randon Lo, Joni Masella, Kathleen Rowe McAllen, Renee Warren

UNDERSTUDIES: Rosalyn Rahn (Narrator), David Asher (Jacob), Doug Voet (Joseph), Kenneth Bryan (Potiphar), James Rich (Pharaoh), Swings: Rosalyn Rahn, John Ganzer

MUSICAL NUMBERS: Prologue, Jacob and Sons/Joseph's Coat, Joseph's Dreams, Poor Poor Joseph, One More Angel in Heaven, Potiphar, Close Every Door, Stone the Crows, Pharaoh's Story, Song of the King, Pharaoh's Dream Explained, Those Canaan Days, The Brothers Came to Egypt/Grovel Grovel, Who's the Thief?, Benjamin Calypso, Joseph All the Time, Jacob in Egypt, Any Dream Will Do, May I Return to the Beginning
   A musical in two acts

General Manager: Theatre Now Inc.; *Press:* Fred Nathan, Francine L. Trevens, Eileen McMahon, Anne S. Abrams, Eric Elice; *Stage Managers:* Michael Martorella, John Fennessy, John Ganzer

* Still playing May 31, 1982. This production opened Off-Broadway at the Entermedia Theatre Wednesday, Nov. 18, 1981 and played 77 performances before moving to Broadway's Royale Theatre.
† Succeeded by: 1. Richard Hilton, 2. Doug Voet, Allen Fawcett

Above: (L) Faye Dunaway, Audrie Neenan in "The Curse of an Aching Heart" *(Terry O'Neill Photo)* **(R) Gordon Stanley, Bill Hutton**
22 **(C), Laurie Beechman (R) and company in "Joseph and the Amazing Technicolor Dreamcoat"** *(Martha Swope Photo)*

MACBETH

By William Shakespeare; Director, Nicol Williamson; Scenery, Kenneth Foy; Costumes, Julie Weiss; Lighting, William Armstrong; Music, Guy Woolfenden; Casting, Lynn Kressel, Kathryn Placzek; Production Coordinator, Lee Blattau; Wardrobe, Millicent Hacker; Presented by Circle in the Square (Theodore Mann, Artistic Director; Paul Libin, Managing Director) at Circle in the Square/Uptown. Opened Thursday, January 28, 1982.*

CAST

First Witch .... Elaine Bromka	Porter .... Rand Bridges
Second Witch .... Bette Henritze	Macduff .... J. T. Walsh
Third Witch .... Tara Loewenstern	Lennox .... Peter Phillips
Duncan .... Tom McDermott	Donalbain .... Mark Herrier
Malcolm .... Ray Dooley	Old Man .... Renato Cibelli
Captain .... Richard Jamieson	First Murderer .... Rik Colitti
Ross .... Paul Falzone	Second Murderer .... Peter McRobbie
Macbeth .... Nicol Williamson	Lady Macduff .... Joyce Fideor
Banquo .... John Henry Cox	Macduff's Son .... Christian Slater
Angus .... Gregory Mortensen	Messenger .... John Wojda
Lady Macbeth .... Andrea Weber	Doctor .... Peter McRobbie
Seyton .... Paul Perri	Gentlewoman .... Elaine Bromka
Fleance .... Peter James	Cream-faced Loon .... Neal Jones

STANDBYS AND UNDERSTUDIES: Richard Jamieson (Macbeth/Macduff), Tara Loewenstern (Lady Macbeth), Peter Phillips (Malcolm), Paul Falzone (Banquo), John Wojda (Lennox/Ross/Murderer), Neal Jones (Angus/Donalbain/Fleance), Gregory Mortensen (Seyton), Renato Cibelli (Duncan), Peter McRobbie (Captain), Elaine Bromka (Lady Macduff), Mark Herrier (Murderer), Rik Colitti (Porter), Tom McDermott (Old Man), Peter James (Macduff's Son), John Henry Cox (Doctor), Bette Henritze (Gentlewoman)

A tragedy performed without intermission.

Company Manager: William Conn; *Press:* Merle Debuskey, David Roggensack; *Stage Managers:* Michael F. Ritchie, Ted William Sowa

* Closed Apr. 4, 1982 after 21 performances and 19 previews.

Nicol Williamson as Macbeth
(David Hartman Photo)

James Earl Jones, Christopher Plummer in "Othello"
(Martha Swope Photo)

OTHELLO

By William Shakespeare; Director, Peter Coe; Scenery, David Chapman; Costumes, Robert Fletcher; Lighting, Marc B. Weiss; Hairstylist, Patrik D. Moreton; Fights staged by B. H. Barry; Music, Stanley Silverman; Casting, Meg Simon/Fran Kumin; A National Artists Management Company production; Production Coordinator, Alecia A. Parker; Assistant to Director, Elliott Woodruff; Props, Clyde Churchill, Jr.; Wardrobe, Carla Lawrence; Hair and Wig Supervisor, Frank Melon; American Shakespeare Theatre production; Presented by Barry and Fran Weissler in association with CBS Video Enterprises by special arrangement with Don Gregory at the Winter Garden Theatre. Opened Wednesday, February 3, 1982.*

CAST

Othello .... James Earl Jones	Gratiano .... Richard Dix
Desdemona .... Dianne Wiest†	Lodovico .... Raymond Skipp
Cassio .... Kelsey Grammer	Montano .... Robert Burr
Iago .... Christopher Plummer	Gentlemen of Cyprus .... Robert Ousley, Harry S. Murphy, Bern Sundstedt
Emilia .... Aideen O'Kelly	Senators of Venice .... Robert Ousley, Harry S. Murphy
Bianca .... Patricia Mauceri	Herald/Soldier .... Kim Bemis
Roderigo .... Graeme Campbell	Servants to Brabantio .... Randy Kovitz, Ellen Newman, Robert Ousley, Bern Sundstedt
Duke of Venice .... Robert Burr	Cypriots .... Ellen Newman, Randy Kovitz
Brabantio .... David Sabin	Officers .... Robert Ousley, Harry S. Murphy, Bern Sundstedt

UNDERSTUDIES: Mel Winkler (Othello), Robert Burr (Iago), Randy Kovitz (Cassio/Gentlemen of Cyprus), Bern Sundstedt (Cassio/Roderico/Herald), Harry S. Murphy (Brabantio), Kim Bemis (Gratiano/Lodovico), Robert Ousley (Duke/Montano), Ellen Newman (Emilia/Desdemona/Bianca)

A tragedy performed in two acts.

General Manager: NAMCO; *Company Manager:* James A. Gerald; *Press:* Seymour Krawitz, Patricia Krawitz, Robert Larkin; *Stage Managers:* Thomas Kelly, Dianne Trulock, Frank Hartenstein, Randy Kovitz

* Closed May 23, 1982 after 122 performances and 5 previews. Production received a 1982 "Tony" Award for Outstanding Reproduction of a Play.
† Succeeded by Cecilia Hart

PUMP BOYS AND DINETTES

Conceived and Written by the company; Scenery, Doug Johnson, Christopher Nowak; Costumes, Patricia McGourty; Lighting, Fred Buchholz; Sound, Bill Dreisbach; Production Coordinator, Sherman Warner; Presented by Dodger Productions, Louis Busch Hager, Marilyn Strauss, Kate Studley, Warner Theatre Productions and Max Weitzenhoffer at the Princess Theatre. Opened Thursday, February 4, 1982.*

CAST

Jackson	John Foley	Rhetta Cupp	Cass Morgan
L. M.	Mark Hardwick	Eddie	John Schimmel
Prudie Cupp	Debra Monk	Jim	Jim Wann

STANDBYS: Rhonda Coullet, Malcolm Ruhl

MUSICAL NUMBERS: Highway 57, Taking It Slow, Serve Yourself, Menu Song, The Best Man, Fisherman's Prayer, Catfish, Mamaw, Be Good or Be Gone, Drinkin' Shoes, Pump Boys, Mona, T.N.D.P.W.A.M., Tips, Sister, Vacation, No Holds Barred, Farmer Tan, Closing Time
   A musical in two acts.

General Management: Dodger Productions; *Press:* Betty Lee Hunt, Maria Cristina Pucci, James Sapp; *Stage Managers:* Mo Donley, Lucia Schliessmann

* Still playing May 31, 1982. This production opened Off Broadway Friday, July 10, 1981 at the Westside Arts Theatre for 20 performances; moved to the Colonnades Theatre Oct. 13, 1981 for 112 performances before its Broadway debut.

THE WORLD OF SHOLOM ALEICHEM

By Arnold Perl; Director, Milton Moss; Stage Movement, Pearl Lang; Music, Stan Free; Musical Arrangements, Earl Shandell; Sets, Karl Eigsti; Lighting, Robby Monk; Costumes, Pearl Somner; Associate Producer, Joseph E. Gilford; Production under the supervision of Larry Arrick; Wardrobe, Alvin Perry, Susan Wright; Hairstylist, Peggy Shierholz; Production Assistant, Rebecca Perl; Casting, Madeline and Joseph Gilford; Presented by Lee Guber and Madeline Gilford at the Rialto Theatre. Opened Thursday, February 4, 1982.*

CAST

Mendele, the book seller	Joe Silver	Defending Angel	Olivia Virgil Harper
"A Tale of Chelm"		Prosecuting Angel	Harris Laskawy
The Melamed, a teacher	Jack Gilford	Angels	Sally-Jane Heit,
		Robin Bartlett, Andy Gale, Renee Lippin, David Lang, Mark Margolis	
Rifkele, his wife	Renee Lippin	"The High School"	
Rabbi David	Harris Laskawy	Aaron Katz	Jack Gilford
Angel Rochele	Robin Bartlett	Hannah, his wife	Sally-Jane Heit
Dodi	Mark Margolis	Moishe, their son	Brian Zoldessy
Goatseller	Sally-Jane Heit	1st Man at the List	Andy Gale
Dodi's Friend	David Lang		
"The Bandit"		The Tutor	Mark Margolis
Bandit	Joe Silver	Woman at the List	Robin Bartlett
Sholom Aleichem	Jack Gilford		
"Bontche Schweig"		Principal	Mitchell Jason
Father Abraham	Arn Weiner	Uncle Maxl	Harris Laskawy
Bontche Schweig	Jack Gilford	Aunt Reba	Renee Lippin
Presiding Angel	Mitchell Jason	Kholyava	David Lang
		2nd Man at the List	Arn Weiner

UNDERSTUDIES: Mark Fleischman, Sherry Lambert
   Performed with one intermission.

General Manager: Ben Sprecher; *Company Manager:* Stephen Arnold; *Press:* Merle Debuskey, David Roggensack, Bruce Cohen; *Stage Managers:* Mortimer Halpern, Sherry Lambert

*Closed Feb. 28, 1982 after 22 performances and 24 previews.

Above: (L) John Schimmel, Cass Morgan, Jim Wann, Debra Monk, John Foley, Mark Hardwick in "Pump Boys and Dinettes" *(Susan Cook Photo)* (R) Harris Laskawy, Renee Lippin, Arn Weier, Jack Gilford, Mark Margolis, David Lang, Sally-Jane Heit, Mitchell Jason in "The World of Sholom Aleichem" *(Martha Swope Photo)*

SPECIAL OCCASIONS

By Bernard Slade; Director, Gene Saks; Scenery, David Jenkins; Costumes, Jennifer von Mayrhauser; Lighting, Tharon Musser; Associate Producers, Martin Cohen, Milly Schoenbaum; Produced in association with Thornhill Productions, Inc.; Props, Joseph P. Harris, Jr., Laura Koch; Wardrobe, Rosie Wells; Hairstylist, Dale Brownell; Production Assistant, Thomas Santopietro; Presented by Morton Gottlieb, Ben Rosenberg, Warren Crane at the Music Box Theatre. Opened Sunday, February 7, 1982.*

CAST

Amy Ruskin .... Suzanne Pleshette
Michael Ruskin .... Richard Mulligan

STANDBYS: Marsha Skaggs, David Jay

A comedy in two acts. The action takes place during the past ten years in various locales in California, New York and Colorado.

General Manager: Ben Rosenberg; *Company Manager:* Martin Cohen; *Press:* Solters/Roskin/Friedman, Milly Schoenbaum, Warren Knowlton, Kevin Patterson; *Stage Managers:* Warren Crane, Kate Pollack

* Closed Feb. 7, 1982 after one performance and 26 previews.

Suzanne Pleshette, Richard Mulligan in "Special Occasions"
(Martha Swope Photo)

NIGHT OF 100 STARS

Written and Produced by Hildy Parks; Director, Clark Jones; Staging, Albert Stephenson; Musical Director, Elliot Lawrence; Settings, Charles Lisanby; Lighting, Bill Klages; Costumes, Alvin Colt; Associate Producer, Lou Del Prete; Production Associate, Linda Finson; Production Supervisor, Alan Hall; Co-Producer, Roy A. Somlyo; Film Segments, John Springer; Special Material, Buz Kohan; Staging for television, Alan Johnson: Musical Supervision, John Morris; Orchestrated by Jonathan Tunick; All Star Band supervised by John Morris; Talent Consultants, Gus Schirmer, Sid Bernstein; Additional Arrangements, Wally Harper, Lanny Myers; Music Coordinator, Peter Howard; Additional Orchestrations, Bill Elton, Tommy Newsom, Tory Zito; Hairstylist, Joe Tubens; Makeup, Joe Cranzano; Associate Director, Enid Roth; Associate Manager, Seymour Herscher; Production Associate, Jodi Moss; Assistant Production Managers, Christopher A. Cohen, Ruth E. Rinklin; Production Assistant, M. Brook Porter; Technical Supervisor, Arthur Siccardi; Wardrobe, Elonzo Dann; Stage Managers, Donald Christy, Peter Aaronson, Raymond Chandler, Jack Horner; Press, Sid Garfield, Mike Hall Associates, Rogers & Cowan; Presented by Alexander H. Cohen at Radio City Music Hall on Sunday evening, February 14, 1982.*

PARTICIPATING ARTISTS

Peter Allen, Steve Allen, June Allyson, Don Ameche, Annie (Allison Smith) and Sandy, Susan Anton, Lucie Arnaz, Beatrice Arthur, Edward Asner, Christopher Atkins, Lauren Bacall, Catherine Bach, Pearl Bailey, Martin Balsam, Priscilla Barnes, Harry Belafonte, Tony Bennett, Milton Berle, Pamela Blair, Tom Bosley, Danielle Brisebois, George Burns, Ellen Burstyn, James Caan, Sid Caesar, James Cagney, Diahann Carroll, Nell Carter, Dick Cavett, Richard Chamberlain, Carol Channing, Cher, Dick Clark, Imogene Coca, Joan Collins, Peter Cook, Bud Cort, Howard Cosell, Christopher Cross, Cathy Lee Crosby, Arlene Dahl, Dance Theatre of Harlem (Lowell Smith, Virginia Johnson), Bette Davis, Sammy Davis, Jr., Pam Dawber, Frances Dee, Robert DeNiro, Colleen Dewhurst, Danny DeVito, Joyce DeWitt, Placido Domingo, Alfred Drake, Doobie Brothers, Sandy Duncan, Nancy Dussault, Linda Evans, Douglas Fairbanks, Jr., Morgan Fairchild, Lola Falana, Peter Falk, Marty Feldman, Jose Ferrer, Peggy Fleming, Jane Fonda, John Forsythe, Phyllis Frelich, Eva Gabor, Anthony Geary, Andy Gibbs, Melissa Gilbert, Lillian Gish, Ruth Gordon, Princess Grace, Farley Granger, Linda Gray, Rocky Graziano, Joel Grey, Charles Grodin, Harry Guardino, Robert Guillaume, Larry Hagman, Margaret Hamilton, Marvin Hamlisch, Valerie Harper, Julie Harris, The Harlem Globetrotters, Goldie Hawn, Helen Hayes, Sherman Hemsley, Florence Henderson, Doug Henning, Judd Hirsch, Dustin Hoffman, Celeste Holm, Lena Horne, Ken Howard, Barnard Hughes, Anne Jeffreys, Ann Jillian, Van Johnson, Louis Jourdan, Howard Keel, Gene Kelly, Deborah Kerr, Richard Kiley, Alan King, Robert Klein, Jack Klugman, Ted Knight, Mayor Edward I. Koch, Burt Lancaster, Frank Langella, Linda Lavin, Michael Learned, Michele Lee, Janet Leigh, Jack Lemmon, David Letterman, Hal Linden, Gina Lollobrigida, Dorothy Loudon, Myrna Loy, Penny Marshall, Mary Martin, James Mason, Gavin MacLeod, Joel McCrea, Ethel Merman, Dina Merrill, Ann Miller, Liza Minnelli, Anna Moffo, Dudley Moore, Mary Tyler Moore, Roger Moore, Paul Newman, Leonard Nimoy, New York Yankees, Jerry Orbach, Al Pacino, Gregory Peck, Anthony Perkins, Miss Piggy, Jane Powell, Robert Preston, Victoria Principal, Anthony Quinn, Charlotte Rae, Tony Randall, Lionel Richie, Jason Robards, Pernell Roberts, Mickey Rooney, The Rockettes, John Rubinstein, Jane Russell, Isabel Sanford, John Schneider, Ricky Schroder, George Segal, William Shatner, Brooke Shields, Sylvia Sidney, Alexis Smith, Rick Springfield, Robert Sterling, James Stewart, Beatrice Straight, Lee Strasberg, Donald Sutherland, Elizabeth Taylor, Daniel Travanti, Cicely Tyson, Liv Ullmann, Peter Ustinov, Ben Vereen, Orson Welles, Robin Williams, Henry Winkler, Henny Youngman, and dancers: David Askler, Gary Gendell, David Gibson, Michael Leeds, Jerry Mitchell, Robert Warners, Anita Ehrler, Mary Sue Finnerty, Philomena Nowlin, Jo Ann Ogawa, Julie Pars, Kathryn Wright

*A Centennial Celebration for the Actors' Fund of America.

COME BACK TO THE 5 & DIME, JIMMY DEAN, JIMMY DEAN

By Ed Graczyk; Director, Robert Altman; Scenery, David Gropman; Costumes, Scott Bushnell; Lighting, Paul Gallo; Sound, Richard Fitzgerald; Casting Director/Assistant to Director, Scott Bushnell; Hairstylist, Gerry Leddy; Manager, Mitzi Harder; Technical Supervisor, Jeremiah J. Harris; Props, Paul Biega; Wardrobe, Ben Wilson; Production Assistant, Roma Friedman; Presented by Dan Fisher, Joseph Clapsaddle, Joel Brykman and Jack Lawrence at the Martin Beck Theatre. Opened Thursday, February 18, 1982.*

CAST

Juanita	Sudie Bond	Edna Louise	Marta Heflin
Sissy	Cher	Martha	Ann Risley
Mona	Sandy Dennis	Alice Ann	Dianne Turley Travis
Joe	Mark Patton	Clarissa	Ruth Miller
Sue Ellen	Gena Ramsel	Joanne	Karen Black
Stella May	Kathy Bates		

UNDERSTUDIES: Ann Risley (Mona/Joanne), Gena Ramsel (Sissy/Stella), Ruth Miller (Juanita), Dianne Turley Travis (Edna), Joey Alan Phipps (Joe)
  A play in two acts. The action alternates between September 30, 1975 and 1955.

General Managers: Joseph Harris, Ira Bernstein, Steven E. Goldstein; *Press:* Jeffrey Richards, C. George Willard, Robert Ganshaw, Ted Killmer, Helen Stern, Richard Humleker; *Stage Managers:* John Brigleb, Jerry Rice

* Closed April 4, 1982 after 52 performances and 4 previews. Originally produced Off Broadway at the Hudson Guild Theatre Feb. 27, 1980 for 30 performances.

LITTLE JOHNNY JONES

Book, Music and Lyrics by George M. Cohan; Adapted by Alfred Uhry; Director, Gerald Gutierrez; Scenery, Robert Randolph; Lighting, Thomas Skelton; Costumes, David Toser; Sound, Abe Jacob; Choreography and Musical Staging, Dan Siretta; Musical Direction, Lynn Crigler; Additional Orchestrations, Eddie Sauter, Mack Schlefer; Dance Arrangements, Russell Warner; Vocal Arrangements and additional Dance Arrangements, Robert Fisher; Musical Consultant, Alfred Simon; Production Associate, Warren Pincus; Production Supervisor, Robert V. Strauss; Props, Paul Mazurek, Charles Zuckerman; Management Assistants, Barbara Softcheck, Beth Fremgen; Wardrobe, Colleen Gieryn, Walter Douglas; Hairstylist, Howard Leonard; Assistant to Director, Jennifer McCray; Casting, Warren Pincus; Assistant Conductor, Don Rebic; Production Assistant, Charles Suisman; Presented by James M. Nederlander, Steven Leber, David Krebs and JFK Center at the Alvin Theatre. Opened Sunday, March 21, 1982.*

CAST

Starter at Hotel Cecil	Jack Bittner	Whitney Wilson	Ernie Sabella
Anthony Anstey	Peter Van Norden	Bellboy	Al Micacchion
Florabelle Fly, Society Editor	Jane Galloway	Johnny Jones, American jockey	Donny Osmond
Timothy D. McGee	Tom Rolfing	Mrs. Kenworth, Goldie's aunt	Anna McNeely
Goldie Gates, copper heiress	Maureen Brennan	Announcer/Capt. Squirvy	Jack Bittner
Sing-Song, Sports Editor	Bruce Chew	Newsboy	David Fredericks

AMERICAN BOYS, PORTERS, SAILORS: Richard Dodd, David Fredericks, James Homan, Gary Kirsch, Bobby Longbottom, Al Micacchion, David Monzione, Keith Savage

AMERICAN GIRLS: Colleen Ashton, Teri Corcoran, Susie Fenner, Linda Gradl, Debra Grimm, Lori Lynott, Annette Michelle, Mayme Paul

STANDBYS AND UNDERSTUDIES: Jamie Torcellini (Johnny), Colleen Ashton (Mrs. Kenworth/Florabelle), Susie Fenner (Goldie), Gary Kirsch (Timothy), Earl Aaron Levine (Anthony/Starter/Announcer/Capt. Squirvy/Sing-Song/Whitney), Tammy Silva, Jonathan Aronson, Jamie Torcellini (Dance Alternates)

MUSICAL NUMBERS: The Cecil in London, Then I'd Be Satisfied with Life, Yankee Doodle Boy, Oh You Wonderful Boy, The Voice in My Heart, Finaletta, Captain of a Ten Day Boat, Goodbye Flo, Life's a Funny Proposition, Let's You and I Just Say Goodbye, Give My Regards to Broadway, Extra! Extra!, American Ragtime, Finale.
  A musical in 2 acts and 8 scenes. The action takes place in England, New York and Saratoga in 1904.

General Management: Marvin A. Krauss Associates; *Assistant Company Manager:* Susan B. Frost; *Press:* Fred Nathan, Eileen McMahon, Francine L. Trevens, Anne S. Abrams; *Stage Managers:* Robert V. Straus, John Actman, Earl Aaron Levine

* Closed March 21, 1982 after 1 performance and 29 previews.

Above: (L) Karen Black, Mark Patton, Sandy Dennis, Sudie Bond, Cher in "Come Back to the 5 & Dime, Jimmy Dean" *(Jean Pagliuso Photo)*
(R) Donny Osmond (C) in "Little Johnny Jones" *(Martha Swope Photo)*

ENCORE

"50 Golden Years of Showstoppers"; Producer-Director, Robert F. Jani; Musical Director, Tom Bahler; Scenery, Charles Lisanby; Lighting, Ken Billington; Staging and Choreography, Adam Grammis, Shozo Nakano, Geoffrey Holder, Linda Lemac, Frank Wagner, Violet Holmes; Costumes, Michael Casey; Conductor, Joseph Klein; Scenic Coordinator, Terry Carriker; Assistants to Producer, Ken Dresser, Nancy Williams, Nance Siemmons, Lauri Warner, Linda Sirkus, Nancy Fager, Stephanie Revesz; Cast Coordinator, Linda Lemac; Hairstylist/Makeup, James Amaral, Peter Bonsignore; Assistant Conductor, Fernando Pasqualone; Presented by Radio City Music Hall Productions for its Golden Jubilee Spectacular at Radio City Music Hall. Opened Friday, March 26, 1982.*

COMPANY

PRINCIPALS: Wendy Edmead, Tom Garrett, Michael Kubala, Kuniko Narai, Deborah Phelan, Justin Ross, Luis Villanueva, Karen Zjemba

ROCKETTES: Lois Ann Alston, Kathy Beatty, Dottie Belle, Susan Boron, Beth Chanin, Barbara Ann Cittadino, Susan Cleland, Eileen Collins, Brie Daniels, Susanne Doris, Jackie Fancy, Deniene Fenn, Alexis Ficks, Prudy Gray, Leslie Gryzko, Jennifer Hammond, Carol Harbich, Cindy Hughes, Stephanie James, Joan Kelleher, Pam Kelleher, Dee Dee Knapp, Judy Little, Sonja Livingston, Mary McNamara, Lynn Newton, Kerri Pearsall, Cindy Peiffer, Gerri Presky, Terry Spano, Pam Stacey, Lynn Sullivan, Susan Theobold, Carol Toman, Pat Tully, Darlene Wendy, Rose Ann Woolsey, Phyllis Wujko

NEW YORKERS: John Aller, David Brownlee, Rick Conant, Dale Furry, Edyie Fleming Geistman, Sonya Hensley, David Michael Johnson, Joe Joyce, Connie Kunkle, Rosemary Loar, Keith Locke, Edward Prostak, Susan Streater, Scott Willis

DANCERS: David Askler, Robert Bolling, Leigh Catlett, Cisco X. Drayton, Larry Lynd, Will Mead, Jackie Patterson, David Roman, Stan Shelmire

PROGRAM

You're at the Music Hall, Encore, Our Scrapbook of Memories, The Glory of Easter, Ohka-No-Zu (Cherry Blossom), Rhapsody in Blue, Showstoppers, Bolero, Fifty Years of American Popular Music, Dancing in Diamonds, That's Entertainment, A Salute to the Music Hall.

Stage Managers: Donald Christy, Jack Horner, Ray Chandler, Peter Aaronson; *Press:* Gifford/Wallace, Keith Sherman

*Still playing May 31, 1982.

Finale of "Encore" Right: Betty Miller, John Vickery, Philip Bosco
in "Eminent Domain"

EMINENT DOMAIN

By Percy Granger: Director, Paul Austin; Scenery, Michael Miller; Costumes, Jennifer von Mayrhauser; Lighting, Lowell Achziger; Production Coordinator, Lee Blattau; Casting, Lynn Kressel; Wardrobe, Millicent Hacker; Props, Frank Jauser; Presented by Circle in the Square (Theodore Mann, Artistic Director; Paul Libin, Managing Director) at the Circle in the Square/Uptown. Opened Sunday, March 28, 1982.*

CAST

Holmes Bradford	Philip Bosco	Stoddard Oates	Scott Burkholder
Katie Bradford	Betty Miller	John Ramsey	Paul Collins
Victor Salt	John Vickery		

A drama in 2 acts and 6 scenes. The action takes place during February 1975 in a university town in the midwest.

Company Manager: William Conn; *Press:* Merle Debuskey, David Roggensack; *Stage Manager:* Michael F. Ritchie

* Closed May 23, 1982 after 57 performances and 11 previews.

AGNES OF GOD

By John Pielmeier; Director, Michael Lindsay-Hogg; Scenery, Eugene Lee; Costumes, Carrie Robbins; Lighting, Roger Morgan; Assistant to Producers, Donna Donaldson; General Assistant, Barbara Hodgen; Wardrobe, Peter Fitzgerald; Props, Sherry Herbert; Casting, Hughes/Moss; Hairstylist, Lyn Quiyou; Presented by Kenneth Waissman, Lou Kramer, Paramount Theatre Productions at the Music Box. Opened Tuesday, March 30, 1982.*

CAST

Agnes .... Amanda Plummer   Mother Miriam Ruth .... Geraldine Page
Dr. Martha Livingstone .... Elizabeth Ashley

UNDERSTUDIES: Susan Riskin (Dr. Livingstone/Mother Ruth), Sally Klein (Agnes)
   A drama in two acts.

General Manager: Edward H. Davis; *Assistant to General Manager:* Dorothy Finn; *Company Manager:* Robb Lady; *Press:* Betty Lee Hunt, Maria Cristina Pucci, James Sapp; *Stage Managers:* Larry Forde, Mark Rubinsky

*Still playing May 31, 1982. Miss Plummer received a 1982 "Tony" Award as Best Featured Actress in a Play.

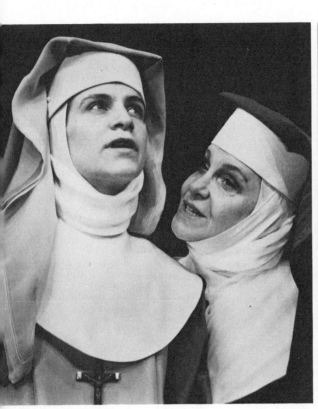 

SOLOMON'S CHILD

By Tom Dulack; Director, John Tillinger; Scenery, Marjorie Bradley Kellogg; Costumes, Jennifer von Mayrhauser; Lighting, Richard Nelson; Management Associate, Thelma Cooper; Assistant to Producers, Faryl Palles; Management Assistant, Penny Peck; Casting, Johnson/Liff Associates, Andrew Zerman; Presented by FDM Productions Inc. (Francois de Menil/Harris Maslansky) at the Little Theatre. Opened Thursday, April 8, 1982.*

CAST

Allen.. John McMartin   Balthazar .... Anthony Zerbe
Joe .... Ellis Williams   Naomi.. Deborah Hedwall
Sam .... Tom Nardini   Liz .... Joanna Merlin
Shelley .... Evan Handler   Trooper .... Mike Houlihan

STANDBYS: John Seitz (Allan/Balthazar), Ilvi Dulack (Naomi), Munson Hicks (Joe/Sam/Trooper)
   A drama in two acts. The action takes place at the present time in the Solomon's summer house in the Catskill Mountains.

General Management: Dorothy Olim Associates; *Assistant Company Manager:* George Elmer; *Press:* Betty Lee Hunt, Maria Cristina Pucci, James Sapp; *Stage Managers:* Franklin Keysar, Robin Kevrick

*Closed April 10, 1982 after 4 performances and 14 previews.

Above: (L) Amanda Plummer, Geraldine Page in "Agnes of God" *(Ken Howard Photo)* **(R) John McMartin, Evan Handler, Joanna Merlin**
in "Solomon's Child" *(Gerry Goodstein Photo)*

MEDEA

Freely adapted from Euripides by Robinson Jeffers; Director, Robert Whitehead; Scenery, Ben Edwards; Costumes, Jane Greenwood; Lighting, Martin Aronstein; Music and Sound, David Amram; Casting, Terry Fay; Props, Michael Gallagher; Wardrobe, Penny Davis; Hairstylist, Robert Cybula; Assistant to Director, Doris Blum; Management Assistants, Lynn Fero, Susan Moritz; Administrative Assistants, Elise Jordan, Jerry R. Moore, Ruth Bogen, Belle Jeanne Stolz; Wigs, Paul Huntley; Presented by Barry and Fran Weissler by arrangement with Kennedy Center and Bunny and Warren Austin at the Cort Theatre. Opened Sunday, May 2, 1982.*

CAST

The Nurse	Judith Anderson	Creon	Paul Sparer
The Tutor	Don McHenry	Jason	Mitchell Ryan
The Children	Jason Kimmell, Christopher Garvin	Aegeus	Peter Brandon
First Woman of Corinth	Pauline Flanagan	Jason's Slave	Lucien Douglas
Second Woman of Corinth	Harriet Nichols	Handmaidens	Emily King, Amy Lovell
Third Woman of Corinth	Giulia Pagano	Attendants to Jason	Wayne Carson, Ralph Roberts
Medea	Zoe Caldwell		

STANDBYS AND UNDERSTUDIES: Guilia Pagano (Medea), Barbara Lester (Nurse/1st Woman), Peter Brandon (Jason), Wayne Carson (Creon/Aegeus/Slave), Ralph Roberts (Tutor), Amy Lovell (2nd Woman), Emily King (3rd Woman), Stephen Garvin (Children)

A tragedy in two acts. The action occurs in front of Medea's house in Corinth.

General Managers: Max Allentuck, Alecia Parker; *Press:* David Powers, Barbara Carroll, Thomas Trenkle; *Stage Managers:* Mitchell Erickson, Stephen Nasuta

* Closed June 27, 1982 after 65 performances and 7 previews. Miss Caldwell received a 1982 "Tony" Award as Best Actress in a Play. Original production opened Dec. 15, 1947 at the National Theatre (now Nederlander Theatre) and played 214 performances with Judith Anderson in the title role for which she received a "Tony."

MASTER HAROLD ... AND THE BOYS

Written and Directed by Athol Fugard; Setting, Jane Clark; Costumes, Sheila McLamb; Lighting, David Noling; Stage Movement, Wesley Fata; Technical Supervision, Theatrical Services; Wardrobe, Alan Eskolsky; Assistant to Director, Russ Lori Rosenweig; Management Assistants, Jane E. Cooper, Edson Scudder, Alix Morrison, Lisa Hogarty; Casting, Meg Simon/Fran Kumin; Yale Repertory Theatre production; Presented by The Shubert Organization, Freyberg/Bloch Productions, Dasha Epstein, Emanuel Azenberg, David Geffen at the Lyceum Theatre. Opened Tuesday, May 4, 1982.*

CAST

Sam	Zakes Mokae	Hally	Lonny Price
Willie	Danny Glover	STANDBYS:	Bill Cobbs, Charles Michael Wright

A drama performed without intermission. The action takes place in the St. Georges Park Tea Room on a wet and windy afternoon in Port Elizabeth, South Africa in 1950.

General Manager: Jose Vega; *Company Manager:* Linda Cohen; *Press:* Bill Evans, Sandra Manley, Leslie Anderson; *Stage Managers:* Neal Ann Stephens, Sally J. Greenhut

* Still playing May 31, 1982. Mr. Mokae received a 1982 "Tony" Award for Best Actor in a Play.

Above: (L) Zoe Caldwell, Judith Anderson in "Medea" *(Jack Buxbaum Photo)* (R) Zakes Mokae, Lonny Price, Danny Glover in "Master Harold ... and the boys" *(Martha Swope Photo)*

THE HOTHOUSE

By Harold Pinter; Director, Adrian Hall; Scenery and Lighting, Eugene Lee; Costumes, William Lane; Associate Producer, Harvey Elliott; Wardrobe, Cheryl Woronoff; Production Assistants, Michael Thompson, Jeffrey Eisenberg, Deborah Elliott; Trinity Square Repertory Company production; Presented by Arthur Cantor and Dorothy Cullman at the Playhouse Theatre. Opened Thursday, May 6, 1982.*

CAST

Roote	George Martin	Lush	Peter Gerety
Gibbs	Richard Kavanaugh	Tubb	Howard London
Lamb	Dan Butler	Lobb	David C. Jones
Miss Cutts	Amy Van Nostrand		

A drama in two acts. The action takes place Christmas morning and night, and moves back and forth from Roote's office, the sitting room, the soundproof room, hallways and stairways throughout the British institution; and finally to the Ministry in London and back.

General/Company Manager: Harvey Elliott; *Press:* Arthur Cantor, Harvey Elliott; *Stage Managers:* Robert Crawley, Ken Bryant

* Closed May 30, 1982 after 29 performances and 7 previews.

IS THERE LIFE AFTER HIGH SCHOOL?

Book, Jeffrey Kindley; Music and Lyrics, Craig Carnelia; Director, Robert Nigro; Based on book of same title by Ralph Keyes; Set, John Lee Beatty; Costumes, Carol Oditz; Lighting, Beverly Emmons; Sound, Tom Morse; Musical Direction and Orchestration, Bruce Coughlin; Associate Producer, Robert Feiden; Casting, Shirley Rich; Assistant to Director, James Kramer; Props, Michael Lynch, Jan Marasek; Wardrobe, Dean Jackson; Hairstylist, Frank Melon; Production Assistants, Marsha Best, Marc Brown; Music Coordinator, Earl Shendell; Presented by Clive Davis, Francois de Menil, Harris Maslansky, 20th Century-Fox Theatre Productions at the Ethel Barrymore Theatre. Opened Friday, May 7, 1982.*

CAST

Raymond Baker, Philip Hoffman, Cynthia Carle, David Patrick Kelly, Alma Cuervo, Maureen Silliman, Sandy Faison, James Widdoes, Harry Groener

UNDERSTUDIES: Scott Bakula, Marcus Olson, Lauren White

MUSICAL NUMBERS: The Kid Inside, Things I Learned in High School, Second Thoughts, Nothing Really Happened, Beer, For Them, Diary of a Homecoming Queen, Thousands of Trumpets, Reunion, High School All Over Again, Fran and Jane, I'm Glad You Didn't Know Me
  A musical in two acts.

General Management: James Walsh; *Company Manager:* Susan Bell; *Press:* Jeffrey Richards, C. George Willard, Ben Morse, Bob Ganshaw, Helen Stern, Ted Killmer, Richard Humleker

* Closed May 16, 1982 after 12 performances and 41 previews.

Above (L) Peter Gerety, George Martin in "The Hothouse" *(Constance Brown Photo)* (R) Top: Raymond Baker, Cynthia Carle, Harry Groener, Philip Hoffman, Alma Cuervo, Below: David Patrick Kelly, James Widdoes (R) *(Peter Cunningham Photo)*

NINE

Book, Arthur Kopit; Adaptation from the Italian, Mario Fratti; Music and Lyrics, Maury Yeston; Director, Tommy Tune; Scenery, Lawrence Miller; Costumes, William Ivey Long; Lighting, Marcia Madeira; Musical Supervision and Orchestrations, Jonathan Tunick; Musical Director, Wally Harper; Choral Composition and Musical Continuity, Maury Yeston; Artistic Associate, Thommie Walsh; Sound, Jack Mann; Hairstylist, Michael Gottfried; Casting, Hughes/Moss; Associate Producer, Mark Beigelman; Presented in association with Shulamith & Michael N. Appell, Jerry Wexler and Michel Kleinman Productions; Props, Michael Durnin; Special Assistant to Mr. Tune, Priscilla Lopez; Technical Coordinator, Richard Siegel; Wardrobe, Judith Giles, Sydney Smith; Presented by Michel Stuart, Harvey J. Klaris, Roger S. Berlind, James M. Nederlander, Francine LeFrak, Kenneth D. Greenblatt at the Forty-sixth Street Theatre. Opened Sunday, May 9, 1982.*

CAST

Guido Contini	Raul Julia	Maria	Jeanie Bowers
Guido at an early age	Cameron Johann	Francesca	Kim Criswell
Luisa	Karen Akers	Venetian Gondolier	Colleen Dodson
Carla	Anita Morris	Giulietta	Louise Edeiken
Claudia	Shelly Burch	Annabella	Nancy McCall
Guido's Mother	Taina Elg	Diana	Cynthia Meryl
Liliane LaFleur	Liliane Montevecchi	Renata	Rita Rehn
Lina Darling	Laura Kenyon	*The Germans:*	
Stephanie Necrophorus	Stephanie Cotsirilos	Gretchen von Krupt	Lulu Downs
Our Lady of the Spa	Kate Dezina	Heidi von Sturm	Linda Kerns
Mama Maddelena, Chief of Chambermaids	Camille Saviola	Olga von Sturm	Dee Etta Rowe
Saraghina	Kathi Moss	Ilsa von Hesse	Alaina Warren Zachary
		Young Guido's Schoolmates	Evans Allen, Jadrien Steele, Patrick Wilcox

STANDBYS AND UNDERSTUDIES: Clifford David (Guido), Cynthia Meryl (Luisa/Liliane), Kim Criswell (Claudia/Carla), Alaina Warren Zachary (Guido's Mother), Colleen Dodson (Our Lady of the Spa), Rita Rehn (Stephanie), Camille Saviola (Saraghina), Lulu Downs (Mama Maddelena), Patrick Wilcox (Young Guido), Julie J. Hafner (Germans), Dorothy Kiara (Italians)

MUSICAL NUMBERS: Delle Donne, Spa Music, Not Since Chaplin, Guido's Song, Coda di Guido, The Germans at the Spa, My Husband Makes Movies, A Call from the Vatican, Only with You, Folies Bergeres, Nine, Ti Voglio Bene/Be Italian, Bells of St. Sebastian, A Man Like You, Unusual Way, Grand Canal, Contini Submits, Tarantella, Every Girl in Venice, Marcia Di Ragazzi, Recitativo, Amor, Only You, Simple, Be On Your Own, I Can't Make This Movie, Getting Tall

A musical in two acts.

General Management: Berenice Weiler/Marilyn S. Miller; *Press:* Judy Jacksina, Glenna Freedman, Angela Wilson, Diane Tomlinson, Susannah Blinkoff; *Stage Managers:* Charles Blackwell, Bruce H. Lumpkin, Nancy Lynch

* Still playing May 31, 1982. Recipient of 1982 "Tony" Awards for Best Musical, Best Score, Best Direction, Best Costumes, and Best Featured Actress in a Musical (Liliane Montevecchi)

Peter Cunningham Photos

Liliane Montevecchi

Karen Akers, Anita Morris Above: (C) Raul Julia

BEYOND THERAPY

By Christopher Durang; Director, John Madden; Settings, Andrew Jackness; Costumes, Jennifer von Mayrhauser; Lighting, Paul Gallo; Music Coordinator, Jack Feldman; Commissioned and originally produced by the Phoenix Theatre; Production Assistant, Fortune Procopio; Technical Coordinator, Theatre Services Inc.; Props, George Green, Robert Bostwick; Wardrobe, Adelaide Laurino; Casting, Mary Colquhoun; Presented by Warner Theatre Productions, Claire Nichtern, FDM Productions, Francois de Menil and Harris Maslansky at the Brooks Atkinson Theatre. Opened Wednesday, May 26, 1982.*

CAST

Bruce	John Lithgow	Charlotte	Kate McGregor-Stewart
Prudence	Dianne Wiest	Bob	Jack Gilpin
Stuart	Peter Michael Goetz	Andrew	David Pierce

STANDBY: James Eckhouse

A comedy in 2 acts and 9 scenes. The action takes place at the present time in a restaurant, Dr. Stuart Framingham's office, Charlotte Wallace's office, and Bruce's apartment.

General Management: Gatchell & Neufeld, Douglas C. Baker; *Company Manager:* Roger Gindi; *Press:* Jeffrey Richards, C. George Willard, Ben Morse, Robert Ganshaw, Helen Stern, Ted Killmer, Richard Humleker; *Stage Managers:* Craig Jacobs, Trey Hunt

* Closed June 13, 1982 after 21 performances and 11 previews. Commissioned and originally produced Off Broadway Jan. 5, 1981 by the Phoenix Theatre for 24 performances.

DO BLACK PATENT LEATHER SHOES REALLY REFLECT UP?

Book, John R. Powers based on his novel; Music and Lyrics, James Quinn, Alaric Jans; Director, Mike Nussbaum; Musical Numbers Staged by Thommie Walsh; Settings, James Maronek; Costumes, Nancy Potts; Lighting, Marilyn Rennagel; Sound, Richard Fitzgerald; Orchestrations and Musical Supervision, Jerome Jay Dryer; Musical Direction and Vocal Arrangements, Larry Hochman; Dance Arrangements, Peter Larson; Production Supervisor, William Gardner; Associate Choreographer, Ronna Kaye; Props, Walter Murphy; Casting, Professional Casting Associates, Alan Coleridge; Wardrobe, Arlene Konowitz; Presented by Mavin Productions Inc., Libby Adler Mages and Daniel A. Golman at the Alvin Theatre. Opened Thursday, May 27, 1982.*

CAST

Eddie Ryan	Russ Thacker	Felix Lindor	Don Stitt
Secretary	Amy Miller	Mike Depki	Peter Heuchling
Becky Bakowski	Maureen Moore	Nancy Ralansky	Karen Tamburrelli
Sister Melanie	Amy Miller	Mary Kenny	Christine Gradl
Sister Lee	Ellen Crawford	Louie Schlang	Jason Graae
Father O'Reilly	Robert Fitch	Sister Helen	Elizabeth Hansen
Virginia Lear	Vicki Lewis	Sister Monica Marie	Catherine Fries

UNDERSTUDIES: Russ Billingsly (Eddie/Felix/Louie), Orrin Reiley (Father O'Reilly/Mike), Catherine Fries (Becky/Nancy/Mary), Amy Miller (Sister Lee/Sister Helen), Carol Estey (Secretary/Sisters Monica, Melanie, Virginia)

MUSICAL NUMBERS: Get Ready Eddie, The Greatest Gift, It's the Nuns, Little Fat Girls, Cookie Cutters, Patron Saints, How Far Is Too Far, Doo-waa Doo-wee, I Must Be in Love, Friends the Best Of, Mad Bombers and Prom Queens, Late Bloomer and Prom Montage, Thank God

A musical in 2 acts and 14 scenes.

General Manager: Richard Horner Associates; *Company Manager:* Bruce Birkenhead; *Press:* Fred Nathan, Eileen McMahon, Louis Sica, Anne S. Abrams

* Closed May 30, 1982 after 5 performances and 15 previews.

Above: (L) Kate McGregor-Stewart, John Lithgow, Dianne Wiest, Peter Michael Goetz in "Beyond Therapy" (R) Russ Thacker (L), Ellen Crawford (C) in "Do Black Patent Leather Shoes Really Reflect Up?" *(Martha Swope Photos)*

THE BEST LITTLE WHOREHOUSE IN TEXAS

Book, Larry L. King, Peter Masterson; Music and Lyrics, Carol Hall; Directed by Peter Masterson and Tommy Tune; Musical Numbers Staged by Tommy Tune; Scenery, Marjorie Bradley Kellogg; Costumes, Ann Roth; Lighting, Dennis Parichy; Music Supervised and Arranged by Robert Billig; Hairstylist, Michael Gottfried; Associate Choreographer, Thommie Walsh; Associate Producers, Bonnie Champion, Danny Kreitzberg; Props, Michael Durin, Douglas R. Siegler; Conductor, Pete Blue; Production Assistant, Jack Tantleff; Assistant to Director, Janie Rosenthal; Wardrobe, Beverly Meyer; Hairstylists, John Barker, Richard Stein; Presented by Stevie Phillips in association with Universal Pictures at the Eugene O'Neil Theatre. Opened Monday, May 31, 1982.*

CAST

Band................ Craig Chambers, Racine Romaguera, Harvey Shapiro, Pete Blue, Chuck Zeuren, Marty Laster	Ginger .... Roxie Lucas
Cowboy/Aggie 71/Photographer/Reporter .... Beau Allen	Beatrice .... Clare Fields
Cowboy/Dogette/Aggie 7/Photographer .... Don Bernhardt	Taddy Jo .... Merilee Magnuson
Cowboy/Aggie 17/Photographer..................... Michael Boyd	Ruby Rae.................................. Diana Broderick
Farmer/Dogette/Aggie 77...................... Andy Parker	Eloise .... Karen Sutherland
Shy Kid/Cameraman/Aggie 21/Photographer/ Reporter............................... Eric Aaron	Durla .... Ruth Gottschall
Miss Wulla Jean .... Louise Quick	Dogette/Aggie 12 .... George Dvorsky
Traveling Salesman/C. J. Scruggs/Chip Brewster/ Governor .... Patrick Hamilton	Dogette/Aggie 11/Governor's Aide .... Joel Anderson
Slick Dude/Soundman/Aggie 1/Leroy Sliney .... Roger Berdahl	Melvin P. Thorpe .... Clinton Allmon
Choir .... Don Bernhardt, Karen Sutherland, Diana Broderick, Merilyn J. Johnson, Clare Fields, George Dvorsky	Melvin Thorpe Singers................... Karen Sutherland, Diana Broderick, Beau Allen, Clare Fields, Eric Aaron, Merilee Magnuson
Angel .... Susann Fletcher	Sheriff Ed Earl Dodd .... Gil Rogers
Shy .... Cheryl Ebarb	Mayor Rufus Poindexter/Senator Wingwoah .... J. Frank Lucas
Jewel................................. Delores Hall	Edsel Mackey .... Robert Moyer
Mona Stangley.................................. Carlin Glynn	Doatsey Mae/Reporter......................... Becky Gelke
Miss Mona's Girls:	T. V. Announcer........................... Larry L. King
Linda Lou .... Valerie Leigh Bixler	Angelette Imogene Charlene .... Mimi Bessette
Dawn .... Mimi Bessette	Angelettes .... Merilee Magnuson, Ruth Bottschall, Karen Sutherland, Diana Broderick, Valerie Leigh Bixler
	Aggie Specialty Dance .... Tom Cashin

UNDERSTUDIES: Becky Gelke (Miss Mona), Ruth Gottschall (Ginger), Robert Moyer (Sheriff/Mayor/Senator/Scruggs), Roxie Lucas (Governor/Doatsey Mae), Mimi Bessette (Angel), Marilyn J. Johnson (Jewel), Roger Berdahl (Mackey/Thorpe), Clare Fields (Shy), Karen Sutherland (Dawn), Andy Parker (Narrator), Patti D' Beck (Swing Dancer)

MUSICAL NUMBERS: Prologue, 20 Fans, A Lil Ole Bitty Pissant Country Place, Girl You're a Woman, Watch Dog Theme, Texas Has a Whorehouse in It, 24 Hours of Lovin', Doatsey Mae, Angelette March, Aggie Song, The Sidestep, No Lies, Good Old Girl, Hard Candy Christmas, Bus from Amarillo A musical in two acts. The action takes place in the State of Texas.

General Management: Schlissel & Kingwill; *Company Manager:* Leonard A. Mulhern; *Press:* Jeffrey Richards, C. George Willard, Robert Ganshaw, Ben Morse, Ted Killmer, Helen Stern, Richard Humleker; *Stage Managers:* Paul J. Phillips, Gerry Burkhardt, Louise Quick

* Closed July 24, 1982 after 63 performances and 9 previews. Original production opened Monday, June 19, 1978 and ran for 1584 performances at the 46th Street Theatre. See THEATRE WORLD Vol. 34.

Carlin Glynn, Delores Hall and band

Miss Mona's Girls

AMADEUS

By Peter Shaffer; Director, Peter Hall; Production Design, John Bury; Associate Scenic Designer, John David Ridge; Associate Lighting Designer, Beverly Emmons; Music Arranged and Directed by Harrison Birtwistle; Production Coordinator, Brent Peek; Assistant Director, Giles Block; Wardrobe, Rosalie Lahm; Special Effects, Chick Silber; Production Assistant, Virlana Tkacz; Sound, Jack Mann; Wigs/Hairstylist, Paul Huntley; Presented by The Shubert Organization (Gerald Schoenfeld, Chairman; Bernard B. Jacobs, President), Elizabeth I. McCann, Nelle Nugent, Roger S. Berlind at the Broadhurst Theatre. Opened Wednesday, December 17, 1980.*

CAST

Antonio Saliere .... Ian McKellen†1	Priest .... Donald C. Moore†4
The Venticelli .... Gordon Gould, Edward Zang	Giuseppe Bonno .... Russell Gold
Salieri's valet .... Victor Griffin	Teresa Salieri, wife of Saliere.................... Linda Robbins†5
Salieri's cook .... Haskell Gordon†2	Katherine Cavalieri, Salieri's pupil .... Michele Farr†6
Joseph II, Emperor of Austria.................. Nicholas Kepros	Constanze Weber, wife of Mozart.......... Amy Irving†7
Johann Kilian von Strack............... Jonathan Moore†3	Wolfgang Amadeus Mozart...................... Peter Firth†8
Count Orsini-Rosenberg .... Patrick Hines	Major Domo .... Philip Pleasants
Baron von Swieten .... Louis Turenne	

Valets ... Ronald Bagden, David Bryant, Rick Hamilton†9, Richard Jay-Alexander, Peter Kingsley, Mark Torres†10
Citizens of Vienna ... Caris Corfman †11, Kristin Rudrud †12, Russell Gold, Haskell Gordon †13, Victor Griffin, Martin LaPlatney †14, John Pankow †15, Michael McCarty †16, Philip Pleasants, Linda Robbins †17

STANDBYS AND UNDERSTUDIES: Daniel Davis (Salieri), Rene Moreno/David Bryant (Mozart), Mary Elizabeth Mastrantonio (Constanze), Philip Pleasants (Joseph II/Venticello/Bonno), Russell Gold (von Strack/van Swieten/Valet), Donald C. Moore (Orsini-Rosenberg), Patrick Tull (Salieri's Cook), Mary A. Dierson (Teresa/Katherina), Robert Langdon-Lloyd (Venticello/Major Domo/Valets)
    A drama in two acts. The action takes place in Vienna in November 1823, and in recall, the decade 1781–1791.

General Management: McCann & Nugent; *Company Manager:* Susan Gustafson; *Press;* Merle Debuskey, William Schelble; *Stage Managers:* Robert L. Borod, Robert Charles, Ellen Raphael, Richard Jay-Alexander

* Still playing May 31, 1982. Recipient of 1981 Tonys for Best Play, Best Director, Outstanding Actor in a Play (Ian McKellen), Outstanding Scenic Design, Outstanding Lighting Design. For original production see THEATRE WORLD Vol. 37.
† Succeeded by: 1. John Wood, Frank Langella, 2. Donald C. Moore, 3. Paul Harding, James Higgins, 4. Michael McCarty, Patrick Tull, 5. Tian King, Linda Robbins, 6. Caris Corfman, Michele Farr, Mary Elizabeth Mastrantonio, 7. Caris Corfman, Michele Farr, Suzanne Lederer, 8. John Pankow, Dennis Boutsikaris, 9. Daniel Watkins, Benjamin Donenberg, 10. Bill Roberts, 11. Michele Farr, Caris Corfman, Mary Elizabeth Mastrantonio, 12. Michele Farr, Kristin Rudrud, Mary A. Dierson, 13. Donald C. Moore, 14. Brad O'Hare, Robert Langdon-Lloyd, 15. Rene Moreno, 16. Donald C. Moore, Michael McCarty, Patrick Tull, 17. Tian King, Linda Robbins

Martha Swope/Van Williams Photos

John Wood, Peter Firth, Amy Irving   Frank Langella (L), Dennis Boutsikaris (R)

ANNIE

Book, Thomas Meehan; Based on "Little Orphan Annie" comic strip; Music, Charles Strouse; Lyrics, Martin Charnin; Director, Mr. Charnin; Musical Numbers/Choreography, Peter Gennaro; Producers, Irwin Meyer, Stephen R. Friedman, Lewis Allen, Alvin Nederland Associates, JFK Center for the Performing Arts, Icarus Productions, Peter Crane; Sets, David Mitchell; Costumes, Theoni V. Aldredge; Lighting, Judy Rasmuson; Musical Direction, Arnold Gross; Dance Music Arrangements, Peter Howard; Orchestrations, Philip J. Lang; Assistant Conductor, Arthur Wagner; Assistant Choreographer, Don Bonnell; Technical Coordinator, Arthur Siccardi; Wardrobe, Adelaide Laurino, Jeane Frisbie; Hairstylists, Ted Azar, Sonia Rivera, Hector Garcia; Assistant to Director, Janice Steele; Props, Abe Einhorn; Production Assistants, Sylvia Pancotti, Stephen Graham; Sandy owned and trained by William Berloni; Original Cast Album, Columbia Records; Presented by Mike Nichols at the Alvin Theatre. Opened Thursday, April 21, 1977; Moved Sept. 16, 1981 to the ANTA Theatre; October 29, 1981 to the Eugene O'Neill Theatre; Dec. 10, 1981 to the Uris Theatre.*

CAST

Molly . . . . Roxanne Dundish	Sandy . . . . Himself
Pepper . . . . Caroline Daly†1	Lt. Ward/Bert Healy/Morgantheau/Brandeis . . . . Richard Ensslen
Duffy . . . . Sherry Dundish	Sophie/Annette/Ronnie Boylan . . . . Shelly Burch†5
July . . . . Martha Byrne†2	Grace Farrell . . . . Kathryn Boule†6
Tessie . . . . Jennine Babo	Drake . . . . Edwin Bordo
Kate . . . . Tara Kennedy†3	Mrs. Pugh/NBC Page/Perkins . . . . Henrietta Valor†7
Annie . . . . Allison Smith	Miss Greer/Bonnie Boylan . . . . Donna Thomason
Miss Hannigan . . . . Marcia Lewis†4	Cecille/Connie Boylan . . . . Marianne Sanazaro
Bundles McCloskey/Ickes/Sound Effects . . . . R. Martin Klein	Oliver Warbucks . . . . Rhodes Reason†8
Apple Seller/Jimmy Johnson/Howe . . . . Timothy Jecko	Rooster Hannigan . . . . Richard Sabellico†9
Dog Catcher/Fred McCracken/Honor Guard . . . . Larry Ross	Lily . . . . Dorothy Stanley
Dog Catcher/Hull . . . . Richard Walker	FDR . . . . Raymond Thorne

UNDERSTUDIES: Becky Snyder (Annie), Raymond Thorne (Warbucks), Roy Meachum (FDR), Lola Powers (Miss Hannigan), Donna Thomason (Grace), Stephanie Vine (Pepper/Duffy/July/Tessie/Kate), Sherry Dundish (Molly), Larry Ross (Rooster), Beth McVey (Lily), Timothy Jecko (Drake), Richard Walker (Healy), Honey (Sandy), Ensemble: Don Bonnell, Mimi Wallace, Roy Meachum

MUSICAL NUMBERS: Maybe, It's the Hard-Knock Life, Tomorrow, We'd Like to Thank You, Little Girls, I Think I'm Gonna Like It Here, N.Y.C., Easy Street, You Won't Be an Orphan for Long, You're Never Fully Dressed without a Smile, Something Was Missing, I Don't Need Anything But You, Annie, A New Deal for Christmas

A musical in 2 acts and 13 scenes. The action takes place December 11–25, 1933 in New York City.

General Management: Gatchell & Neufeld, Douglas C. Baker; *Company Manager:* Sandy Carlson; *Press:* David Powers, Barbara Carroll; *Stage Managers:* Brooks Fountain, Barrie Moss, Roy Meachum, Larry Mengden

* Still playing May 31, 1982. For original production, see THEATRE WORLD Vol. 33. Recipient of 1977 NY Drama Critics Circle and "Tony" Awards for Best Musical.
† Succeeded by: 1. Stephanie Vine, 2. Becky Snyder, 3. Nicole Nowicki, 4. Ruth Kobart during vacation, 5. Beth McVey, 6. Anne Kerry, Lauren Mitchell, 7. Lola Powers, 8. Harve Presnell, 9. Guy Stroman during vacation.

Martha Swope Photos

Sandy, Allison Smith

Allison Smith, Harve Presnell, Sandy

BARNUM

Music, Cy Coleman; Lyrics, Michael Stewart; Book, Mark Bramble; Directed and Staged by Joe Layton; Scenery, David Mitchell; Costumes, Theoni V. Aldredge; Lighting, Craig Miller; Sound, Otts Munderloh; Orchestrations, Hershy Kay; Vocal Arrangements, Cy Coleman, Jeremy Stone; Music Director, Peter Howard; Production Supervisor, Mary Porter Hall; Hairstylists, Ted Azar, Chris Calabrese, Vincent Esoldi, Adele Rubin; Technical Supervisor, Peter Feller; Assistant to Producers, Erik P. Sletteland; Wardrobe, Mary P. Eno; Production Assistants, Michael Gill, Marsha Best; Assistant Conductor, Gregory J. Dlugos, Peter Phillips; Assistant to Director, John Mineo; Props, Ed Slaggert; Original Cast Album, CBS Masterworks Records; Presented by Judy Gordon, Cy Coleman, Maurice Rosenfield, Lois F. Rosenfield in association with Irvin Feld and Kenneth Feld at the St. James Theatre. Opened Wednesday, April 30, 1980.*

CAST

Phineas Taylor Barnum	Jim Dale†1
Chairy Barnum	Glenn Close†2
Ringmaster/Julius Goldschmidt/James A. Bailey	William C. Witter†3
Chester Lyman/Humbert Morrissey	Terrance V. Mann†4
Joice Heth	Terri White†5
Amos Scudder/Edgar Templeton	Kelly Walters†6
Lady Plate Balancer	Catherine Carr†7
Lady Juggler	Barbara Nadel†8
Chief Bricklayer	Edward T. Jacobs†9
White-face Clown	Andy Teirstein†10
Sherwood Stratton	Dirk Lumbard†11
Mrs. Stratton	Sophie Schwab†12
Tom Thumb	Leonard John Crofoot
Susan B. Anthony	Karen Trott
Jenny Lind	Marianne Tatum†13
One-Man Band	Steven Michael Harris
Wilton	Bruce Robertson†14
Lady Aerialist	Robbi Morgan†15
Pianists	Karen Gustafson, Gregory J. Dlugos

STANDBYS AND UNDERSTUDIES: Harvey Evans/Jess Richards (Barnum), Suellen Estey (Chairy/Jenny), Andrea Wright (Jenny), Karen Trott (Chairy), R. J. Lewis (Lyman), Steven Michael Harris (Ringmaster/Bailey/Goldschmidt/Scudder), Fred Feldt (Stratton/Templeton/Morrisey/Tom Thumb), Mary Testa (Joice), Navarre Matlovsky (Wilton), Ensemble; Mary Testa, Jerry Mitchell, Fred Feldt, Paula Grider

MUSICAL NUMBERS: There's a Sucker Born Every Minute, Thank God I'm Old, The Colors of My Life, One Brick at a Time, Museum Song, I Like Your Style, Bigger Isn't Better, Love Makes Such Fools of Us All, Out There, Come Follow the Band, Black and White, Prince of Humbug, Join the Circus
A musical in two acts. The action takes place all over America and the major capitals of the world from 1835 through 1880

General Manager: James Walsh; *Company Manager:* Susan Bell; *Press:* David Powers, Barbara Carroll, Tom Trenkle; *Stage Managers:* Mary Porter Hall, John Beven, Michael Mann, Fred Feldt

* Closed May 16, 1982 after 854 performances and 26 previews. Recipient of 1980 "Tonys" for Best Actor in a Musical (Jim Dale), Best Scenic Design, Best Costumes. For original production see THEATRE WORLD Vol. 36.
† Succeeded by: 1. Tony Orlando during vacation, Mike Burstyn, 2. Catherine Cox, Deborah Reagan, 3. Terrence V. Mann, Kelly Walters, 4. R. J. Lewis, R. Robert Melvin, 5. Lillias White, 6. Richard Gervais, 7. Missy Whitchurch, 8. Mary Testa, Andrea Wright, 9. Fred Garbo Garver, Navarre Matlovsky, 10. Marshall Coid, 11. R. J. Lewis, 12. Andrea Wright, 13. Suellen Estey during vacation, Catherine Gaines, 14. R. J. Lewis, 15. Colleen Flynn

Martha Swope Photos

Catherine Cox, Tony Orlando

Mike Burstyn

Phyllis Frelich, John Rubinstein   Phyllis Frelich, Peter Evans

CHILDREN OF A LESSER GOD

By Mark Medoff; Director, Gordon Davidson; Set, Thomas A. Walsh; Costumes, Nancy Potts; Lighting, Tharon Musser; Associate Producers, William P. Wingate, Kenneth Brecher; Wardrobe, Jim Hodson; Technical Supervisor, Arthur Siccardi; Assistant to Producers, Leslie Butler; Assistant to Director, April Webster; Production Assistant, Neila Ruben; Management Assistant, Jane E. Cooper; Sign Language Consultant, Lou Fant; Interpreters, Jean Worth, Susan Freundlich; Center Theatre Group/Mark Taper Forum production; Presented by Emanuel Azenberg, The Shubert Organization, Dasha Epstein, Ron Dante at the Longacre Theatre. Opened Sunday, March 30, 1980.*

CAST

Sarah Norman	Phyllis Frelich	Mrs. Norman	Scotty Bloch†3
James Leeds	John Rubinstein†1	Lydia	Julianne Gold†4
Orin Dennis	Lewis Merkin	Edna Klein	Lucy Martin
Mr. Franklin	William Frankfather†2		

STANDBYS: Janice I. Cole/Julianna Fjeld (Sarah), Robert Steinberg/Michael Keys-Hall (James), Mary Vreeland (Lydia), Ron Trumble, Jr./Patrick D'Avanzo (Orin), Mike Mearian (Franklin), Jill Andre (Edna/Mrs. Norman)
A drama in two acts. The action takes place at the present time.

General Manager: Jose Vega; *Company Manager:* Barbara Darwall; *Press:* Bill Evans, Sandra Manley, Howard Atlee, Leslie Anderson; *Stage Managers:* Peter von Mayrhauser, Judith Binus

* Closed May 16, 1982 after 887 performances and 9 previews. Recipient of 1980 "Tonys" for Best Play, Best Actress (Phyllis Frelich), Best Actor (John Rubinstein). For original production see THEATRE WORLD Vol. 36.
† Succeeded by: 1. Robert Steinberg, David Ackroyd, Peter Evans, James N. Stephens, 2. Howard Brunner, 3. Augusta Dabney, 4. Janice I. Cole

Martha Swope Photos

A CHORUS LINE

Conceived, Choreographed and Directed by Michael Bennett; Book, James Kirkwood, Nicholas Dante; Music, Marvin Hamlisch; Lyrics, Edward Kleban; Co-choreographer, Bob Avian; Musical Direction/Vocal Arrangements, Don Pippin; Associate Producer, Bernard Gersten; Setting, Robin Wagner; Costumes, Theoni V. Aldredge; Lighting, Tharon Musser; Sound, Abe Jacobs; Music Coordinator, Robert Thomas; Orchestrations, Bill Byers, Hershy Kay, Jonathan Tunick; Assistant to Choreographers, Baayork Lee; Musical Director, Robert Rogers; Wardrobe, Alyce Gilbert; Production Supervisor, Jason Steven Cohen; Original Cast Album, Columbia Records; New York Shakespeare Festival production; Presented by Joseph Papp in association with Plum Productions at the Shubert Theatre. Opened Sunday, October 19, 1975.*

CAST

Roy	Don Mirault†1	Don	Dennis Edenfield†9
Kristine	Kerry Casserly†2	Bebe	Rene Ceballos†10
Sheila	Susan Danielle	Connie	Lauren Tom†11
Val	Mitzi Hamilton	Diana	Chris Bocchino†12
Mike	Buddy Balou†3	Al	Jerry Colker
Butch	Roscoe Gilliam	Frank	Philip C. Perry
Larry	J. Richard Hart	Greg	Danny Weathers
Maggie	Marcia Lynn Watkins†4	Bobby	Matt West
Richie	Kevin Chinn	Paul	Rene Clemente†13
Tricia	Diane Fratantoni	Vicki	Joanna Zercher†14
Tom	James Young	Ed	Jon Michael Richardson†15
Zach	Tim Millett†5	Jarad	Morris Freed†16
Mark	Danny Herman	Linda	Tracy Shayne†17
Cassie	Deborah Henry†6	Sam	Troy Garza†18
Judy	Jannet Moranz†7	Jenny	Catherine Cooper†19
Lois	Ann Louise Schaut†8	Ralph	T. Michael Reed†20

UNDERSTUDIES: Jerry Colker (Mike), Catherine Cooper (Cassie/Sheila/Val), Michael Danek (Zach), John Dolf (Mike/Mark/Larry), Thia Fadel (Cassie/Sheila/Judy), Diane Fratantoni (Diana/Val/Connie/Maggie/Bebe), Morris Freed (Mark), Troy Garza (Mike/Mark/Paul/Larry/Al), Roscoe Gilliam (Richie), J. Richard Hart (Mike/Al), Danny Herman (Mike), Bradley Jones (Bobby/Greg), Evan Pappas (Larry/Al/Paul), Peggy Parten (Judy/Kristine), Philip C. Perry (Mark/Don/Al), Tracy Shayne (Bebe/Diana/Maggie), Dorothy Tancredi (Maggie/Bebe), James Young (Al/Zach/Mike/Greg)

MUSICAL NUMBERS: I Hope I Get It, I Can Do That, and. . . ., At the Ballet, Sing!, Hello 12 Hello 13 Hello Love, Nothing, Dance 10 Looks 3, Music and the Mirror, One Tap Combination, What I Did For Love, Finale

A musical performed without intermission. The action takes place in 1975 during an audition in the theatre.

General Manager: Robert Kamlot; *Company Manager:* Bob MacDonald; *Press:* Merle Debuskey, William Schelble, Richard Kornberg; *Stage Managers:* Tom Porter, Wendy Mansfield, Morris Freed, Bradley Jones

* Still playing May 31, 1982. Cited as Best Musical by NY Drama Critics Circle, winner of 1976 Pulitzer Prize, 1976 "Tonys" for Best Musical, Best Book, Best Score, Best Direction, Best Lighting, Best Choreography, Best Musical Actress (Donna McKechnie), Best Featured Actress and Actor in a Musical (Kelly Bishop, Sammy Williams), and a Special Theatre World Award was presented to each member of the creative staff and original cast. See THEATRE WORLD Vol. 31.
† Succeeded by: 1. Evan Pappas, 2. Christine Barker, 3. Cary Scott Lowenstein, 4. Pam Klinger, 5. David Thome, Tim Millett, 6. Cheryl Clark, Pamela Sousa, 7. Melissa Randel, 8. Catherine Cooper, 9. Michael Weir, Michael Danek, 10. Pamela Ann Wilson, 11. Lily-Lee Wong, 12. Diane Frantantoni, Dorothy Tancredi, 13. Timothy Wahrer, Rene Clemente, Tommy Aguilar, 14. Tracy Shayne, Terry Lombardozzi, Peggy Parten, 15. Kevin Backstrom, Morris Freed, 16. Troy Garza, 17. Karen Curlee, Tracy Shayne, 18. John Dolf, 19. Kathleen Moore, Thia Fadel, 20. Bradley Jones

Martha Swope Photo

The cast in the finale

DANCIN'

Conceived, Directed and Choreographed by Bob Fosse; Scenery, Peter Larkin; Costumes, Willa Kim; Lighting, Jules Fisher; Associate Producer, Patty Grubman; Music Conducted and Arranged by Gordon Lowry Harrell; Orchestrations, Ralph Burns; Sound, Abe Jacob; Hairstylist, Romaine Greene, Cristofer Shihar, James Nelson; Wardrobe, Joseph Busheme, Don Brassington; Production Assistant, Vicki Stein; Assistants to Mr. Fosse, Kathryn Doby, Christopher Chadman, Gwen Verdon; Associate Conductor, Michael Camilo; Props, Mitchell Walling, Charles Zuckerman; Management Assistant, Barbara Softcheck; Presented by Jules Fisher, The Shubert Organization and Columbia Pictures at the Broadhurst Theatre. Opened Monday, March 27, 1978; moved to the Ambassador Theatre Dec. 4, 1980.*

CAST

Hinton Battle †, Eileen Casey, Christine Colby, Bruce Anthony Davis, Clif de Raita, Wendy Edmead, Janet Eilber, Gail Mae Ferguson, Richard Korthaze, Michael Kubala, P. J. Mann, Michael Ricardo, Terri Treas, Chet Walker, Robert Warners, Barbara Yeager

MUSICAL NUMBERS: Prologue (Hot August Night), Crunchy Granola Suite, Mr. Bojangles, Chaconne, Percussion, Ionisation, I Wanna Be a Dancin' Man, Big Noise from Winnetka, If It Feels Good Let It Ride, Easy, I've Got Them Feelin' Too Good Today Blues, Was Dog a Doughnut, Sing Sing Sing, Here You Come Again, Yankee Doodle Dandy, Gary Owen, Stouthearted Men, Under the Double Eagle, Dixie, When Johnny Comes Marching Home, Rally Round the Flag, Pack Up Your Troubles, Stars and Stripes Forever, Yankee Doodle Disco, Dancin'
    A "musical entertainment" in 3 acts and 13 scenes.

General Managers: Marvin A. Kraus, Gary Gunas, Eric Angelson, Steven C. Callahan; *Company Managers:* G. Warren McClane, Sue Frost; *Press:* Merle Debuskey, Leo Stern, William Schelble; *Stage Managers:* Peter B. Mumford, Karen DeFrancis, Richard Korthaze
* Closed June 27, 1982 after 1774 performances and 13 previews. Recipient of 1980 "Tony's" for Best Choreography, Best Lighting. For original production, see THEATRE WORLD Vol. 34.
† During the season members of the cast were succeeded by John DeLuca, Lisa Embs, Bill Hastings, Edmund LaFosse, Dana Moore, Stephen Moore, Maryann Neu, Cynthia Onrubia, Adrian Rosario, Beth Shorter, Laurie Dawn Skinner, Penny Fekany, Laurent Giroux, Jodi Moccia, Keith Keen, Gale Samuels, Ciscoe Bruton, Lloyd Culbreath, Spence Ford, Bebe Neuwirth, Alison Sherve, Sharon Brooks, David Thome, Charles Ward, Kathryn Ann Wright

DEATHTRAP

By Ira Levin; Director, Robert Moore; Set, William Ritman; Costumes, Ruth Morley; Lighting, Marc B. Weiss; Wardrobe, Mariana Torres; Assistant to Director, George Rondo; Assistants to Producers, Dorothy Spellman, Jean Bankier; Props, Bruce Becker, Eoin Sprott; Presented by Alfred de Liagre, Jr. and Roger L. Stevens at the Music Box Theatre. Opened Sunday, February 26, 1978; moved to Biltmore Theatre Jan. 5, 1982.*

CAST

Sidney Bruhl	John Wood†1	Helga ten Dorp	Marian Winters†3
Myra Bruhl	Marian Seldes	Porter Milgrim	Richard Wood†4
Clifford Anderson	Victor Garber†2		

STANDBYS: Donald Barton (Sidney), Patricia Guinan (Myra/Helga), Ernest Townsend/David Sederholm (Clifford)
    A "comedy thriller" in 2 acts and 6 scenes. The action takes place at the present time in Sidney Bruhl's study in the Bruhl home in Westport, Connecticut.

General Manager: C. Edwin Knill; *Company Manager:* Constance Coble; *Press:* Jeffrey Richards, Ben Morse, Robert Ganshaw, Ted Killmer, C. George Willard, Helen Stern, Richard Humleker; *Stage Managers:* Robert St. Clair, Steven Shaw

* Closed June 13, 1982 after 1793 performances and 6 previews. For original production, see THEATRE WORLD Vol. 34.
† Succeeded by: 1. Patrick Horgan, Stacy Keach, John Cullum, Robert Reed, Farley Granger, 2. Daren Kelly, Steve Bassett, Michael McBride, 3. Elizabeth Parish, 4. William LeMassena

Above: (L) "Benny's Number" in "Dancin'" *(Martha Swope Photo)* (R) Marian Seldes, Ernest Townsend, Farley Granger, William LeMassena, Elizabeth Parrish in "Deathtrap" *(Sy Friedman Photo)*

EVITA

Lyrics, Tim Rice; Music, Andrew Lloyd Webber; Director, Harold Prince; Choreography, Larry Fuller; Set/Costumes/Projections, Timothy O'Brien, Tazeena Firth; Executive Producers, R. Tyler Gatchell, Jr., Peter Neufeld; Orchestrations, Hershy Kay, Andrew Lloyd Webber; Musical Director, Paul Gemignani; Lighting, David Hersey; Sound, Abe Jacob; Production Associates, Tim Rice, Andrew Lloyd Webber; Assistant Musical Director, Edward Strauss; Props, George Green Jr., George Green III; Assistant Conductor, Uel Wade; Casting, Joanna Merlin; Projects Coordinator, Arlene Caruso; Wardrobe, Adelaide Laurino; Hairstylist, Richard Allen; Production Assistant, Wiley Hausam; Original Cast Album, MCA Records; Presented by Robert Stigwood in association with David Land at the Broadway Theatre. Opened Tuesday, September 25, 1979.*

CAST

Evita .... Patti LuPone†1,Terri Klausner†2	Peron's Mistress .... Jan Ohringer†5
Che .... Mandy Patinkin†3	Magaldi .... Mark Syers†6
Peron .... Bob Gunton†4	Children .... Tammy Amerson,

Megan Forste, Lilo Grunwald, Colette Sena Heyman, Michael Pastryk, Christopher Wooten

PEOPLE OF ARGENTINA: Dennis Birchall, Susan Cella, Frank Cruz, Kim Darwin, Al DeCristo, Anny DeGange, Scott Fless, Robert Frisch, Carole Garcia, Robert Heitzinger, Robert Hendersen, Ken Hilliard, Michael Hayward-Jones, Robert Logan, Jack Neubeck, Amy Niles, Marcia O'Brien, Joanie O'Neill, Nancy Opel, Dawn Perry, Cassie Rand, Morgan Richardson, Drusilla Ross, Davia Sacks, James Sbano, David Staller, Michelle Stubbs, Wilfredo Suarez, Susan Terry, Claude Tessier, Leslie Tinnaro, Ian Michael Towers, Philip Tracy, Kenneth W. Urmston, Mark Waldrop, John Yost

UNDERSTUDIES: Susan Cella (Eva), James Sbano (Che), Robert Frisch (Peron), Jack Neubeck (Magaldi), Amy Niles (Peron's Mistress)

MUSICAL NUMBERS: A Cinema in Buenos Aires, Requiem for Evita, Oh What a Circus, On This Night of a Thousand Stars, Eva Beware of the City, Buenos Aires, Goodnight and Thank You, Art of the Impossible, Charity Concert, I'd Be Surprisingly Good for You, Another Suitcase in Another Hall, Peron's Latest Flame, A New Argentina, On the Balcony of the Casa Rosada, Don't Cry for Me Argentina, High Flying Adored, Rainbow High, Rainbow Tour, The Actress Hasn't Learned, And the Money Kept Rolling In, Santa Evita, Waltz for Eva and Che, She Is a Diamond, Dice Are Rolling, Eva's Final Broadcast, Montage, Lament

A musical in two acts. Based on the life of Eva Peron, second wife of Argentina dictator Juan Peron.

General Manager: Howard Haines; *Company Manager:* John Caruso; *Press:* Mary Bryant, Philip Rinaldi; *Stage Managers:* George Martin, John Grigas, John-David Wilder, Kenneth W. Urmston

* Still playing May 31, 1982. Winner of 1980 NY Drama Critics Circle Award for Best Musical, 7 "Tonys" for Best Musical, Best Actress (Patti LuPone), Best Direction, Score, Book, Lighting, and Best Featured Actor in a Musical (Mandy Patinkin). For original production, see THEATRE WORLD Vol. 36.

† Succeeded by: 1. Derin Altay, Loni Ackerman, 2. Nancy Opel (matinees), 3. James Stein, Anthony Crivello, 4. David Cryer, 5. Cynthia Hunt, 6. James Whitson

Martha Swope Photo

(C) David Cryer, Loni Ackerman, (R) Anthony Crivello

FORTY-SECOND STREET

Songs, Harry Warren, Al Dubin; Book, Michael Stewart, Mark Bramble; Based on novel by Bradford Ropes; Direction/Choreography, Gower Champion; Scenery, Robin Wagner; Costumes, Theoni V. Aldredge; Lighting, Tharon Musser; Musical Direction/Vocal Arrangements, John Lesko; Orchestrations, Philip J. Lang; Dance Arrangements, Donald Johnston; Casting, Feuer & Ritzer; Sound, Richard Fitzgerald; Dance Assistants, Karin Baker, Randy Skinner; Assistants to Producer, Craig Hoffman, Jon Maas; Wardrobe, Gene Wilson, Kathleen Foster; Assistant to Director, Larry Carpenter; Assistant Conductor, Donald Johnston; Hairstylists, Ted Azar, Robert DiNiro, Dale Brownell, Anne Sampogna, Kelvin Trahan, Donna Manasia, Manuel Rodriguez; Staff Assistants, Bonnie Warschauer, Marcia Goldberg; Assistant Musical Director, Bernie Leighton; Casting, George Connolly; Props, Leo Herbert, Edward Burden; Original Cast Album by RCA Records; Presented by David Merrick at the Winter Garden Theatre. Opened Monday, August 25, 1980; moved to Majestic Theatre March 30, 1981.*

CAST

Andy Lee	Danny Carroll	Lorraine	Ginny King†5
Oscar	Robert Colston	Phyllis	Jeri Kansas†6
Mac	Stan Page	Julian Marsh	Jerry Orbach†7
Annie	Karen Prunczik†1	Dorothy Brock	Tammy Grimes†8
Maggie Jones	Carole Cook†2	Abner Dillon	Don Crabtree
Bert Barry	Joseph Bova	Pat Denning	James Congdon†9
Billy Lawlor	Lee Roy Reams†3	Thugs	Stan Page, Ron Schwinn
Peggy Sawyer	Wanda Richert†4	Doctor	Stan Page

UNDERSTUDIES AND STANDBYS: Sheila Smith/Charlotte Fairchild (Dorothy/Maggie), Stephen G. Arlen (Marsh), Mary Cadorette (Peggy), Nikki Sahagen (Peggy), Joel Blum (Billy), Bill Nabel (Bert), Don Percassi (Andy), Stan Page (Abner/Pat), Barbara Mandra (Annie), Bernie Leighton (Oscar), Debra Piliavento, Lorraine Person (Phyllis/Lorraine), Ensemble: Lorraine Person, Yvonne Dutton, Jon Engstrom, Christopher Lucas, Kelli McNally, Lizzie Moran, Debra Pigliavento

ENSEMBLE: Doreen Alderman, Dennis Angulo, Carole Banninger, Steve Belin, Joel Blum, Mary Cadorette, Pam Cecil, Ronny DeVito, Rob Draper, Brandt Edwards, Sharon Ferrol, Cathy Greco, Kim Morgan Greene, Christine Jacobsen, Jack Karcher, Billye Kersey, Karen Klump, Terri Ann Kundrat, Neva Leigh, Gail Lohla, Barbara Mandra, Shan Martin, Maureen Mellon, Sandra Menhart, Bill Nabel, Don Percassi, Michael Ricardo, Lars Rosager, Linda Sabatelli, Nikki Sahagen, Ron Schwinn, Maryellen Scilla, Yveline Semeria, Robin Stephens, David Storey

MUSICAL NUMBERS: Audition, Young and Healthy, Shadow Waltz, Go into Your Dance, You're Getting to Be a Habit with Me, Getting Out of Town, Dames, I Know Now, We're in the Money, Sunny Side to Every Situation, Lullaby of Broadway, About a Quarter to Nine, Pretty Lady, Shuffle Off to Buffalo, 42nd Street

A musical in 2 acts and 16 scenes. The action takes place during 1933 in New York City and Philadelphia.

Company Manager: Leo K. Cohen; *Press:* Solters/Roskin/Friedman, Milly Schoenbaum, Warren Knowlton, Kevin Patterson; *Stage Managers:* Steve Zweigbaum, Barry Kearsley, Jane E. Neufeld, Debra Pigliavento

* Still playing May 31, 1982. Recipient of 1981 "Tonys" for Best Musical, and for Outstanding Choreography. For original production, see THEATRE WORLD Vol. 37.
† Succeeded by: 1. Clare Leach, 2. Charlotte Fairchild during vacation, Peggy Cass, 3. Ken Prescott during vacation, 4. Nancy Sinclair, Karen Prunczik, Mary Cadorette, Gail Benedict, Lisa Brown, 5. Gail Lohla, 6. Barbara Mandra, 7. Stephen G. Arlen during vacation, 8. Charlotte Fairchild during vacation, Millicent Martin, 9. Stephen G. Arlen

Martha Swope Photos

Lee Roy Reams and chorus   Peggy Cass and chorus

LENA HORNE: THE LADY AND HER MUSIC

Musical Direction, Harold Wheeler; Scenery, David Gropman; Costumes, Stanley Simmons; Lighting, Thomas Skelton; Musical Conductor, Coleridge T. Perkinson; Musical Consultant, Luther Henderson; Hairstylist, Phyllis Della; Miss Horne's Wardrobe, Giorgio Sant'Angelo; Production Staged by Arthur Faria; Production Assistant, Brenda Braxton; Assistant Conductor, Linda Twine; Recorded by Qwest Records; Presented by James M. Nederlander, Michael Frazier, Fred Walker in association with Sherman Sneed and Jack Lawrence at the Nederlander Theatre. Opened Tuesday, May 12, 1981.*

COMPANY

LENA'S TRIO: Grady Tate (Drums), Steve Bargonetti (Guitar), Bob Cranshaw (Bass)

THE COMPANY: Clare Bathe, Tyra Ferrell, Vondie Curtis-Hall, Deborah Lynn Bridges (Alternate), Peter Oliver-Norman (Alternate)

MUSICAL NUMBERS: Life Goes On, I'm Going to Sit Right Down, Stormy Weather, As Long as I Live, Push de Button, Fly, I'm Glad There Is You, That's What Miracles Are All About, From This Moment On, Just One of Those Things, Love, A Lady Must Live, Where or When, Surrey with the Fringe on Top, Can't Help Lovin' Dat Man of Mine, Copper Colored Gal of Mine, Deed I Do, I Got a Name, If You Believe, Lady with a Fan, Raisin' the Rent, Watch What Happens, I Want to Be Happy, Better Than Anything
  Performed with one intermission.

General Manager: James Walsh; *Company Manager:* Sheila R. Phillips; *Press:* Solters/Roskin/Friedman, Joshua Ellis, Cindy Valk; *Stage Managers:* Joe Lorden, Jack Gianino

* Closed June 30, 1982 after 333 performances and 19 previews. Miss Horne received a 1981 Special Tony Award and a special Citation from the New York Drama Critics Circle for her performance.

Martha Swope Photo

 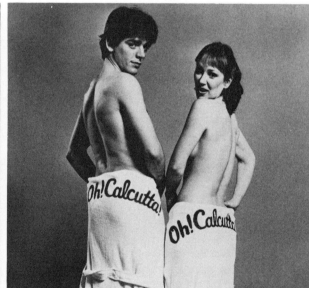

OH! CALCUTTA!

Devised by Kenneth Tynan; Conceived and Directed by Jacques Levy; Contributors, Robert Benton, David Newman, Jules Feiffer, Dan Greenberg, Lenore Kandel, John Lennon, Jacques Levy, Leonard Melfi, Sam Shepard, Clovis Trouille, Kenneth Tynan, Sherman Yellen; Music and Lyrics, Robert Dennis, Peter Schickele, Stanley Walden, Jacques Levy; Choreography, Margo Sappington; Musical Director, Stanley Walden; Scenery and Lighting, Harry Silverglat Darrow; Costumes, Kenneth M. Yount; Supervised by James Tilton; Musical Conductor, Norman Bergen; Sound, Sander Hacker; Assistant to Director, Nancy Tribush; Projected Media Design, Gardner Compton; Live Action Film, Ron Merk; Production Assistants, Marcia Edelstein, Andrea Ladik; Assistant Musical Conductor, Dan Carter; Technical Directors, Thomas Healy, Charles Moran; Wardrobe, Susan J. Wright, Melissa Davis; Props, James Tilton; Presented by Hillard Elkins, Norman Kean and Robert S. Fishko at the Edison Theatre. Opened Friday, September 24, 1976.*

CAST

Daryl Adams, Deborah Bauers, Jacqueline Carol, Charles E. Gerber, Cheryl Hartley, David Heisey, Nick Mangano, Ann Neville, Dara Norman, Thom Pieczara, Lee Ramey, Julie Ridge, Sean Sullivan

MUSICAL NUMBERS AND SKITS: Taking Off the Robe, Will Answer All Sincere Replies, Playin' Jack and Jill, The Paintings of Clovis Trouille, Much Too Soon, Dance for George, Delicious Indignities, Was It Good For You Too?, Suite for 5 Letters, One on One, Rock Garden, Spread Your Love Around, Love Lust Poem, Four in Hand, Coming Together Going Together
  An "erotic musical" in Two acts.

Company Manager: Doris J. Buberl; *Press:* Les Schecter, Barbara Schwei; *Stage Managers:* Ron Nash, Maria DiDia
*Still playing May 31, 1982. For original production, see THEATRE WORLD Vol. 33.

Above: (L) Lena Horne (R) Lee Ramey, Cheryl Hartley in "Oh! Calcutta!"

THE PIRATES OF PENZANCE

Lyrics, W. S. Gilbert; Music, Arthur S. Sullivan; Director, Wilford Leach; Music Adapted and Conducted by William Elliott; Choreography, Graciela Daniele; Scenery, Bob Shaw, Wilford Leach; Supervised by Paul Eads; Costumes, Patricia McGourty; Hairstylist/Makeup, J. Roy Helland; Lighting, Jennifer Tipton; Sound, Don Ketteler; Production Supervisor, Jason Steven Cohen; Wardrobe, Barrett Hong; Assistant to Director, John Albano; Production Assistant, Chris Sinclair; Pirate Boat Designed by Jack Chandler; Associate Conductor, Susan Anderson; Props, Robert Bostwick; Original Cast Album by Elektra/Asylum Records; New York Shakespeare Festival production; Presented by Joseph Papp; Opened at Uris Theatre, Thursday, January 8, 1981; moved to the Minskoff Theatre Aug. 12, 1981.*

CAST

Pirate King	Kevin Kline[†1]	
Samuel, His lieutenant	Stephen Hanan[†2]	
Frederic	Rex Smith[†3]	
Ruth, a pirate maid	Estelle Parsons[†4]	
Major-General Stanley	George Rose[†5]	

Edith . . . . Alexandra Korey[†6]
Kate . . . . Marcie Shaw[†7]
Isabel . . . . Wendy Wolfe[†8]
Mabel . . . . Linda Ronstadt[†9]
Sergeant . . . . Tony Azito[†10]

PIRATES AND POLICE: Dean Badolato, Mark Beudert, Scott Burkholder, Walter Caldwell, Tim Flavin, Nick Jolley, George Kmeck, Phil LaDuca, Daniel Marcus, G. Eugene Moose, Jeff McCarthy, Joseph Neal, Walter Niehenke, Joe Pichette, Ellis Skeeter Williams, James Caddell, Don Goodspeed, Wally Kurth, Morgan MacKay, Robert Polenz, Michael Scott, Martin Walsh, Mark Watson

UNDERSTUDIES: Walter Niehenke/Jeff McCarthy (Pirate King), G. Eugene Moose (Samuel), Wendy Wolfe (Ruth), Mark Beudert, Scott Burkholder (Frederic), Nancy Heikin (Edith), Joe Pichette (Stanley), Daniel Marcus (Sergeant), Kathy Morath (Mabel), Bonnie Simmons (Kate), Maria Guida (Isabel), Swings: Roy Alan, Robert Polenz, Dinna Lee Marshall, Valerie Piacenti

MUSICAL NUMBERS: Pour the Pirate Sherry, When Frederic Was a Little Lad, Oh Better Far to Live and Die, False One You Have Deceived Me, Climbing over Rocky Mountain, Stop Ladies Pray!, Is There Not One Maiden Breast, Poor Wandering One, What Ought We To Do?, How Beautiful Blue Sky, We Must Not Lose Our Senses, Hold Monsters!, I Am the Model of a Modern Major-General, Men of Dark and Dismal Fate, Dry the Glistening Tear, Then Frederic, When the Foeman Bares His Steel, Now for the Pirates Lair, When You Had Left Our Pirate Fold, My Eyes Are Fully Open, My Heart's on Fire, All Is Prepared, Stay Frederic, Sorry Her Lot, No I Am Brave, When a Felon's Not Engaged to His Employment, A Rollicking Band of Pirates We, With Cat-Like Tread, Hush! Not a Word!, Sighing Softly to the River, Finale.

An operetta in two acts.

General Manager: Robert Kamlot; *Company Manager:* Rheba Flegelman; *Press:* Merle Debuskey, Richard Kornberg, Anthony Sherwood, Ed Bullins, Dennis Thread; *Stage Managers:* Frank DiFilia, Bonnie Panson, Roy Alan

* Still playing May 31, 1982. Recipient of 1981 "Tony" for Outstanding Reproduction of a Musical, Outstanding Actor in a Musical (Kevin Kline), Outstanding Direction, and a Special Citation from the New York Drama Critics Circle. For original NY production, see THEATRE WORLD Vol. 37.

† Succeeded by: 1. Treat Williams, Gary Sandy, James Belushi, 2. Walter Niehenke, 3. Robby Benson, Patrick Cassidy, Rex Smith, Peter Noone, 4. Kaye Ballard, 5. George S. Irving for 3 months, 6. Nancy Heikin, 7. Bonnie Simmons, 8. Maria Guida, 9. Karla DeVito, Maureen McGovern, Kathryn Morath for vacation, Pam Dawber for 2 weeks, 10. David Garrison for 3 months

Martha Swope Photo

Kaye Ballard, George Rose, Gary Sandy, Maureen McGovern, Patrick Cassidy

SOPHISTICATED LADIES

Concept, Donald McKayle; Based on music of Duke Ellington; Director, Michael Smuin; Musical Staging and Choreography, Donald McKayle, Michael Smuin; Co-Choreographer/Tap, Henry LeTang; Musical Director, Mercer Ellington; Set, Tony Walton; Costumes, Willa Kim; Lighting, Jennifer Tipton; Sound, Otts Munderloh; Hairstylists, Howard Leonard, Danny Wintrobe; Orchestrations, Al Cohn; Musical and Dance Arrangements, Lloyd Mayers; Vocal Arrangements, Malcolm Dodds, Lloyd Mayers; Associate Choreographer, Bruce Heath; Assistant Choreographer, Mercedes Ellington; Musical Consultant-/Additional Arrangements, Paul Chihara; Wardrobe, Jennifer Bryan; Production Assistants, Michael Harrod, Mark Saraceni; Casting, Julie Hughes/Barry Moss; Assistant Conductor, Frank Owens; Props, Paul Biega, Tom Ciaccio; Management Assistants, Nancy Simmons, Bruce Klinger; Original Cast Album by RCA Records; Presented by Robert S. Berlind, Manheim Fox, Sondra Gilman, Burton L. Litwin, Louise Westergaard in association with Belwin Mills Publishing Corp. and Norzar Productions at the Lunt-Fontanne Theatre. Opened Sunday, March 1, 1981.*

CAST

Hinton Battle†1
Gregg Burge†2
Gregory Hines†3
Judith Jamison
Mercedes Ellington

Terri Klausner†4
P. J. Benjamin†5
Phyllis Hyman
Priscilla Baskerville

SOPHISTICATED LADIES AND GENTLEMEN: Leslie Dockery, Mercedes Ellington, Darcy Phifer, Christina Saffran, Adrian Bailey, Calvin McRae, Richard Pessagno, T. A. Stephens

UNDERSTUDIES AND STANDBYS: Alan Weeks (Mr. Hines), Anita Moore/Naomi Moody (Miss Hyman), Naomi Moody (Miss Baskerville), Adrian Bailey/Jeff Veazey (Mr. Hines), Valarie Pettiford/Mercedes Ellington (Miss Jamison), Christina Saffran/Denise DiRenzo (Miss Drake), Calvin McRae/Rick Pessagno (Mr. Benjamin)

MUSICAL NUMBERS: I've Got to Be a Rug Cutter, Music Is a Woman, The Mooche, Hit Me with a Hot Note, Love You Madly, Perdido, Fat and Forty, It Don't Mean a Thing, Bli-Blip, Cotton Tail, Take the A Train, Solitude, Don't Get Around Much Anymore, I Let a Song Go Out of My Heart, Caravan, Something to Live For, Old Man Blues, Drop Me Off in Harlem, Rockin' in Rhythm, Duke's Place, Diminuendo in Blue, In a Sentimental Mood, I'm Beginning to See the Light, Satin Doll, Just Squeeze Me, Dancers in Love, Echoes in Harlem, I'm Just a Lucky So-and-So, Hey Baby, Imagine My Frustration, Kinda Dukish, Ko Ko, I'm Checking Out Goombye, Do Nothing 'Til You Hear from Me, I Got It Bad and That Ain't Good, Mood Indigo, Sophisticated Lady, Finale
   A musical entertainment in two acts.

General Managers: Joseph P. Harris, Steven E. Goldstein, Peter T. Kulok; *Press:* Fred Nathan, Eileen McMahon, Francine L. Trevens, Anne Abrams, David Diamond; *Stage Managers:* Martin Gold, Carlos Gorbea, Kenneth Hanson

* Still playing May 31, 1982. Recipient of 1981 "Tonys" for Outstanding Featured Actor in a musical (Hinton Battle), and Outstanding Costume Design. For original production, See THEATRE WORLD Vol. 37.
† Succeeded by: 1. Michael Scott Gregory, 2. Gary Chapman, 3. Maurice Hines, 4. Donna Drake, 5. Don Correia.

Kenn Duncan Photos

Don Correia, Donna Drake

(C) Judith Jamison, Maurice Hines

SUGAR BABIES

Conceived by Ralph G. Allen, Harry Rigby; Book, Ralph G. Allen; Based on traditional material; Music, Jimmy McHugh; Lyrics, Dorothy Fields, Al Dubin; Additional Music and Lyrics, Arthur Malvin; "Sugar Babies Bounce" by Jay Livingston and Ray Evans; Staged and Choreographed by Ernest Flatt; Sketches Directed by Rudy Tronto; Production Supervisor, Ernest Flatt; Associate Producer, Jack Schlissel; Scenery and Costumes, Raoul Pene du Bois; Lighting, Gilbert V. Hemsley, Jr.; Vocal Arrangements, Arthur Malvin, Hugh Martin, Ralph Blane; Musical Director, Glen Roven; Orchestrations, Dick Hyman; Dance Music Arrangements, Arnold Gross; Associate Producers, Frank Montalvo, Thomas Walton Associates; Assistant Choreographer, Toni Kay; Associate Conductor, Bill Grossman; Wardrobe, Florence Aubert, Irene Ferrari; Hairstylists, Stephen LoVullo, Vincent Tucker, Frank Paul, Joe Anthony, Juan DeJuan; Props, Elias Bergman; Casting, Elizabeth R. Woodman; Presented by Terry Allen Kramer and Harry Rigby in association with Columbia Pictures at the Mark Hellinger Theatre. Opened Monday, October 8, 1979.*

CAST

Mickey Rooney†1, Ann Miller†3, Scot Stewart, Richard Galuppi, Jane Summerhays, Ronn Lucas, Tom Boyd, Michael Allen Davis†4, Peter Leeds, Chaz Chase†5, Maxie Furman†2

GAIETY QUARTET: Hank Brunjes, Bob Heath, Eddie Pruett, Michael Radigan, Ken Mitchell (Alternate)

SUGAR BABIES: Carol Ann Basch, Carole Cotter, Kimberly Dean, Kaylyn Dillehay, Candy Durkin, Chris Elia, Jeri Kansas, Robin Manus, Faye Fujisaki Mark, Melanie Montana, Regina Newsome, Linda Ravin, Michele Rogers, Rose Scudder, Alternates: Laurie Sloan, Laurie Jaeger

STANDBYS AND UNDERSTUDIES: Maxie Furman (Mr. Rooney), Jane Summerhays (Miss Miller), Tom Boyd (Mr. Rooney), Rose Scudder (Miss Miller), Michele Rogers/Chris Elia (Miss Summerhays), Tom Boyd (Mr. Furman), Richard Galuppi/Tom Boyd (Mr. Leeds), Michael Radigan (Mr. Stewart), Hank Brunjes (Mr. Boyd)

SONGS AND SKETCHES: A Memory of Burlesque, A Good Old Burlesque Show, Welcome to the Gaiety, Let Me Be Your Sugar Baby, Meet Me 'Round the Corner, I Want a Girl, Travelin', In Louisiana, I Feel a Song Comin' On, Goin' Back to New Orleans, Home Sweet Home, Feathered Fantasy, Sally, Scenes from Domestic Life, A Very Moving Love Story, Don't Blame Me, Orientale, Little Red Schoolhouse, Springboard Sisters, Sugar Baby Bounce, Mme. Rentz and Her All Female Minstrels, Mr. Banjo Man, Candy Butcher, Girls and Garters, Exactly Like You, Court of Last Resort, In a Greek Garden, Warm and Willing, Presenting Madame Alla Gazaza, Tropical Madness, Cuban Love Song, Cautionary Tales, Bon Appetit, Old Glory, You Can't Blame Your Uncle Sammy

A "burlesque musical" in two acts.

General Management: Alan Wasser; *Press:* Harry Luhrman, Terry M. Lilly, Bill Miller, Kevin P. McAnarney; *Stage Managers:* Kay Vance, Bob Burland, David Campbell

* Closed Aug. 28, 1982 after 1208 performances and 8 previews. For original NY production see THEATRE WORLDS Vol. 36.
† Succeeded by: 1. Joey Bishop, Rip Taylor, Eddie Bracken during vacations, 2. Sammy Smith during vacation, 3. Helen Gallagher during vacation, 4. and 5. Ronn Lucas during vacations

Martha Swope Photos

Mickey Rooney and the Sugar Babies

Mickey Rooney, Ann Miller

WOMAN OF THE YEAR

Book, Peter Stone; Based on MGM film by Ring Lardner, Jr., Michael Kanin; Music, John Kander; Lyrics, Fred Ebb; Director, Robert Moore; Musical Staging, Tony Charmoli; Settings, Tony Walton; Costumes, Theoni V. Aldredge; Lighting, Marilyn Rennagel; Sound, Abe Jacob; Musical Direction/Vocal Arrangements, Donald Pippin; Orchestrations, Michael Gibson; Dance Arrangements, Ronald Melrose; Animations, Michael Sporn; Assistant to Mr. Charmoli, Ed Nolfi; Hairstylists, Masarone, Paul Warden; Assistant to Producers, Donald Martocchio; Production Assistant, Michael Gavenchak; Wardrobe, Stephanie Edwards; Assistant to Director, George Rondo; Production Associate, Melinda Sherwood; Props, Munro Gabler; Original Cast Album by Arista Records; Presented by Lawrence Kasha, David S. Landay, James M. Nederlander, Warner Theatre Productions/Claire Nichtern, Carole J. Shorenstein, Stewart F. Lane at the Palace Theatre. Opened Sunday, March 29, 1981.*

CAST

Chairperson	Helon Blount	Ellis McMaster	Rex Hays
Tess Harding	Lauren Bacall†1	Abbott Canfield	Lawrence Raiken†5
Floor Manager	Michael O'Gorman	Maury	Rex Everhart
Chip Salisbury	Daren Kelly†2	Helga	Grace Keagy
Gerald	Roderick Cook	Alexi Petrikov	Eivind Harum†6
Pinky Peters	Gerry Vichi	Cleaning Women	Helon Blount, Marian Haraldson
Phil Witaker	Tom Avera†3	Jan Donovan	Marilyn Cooper†7
Sam Craig	Harry Guardino†4	Larry Donovan	Jamie Ross†8

CHORUS: DeWright Baxter, Joan Bell, Helon Blount, Mark Bove, Sergio Cal, James Fatta, Richard Glendon-Larson, Marian Haraldson, Nina Hennessey, Paige Messman, Michael O'Gorman, Elyssa Paternoster, Daniel Quinn, Bubba Dean Rambo, Swings: Dennis Batutis, Ed Nolfi, Deborah Roshe

UNDERSTUDIES: Jamie Ross/Timothy Jecko (Sam), Marian Haraldson (Helga), Mark Bove (Alexi), Richard Glendon-Larson (Chip), Ralston Hill (Phil/Ellis/Larry), Michael Davis (Gerald/Abbott/Maury), Paige Massman (Jan)

MUSICAL NUMBERS: Woman of the Year, Poker Game, See You in the Funny Papers, You're Right, Shut Up Gerald, So What Else Is New?, One of the Boys, Table Talk, The Two of Us, It Isn't Working, I Told You So, I Wrote the Book, Happy in the Morning, Sometimes a Day Goes By, The Grass Is Always Greener, We're Gonna Work It Out

A musical in 2 acts and 15 scenes. The action takes place at the present time.

General Management: Marvin A. Krauss Associates; *Company Manager:* G. Warren McClane; *Press:* Merle Debuskey, Diane Judge; *Stage Managers:* Robert V. Straus, Joel Tropper, Pat Trott

* Still playing May 31, 1982. Recipient of 1981 "Tonys" for Best Musical Book, Best Score, Outstanding Actress in a Musical (Lauren Bacall), Outstanding Featured Actress in a Musical (Marilyn Cooper). See THEATRE WORLD Vol. 37.
† Succeeded by: 1. Raquel Welch, 2. John Hammill during vacation, 3. Mace Barrett, 4. Jamie Ross, 5. John Hillner, 6. George de la Pena, 7. Carol Arthur during vacation, 8. Ralston Hill, Timothy Jecko

Martha Swope Photos

Lauren Bacall

Lauren Bacall and chorus

OPENED AND CLOSED IN PREVIEWS

THE LITTLE PRINCE AND THE AVIATOR

Book, Hugh Wheeler; Based on "The Little Prince" by Antoine de Saint-Exupery; Music, John Barry; Lyrics, Don Black; Director, Jerry Adler; Choreography, Billy Wilson; Scenery, Eugene Lee; Costumes, Christa Scholtz; Lighting, Roger Morgan; Vocal Arrangements/Musical Direction, David Friedman; Orchestrations, Don Walker; Dance Music Arrangements, Grant Sturiale; Environmental Sound, Kirk Nurock; Sound, Robert Kerzman; Sound Effects, Gary Harris; Production Coordinator, Jule Foster; Casting, Cheryl Raab, Nina Katzander; Production Assistants, Douglas Colby, Steven Gregory; Associate Conductor, Richard Vitzhum; Hairstylist/Makeup, Angela Gari; Wardrobe, Josephine Zampedrie; Props, Leo Herbert; General Manager, GRQ Productions/Gene Wolsk, Cheryl Raab; Stage Managers, Zoya Wyeth, B. J. Allen, Allan Sobek; Press, Merle Debuskey, Leo Stern, Jan Greenberg; Presented by A. Joseph Tandet at the Alvin Theatre on December 31, 1981. Closed January 17, 1982 after 20 previews.

CAST

Little Prince . . . . Anthony Rapp	Pilot/Drunkard . . . . Larry G. Bailey
Toni . . . . Michael York	Pilot/Vulture . . . . Kenneth D. Ard
Suzanne/Little Rose . . . . Ellen Greene	Pilot . . . . Fred C. Mann III
Georges/Fennec . . . . David Purdham	Lotus Club Girls . . . . Brooks Almy,
	Lynn Gendron, Robin Kensey, Diana Laurenson
Snake/Pilot . . . . Chip Garnett	Ahmed/Georges as a child . . . . Lee Gordon
Cactus . . . . Joe DeGunther	Nurse . . . . Brooks Almy
Rose . . . . Janet Eilber	Suzanne as a child . . . . Jennifer Fetten
Pilot/Lamplighter . . . . Mark Dovey	Businessman . . . . Edward Conery
Pilot/Cap. Juby Pilot/King . . . . Alan Gilbert	
Pilot/Juby Pilot/Conceited Man . . . . Robert Hoshour	

UNDERSTUDIES: Edward Conery (Toni/Georges), Brooks Almy (Suzanne), Tori Brenno (Rose), Jonathan Ward (Little Prince/Little Georges), Swings: Tori Brenno, James Boyd Parker.

MUSICAL NUMBERS: Par Avion, Power Comes Power Goes, I Pity the Poor Parisiennes, Making Every Minute Count, Made for Each Other, Wind Sand and Stars, First Impressions, A Day Will Never Be the Same, I've Got You to Thank for All This, I Don't Regret a Thing, We Couldn't We Mustn't We Won't, Watch Out for the Baobabs, I Like My Misfortunes to Be Taken Seriously, Volcano Song, More Than Just a Pretty Flower, Playground of the Planets, It Was You, Grain of Sand, Sunset Song, Little Prince, Stars Will Be Laughing
  A musical in two acts. The action takes place in the Sahara Desert, Paris, and Asteroid B6-12 during the years 1911–1928.

Martha Swope Photos

Anthony Rapp, Michael York, Chip Garnett   Ellen Greene, Michael York

PRODUCTIONS FROM PAST SEASONS THAT CLOSED THIS SEASON

Title	Opened	Closed	Performances
Gemini	5/21/77	9/5/81	1819
Deathtrap	2/26/78	6/13/82	1793
Ain't Misbehavin'	5/9/78	2/21/82	1604
The Best Little Whorehouse in Texas	4/17/78	3/27/82	1584
They're Playing Our Song	2/11/79	9/6/81	1082
The Elephant Man	4/19/79	6/28/81	916
Children of a Lesser God	3/30/80	5/16/82	887
Barnum	4/30/80	5/16/82	854
A Day in Hollywood/A Night in the Ukraine .	5/1/80	9/27/81	588
Morning's at Seven	4/10/80	8/16/81	564
Fifth of July	11/5/80	1/24/82	511
March of the Falsettos	3/27/81	1/31/82	298
I Can't Keep Running in Place	5/14/81	10/25/81	187
The Little Foxes	5/7/81	9/6/81	123

OFF BROADWAY

THREE MUSES THEATRE Tuesday, June 2, 1981 (2 performances)
SPOON RIVER ANTHOLOGY Excerpts from Edgar Lee Master; Director, Charles Repole; Set, Rob Hamilton; Costumes, Debbie Ann Thompson. **CAST:** Dennis Black, Lee Geisel, Lillian Graff, Paul F. Hewitt, Christine Jennings

PLAYERS THEATRE Wednesday, June 3–August 2, 1981 (70 performances) Gordon Crowe presents:
THE BUTLER DID IT By Walter Marks and Peter Marks; Director, Doug Rogers; Scenery, Akira Yoshimura; Lighting, Gregg Marriner; Costumes, Merrill Cleghorne; Production Coordinator, Barbara Carroll; Company Manager, Patricia Crowe; Press, Jeffrey Richards, C. George Willard, Robert Gansha; Ben Morse, Helen Stern, Ted Killmer, Stanley Evans, Richard Humleker; Stage Managers, Robert Vandergriff, Karen McLaughlin; Casting, Group 3, Patricia Crowe; Technical Director, Steve Shereff; Wardrobe, Henry DeGulis. **CAST:** Gordon Connell (Raymond), John Monteleone (Aldo), Gerrianne Raphael (Angela), Patricia Kalember (Victoria), Alan Mixon (Anthony), John Hallow (Det. Mumford), Understudy: Karen McLaughlin
A comedy thriller in 2 acts and 6 scenes.

CIRCLE IN THE SQUARE/DOWNTOWN Opened Wednesday, June 3, 1981.* Elliot Martin presents the Long Wharf Theatre Production of:
AMERICAN BUFFALO By David Mamet; Director, Arvin Brown; Setting, Marjorie Bradley Kellogg; Costumes, Bill Walker; Lighting, Ronald Wallace; Technical Director, David McWilliams; Props, Michael Urban; Management Associate, Jack Tantleff; Production Associates, David Lancaster, Linda Giannini; Wardrobe, Mary Lou Rios; Casting, Marjorie Martin; Press, Jeffrey Richards, Ben Morse, C. George Willard, Robert Ganshaw, Helen Stern, Ted Killmer

CAST

Donny Dubrow . . . . Clifton James†1
Bobby . . . . Thomas Waites†2
Walter Cole (Teacher) . . . . Al Pacino
Standbys: Jose Santana, Ralph Monaco

A drama in two acts. The action takes place at the present time in Don's Resale Shop (Junkshop) on a Friday.

* Closed July 11, 1982 after 276 performances and 13 previews. Suspended from Oct. 31, 1981 to Thursday, Feb. 25, 1982. Original Broadway production opened Feb. 16, 1977 at the Barrymore Theatre and played 135 performances. See THEATRE WORLD, Vol. 33.
†Succeeded by: 1. J. J. Johnston, 2. James Hayden, Bruce MacVittie

TYSON STUDIO Friday, June 5–20, 1981 (16 performances) MRT Productions and Empire Stage Players present:
YOUNG BUCKS By John Kunik; Director, George Mead; Set, Vittorio Capecce; Costumes, Walker Hicklin; Lighting, Andrea Wilson; Sound, John North; Props, Shoestring Theatrical Properties; Executive Producers, Steven Smith, Michael Tylo, Don Hampton; Stage Managers, James Bohr, Gordon Juel; Technical Director, Blaise Corrigan; Art Director, Cheryl Podgorski; Props/Wardrobe, Andy Toleando; Press, Fred Hoot, Grace Harvey. **CAST:** Richard Bekins (Bruce), William Cain (Lloyd), Tim Choate (Keith), Dave Florek (Russ), David Haller (Bobby), K. C. Kelly (Jeff), Charley Lang (John), Bill Randolph (Dave), Christopher Rich (Tom), Victor Talmadge (Stan), Jeffrey Waid (Kevin)
A play in 2 acts and 4 scenes. The action takes place at the present time at a high school district basketball tournament at a midwestern university.

Gerrianne Raphael, Patricia Kalember, Alan Mixon in "The Butler Did It" *(Stephanie Saia Photo)*

ASTOR PLACE THEATRE Tuesday, June 9–21, 1981 (15 performances) Jonathan Reinis and Arthur Cantor present:
SHAY DUFFIN AS BRENDAN BEHAN Written and adapted from the works of Brendan Behan by Shay Duffin; Director, Denis Hayes; Set and Lighting, Joe Behan; Stage Manager, Larry Bussard; General Manager, Arthur Cantor; Company Manager, Harvey Elliott; Press, Jeffrey Richards, C. George Willard, Robert Ganshaw, Ben Morse, Helen Stern, Ted Killmer, Richard Humleker
Presented in two parts.

HORACE MANN THEATRE Wednesday, June 10– July 5, 1981 (28 performances) The Center for Theatre Studies at Columbia University presents:
WELDED By Eugene O'Neill; Director, Jose Quintero; Producer, Andrew B. Harris; Set and Costumes, Quentin Thomas; Technical Director/Lighting, Michael Valentino; Costume Coordinator, Carolyn J. Baehr; Assistants to the Director, John Handy, Richard C. Tunis, Harland Meltzer; Stage Managers, Michael O'Gara, Elizabeth Diamond, Carolyn Baehr; General Manager, Jeffrey Rosenstock; Assistants to Producer, Simone DeKoven, W. David Anderson; Casting, Richard Rosenwald, Maryellen Kernaghan; Press, Peter Cromarty, Shirley Herz

CAST: Philip Anglim (Michael Cape), Ellen Tobie (Eleanor), Court Miller (John), Laura Gardner (A Woman)
A drama in 3 acts and 4 scenes, performed without an intermission. The action takes place in a studio apartment, a library, and a bedroom.

URBAN ARTS THEATRE Wednesday, June 10–August 2, 1981 (52 performances) The Glines Inc. presents:
NIAGARA FALLS By Victor Bumbalo; Directed by Mr. Bumbalo; Set, Christopher Hacker; Costumes, George Whitmore; Lighting, Curt Ostermann; Producers, Barry Laine, Candida Scott Piel; Stage Managers, James Ross Smith, Dorothy Chansky; Press, Barry Laine

CAST: "American Coffee": Teri Keane (Connie Poletti), Joseph Rose (Johnny Poletti) "The Shangri-La Motor Inn": Veronica McAuley (Jackie Ventura), William Castleman (Fred Heneberry), Dan Lauria (Vinnie Ventura)

Clifton James, Al Pacino, Thomas Waites in "American Buffalo" *(Peter Cunningham Photo)*

BOUWERIE LANE THEATRE Thursday, June 11–28, 1981. (12 performances) Charlotte Bunin and Irene Kearney present:

THE WONDERFUL ICE CREAM SUIT By Ray Bradbury; Director, William E. Hunt; Set and Lighting, Francis J. Kiman; Costumes, Pamela C. Kiman; Original Music, Raoul Alphonse; Sound, George Jacobs; Assistant to Producers, Peter Bush; Stage Manager, Bill Edwards; Press, Francine L. Trevens, Freelance Talents

CAST: Ivonne Coll (Ruby), Elisa De La Roche (Celia), Tony Diaz (Dominiguez), Edward Estrada (Leo), Felipe Gorostinza (Manulo), Marty Greene (Shumway), Karl Jiminez (El Toro), Ricardo Matamoros (Gomez), Hector Mercado (Vamenos), Paul-Felix Montez (Villanazul), Walter Valentino (Martinez)

A comedy in two acts. The action takes place in a big city on a warm summer evening.

CHERRY LANE THEATRE Friday, June 12, 1981–January 31, 1982 (269 performances)* Howard Feuer, Jeremy Ritzer, Lawrence Gordon, Sidney Shlenker present:

ENTERTAINING MR. SLOANE By Joe Orton; Director, John Tillinger; Set, Mark Haack; Lighting, David N. Weiss; Costumes, Bill Walker; This production originally produced by Penumbra Productions (Michael Houlihan, Executive Producer); Wardrobe, Barbara Perkins; Technical Director, William Camp; Props, Leslie Moore; Company Manager, Erik Murkoff; Stage Managers, Kevin Mangan, Richard Eddon; General Manager, Albert Poland; Press, Fred Nathan, Eileen McMahon, Patt Dale, Anne S. Abrams

CAST

Kath	Barbara Bryne
Sloane	Maxwell Caulfield†1
Kemp	Gwyllum Evans
Ed	Joseph Maher†2

STANDBYS: Eda Seasongood (Kath), Richard Eddon (Sloane), Richard Lupino (Ed/Kemp) A drama in three acts. The action takes place at the present time in the home of Kath and her father Kemp.

* This production played 20 performances at Westside Mainstage from May 14–June 7, 1981.
†Succeeded by: 1. Richard Eddon, Brad Davis, 2. Jerome Dempsey

ENTERMEDIA THEATRE Tuesday, June 16–July 26, 1981 (42 performances) Kenneth Waissman with Edward Mezvinsky and Sidney Shlenker presents:

EL BRAVO! With Book by Jose Fernandez and Thom Schiera; Music and Lyrics, John Clifton; Based on a story by Jose Fernandez and Kenneth Waissman; Direction and Choreography, Patricia Birch; Scenery, Tom Lynch; Costumes, Carrie Robbins; Lighting, Neil Peter Jampolis; Sound, Tom Morse; Vocal and Dance Arrangements/Musical Supervision, Louis St. Louis; Orchestrations, Michael Gibson, Gary Anderson; Musical Direction/Vocal Arrangements, Herbert Kaplan; Associate Producer, Barry Greene; Casting, James Kramer & Associates; Production Assistant, Mark Schorr; Assistant to Director, Peggy Peterson; Assistant to Choreographer, Greg Rosatti; Wardrobe, Danajean Cicerchi; Props, Liam Herbert; General Assistant, Barbara Hodgen; Assistant to Producer, Donna Donaldson; General Manager, Edward H. Davis; Stage Managers, Michael Martorella, David Piel; Press, Betty Lee Hunt, Maria Cristina Pucci, James Sapp

CAST: Aurelio Padron (Pepe "El Bravo" DeMarco), Chamaco Garcia (Beggar), Dennis Daniels (Alan), Charlie Serrano (Juanito), Ray DeMattis (Honest John), Keith Jochim (Sgt. Noble), Michael Jeter (Cruikshank), Venesa Bell (Kitty), Starr Danias (Annabelle), Frank Kopyc (Fr. Tucker), Lenka Peterson (Mrs. Krekelberg), Yamil Borges (Mariana), Olga Merediz (Aunt Rosa), Ray Stephens (Willy), Duane Bodin (Narrator/Louie), Jesse Corti (Jose), S. J. Davis (Betty), Julia Lema (Julia), Alaina Warren Zachary (Duchess), Jenifer Lewis (Officer Walker), Stephen Jay (Officer Chase), Quitman Fludd III (Officer Cruz), Swings: Leilani Jones, Greg Rosatti

MUSICAL NUMBERS: El Bravo, Cuchifrito Restaurant, Que Pasa, Honest John's Game, Chiquita Bonita, Shoes, Hey Chico, Criminal, He Says, Talent Contest, Gotta Get Out, Adios Barrio, Fairy Tales, Torture, That Latin Lure, Congratulations!, Bailar!, And Furthermore, Finale

A musical in 2 acts and 14 scenes with a prologue. The action takes place "once upon a time in El Barrio, somewhere in New York City."

Barbara Bryne, Brad Davis in "Entertaining Mr. Sloane"
(Martha Swope Photo)

WONDERHORSE THEATRE Thursday, June 18–28, 1981 (12 performances) David J. Rothkopf presents:

CLOSE ENOUGH FOR JAZZ With Book and Lyrics by Joseph Keenan; Music, Scott Steidl; Created by Joseph Keenan, David Rothkopf; Director, David Rothkopf; Musical Director, Douglas Bernstein; Vocal Arrangements, Scott Steidl, Douglas Bernstein; Set and Lights, Bill Motyka; Costumes, Amanda Klein; Choreography, Mary Duncan; Production Associate, Cindy Gasparri; General Managers, Bob Buckley, Douglas Urbanski, Stephen Wells; Stage Managers, Howard R. McBride, Cheryl Singleton; Press, Fred Hoot, Carol Jackson, Steven Grenyo

CAST: Susan J. Baum, Stephen Berenson, Mary Duncan, Debra Jacobs, Joe Joyce, Nina Hennessey, Dietrich Snelling

MUSICAL NUMBERS AND SKETCHES: Close Enough for Jazz, Required Reading, Somebody Else/First Interlude, A Playwright Remembered, Dressing Room, The Post, Paperback Writer, This Is It/Second Interlude, Corporate Choreography, Anyone Else/Third Interlude, Don't Quote Me, Ballad/Fourth Interlude, What I'm Looking For/Fifth Interlude, Nobody Else/Final Interlude

A musical comedy revue in two acts.

WESTSIDE ARTS THEATRE/DOWNSTAIRS Thursday, June 18–July 19, 1981. (37 performances) Spencer Tandy, Joseph Butt and Peter Alsop present:

THE HEEBIE JEEBIES By Mark Hampton and Stuart Ross; Script and Production Adviser, Vet Boswell; Direction and Musical Staging, Stuart Ross; Scenery, Michael Sharp; Costumes, Carol Oditz; Lighting, Richard Winkler; Musical Supervision, Howard A. Roberts; Vocal Direction, Elise Bretton; Orchestrations, Christopher Bankey; Associate Choreographer, Terry Rieser; Produced in association with Dale Ward, Doug Cole; Props, John Kilner; Assistant to Producers, Margie Stanko; Hairstylist, Louis-Vincent; General Management, Dorothy Olim Associates; Associate, Thelma Cooper; Company Manager, George Elmer; Stage Managers, Robert Bennett, Michael Trueman; Press, Jeffrey Richards, Robert Ganshaw, Ben Morse, Helen Stern, C. George Willard, Ted Killmer, Richard Humleker, Stanley Evans

CAST: Memrie Innerarity (Martha Boswell), Audrey Lavine (Vet Boswell), Nancy McCall (Connee Boswell), Mary-Cleere Haran (Understudy)

A musical tribute to the Boswell Sisters in two acts, reprising their many hits.

Olga Merediz, Keith Jochim, Michael Jeter, in "El Bravo!"
(Sam Siegel Photo)

PROVINCETOWN PLAYHOUSE Tuesday, June 23–July 12, 1981 (23 performances) Kevin Gebhard presents:
OSCAR REMEMBERED A monodrama starring Maxim Mazumdar; Set Design, Tom H. John; Lighting Design, Richard Winkler; Production Supervisor, Larry Fuller; Assistant to Producer, Patricia Butterfield; Wardrobe, Deborah Lowman; Management Associate, Thelma Cooper; General Management, Dorothy Olim Associates; Company Manager, George Elmer; Stage Manager, Bill Hare; Press, Jeffrey Richards, Ben Morse, C. George Willard, Robert Ganshaw, Helen Stern, Ted Killmer, Stanley Evans, Richard Humleker
Performed in two parts: The Years 1892 to 1895, and Some Years after Oscar Wilde's Death.

PERRY STREET THEATRE Wednesday, June 24–July 26, 1981 (28 performances) Horizon Theatre presents:
EXTENUATING CIRCUMSTANCES By Dick Brukenfeld; Directed by the author; Set, Carole Lee Carroll; Costumes, Edi Giguere; Lighting, Victor En Yu Tan; Music, Joseph Blunt; Props, Adrienne Dornbusch; Wardrobe, Cheryl Warrenoff; Production Assistant, John Shepard; Production Supervisor, Sam Ellis; General Managers, Di Dia/Fiore Productions; Company Manager, Vito Perri; Stage Manager, C. L. Ringelstein; Press, Faith Geer

CAST: Glenn Cabrera (1st Official/Ko Soo Tee/Servant/Boatman), Willy Corpus (Linguist), Thomas Ikeda (Tseang), Eric Loeb (Capt. Cowpland), Tom Matsusaka (Pan Yu), Michael Albert Mantel (Frank), David Reinhardsen (Nick/Tony), Isao Sato (2nd Official/Peng/Bailiff), Stewart Schwartz (George Gruber), Edward Seamon (Wilcocks), Hal Studer (Lewis), Ginny Yang (Asay/Ko Leang She)
A play in 2 acts and 12 scenes. The action takes place in Canton, China in 1821 and is based on an actual incident.

JONES BEACH THEATRE Tuesday, June 30–September 6, 1981 (56 performances) Richard Horner Associates (Richard Horner-Lynne Stuart) in association with Long Island State Park and Recreation Commission present:
DAMN YANKEES Based on novel "The Year the Yankees Lost the Pennant" by Douglass Wallop; Book, George Abbott, Douglass Wallop; Music and Lyrics, Richard Adler, Jerry Ross; Direction and Choreography, Frank Wagner; Scenery and Costumes, Robert Fletcher; Lighting, Marc B. Weiss; Musical Director, Joseph Klein; Executive General Manager, Malcolm Allen; Assistant Choreographer, Marsha Wagner; Production General Manager, Stanley D. Silver; Casting, Lynne Stuart; Props, Jack Cassidy; Associate Conductor, Douglas Finney; Hairstylist, James Nelson; Wardrobe, Arlene Konowitz, Heather Haven; Production Coordinator, Jack Kauflin; Assistant Company Manager, Roger Sherman; Stage Managers, Valentine Mayer, Nicholas Russiyan; Press, Bob Ullman, James Radiches

CAST: Julienne Marie (Meg), Paul Merrill (Joe/Boyd) Eddie Bracken (Applegate), Barbara Kossen (Sister), Mara "Mutzie" Landi (Doris), Joe Namath (Joe Hardy), Ronald Earl Gattis (Henry), Anthony Inneo (Sohovik), Clyde Laurents (Smokey), David E. Mallard (Vernon), Robert Nichols (Van Buren), Paul V. Ames (Rocky), Alyson Reed (Gloria), Jordan Bowers (Lynch/Weston/Commissioner/Announcer), Thomas Ruisinger (Welch), Susan Elizabeth Scott (Lola), D. Peter Samuel (Postmaster)

ENSEMBLE: Paul V. Ames, Bill Badolato, Melinda Black, Jordan Earl Grattis, Anthony Inneo, Clyde Laurents, Judith M. Laxer, Kathleen Mahony-Bennett, David E. Mallard, Paul R. Nunes, Mimi Quillin, D. Peter Samuel, Lynne Savage, Mary Leigh Stahl, Sandra L. Turner, Zachary Wilde, Scott Willis, Swings: Thomas LoMonaco, Debra Lyman
STANDBYS AND UNDERSTUDIES: Mary Leigh Stahl (Meg/Sister/Doris/Weston), D. Peter Samuel (Joe Hardy), Clyde Laurents (Applegate), Melinda Black (Lola), Kathleen Mahony-Bennett (Gloria), Jordan Bowers (Joe Boyd/Welch), Paul V. Ames (Van Buren), Ciscoe Bruton II (Henry), Bill Badolato (Sohovic), Ronald Earl Gattis (Vernon), Anthony Inneo (Rocky/Smokey), Zachary Wilde (Lynch), Paul R. Nunes (Postmaster), Scott Willis (Commissioner)
A musical in 2 acts and 18 scenes. For original Broadway production, see THEATRE WORLD Vol. 11.

Tom Matsusaka, Ginny Yang, Nicholas Saunders, David Reinhardsen, Eric Loeb, Edward Seamon, Michael Albert Mantel in "Extenuating Circumstances" *(Stephanie Saia Photo)*

WESTSIDE ARTS THEATRE/CABARET SPACE Friday, July 3–12, 1981 (12 performances) '81 Theatre Inc. presents:
WHAT THE BUTLER SAW By Joe Orton; Director, Jonathan Davenport; Set, Robert Berg; Costumes, Jim Stewart; Lighting, Terry Alan Smith; Hairstylist/ Makeup, Stephen Procci; Executive Producer, Nelson Denis; Technical Director, Michael Gallagher; Production Assistant, Mia Katigbak; General Managers, Chris Silva, Michael Thomas Lord, Stephen Dailey, Will Dailey; Stage Managers, Greta Minsky, John E. C. Doyle; Press, Jeffrey Richards, Robert Ganshaw, Ben Morse, C. George Willard, Helen Stern, Ted Killmer, Stanley Evans, Richard Humleker

CAST: Harry Reems (Dr. Prentice), Holly Woodlawn (Geraldine Barclay), le Clanche du Rand (Mrs. Prentice), Jonathan Goldwater (Nicholas), George Lloyd (Dr. Rance), Brandon Brady (Sgt. Match), Understudies: Edward Conery, Staci Sweeden, John E. C. Doyle
A comedy in two acts. The action takes place in a room in a private clinic.

WONDERHORSE THEATRE Thursday, July 9–19, 1981 (12 performances) Gemini Theatre presents:
BUTTERFLIES ARE FREE By Leonard Gershe; Director, Laurie Eliscu; Set, Ellenmarie Jervey, Jerry Corrigan; Lighting, Bruce A. Kraemer; Costumes, Joe Panko; Sound, Hal Schuler; Stage Manager, Chet Fasulo

CAST: Marc Geller (Don Baker), Jacquie Porter (Jill Tanner), Mae Munroe (Mrs. Baker), Michael McKenzie (Ralph Austin)
A comedy in two acts. The action takes place in Don Baker's apartment on East 11th Street in New York in 1968.
(No photos submitted)

Joe Namath, Susan Elizabeth Scott in "Damn Yankees" *(Martha Swope Photo)*

ORPHEUM THEATRE Opened Tuesday, July 14, 1981.* Frank Gero, Mark Gero, Mitchell Maxwell, Alan J. Schuster, Frederick Zollo present the WPA Theatre (Kyle Renick, Producing Director) production of:
KEY EXCHANGE By Kevin Wade; Director, Barnet Kellman; Set, Terry Ariano; Costumes, Robert Wojewodski; Lighting, Frances Aronson; Associate Producers, Fred H. Krones, Nicholas Paleologos; Sound, Michael Jay; Assistant to Producers, Jonathan Gero; Company Manager, Ronnie Gallion; Press, Solters/Roskin/Friedman, Milly Schoenbaum, Warren Knowlton, Kevin Patterson

CAST

Michael .... Mark Blum
Philip .... Ben Masters
Lisa...................................... Brooke Adams†
Understudies: Robert Schenkkan, Sofia Landon

A comedy in 2 acts and 9 scenes. The action takes place at the present time in New York's Central Park from Sunday, June 20, to Sunday, August 8.

* Closed May 16, 1982 after 352 performances. Originally produced at the WPA Theatre Thursday, June 4, 1981 for 20 performances.
† Succeeded by Priscilla Lopez

LION THEATRE Thursday, July 23–August 2, 1981 (12 performances) Lion Theatre Company and South Street Theatre present:
VILLAGER By Ron McLarty; Director, John Guerrasio; Setting, Linda Skipper; Costumes, Bud Santora; Lighting, Norman Coates; Stage Managers, Louise Miller, Leslie Friedman; Production Assistant, Megan Spurdle; Press, Jeffrey Richards, C. George Willard, Stanley Evans

CAST: Bob Horen (Gaston Means), Barney Martin (Jess Smith), Winston May (Harry Daugherty), Roy Poole (Warren G. Harding), Kate Wilkinson (Florence Harding), Janet Zarish (Nan Britton)

A play in two acts. The action takes place over a period of several months early in 1923 in a sitting room adjacent to the bedroom of Florence Harding in The White House.

THE COMMON AT ST. PETER'S CHURCH Tuesday, August 4–16, 1981 (16 performances) American Theatre Exchange presents:
TELEMACHUS CLAY By Lewis John Carlino; Artistic Director/-Choreographer, George Stevenson; Lighting, Michael Meier; Stage Manager, Frank Montano; Sound, Judith Millman; Set, George Stevenson; Props, Joan Valentina; Press, Aaron Ross, Dennis Morton

CAST: Dennis Morton, Garret Jorden, Dianne Sally Lusk, Joanne Grace Voss, Juff Blaufarb, Lenny Pass, Nancy Martin, Peter A. Perrone, Aaron Ross, Claire Clark, Joseph Henderson, George Stevenson

SOUTH STREET THEATRE Tuesday, August 11–15, 1981 (7 performances and 19 previews) Graham Leader in association with Paul Posnick presents:
PEEP By James Murray; Director, Dorothy Lyman; Set, Mark Haack; Lighting, David N. Weiss; Costumes, Margarita Delgado; General Manager, Mike Houlihan; Assistant Director, Emelise Aleandri; Choreographer, William Herter; Wardrobe, Jill Exly; Props, Leslie Moore, Roni Gallion; Technical Director, Kevin Mangan; Stage Managers, Sherry Cohen, Devon O'Brien; Press, Fred Nathan, Patt Dale, Eileen McMahon, Elissa Leone
CAST: Anna Maria Horsford (Amazon), Linda Lee Johnson (Roxanne), Jill Larson (Charlene), Denise Lute (Nanette), Devon O'Brien (New Girl), Jacqueline M. Sedlar (Sophia), Sioux Saloka (Blue)

A play in 2 acts and 4 scenes. The action takes place in the Fantasy Theatre on 42nd Street in New York during the summer.

Mark Blum, Priscilla Lopez, Ben Masters in "Key Exchange"
(Carol Rosegg Photo)

WESTSIDE MAINSTAGE Tuesday, August 11–September 4, 1981 (16 performances) Boston Common (Ronald Hunter, Artistic Director) presents:
COMANCHE CAFE/DOMINO COURTS By William Hauptman; Director, Ronald Hunter; Scenery, Reagan Cook; Costumes, Alan H. Weitzman; Lighting, David Crist; Music Coordinator, Steven J. Matay; Stage Manager, David Pratt; Press, Owen Levy

CAST: "Comanche Cafe": Eliza DeCroes (Ronnie), Dorothi Fox (Mattie). The action takes place in the 1930's in a roadside diner in Southern Oklahoma. "Domino Courts": Donald Silva (Floyd), Eliza DeCroes (Ronnie), James Laurence (Roy), Judith McIntyre (Flo). The action takes place in 1939 somewhere in the Dustbowl of Southern Oklahoma in one of the cabins of the Domino Tourist Courts.

ONSTAGE THEATRE Monday, August 17–November 11, 1981 (101 performances) The Bosom Buddies Company presents:
JERRY'S GIRLS By Jerry Herman and Larry Alford; Staged and Directed by Larry Alford; Musical Direction, Cheryl Hardwick; Set and Lighting, Hal Tine; Costumes, Bernard Johnson; Choreography, Sharon Halley; Vocal Arrangements, John Visser; Stage Managers, Gene Bland, Todd Fleischer; General Manager, Leonard A. Mulhern; Company Manager, Jack Tantleff; Technical Director, Dan Niccum; Press, Ted Hook, Walt Veasey

CAST: Evalyn Baron, Alexandra Korey, Leila Martin, Pauletta Pearson, Jerry Herman
A musical revue in two acts starring the music and lyrics of Jerry Herman.

Pauletta Pearson, Jerry Herman, Evalyn Baron, Alexandra Korey, Leila Martin in "Jerry's Girls"

5

Craig Smith in "Something Cloudy, Something Clear"
(Gerry Goodstein Photo)

SARGENT THEATRE Wednesday, August 19–September 26, 1981 (16 performances) American Theatre of Actors presents:
RAFT By Al Capa; Director, John Daines; Set and Lighting, Joe Ray; Stage Manager, Tresa Davidson

CAST: Ross Fenton, Frank Stoegerer, Vera Lockwood, Leith Symington, Natalie Priest, Brian Watson

BOUWERIE LANE THEATRE Monday, August 24, 1981–March 13, 1982 (51 performances) Jean Cocteau Repertory (Eve Adamson, Artistic Director) presents:
SOMETHING CLOUDY, SOMETHING CLEAR By Tennessee Williams; Director, Eve Adamson; Set and Costumes, Douglas McKeown; Lighting, Giles Hogya; Choreography, Richard Peck; Assistant to Director, Marcello Gobelli; Production Assistant, Jessica Lanier; Stage Manager, Mark S. Henry

CAST: Craig Smith (August), Elton Cormier (Kip), Dominique Cieri (Clare), David Fuller (Merchant Seaman), John Schmerling (Maurice Fiddler), Phyllis Deitschel (Celeste Fiddler), Meg Fisher (Caroline Wales)
A drama in two acts. The action takes place during the late summer of 1940 in Provincetown, Mass.

COLONNADES THEATRE Friday, August 27–September 12, 1981 The Colonnades Theatre Lab presents:
THREE BY PIRANDELLO "The Man with the Flower in His Mouth," "The Jar," "The License"; Director, Michael Simone; Set, Joe Moblia; Costumes, Michael Hite; Lighting, Fred Jason Hancock; Stage Manager, Kate Hancock; Press, Jeffrey Richards, Robert Ganshaw, Richard Dahl

CAST: Danny DeVito, Val Dufour, Sam Locante, Angela Pietropinto, Antonio Sordi, Louise Contella, Amy Epstein, Charles Laulette, Pat Maniccia, Judi Mark, Steve Mendillo, Steve Parris, Gene Santarelli

John Getz, Leslie Lyles in "Sea Marks" *(Carol Rosegg Photo)*

WESTSIDE MAINSTAGE Wednesday, September 9–19, 1981 (13 performances) Richard Goodwin and Gale Salus present:
THE KILLING OF SISTER GEORGE By Frank Marcus; Director, Gale Salus; Scenery, Angelyn Wood; Lighting, Dana Bate; Costumes, Midge Gilman; Stage Managers, Kevin Harnett, Susan Elizabeth Mowrer; Press, Shirley Herz, Peter Cromarty, Sam Rudy
CAST: Susan Morgenstern (Sister George), Julie Nelson (Childie McNaught), Janie Tamarkin (Mrs. Croft), Aurelia DeFelice (Madame Zenia), Understudies: Gale Salus, Susan Elizabeth Mowrer
A drama in three acts. The action takes place in the living room of June Buckridge's flat on Devonshire Street, London.

UKRANIAN HALL Monday, September 14–27, 1981 (12 performances) Wayne Clark, Ronnie Britton and Robert Speller present:
TOULOUSE Written and directed by Ronnie Britton; Choreography, Robert Speller; Musical Direction/Orchestrations, Keith Ripka; Decor, Anthony Cava; Costumes, Bob Thompson; Lighting, Nina Votolato; Assistant Musical Director, Patrick Hays; Stage Manager, Schorling Schneider

CAST: Richard Rescigno (Toulouse-Lautrec), Beverly Gold (Suzanne), Molly Stark (Mme. Jardin), Linda David (Darnelle), Faye Cameron (Yvette Guilbert), Monte Ralstin (Bourges), Susie Vaughan Raney (Claudine), Amy Ryder (Colette), Christopher LeBlanc (Gabriel), Barbara Rouse (Daphne), Valerie Adami (La Goulue), Lana Fevola (Jane Avril), Louis Baldonieri (Valentine), Louise Claps (Mimi), Gerta Grunen (Countess), Andrew Krawetz (Police Chief), Scott Wakefield (Stephen), William Kase (Joseph), Bruno Damon (Bartender), Mark Enis (Claude), James Coleman (Philippe), Michael Del Rio (Pierre), Charlotte d'Amboise (Lulu), Sandra Aldin (Marie), Clayton Sauer (Robert), Thom Stickney (Roland), Marla Kassoff (Simone), Fay Reed (Charlotte), Lory Marcosson (Belle), Schorling Schneider (Gele), Tracy Osuna (Ileana), Franck Mariglio (Marcel), Jose Andres Ocampo Cano (Jacques), Marla Graham (Fifi), Matthew Sullivan (Mircea)
A musical in two acts and nine scenes. The action takes place in Paris in August and October of 1891.

PLAYERS THEATRE Thursday, September 24–November 15, 1981 (59 performances) Dana Matthow and Deborah Matthow present:
SEA MARKS By Gardner McKay; Director, John Stix; Scenery, Leslie Taylor, Dale Jordan; Costumes, Richard Hornung; Lighting, Todd Elmer; General Management, Dorothy Olim Associates; Company Manager, George Elmer; Management Associate, Thelma Cooper; Wardrobe, Deborah Lowman; Production Assistant, Ted Reinert; Stage Manager, Tom Picard; Press, Bruce Cohen

CAST: John Getz (Colm Primrose), Leslie Lyles (Timothea Stiles)
A drama in two acts. The action takes place at the present time in Ireland, and in Liverpool, England.

THEATRE EAST Tuesday, September 22–November 15, 1981 (64 performances). Three additional performances were given December 17–19, 1981 at Jan Hus House. Ruth Kalkstein presents:
CHEKHOV ON THE LAWN By Elihu Winer; Direction, Mr. Winer; Scenery and Lighting, Joe Ray; Stage Manager, Lori Styler; General Manager, Richard Horner Associates; Company Manager, Roger Sherman; Press, David Lipsky

CAST: William Shust as Anton Chekhov.
Performed in two parts. The action takes place on the lawn of Chekhov's home in Yalta on the afternoon of April 17, 1900.

TYSON STUDIO Friday, September 25–October 10, 1981 (12 performances) Carol Jackson presents:
TWO ONE-ACT PLAYS By Anna Marie Barlow; Director, Philip Gushee; Design, Quentin Thomas; Stage Managers, Rosemary Richardson; Press, Fred Hoot, Ken Munzing

CAST: "A Limb of Snow" with Richard Fancy (Jim), Cheryl Henderson (Hannah). "The Meeting" with Elizabeth Davis (Nancy), George Babiak (Boy), Richard Fancy (Frank)

ACTORS PLAYHOUSE Sunday, September 27–October 25, 1981 (23 performances) Karen B. Gromis and Bunny Adir Ltd. present:
EVERYBODY'S GETTIN' INTO THE ACT By Bob Ost; Staged by Darwin Knight; Musical Director, William McCauley; Musical Arrangements, Curtis Blaine; Scenery, Frank J. Boros; Costumes, Dianne Finn Chapman; Lighting/Stage Manager, Ric Barrett; Presented in Association with Goz Enterprises Inc.; Hairstylist, Daniel Mendez; Stage Manager, Julie Oliveri; Wardrobe, Carla Froeberg; Press, Fred Nathan, Patt Dale, Eileen McMahon, Jan Greenberg, James Rich, Anne Abrams

CAST: Ann Hodapp, Bill McCauley, Leilani Mickey, Tuck Milligan, Ross Petty, Julie Oliveri (Understudy)

MUSICAL NUMBERS: Everybody's Gettin' into the Act, That First Hello, Perfection, Too Good, So Close, Steppin' Back, I'm Available, Love Me Just a Little Bit, Love Duet, Looks Like Love, You Never Take Me Anywhere, Yes I See the Woman, To Wit, A Party in Southampton, It Always Seems to Rain, Never Never, Keepin' It Together, Ballad of the Victim, Alive and Well, Valse Triste, And I'm There!, Don't I Know You?
  "A Contemporary Vaudeville" in 2 acts and 7 scenes with a prologue and epilogue.

ASTOR PLACE THEATRE Wednesday, September 30–October 18, 1981 (23 performances) David Jones and George Barimo present:
PARTICULAR FRIENDSHIPS By Bill Elverman; Director, Dennis Rosa; Scenery and Costumes, Ben Shecter; Lighting, Craig Miller; Original Music, William D. Brohn; Assistant Director, Mark Menard; Wardrobe, Davette Pitts; Management Associate, Thelma Cooper; General Management, Dorothy Olim Associates; Company Manager, George Elmer; Stage Managers, Perry Cline, Betsy Tooker; Press, Jeffrey Richards, Robert Ganshaw, C. George Willard, Ben Morse, Helen Stern, Ted Killmer, Stanley Evans, Richard Humleker; Hairstylist, Milton Buras; Makeup, Barbara Armstrong

CAST: Luke Reilly (Avery Graham), Julie Kavner (Brooke Silver), Understudies: Betsy Tooker, Cotter Smith
  A play in two acts. The action takes place at the present time in Avery's New York City apartment.
  Stephanie Saia Photo

MARTINIQUE THEATRE Wednesday, October 7–25, 1981 (23 performances and 6 previews) The Kleist Company presents:
THE BROKEN PITCHER By Heinrich von Kleist; New Translation, Jon Swan; Director, Carl Weber; Production and Lighting Design, Wolfgang Roth; Costumes, Dean H. Reiter; Production sponsored by Goethe House; Production Assistants, Nina Stern, Edward LeViseur; General Manager, Lily Turner; Stage Managers, John Weeks, Roy Cockrum

CAST: Barbara Wild (Lisa), Marylouise Burke (Margaret), George Ede (Adam/Village Justice), Larry Pine (Link, a clerk), Roy Cockrum (Servant), Richard M. Davidson (Walter/District Judge), Sylvia Short (Mistress Martha Rull), Marta Heflin (Eve, her daughter), Thomas Carson (Veit Puddle), Gary Kingsolver (Ruprecht, his son), Norman Marshall (Constable), Angela Pietropinto (Mistress Bridget)
  A comedy performed without intermission. The action takes place in a Dutch village near Utrecht in 1808.

Ross Petty, Leilani Mickey, Tuck Milligan, Ann Hodapp in "Everybody's Gettin' into the Act" *(Linnea Beason Photo)*

THEATER AT ST. PETER'S CHURCH Thursday, October 8–13, 1981 (7 performances) Allen Grossman, Karl Allison and Nan Pearlman in association with the Common at St. Peter's Church present:
DOUBLE FEATURE With Book, Music and Lyrics by Jeffrey Moss; Director, Sheldon Larry; Choreography, Adam Grammis; Scenery, Stuart Wurtzel; Costumes, Patrizia von Brandenstein; Lighting, Marilyn Rennagel; Hairstylist, Patrik D. Moreton; Musical Arrangements and Orchestrations, Michael Starobin; Musical Director, Michael Lee Stockler; Additional Dance Arrangements, Glen Roven; Assistant Choreographer, Tina Paul; General Management, Kingwil Office; Company Manager, Al Isaac; Production Assistant, Eric Elice; Assistant to Director, Bill Hegeman; Production Associates, Bill Rosenfield, Jim Parker; Assistant to Producers, Lawrence Katen; Props, John Doyle; Casting, Meg Simon/Fran Kumin; Press, Jeffrey Richards, Robert Ganshaw, C. George Willard, Ben Morse, Helen Stern, Ted Killmer, Stanley Evans, Richard Humleker

CAST: Pamela Blair (Christine), Carole Shelley (Margaret), Stephen Vinovich (Alan), Don Scardino (John), Michael Kubala (He), Tina Paul (She)

MUSICAL NUMBERS: Just as It Should Be, Morning, Double Feature, When I Met Her, What If I Asked You for a Dance?, We Saw a Movie Together, How's It Gonna End?, One Step at a Time, The First Touch of Autumn, Wallpaper, Our Last Dance Together, A Little Bit of This
  A musical in two acts. The action takes place in New York City at the present time.

CHERNUCHIN THEATRE Thursday, October 9–24, 1981 (16 performances) Alpha Theatre Productions presents:
A SONG FOR ALL SAINTS By James Lineberger; Director, George Schwimmer; Assistant Producer, Irene Klein; Set, Robert Alan Harper; Lighting, Gianno Chiofalo; Costumes, Mary Ellen Bosche; Technical Director, Robert Falls; Props, Katherine Stives; Stage Manager, Shari Goldstein; Press, Free Lance Talents

CAST: Ralph Wakefield (Leroy Faggart), Victor Ferrer (Spanky), Marna Fran Deitch (Alfalfa), Michael Waite (Froggy), Susan Lowden (Darla), Ron Mychal Hayes (Stymie), Bonnie Saks Black (Farina), Miles Mason (Buckwheat), Frances Barnes (Estelle), Kathleen Kellaigh (Ann), Kevin Kelly (Howard), Kari Page (Yolanda)

Julie Kavner, Luke Reilly in "Particular Friendships"

Kevin Bacon, Orson Bean, Mark Keyloun in "40- Deuce" *(Bob Kiss Photo)*

PERRY STREET THEATRE Friday, October 9–25, 1981 (19 performances and 23 previews) Steven Steinlauf presents:
FORTY-DEUCE By Alan Bowne; Director, Tony Tanner; Scenery, Dan Leigh; Lighting, Craig Miller; Costumes, Gary Lisz; Associate Producer, Anne Thomson; Casting, Leonard Finger; Production Assistant, Alan Rish; Assistants to Producer, Myra Scheer, Richard Schiff; Mangement, Gilbert A. Wang/Frank Zimmerman & Co.; Stage Manager, Ryan Kelly; Press, Judy Jacksina, Glenna Freedman, Dolph Browning, Angela Wilson

CAST: John Noonan (John Anthony), Harris Laskawy (Augie), Ahvi Spindell (Mitchell), Kevin Bacon (Ricky), Tommy Citera (Crank), Mark Keyloun (Blow), Carol-Jean Lewis (Dealer), Bo Rucker (Dealer), Orson Bean (Roper), Understudies: Grant Forsberg (Blow/Ricky), Michael Arkin (Roper/Augie), Anthony Barrile (Mitchell/Crank/John)
    A drama in 2 acts and 4 scenes. The action takes place at the present time in a hotel on Eighth Avenue in the Times Square area, New York City.

PROVINCETOWN PLAYHOUSE Tuesday, October 13–November 15, 1981 (40 performances) Gintare Sileika and Linda Laundra present the Writers Theatre production of:
MY OWN STRANGER Adapted from the writings of Anne Sexton by Marilyn Campbell; Conceived and Directed by Linda Laundra; Scenery, Christina Weppner; Costumes, Clifford Capone; Lighting, Robby Monk; Original Music, Richard Kassel; General Manager, Kevin Dowling; Production Coordinator, David Laundra; General Management, Ad Ventures; Hairstylist, Jerry Pritchet; Casting, Thomas M. Fontana; Stage Manager, Becky Wold; Press, Gifford/Wallace Inc., Keith Sherman

CAST: Marilyn Campbell, Nancy-Elizabeth Kammer, Pat Lysinger, Understudy: Emily Nash
    Performed with one intermission.

ST. CLEMENT'S THEATRE Wednesday, October 14–December 19, 1981 (68 performances) M. G. I. and Scott Bushnell in association with the Los Angeles Actors' Theatre presents:
TWO BY SOUTH Written by Frank South; Director, Robert Altman; Scenery, John Kavelin; Lighting, Barbara Ling; Original Songs, Danny Darst; Production Assistant, Margie Stanko; Technical Director, Gary Jennings; General Manager, M.G.I.; Company Manager, Doug Cole; Stage Manager, John Brigleb; Press, Jeffrey Richards, Ben Morse, C. George Willard, Robert Ganshaw, Helen Stern, Ted Killmer, Richard Humleker, Stanley Evans

CAST: "Precious Blood": Guy Boyd, Alfre Woodard. "Rattlesnake in a Cooler": Leo Burmester, Danny Darst

WESTSIDE MAINSTAGE Wednesday, October 14–November 1, 1981 (12 performances) Fred Crecca presents:
A PRAYER FOR MY DAUGHTER By Thomas Babe; Director, Joseph Ragno; Assistant Director, Odessa David; Set, Regan Cook; Lighting, Richard Sheppard; Stage Manager, Lisa Ledwich; Press, Fred Crecca

CAST: Jeb Ellis-Brown (Jimmy), M. Patrick Hughes (Kelly), Aleks Shaklin (Jack), Harvey Siegel (Sean)
    A drama in two acts. The action takes place at the present time in the detective squad room of a New York City police precinct.

LAMBS THEATRE Wednesday, October 21, 1981–April 11, 1982 (193 performances) Philip M. Getter presents:
COTTON PATCH GOSPEL Book, Tom Key, Russell Treyz; Based on "The Cotton Patch Version of Matthew and John" by Clarence Jordan; Music and Lyrics, Harry Chapin; Director, Russell Treyz; Musical Director, Tom Chapin; Scenery, John Falabella; Lighting, Roger Morgan; Associate Producer, Louis F. Burke; Production Assistant, Sue Anne Kershenson; General Management, Theatre Now, Inc.; Company Manager, Charlotte Wilcox; Stage Manager, Mark Rubinsky; Press, Susan L. Schulman, Claudia McAllister, Sandi Kimmel

CAST

Tom Key	The Cotton Pickers
Scott Ainslie	Michael Mark
Pete Corum	Jim Lauderdale

MUSICAL NUMBERS: Somethin's Brewin' in Gainesville, I Did It, Mama Is Here, It Isn't Easy, Sho' Nuff, Turn It Around, When I Look Up, There Ain't No Busy Signals/Spitball, We're Going to Atlanta, What Does Atlanta Mean to Me, Are We Ready?, You Are Still My Boy, We Got to Get Organized, We're Gonna Love It, Jubilation, Agony Round, I Wonder
    A musical in two acts. The action takes place "here and now."

VANDAM THEATRE Thursday, October 22–November 1, 1981 (10 performances) Gemini Theatre presents:
SUMMERTREE By Ron Cowen; Director, Howard Rossen; Production Design, Jerry Corrigan; Sound, Hal Schuler; Stage Manager, Laurence P. Clement

CAST: Marc Geller (Young Man), Brad Karnes (Little Boy), Joanne Jacobson (Mother), Bill Rowley (Father), Anne Howard (Girl), Alec Baldwin (Soldier)
    A drama in two acts. The action takes place at the present time.

Tom Key (front) in "Cotton Patch Gospel" *(Martha Swope Photo)*

RICHARD ALLEN CENTER Friday, October 23, 1981–January 3, 1982 (59 performances) Moved to Actors Playhouse January 15–May 30, 1982 (117 performances) The Glines presents
TORCH SONG TRILOGY By Harvey Fierstein; Director, Peter Pope; Producer, Lawrence Lane; Production Manager, Penny Landau; Technical Director, Richard Wittenmyer; Scenery, Leon Munier; Costumes, Mardi Philips; Lighting, Scott Pinkney; Musical Direction and Arrangements, Ned Levy; Original Music, Ada Janik; Production Assistants, Vincent Arbona, Larry Bussard, Giani Siri; General Manager, Lawrence Lane; Company Manager, Judy Thomas; Stage Managers, John Handy, William Castleman; Press, Free Lance Talents, Francine L. Trevens, David Mayhew, Fred Nathan

CAST

Arnold Beckoff	Harvey Fierstein
Ed	Joel Crothers†1
Lady Blues/Laurel	Diane Tarleton
Alan	Paul Joynt
David	Matthew Broderick†2
Mrs. Beckoff	Estelle Getty

Understudy: Casey Wayne

PART I: The International Stud, **PART II:** Fugue in a Nursery, **PART III:** Widows and Children First!
Performed with two intermissions.

† Succeeded by: 1. Court Miller, 2. Fisher Stevens

Ken Howard Photo

LION THEATRE Monday, October 26–December 27, 1981 (56 performances) Prism Theatre (Stephen Stewart-James, Producer) in association with Harold Bligh presents:
AMIDST THE GLADIOLAS By Vito A. Gentile, Jr.; Director, Ron Comenzo; Set, Robert R. Yodice; Lighting, Paul Everett; Costumes, Sam Fleming; Sound Tom Gould; Production Manager, Arturo Proazzi; Costume Coordinator, Eileen Madison; Wardrobe, Terry Sommer; Technical Director, Bernadette Wise; Stage Managers, D. C. Rosenberg, Kathleen Marsters

CAST: Esther Brandice (Rosa), Sally-Jane Heit (Connie), Dorothy Holland (Francine), Estelle Kemler (Phyllis), Dina Paisner (Jenny), Joe Palmieri (Sammy), Rosemary Prinz (Maryanne), James Selby (Bernard), Charlotte Volage (Understudy)
A play in two acts. The action takes place at the present time in the Gold Room of the Lucchese Funeral Home in Brooklyn, NY.

THE GRAND GALLERY Thursday/Friday, October 29–30, 1981 (2 performances) The President, Board of Governors, Joseph Kesselring Award Committee of the National Arts Club present:
PRISM BLUES By Susan Charlotte; Director, Michael Parva; Set, Carl Hagmueller; Costumes, Ann Morrell; Lighting, Craig Kennedy; Sound, Robert Lochow; Stage Mangers, Laurie B. Clark, Howard P. Lev, Desiree Conte

CAST: Victoria Lanman (Sara), Regina Taylor (Cookie), Jean Anderson (Mrs. Weiss), Juanita Bethea (Mrs. Roberts), Yvette Freeman (Johnson), Myra Anderson (Daniels), Erma Campbell (Captain), Kymberly Schwartz (Denise), Debora (Inmate Taylor), John Hotard (David Brooks), Gary Mitchell (Williams/Court Attendant), F. David Halpert (Mr. Weiss/District Attorney)
A drama in two acts. The action takes place during the present and in the past.

Diane Tarleton, Paul Joynt, Harvey Fierstein, Matthew Broderick, Court Miller, Estelle Getty in "Torch Song Trilogy"

AMERICAN THEATRE OF ACTORS Friday, October 30–November 21, 1981 (18 performances) Actors' and Directors' Theater Inc. presents:
THE HEIRESS By Ruth and Augustus Goetz; Suggested by Henry James' novel "Washington Square"; Director, Nell Robinson; Setting, Joseph A. Varga; Lighting, Scott Pinkney; Costumes, Mary I. Whitehead; Technical Director, Randall Etheredge; Stage Managers, Stacey April, Jan Pessin; Press, Shirley Herz, Sam Rudy, Peter Cromarty

CAST: Jan Pessin (Maria), Miller Lide (Dr. Sloper), Lois Diane Hicks (Lavinia Penniman), Roxana Stuart (Catherine Sloper), Ruth Ann Norris (Elizabeth Almond), Scott Bingham (Arthur Townsend), Wendy Matthews (Marian Almond), Robin Thomas (Morris Townsend), Jacque Dean (Mrs. Montgomery)
A drama in 2 acts and 7 scenes. The action takes place in the front parlor of Dr. Sloper's home on Washington Square in New York City during 1850–1853.

HAROLD CLURMAN THEATRE Sunday, November 1–22, 1981 (25 performances) The Women's Ensemble presents:
TAKEN IN MARRIAGE By Thomas Babe; Director, Russ Weatherford; Choreography, Arthur Goldweit; Lighting, Stephen and Candace Solie; Assistant to Director, Ann Clay; Hairstylist, Larry Brescia; Props, Cindy Holden, Chris Robinson; Technical Director, Sam Gonzalez; General Management, Soloway/Francis; Company Manager, Brian Dunbar; Stage Manager, D. King Rodger; Press, Shirley Herz, Sam Rudy, Peter Cromarty

CAST: Prudence Sherman (Dixie Avalon), Sammi Gavich (Annie), Carolyn Kennedy (Andrea), Patricia Newcastle (Ruth Chandler), Barbara LeBrun (Aunt Helen)
A drama in two acts. The action takes place at the present time in a small town in New Hampshire.

Dorothy Holland, Dina Paisner in "Amidst the Gladiolas"
(Gary Schoichet Photo)

WONDERHORSE THEATRE Wednesday, November 4–29, 1981 (28 performances) Andrew Harris presents:
COWBOY MOUTH (IN CONCERT) By Sam Shepard and Patti Smith; Director, George Ferencz; Music by the company; Lyrics, Sam Shepard, Patti Smith; Technical Director, Thomas Rees; Lighting, Mark Weingartner; Costumes, Schnoz & Schnoz; Assistant Director, Virlana Tkacz; Production Coordinator, Carolyn Baehr; Stage Manager, Marilyn Skow; Press, Shirley Herz, Peter Cromarty

CAST: Brooks McKay (Slim), Annette Kurek (Cavale), Robert E. Barnes, Jr. (Lobster Man)
    Performed in two acts.

ACTORS AND DIRECTORS THEATRE Friday, November 6–29, 1981 (20 performances) The New York Theatre Studio (Richard V. Romagnoli, Artistic Director; Cheryl Faraone, Managing Director) present:
CUBISTIQUE By Tom Cone; Director, Ted Walch; Set, Loy Arcenas, Gerard P. Bourcier; Costumes, Louise Martinez; Lighting, John Hickey; Sound, Gary Massey; General Manager, Moss Hassell; Choreographer, Maria Zannieri; Dialect Coach, Tim Monich; Technical Director, Dennis Runge; Stage Managers, David Thalenberg, Sally Burnett, Rebecca Pease; Press, Ed Callaghan, Burnham/Callaghan Associates.

CAST: John Barone (Jean), Brenda Wehle (Francis), Susan Sharkey (Annie). The action takes place in a Paris salon in the early 1920's.

FRUGAL REPAST By Sheldon Rosen; Director, Dorothy Lyman.

CAST: Susan Sharkey (Baggy), James Greene (Raggy). The action takes place on a street corner. Suggested by a 1904 Pablo Picasso etching "The Frugal Repast."

SOUTH STREET THEATRE Sunday, November 8, 1981—January 31, 1982 (62 performances) Jean Sullivan, Michael Fischetti present:
THE STRONGER By August Strindberg; Translated by George Springer; Director, Gene Nye; Set, Bob Phillips; Costumes, Amanda Klein; Lighting, Malcolm Sturchio; Sound, Amy Steindler; General Manager, Eleanor Meglio; Stage Managers, Leslie Moore, Ronna Levy; Press, Jeffrey Richards Associates, Ted Killmer.

CAST: Jean Sullivan (Miss X), Phyllis Somerville (Mrs. Y), Ronna Levy (Waitress).
    The action takes place in a ladies' cafe in Stockholm, Sweden on a Christmas Eve in the 1880's.

HUGHIE By Eugene O'Neill; Director, Gino Giglio.

CAST: Frank Geraci (Night Clerk), Michael Fischetti (Erie Smith).
    The action takes place at 3 A.M. in the lobby of a NYC mid-town hotel during the summer of 1928.

ASTOR PLACE THEATRE Monday, November 9–15, 1981 (8 performances and 8 previews) Baraboo Productions present:
FIGHTING BOB By Tom Cole; Director, Sharon Ott; Scenery, Laura Maurer; Lighting, Rachel Budin; Costumes, Susan Tsu; Music, Mark Van Hecke; Wigs and Hairstyles, Charles Lo Presto; Props, Ellen Dorsey; Production Assistant, Tom Burke; Wardrobe, Cathay Brackman; Executive Assistant, Susan Dorsey; General Manager, Robert S. Fishko; Company Manager, Margay Whitlock; Stage Manager, Marjorie Horne; Press, Jeffrey Richards, Robert Ganshaw, C. George Willard, Ben Morse, Helen Stern, Ted Killmer, Stanley Evans, Richard Humleker

CAST: John P. Connolly (Teacher), Sonja Lanzener (Belle Case LaFollette), Eugene J. Anthony (Robert M. LaFollette), David E. Chadderdon (General George Bryant/Philetus Sawyer), Paul Meacham (Deacon John Z. Saxton/Theodore Roosevelt)
    A play in three acts. The action takes place at the present time in a nightschool classroom.

Frank Geraci, Michael Fischetti in "Hughie" *(Susan Cook Photo)*

WESTSIDE ARTS/CHERYL CRAWFORD THEATRE   Monday, November 9, 1981—January 31, 1982 (128 performances). This production had played 170 performances at the Playwrights Horizons. Mary Lea Johnson, Francine LeFrak, Martin Richards, Warner Theatre Productions Inc. present the Playwrights Horizons production of:
MARCH OF THE FALSETTOS By William Finn; Director, James Lapine; Set, Douglas Stein; Costumes, Maureen Connor; Lighting, Frances Aronson; Orchestrations/Musical Direction, Michael Starobin; Associate Producer, Sam Crothers; Original Cast Album by DRG Records; Wardrobe, Rachel Chanoff; Assistant to Director, Lynda Lee Burks; General Management, Gatchell & Neufeld; Company Manager, Roger Gindi; Stage Managers, Trey Hunt, William L. McMullen; Press, Jeffrey Richards, Robert Ganshaw, Ben Morse, Helen Stern, C. George Willard, Ted Killmer, Richard Humleker, Stanley Evans

CAST

Marvin	Michael Rupert
Trina, his ex-wife	Alison Fraser
Jason, his son	Gregg Phillips
Whizzer Brown, his lover	Brent Barrett
Mendel, his psychiatrist	Chip Zien

UNDERSTUDIES: Ralph Bruneau (Mendel/Marvin/Whizzer), Emily Grinspan (Trina), James Kushner (Jason)
MUSICAL NUMBERS: 4 Jews in a Room Bitching, A Tight-Knit Family, Love Is Blind, The Thrill of First Love, Marvin at the Psychiatrist, This Had Better Come to a Stop, Please Come to My House, Jason's Therapy, A Marriage Proposal, Trina's Song, March of the Falsettos, Chess Game, Making a Home, The Games I Play, Marvin Hits Trina, I Never Wanted to Love You, Father to Son
    A musical performed without intermission.

Susan Cook Photo

**Chip Zien, Gregg Phillips, Michael Rupert, Alison Fraser, Brent Barrett
in "March of the Falsettos"**

URBAN ARTS THEATRE Sunday, November 15–29, 1981 (18 performances and 3 previews) Julianne Boyd presents:
THE COLLYER BROTHERS AT HOME and PERIOD PIECE
By Mark St. Germain; Director, Julianne Boyd; Costumes, Christina Weppner; Scenery, Reagan Cook; Lighting, Rick Belzer; Sound, Regina M. Mullen; Original Music, Martha Worth Micci; Musical Direction, Michael Ward; Casting, Ellen Madison; Production Assistant, Charles Mandracchia; Makeup, Peg Schierholz; Stage Managers, Renee F. Lutz, Jane Unger; Press, Amelise Aleandri

CAST: "The Collyer Brothers at Home": Wyman Pendleton (Langley Collyer), Fred Sadoff (Homer Collyer). "Period Piece": Wyman Pendleton (Teddy Cantell), Fred Sadoff (Harrison Budds)

47th STREET THEATRE Wednesday, November 18–29, 1981 (12 performances) Carnes & Allen present:
CHANTECLER With Book and Lyrics by Anthony A. Piano; Based on Edmond Rostand play; Music, Michael R. Colichio; Director, Edward Berkeley; Choreography, Nora Peterson; Musical Direction, Robert Goldstone; Musical Arrangements, Michael R. Colicchio; Costumes, Beth Kuhn; Production Design, John Kasarda; Lighting, Gregory MacPherson; Fight Choreography, Bill Campbell; Technical Director, Joel Howard; Assistant Choreographer, Isabel Menson; Stage Managers, Scott Lafever, Uriel Menson; Press, Becky Flora

CAST: Jeanne Allen (Mme. Guinea Hen), Gary Barker (Duck/Briffaut/Owl/Oestereich), James Beaumont (Mr. Peacock/Owl/Spirit of the Forest), Ralph Bruneau (Chantecler), Bill Campbell (Peregrine Pigeon/White Pile/Owl), Kate Dezine (Ondine), Rick Friesen (Gaspar/Scops), Isabel Glasser (Cat), Gigi Hageman (Goose/Creature of the Forest), D. Michael Heath (Turkey/Nightingale), Gary Jaketic (Georges/Owl/Magyar), Donna Jones (Bichette/Creature of the Forest), Tom Lantzy (Raven), Steven Memel (Rooster/Bubo Ignavus/Phantom Bantam), Anne Parks (Mrs. Peacock/Creatures of Forest), Sandy Perrill (Madelaine/Doe), Chad Restum (Marius/Owl/Rat), Tom Rolfing (Patou), Debra Stricklin (Therese/Raccoon),

A musical in two acts. The action takes place at the present time in a barnyard and surrounding forest in Gascony, France, during the summer and autumn. (No photos available)

MARTIN THEATRE Sunday, November 24–29, 1981 (8 performances) Performing Arts Repertory Theatre (Jay Harnick, Artistic Director) presents:
SUSAN B! With Book by Jules Tasca; Lyrics, Ted Drachman; Music, Thomas Tierney; Director, John Henry Davis; Choreography, Haila Strauss; Musical Direction, Harrison Fisher; Costumes, David Robinson; Settings, Jack Stewart; Stage Manager, Alan Easterby; Press, Charles Hull

CAST: Lillian Byrd (Susan), Frank Groseclose (Greeley/Daniel), Julianne Ross (Guelma), Kathleen McGrath (Lucy/Elizabeth), Greg Gunning (Aaron/Tasche), Larry Cahn (Parker)
A musical performed without intermission

TYSON STUDIO Friday, November 27—December 13, 1981 (16 performances) Empire Stage Players Inc. present:
STUNNING ACHIEVEMENTS IN IOWA By Mark D. Kaufmann; Director, Norman Morrow; Executive Producer, Earl Arremis Johnson; Set and Lighting, Bob Briggs; Costumes, Denise Galonsky; Sound, Raymond Benson; Props, Diane Waller; Assistant to Director, Rita Montone; Administrative Assistant, Adriane Hoard; Technical Director, Blaise Corrigan; Art Director, Pamela Hampton; Stage Managers, Kelly Carty, Joe White; Press, Fred Hoot, Ken Munzing

CAST: Vince Carroll (Arnold), Eugene Pressman (Estes), Paul Carlin (Vic), Jo Deodato Clark (Polly), Cynthia Bock (Esther), Eloise Iliff (Elizabeth), Nancy Ward (Doris)

A play in 2 acts and 5 scenes. The action takes palce during the mid-1970's in the dining room of a farmhouse in Iowa.

Wyman Pendleton, Fred Sadoff in "Period Piece"
(Cathryn Williams Photo)

AMDA STUDIO ONE Friday, November 27—December 20, 1981 (20 performances) Bandwagon presents:
SOMETHING FOR THE BOYS With Music and Lyrics by Cole Porter; Book, Herbert and Dorothy Fields; Concept-Direction-Choreography, Tod Jackson; Musical Direction, Bruce Kirle; Producer, Jerry Bell; Scenery and Lighting, Patrick Dearborn; Costumes, Jim Lowe; Hairstylist, Glenn Conn; Vocal and Dance Arrangements, Bruce Kirle; Orchestrations, David Caldwell; General Manager/Sound, Jon Hutcheson; Stage Managers, James Lockhart, Robert Strickstein; Props, Faith Houston; Technical Director, Jean-Pierre LaPlanche; Assistant Director, Robin Lee; Assistant Choreographer, Carol Estey; Assistant Musical Director, David Caldwell; Assistant to Producer, Bill Ferry; Production Coordinator, Sandra Starr; Press, Betty Lee Hunt, Maria Cristina Pucci, James Sapp

CAST: Austin Adams (Patrick), David Robert Adams (Paul), Karen Babcock (Sarah), Carleton Carpenter (Harry), Joseph Culliton (Roger), James Herriges (John), T. J. Hicks (Charles), Patti Karr (Chiquita), Frank Kosik (Robert), Wade Laboissonniere (David), MacKenzie Lee (Rocky), Rosemary Loar (Betty Jean), Judith McConnell (Melanie), Robert McNamara (Tobias), Virginia Martin (Blossom), James Maxwell (Allen), Darleigh Miller (Ann), P. J. Nelson (Mrs. Grubbs), Kari Seier (Barb ara), Llewellyn Thomas (Col. Grubbs), Scott Willis (Laddie)

MUSICAL NUMBERS: Prologue, See That You're Born in Texas, When My Baby Goes to Town, Something for the Boys, When We're Home in the Range, Could It Be You?, Hey Good Lookin', He's a Right Guy, Leader of a Big Time Band, I'm in Love with a Soldier Boy, There's a Happy Land in the Sky, By the Mississiniwah, Finale
A musical in 2 acts 11 scenes with prologue.

Patti Karr, MacKenzie Lee, Virginia Martin, Robert McNamara, Carleton Carpenter in "Something for the Boys"
(Patrick Dearborn Photo)

John Cullum as Whistler

WESTSIDE MAINSTAGE Friday, November 27—December 13, 1981 (12 performances) The Actors Collective presents:
THE POKEY By Stephen Black; Director, Morgan Sloane; Set, Bill Motyka; Costumes, Bebe Shamash, Lynne Born; Lighting, Jonathan Ruttenberg; Sound, Janet Crane, Alan Woolf; Production Managers, Charles G. Bergwin, Randy Osofsky; Production Assistants, Katherine Boshamer, Wendy Way; Stage Manager, Melissa Davis; Press, Owen Levy

CAST: Lynne Born (Young Woman), Perry Jon Pirkkanen (Young Man)

PROVINCETOWN PLAYHOUSE Sunday, December 6, 1981—January 3, 1982 (34 performances) Frank Gero and Mark Gero in association with Hori Productions of Tokyo present:
JOHN CULLUM AS WHISTLER By Lawrence and Maggie Williams; Adapted from the novel "I, James McNeill Whistler" by Lawrence Williams; Director, Jerome Kilty; Scenery and Costumes, David Gropman; Scenic and Costumes Supervisor, Keith Gonzalez; Lighting, William Armstrong; Production Supervisor, Bob D. Bernard; Assistant to Producers, Jason Gero; Company Manager, Ronni Galion; Stage Manager, Elise Warner; Press, Shirley Herz, Sam Rudy, Peter Cromarty
James McNeill Whistler and others played by John Cullum with one intermission.

ACTORS AND DIRECTORS THEATRE Monday, December 7–31, 1981 (27 performances and 6 previews) Miranda Smith presents:
MAGIC TIME By James Sherman; Director, Henry Hoffman; Scenery, Karen Gerson; Costumes, Sue Ellen Rohrer; Lighting, Juan Acevedo-Lucio; Titlesong by Karen Manno, Jonathan Rosen; Props, Jonathan Rosen; Fencing Choreographer, Rick Casoria; General Manager, Miranda Smith; Press, Jeffrey Richards, Robert Ganshaw, Ted Killmer

CAST: Richard Levine (Larry/Laertes), Judy Tate (Joan/Stage Manager), Robin Chadwick (Alan/Polonius), Ivar Brogger (Scott/Claudius), Rick Casorla (Chris/Horatio), Elizabeth Burr (Laurie/Ophelia), Karen Ingenthron (Ann/Gertrude), Richard Marion (David/Hamlet), Meg Van Zyl (Understudy)
Performed without intermission. The action takes place backstage in a dressing room on Sunday night before Labor Day 1974.

THE OPEN EYE Thursday, December 10–20, 1981 (12 performances and 5 previews) Shari Upbin and Georgene Callahan present:
VINCENT By Christopher Consani; Based on "Vincent van Gogh: The Lark and the Crow"; Director, Shari Upbin; Visual Design; Jonathan Yarus; Settings, David Woolard; Costumes Michael Johnson; Lighting, Ortansa Lebadaru; Original Music, Joel Silberman; Production Coordinators, James Vaughn, Scott Bloom; Technical Director, Daphne Groos; Press, Betty Lee Hunt, Maria Cristina Pucci, James Sapp

CAST: Christopher Consani (Vincent van Gogh), Lou Liotta (Theo/Father/Paul Gauguin)
The action takes place at the end of Vincent's life in Auvers, near Paris, in 1890 . . . and in recall. Performed with one intermission.

VILLAGE GATE UPSTAIRS Monday, December 14, 1981—March 28, 1982 (120 performances and 27 previews) Cameron Mackintosh, Hinks Shimberg in spite of Art D'Lugoff present:
TOMFOOLERY The words and music of Tom Lehrer; Adapted by Cameron Mackintosh and Robin Ray; Directors, Gary Pearle, Mary Kyte; Setting, Tom Lynch; Costumes, Ann Emonts; Lighting, Robert Jared; Musical Direction, Eric Stern; Musical and Vocal Arrangements, John McKinney; Original Musical Arrangements, Chris Walker; Wardrobe, Miriam Nieves; Sound, Jane Pipik; Production Assistant, Douglas Cox; General Manager, Albert Poland; Company Manger, Nancy Nagel; Stage Managers, Alice Galloway, Connie Coit; Press, Solters/Roskin/Friedman, Milly Schoenbaum, Kevin Patterson

CAST: MacIntyre Dixon, Joy Franz, Jonathan Hadary, Donald Corren, Standbys: Connie Coit, Michael McCormick

MUSICAL NUMBERS: Be Prepared, Poisoning Pigeons, I Wanna Go Back to Dixie, My Home Town, Pollution, Bright College Days, Fight Fiercely Harvard, The Elements, Folk Song Army, In Old Mexico, She's My Girl, When You Are Old and Grey, Verner von Braun, Who's Next, I Got It from Agnes, National Brotherhood Week, So Long Mom, Send the Marines, Hunting Song, Irish Ballad, New Math, Silent E, Oedipus Rex, I Hold Your Hand in Mine, Masochism Tango, Old Dope Peddler, Vatican Rag, We Will All Go Together
Performed in two acts.

Martha Swope/Carol Rosegg Photo

Donald Corren, Jonathan Hadary, Joy Franz, MacIntyre Dixon in "Tomfoolery"

ST. PETER'S HALL Sunday, December 13, 1981—January 10, 1982 (18 performances) The Shaliko Company presents:
THE MIDNIGHT VISITOR By Daniel Mark Epstein; Director, Leonardo Shapiro; Set, Bil Mikulewicz; Costumes, Kenneth Yount; Lighting, Candice Dunn; Technical Director, Dave Fish; Casting, David Rubin; General Management, Nexus Theatre Associates Ltd./Clyde Kuemmerle; Stage Managers, Rob Schoenbohm, Geoffrey Miller, John Goldstein; Press, Shirley Herz, Sam Rudy, Peter Cromarty

CAST: Walt Gorney (Cyrus), Cecil MacKinnon (Bridget), Nada Rowand (Helen), Lisa Pelikan (Mary), Susan Lynch (Franny), Robert Schenkkan (Sebastian), Understudies: Lucy Winner, Geoffrey Miller
A drama in two acts. The action takes place in the living room of a country house on a late evening in early January. It has been snowing all day.

HAROLD CLURMAN THEATRE Tuesday, December 15, 1981—January 3, 1982 (22 performances) Aristotle Productions presents:
HEAD OVER HEELS With Book by William S. Kilborne, Jr. and Albert T. Viola; Based on play "The Wonder Hat" by Kenneth Sawyer Goodman and Ben Hecht; Music, Albert T. Viola; Lyrics, William S. Kilborne, Jr.; Director, Jay Binder; Musical Numbers Staged by Terry Rieser; Executive Producers, Leonard Soloway, Allan Francis; Associate Producer, Joseph M. Sutherin; Scenery and Costumes, John Falabella; Lighting, Jeff Davis; Musical Direction/Vocal Arrangements, Herbert Kaplan; Orchestrations/Musical Supervision, John Clifton; Hairstylist, Jerry Leddy; Makeup, John Richardson; Production Assistants, Philip Funkenbusch, Karen Moseska; General Management, Soloway & Francis; Company Manager, Brian Dunbar; Stage Managers, Laura deBuys, John Philip; Press, Shirley Herz, Sam Rudy, Peter Cromarty

CAST: John Cunningham (Punchinello), Dennis Bailey (Harlequin), Elizabeth Austin (Columbine), Charles Michael Wright (Pierrot), Gwyda DonHowe (Nurse)

MUSICAL NUMBERS: New Loves for Old, Perfection, I'm in Love, Aqua Vitae, Nowhere, Finaletto, Castles in the Sand, As If, Could He Be You?, Lullabye to Myself, How Do You Keep Out of Love?, Finale.
A musical in two acts. The action takes place on a moonlit evening.

THEATRE AT ST. PETER'S CHURCH Tuesday, December 22, 1981—January 24, 1982 (30 performances) The Praxis Group presents:
FRANCIS With Book by Joseph Leonardo; Lyrics, Kenny Morris; Music, Steve Jankowski; Director, Frank Martin; Sets, Neil Bierbower; Lighting, Thomas Bowen; Costumes, Martha Kelly; Musical Direction and Arrangements, Larry Esposito; Assistant to Director, Patrice Braun; Wardrobe, Fran Miksits; Props, Stan Chervin; General Management, Dorothy Olim Associates; Company Manager, George Elmer; Management Associate, Thelma Cooper; Stage Managers, William Hare, Chuck Newcombe; Press, Shirley Herz, Sam Rudy, Peter Cromarty

CAST: John Dossett (Francis Bernadone), K. C. Wilson (Old Rufino), Lloyd Battista (Pope/Francis' Father), Tanny McDonald (Francis' Mother), Donna Murphy (Clare de Favorone), Kenny Morris (Leo), Cris Groenendaal (Bernard de Quintavalle), Ron Lee Savin (Father Silvestro), Paul Browne (Juniper), Whitney Kershaw (Agnes), Deborah Bendixen (Pacifica), Tom Rolfing (Elias Bombarone of Cortono), Understudies: Deborah Bendixen (Clare/Pica), Chuck Newcombe (Juniper/Leo/Silvestro), Ron Lee Savin (Rufino)

MUSICAL NUMBERS: Miracle Town, The Legend of Old Rufino, The Legend of King Arthur, Serenade, Canticle of Pleasure, I'm Ready Now!, The Fire in My Heart, Ballet San Damiano, For the Good of Brotherhood, New Madness, Bidding the World Farewell, Oh Brother, All the Time in the World, Walking All the Way to Rome, Two Keys, The Road to Paradise, Francis, Praises to the Sun
A musical in two acts. The action takes place during the 12th Century in Umbria, a province of Central Italy.

Lloyd Battista, John Dossett in "Francis" *(Martha Swope Photo)*

WONDERHORSE THEATRE Wednesday, January 6–30, 1982 (20 performances) Fields Repertory Productions presents:
ANGEL CITY By Sam Shepard; Director, Kevin O'Connor; Setting, Jon J. Terzis; Movement, Karen Azenberg; Costumes, Carla Kramer; Lighting, Dorian Vernacchio; Stage Managers, Lisa DiFranza, Harriett Kittner; Press, Burnham/Callaghan Associates

CAST: Paul D'Amato (Lanx), Frank Licato (Rabbit), William Olland (Wheeler), Rich Hallman (Tympani), Joanne Hoersch (Miss Scoons), Nick Stern (Sax)
A play in two acts.

NEW YORK STAGEWORKS Wednesday, January 6–30, 1982 (5 performances) Cecily and Craig LaPlount, Nick Roberts, and Terpy Alan Smith present:
THE BRIDGE TO LATONIA By Marc B. Berman; Director, Susan Gregg; Production Manager, Scott Evans; Production Assistants, Bruce Thomson, Shelly White; Lighting, Terry Alan Smith; Associate Producer, Cynthia Nash; General Manager, George Morelli; Stage Managers, Hazel Norris, Kevin Ryan, Elinor Nauen

CAST: Joan Wooters (Beverly), Robert Frederick (Casey), Tony Pasqualini (Monte), Sarah Brooke (Peach). The action takes place at the present time in a house in Cincinnati on a rainy night.

THE SKIRMISHERS By John Bishop; Director, Ted Bank
CAST: Christopher Goutman (Alan), Diane Heles (Stoni), Eddie Jones (Ralph). The action takes place at the present time in New York City.

Eddie Jones, Diane Heles, Christopher Goutman in "The Skirmishers"

MERCER STREET THEATRE January 6–24, 1982 (11 performances) Echo Stage (Martin Nordal, Artistic Director) presents:
GHOSTS By Henrik Ibsen; Translated by Michael Meyer; Director, Martin Nordal; Set, Mina Albergo; Lighting, Leon di Leone; Costumes, David Craven; Production Manager, Mitchell Mills

CAST: Jorelle Crona (Regina), Victor Talmadge (Oswald), Jane Hamilton (Mrs. Alving), G. Leslie Muchmore (Engstrand), Rob Pherson (Manders)

WONDERHORSE THEATRE Thursday, January 7–31, 1982 (16 performances) Cherubs Guild presents:
INVITATION TO A MARCH By Arthur Laurents; Director, Hillary Wyler; Producers, Carol Avila, Lesley Starbuck; Set, James Stewart, Lighting, Jo Mayer; Costumes, Margie Peterson; Original Music, Stephen Sondheim; Props, Dianne Pobuda; Technical Director, John Sawitsky; Stage Managers, Laura Balboni, Georganne Rogers; Press, Shirley Herz, Sam Rudy, Peter Cromarty

CAST: Rebecca Taylor (Camilla), Marilyn Alex (Lily), Paul Marchand (Cary), Vivien Landau (DeeDee), Daniel Stewart (Schuyler), Varley O'Connor (Norma), Timothy B. Lynch (Aaron), David Bailey (Tucker)
A play in three acts. The action takes place on the South Shore of Long Island during the summer of 1960.

ASTOR PLACE THEATRE Thursday, January 7–24, 1982 (21 performances and 14 previews) Elena Latici, Charles Hollerith, Jr., Max Weitzenhoffer, David Jones present:
THE GOOD PARTS By Israel Horovitz; Director, Barnet Kellman; Setting, David Jenkins; Costumes, Robert Wojewodski; Lighting, Roger Morgan; Sound, Michael Jay; Casting, Elizabeth R. Woodman; Wardrobe, Lucy Brackell; Props, Leslie Moore; General Manager, Albert Poland; Company Manager, Louise M. Bayer; Stage Managers, Amy Pell, Dorothy French; Press, Solters/Roskin/Friedman, Milly Schoenbaum, Claudia McAllister, Kevin Patterson

CAST: Robert DeFrank (Men of Greece), Nancy Mette (Women of Greece), Tony Roberts (Brian "Sonny" Levine), Stephen Strimpell (Eugene Jacoby), Cecilia Hart (Maxine/Brenda), Judy Graubart (Eloise/Mildred), Understudies: Dorothy French, Gerry Bamman
A comedy in two acts. The action takes place at the present time in Greece.

PLAYERS THEATRE Sunday, January 10, 1982 (1 performance and 13 previews) Paul Streitz presents:
OH, JOHNNY With Music and Lyrics, Gary Cherpakov; Book and Lyrics, Paul Streitz; Musical Director/Vocal and Dance Arrangements, Robert Marks; Director/Choreographer, Alan Weeks; Associate Producer, Stephen Harausz; Set, Jim Chestnutt; Lighting, Toni Goldin; Assistant to Mr. Weeks, Sara Lindsey; Assistant Choreographer, David Lang; Makeup, Suki Vasquez; Art Director, Paul Streitz; Wardrobe, Julie Webster; Technical Director, Ted Ciganik; Technical Coordinator, Barry Arnold; Hairstylist, Michael Weeks; Production Assistant, Dendrie Taylor; Assistant to Producer, Victor Lukas; Stage Managers, Robert O'Rourke, Joe Joyce; Press, Jeffrey Richards, C. George Willard, Robert Ganshaw, Helen Stern, Ted Killmer, Richard Humleker

CAST: Michael Crouch (Johnny), Christine Joy (White Lotus), Nazig Edwards (Lili), Brad Miskell (Gopher), Janet Wong (One China), Jerry Coyle (Col. Sitright), Joey Ginza (General Ko), Katherine Lench (Trio), Sally Yorke (Trio), Janet Donohue (Trio), David C. Wright (Soldier), Clayton Davis (Soldier), Robert Kellett (Soldier), Marina Chamlin (Swing), Joe Joyce (Soldier/Swing)
A musical in two acts. The action takes place a long time ago when this country was much younger than it is today.

Cecilia Hart, Tony Roberts, Judy Graubart in "The Good Parts"

TYSON STUDIO Wednesday, January 13–24, 1982 (12 performances) Empire Stage Players presents:
PASS WITH CARE By Shelby Brammer; Direction by Miss Brammer; Production Design, Bob Briggs, John North; Executive Producers, Pat Robertson, Don Hampton; Company Manager, Peter Pope; Art Director, Pamela Hampton; Production Assistants, Karen MacIntyre, Jackie Albracht, Clint Reeves; Stage Manager, Kelly Carty; Press, Fred Hoot, Ken Munzing

CAST: Rita Montone (Abra), Lewis Black (Jack), Ken Hardeman (Jimmy John), Marc Clark (Ben), Christopher Rich (Danny), Joe White (Peter), Karen MacIntyre, Jackie Albracht (Ladies in back seat)
A prologue and five scenes performed without intermission. The action takes place in 1966 and 1972.

WESTSIDE MAINSTAGE Wednesday, January 13–February 6, 1982 (16 performances) Boston Common in association with Donna Betts presents:
DUSTOFF By Bruce King; Director, Jan Bowes; Set, Mike Boak; Costumes, Margaret Yule; Lighting, Wayne Lawrence; Sound, Eric Toline; Props, Thomas Abrams; Stage Manager, Terre Lintner; Press, Owen Levy

CAST: James Laurence (Jawbone), Tino Juarez (Breed), Darrell Troutman (Shank), Ted Minos (Chinatown), Bo Rucker (Pimp), Scott Wakefield (Homer), Dan Lauria (Top), Walt Willey (Jeb), Camila Cabrerra (Lee), Bea Soong (Lin)
A drama in three acts. The action takes place during 1970 in a hut of a medical evacuation unit in Vietnam.

Scott Wakefield, Bo Rucker, Ted Minos, Daryl Troutman, Jim Laurence (smoking) in "Dustoff" *(Images Plus Photo)*

PALSSON'S Friday, January 15, 1982 and still playing May 31, 1982. Michael Chapman presents:
FORBIDDEN BROADWAY By Gerard Alessandrini; Director, Michael Chapman; Original Lyrics, Gerard Alessandrini; Music Supervisor, Pete Blue; Pianist/Musical Arrangements, Fred Barton; Press, Solters/Roskin/Friedman, Josh Ellis, Cindy Valk, Becky Flora

CAST: Gerard Alessandrini, Bill Carmichael, Nora Mae Lyng, Wendee Winters, Fred Barton
  A musical comedy satire.

THE WOODEN O Wednesday, January 20–February 20, 1982 (12 performances) The Wooden O presents:
HOOFERS By Clif Dowell and Eduardo Angulo; Director, Clif Dowell; Choreography, Tod Miller, Germaine Salsberg; Musical Direction, Faser Hardin; Musical Arrangements, Eduardo Angulo and Faser Hardin; Set, Neil Jacob; Costumes, Nancy Steele; Lighting, Alan Sporing; Stage Manager, Robert Carver; Press, Max Eisen, Maria Somma, Reva Cooper

CAST: Richard Atkins (George), Tod Miller (Jack), Virginia Seidel (Jill)

MUSICAL NUMBERS: The Wedding Cake, Watch After Jill, When Love Looks into Your Heart, Hoofers, Mailman's Valentine, Jack of All Trades, Have We Gotta Show, I Gotta Tango to Do, Yankee Come Home, At the Savoy Grill, Why Should a Guy Cry, Syncopated Lady, Women, One Jack
  A musical in two acts.

SOUTH STREET THEATRE Sunday, January 24–February 7, 1982 (21 performances) Penumbra Productions (Mike Houlihan, Executive Producer; John Tillinger, Artistic Director) and South Street Theatre (Jean Sullivan, Michael Fischetti, Artistic Directors) present:
THE BRIXTON RECOVERY By Jack Gilhooley; Director, Mike Houlihan; Set, Mark Haack; Lighting, Robert Giffin; Costumes, Kristina Watson; Music Supervision, George Clinton; Casting, Bonnie G. Timmerman; Props, Leslie Moore; Technical Director, Bob Adams; Production assistant, Barbara Perkins; General Manager, Ken Bryant; Stage Manager, Kevin Mangan; Press, Jeffrey Richards, C. George Willard, Ted Killmer

CAST: William Russ (Mickey "Spider" McGuire) succeeded by Tom McLaughlin, Hazel Medina (Shirley), Standbys: Tom McLaughlin, Barbara Perkins
  A drama in 2 acts and 4 scenes. The action takes place during a spring of the late 1970's in Shirley's flat in the Brixton section of London.

AMDA STUDIO ONE Sunday, January 24–February 14, 1982 (14 performances) New York Theatre Studio (Richard V. Romagnoli, Artistic Director; Cheryl Faraone, Managing Director presents the American premiere of:
THE SOUL OF THE WHITE ANT By Snoo Wilson; Director, Richard V. Romagnoli; Original Music, James Petosa; Sets, Gerard P. Bourcier; Costumes, Karen Matthews; Sound, Gary Massey; Lighting, John Hickey; Production Manager, Moss Hassell; Assistant to Director, Sally Burnett; General Manager, Gary Pollard; Technical Director, Dennis Runge; Stage Manager, Rebecca Pease; Press, Patt Dale, Jim Baldassare

CAST: Ellen Greenfield (Edith), Megan Bagot (June), Mary Jay (Mabel de Wet), John Gillis (Pietr de Groot), Daniel Szelag (Eugene Marais), Alan Coates (Julius)
  A drama in six scenes, performed without intermission. The action takes place at the present time in Excelsis, a small town in the Transvaal region of South Africa near Johannesburg.

Bill Carmichael, Wendee Winters, Gerard Alessandrini, Nora Mae Lyng in "Forbidden Broadway" *(Eric Stephen Jacobs Photo)*

ENSEMBLE STUDIO THEATRE Thursday, January 28–February 14, 1982 (24 performances) The Ensemble Studio Theatre (Curt Dempster, Artistic Director; Deborah Dahl, Managing Director) presents:
THE HOUSE ACROSS THE STREET By Darrah Cloud; Director, Bruce Levitt; Set, Brian Martin; Costumes, Deborah Shaw; Lighting, Richard Lund; Sound, Bruce Ellman; Production Supervisor, David S. Rosenak; Props, Gabelle Aarons; Casting, Billy Hopkins; Technical Director, Nicholas R. Miller; Stage Managers, K. Siobhan Phelan, Joan Ungaro; Press, Shirley Herz, Peter Cromarty, Sam Rudy

CAST: Cordis Heard (Lillian Fortune), Jane Hoffman (Grandma Fortune), Sarah Inglis (Donna Fortune), Stephen Baccus (Donald Fortune), Lewis Arlt (Don Fortune, Sr.), Bill Swikowski (Norman Bird)
  A "bizarre comedy" in two acts. The action takes place at the present time in a household in a Chicago suburb.

PROVINCETOWN PLAYHOUSE Wednesday, January 27–May 16, 1982 (127 performances) Burton Greenhouse presents:
KILLER'S HEAD By Sam Shepard; Directed by Tony Barsha; With Perry Lang as Mazon. This play was not performed after opening night and six previews.

THE UNSEEN HAND By Sam Shepard; Director, Tony Barsha; Sets, Dorian Vernacchio; Costumes, Allison Connor; Lighting, Anne E. Militello; Sound, James Hardy; Assistant to Director, Annette Barbasch; General Management, Casa Verde Productions; Stage Managers, Dan Ziegler, Walter Hadler; Press, Patt Dale, Jim Baldassare

CAST

Blue Morphan	Beeson Carroll
Willy the Space Freak	Deirdre O'Connell
Cisco Morphan	Michael Brody
The Kid	David Watkins
Sycamore Morphan	Walter Hadler

Deirdre O'Connell, Beeson Carroll in "The Unseen Hand"
(Gerry Goodstein Photo)

Christine Andreas, D'Jamin Bartlett in "Alec Wilder"
(Carol Rosegg Photo)

VINEYARD THEATER   Wednesday, February 3–21, 1982 (20 performances) The Production Company (Norman Rene, Producing Director) in association with Vineyard Theater (Barbara Zinn, Artistic Director) present:
ALEC WILDER: CLUES TO A LIFE conceived: by Barbara Zinn and Elliot Weiss; Director, Norman Rene; Setting, Jane Thurn; Costumes, Oleksa; Lighting, Debra J. Kletter; Musical Arrangements, Elliot Weiss; Choreographer, Louise Quick; Musical Director, E. Martin Perry; Stage Manager, Susi Mara; Press, Bruce, Cohen

CAST: Christine Andreas, D'Jamin Bartlett, Keith David, Craig Lucas

MUSICAL NUMBERS: A Child Is Born, The Echoes of My Mind, Photographs, That's My Girl, Ellen, Unbelievable, Give Me Time, Where Is the One?, Don't Deny, Moon and Sand, I'd Do It All Again, Lovers and Losers, I'll Be Around, While We're Young, Night Talk, The Wrong Blues, I've Been There, Rain Rain, Blackberry Winter, Trouble Is a Man, You Wrong Me, The Worm Has Turned, It's So Peaceful in the Country, Did You Ever Cross Over to Sneden's, Mimosa and Me, I See It Now
   A musical entertainment in two parts.

WEST END THEATRE   Thursday, February 4–21, 1982 (15 performances) Mark Levine presents:
A TRINITY By Guy Hoffman; Director, Jo Bellomo; Set, Robert W. Mogel; Lighting, Jeffrey McRoberts; Artist, Lawrence R. Gendron; Stage Manager, Josephine Steinway; Press, Louis Gignac

CAST: Annette Mayo (The Princess), Allan Benjamin (The Father), Gene Canfield (The Cowboy)
   A play without intermission. The action takes place "somewhere in the universe."

Seated: Roger Forbes, Bill Moor, Standing: John Braden, Gavin Reed in "Potsdam Quartet" *(Susan Cook Photo)*

PERRY STREET THEATRE   Thursday, February 4–28, 1982 (27 performances) Prism Theatre (Ron Comenzo and Stephen Stewart-James, Artistic Directors) presents:
SHEEPSKIN AND BOTTOM OF THE NINTH Two plays by Victor L. Cahn; Director, Victor Argo; Set, Patrick Mann; Costumes, Sam Fleming; Lighting, John Tissot; Sound, Eloida G. Hulbert; Casting, Kathleen Marsters; Wardrobe, Michele Dorosho: Props, Maureen T. Boler; Stage Managers, Janet Friedman, Carol Klein; Press, Hunt/Pucci Associates, James Sapp

CAST: "Sheepskin": Ed Setrakian (Prof. Hardy), Rochelle Parker (Helen Hardy), Patricia Kalember (Linda Tipton). The action takes place at the present time in the living room of the Hardy house on the campus of a New England university.

"Bottom of the Ninth": Lou Miranda (Frank), Emmett O'Sullivan-Moore (Henry). The action takes place in March of 1980 during the first game of spring training.

LION THEATRE   Monday, February 8–28, 1982 (24 performances) New York Theatre Workshop (Stewart Graham, Chairman) presents:
THE POTSDAM QUARTET By David Pinner; Director, Jacques Levy; Producers, Alison Clarkson, Stephen Graham; Set, Hugh Landwehr; Casting, Johnson-Liff Associates; Costumes, Lindsay W. Davis; Lighting, Robby Monk; Sound, Frank Vince; Production Assistant, Bess O'Brien; Props, Ron Burns; Stage Managers, Nancy Kohlbeck, Robert Alan Morrow; Press, Judy Jacksina, Glenna Freedman, Angela Wilson, Diane Tomlinson

CAST: George Kyle (Russian Soldier), John Braden (Aaron Green), Roger Forbes (Douglas Swift), Gavin Reed (Ronald Taylor), Bill Moor (John Healey)
   A comedy-drama in two acts. The action takes place in 1945 in an anteroom at the Potsdam Conference.

GREEK THEATRE OF NEW YORK   Wednesday, February 10–March 7, 1982 (21 performances) The Greek Theatre of New York (Yannis Simonides, Artistic Director; Wendy Bustard, Managing Director) presents:
HAPPY SUNSET, INC. By Manolis Korres; Translated by Linda and Alkis Papoutsis; Director, Alkis Papoutsis; Set, Robert U. Taylor; Costumes, Amanda J. Klein; Lighting, Andrea Wilson; Production Manager, Gary Walter; Technical Director, Jeffrey Berzon; Props/Wardrobe, Maryanne Griffiths; Production Assistant, Jeffrey Coldren; Stage Managers, Duane Fletcher, Rob Lane; Press, Mary Philis

CAST: Douglas Andros (Mourtos), Lee Beltzer (Kouris), Peter Carew (Tsilias), Olga Druce (Naka), Ronald Durling (Gen. Vergis), Marlea Evans (Olga), Leslie Goldstein (Loupas), Aphroditi Kolaitis (Rena), Frank Nastasi (Tryphon), Nikos Kontomanolis (Kosmas), Vera Lekas (Mrs. Kouris), Joan Neuman (Katina), Madeline Shaw (Evanthia), Constance Stellas (Fofie/Sophia)
   A play in three acts. The action takes place at the present time in a home for the elderly in a suburb of Athens, Greece.

ALL SOULS CHURCH FELLOWSHIP HALL   Friday, February 12–March 1, 1982 (12 performances) All Souls Players presents:
LANDSCAPE/SILENCE/NIGHT By Harold Pinter; Director, Henry Levinson; Production Manager, Martha Levinson; Press, Peter Sauerbrey

CAST: "Landscape": Carol Poppenger (Beth), Evan Thompson (Duff). "Silence": Richard Voights (Rumsey), Maureen Kerrigan (Ellen), John Berrier (Bates). "Night": Evan Thompson (Man), Carol Poppenger (Woman)
   Three short plays performed with one intermission.

WONDERHORSE THEATRE   Monday, February 15–28, 1982 (14 performances and 7 previews) Riverside Productions in association with Union Square Theatre (Lee Pucklis, Producing Director; Evadne Giannini, Artistic Director) presents:
CLOWNMAKER By Richard Crane; Director, Isaiah Sheffer; Settings, Barbara Miller, Daniel Michaelson; Costumes, Daniel Michaelson; Lighting, Arden Fingerhut; Special Consultant, Igor Youskevitch; Wardrobe, Cindy Flowers; Stage Managers, Gary Stein, Con Roche; Press, Seymour Krawitz, Robert Larkin

CAST: Jerome Dempsey (Sergei Diaghilev), Stephen Lang (Vaslav Nijinsky), Ann Sachs (Romola De Pulsky), Dennis Bacigalupi (Alexandrov/Astruc/Dmitri/Massine), Kevin McClarnon (Prince Lvov/Bolm/Vassily), Alexandra O'Karma (Olga/Karsavina/-Mimi/Anna/Vera), Understudies: Con Roche, Bertina Johnson
A play in two acts. The action takes place between 1909 and 1928.

HAROLD CLURMAN THEATRE   Tuesday, February 16–March 21, 1982 (30 performances) Jack Garfein presents:
CHUCKY'S HUNCH By Rochelle Owens; Director, Elinor Renfield; Setting, Abe Lubelski; Lighting, Peter Kaczorowski; Costumes, Carla Kramer; Sound, Paul Garrity; Associate Producer, Byron Lasky; Stage Manager, Marc Cohen; Press, Burnham-Callaghan Associates, Edward T. Callaghan

CAST: Kevin O'Connor (Chucky Craydon)

THEATRE AT ST. CLEMENT'S   Wednesday, February 17–March 7, 1982 (16 performances) Theatre at St. Clement's (Michael Hadge, Artistic Director; Stephen Berwind, Managing Director) presents:
PHILISTINES By Maxim Gorky; Adapted and Directed by Michael Landrum; Set, Lou Anne Gilleland; Lighting, Victor En Yu Tang; Costumes, Carla Kramer; Technical Director, Melanie Hulse; Props, Kim Petrosky; Stage Managers, Tony Berk, Nona Waldeck

CAST: Gina Barnett (Lena), J. D. Clarke (Doctor), Tom Everett (Nil), Clark Gordon (Perchikhin), Martha Greenhouse (Akulina), Rudy Hornish (Teterev), Jennifer Houlton (Polya), Suzanne La-Croix (Stepanida), Janice Lathen (Tzvataeva), Stephen Mellor (Peter), Bob Morrisey (Shishkin), Seymour Penzner (Bezsemenov), Susan Stevens (Tanya), Nona Waldeck (Understudy)
A play in 2 acts and 4 scenes. The action takes place during the autumn of 1902 in a provincial Russian town.

WESTSIDE ARTS THEATRE   Wednesday, February 17–May 23, 1982 (111 performances) Harold DeFelice/Louis W. Scheeder with J.N.H. Ventures Inc. and Margo Lion present:
HOW I GOT THAT STORY By Amlin Gray; Director, Carole Rothman; Scenery, Patricia Woodbridge; Costumes, Carol Oditz; Lighting, Pat Collins; Sound, Gary Harris; Choreography, John Lone; Original music and sound effects composed and performed by Bob Gunton; Production Assistant, Judith Ann Chew; Management Assistant, Karen Berry; General and Company Managers, Buckley, Urbanski & Wells; Stage Manager, Fredric H. Orner; Press, Bob Ullman, Richard Kornberg

CAST

The Reporter.............................. Don Scardino
The Historical Event .... Bob Gunton
    Performed with one intermission.

(back) Gene O'Neill, K. C. Kelly, David Kimball, John Finn, (front) Anthony Risoli, George Taylor, Ben George, Thick Wilson in "Last of the Knucklemen" *(Ilene Jones Photo)*

AMERICAN THEATRE OF ACTORS   Wednesday, March 3–27, 1982 (16 performances) American Theatre of Actors (Manes Jennings, Artistic Director) and Tejas Productions present:
THE LAST OF THE KNUCKLEMEN By John Powers; Director, Peter Masterson; Set and Lighting, Kevin Hickson; Assistant Director, Carlin Glynn; Associate Producer, John Roddick; Staged Fights, Normand Beauregard; Stage Managers, Peter J. Taylor, Suky Aronoff; Press, Susan L. Schulman

CAST: David Kimball (Mad Dog), Anthony Risoli (Horse), Ben George (Pansy), John Finn (Tassie), Gene O'Neill (Tom), K. C. Kelly (Monk), Thick Wilson (Methusalah), George Taylor (Tarzan), Gary Klar (Carl)
A drama in 3 acts and 6 scenes. The action takes place at the present time in a bunkhouse in a Northwest Australia mining camp where the average temperature is 120 degrees.

ACTORS AND DIRECTORS THEATRE   Sunday, March 7–28, 1982 (26 performances) The Production Company (Norman Rene, Artistic Director) presents:
THE CHINESE VIEWING PAVILION By Gus Kaikkonene; Director, John Roach; Sets, Jane Thurn; Costumes, Walter Hicklin; Lighting, Bill Armstrong; General Manager, Margi Rountree; Press, Judy Jacksina, Glenna Freedman, Angela Wilson, Diane Tomlinson; Stage Manager, Tracy B. Cohen

CAST: George Lloyd (Rose Cardone), Lynn Cohen (Lynn Cohen), Laural Merlington (Melody Sangsue), Max Mayer (Richard Cardone), Bill Sadler (Hector), Robb Webb (Paul Reinclaud), Roscoe Born (Keith), Lillie Robertson (Lily)
A play in 2 acts and 4 scenes. The action takes place over the course of 5 years in a Chinese viewing pavilion on a farm near the Delaware River.

Bob Gunton, Don Scardino in "How I Got That Story"
(Gerry Goodstein Photo)

HAROLD CLURMAN THEATRE Sunday, March 7–21, 1982 (16 performances) Jack Garfein, Artistic Director, presents:
BIRDBATH By Leonard Melfi; Director, Tom O'Horgan; General Manager, Soloway & Francis, Brian Dunbar; Production Coordinator, Annette Holloway; Technical Director, Sam Gonzalez; Stage Managers, David Marc, Agapi Stassinopoulos; Associate Producer, Byron Lasky; Press, Burnham-Callaghan, Edward T. Callaghan

CAST: Kevin O'Connor (Frankie Basta), Barbara eda-Young (Velma Sparrow)

CROSSING THE CRAB NEBULA By Lewis Black; Director, William Peters; Assistant Director, Sarah Albertson;
CAST: Kevin O'Connor (Booney), Peter Crombie (Radio), Barbara eda-Young (Mirage)

NAT HORNE THEATRE Thursday, March 11–April 4, 1982 (20 performances) King Stuart Productions presents:

I TAKE THESE WOMEN With Book by J. J. Coyle; Music, Robert Kole; Lyrics, Sandi Merle; Directed and Staged by Mr. Coyle; Scenery, Ernest A. Smith; Lighting, Paul B. Fadoul; Musical Direction/Incidental Music, Nathan Hurwitz; Assistant Musical Director, Howard Sperling; Costumes, Guy Tanno; Stage Manager, Ed Strum.
CAST: Jane Altman (Mary), Jean Barlow (Annie), Judi Mann (Jane), Lew Resseguie (Guy), Richard-Charles Hoh (Jim), Robert Cooner (Jack). **MUSICAL NUMBERS:** Adultery, Annie's Lament, I Am Yours, Soliloquy, Why, This Is My House, Common Sense, I Took These Women, Yesterday's Champagne, Incomprehensible, I Like Her, You Turn Me On, On My Own. In 2 acts and 6 scenes with prologue. The action takes place at Easter time in 1970.

28th STREET PLAYHOUSE/ACTORS OUTLET March 12–April 11, 1982 (24 performances) Metropolitan Theatre Alliance (Paul Leavin, Artistic Director) presents:

OCCUPATIONS By Trevor Griffiths; Director, James Traub with Melody James; Set, Jack Chandler; Lighting, Dan Kinsley; Costumes, Amanda Aldridge; Sound, Charles Koeppel; Stage Manager, Barbara Bellas.

CAST: Ellen Barber (Angelica), Cynthia Hayden (Polya), Harris Laskawy (Kabak), Time Winters (Libertini), Chris Caraso (Gramsci), Anthony Gialmo (D'Avanzo), Dino Laudicina (Terrini), John Tarrant (Valetta).
  A drama in 2 acts. The action takes place during 1920 in Turin, Italy.

ASTOR PLACE THEATRE Sunday, March 14–April 11, 1982 (33 performances) Raphael D. Silver presents:
MAYBE I'M DOING IT WRONG With Music and Lyrics by Randy Newman; Conceived and Directed by Joan Micklin Silver; Musical Direction/Arrangements, Michael S. Roth; Dance Direction, Eric Elice; Setting, Heidi Landesman; Costumes, Hilary Rosenfeld; Lighting, Fred Buchholz; Production Assistant, Susannah Blinkoff; Wardrobe, April Briggs; Props, David Michael Kenney; Assistant to Producer, Judith Lynn Brown; General Management, Dorothy Olim Associates; Company Manager, George Elmer; Stage Manager, Richard Elkow; Press, Jeffrey Richards, Robert Ganshaw, Ted Killmer, Ben Morse, Helen Stern, C. George Willard, Richard Humleker

CAST: Mark Linn-Baker, Patti Perkins, Larry Riley (succeeded by Clent Bowers), Deborah Rush, Understudies: Eric Elice, Marilyn Pasekoff

MUSICAL NUMBERS: Sigmund Freud's Impersonation of Albert Einstein in America, My Old Kentucky Home, Birmingham, Political Science, It's Money That I Love, Jolly Coppers on Parade, Caroline, Simon Smith and the Amazing Dancing Bear, Love Story, Tickle Me, Maybe I'm Doing It Wrong, Debutante's Ball, Burn On, Pants, God's Song, They Just Got Married, A Wedding in Cherokee County, Yellow Man, Girls in My Life, Rider in the Rain, Mama Told Me Not to Come, Old Man, Lonely at the Top, Mr. President, Sail Away, Theme from Ragtime, Marie, I Think It's Going to Rain Today, Let's Burn the Cornfield, Davy the Fat Boy, You Can Leave Your Hat On, Rollin', Short People, I'll Be Home, Dayton, Ohio 1903

back: William Thomas, Jr., Kevin Bacon, Miles Chapin, Page Moseley, Gedde Watanabe, front: Bronson Pinchot, David Naughton, Blanche Baker, Albert Macklin in "Poor Little Lambs" *(Gerry Goodstein Photo)*

THEATRE AT ST. PETER'S CHURCH Sunday, March 14–May 16, 1982 (73 performances) The Theatre of St. Peter's Church (Edmund Anderson, Executive Director; Arthur W. Pearson, Program Director) presents:
POOR LITTLE LAMBS By Paul Rudnick; Director, Jack Hofsiss; Producer, Richmond Crinkley; Sets, David Jenkins; Costumes, William Ivey Long; Lighting, Beverly Emmons; Sound, T. Richard Fitzgerald; Stage Movements, Peter Anastos; Musical Consultant, Bob Brush; Associate Producer, Scott Steele; Production Associate, Alison Clarkson; Assistant to Director, Keith Edmondson; Wardrobe, Beckie DeLong; Props, Michael Grief; Production Coordinator, Diane Asadorian; General Manager, Mario DeMaria; Company Manager, John Parsons; Casting, Mary Colquhoun; Stage Managers, Janet Beroza, Scott Barnes; Press, Betty Lee Hunt, Maria Cristina Pucci, James Sapp

CAST: Bronson Pinchot (Stu Arnstine), Albert Macklin (Ricky Hochieser), David Naughton (Davey Weldman), Kevin Bacon (Frank Wozniak), Miles Chapin (Jack Hayes), William Thomas, Jr. (Ike Ennis), Gedde Watanabe (Itsu Yoshiro), Page Moseley (Drew Waterman Reed), Blanche Baker (Claire Hazard), Scott Barnes (Understudy)

MUSICAL NUMBERS: Mother of Men, When My Sugar Walks Down the Street, I Married an Angel, Bright College Years, Love for Sale, Undertaker, Boola, Bingo, Good Night Poor Harvard, Down the Field, Bull-dog, We're Saving Ourselves for Yale, When the Summer Moon Comes Along, You'll Have' to Put a Nightie on Aphrodite, The Whiffenpoof Song
  A musical in two acts. The action takes place during the current academic year at Yale University, New Haven, Connecticut.

Patti Perkins, Mark Linn-Baker in "Maybe I'm Doing It Wrong"
(Stephanie Saia Photo)

SOUTH STREET THEATRE   Monday, March 15–27, 1982 (14 performances) Magpie Productions in association with David G. Watson presents:
SCENES DEDICATED TO MY BROTHER and WHAT PEOPLE DO WHEN THEY'RE ALL ALONE Two plays by Joel Homer; Director, Maggie L. Harrer; Lighting, Joshua Dachs; Sets, Joshua Dachs, Maggie L. Herrer; Costumes, Sara Denning; Sound, Paul Garrity; Casting, Mary Ellen Mulcahy; Technical Director, Richard Langbauer; Stage Manager, Renee F. Lutz; Press, Judy Jacksina, Glenna Freedman, Angela Wilson, Diane Tomlinson

CAST: "Scenes Dedicated to My Brother": Jack Fogarty (Father), Stephen Hamilton (Older Son), Joel Fredrickson (Younger Son), Suzanne Johnson (Woman's Voice). The action takes place during the present and past in Father's home.

"What People Do When They're All Alone": Patti Karr. The action takes place at the present time in the woman's apartment.

DOUGLAS FAIRBANKS THEATRE   Wednesday, March 24–April 25, 1982 (30 performances and 15 previews. Inaugural production in this newly-constructed theatre) Lucille Lortel and Mortimer Levitt in association with Burry Fredrik and Haila Stoddard present:
CATHOLIC SCHOOL GIRLS By Casey Kurtti; Director, Burry Fredrik; Associate Producer, Ben Sprecher; Setting, Paul Leonard; Lighting, Paul Everett; Costumes, Sigrid Insull; Production Manager, Paul Everett; General Manager, Ben Sprecher; Assistant Company Manager, Steven Deshler; Stage Managers, Melissa Davis, Vandra Thorburn; Press, Jeffrey Richards, Robert Ganshaw, Ted Killmer, Ben Morse, Helen Stern, C. George Willard

CAST: Lynne Born (Elizabeth McHugh/Sister Mary Thomasina), Maggie Low (Wanda Sluska/Sister Mary Agnes), Shelley Rogers (Maria Theresa Russo/Sister Mary Germaine), Christine von Dohln (Colleen Dockery/Sister Mary Lucille), Vandra Thorburn (Understudy)
A comedy in two acts.

WESTSIDE MAINSTAGE   Thursday, March 25–April 16, 1982 (16 performances) Jerry McGee and Jerome Dempsey present:
HOMEBOYS By John Lordan; Directed by Mr. Lordan; Set, Bill Bartelt; Lighting, Gregg Marriner; Costumes, Ruettiger; Technical Director, John Schulz; Stage Manager, Judith Mayer; Press, Shirley Herz, Sam Rudy, Peter Cromarty

CAST: Billy Padget (Joe), Tony Simotes (Charlie), Mark Clifford Smith (Willie), Judy Rice (Sue)
A play in two acts. The action takes place at the present time in Joe's home.

HAROLD CLURMAN THEATRE   Friday, March 26–April 11, 1982 (12 performances) Ron Barba and Ruth Preven in association with DiDia/Fiore Productions present:
MEEGAN'S GAME By Elliott Caplin; Director, Gary Bowen; Scenery, Reagon Cook; Costumes, Susan J. Wright; Lighting, Jeffrey McRoberts; Technical Director, Sam Gonzalez; Production Assistants, Adrienne Dornbusch, Susan Jacobs; Management Associate, Rosemary Carey; Stage Managers, Carol Klein, Richard Battaglia; Press, Bruce Cohen

CAST: Linda Barnhurst (Vera), Richard Battaglia (Waiter), Aida Berlyn (Minerva), Nick Ferrari-Ferris (Charley), Marshall Hambro (Doc), Ron Harper (Dutch), M. Patrick Hughes (Meegan), Bernie Rachelle (Rabbi), Greg Spagna (Anthony), Carlotta Sherwood (Madie).
A drama in two acts. The action takes place on a Saturday night of June 1981 in the Bronx, New York.

Lynne Born, Maggie Low, Shelley Rogers, Christine Von Dohln in *"Catholic School Girls" (Stephanie Saia Photo)*

VANDAM THEATRE   Tuesday, March 30, 1982 (1 performance and 15 previews) John Stark presents:
ONE NIGHT STAND By Carol Bolt; Director, Raymond Homer; Associate Producer, Nola J. Hague; Setting and Lighting, James Charles; Costumes and Props, Robin Leslie Mann; Stage Manager, Rosemary Richardson; Press, Fred Hoot, Ken Munzing

CAST: Sherry Arell (Sharon), Florence Barrett (Daisy), Hugh Karraker (Rafe)
A comedy-thriller in two acts.

WONDERHORSE THEATRE   Wednesday, March 31–April 18, 1982 (16 performances) TRG Repertory Company (Marvin Kahan, Artistic Director; Anita Pintozzi, Associate Producer) presents:
THE EVANGELIST With Book, Music and Lyrics by Al Carmines; Director, William Hopkins; Producer, Marvin Kahan; Musical Director, Ernest Lehrer; Set, Peter Harrison; Lighting, Craig Kennedy; Costumes, Paula Iasella; Choreographer, Ellen Krueger; Assistant Choreographer, Patricia Steigauf; Production Assistants, Ali Croluis, Allan Scherer; Stage Managers, Chris Cade, Ed Cachianes; Press, Jan Greenberg, Susan Leaming

CAST: Paul Farin (Ben), Keith Baker (Garland), Carlo Thomas (Bishop), Kate Ingram (Florrie), Judith Moore (Mathilda), Donna Bullock (Raven), Miles Herter (McKeechen), Kevin Jones (Ernest), Judy Soto (Selina), Barbara Swift (Sister Elizabeth), Lee Teplitzky (Ragged Bumpus), Megan Lynn Thomas (Betsy)

MUSICAL NUMBERS: Hymns from the Darkness, Everything God Does Is Perfect, Holy Ghost Ride, I Was a Black Sheep, Home, I Am a Preacher of the Lord, Remember Joplin, Omaha I'm Here, Cardboard Madonna, Blame It on the Moon, Little Children on the Grass, Clinging to the Rock, Goodbye, The Brother Blues, Serenade, I Love You, Do I Do It Through God?, Buds of May, Men Are Men, We're Going to Des Moines, Who Is She?, Garland Is My Man, I Am an Evangelist, The Light, Navajo Woman, Raven the Magnet, Home
A musical in 2 acts and 8 scenes. The action takes place during the summer of 1924 in St. Joseph, Mo., Omaha, Neb., and Des Moines, Iowa.

Kate Ingram, Keith Baker, Judith Moore in "The Evangelist" *(Carol Rosegg Photo)*

Reed Birney, Patricia Mauceri, Stefano Loverso in "Bella Figura"
(Ken Howard Photo)

ENSEMBLE STUDIO THEATRE April 1–25, 1982 (20 performances) The Ensemble Studio Theatre (Curt Dempster, Artistic Director; Deborah Dahl, Managing Director) in association with David S. Rosenak presents:
BELLA FIGURA By Brother Jonathan; Director, John Schwab; Set, Brian Martin; Costumes, Madeline Cohen; Lighting, Todd Elmer; Sound, Bruce Ellman; Incidental Music, Seymour Barab; Technical Director, Nicholas R. Miller; Casting, Billy Hopkins, Doug Aibel; Assistant to Director, Mary A. Kelly; Stage Managers, K. Siobhan Phelan, Joan Ungaro; Press, Shirley Herz, Sam Rudy, Peter Cromarty

CAST: Reed Birney (Brother Philip), Dominic Chianese (Monsignor Zaniol), James Greene (Prof. Hoffman), Patricia Mauceri (Beatrice Colmar), Stefano Loverso (Virginio Ferrari), Jo Henderson (Sophie Hoffman).
A drama in 2 acts and 15 scenes. The action takes place in Venice during the late spring of 1962.

KOZO THEATRE Sunday, April 4–18, 1982 (16 performances and 4 previews) Kozo Theatre Development Corp. (James A. Simpson, Artistic Director) presents:
BAAL By Bertholt Brecht; New English version by Peter Mellencamp; Directed and Conceived by James A. Simpson; Musical Director, Mile Nolan; Set and Lighting, Jane Musky; Costumes, Nina Moser; Slides, Debbie Huff; Hairstylist, Doris Bedell; Choreography, Bonnie Zimering; Technical Director/Stage Manager, David Prittie; Associate Producers, Jody Gelb, Jerry Levine; Assistant Stage Manager, Jeff Shoemaker; Press, Susan Bloch, Adrian Bryan-Brown, Ellen Zeisler, Ron Jewell

CAST: Keith Druhl (Meck), Jody Gelb (Emily), Eve Bennett Gordon (Sophie), Zach Frenier (Baal), Frank Hankey (Detective), Steve Hofvendahl (Lupu), Tara King (Louise), Bruce McVittie (Joe), Gary Morabito (Ekart), Dan Moran (Bum), Karen Tull (Johanna), Understudies: Bill Habeeb, Lin Ciangio

Polly Pen, Sandra Wheeler, Alan Brasington in "Charlotte Sweet" *(Elizabeth Wolynski Photo)*

THREE MUSES THEATRE Tuesday, April 6–25, 1982 (18 performances) Jo Anne Vallier and Joseph Feury present:
BAGS With Book and Lyrics by Elizabeth Perry; Composer/Musical Director, Robert Mitchell; Scenery, John Falabella; Costumes, David Murin; Lighting, David Segal; Directed and Choreographed by Wally Strauss; Director's Assistants, Maggy Gorrill, Carole D'Andrea; Casting, Sue Hessel; Props/Wardrobe, Lisa Blackwell; Stage Manager, Bill Buxton; Press, Shirley Herz, Sam Rudy, Peter Cromarty

CAST: Peggy Atkinson (Mrs. Rodriguez), Michael Blevins (Dangerous/Dealer), Juanita Fleming (Ms. Head), Don Gantry (Gus Rinalto), Maggy Gorrill (Lucky), Tiger Haynes (Bobby), Audre Johnston (Magda), Susan Kaslow (Badmouth/Sabrett's Woman), Stephani Low (Kiria), Thom McCleister (Buyer/Sonny/Demolition Man), Brian Sutherland (Cop/Mambo), Fiddle Viracola (Meg), Michael Zaslow (Dr. Sheinberg)

MUSICAL NUMBERS: It's Mine, I Was Beautiful, Bobby's Songs, The Clean Ones, Lady Wake Up, This Is Where We Met, So Much for Marriage, Honky Jewish Boy, Out on the Streets, Street People's Anthem, Lucky Me, Song to Endangered Species, Street Corner Song, Schwesters, The Freedom Song
A musical in 2 acts and 11 scenes. The action takes place at the present time in New York City.

ACTORS' AND DIRECTORS' THEATER Thursday, April 8–25, 1982 (15 performances) Actors' and Directors' Theater (Nell Robinson, Artistic Director; Ruth Ann Norris, Managing Director) presents:
DIVINE FIRE By Kenneth Ludwig; Director, Nell Robinson; Scenery, Joseph A. Varga; Costumes, Mary I. Whitehead; Lighting, Scott Pinkney; Technical Director, Randall Etheredge; Stage Managers, Linda J. Shiers, Suzanne O'Hare, James Sigler; Press, Shirley Herz, Sam Rudy, Peter Cromarty

CAST: Brian Evers (Abelard), Wendy Rosenberg (Heloise), Arthur Burns (Bernard), John High (Narrator/Suger), Robert McFarland (Fulbert), Charles Shaw-Robinson (Louis), Allen Swift (Pope Innocent II), Thomas Moran (Pierre), Ruth Ann Norris (Denise), Michael Fantacci (Benjamin), Paul Fouquet (Jacques), Richard Bitsko (Robert), Lisa Loving (Bett), Erick Avari (Zani), Lois Diane Hicks (Peasant), Ryan Listman (Peasant/Servant), Wendy Matthews (Marie)
A drama in 2 acts and 15 scenes. The action takes place in France during the first half of the Twelfth Century.

CHERNUCHIN THEATRE Tuesday, April 13–May 1, 1982 (16 performances and 4 previews) American Theatre of Actors (James Jennings, Artistic Director) presents:
CHARLOTTE SWEET with Libretto by Michael Colby; Music, Gerald Jay Markoe; Director, Edward Stone; Choreographer, Dennis Dennehy; Staging, Dennis Dennehy, Edward Stone; Lighting, Jason Kantrowitz; Musical Director, Polly Pen; Musical Coordinator, Randy Parrish; Project Producer, Ruthanne Patterson; Hairstylist, Diane Balmer; Production Assistant, Ann-Marie Perreault; Technical Director, Bob Briggs; Stage Managers, Peter Weicker, Michelle Roberts; Press, Fred Hoot, Ken Munzing
CAST: Michael McCormick (Harry Host), Mara Beckerman (Charlotte Sweet), Christopher Seppe (Ludlow Land Grimble), Michael Dantuono (Bob Sweet), Alan Brasington (Barnaby Bugaboo), Sandra Wheeler (Katinka Bugaboo), Virginia Seidel (Cecily Mackintosh), Polly Pen (Skitzy Scofield)
MUSICAL NUMBERS: At the Music Hall, Charlotte Sweet, A Daughter for Valentine's Day, Forever, Liverpool Sunset, Layers of Underwear, Quartet Agonistes, Circus of Voices, Keep It Low, Bubbles in Me Bonnet, Vegetable Reggie, My Baby and Me, A-Weaving, Your High Note, Katinka, The Darkness, On It Goes, You See in Me a Bobby, Christmas Buche, The Letter, Good Things Come, It Could Only Happen in the Theatre, Lonely Canary, Queenly Comments, Surprise Surprise, The Reckoning, Farewell to Auld Lang Syne
A musical in two acts. The action takes place in turn-of-the-century England.

BALDWIN THEATRE Wednesday, April 14–May 2, 1982 (15 performances)
HEDDA GABLER By Henrik Ibsen; Director, Michael Morrows; Set, Mr. Morrows; Lighting, Scott Sorrel; General Manager, Karen Alkofer; Hairstylist/Makeup, Robin Oka; Stage Managers, Mathias Holzman, Bill Seide, Marc Silber; Press, Fred Hoot, Ken Munzing

CAST: Karen Alkofer (Berte), Richard Costabile (George), Mimi Rogers Weddell (Aunt Julia), Karen Cannady (Thea), Anita Sorel (Hedda), Keith Walters (Ejlert), John King (Judge Brack)
A drama in 2 acts and 4 scenes. The action takes place in the Tesman's villa in Oslo during 1891.

THEATRE AT ST. CLEMENT'S Thursday, April 15–May 9, 1982 (16 performances)
MAIDEN STAKES By David Libman; Director, Anita Khanzadian; Scenery, Gary Jennings; Lighting, Dale Jordan; Costumes, Margo LaZaro; Sound, Peter Kallish; Stage Manager, Neile Weissman; Press, Stephen Berwind

CAST: Eddie Jones (Tarsh), Barbara eda-Young (Margo Crosby), Victor Arnold (Boogler), Ira Lewis (Lawyer)
The action takes place in Boog and Tarsh's apartment in the Bay Ridge section of Brooklyn.

ORPHEUM THEATRE Thursday, April 15–May 1, 1982 (9 performances) Rooty Kazooty presents:
BROKEN TOYS! By Keith Berger; Director, Carl Haber; Assistant Director, Alan Preston; Sets, Lisa Beck; Lighting, Kevin Jones; Costumes, Mara Lonner, Karen Dusenberg; Music/Arrangements, Eric Kupper; Hairstylists/Makeup, A. Vernon Keech, Don Mikula, Lucille Reader; Stage Manager, Bill Szymansky; Press, Shirley Herz, Sam Rudy, Peter Cromarty

CAST: Elizabeth Wren Arthur (Melissa), Keith Berger (Rooty Kazooty), Nerida Normal (Kanga), Oona Lind (Big Dolly), Maria Pessino (Kandy), Lonnie Lichtenberg (Randy), Daud Svitzer (Golly), Lucille (Pretty Polly), Johnny Seitz (3-D Jesus)
A musical in two acts. The action takes place at the present time in the bedroom and attic of a suburban house.

VANDAM THEATRE Thursday, April 15–25, 1982 (12 performances) T. L. Boston presents:
TWO By Fredricka Weber; Music and Lyrics, Misha Segal, Fredricka Weber; Director, Raymond Homer; Choreographer, Barbara Hanks; Scenery, Seth Price; Lighting, Deborah Tulchin; Musical Director, Michael Stockler; Orchestrations, Doug Katsaros; Stage Manager, David H. Bosboom; Props, Leslie Moore; Wardrobe, Robert Galloway; Press, Fred Hoot, Ken Munzing

CAST: Joe Godfrey (Dickie), Evelyn Page (Mother), Charles C. Welch (Father/Uncle Bud), Fredricka Weber (Frannie), Townspeople: Viki Boyle, Shaun Bushnell, Dennis Sullivan, Shaver Tillitt

MUSICAL NUMBERS: Illinois, It Might Fall Off, What Is Normal, We Do Have, I've Got a Secret, Stop the Slushing, I'll Be a Hairstylist to the Movie Stars, The Answer to Life Is Death, Ain't She Sweet, Children Today, I Did It!, Frannie, Do the Opposite, I Feel Like I Lost Something, One Door Opens, My God Laughs, Don't Lose That Spark
The action takes place during the 1940's in the small Illinois towns of Dwight and Beardstown.

T. L. Boston Photo

Victor Arnold, Barbara eda-Young in "Maiden Stakes"

TOWN HALL Friday, April 16–18, 1982 (3 performances) Executive VI (Otis Chestnut, Robert Williams, Donald Prince, David Bey, Oscar Lewis, James Pettis) presents:
GOD'S TROMBONES By James Weldon Johnson; Director, James Pettis; Costumes, Leither Ligon; Hairstylist, Peccolia Turner; Press, Howard Atlee Associates

CAST: Maxwell Glanville (Pastor), Shirley A. Reed (Soloist), The James Pettis Singers (under the direction of James Pettis): Lola Underwood, Leither Ligon, Naomi Golf, Lorraine Stancil, Mae Smith, Gracie Hyman, Elijah Bennett, Everett Jenkins, Marian Taylor, David Williams,
STANDBYS: Everett Ensley, Annie Stancil, Lola Underwood
A series of seven sermons glorifying God and the Bible and adapted in the rhythmic style of standard hymns and melodies performed with one intermission.

WONDERHORSE THEATRE Sunday, April 18–May 8, 1982 (15 performances) Cherubs Guild presents:
MASQUE and DACHA Two plays by Michael Dinwiddie; Director, Leslie Hurley; Sets, Edmond Ramage; Lighting, Jo Mayer; Original Music, Mudra Lipari; Costumes, Martin Pakledinaz; Producers, Carol Avila, Lesley Starbuck, Hillary Wyler; Stage Manager, Peggie Lowenberg; Press, Shirley Herz, Sam Rudy, Peter Cromarty

CAST: "Masque": Kurt Schlesinger (Brian), Cheryl Emanuel (Emilie), Yvonne Warden (Mme. Avant). The action takes place on the balcony of a ballroom in the 1850's New Orleans. "Dacha": Yvonne Warden (Nana), Kim Yancey (Kathy). The action takes place at the present time in a Harlem brownstone.

Fredricka Weber (L), Charles C. Welch (R) in "Two"

Lisa Kable, Lisa Reed, Nina Levine in "Best All 'Round"
(*Gerry Goodstein Photo*)

PLAYERS THEATRE   Thursday, April 22–25, 1982 (6 performances and 7 previews) The Dynamite Limited Partnership presents:
T.N.T. (Tricephalous Neurosyllogistic Training) By Richard Morrock; Director, Frank Carucci; Musical Numbers Staged by Mary Lou Crivello; Musical Direction/Arrangements, William Gladd; Scenery and Lighting, Ernest Allen Smith; Costumes, Susa J. Wright; Production Coordinator, Shari Goldstein; Production Assistant, David Diamond; Management Associate, Rosemary Carey; General Managers, DiDia/Fiore Productions; Stage Managers, Irene Klein, Gabriel Barr; Press, Free Lance Talents, Francine L. Trevens, David Mayhew

CAST: Steven F. Hall (Grant), Mary Anne Dorward (Bonnie), Regis Bowman (Max), Joanne Bradley (Fran), Kenneth Boys (Bill), Mary Garripoli (Debbie), Bill Boss (Jonathan), Gabriel Barre (Jerry), Christine Campbell (Marie), Natalie Strauss (Gail)

MUSICIAL NUMBERS: Why?, Tricephalous You, Life Is a Four-Letter Word, A Casual Kind of Thing, Previous Lives, Where Have I Been?, Mantra, Id Superego, Longing for Someone, I'm O.K. You're O.K., Meat Market, The Secret of Life
   A musical in 2 acts and 5 scenes. The action takes place at the present time in the college auditorium, and the cafeteria.

PERRY STREET THEATRE   Monday, April 26–May 30, 1982 (28 performances) Prism Theatre (Ron Comenzo, Carol Drake, Producers) presents:
BEST ALL 'ROUND By Marsha Sheiness; Director, Stephen Stewart-James; Set, Patrick Mann; Lighting, Paul Everett; Costumes, Sam Fleming; Sound, Eloida G. Hulbert; Production Manager, Thomas Bothwell; Wardrobe, Michele Doroshow; Wigs, Bob Kelley; Stage Manager, Susanne Jul; Press, Clarence Allsopp

CAST: Nina Levine (Michael Lee), Lisa Reed (Nickie), Lisa Kable (Kay), Understudies: Anna Mulkey (Kay), Mary Caton (Michael/-Nickie)
   A play in two acts. The action takes place in Corpus Christi, Texas during 1957–58.

500 THEATRE ROW   Monday, April 26–May 19, 1982 (12 performances) Hudson Spring Productions presents:
FRENCH GRAY By Josef Bush; Director, Jeff Glickman; Performed by Sheri Myers.
   The confession of the Widow Capet, formerly Marie Antoinette of France, as she prepares to meet her end at the hands of justice.

CHERRY LANE THEATRE   Wednesday, May 5–June 20, 1982 (55 performances and 3 previews) William Bixby, Jr. in association with Edwin W. Schloss and Abigail Franklin presents:
CAST OF CHARACTERS By Ruth Draper; Director, David Kaplan; Lighting, Stuart Duke; Costumes, Dunya Ramicova; Production Assistants, Meghan Robinson, William Watkins; Production Supervisor, Neil Mazzella; General Manager, Abigail Franklin; Stage Manager, Nora Peck; Press, Fred Nathan, Eileen McMahon, Louis Sica, Anne S. Abrams
   A one-woman performance in two parts with selections from the repertoire of the late Ruth Draper. The program was selected from Three Women and Mr. Clifford, The Italian Lesson, A Scottish Immigrant at Ellis Island, The Actress, A Class in Greek Poise, The French Dressmaker, A Children's Party, In the Court of Philip IV, Four Imaginary Folk Songs, In a Church in Italy.

AMERICAN RENAISSANCE THEATER   Thursday, May 6–29, 1982 (16 performances) Tom Greene III, Anthony P. Galli and Jessie B. Greene present:
BASEBALL WIVES By Grubb Graebner; Director, Gloria Maddox; Scenery and Costumes, John Falabella; Lighting, Jeff Davis; Sound, Gordon Kupperstein; Casting, Margo McKee; Consulting Producers, Soloway & Francis; Stage Manager, Julienne Fisher; Press, Shirley Herz, Sam Rudy, Peter Cromarty

CAST: Lynn Goodwin (Becky), Patti Karr (Doris), Marcella Lowery (Janelle). A play in two acts. The action takes place at the present time throughout the professional baseball season from early spring to late fall.

Marcella Lowery, Lynn Goodwin, Patti Karr in "Baseball Wives"
(*Carol Rosegg Photo*)

NAMELESS THEATRE   Thursday, May 6–23, 1982 (12 performances) Patrick J. Byrne presents:
LA RONDE By Arthur Schnitzler; Director, James Leggi; Set and Lighting, Donald L. Brooks; Music, Arnold Black; Costumes, Maxine Moffett; Technical Director, Donald Chan; Stage Manager, Ray Healey; Press, Julienne Fisher

CAST: Laurie Oudin (Whore), Steve Kollmorgen (Soldier), Beth Friend (Parlow Maid), John G. Moraitis (Young Man), Janet Bailey (Young Wife), Doug Blackburn (Husband), Marcia Blau (Little Miss), Robert Shea (Poet), Judy Levitt (Actress), Ryan Thomas (Count)
   A play in two acts. The action takes place in Vienna in the 1890's.

VANDAM THEATRE   Wednesday, May 12, 1982 and still playing May 31, 1982. Lester Lockwood, Sr. and Lester Lockwood, Jr. present:
THE SIX O'CLOCK BOYS By Sidney Morris; Director, Raymond Homer; Set and Costumes, Helen Lockwood; Lighting, Angus Moss; Casting, Kathy Lockwood; General Manager, Lily Turner; Stage Manager, Lisa Ledwich; Press, Howard Atlee, Ellen Levene, Barbara Atlee

CAST: Vera Lockwood (Gabie), Johnnie Collins III (Monday Night Boy) succeeded by Dan Freedman, Jack Couch (Tuesday Night Boy) succeeded by Lee Collings, Scott Stevensen (Wednesday Night Boy) succeeded by James Nixon
   A drama in two acts. The action takes place in the early 1970's in Gabie's room in the Endicott, a welfare hotel in New York City.

SOUTH STREET THEATRE   Thursday, May 17–June 20, 1982 (19 performances) Kevin C. Donahue and John Hart Associates in association with South Street Theatre (Jean Sullivan, Producing Director) present:
BOOTH By Robert A. Morse; Director, Christopher Catt; Scenery, David Chapman; Lighting, Frances Aronson; Costumes, Lindsay Davis; Musical Sequences, David Spangler; Combat Choreography, A. C. Weary; Sound, Lewis Mead; Artistic Adviser, Tim Lovejoy; Wardrobe, Caroleann Runion; Production Assistant, Brian Johnson; Wig and Hairstylist/Makeup, Ester Teller; Assistant to Producers, Cathy Donahue; Casting, Hughes/Moss, Phil DiMaggio; Company Manager, Ron Aja; Stage Managers, Renee F. Lutz, Kirk Jackson; Press, Howard Atlee, Ellen Levene, Barbara Atlee

CAST: Michael Nouri (Edwin Booth), Michael Connolly (Junius Booth), Steve Bassett (John Matthews), Jane Cronin (Laura Keene), Howard Korder (John McCullough), Peter Boyden (Harry Hawk), John Glover (John Wilkes Booth)
   A drama in two acts. The action takes place in New York City, Washington, D.C., Boston, Maryland and Virginia from November 1863 through April 1965.

ACTORS STUDIO   Tuesday, May 18–31, 1982 (12 performances)
CHILDREN OF DARKNESS By Edwin Justus Mayer; Director, Arthur Sherman; Set, Matthew C. Jacobs; Lighting, Phil Monat; Costumes, Martha Hally; Production Coordinator, Sam Coppola; Associate Director, Carmine R. Pontilena; Assistant to Director, Lisa Ungar; Production Assistant, Jackie Slotkin; Assistant Production Coordinator, John Kassan; Stage Managers, Dorothy French, Marie Scampmini

CAST: Edmund Lyndeck (Snap), Tom Paliferro (Bailiff), Joseph Culp (Cartwright), Joseph Tobin (Fierce), Fred Coffin (Jonathin Wild), Ron Leibman (Count LaRuse), Mary Joan Negro (Laetitia), Patrick O'Neal (Lord Wainwright), David Parker, David Daniel
   A drama in 3 acts. The action takes place in a room in the "undersheriff's" house which adjoins New Gate Prison, London in 1725. (No Photo available)

James Nixon, Vera Lockwood in "Six O'Clock Boys"
(Lester Lockwood, Jr. Photo)

WEST END THEATRE   Saturday, May 22–June 12, 1982 (12 performances) The Facemakers present:
SHE LOVES ME With Book by Joe Masteroff; Lyrics, Sheldon Harnick; Music, Jerry Bock; Based on play by Miklos Laszlo; Director, Owen Thompson; Music Director, John Walter; Musical Consultant, Caryl M. Ginsburg; Costumes, Jennie Cleaver; Set and Lighting, Michael E. Golden, Walter Plinge; Stage Manager, Michael E. Golden

CAST: Matthew Douglas Anton (Maraczek), Michael Barbieri (Sipos), Susan C. Carey (2nd Customer/Dance Captain), Shira Flam (Amalia), David H. Hamilton (Georg Nowack), Bambi Jones (Miss Ritter), Bill MacNulty (Keller), Brad Negbaur (Arpad), Toby Parker (Waiter), Ashton Phillips (Violinist), Owen Thompson (Kodaly), Frances Ellen Thorpe (3rd Customer), Lisa Ward (1st Customer)
   A musical in two acts.

Michael Nouri, John Glover in "Booth"
(Susan Cook Photo)

69

DOUGLAS FAIRBANKS THEATRE   Thursday, May 27–June 13, 1982 (22 performances) Kyle Renick and Gene Persson in association with Miranda Smith present the WPA Theatre production of:
THE FREAK By Granville Wyche Burgess; Director, Stephen Zuckerman; Set, Christina Weppner; Costumes, Susan Denison; Lighting, Richard Winkler; Casting, Darlene Kaplan; Production Assistant, William L. McMullen; Props, Carol Kalil; Company Manager, David Jannone; Stage Managers, Melissa Davis, Vandra Thorburn; Press, Jeffrey Richards, Robert Ganshaw, Ted Killmer, Ben Morse, Helen Stern, C. George Willard, Richard Humleker

CAST: James Rebhorn (Dr. Wesley Ketchum), James Greene (Squire Cayce), Peter J. Saputo (Charlie Dietrich), Polly Draper (Gertrude Cayce), Dann Florek (Edgar Cayce), Richard Patrick-Warner (Dr. Philip Barber), Eddie Jones (Dr. Joe Quigly), William Riker (Dr. Furman Shepherd)
   A drama in 3 acts and 10 scenes. The action takes place in Hopkinsville, Ky. from late summer of 1910 to early spring of 1911.

Eddie Jones, Richard Patrick-Warner, James Greene, William Riker, Dann Florek in "The Freak" *(Peter Cunningham Photo)*

Brian Murray in "The Arcata Promise"

NO SMOKING PLAYHOUSE   May 27–June 12, 1982 (12 performances) Brockman Seawell presents:
THE ARCATA PROMISE By David Mercer; Director, Geoffrey Sherman; Costumes, Sam Fleming; Set, C. L. Hundley; Lighting, Ed Matthews; Production Coordinator, Thomas J. Rees; Stage Managers, Scott Lane, Penelope Demos.
CAST: Kermit Brown (Tony Greeves), Lisa Carlin (Laura), Brian Murray (Theodore Gunge). A play in two acts and four scenes. The action takes place in the past and present in Theodore Gunge's basement flat, and his Chelsea flat.

WONDERHORSE THEATRE   Thursday, May 27–July 4, 1982 (20 performances) Mirabel Productions and Chris Silva present:
TOUCHED By Stephen Lowe; Director, Richard Seyd; Set, Michael Gallagher; Costumes, Edi Giguere; Lighting, Vincent Lalomia; Hairstylist/Makeup, Sigrid Wurschmidt; Wardrobe, Linda Wager; Assistant Director, Jim Piddock; General Manager, Chris Silva; Stage Managers, Leslie Moore, Kym Moore, Elena Rivera; Press, Burnham-Callaghan Associates

CAST: Jennifer Sternberg (Sandra), Blanche Cholet (Mary), Elly Huber (Betty), Mark Smith (Johnny), Jane Darby (Joan), Wendy Ann Finnegan (Pauline), Alexandra Gersten (Bridie), Steve Coats (Keith), John Swindells (Harry), Martha Farrar (Mother)
   A drama in 2 acts and 9 scenes. The action takes place in and around Nottingham, England during the one hundred days between victory in Europe and victory in Japan in 1945.

Elly Huber, Jennifer Sternberg in "Touched"
(Carol Rosegg Photo)

OFF BROADWAY SERIES
Amas Repertory Theatre

Founder/Artistic Director, Rosetta LeNoire; Administrator/Business Manager, Gary Halcott; Administrator, Jerry Lapidus

Thursday, October 22–November 15, 1981 (16 performances)
WILL THEY EVER LOVE US ON BROADWAY written and composed by Osayande Baruti in consultation with Coleridge-Taylor Perkinson and Mabel Robinson; Musical Director/Dance, Vocal and Instrumental Arranger, Coleridge-Taylor Perkinson; Conductor, Fred Gripper; Set, Thomas Barnes; Lighting, John Enea; Costumes, Judy Dearing; Stage Managers, Steven D. Nash, Paul Reggio; Wardrobe, Floyd Hill; Production Consultant, Chuck Patterson; Technical Assistant, Darren McGill
CAST: J. Herbert Kerr, Jr. (Kwame Kombs), Marva Hicks (Jessie Day), L. Edmond Wesley (Sam Johnson), Roma Maffia (Rosita Consuela Rialto), William Lucas (I. A. Prince), Ed Battle (Rafael Fredericks), Fred Gripper (Rehearsal Pianist), Valencia Edner (Savanna Fredericks), Melodee Savage (Cast Member), James Judy (Ivan Dierch), Dwayne Grayman (George Jenkins) A musical in 2 acts. The action takes place on the stage of a Broadway theatre in 1981.

Wednesday, February 4–28, 1982 (16 performances)
THE WINDS OF CHANGE by Franklin C. Tramutola; Composer, Joseph D. D'Agostino; Lyricist, Gary Romero; Musical Director/Keyboards/Vocal and Instrumental Arrangements, Lea Richardson; Associate Musical Director/Keyboards/Dance and Instrumental Arrangements, Daryl M. Waters; Set, Tom Barnes; Lighting, Ronald L. McIntyre; Costumes, Judy Dearing; Directed and Staged by William Michael Maher; Technical Director, Edward Goetz; Wardrobe, Richard Rodriguez; Stage Managers, Steven D. Nash, James Knight, Darren McGill

CAST: Richard T. Alpers (Mr. Holmes), Susan Berkson (Mrs. Holmes), Terry Kirwin (Ned Vann), Steve Correia (Master/Reporter), Nick DiVirgilio (Michaelko), Marjorie Gayle Edwards (Dance/Reporter's Assistant), Jimmy Foster (Master/Managing Editor), Donald Grimme (Master/Reporter), Sonya Hensley (Nonnie/Sandy/Reporter's Assistant), Vicki Juditz (Lolo/Reporter's Assistant), Jon-David Kibbe (Eddy/Reporter/Master), Dinah Lenney (Mary Olcott), Robin Oxman (Hannah/Reporter's Assistant), Jack Sevier (Col. Olcott), Molly Stark (H. P. Blavatsky) A musical in 2 acts and 15 scenes with a prologue and epilogue. The action takes place between 1872 and 1879 in New York City.

Thursday, April 15–May 9, 1982 (16 performances)
FIVE POINTS by Lawrence Holder; Music and Lyrics, John Braden; Musical Director/Arranger, Steven Oirich; Director/Stager, William Michael Maher; Choreographer, Keith Rozie. Technical Director, Adam Hart; Set, Tom Barnes; Lighting, Gregg Marriner; Costumes, Gabriel Berry; Pianist, Bill Hindin; Wardrobe, Pamela Reeves; Stage Managers, Paul Duffy, Jim Griffith, Kuan Mangle; Hairstylist/Makeup, Lawrence Long
CAST: Larry Campbell (Pete Williams), Marjorie Gayle Edwards (Ensemble), Joseph Fugett (Juba), J. Herbert Kerr, Jr. (Johnnie Night), Robert Lydiard (Jack Diamond), Cynthia McPherson (Ethel Myrrh), Valois Mickens (Ensemble), Nicky Paraiso (Fong), Tonya Pinkins (Arnabelle), Rochelle Parker (Lena), Bertin Rowser (Ensemble), Robert Vaucresson, Jr. (Ensemble) A musical in 2 acts and 10 scenes. The action takes place in the Five Points district of New York City during the 1840's.

American Jewish Theatre

92nd Street YM-YWHA

Artistic Director, Stanley Brechener; Assistant to Director, J. B. Nader; Resident Director, Dan Held; New Play Program, Leslie Goldstein; Technical Director, Kevin L. Ash; Audience Development, Norman Golden; Production Coordinator, J. B. Nader

Thursday, Sept. 17–Oct. 25, 1981 (24 performances)
IN THE MATTER OF J. ROBERT OPPENHEIMER by Heinar Kipphardt: Translated by Ruth Speirs; Director, Robert Brink; Stage Manager, Nancy Kohlbeck. CAST: Frank Anderson, Herman Arbeit, Craig Augustine, Arthur Burns, Tommy Canary, Tom Cipolla, Wally Duquet, Davis Hall, Warrington Winters, Gordon Jones, Dane Knell, Terry Layman, John O'Creagh, Doug Roberts, Albert Sinkys, Jerry Terheyden, Jennifer L. Thompson
Saturday Nov. 14–Dec. 20, 1981 (24 performances)
HOUSE MUSIC by Hans Sah; Director, Geoffrey Sherman; Music and Lyrics, Alan Menken; Set and Lighting, Paul Wonsek; Stage Manager, Greta Minsky; Costumes, Barbara Weiss. CAST: Clement Fowler, Robert Blumenfeld, Shirin Trainer, Jean Hackett, Brian Zoldessy, Elaine Grollman, Eberle Thoman, Waltrudis Buck, Jack Poggi, Sol Frieder, George Buck, Albert S. Bennett, Fran Anthony
Saturday, Jan 16–Feb. 21, 1982 (24 performances)
THE PRICE by Arthur Miller; Director, Dan Held; Set, Tony Castrigno; Costumes, Karen Hummel; Stage Manager, Leslie Gold-

stein. CAST: Michael M. Ryan, Joan Copeland, Joseph Buloff, David Gale
Saturday, March 6–April 18, 1982 (24 performances)
THE KEYMAKER by Nat Teitel; Director, Stanley Brechner; Set, Peter Wingate; Lighting, Helen Gatling; Costumes, Barbara Weiss; Stage Manager, Anne Cowett.
CAST: Carol Teitel, Mark Nelson, Lloyd Battista, Sasha von Scherler, Norman Golden, Conrad L. Osborne, Aphroditi Kolaitis, Earl Hammond, Cecile Callan, Robert Blumenfeld, Jacqueline Barsh
Saturday, May 1–June 13, 1982 (24 performances)
THE RASPBERRY PICKER by Fritz Hochwalder; Director, Dan Held; Set, Tony Castrigno; Lighting, Helen Gatling, Costumes, Karen Hummel, Stage Managers, Debbie Acquavella, Eli Shurany. CAST: Frank Borgman, Annie Combs, John Fiedler, Earl Hammond, Anita Keal, Jan Meredith, Fred Miller, Lee Moore, Joe Ponazecki, Larry Swansen, Nicholas Saunders, Norman Golden

Above: (L) Molly Stark, Jack Sevier in "The Winds of Change" *(JWL Photo)* (R) Joan Copeland, Joseph Buloff, Michael Miller in "The Price" *(Gerry Goodstein Photo)*

American Place Theatre

Eighteenth Season

Director, Wynn Handman; Associate Director, Julia Miles; General Manager, Joanna Vedder; Assistants to Directors, Elaine DeLeon, Bonnie Keyes, Martha Fischer; Casting, Bonnie Timmerman, Barbara Clamon, Alison Rose; Press, Jeffrey Richards, Robert Ganshaw, Helen Stern, Ted Killmer

Tuesday, June 2–14, 1981 (12 performances)
THE FUEHRER BUNKER by W. D. Snodgrass; Director, Carl Weber; Music and Chorus Supervision, Richard Peaslee; Musical Director and Accordionist, William Schimmel; Costumes, K. L. Fredericks; Lighting, Daniel C. Abrahamsen; Assistant Director, Gordon Edelstein; Technical Director, Frank McAlister; Production Assistant, Lisa Salomon; Stage Managers, W. Scott Allison, Joseph S. Kubala. CAST: Larry Block (Martin Bormann), Catherine Byers (Magda Goebbels), Thomas Carson (Heinrich Himmler), Paul Collins (Joseph Goebbels), Jerome Dempsey (Herman Goering), Annette Kurek (Eva Braun), Carl Low (Leader/Gotthard Heinrici), Robert Stattel (Adolf Hitler)
Performed without intermission.

Monday, October 19–November 1, 1981 (16 performances)
GRACE by Jane Stanton Hitchcock; Director, Peter Thompson; Set, William Barclay; Lighting, Phil Monat; Costumes, David Griffin; Assistant to Director, Joan Thompson; Production Assistants, Joseph Onorato, Ed Shockley; Wardrobe, K. L. Fredericks; Stage Manager, Nancy Harrington
CAST: Scotty Bloch (Grace), Catherine Byers (Mae), Rino Thunder (Indian), Karen Looze (Rose), Jane Fleiss (Sissy), Emmanuel Yesckas (Dino), James Higgins (Patterson), Hope Cameron (Mrs. Meers) A play in 2 acts and 3 scenes. The action takes place at the present time in Oklahoma City, Oklahoma and in Tucson, Arizona.

Tuesday, December 8–20, 1981 (14 performances and 5 previews)
BEHIND THE BROKEN WORDS with Roscoe Lee Browne and Anthony Zerbe as creators and co-stars in a theatre piece that presents a poetic journey into some of America's outstanding literary works. Performed in two parts.

Thursday, February 25–March 21, 1982 (28 performances and 26 previews) Roger S. Berlind and John Wulp present:
LYDIE BREEZE by John Guare; Director, Louis Malle; Scenery, John Wulp; Costumes, Willa Kim; Lighting, Jennifer Tipton; Music, Glen Roven; Assistant to Director, James Bruce; Wardrobe, K. L. Fredericks; Hairstylist, Karole Coeyman; Casting, Juliet Taylor, John Lyons; Technical Supervisor, DCA Design Associates; General Managers, Elizabeth I. McCann, Nelle Nugent; Production Coordinator, Brent Peek; Company Manager, Gintare Sileika; Stage Managers, Jay Adler, Scott Allen; Press, Robert Ullman, Louise Ment
CAST: Ben Cross (Jeremiah Grady), Roberta Maxwell (Beaty), Cynthia Nixon (Lydie Hickman), Madeleine Potter (Gussie Hickman), Josef Sommer (Joshua Hickman), Robert Joy (Jude Emerson), James Cahill (Lucian Rock) A drama in two acts. The action takes place on Nantucket Island during September of 1895.

Thursday, March 25–April 11, 1982 (15 performances)
The Women's Project in association with Portland Stage Company presents:
THE DEATH OF A MINER by Paul Cizmar; Director, Barbara Rosoff; Set, Leslie Taylor; Lighting, Arden Fingerhut; Costumes, Heidi Hollmann, Susan J. Wright; Lighting Associate, Dale Jordon; Wardrobe, K. L. Fredericks; Props, Roger Y. Edes; Technical Director, Ken Brown; Stage Manager, Vincent A. Feraudo
CAST: Mary McDonnell (Mary Alice), Cotter Smith (Jack), Margaret MacLeod (Sallie), Kristin Jolliff (Winona), Dave Florek (Pete), John Griesemer (Chester), Shaw Purnell (Bonnie Jean), Ritch Brinkley (Barney), Douglas Gower (Dale), Steven Loring (Joseph) The action takes place at the present time in a coal-mining town in Appalachia.

Wednesday, March 31–April 11, 1982 (8 performances and 6 previews)
The Women's Project presents:
THE BROTHERS by Kathleen Collins; Director, Billie Allen; Set, Christina Weppner; Costumes, K. L. Fredericks; Lighting, Ann Wrightson; Music, Michael Minard; Stage Managers, Nancy Harrington, Duane Jones, Cheryl D. Singleton
CAST: Josephine Premice (Danielle Edwards), Trazana Beverley (Marietta Edwards), Duane Jones (Norrell), Janet League (Lillie Edwards), Leila Danette (Rosie Gould), Marie Thomas (Letitia Edwards), Seret Scott (Caroline Edwards), Duane Jones (Doctor/Voice of Newscaster)
Performed without intermission. The action takes place in the mind of Danielle Edwards—past, present and future.

Thursday, April 15–18, 1982 (5 performances)
The Acting Company (John Houseman, Producing Artistic Director; Artistic Directors,
Michael Kahn, Alan Schneider; Executive Producer, Margot Harley) presents:
TWELFTH NIGHT by William Shakespeare; Director, Michael Langham; Set and Costumes, Desmond Heeley; Lighting, John Michael Deegan; Music Composed and Directed by David Erlanger; Choreography, Becky Borczon; Stage Fights, Jake Turner; Wigs, Charles LoPresto; Wardrobe, Marcia Ellen Cohen; Props, T. Wiley Bramlett; Stage Managers, Don Judge, Kathleen B. Boyette; Press, Fred Nathan, Anne S. Abrams
CAST: Patrick O'Connell (Orsino), Casey Biggs (Sebastian), Barry Heins (Antonio), Ray Virta (Valentine/Friar), Richard S. Iglewski (Sir Toby Belch), Paul Walker (Sir Andrew Aguecheek), Jeffrey Rubin (Malvolio), Brian Reddy (Fabian/Sea Captain), Tommy Bramlett (1st Sailor/2nd Officer), Daniel Wirth (Curio/1st Officer), Philip Goodwin (Feste), Michele-Denise Woods (Olivia), Pamela Nyberg (Viola), Lynn Chausow (Maria), Ronna Kress (Servant)
Performed in two acts.

Tuesday, April 20–24, 1982 (6 performances)
THE COUNTRY WIFE by William Wycherley; Director, Garland Wright; Sets, Jack Barkla; Costumes, Judith Dolan; Lighting, Dennis Parichy; Assistant to Director, Randolph Foerster
CAST: Casey Biggs (Mr. Horner), Philip Goodwin (Dr. Quack), Barry Heins (Horner's Servant), Brian Reddy (Sir Jasper Fidget), Pamela Nyberg (Lady Fidget), Ronna Kress (Mrs. Dainty Fidget), Patrick O'Connell (Harcourt), Daniel Wirth (Dorilant), Paul Walker (Sparkish), Richard S. Iglewski (Pinchwife), Michele-Denise Woods (Alithea), Lynn Chausow (Margery Pinchwife), Becky Borczon (Lucy), Pamela Tucker-White (Mrs. Squeamish), Bonnie Bowers (Old Lady Squeamish), Jeffrey Rubin (Bookseller), Ray Virta (Servant/Tradesman)
Presented in two acts.

Sunday, May 23, 1982 - Aug. 22, 1982 (83 performances and 8 previews).
THE REGARD OF FLIGHT by Bill Irwin; Original Music, Doug Skinner; Lighting, Joan Arhelger; Wardrobe, K. L. Fredericks; Production Assistants, Carroll Cartwright, Richard Hester; Stage Managers, Nancy Harrington, Larry Woodbridge
CAST: Doug Skinner, Bill Irwin, Michael O'Connor
Performed without intermission.

Roberta Maxwell, Cynthia Nixon in "Lydie Breeze"
(Gerry Goodstein Photo)

Casey Biggs, Lynn Chausow in "The Country Wife"
(Diane Gorodnitzki Photo)

American Renaissance Theater

Artistic Director, Robert Elston; Associate Director, Elizabeth Perry; Artistic Adviser, Susan Reed

June 4 and 13, 1981 (2 performances)
WOMEN OF IRELAND in poetry, song and dance, performed by Susan Reed and Bambi Linn

June 5 and 11, 1981 (2 performances)
WHERE WORDS OF ALL THE WORLD'S POETS GO a program of black poetry and song with jazz combo; Director, Pat White; Starring Darryl Alladice

June 6, 7 and 14, 1981 (3 performances)
NOTES by and with Robert Elston; Directed by Elizabeth Perry

June 6 and 12, 1981 (2 performances)
PORTRAIT OF A MAN compiled and starring Robert Elston in a collage of poetry and song: Directed by Anita Khanzadian

Wednesday, June 17–July 9, 1981 (2 performances of each play)
SALON PERFORMANCES OF CLASSIC PLAYS: ANTIGONE by Sophocles; Translated by Dudley Fitts, Robert Fitzerald; Director, Stephen Berwind; with Robert Elston, Joseph Adams, Molly Adams, Donna Davis, Sally Dunn, Davis Hall, Ira Lewis, Bernard Mantell, Stephen Berwind. **DON JUAN** by Moliere; Director, Lise Liepmann; Assistant to Director, Mimi Huntington; with Davis Hall, Michael Bahr, Maggie Benson, Alex Simmons, Bernard Mantell, Will Osborne, Sims Wyeth, Irene Wagner, Deborah Genninger, Brian Muirhill. **JOHN GABRIEL BORKMAN** by Ibsen; Director, Anita Khanzadian; Stage Manager, Jaclyn Ferraro; with Eloise Iliff, Mimi Huntington, Elizabeth Perry, Merriman Gatch, Davis Hall, Brandwell Teuscher, Herman Arbeit, Irene Wagner. **LIGHT UP THE SKY** by Moss Hart; Director, Amie Brockway; Stage Manager, Leone Fogel; with Rhoda Carol Fairman, Jim Secrest, Judith Lesley, Richard Henson, Molly Adams, Will Osborne, Herman O. Arbeit, Bernard Mantell, Anita Keal, Ed Hyland, Davis Hall

July 22–24, 1981 (3 performances)
DREAMBOATS by Irene Wagner; Director, Carol Williard; Set, John Zaugg; Stage Manager, Bill Gerdes; with Jan Marks, Irene Wagner, Douglas Popper, Bernie Mantell, Will Osborne, Davis Hall, Alex Simmons, Sims Wyeth. The action takes place in "the relative present" over the course of two years.

September 2–4, 1981 (3 performances)
SAINT JOAN OF ARC AND THE STAND-UP COMEDY ACT with Rhoda Carroll and Alex Simmons

Oct. 18–Nov. 20, 1981 (20 performances)
AFTER MANY A SUMMER a contemporary adaptation of Chekhov's "The Seagull" written and directed by Robert Elston; Music, Robert Mitchell; Costumes, Susan Reed; Lighting, David Shepherd; Set, Ernie Schenk; Stage Manager, Jaclyn Ferraro; with Gene Gross (Peter), Richard Santino (Neil), Jody Cerrone (Marcia), Will Osborne (Seymour), Sally Dunn (Nina), Bea Boyle (Paula), Berkeley Harris (Dr. Dorn), Ned Farster (John), Beverlee McKinsey (Irene), Robert Elston (Alexander). Performed with two intermissions. The action takes place on a lake in Maine during the 1960's.

Nov. 19–Dec. 13, 1981 (20 performances)
DON JUAN by Moliere; Director, Lise Liepmann; Set, Angelyn Wood; Lighting, Mike Grimes; Costumes, Marilyn Downs; Sound, Ron Gold; Assistant Director, Sandy Allen; Stage Managers, Dyana Lee, Rory Lance; with Michael Bahr (Sganarelle), Sims Wyeth (Gusman/Peter/Don Alonso), Robert Brandt (Don Juan), Merriman Gatch (Dona Elvira), Irene Wagner (Charlotte), Deborah Genninger (Mathurine/La Violette), Rory Lance (La Ramee/Poor Man), Bernie Mantell (Don Carlos/Statue), Brian Muirhill (Dimanche), Richard Henson (Don Luis). Performed with one intermission.

Monday, December 14, 1981 (1 performance)
CHRISTMAS REVUE with Ron Gold, Susan Reed, Donna Dailey, Judith Lesley, Robert Keiber & Friend, Sue Renee Bernstein, Darryl Alladice, Robert Elston, Erica Kaplan

Jan. 7–Feb. 6, 1982 (12 performances)
STORY TIME by Stan Edelman; Director, Susan Einhorn; with Judy Bohannon (Rosalie), Janni Brenn (Ruby), Randy Jones (Joe). The action takes place in Ruby's diner at the present time. **AMOS AND ISAIAH** by David Libman; Director, Neile Weissman; with David Libman (Belkin), Molly Adams (Nurse), Merriman Gatch (Burn), Ernie Shank (Morrissey), Hugh Hurd (Isaiah Potts), Neile Weissman (Rabbi Amos Levy). **PROLOGUE:** Hugh Hurd (God), Ernie Shank (Adam), Molly Adams (Eve), David Libman (Serpent-/Dolour), Neile Weissman (Angel/Holy Ghost), Merriman Gatch (Misery) **MAN AROUND THE HOUSE** by Joe Julian; Director, Lynn Thomson; with Jill Andre (Ruth), Sean Mullane (Matthew), Lourdes Sanchez-Vargas (Mercedes), Fisher Stevens (Dave), Michael Bahr (Joe), Aurelia DeFelice (Clare), Francis Reilly (Cop/-Narrator) **GIANTS** by Melvin H. Freedman; Director, Stephen Berwind; with Thurman Scott (Sam Gray Ash), Merriman Gatch (Myra Anthony), Robert Elston (Steven Saks), Chaz Denny (Tod Greenleaf), Cathy Jewell (Dorothy Kane), Douglas Popper (Walter Minotti)

Amistad World Theatre

Samuel P. Barton, Artistic Director; Shirley Fishman, Managing Director

N.E.T.W.O.R.K. October 1–November 1, 1981 (20 performances)
THE FLIES by Jean Paul Sartre; Director, Samuel P. Barton; Choreography, Otis Sallid; Original Music, Cornelia Post; Lighting, William Plachy; Costumes, Neil Cooper; Sound, Tom Spohn; Set/Costumes, Samuel P. Barton; Makeup, Diane Bailey; Hairstylist, Freddy Chevere; Masks, Townsend Post. CAST: Leon Morenzie (Zeus), Helmar Augustus Cooper (Aegistheus), Petie Trigg Seale (Clytemnestra), Linda Thomas Wright (Electra), Hector Mercado (Orestes), Peter Yoshida (Tutor), Onike (High Priestess/Fury), John Davis (Soldier), Earl Arthur Imbert (Soldier/Fury), Gloria Irizarry, Sol (Old Women), Nancy Hamada (Aricie/Fury), Marcelino Rosado (Idiot/Segestes), Stuart Smith (Boy on leash), Nicky Kay (Young Boy), Gerry Igarashi (Young Woman), Townspeople/Flies: Kim Yancey, Annette Bland, Fay Burrell, Maritza Rivera, Esther Ryvlin, Darious Perry Barrett, Eugene Nesmith. Performed in 3 acts and 5 scenes.

November 19–December 20, 1981 (16 performances)
THE WHO GETS SLAPPED by Leonid Andreyev; Director, Alba Oms; Costumes, Neil Cooper; Set, Samuel P. Barton; Lighting, Karen Singleton; Stage Managers, Charles Douglass, Tano. CAST: Jaime Sanchez (He), Leon Morenzie (Mancini), Helmar Augustus Cooper (Briquet), Ilka Tanya Payan (Zinida), Nile Yazici (Consuelo), Josh Cruze (Bezano), Emmanuel Yeskas (Gentleman), Daniel Snow (Regnard), Jeffrey Joseph (Jackson), Michael G. Chin (Polly), Stuart Smith (Tilly), Marcelino Rosado (Willie), Yamila Constantina (Angelica). Performed with two intermissions.

January 14–February 14, 1982 (20 performances)
MULATTO by Langston Hughes; Director, Samuel P. Barton; Choreography, Otis A. Sallid; Music, Cornelia J. Post; Lighting, Karen Singleton; Costumes, Neil Cooper; Set, Samuel P. Barton; Sound, Valeria Ferrand; Stage Managers, Thomas J. Podiak, Tano. CAST: John A. Bakos (Col. Norwood), Betty Vaughn (Cora), Christopher Moore (William), Sharon Dennis (Sallie), Phil DiPietro (Robert), Helmar Augustus Cooper (Sam), Stanley Harrison (Fred), Jeffrey Joseph (Mose), Yvonne Whitley (Marybell), Stuart Smith (Bubba), Robert Moseley (Talbot), David Lough (Storekeeper), Richard Mooney (Undertaker), Steven Fertig (Undertaker's Helper), Cornelia J. Post (Livonia), Kim Yancey (Young Cora), Susan Jane Wright (Mrs. Norwood), Field Hands: Antonio Aponte, Jon Furbert, Cliff Terry. A drama in two acts.

Above: (L) Beverlee McKinsey, Robert Elston in "After Many a Summer" *(Ernie Schenk Photo)* (R) Ilka Payan, Jaime Sanchez in "He Who Gets Slapped" *(Don Ventura Photo)*

Ark Theatre Company

Directors, Donald Marcus, Lisa Milligan, Bruce Daniel; Director of Development, Mary Keil; Associate Director, David Trainer

Thursday, March 4–April 4, 1982 (20 performances)
THE MIDDLE AGES by A. R. Gurney, Jr.; Director, Donald Marcus; Set, John Falabella; Costumes, Gail Brassard; Lighting, Heather Carson; Props, Roderick Thompson; Assistants to Producers, Stacey April, Susan Feltman; Wardrobe, Pam Peterson; Casting, Jim Peacock; Stage Managers, Margaret Hahn, David Ness.
CAST: Jack Gilpin (Barney), Carolyn Mignini (Eleanor), Steven Gilborn (Charles, Barney's father), Pat Lavelle (Myra, Eleanor's mother). A play in two acts. The action takes place in the trophy room of a men's club in a large city over a span of time from the mid-forties to the early eighties.

Thursday, May 13–June 13, 1982 (20 performances)
UNHEARD SONGS by Percy Granger; Director, Charles Morey; Scenery, Roderick P. Thompson; Costumes, Elizabeth P. Palmer; Lighting, Ann Wrightson; Assistant Producers, Ken Schwenker; Wardrobe, Ivelisse Diaz; Casting, Donna Isaacson; Stage Managers, Thom Mangan, Kathy Ponvert
CAST: "Solitude Forty" with Richard Mathews (Anders Fritzen), Thomas A. Carlin (Emil Mapes).The action takes place at the present time in the North Woods of Minnesota. "Vivien" with Paul Austin (Vivien Hogan), Richmond Hoxie (Paul Hogan), Dana Ivey (Mrs. Tendesco). The action takes place at the present time.

Circle Repertory Company

Marshall W. Mason, Artistic Director
Thirteenth Season

Producing Director, Porter Van Zandt; Business Manager, Paul S. Daniels; Associate, Glynn Lowrey; Dramaturg, John Bishop; Literary Manager, B. Rodney Mariott; Casting, John Bard Manulis; Assistant to Mr. Mason, Glenna L. Clay; Production Manager, Alice Galloway; Stage Managers, Jody Boese, Fred Reinglas, Rob Gomes; Props, Claudia Silver; Press, Richard Frankel, Jane Brandmeir, Reva Cooper

Thursday, June 11–July 5, 1981 (39 performances)
A TALE TOLD By Lanford Wilson; Director, Marshall W. Mason; Set, John Lee Beatty; Costumes, Laura Crow; Lighting, Dennis Parichy; Sound, Chuck London; Assistant Director, John Bard Manulis; Stage Manager, Fred Reinglas
CAST: Nancy Killmer (Viola Platt), Patricia Wettig (Olive), Helen Stenborg (Netta), Elizabeth Sturges (Lottie), Michael Higgins (Eldon), Timothy Shelton (Buddy), Lindsey Ginter (Emmett Young), Jimmie Ray Weeks (Harley Campbell), Fritz Weaver (Mr. Talley), Laura Hughes (Avalaine Platt), David Ferry (Timmy), Trish Hawkins (Sally) A drama in two acts. The action takes place during the early evening of Independence Day 1944 in the front parlor of the Talley Place, a farm near Lebanon, Missouri.

Tuesday, August 4–30, 1981. (32 performances)
THE DIVINERS by Jim Leonard, Jr.; Directors, B. Rodney Marriott, Porter Van Zandt; Set, John Lee Beatty; Lighting, Dennis Parichy; Costumes, Jennifer von Mayrhauser; Stage Manager, M. A. Howard
CAST: Gary Berner succeeded by William Hurt (Melvin), Jack Davidson (Basil), Rob Gomes (Dewey) Stephanie Gordon (Norma), Deborah Hedwall (Goldie), Laura Hughes (Darlene), Nancy Killmer (Luella), Robert Macnaughton (Buddy), Timothy Shelton (C. C.), Jimmy Ray Weeks (Ferris), Patricia Wettig (Jennie Mae), Rosemary Sykes (alternate Jennie Mae) A drama in two acts. The action takes place during the early 1930's in the homes, fields and public gathering places of the mythical Southern Indiana town of Zion, population 40.

Wednesday, October 7–November 22, 1981 (54 performances)
THREADS by Jonathan Bolt; Director, B. Rodney Marriott; Set, David Potts; Costumes, Joan E. Weiss; Lighting, Craig Miller; Sound, Chuck London, Stewart Werner; Music, Stephen Lockwood, Patricia Lee Stotter; Stage Managers, Jody Boese, Fred Reinglas, Kate Stewart; Props, Tim Morse; Wardrobe, Alice Connorton
CAST: Ben Siegler (David Owens), Jonathan Hogan (Clyde Owens), Roger Chapman (Pete), Jo Henderson (Sally Owens), William Andrews (Abner Owens), Nancy Killmer (Jesse Sykes), David Morse (Nub), Patricia Wettig (Janine), Alice Connorton (Voice of neighbor), Understudies: Nancy Killmer (Sally), Patricia Wettig (Jesse), David Morse (Clyde) A drama in three acts. The action takes place during the summer of 1965 in Alamance Springs, a small mill town in the Piedmont hills of North Carolina.

Wednesday, December 30, 1981–February 11, 1982 (49 performances)
CONFLUENCE: Three One-Act Plays; Set, Bob Phillips; Costumes, Joan E. Weiss; Lighting, Mal Sturchio; Sound, Chuck London, Stewart Werner; Production Manager, Michael Spellman; Props, Susan Freel, Hannah Murray; Wardrobe, Ellen Conway; Stage Managers, Jody Boese, Fred Reinglas, Kate Stewart
THYMUS VULGARIS by Lanford Wilson; Director, June Stein.
CAST: Pearl Shear (Ruby), Katherine Cortez (Evelyn), Jeff McCracken (The Cop). The action takes place at the present time in a trailer park in Palmdale, California. (Because of illness, this play was canceled from Jan. 31, 1982)
CONFLUENCE by John Bishop; Director, B. Rodney Mariott.
CAST: Jimmie Ray Weeks (Chuck), Katherine Cortez (Kathy), Edward Seamon (Earl), The action takes place at the present time in the small town of Confluence, Pennsylvania during the summer.

AM I BLUE by Beth Henley; Director, Stuart White. CAST: Jeff McCracken (John Polk Richards), June Stein (Ashbe Williams), Pearl Shear (Hilda), Jimmie Ray Weeks (Barker), Edward Seamon (Bum), Ellen Conway (Hippie), Katherine Cortez (Whore). The action takes place in New Orleans in 1968.

Wednesday, March 10–April 11, 1982 (39 performances)
SNOW ORCHID by Joe Pintauro; Director, Tony Giordano; Set, Hugh Landwehr; Costumes, David Murin; Lighting, Dennis Parichy; Sound, Chuck London, Stewart Werner; Production Manager, Michael Spellman; Stage Manager, Bill Kavanagh
CAST: Ben Siegler (Blaise), Robert LuPone (Sebbie), Olympia Dukakis (Filumena), Peter Boyle (Rocco) A drama in two acts. The action takes place during 1973 in the house of the Lazarra family in the Greenpoint section of Brooklyn.

ENTERMEDIA THEATRE
Wednesday, March 10–April 4, 1982 (16 previews only)
Circle Repertory presents:
RICHARD II by William Shakespeare; Director, Marshall W. Mason; Sets, Karl Eigsti; Costumes, Laura Crow; Lights, Dennis Parichy; Music, Norman L. Berman; Sound, Chuck London Media; Production Manager, Michael Spellman; Company Manager, Roger Gindi; Stage Managers, Jody Boese, Fred Reinglas, Ginny Martino, Kelly Connell, Tim Morse; Technical Director, Joe Sabo; Wardrobe, Rose Wells; Props, Susan Freel, Koko Chalfant; Assistant Director, William Becvar; Fight Director, Peter Nels
CAST: William Hurt (Richard II), Michael Higgins (Duke of Lancaster), Stephanie Gordon (Duchess of Gloucester), Richard Cox (Henry Bolingbroke), Bill Carr (Lord Willoughby), Gary Berner (Lord Berkeley), John Dossett (Duke of Aumerle), Edward Seamon (Duke of York), Michael Ayr (Thomas Mowbray/Exton), Ken Kliban (Lord Marshall Green/Abbot of Westminster), Charles T. Harper (Bushy/Groom), Lindsay Crouse (Queen to Richard), Jack Davidson (Earl of Northumberland), Jimmie Ray Weeks (Lord Russ), Lou Liberatore (Servant), Tim Morse (Servant), Roger Chapman (Bagot), Timothy Busfield (Hotspur), Jonathan Bolt (Welsh Captain/Bishop of Carlisle), Ellen Conway (Queen's Lady), Jacqueline Brookes (Duchess of York), Understudies: Richard II (Michael Ayr), Bill Carr (Mowbray/Exton/Don), Katherine Cortez (Queen) Performed with one intermission.

Friday, March 12–April 4, 1982 (16 performances in repertory with "Richard II")
THE GREAT GRANDSON OF JEDEDIAH KOHLER by John Bishop; Directors, John Bard Manulis, Marshall W. Mason; Music and Songs, Jonathan Holtzman; Press, Reva Cooper CAST: Jake Dengel (Death) Michael Ayr (Jed Kohler), Ken Kliban (Leon/-Blake), Gary Berner (Shorty/Doc), Edward Seamon (Father/-Jedediah/Cop), Trish Hawkins (Mother/Nancy), Katherine Cortez (Bobbi), Jonathan Bolt (Graham/Ronald), William Hurt (Ike McKee/Henry Jarvis), Lou Liberatore (Johnny Two-Deuce), Tim Morse (Frank), Jimmie Ray Weeks (Brother), Jack Davidson (Jack Beck/Prescott Man/Coach Torsi), Roger Chapman (Joe Goldman), Charles T. Harper (Wally Silver), Charles T. Harper (Understudy)
A drama in two acts. The action takes place at the present time in the City, the Suburbs, Las Vegas, and the Old West.

Ben Siegler, Roger Chapman, Jo Henderson, Jonathan Hogan, Patricia Wettig, David Morse, Nancy Killmer in "Threads" Above: Steven Gilborn, Jack Gilpin in "The Middle Ages" *(Ken Schwenker Photo)*

Robert Macnaughton, Timothy Shelton in "The Diviners" Above: Michael Higgins, Fritz Weaver, Elizabeth Sturges in "A Tale Told"

Edward Seamon, Jimmie Ray Weeks in "Confluence"
(Gerry Goodstein Photos)

Lindsay Crouse, William Hurt in "Richard II"

Equity Library Theatre

George Wojtasik, Managing Director
Thirty-ninth Season

Production Director, Lynn Montgomery; Business Manager, Claude H. Maluenda; Informals Producer, Julie Ellen Prusinowksi; Production Coordinator/Informals Producer. Stephanie Brown; Technical Director, John Patterson Reed, Richard Malone; Costumer, Ken Brown; Staff Assistant Musical Director, Nelson C. Huber; Sound, Hal Schuler; Theatre Manager, Patrick J. Casey; Press, Lewis Harmon

Thursday, September 24–October 11, 1981 (24 performances)
KING OF HEARTS by Jean Kerr and Eleanor Brooke; Director, Richard Mogavero; Set, Barry Axtell; Costumes, M. David Scott; Lighting, Michael White; Stage Managers, David Semonin, Rebecca Ditzler, Robert Boyle; Props, Shirley Hinkamp. For original production, see THEATRE WORLD Vol. 10.
CAST: Alice Elliott (Dunreath), Dugg Smith (Larry), J. B. Waters (Jeniella), Joel Weiss (Mike), Dennis Predovic (Francis), Richard Marr (Joe), Douglas Parvin (Norman), Robert Boyle (Hobart), Benjamin Bernouy (Billy), George C. Simms (Policeman), Sabra (Happy)
A comedy in three acts. The action takes place in Larry Larkin's studio in New York City in the mid-fifties.

Thursday, October 29–November 22, 1981 (32 performances)
SEESAW with Book by Michael Bennett; Music, Cy Coleman; Lyrics, Dorothy Fields; Based on play "Two for the Seesaw" by William Gibson; Director, Yvonne Ghareeb; Choreography, Cheryl Carty; Scenery, D. Alan Bradford; Lighting, Chester M. Pule; Musical Direction, Joel Silberman; Costumes, Nance McQuigg; Assistant to Director, Susan Farwell; Stage Managers, Janet Friedman, David H. Bosboom, Tom Nicholas; For original production, see THEATRE WORLD Vol. 29.
CAST:Bill Tatum (Jerry Ryan), Diana Szlosberg (Gittel Mosca), Richard Ruth (David), Jennifer Smith (Sophie), Kevin Rogers (Julio), Joe Tonti (Oscar), Marla Singer (Nurse), Deborah Unger (Ethel), and citizens of New York: Mary Lou Crivello, Lester Holmes, Timothy G. McInerney, Marla Singer, Jennifer Smith, Bruce Warren, Thom Warren, Karen Ziemba, Kathryn Anne, Chelli Jackson, Roger Keiper, Joe Tonti, Kevin Rogers, Deborah Unger
A musical in 2 acts and 17 scenes. The action takes place in New York City.

Thursday, December 3–20, 1981 (24 performances)
TEN LITTLE INDIANS by Agatha Christie; Director, Philip Giberson; Set, Reagan Cook; Costumes, Ann Hould-Ward; Lighting, Wayne S. Lawrence; Sound, Judy Baldwin; Props, Pat Pearce; Stage Managers, Pamela Edington, Eddas Bennett, Donald A. Davis
CAST: Charles Hudson (Rogers), Joan Turetzky (Mrs. Rogers), Arland Russell (Fred Narracott), Kathryn Boule (Vera), Marcus Smythe (Philip), Albert Macklin (Anthony), Patrick Tull (Blore), Robert McFarland (Gen. MacKenzie), Judith Tillman (Emily), Fred Miller (Sir Lawrence Wargrave), Frank Vohs (Dr. Armstrong), Stockman Barner (A Voice) A mystery drama in 3 acts and 5 scenes. The action takes place in the living room of a house on Indian Island off the coast of Devon, England, during August of 1937.

Thursday, January 7–31, 1982 (32 performances)
STREET SCENE an American opera based on Elmer Rice's play; Music, Kurt Weill; Book, Elmer Rice; Lyrics, Langston Hughes; Director, Robert Brink; Musical Direction, Jeffrey Lewis; Scenery, James Morgan; Lighting, Jeffrey Schissler; Choreography, Piper Pickrell; Costumes, Karen Gerson; Production Assistant, Hilary Rappaport; Wardrobe, Jeanne Marie English, Terriayn Winter, Sheila Wormer; Props, Regina Wrubel; Stage Managers, Mark Schorr, Louise Reed, Sheila Mathews. For original Broadway production, see THEATRE WORLD Vol. 3.
CAST: Leslie Anders (Larua), Fred Barrows (Steve), Albert S. Bennett (Abraham), Jak Brami (Vincent), Michael Brian (Workman), Gloria Boucher (Jennie), Jenifer Burkhart (Neighbor), Bruce Butler (Henry), Nancy Cameron (Emma), Joe Antony Cavise (Dick), Tom Cipolla (Lippo), Michel Cullen (Officer Murphy), David Dollase (Carl), Greg Everett (Workman), Jim Fitzpatrick (Policeman), Bruce W. Fuller (Old Clothes Man), Sue Anne Gershenson (Rose), Terry Greiss (City Marshall), Steve Gunderson (Daniel), Don Harrington (George), D. Michael Heath (Sam), Jane Ives (Shirley), Katherine Meloche (Mae), Deborah Moldow (Nursemaid), Howard Pinhasik (Harry), Casper Roos (Frank), Jane Seaman (Anna), Mimi Sherwin (Greta), Dawn Spare (Laura), Robert Stillman (Workman), Frank Stoeger (Fred), Gail Titunik (Nursemaid), Robert Weed (Charlie), Sandra Wheeler (Olga), Robert York (Willie) A musical in two acts. The action takes place on a sidewalk in New York City on June 15, 1947.

Thursday, February 11–28, 1982 (24 performances)
LYSISTRATA by Aristophanes; Director, Alan Fox; Music, Richard Weinstock; Scenery, Peter Harrison; Lighting, Richard Dorf-

man; Choreography, Harry Streep III; Costumes, George Vallo; Masks, Scott Clement; Wardrobe, Evelyn Greene, Kathleen Mulligan; Stage Managers, Kathleen Marsters, Lena Boyd, Chris Fielder CAST:Deborah Allison (Myrrhine), Scott Campbell (Cinesias), Deborah (Didi) Charney (Acharnian Woman), Jeanne Cullen (Athenian Woman), Roy Doliner (Athenian Leader), Maralyn Dossey (Stratylis), Samuelle Easton (Ismene), Anthony Fallon (Spartan Herald), Ryon C. Garee (Spartan Ambassador), Steven Greenberg (Athenian Elder), Kenneth Hughes (Dance Soloist), Todd Jamieson (Athenian Elder), Karen Lamb (Athenian Woman), Gerald Lancaster (Magistrate), Howard McMaster (Athenian Elder), Brian O'Halloran (Elder), Cynthia Sophiea (Lampito), Madelon Thomas (Lysistrata), Beatrice Wells (Calonice), Trish Weyenberg (Corinthian Woman)

Thursday, March 11–April 4, 1982 (32 performances)
NYMPH ERRANT with Music and Lyrics by Cole Porter; Book, Romney Brent; From novel by James Laver; Director, Clinton J. Atkinson; Choreography, Dennis Dennehy; Musical Direction/Arrangements, Donald Sosin; Musical Staging, Dennis Dennehy, Clinton J. Atkinson; Sets, Johniene Papandreas; Costumes, Marie Anne Chiment; Lighting, Scott Pinkney; Wardrobe, Kathleen Mulligan; Makeup, Steve Terry; Hairstylists, Janetta Turner, Ross Michaels; Stage Managers, Ross Michaels, Julie Daye; Press, Louis Harmon CAST: Lili Arbogast (Mme. Arthur), Michael Ashton (Ensemble), Susan Berkson (Edith/Ensemble), Lynne Charnay (Cocotte), Rick DeFilipps (Ensemble), Diane Drielsma (Henrietta), Barry Ford (Rev. Pither), Philip Galbraith (Hercule), P. J. Galbraith (Ensemble), Avril Gentles (Mrs. Bramberg), George Gitto (Andre), Eva Grant (Ensemble), Larry Grey (Alexei), Joe Hart (Winthrop), Josie Lawrence (Bertha), Andrea Lee (Ensemble), Boncalla Lewis (Haidee Robinson), Kathleen Mahony-Bennett (Evangeline), Gerry McCarthy (Madeline), Nancy Meadows (Winnie/Feliza), Steven J. Parris (Constantine), Robert Edward Riley (Joe), Enid Rogers (Aunt Ermyntrude/Miss Pratt), Joanna Seaton (Joyce Arbuthnot-Palmer), Lee Sloan (Kassim), Ric Stoneback (Ali), Cynthia Thole (Ensemble), Barbara Tobias (Ensemble), Michael Vita (Count), Molly Wassermann (Bessie)
A Musical in 2 acts and 11 scenes.

Thurdsay, April 15–May 2, 1982 (24 performances)
TEACH ME HOW TO CRY by Patricia Joudry; Director, Don Price; Scenery, Joe Mobilia; Costumes, Richard von Ernst; Lighting, Susan A. White; Props, Susan Haynie; Production Assistant, Jerry Lucas; Stage Managers, Ellen Feldman, Patrice Thomas; Technical Director, John Patterson Reed
CAST: Elinor Basescu (Mrs. Grant), Lynn Watson (Miss Robson), Jolene Adams (Melinda Grant), Jennifer Taylor (Polly Fisher), Stephen McDonough (Bruce Mitchell) succeeded by Bill Randolph, Emily Hacker (Anne), Cindie Lovelace (Eleanor), Gerry Goodman (Will Henderson), Helen-Jean Arthur (Mrs. Henderson), Alan Zampese (Mr. Henderson)
A play in 2 acts and 10 scenes. The action takes place in Middle America in early spring.

Thursday, May 13–June 6, 1982 (32 performances)
APPLAUSE with Book by Betty Comden and Adolph Green; Based on film "All About Eve" and original story by Mary Orr; Music, Charles Strouse; Lyrics, Lee Adams; Staged and Directed by Leslie Eberhard; Musical Direction, J. T. Smith; Choreography, David Holdgreiwe; Scenery, Philip Louis Rodzen; Costumes, Lee Danser; Lighting, David N. Weiss; Wardrobe, Otis Gustafson; Props, Richard A. Mayora; Production Assistant, Jerry Lucas; Assistant Choreographer, Marshall Hagins; Stage Managers, Kevin R. Chapman, Richard Costabile, Frances Miksits
CAST: Lewis Arlt (Bill Sampson), Jon Breuer (Announcer), Channing Chase (Karen Richards), John Delph (Stan Harding), Marshall Hagins (Danny Burns), Charles T. Harper (Duane), Beth Leavel (Bonnie), Sean McGuirk (Bert), Philip William McKinley (Peter), Paul Merrill (Howard Benedict), Scott Robertson (Buzz Richards), Renee Roy (Margo Channing), Karen Stefko (Eve Harrington), Dean G. Watts (Bob), Ensemble: Diana Baer, Jon Breuer, Paul Cavin, Jenean Chander, Tracy Dodrill, Marshall Hagins, Marv Lawson, Laurie Leabu, Janice Lindberg, Amelia Marshall, John Milne, Patrick Parker, Jon Reininga, Dean G. Watts, Bradd Wong
A musical in 2 acts and 15 scenes.

Gary Wheeler Photos

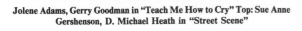

Jolene Adams, Gerry Goodman in "Teach Me How to Cry" Top: Sue Anne Gershenson, D. Michael Heath in "Street Scene"

Lewis Arlt, Renee Roy, Channing Chase, Scott Robertson, Charles T. Harper in "Applause" Top: Kathleen Mahony-Bennett, Lee Sloan in "Nymph Errant"

CSC/Classic Stage Company

Fifteenth Season

Artistic Director, Christopher Martin; Managing Director, Stephen J. Holland; Business Manager, Claudia Lee; Assistant Managing Director, Dan J. Martin; Administrative Assistant, Susan Stern; Production Manager, Robert Holley; Technical Director, Marc Malamud; Stage Manager/Props, Christine Michael; Dramaturg, Karen Sunde; Associate Director, Brian Lawson; Resident Composer, Noble Shropshire; Costumer, Miriam Nieves; Assistant to Artistic Director, Susan McCloskey

COMPANY: David Aston-Reese, John Camera, Ray Dooley, Patrick Egan, Ginger Grace, Brian Lawson, Douglas Moore, Patricia O'Donnell, Carol Schultz, Noble Shropshire, David Snizek, Tom Spackman, Tom Spiller, Robert Stattel, Karen Sunde

PRODUCTIONS: Ibsen's "Peer Gynt I" and "Peer Gynt II," Chekhov's "Cherry Orchard," Shakespeare's "King Lear," and Strindberg's "Ghost Sonata."

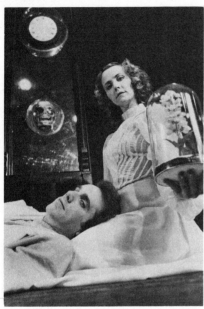

Tom Spackman, Ginger Grace in "Ghost Sonata"
(Gerry Goodstein Photo)

Classic Theatre

Executive Director, Nicholas John Stathis; Artistic Director, Maurice Edwards

September 10–October 4, 1981 (16 performances)
THE PARIS OF JEAN COCTEAU conceived and staged by Myriam Degan; Producer, Nicholas John Stathis; Musical Director, Robert Cornman; Costumes/Lighting, Myriam Degan; General Manager, Lawrence Gilligan; Stage Managers, Janet Struzik, Carol Sussman; Production Assistant, David Presby; Press, Sonia Dressner; Music of Milhaud, Honegger, Poulenc, Satie
CAST: Cindy Beall, Barbara Creed, Maurice Edwards, Frances Ford, Michael Hermanski, Wallace King, Eleni Lambros, Patrick Reilly

An evening of theatre, dance, pantomime and songs based on original texts by Jean Cocteau, including his one-act play "The School for Widows."

October 15–November 18, 1981 (16 performances)
TANGO by Slawomir Mrozek; Director, Jerry Gelb; Producer, Nicholas John Stathis; Set, Bob Phillips; Lighting, Mal Sturchio; Costumes, Amanda Klein; General Manager, Lawrence Gilligan; Stage Managers, Michael J. Kondrat, Andrea Grober; Choreography, Carol Alexander
CAST: Irma St. Paule (Eugenia), Laurence Rush (Eddie), Jack Banning (Eugene), Jan A. Notzon (Arthur), Marina Stefan (Eleanor), Emilio Del Pozo (Stromil), Antoinette Cendoma (Ala). A play in 3 acts. The action takes place in a loft at 114 West 14th Street, New York City.

January 21–February 14, 1982 (16 performances)
EVIL SPIRIT by Alexandre Shirvanzade; Translated from the Armenian by Nishan Parlakian; Director, Joseph S. King; Producer, Nicholas John Stathis; Design, Donald L. Brooks; Lighting, Jeffrey Schneider; Sound, John Kirton; General Manager, Lawrence Gilligan; Stage Managers, Malcolm D. Ewen, Jackie Van den Bodenkamp
CAST: Krikor Satamian (Kijh-Taniel), Laura McDonald (Sona as a child), Grace Bentley (Shoosan) Heidi Herz (Manan), Heather Nicole Rose (Zarig), Page Seaman (Vartush), Jeffrey Kurz (Vosgan), Holly Hawkins (Sona), Billie Brenan (Zarnishan), Arthur Barsamian (Garabed), Marla Sterling (Chavahir), Paul Detrick (Murad), Irma St. Paule (Miansaz). Performed with two intermissions. The action takes place at the turn of the century.

April 15–May 2, 1982 (12 performances)
HE, SHE, SHAW two one-act plays by George Bernard Shaw; Director, Jonathan Amacker; Set, Roger Benischek; Lighting, Michael M. Bergfeld; Costumes, McKay Coble-Randall; Assistant Director, Sonia Dressner; Stage Managers, Virginia Jones, Mark Shoemaker.
CAST: "Augustus Does His Bit" with Earle Edgerton (Lord Highcastle), Richard Carlow (Clerk), Dawn Couch (Lady). The action takes place in 1915 in a recruiting office in the town hall of Little Pifflington, England. "The Man of Destiny" with William March (Napoleon), Richard Carlow (Giuseppe Grandi), Jess R. Stevens (Lieutenant), Dawn Couch (Lady). The action takes place on May 12, 1796 at an inn in the village of Tavazzano in Northern Italy.

Frank Silvera Writers' Workshop

Artistic Director, Garland Lee Thompson; Acting Managing Director, Sharon Finley; Casting, Dianne Kirksey; ATAC Coordinator, Karen Perry; Administrative Assistants, Shelley Renee Crosby, Jerry Maple, Jr.; Writer in Residence, Bheki Langa

January 28–April 11, 1982 (44 performances)
THE CONTRACT by Nathan Ross Freeman; Director, Wyatt Paul Davis; Music, Julius E. McCullough; Wardrobe, Ali Davis; Props, Anthony Smith; Stage Managers, Zebedee Collins, Gregoriann Daly; Sound, Euston James, Garland Thompson, Jr.; Set/Technical Director, DeWarren Moses; Costumes, Karen Perry; Associate Producer, Artyann Coleman; Vocals, Julius E. McCullough, Yvonne Gardner
CAST: Noble Lee Lester (Rev. Jamison), Timothy W. Simonson (Christ), Phyllis Stickney (Gem)

April 29–May 16, 1982 (12 performances)
WHATEVER HAPPENED TA AMOS N' ANDY? by William Electric Black; Director, Pat White; Producer, Garland Lee Thompson; Associate Producer, Jerry Maple, Jr.; Set, Paul Davis; Lights, Zebedee Collins; Sound, Garland Thompson, Jr.; Costumes, Karen Perry; Wardrobe, Lorri Richardson; Production Assistants, Anthony Smith, Paul Zimmerman; Props, Rocco Clark Bey, Reeva Dinez; Stage Managers, Zebedee Collins, Gregoriann Daly, Euston James.
CAST: Rob Ashley Bowles (Calhoun/Detective), Eldon Bullock (Amos), Margaret Bynum (Sapphire/Maid), Helmar Augustus Cooper (Andy), Gregory Holtz, Sr. (Lightnin'/Butch/Butler), Dorothi Fox (Moma/Moma Buktu/Carla Starr/Cleaning Woman), William Williams (Kingfish/Wino/Cameraman). A play in two acts.

Noble Lee Lester in "The Contract" *(Bert Andrews Photo)*

Hudson Guild Theatre

David Kerry Heefner, Producing Director; General Manager, Daniel Swee; Business Assistant, John Fisher; Production Stage Manager, Edward R. Fitzgerald; Technical Director, Charles Owen; Press, Susan Chicoine

Wednesday, November 11–December 13, 1981 (28 performances)
SLEEP BEAUTY by Arthur Meryash; Directors, Jordan Deitcher, Arthur Feinsod; Setting, Roger Mooney; Costumes, Edi Giguere; Lighting, Paul Wonsek; Production Assistant, Carol Klein
CAST: Clarice Taylor (Augustina Cooper), Charles Henry Patterson (Joe Boyle), Tom Everett (Chuck Whitfield)
A play in 2 acts and 6 scenes. The action takes place at the present time in Joe Boyle's apartment at the rear of an old duplex in Oakland, California.

Sunday, January 17–31, 1982 (28 performances)
BESIDE THE SEASIDE by Stephen Temperley; Director, Vivian Matalon; Setting, William Ritman; Costumes, David Loveless; Lighting, Richard Nelson; Wig and Hairstylist, Paul Huntley; Song "Wonderful Child" by Lee Goldsmith and Roger Anderson, sung by Michael Hayward Jones; Production Assistant, Robert Nolan; Assistant to Director, Charles Blasius; Wardrobe, Janice Lathen; Props, LouAnne Gilleland; General Manager, Daniel Swee; Stage Manager, Edward R. Fitzgerald.
CAST: Leslie O'Hara (Claudia), Charlotte Moore (Anna), Cinder (Toby), Harry Groener (Jimmy), Jack Ryland (Max), Kathryn C. Sparer (Molly).
A comedy in 2 acts and 4 scenes. The action takes place during August of 1924 in a section of the garden of Undercliff House, Sandgate, on the Southeast Coast of England.

Thursday, February 4–13, 1982 (12 performances)
VAMPS AND RIDEOUTS with Music by Jule Styne; Material adapted by Phyllis Newman, James Pentecost; Conceived by Phyllis Newman; Director, James Pentecost; Musical Direction and Arrangements, Eric Stern; Musical Staging, Dennis Dennehy; Scenery, Lawrence Miller; Costumes, Cynthia O'Neal; Lighting, David H. Murdock; Production Assistant, Mary Rindfleisch; Stage Manager, Buzz Cohen

CAST: Phyllis Newman, George Lee Andrews, Pauletta Pearson
MUSICAL NUMBERS: It's a Perfect Relationship, I Met a Girl, People, Marriage Medley, Long Before I Knew You, The Party's Over, Let's See What Happens, Ambition, I'm the Greatest Star, Never Never Land, Make Someone Happy, Just in Time, Little Rock, Shoo In, My Fortune Is My Face, Guess I'll Hang My Tears Out to Dry, Hey Look No Crying, My Own Morning, Some People, Let Me Entertain You, All I Need Is the Girl, Women's Medley, The Music That Makes Me Dance, Together
A musical entertainment performed with one intermission.

Wednesday, February 24–April 21, 1982 (28 performances)
WONDERLAND by Margaret Keilstrup; Director, David Kerry Heefner; Set and Lighting, Paul Wonsek; Costumes, Bob Graham; Production Assistant, Debra Acquavella; Props, Jonathan Wilson; General Manager, Daniel Swee; Technical Director, Charles Owen; Stage Manager, Edward R. Fitzgerald
CAST: Dennis Bailey (Stephen Terrill), Thomas A. Carlin (Pop Heron), Debra Mooney (Leah Heron), Alice Drummond (Minnie Pierce)
A play in two acts. The action takes place at the present time on a late September night, in The Plainsman, an old hotel.

Wednesday, April 14–May 9, 1982 (28 performances)
EMIGRES by Slawomir Mrozek; Director, Thomas Gruenewald; Set, James Leonard Joy; Costumes, Mariann Verheyen; Lighting, Jeff Davis; General Manager, Daniel Swee; Props, Jill Frizsell; Production Assistant, Mari Schatz; Stage Manager, Edward R. Fitzgerald
CAST: David Leary, Sam Tsoutsouvas
A play in two acts. The action takes place at the present time in a basement.

Leslie O'Hara, Jack Ryland, Harry Groener, Charlotte Moore in "Beside the Seaside"
(Martha Swope Photo)

Debra Mooney, Dennis Bailey, Thomas A. Carlin, Alice Drummond in "Wonderland" *(Ken Howard Photo)*

Henry Street Settlement's New Federal Theatre

Twelfth Season

Producers, Woodie King, Jr., Steve Tennen; Executive Director, Dr. Niathan Allen; Production Coordinator, Tsehaya D. A. Smith; Production Manager, Robert Edmonds; Production Secretary, Annie Brown; Technical Director, Bonnie Becker; Props, Sam Singleton; Wardrobe, Ali Davis; Project Coordinator, Jeanne D. Nutter; Sound, Richard Arnold; Hairstylist, Walter Thomas; Press, Warren Knowlton

LOUIS ABRONS ARTS FOR LIVING CENTER

June 18–August 9, 1981 (32 performances)
ZORA and WHEN THE CHICKENS CAME HOME TO ROOST by Laurence Holder; Director, Allie Woods; Set, Robert Edmonds; Costumes, Judy Dearing; Lights, Allen Lee Hughes; Stage Manager, Gwendolyn M. Gilliam. CAST: "Zora" with Phylicia Ayers-Allen. The action takes place in a bus terminal on Christmas of 1949. "When the Chickens Came Home to Roost" with Kirk Kirksey (Elijah Muhammad), Denzel Washington (Malcolm Shabazz)

July 16–August 2, 1981 (12 performances)
STEAL AWAY by Ramona King; Director, Anderson Johnson; Set, Llewellyn Harrison; Costumes, Judy Dearing; Lighting, Shirley Prendergast; Stage Manager, Ed Cambridge. CAST: Joyce Sylvester (Tracyada), Minnie Gentry (Stella), Beatrice Winde (Sudy), Estelle Evans (Redd), Juanita Clark (Jade), Dorothi Fox (Blu). A play in 2 acts and 5 scenes. The action takes place in Chicago in the early 1930's in Stella Kyzer's home and in the Chicago Savings and Loan Bank.

October 22–November 8, 1981 (12 performances)
THE BLACK PEOPLE'S PARTY by Earl Anthony; Director, Norman Riley; Set, Llewellyn C. Harrison; Costumes, Judy Dearing; Lighting, Marshall Williams; Music, Norman Riley; Sound, Richard Johnson; Stage Manager, Dwight R. B. Cook. CAST: Ronald Willoughby (Carter), Hunter Cain (O'Ryan), P. Anderson Scott (Reggie), Gregory Miller (Chocezi), Lucy Holland (Tee), Jane Scott (Paulette), John J. J. Cole (Chairman Richard), Andre (Cochise) Worthy (Sherman), Rickey Arnold (Alvin). A play in 2 acts.

January 7–24, 1982 (12 performances)
DREAMS DEFERRED by Laurence Holder; Director, Allie Woods; Set, Pete Caldwell; Costumes, Judy Dearing; Lighting, Marshall Williams; Sound, Carol Bauman; Stage Manager, C. L. Ringelstein. Music, Julius Williams. CAST: Erma Campbell (Martine), Nathaniel Ellis (Sadness), Kim Sullivan (Homer), Clebert Ford (Elder), Phyllis Yvonne Stickney (Kim), Kathleen Morrison (Ovid), Michael Alson (Leon). A play in two acts. The action takes place in the cafeteria of the Harlem "Y" in 1935 and 1943.

January 15–31, 1982 (12 performances)
KEYBOARD by Matt Robinson; Director, Shauneille Perry; Set, Robert Edmonds; Costumes, Judy Dearing; Lighting, Sandra Ross; Sound, Regge Life; Stage Manager, Dwight R. B. Cook; Choreography, Otis A. Sallid. CAST: Cleavon Little (Keyboard), Zaida Coles (Marguerite), Giancarlo Esposito (Skippy), Andre Robinson, Jr. (Tweety), John Outlaw (Paul), Lex Monson (Rev. Rideout), Louise Stubbs (Orabelle). A play in 2 acts and 3 scenes. The action takes place in the home of the Higgins family, and in Mt. Moriah Baptist Church.

February 11–28, 1982 (12 performances)
LA CHEFA by Tato Laviera; Set, Miguel Aguilar, Carmelo Montalvo; Costumes, Judy Dearing; Lighting, Lynne Reed; Sound, Richard Henry Arnold, Jr.; Stage Manager, C. L. Ringelstein; Music, Tato Laviera; Performed by Eddie Conde. CAST: Alfonso Manosalvas (Buenportorro), Denia Brache (Chefa), Nelson Landrieu (Notario), Bob Bella (Sefardi), Michael Yanez (Futuro), Mark Keeler (Father Janer), Elizabeth Longo (Chencha), Arlene Roman (I-Love-Lucy), Eddie Conde (Papo Tio), Ken Bush (Paul Lee). The action takes place during the early 1950's on the Lower East Side.

March 18–April 4, 1982 (12 performances)
PAPER ANGELS by Genny Lim; Director, John Lone; Set, Karen Schulz; Costumes, Susan Hilferty; Lighting, Paul Gallo; Sound, Carol E. Bauman; Assistant Director, Alice Jankowiak; Stage Manager, C. L. Ringelstein; Original Music composed and performed by John Lone. CAST: Kitty Mei-Mei Chen (Ku-Ling), Matthew Grana (Henderson), William Hao (Lum), Lilah Kan (Chin-Moo), Mia Katigbak (Mei-Lai), Steve Monroe (Interrogation Officer/Warden/Guard/Man on Ship), Jean Kay Sifford (Matron/Sister Mary), Toshi Toda (Lee), Ching Valdes (Chang-Li-Ti/Chan/Kitchen Help/Other Woman), Victor Wong (Chin-Gung), Henry Yuk (Fong). The action takes place in 1915 at Angel Island Immigration Detention Center in San Francisco Bay.

HARRY DEJUR HENRY STREET PLAYHOUSE

September 18–October 4, 1981 (12 performances)
LOUIS with Book and Lyrics by Don Evans; Music, Michael Renzi; Director, Gilbert Moses; Choreography, Billy Wilson; Musical Direction/Arrangement, Danny Holgate; Lighting, Shirley Prendergast; Costumes, Judy Dearing; Stage Manager, Harrison Avery; Conductor, Neal Tate; Press, Howard Atlee. CAST: Tiger Haynes (Papa Jazz), Donna Ingram (Urchin/Cora/Sarah), Assata Hazell (Urchin/Flora), Alde Lewis, Jr. (Urchin), Debbie Allen (Daisy), Mel Edmundson (Willie), Don Jay (Bennie), Eugene Little (Man), Marcella Lowry (Mayann), Ken Page (Joe Oliver), Rickey Powell (Gabe), Renee Rose (Adora), Lynn Sterling (Sally), Jeffrey V. Thompson (Frenchman), Andy Torres (Otis), Skip Waters (Buddy), Northern J. Calloway (Louis), Ernestine Jackson (Lil). A musical based on the early career of Louis Armstrong.

October 9–25, 1981 (12 performances)
BOY AND TARZAN APPEAR IN A CLEARING by Amiri Baraka; Director, George Ferencz; Music, Hugh Masekela; Set, George Ferencz; Costumes, Sally J. Lesser; Lighting, Marshall Williams; Multi-Media Design/Direction, Allan Siegel; Stage Manager, Bonnie L. Becker. CAST: Rod McLucas (Boy), Jack R. Marks (Tarzan), Willie Carpenter (Stan), Rosita Broadous (Mary), James Pickens, Jr. (Mkazi), Christine Campbell (Ayanna), Yusef Iman (Chauffeur), Selaelo Maredi, Seth Sibanda (Chorus), in film: Ellen Dolan, Josh Warby, Doctor Ed, Nandi Lolita Lebron Cepeda Broadous

December 1–21, 1981 (12 performances)
CHILD OF THE SUN with Book, Music, Lyrics by Damien Leake; Director, Harold Scott; Choreography/Musical Staging, Otis Sallid; Associate Producer, Chapman Roberts; Set, John Scheffler; Costumes, Judy Dearing; Lighting, Shirley Prendergast; Sound, Regge Life; Dance/Musical Arrangements, Frederic Gripper; Musical Director/Conductor, Lea Richardson; Musical Supervisor, Chapman Roberts; Associate Musical Director, William Foster McDaniel. CAST: Kevin Harris (Joe), Nat Morris (James), Jackee Harry (Cassie), Pauletta Pearson (Marilyn), Count Stovall (Trinity), Gordon Heath (Jake), Raymond Patterson (Jesse), Yolanda Lee (Maggie), Alistair Butler, David Cameron, Bar Dell Conner, Leslie Dockery, Jacqueline Gilliard, Diane Hayes, Dyane Harvey, Sonya Hensley, Perry Moore

February 25–March 13, 1982
WHO LOVES THE DANCER by Rob Penny; Director, Shauneille Perry; Set, Robert Edmonds; Costumes, Judy Dearing; Lighting, Sandra Ross; Vocal Arranger, Cliff Terry; Sound, Regge Life; Choreographer, Bob Johnson; Assistant Director, Elizabeth Van Dyke; Stage Manager, Dwight R. B. Cook; Original Music, Cliff Terry and Terrance Terry Ellis. CAST: Giancarlo Esposito (Ken), Louise Stubbs (Thelma), Jewel Brimage (Marcella), Peter Wise (Roy Lee), Rosanna Carter (Big Momma), Kim Weston-Moran (Cookie), Andre Robinson, Jr. (Ray), Martin D. Pinckney (Moon), Cliff Terry (Dickey), Terrance Terry Ellis (Bobby), Kevin Hall (L'il Earl), Richard H. Arnold, Jr. (Tank), Sloan Robinson (Chandra), Richard Gant (Garrett), Aissatou Parks, Natalie Ryder (Girls), Steven Cruz (Understudy). A play in two acts and 24 scenes. The action takes place in Pittsburgh, Pa., during the summer of 1956.

November 20–December 6, 1981 (12 performances)
A DAY OUT OF TIME by Alan Foster Friedman; Music by Mr. Friedman; Director, Harold Guskin; Set, David Weiss; Costumes, Judy Dearing; Lights, Lynne Reed; Sound, Jerry Kornbluth; Stage Manager, C. L. Ringelstein.
CAST: Tim Donoghue (Ryder), George Cocorelis (Nikos), Tom Mardirosian (Haroutoon), Barbara Tirrell (Araxie), Jim Shankman (Stephan), Betsy Aidem (Miriam), James Hendricks (Klimenko), Jerry Matz (Rizhie), Robert Silver (Mordecai), Carol Nadell (Hannah), Ted Geislinger (Berel), John Capodice (Cione), Robert S. Reiser (Peddler). A play in two acts. The action takes place during October of 1906 in a second floor holding room in the Immigration Center on Ellis Island.

April 1–18, 1982 (12 performances)
THE WORLD OF BEN CALDWELL by Ben Caldwell; Director, Richard Gant; Costumes, Myrna Colley-Lee; Set, Llewellyn Harrison; Lighting, Lynne Reed; Sound, Regge Life; Choreography, Sloan Robinson; Stage Manager, Debbie Weiner CAST: Steve Coats, Morgan Freeman, Terria Joseph, Dianne Kirksey, Kirk Kirksey, Garrett Morris, Reginald Vel Johnson. Presented with one intermission.

Giancarlo Esposito, Zaida Coles, Andre Robinson, Jr., Cleavon Little in "Keyboard" *(Bert Andrews Photo)*

Richard Gant, Giancarlo Esposito, Sloan Robinson in "Who Loves the Dancer" *(Bert Andrews Photo)*

INTAR/International Arts Relations

Artistic Director, Max Ferra; Managing Director, Dennis Ferguson; General Administrator, Janet L. Murphy; Projects Coordinator, Vivian Diaz; Playwrights Lab Director, Maria Irene Fornes; Press, Clarence Allsopp, Miriam Fernandez Soberon

Thursday, July 30–August 24, 1981 (28 performances)
BODY BAGS by tee Saralegui; Director, Melvin Van Peebles; Set and Costumes, Ken Holaman; Lighting, Larry Crimmins; Sound, David S. Rapkin; Casting, David Rubin; Assistant to Director, Mario Van Peebles; Technical Director, Judy Snyder; Props, Patrick Ferruccio; Stage Manager, John N. Concannon
CAST: Donna Pescow (Anita), John Snyder (Johnny), Jaime Tirelli (Lou)
A play in two aacts.

October 17–November 22, 1981 (23 performances)
CRISP! a musical conceived by Max Ferra and Dolores Prida; Based on "Los Intereses Creados" by Jacinto Benavente; Book and Lyrics, Dolores Prida; Music, Manuel Del Fuego; Director, Max Ferra; Musical Director, Tania Leon; Choreographer, Daniel Lewis; Set, Larry Brodsky; Costumes, Debra Stein; Lighting, Tom Hennes; Casting, David Rubin; Assistant to Director, Winston Gonzalez; Technical Director, Seth Price; Stage Managers, Gail A. Burns, Charles Douglass, Wanda DeJesus.

CAST: Manuel Martinez, Cintia Cruz, Dain Chandler, Juan Vaquer, Mary Stout, Felipe Gorostiza, C. J. Critt, Antonia Rey, Sandra Nieves, Edward Paul Allen, Brent Collins, Stephen Rosario, Kenya Benitez, Jose Maldonado, Understudies: Wanda DeJesus, Charles Douglass
A musical in 2 acts and 10 scenes. The action takes place in an imaginary country at the beginning of an imaginary century.
April 1–25, 1982 (27 performances)
THE EXTRAVAGANT TRIUMPH OF JESUS CHRIST, KARL MARX, AND WILLIAM SHAKESPEARE by Fernando Arrabal; Translated by Miguel Falquez-Certain; Director, Eduardo Manet; Set/Costumes, Randy Barcelo; Lighting, Cheryl Thacker; Sound, Paul Garrity; Casting, David Rubin; Stage Manager, Gail A. Burns.
CAST: Betty LaRoe (Noemi), Naseer El-Kadi (Garapito/Accos), Ron Faber (Tallarin/Samir), Cecilia Flores (Elisee), Thomas Kopache (Ioga), Madeleine LeRoux (Ziza), Brian Rose (Cis), Philip Gordon (Understudy). A tragicomedy in two acts.

Center: (L) Antonio Rey, Manuel Martinez in "Crisp!" *(Gary Schoichet Photo)* (R) Betty LaRoe, Ron Faber in "The Extravagant Triumph . . ." *(Rafael Llerena Photo)*

Jewish Repertory Theatre

Seventh Season

Artistic Director, Ran Avni; Literary Adviser, Edward M. Cohen; Company Manager, Patricia Jenkins

September 10–27, 1981 (12 performances)
INCIDENT AT VICHY by Arthur Miller; Director, Ran Avni; Sets, Adalberto Ortiz; Costumes, Edi Giguere; Lighting, Carol B. Sealey; Props, Marion Mooney; Assistant Director, Patricia Jenkins; Technical Director, Jeffrey Ross Norberry; Stage Manager, Mitchell Maglio. CAST: Ward Asquith, Harold Alvarez, Donald J. Hoffman, Mark Fleischman, Bernie Rachelle, Fred Sanders, Michael Albert Mantel, Thomas Scott Nonnon, Frank Anderson, Robert Davis, Ted Polites, Donald Ilko, Robin Chadwick, William Brenner, Erick Avari, Hal Studer, Nicholas B. Daddazio

October 24–November 19, 1981 (20 performances)
AWAKE AND SING! by Clifford Odets; Director, Lynn Polan; Set, Jeffrey Schneider; Costumes, Karen Hummel; Lighting, Carol B. Sealey; Technical Director, Ted Ciganik; Sound, Andrew Howard; Props, Dennis Krick; Stage Managers, Richard D. Polak, Melissa Thea. CAST: Michael Albert Mantel, Alan Brandt, Ellen Barber, Michael Marcus, Vera Lockwood, Chris Manor, James Goodwin Rice, Herbert Rubens, David Wohl

December 5, 1981–January 3, 1982 (20 performances)
ELEPHANTS by David Rush; Director, Edward M. Cohen; Set, Geoffrey Hall; Costumes, Jessica Fasman; Lighting, Dan Kinsley; Sound, Andrew Howard; Props, Teri Davidson; Stage Managers, Barry Katz, Franklin Heller, Erick Kohner. CAST: Lee Wallace (Henry Leider), Marilyn Chris (Woman), Richard Niles (Ben Leider). A drama in two acts. The action takes place in an apartment built into a synagogue on the near north side of Chicago.

February 6–March 7, 1982 (20 performances)
DELMORE an evening of two one-act plays; Director, Florence Stanley; Sets, Ken Rothchild; Costumes, Linda Vigdor; Lighting, Carol B. Sealey; Sound, Andrew Howard; Assistant Director, Bo Walker; Stage Managers, Lisa Ledwich, Scott A. Wiscamb. CAST: "Luna Park" by Donald Margulies; Based on Delmore Schwartz's story "In Dreams Begin Responsibilities" with Barbara Glenn Gordon (Rose), Willie Reale (Delmore), David Wohl (Harry), Susan Merson (Young Rose). "Shenandoah" by Delmore Schwartz, with Stephen Stout (Shenandoah), Lydia Stryk (Elsie), Susan Merson (Edna), Maurice Sterman (Jacob), David Wohl (Walter), Michele Ferber (Bertha), Scott Bloom (Harry), Robert Davis (Jack), Shirley Rickards (Sarah), Stephen Singer (Nathan), Joel Swetow (Dr. Adamson)

April 10–May 9, 1982 (20 performances)
PANTAGLEIZE by Michel de Ghelderode; Translated by George Hauger; Director, Anthony McKay; Set, Michael C. Smith; Costumes, Marie Ann Chiment; Lighting, Dan Kinsley; Music and Lyrics, Barbara Schottenfeld; Stage Managers, Franklin Heller, Tresa Davidson. CAST: Joel Bernstein, Philip Brown, Bernard Tato, Kenneth Norris, James DeMarse, Jeffrey Ware, Ellen Barber, Mark Henderson, Peter Smith, Joseph Jamrog, Michael Marcus, Lawrence Lippert

May 29–June 27, 1982 (20 performances)
VAGABOND STARS with Book by Nahma Sandrow; Music, Raphael Crystal; Based on material from the Yiddish theatre; Lyrics, Alan Poul; Director, Ran Avni; Choreographer, Bick Goss; Sets, Jeffrey Schneider; Costumes, Karen Hummel; Lighting, Phil Monat; Musical Direction/Arrangements, Raphael Crystal; Stage Managers, Penny Landau, Dale Copps. CAST: Herbert Rubens, Dana Zeller-Alexis, Steve Sterner, Susan Victor, Steve Yudson. A musical in two acts.

Susan Merson, Willie Reale, David Wohl in "Delmore"

Marilyn Chris, Lee Wallace in "Elephants"

The Labor Theater

Producer, Bette Craig; Director, C. R. Portz

ST. PETER'S HALL

October 22–November 22, 1981 (24 performances)
YOURS FOR THE REVOLUTION, JACK LONDON by C. R. Portz; Stage Manager, Scott Robbe; Props and Set, Jennifer Long; Music Coordinator, Martin Burman; Press, Valerie Warner. CAST: Chuck Portz. A play in 2 acts and 3 scenes. The action takes place in Jack London's Oakland, California, study in 1901, and on his Sonoma Valley ranch in 1913 and 1916.

April 2–4, 1982 (4 performances)
THE BOTTOM LINE by C. R. Portz; Musical Direction, Martin Burman; Choreography, Suzan Moss; Design, Jenny Long; Costumes, K. L. Fredericks; Production Assistants, Noel Richetti, Claudia Schwartz; Stage Manager, Eric Grosshans. CAST: Martin Burman, Gussie Harris, Marcia McIntosh, David Ossian, Guy Sherman

May 6–June 5, 1982 (24 performances)
THE BAYSIDE BOYS by C. R. Portz; Director, Mr. Portz; Set, Lynda Wormell; Lighting, Bruce A. Kramer; Costumes, K. L. Fredericks; Stage Managers, James Sweeney, Eric Grosshans. CAST: Larry Fleischman, Chuck Griffin, Philip Levy, Al Mizgalski, Marvin Pearl, Scott Robbe, Ron Ryan, Ralph Santinelli, Kitty Troll, Bruce Willis

Chuck Portz in "Yours for the Revolution, Jack London"

Lion Theatre Company

Artistic Director, Gene Nye; Producing Director, Eleanor Meglio; Production Manager, Stacey April; Technical Director, Carl Keator; Props, David Anthony; Administrative Assistant, Ninetta Remley; Stage Manager, Marc Elliott Field; Press, Burnham-Callaghan Associates, Lynda C. Kinney

April 21–June 27, 1982 (70 performances)
In repertory: ROMEO AND JULIET by William Shakespeare; (26 performances) Choreography, Betsy Marrion; Music, Alexander Peskanov; Fight, Michael Arabian; Special Millinery, Penny Howell; Hairstylist, Daniel Paul Platten; Masks, Catherine Gollner; Costumes, Charlotte Sorre. CAUCASIAN CHALK CIRCLE by Bertolt Brecht; (26 performances) English Version, Eric Bentley; Costumes, Charlotte Sorre; Music, Albert Tepper; Musical Direction/Percussion, Scott Kanoff; Film, Rip Wilson. KITTY HAWK by Len Jenkin; (18 performances) Costumes, Jonathan Bixby. For all three productions: Director, Gene Nye; Lighting, William D. Anderson; Set, Linda Skipper

CAST: (Lion Theatre Ensemble) David Anthony, Michael Arabian, William Brenner, Maria Cellario, Dorothy Fradera, Janice Fuller, George Gale, Robert Hock, Scott Kanoff, Ann-Sara Matthews, Keith McDermott, David Morgand, Jay Natelle, Peter Noel-Duhamel, Ennis Smith, Ronald Willoughby, Nan Wray, and Debra Lee Babcock, Alice King, Geoffrey Sharp, Charles Tuthill

**Right: Ann-Sara Mathews, Keith McDermott
in "Romeo and Juliet"**

LOOM/Light Opera of Manhattan

June 1, 1981–May 31, 1982
Thirteenth Season

Producer-Director, William Mount-Burke; Associate Director, Raymond Allen; Choreographer, Jerry Gotham; Assistant Musical Director/Pianist, Brian Molloy; Assistant Conductor/Organist, Stanley German; Special Coaching, Dr. John Mizell; Administrator, Charles H. Startup; Wardrobe, Brenda D. Jones; Stage Managers, Jerry Gotham, Richard Perry; Press, Peggy Friedman

COMPANY

Raymond Allen, Robert Baker, Elizabeth Burgess-Harr, Joyce Bolton, Lloyd Harris, Eleanore Knapp, Ann J. Kirschner, Jacqueline Kroschell, Sylvia Lanka, Ethelmae Mason, Anthony Michalik, Vaskek Pazdera, Gary Pitts, Irma Rogers, Stephen Rosario, Cheryl Savitt

PRODUCTIONS

The Student Prince, The Mikado, The Pirates of Penzance, The Sorcerer, H.M.S. Pinafore, Ruddigore, The Desert Song, The Red Mill, Babes in Toyland, Princess Ida, The Grand Duke, The Yeoman of the Guard, The Merry Widow, A Night in Venice

Center: (L) Stephen Rosario, Cheryl Savitt in "A Night in Venice" (R) Raymond Allen, Robert Barker, Joyce Bolton in "The Sorcerer"
(Joseph Tenga Photos)

Manhattan Theatre Club

Tenth Season
Artistic Director, Lynne Meadow; Managing Director, Barry Grove; Associate Artistic Director, Douglas Hughes; General Manager, Connie L. Alexis; Audience Development Director/Press, Patricia Cox; Press Associate, Bob Burrichter; Business Manager, Victoria B. Bailey; Literary Manager, Jonathan Alper; Casting Directors, Deborah Brown, Donna Isaacson; Production Manager, Peter Glazer; Technical Director, Brian Lago

MTC/DOWNSTAGE

June 2–July 3, 1981 (44 performances)
HUNTING SCENES FROM LOWER BAVARIA by Martin Sperr; Translated by Christopher Holme; Dramaturg, Jonathan Alper; Director, Ulrich Heising; Set, Karen Schulz; Costumes, William Ivey Long; Lighting, Marc B. Weiss; Production Assistant, Lisa Anne Wilson; Assistant to Director, Johan Rainer; Stage Managers, Richard Elkow, John Beven. CAST: Marge Redmond (Barbara), Dominic Chianese (Boney), Jack Davidson (Mayor), Michael Burg (Priest), Suzanne Costallos (Maria), Raymond Barry (Volker), Paul McCrane (Rovo), Sasha von Scherler (Butcher's Widow), Tom Kopache (George), Pippa Pearthree (Tonka), Ann Lange (Paula), Christine Rose (Zenta), John Pankow (Abram), John Beven (Max), David Saint (Standby)

A play in two acts. The action takes place in and about the small village of Reinod, Lower Bavaria, during the late summer of 1948.

MTC/UPSTAGE

Tuesday, June 9–July 3, 1981 (28 performances)
HARRY RUBY'S SONGS MY MOTHER NEVER SANG co-conceived by Michael S. Roth and Paul Lazarus; Based on an original idea by Michael S. Roth; Director, Paul Lazarus; Choreography, Douglas Norwick; Orchestration and Musical Direction, Michael S. Roth; Set, Jane Thurn; Costumes, Christa Scholtz; Lighting, F. Mitchell Dana; Stage Managers, Esther Cohen, Betsy Nicholson
CAST: Indira Christopherson, Peter Frechette, I. M. Hobson, Owen S. Rachleff. (Standby) A tribute to Harry Ruby performed without intermission.

MTC/UPSTAGE

Tuesday, October 20–November 22, 1981 (40 performances)
THE RESURRECTION OF LADY LESTER by OyamaO; Director, Andre Mtumi; Set, Kate Edmunds; Costumes, Rita Ryack; Lighting, William Armstrong; Stage Manager, Alan Fox; Musical Director/Original Compositions/Arrangements, Dwight Andrews
CAST: Obaka Adedunyo (Lincoln/Slump/Pooky), Larry Bryggman (Tramb/Major/Manager), Randy Danson (White Marie/W-.I.B.), Arthur French (Booboo/Sgt. Tweed), Yvette Hawkins (Miss Lady/Lady Day), Carol-Jean Lewis (Sarah/Tuta/Agatha), Cleavon Little (Lester Young), Otis Young-Smith (Swoop/Mouse/Bo/-Grand Marshall)
MUSICAL NUMBERS: Ain't No Place Like the Open Road, Birdland Jam, Come and Go to That Land, Darn That Dream, Dried Up Corncob Blues, Goodbye Pork Pie Hat, Lester Leaps In, Lester's Death Music, Lush Life, Miss Lady Ballad, Three Little Words

MTC/DOWNSTAGE

Tuesday, October 20–November 29, 1981 (47 performances)
CROSSING NIAGARA by Alonso Alegria; Director, Andre Ernotte; Set and Costumes, Santo Loquasto; Lighting, Jennifer Tipton; Associate Artistic Director, Douglas Hughes; General Manager, Connie L. Alexis; Casting, Deborah Brown; Stage Managers, John Beven, James McC-Clark.
CAST: Alvin Epstein (Blondin), Paul McCrane (Carlo), Standbys: James Burge (Blondin), John Geter (Carlo)

A play in 2 acts and 5 scenes. The action takes place in Blondin's rooms in Niagara Falls, N.Y., and over the Falls on August 18, 1859.

MTC/UPSTAGE

Tuesday, November 3–22, 1981 (18 performances) Returned Tuesday, December 1–20, 1981 for 24 additional performances.
AND I AIN'T FINISHED YET by Eve Merriam; Director, Sheldon Epps; Musical Director-Arranger, Patti Brown; Set, Kate Edmunds; Costumes, Judy Dearing; Lighting, Robby Monk; Production Assistant, Daniel Kanter; Wardrobe, William Michael Vick; Stage Managers, Jason LaPadura, Susi Mara
CAST: Lynne Thigpen (Ex-Slave/Ida B. Wells/Sister Tessie/Gertrude "Ma" Rainey/Hannah Tutson/Jackie "Moms" Mabley/Fannie Lou Hamer), Stanley Ramsey (Mason/Newsboy/Black Preacher/Aaron Henry), Robin Karfo (Young Southern Girl/Mason's Wife/Conductor/Mrs. Gary), Bo Smith (Mason/Judge/Investigator/Reporter), Patti Brown (Lady at the piano)
Performed without an intermission.

MTC/DOWNSTAGE

Wednesday, December 23, 1981–January 24, 1982 (45 performances)
NO END OF BLAME 'Scenes of Overcoming' by Howard Baker; Director, Walton Jones; Set, Tony Straiges; Costumes, Christa Scholtz; Lighting and Projections, Donald Edmund Thomas; Bela's Cartoons, Gerald Scarfe; Grigor's Drawings, Clare Shenstone; Wardrobe, Kate Amendola; Assistant to Director, Elizabeth Bailey; Stage Managers, Robert Kellogg, Betsy Nicholson
CAST: Elizabeth Norment (Peasant/Tea Woman), Joe Grifasi (Grigor Gabor), Michael Cristofer (Bela Veracek), Ralph Byers (Soldier/Art Student/Comrade/John Lowry/Airman/Male Nurse), Gene O'Neill (Hungarian Soldier/Art Student/Airman/Mr. Mik/Male Nurse), George Ede (Hungarian Officer/Comrade/Anthony Diver), John C. Vennema (Red Soldier/GPU Man/Customs Officer/Bob Stringer/Male Nurse), Michael Gross (Red Soldier/Billwitz/Frank Deeds/Hoogstraten), Keith Reddin (Red Soldier/Art Student/Comrade/Airman/Dockerill), Robin Bartlett (Stella/Airwoman/Dr. Glasson), Patricia Hodges (Comrade/Airwoman), Caitlin Clarke (Ilona/Secretary), George Hall (Gardener/Airman/Sir Herbert Strubenzee/Male Nurse), Standbys: Elizabeth Norment, John C. Vennema
A drama in 2 acts and 13 scenes. The action takes place from 1918 to 1973.

MTC/UPSTAGE

Sunday, January 31–February 21, 1982 (42 performances)
STRANGE SNOW by Steve Metcalfe; Director, Thomas Bullard; Set, Atkin Pace; Costumes, Nan Cibula; Lighting, Cheryl Thacker; Casting, Deborah Brown; Production Assistant, Amy Sicular; Stage Managers, Loretta Robertson, Mari S. Schatz
CAST: Dann Florek (Megs), Kaiulani Lee (Martha), Christopher Curry (David)
A comedy-drama in two acts. The action takes place within a 24 hour period in the Flanagan home.

MTC/DOWNSTAGE

Tuesday, February 23–March 28, 1982 (56 performances)
SALLY AND MARSHA by Sybille Pearson; Director, Lynne Meadow; Set, Stuart Wurtzel; Costumes, Patricia McGourty; Lighting, Marc B. Weiss; Wardrobe, Kate Amendola; Assistant to Director, Susan Fenichell; Stage Managers, Tom Aberger, Daniel L. Kanter
CAST: Bernadette Peters (Sally), Christine Baranski (Marsha)
A play in two acts. The action takes place at the present time over a period of seven months in a New York City West Side apartment.

MTC/UPSTAGE

Sunday, March 28–April 18, 1982 (48 performances)
LIVIN' DOLLS by Scott Wittman and Marc Shaiman; Conceived by Scott Wittman; Director, Richard Maltby, Jr.; Musical Staging, Scott Wittman, Richard Maltby, Jr.; Musical Direction/Vocal Arrangements, Marc Shaiman; Costumes, Timothy Dunleavy; Set, John Lee Beatty; Lighting, Pat Collins; Sound, D. Perry Brandston; Hairstylist/Makeup, Charles Elsen, Dennis Bergevin; Production Assistant, David K. Rodger; Wardrobe, Theresa Snider; Stage Managers, Susan Green, Morton Milder
CAST: Linda Hart (Babe), Zora Rasmussen (Blabby Betty), Deborah Van Valkenburg (Candi), Lisa Embs (Fifi), Kim Milford (Poindexter), James Rich (Paul), Tom Wiggin (Rip Curl)
MUSICAL NUMBERS: Waiting for Our Wave, Love Come A-Callin', Girls, A Livin' Doll, Nobody's Valentine, Lifesaver, Down in the Sand, Something Special, Poindexter's Lament, Round About Midnight, Wipeout at Panic Point, There's a Girl, Lost in Space, G. I. Joe, No Questions Asked, Finale
A musical play in two acts. The action takes place during a fabulous two-week vacation in Hawaii.

MTC/DOWNSTAGE

Wednesday, April 28–May 23, 1982 (48 performances)
GARDENIA by John Guare; Director, Karel Reisz; Composer, Glen Roven; Set, Santo Loquasto; Costumes, Ann Roth; Lighting, Craig Miller; Hairstylist/Makeup, Peg Schierholz; Wardrobe, C. L. Ringelstein; Stage Managers, Stephen McCorkle, Wendy Chapin
CAST: Sam Waterston (Joshua Hickman), JoBeth Williams (Lydie Breeze), Edward Herrmann (Amos Mason), James Woods (Dan Grady), R. J. Burke (Jeremiah Grady), Jarlath Conroy (Ambrose O'Malley)

A drama in two acts. The action takes place on a Nantucket beach in early June of 1875, and in a Charlestown prison in December of 1884.

MTC/UPSTAGE

Sunday, May 16–30, 1982 (32 performances)
SCENES FROM LA VIE DE BOHEME by Anthony Giardina; Director, Douglas Hughes; Set, Adrianne Lobel; Costumes, Rita Ryack; Lighting, Craig Miller; Wardrobe, Lisa Anne Wilson; Assistant to Director, David Saint; Stage Managers, Jason LaPadura, Susi Mara
CAST: Jed Cooper (Malcolm), Michael Kaufman (Paul), John Christopher Jones (Jacob), Mary Elaine Monti (Deanna), Daniel Gerroll (John), Cornelia Mills (Una), John Shepard (Man with Una), Robin Karfo (Joria), Susi Mara (Madeline)

A play in three acts. The action takes place from January 1979 to January 1982.

Right: Cleavon Little, Yvette Hawkins in "The Resurrection of Lady Lester" Below: Bernadette Peters, Christine Baranski in "Sally and Marsha"

Sam Waterston, James Woods, JoBeth Williams in "Gardenia" Above: Joe Grifasi, Michael Cristofer, Caitlin Clarke in "No End of Blame"

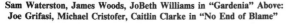

Paul McCrane, Alvin Epstein in "Crossing Niagara"
Gerry Goodstein Photos

85

Manhattan Punch Line

Fourth Season

Artistic Director, Steve Kaplan; Executive Director, Mitch McGuire; Producing Director, Jerry Heymann; General Manager, Mark Richard; Development, Candace Cohen; Press, Sandi Kimmel, Fred Hoot

September 17–October 18, 1981 (20 performances)
BADGERS by Donald Wollner; Director, Ellen Sandler; Set, Nancy Tobias; Costumes, Gayle Everhart; Lighting, John Hickey; Assistant Director, Pam Perrell; Technical Director, Gordon Ahlstrom; Stage Manager, Joseph Westerfield. **CAST:** Stephanie Murphy (Jessica), Matthew Penn (Leo), Gabriel Yorke (Doug), Peter E. Green (Richard), Derek Hoxby (Bob), Adam Lefevre (Jim), Steve Beauchamp (Ken), Dee Ann Sexton (Charlayne). A play in two acts. The action takes place over 4 days in the spring of 1967 at the University of Wisconsin.

October 29–November 29, 1981 (20 performances)
THE COARSE ACTING SHOW by Michael Green; Four one-act plays directed by Jerry Heymann; Set, Reagan Cook; Costumes, Ann Hould-Ward; Lighting, Gregory C. McPherson; Music, Bill Schimmel; Technical Director, D. Arthur Runge; Stage Manager, Stacy Fleischer. **CAST:** Reathel Bean (Cogsworth), Brad Bellamy (Adolph), Robert Alan Beuth (Pick), Victoria Boothby (Phoenicia), Jim DeMarse (Ted), Arthur Erickson (Neil), Ellen Fiske (Maureen), Carrick Glenn (Brenda), Steve Kaplan (Irwin), Larry Kleinstein (Larsy), Danny Meisner (Howie), Bruce Mower (George), S. Barkley Murray (Eleanor), Bruce Pachtman (Barney), Brian Rose (Burt), Selma Rosenblatt (Marilyn), F. L. Schmidlapp (Stantz), Joel Simon (Ira), Judith Thomas (Lucy), Rick Weatherwax (Willard). The plays are Henry X (Part 7), Streuth, The Cherry Sisters, Il Fornicazione.

December 17, 1981–January 11, 1982 (20 performances)
AN ITALIAN STRAW HAT by Eugene Labiche and Marc-Michel; Translated by Jerry Heymann; Director, Steve Kaplan; Set, Joseph Varga; Costumes, David Robinson; Lighting, Gregory Chabay; Music, William Schimmel; Technical Director, Derald Plumer; Stage Manager, Michael O'Boyll. **CAST:** Warren Sweeney (Felix), Lynn Weaver (Virginie), Tom Sleeth (Vezinet), John Rothman (Fadinard), Arthur Erickson (Emile), Eileen Albert (Anais), Robert Dale Martin (Nonancourt), Getchie Argetsinger (Helene), Tom Shelton (Bobin), Nevada Barr (Clara), Gordon G. Jones (Tardiveau), Mike Brennan (Achille), Lizabeth Pritchett (Baroness), Rebecca Locke (Servant), Judy Thomas (Clothilde), Ron Johnston (Beauperthuis), People of France; David Barbee, Nancy Blum, Mike Lisenco, Alan J. Ross. The action takes place in Paris.

January 29–February 28, 1982 (20 performances)
FEROCIOUS KISSES by Gil Schwartz; Director, Josh Mostel; Set, Geoffrey Hall; Costumes, Amanda Aldridge; Lighting, Dennis Size; Technical Director, Barney Baker; Stage Manager, Lawrence Berrick. A play in two acts. The action takes place in a New York hotel suite, and a Los Angeles hotel suite.

March 25–May 10, 1982 (41 performances)
THE ROADS TO HOME by Horton Foote; Director, Calvin Skaggs; Set, Oliver D'Arcy; Costumes, Edi Giguere; Lighting, Richard Dorfman; Stage Manager, Ellen Sontag; General Manager, Mark Richard.
CAST: Carol Fox (Mabel), Rochelle Oliver (Vonnie), B. Hallie Foote (Annie), Greg Zittel (Mr. Long), Jess Osuna (Jack), Jon Berry (Eddie), Ron Marr (Dave), James Paradise (Cecil), Tony Noll (Greene). Three related one-act plays. The action takes place in 1924 and 1928 in Houston and Austin, Texas.

May 21–June 14, 1982 (20 performances)
WHAT A LIFE! by Clifford Goldsmith; Director, Jerry Heymann; Set, Johniene Papandreas; Costumes, Lorraine Calvert; Lighting, Gregory C. MacPherson; Stage Manager, Anne Cowett; General Manager, Mark Richard. **CAST:** Anne Gartlan (Miss Shea), Tom Rolfing (Mr. Nelson), Robert Ott Boyle (Mr. Patterson), Fay Gold (Miss Pike), Jerry Stein (Student), Nancy Kawalek (Wilma), George Bakos (Student), Nancy Shull (Miss Eggleston), Lori Luzynski (Miss Johnson), Rusty Jacobs (Henry Aldrich), Karyn Lynn Dale (Barbara), Anne Jamison (Gertie), Richard Marr (Mr. Bradley), Betty Gardham (Miss Wheeler), Brad Spencer (George), Rusti Moon (Mrs. Aldrich), Mitch McGuire (Mr. Ferguson). A comedy in three acts. The action takes place in the principal's office of Central High School.

Cathryn Williams Photos

Rochelle Oliver, Carole Fox, B. Hallie Foote in "The Roads to Home"

Mitch McGuire, Anne Gartlan in "What a Life!"

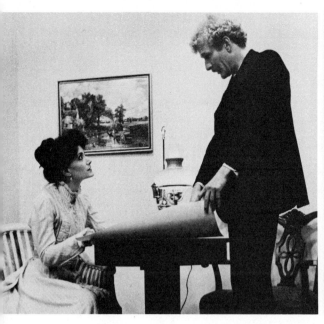

The Meat and Potatoes Company

Sixth Season

Artistic Director, Neal Weaver; Administrative Director, Jane Dwyer; Production Manager, Ann Folke; General Manager, Bonnie Arquilla; Press, Helen Hafner, Penny Watkins

ALVINA KRAUSE THEATRE

June 11–July 5, 1981 (20 performances)
FASNACHT DAY by John Speicher; Director, James E. Dwyer; Set, Bob Phillips; Costumes, Susan Cox; Lighting, Jeff Robbins; Stage Manager, Kevin Osborne. CAST: Margaret Donohue (Helen), Jay Devlin (Tommy), Lisa Cosman (Mother), Donald Pace (Doctor), Jeanne Schlegel (Grandmother), Evan Thompson (Father). A play in two acts. The action takes place at the present time in a small city in Eastern Pennsylvania.

July 15–August 8, 1981 (20 performances)
CAFE FANTASIO written and directed by Neal Weaver; Set/Costumes, Jan Finnell, Eric Thomann; Stage Manager, Jeffery L. Robbins. CAST: Catherine Roth (Becky), Tobin Wheeler (Leon), Alvin Railey (Toby), Dustyn Taylor (Friz), Richardson Taylor (Tom), James Chesson (Val), Sally Prager (Gina), Kevin Osborne (Tony), Lisa Cosman (Grace), Alan R. Schleyer (Roger), Elliot Landen (Otis), Frank Ciraci (Paul), Julia Palmore (Dorothea), Jamie Bowman (Johanna), Jeffrey L. Robbins (Fred), Karli Dwyer or Laura Spitler (Lisa), Olaf Peterson (George). A play in two acts. The action takes place at the Cafe Fantasio during 1965 in the East Village of NYC.

September 9–October 4, 1981 (20 performances)
MAN AND SUPERMAN by George Bernard Shaw; Director, Neal Weaver; Sets, Mr. Weaver; Lighting, Terry H. Wells; Stage Managers, Elliott Landen, Mikal Atwell. CAST: Joel Parsons (Roebuck), Mikal Atwell (Parlormaid), Anthony Moore (Octavius), Stephen Ahern (Tanner), Tessa M. Mills (Mrs. Whitefield), Elissa Napolin (Ann), Lisa Cosman (Miss Ramsden), Terri Price (Violet), Spike Steingasser (Straker), Malachy Cleary (Hector), Donald Pace (Mr. Malone)

October 15–November 8, 1981 (20 performances)
UNCLE VANYA by Anton Chekhov; Direction and Design, Neal Weaver; Stage Manager, Jerome Hoffman; Press, Penny Watkins. CAST: Lisa Cosman (Marina), Richard Bourg (Astrov), Evan Thompson (Vanya), Elliott Landen (Alexandre), Barbara Leto (Andreyevna), Sally Prager (Sonia), James Cimino (Waffles), Tessa Mills (Vanya's mother), Jerome Hoffman (Yefim)

November 19–December 20, 1981 (20 performances)
THE COUNT OF MONTE CRISTO by Charles Fechter and James O'Neill; Design and Direction, Neal Weaver; Fight Director, Michael Arabian; Music Coordinator, Anthony Moore; Stage Managers, Penny Weinberger, Richard Goemann. CAST: Elliott Landen (Morel), Brian Doughty (Pamphile), Michael Fantacci (Fernand), Richard Goemann (Fisherman), Anne-Marie Hackett (Peasant), Nancy Hammill (Mercedes), Jerome Hoffman (Danglars), Carol Julian (Mlle. Dangler), Adam Kilgour (Foria), Jim Knobeloch (Albert), Anthony Moore (Villefort), Kevin Osborne (Caderousse), William Perley (Edmund), Jim Scholle (Soldier), Ronn Tombaugh (Noirtier), Scott Winters (Vierry)

January 14–February 14, 1982 (20 performances)
TWELFTH NIGHT by William Shakespeare; Director, Harris Laskawy; Set, Bill Wells; Lighting, Sarkis; Sound, Anthony White; Stage Manager, Bill Wells. CAST: William Preston (Feste), James Horan (Orsino), Janet Maylie (Viola), James Maxwell (Sebastian), Jana Robbins (Olivia), Michael Howard (Sir Toby), Richard Vernon (Malvolio), Lizette Gordon-Smith (Maria), Patrick Husted (Sir Andrew), Phil Rosenthal (Fabian), Ken Stirbl (Antonio), Harvey Wilson (Sea Captain), Mark Johnson (Valentine), Richard Goemann (Curio), Harvey Wilson (Priest), Lisa Contadino (Handmaiden), Mark Johnson, Richard Goemann (Sailors)

February 25–March 28, 1982 (20 performances)
DOUBLE DUTCH by Marilyn Seven; Director, Neal Weaver; Set, Stephen Caldwell; Lighting, Lisa Grossman; Stage Manager, Michael Goldman. CAST: Constance Boardman (Marylou), Brad Bowton (Skip), Eddie Eng (Makoto), Marilyn Hiratzka (Judy), Machiko Izawa (Yukiko), E. D. Miller (Belford), Mustafa Noor (Akira), Judy Canon Ott (Taeko), Gerri Igarashi (Haruko), Olaf Peterson (Biff), Peter Yoshida (Yoshito). A drama in 3 acts. The action takes place during 1941 and 1942 in Yoshito's home, and in an internment camp.

April 9–May 9, 1982 (20 performances)
LADIES IN RETIREMENT by Reginald Denham and Edward Percy; Director, Jon Teta; Set, Neal Weaver; Costumes, Lisa Cosman; Stage Managers, Michael E. Golden, Anne-Marie Hackett. CAST: Toni Genfan Brown (Sister Teresa), Lisa Cosman (Leonora), Terry Ashe Croft (Ellen), Elaine Eldridge (Louise), Anne-Marie Hackett (Lucy), Edward Hyland (Albert), Irma St. Paule (Emily)

May 20–June 20, 1982 (20 performances)
SPRING'S AWAKENING by Frank Wedekind; Director, Neal Weaver; Set, Bonnie Arquilla; Costumes, Ronn Tombaugh; Lights, Hal Haner; Stage Managers, Steve Fischer, Darren J. McGregor, Richard Payne.
CAST: Timothy Bennett, Toni Genfan Brown, Greg Delaney, Steve Fischer, Joseph Foulon, Michelle Giannini, Ann Gentry, Anne-Marie Hackett, Hal Haner, Sue Jacobson, Neal Jones, Elliott Landen, Darren J. McGregor, Dale Merchant, Richard Payne, Steve Rapella, Robert K. Reddy, Alan Robinson, Ronn Tombaugh, Susan Treadwell, Jim Vopelak.

Top: (L) Barbara Leto, Richard Bourg in "Uncle Vanya" (R) Mustafa Noor, Peter Yoshida in "Double Dutch" *(Herb Fogelson Photos)*

A SOLDIER'S PLAY

By Charles Fuller; Director, Douglas Turner Ward; Scenery, Felix E. Cochren; Costumes, Judy Dearing; Lighting, Allen Lee Hughes; Sound, Regge Life; Props, Lisa L. Watson; Wardrobe, Marcia L. Belton; Sound, Harry Aikens; Production Assistant, Janice C. Lane; Technical Director, Rodney J. Lucas; Stage Managers, Clinton Turner Davis, Femi Sarah Heggie; Press, Howard Atlee, Bill Evans, Barbara Atlee CAST: Tech/Sgt. Vernon C. Waters, Adolph Caesar, Pvt. James Wilkie, Steven A. Jones, Capt. Charles Taylor, Peter Friedman, Pvt. Tony Smalls, Brent Jennings, Cpl. Bernard Cobb, Eugene Lee, Capt. Richard Davenport, Charles Brown, Pfc. Melvin Peterson, Denzel Washington, Pvt. C. J. Memphis, Larry Riley†, Cpl. Ellis, James Pickens, Jr., Lt. Byrd, Cotter Smith, Pvt. Louis Henson, Samuel L. Jackson, Capt. Wilcox, Steven Zettler

UNDERSTUDIES: Cotter Smith (Taylor), James Pickens, Jr. (Davenport/Peterson)
A drama in two acts. The action takes place in 1944 in Fort Neal, Louisiana.
* Still playing May 31, 1982. Recipient of 1982 Pulitzer Prize, and New York Drama Critics Circle citation as Best New American Play.

† Succeeded by David Alan Grier.

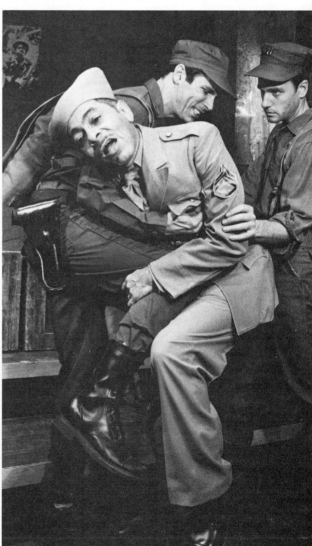

Brent Jennings, Eugene Lee, Denzel Washington, Samuel L. Jackson,
Larry Riley, front: Adolph Caesar, Peter Friedman Above:
Denzel Washington, Charles Brown

Adolph Caesar, Cotter Smith, Steven Zettler

Negro Ensemble Company

Douglas Turner Ward, Artistic Director
Fourteenth Season
Managing Director, Leon B. Denmark; Production Manager, Karen E. Johnson; Administrative Manager, William Edwards; Consultant, Gerald S. Krone; Wardrobe, Arneice McWilliams; Sound, Harry Aikens; Production Assistant, Janice Lane; Technical Director, Rodney J. Lucas; Press, Howard Atlee, Bill Evans, Jim Baldassare

THEATRE FOUR
Saturday, June 20–July 26, 1981 (44 performances)
ZOOMAN AND THE SIGN by Charles Fuller; Director, Douglas Turner Ward; Scenery, Rodney J. Lucas; Costumes, Shirley Prendergast; Lighting, Judy Dearing; Stage Managers, Clinton Turner Davis, Femi Sarah Heggie
CAST: Giancarlo Esposito (Zooman), Mary Alice (Rachel Tate), Carl Gordon (Emmett Tate), Ray Aranha (Reuben Tate), Alvin Alexis (Victor Tate), Terrance Terry Ellis (Russell Odoms), Steven A. Jones (Donald Jackson), Frances Foster (Ash Boswell), Carol Lynn Maillard (Grace Georges), Phylicia Ayers-Allen (Understudy)
A drama in 2 acts. The action takes place at the present time in Philadelphia, Pa., in the home of Rachel and Reuben Tate, the street outside, and various other locations.

NEC/CHERRY LANE THEATRE
Wednesday, March 24–April 25, 1982 (31 performances)
COLORED PEOPLE'S TIME by Leslie Lee; Director, Horacena J. Taylor; Scenery, Felix E. Cochren; Costumes, Myrna Colley-Lee; Lighting, Shirley Prendergast; Sound, Gary Harris; Wardrobe, Viki Jones; Props, Garland Thompson, Jr., Eric Mungen; Production Assistant, Janice C. Lane; Technical Director, Rodney J. Lucas; Assistant Director, Fred Tyson; Company Manager, Susan E. Watson; Stage Managers, Femi Sarah Heggie, Chester A. Sims; Press, Howard Atlee, Barbara Atlee
CAST: L. Scott Caldwell, Chuck Cooper, Robert Gossett, Jackee Harry, Juanita Mahone, Debbi Morgan, Charles H. Patterson, Charles Weldon, Curt Williams
A play in 2 acts and 13 scenes, with a prologue and epilogue. The action takes place in the U.S. from 1859 to 1956.

L. Scott Caldwell, Charles Weldon in "Colored People's Time"
Left: Alvin Alexis, Giancarlo Esposito in "Zooman and the Sign"

A Woman's Project

Producer, John Brick; Co-ordinators, Leslie (Hoban) Blake, Terrence Christgau, Bonnie Young
NEW YORK THEATER ENSEMBLE
November 5–22, 1981 (12 performances)
HAPPY ENDINGS by Abigail Quart; Director, Leslie (Hoban) Blake; Set, Patrick Angus; Lighting, Patricia McGillicuddy; Costumes, Sara; Sound, Chris Fish, Frank Berman; Mask, Stephen Caldwell; Stage Manager, David Oberon. CAST: Allen Barone (Erskine/Roger), Cly Fowkes (Gopher Girl/Joan), Susan Frazer (Beauty/Angela), Phillip Hershberger (Beast/Tom), Lisa Nicole Wolpe (Edie/Ann), John Imro (Harvey/Zaniel)
January 7–31, 1982 (16 performances)
THE MENAECHMI by Plautus; Adaptation/Direction, Leslie (Hoban) Blake; Set, Jacqueline Allen; Costumes, Jeffrey Wallach; Choreography, Barbara (Babs) Brogan; Lighting, Linda Young; Sound, Chris Fish; Stage Manager, Angie Pappas. CAST: Allen Barone (Menaechmus II/Thug), Jeri Lynn Cohen (Desiree), Laurence Gleason (Messenio), Michael E. Hermanski (Menaechmus I), Susan Mitchell (Milphiddipa), Foster Padway (Mixmaster/Decio/Doctor), Maggie Scott (Domina), Jeffrey Shoemaker (Peniculus/Old Man)
April 15–May 9, 1982 (16 performances)
THE ROVER by Aphra Behn; Adaptation/Direction, Leslie (Hoban) Blake; Assistant Director/Costumes/Set, Bruce Thomson; Wardrobe, Marjorie Dundas, Jeffrey Wallach; Fight Director, Peter Moore; Choreographer, Beth Kurtz; Lighting, Peter Andros; Original Music, David Sherman; Technical Director, Roy Martin; Stage Managers, Ken Lowstetter, Lesley Kahn. CAST: Michael Adler (Blunt), Garry Apple (Officer), Barbara Bornmann (Valeria), Elizabeth Bove (Angelica), Kay Colburn (Florinda), Stephen Cross (Antonio), Cly Fowkes (Hellena), Jack Gooden (Pedro), Lynn Homa (Lucetta), Suzi List (Dancer), Grace Lozzi (Bianca), Teel J. Michaels (Officer), Peter Moore (Belville), Andrew Potter (Willmore/The Rover), Philip Rosenberg (Stephano), Loretta Rotunno (Moretta), Connor Smith (Frederick), Georgette Tashji (Dancer), Jack Thomas (Officer), Lesley Kahn (Understudy)

Connor Smith, Michael Adler, Kay Colburn in "The Rover"
(Jim Manley Photo)

No Smoking Playhouse/Merry Enterprises Theatre

Sixth Season

Artistic Director, Norman Thomas Marshall; Associate Directors, George Wolf Reily, John Von Hartz; General Manager, Edward R. F. Matthews; Press, Anne Einhorn, Adam Redfield; Special Projects Director, Frank Girardeau

July 9–26, 1981 (12 performances)
Merry Enterprises Theatre and City Gates Theatre present:
THE COUNTRY WIFE by William Wycherley; "Rudely Adapted and Directed by Phil Davis"; Set, Nicholas Vizzini, Edmund McCarthy; Costumes, Marla Kaye; Lighting, Leslie Ann Kilian; Production Manager, Joan M. Mayer. CAST: Gary Cox, Jyll Stein, Alan Bluestone, Syl Rich, Brad Gorman, Rona Katzker, Richard Litt, Fay Bright, George Wolf Reily, Ann Citron, Steven Salter, Cindy Reynolds, Katherine Gowan, Lisa Ann Getzler, J. Michael Craig

Nobember 18–December 6, 1981 (20 performances)
THE WOULD-BE GENTLEMAN by Moliere; Adapted by Bobby Clark; Director, Marvin Einhorn; Set, Vittorio Capecce; Costumes, Van Ramsey; Lighting, Edward R. F. Matthews; Sound, Nicholas Vizzini; Production Manager, Sheila Mathews; Technical Director, Ted Reinert; Fencing Choreographer, Marc Krone; Choreographer, Olivia Negron; Wardrobe, Marla Kaye; Props, Bernett Belgraier; Stage Managers, Sheila Mathews, Marjorie Golden. CAST: George Babiak (Singer), Alan Bluestone (Tailor), Greg Fellows (Raymond/-Criquet), Marjorie Golden (Singer), Malcolm Gray (Jourdain), Diane Heles (Dorimene), Cheryl Henderson (Nicole), Mary Elizabeth Horowitz (Lucille), Marc Krone (Marcel), Steven Lovett (Cleonte), Michael Makman (Fencing Master), Olivia Negron (Mlle. Valere), Robert B. Putnam (Baptiste), George Wolf Reily (Philosopher), Sylvester Rich (Covielle), Mike Rogers (Dancing Master), Cathy Roskam (Mme. Jourdain), Jeanmay Spence (Singer), Casey Walters (Music Master), Eric Zwener (Count Dorante)

February 4–28, 1982 (20 performances)
THE UNICORN by Michael Kimberley; Director, Norman Thomas Marshall; Set, Tom Schwinn; Lighting, Edward R. F. Matthews; Costumes, Marla R. Kaye; Technical Director, Marc Krone; Stage Managers, Alan Bluestone, William Nickerson; Press, Alpert-/LeVine, Alan Hale. CAST: Hansford Rowe (Harry), Adam Redfield (Billy), Ed VanNuys (Louie), Janie Kelly (Madge). The action takes place in a Chicago residential hotel.

April 15–May 9, 1982 (20 performances)
A MIDSUMMER NIGHT'S DREAM by William Shakespeare; Director, George Wolf Reily; Set, Beate Kessler; Costumes, Jean Zarzour; Lighting, Edward R. F. Matthews; Music, Steve Cohen; Choreographer, Eden Lee Murray; Technical Director, Ted Reinert; Stage Managers, Marla R. Kaye, Betty Berkowitz.
CAST: George Babiak (Starveling), June Ballinger (Titania/Hippolyta), Peter Blaxill (Egeus/Philostrate), Mary Kay Dean (Helena), Susana Falcon (Moth), Malcolm Gray (Bottom), Marc Krone (Lysander), Edmund McCarthy (Snug), Eden-Lee Murray (Hermia), Ted Reinert (Snout), Ruthie Rosenfeld (Cobweb), W. B. Ross (Flute), Suzy Sharp (Peaseblossom), Jean May Spence (Mustardseed), Jyll Stein (Puck), Lou Trapani (Quince), Steve Pudenz (Theseus/Oberon), Eric Zwemer (Demetrius)

Adam Redfield in "The Unicorn"
(Marvin Einhorn Photo)

Ron McLarty, Christine Baranski in "Operation Midnight Climax" *(Bert Andrews Photo)*

Off Center Theatre

Fourteenth Season

Executive Director, Tony McGrath; Administrative Director, Abigail Rosen; Assistant, Mitch Levine; Art Director, Nancy Johnson; Dramaturge, Stanley Seidman; Press, Ted Goldsmith

October 21–November 14, 1981 (20 performances)
MacRUNE'S GUEVARA by John Spurling; Director, Larry Loonin; Set/Lighting, Whitney Quesenbery; Costumes, Nancy Johnson; Assistant Director, Lisa DiFranza; Sound, John Marshall; Stage Managers, Jerry Litwin, Mitch Levine. CAST: Bill Olland (Edward Hotel), Juan Wolf (Che Guevara), Bob Fass (MacRune), Robin Sagon (Narrator), Harriett Kittner (Tania), Georgia Harrell (Isabella), John Elejalde (Joaquin), Carlos Cardona (Raimundo), Allen Rockwerk (Felipe), David Melville (Coco)

November 19–December 6, 1981 (16 performances)
OPERATION MIDNIGHT CLIMAX by Neal Bell; Director, Thomas Babe; Set/Costumes, Mike Boak; Lighting, Greg MacPherson; Technical Director, Ted Ciganik; Stage Managers, Bill Fears, Roderick Spencer.
CAST: Christine Baranski (Angela), Dominic Chianese (Zeb), Richmond Hoxie (Guy), Ron McLarty (Mac)

December 9–23, 1981 (13 performances)
BITING THE APPLE by Tony McGrath and Stanley Seidman; Director, Mr. McGrath; Choreographer, Jeff Edmund; Musical Director/Pianist, Adele Dinerstein; Set, Jim Hardy; Lighting, Annette Purnell; Composer, Adam Penenberg; Stage Manager, Mitchell Levine. CAST: Dahlia Benson (Cora), Celia Bressack (Constance), Sidney Howell (Tom Arrow), Charles Nicholson (Arnold), Lawrence Redmond (Perry), Carver St. John (Stage Manager)

January 29–February 20, 1982 (20 performances)
A MAD WORLD, MY MASTERS by Barrie Keeffe; Director, Frederick K. Van Patten; Set, LouAnne Gilleland; Lighting, Whitney Quesenbery; Costumes, Nancy Johnson; Sound, Tom Gould; Stage Managers, Jerry Litwin, Paula Barish. CAST: Steve Coats (Charlie), Douglas Fisher (Horace), Matthew Gottlieb (Fox), Michael Grodenchik (Sprightly), Georgia Harrell (Janet), Leslie Harrell (Grandma), Lucinda Hitchcock-Cone (Vi), Allen C. Kennedy (Dr. O'Flaherty), Jerry Matz (Ronald), Vinnie Platania (Bert)

May 27–June 13, 1982 (16 performances)
HELLO ... I'M NOT IN RIGHT NOW with book, music and lyrics by Barbara Schottenfeld; Director, Mitchell Ivers; Set, Ursula Belden, Rob Hamilton; Costumes, Cinthia Waas; Lighting, Whitney Quesenbery; Musical Director, Andrew Howard; Choreographer, David Storey; Sound, Tom Gould; Orchestrations, Robert Merken; Vocal Director, Neil Semer; Production Assistant, Pamela Pennenberg; Stage Managers, Jerry Litwin, Louise Hochberg. CAST: Ralph Bruneau (Josh), Bev Larson (Susan), Barbara Schottenfeld (Abby)

Theater of The Open Eye

Tenth Season

Artistic Director, Jean Erdman; Executive Director, Nola Hague; Technical Director, Seth Price, Daphne Groos; Business Manager, William Waters: Literary Manager, Lee Teneyck, Robert Walter; Administrative Assistant, Alice Nedos; Press, Ann Scofield, Amie Brockway; Production Manager, Clayton Campbell

June 16–28, 1981
THE SHINING HOUSE from a ritual of pagan Hawaii; Direction/Choreography, Jean Erdman; Set, Paul Jenkins; Songs/Electronic Score, Michael Czajkowski; Libretto, Christopher Millis; Masks, Ralph Lee; Costumes, Kevin Woodworth; Set, Trueman Kelley; Lighting, Gregg Marriner; Sound, Gary Harris; Stage Manager, Tony Davis. CAST: Nancy Allison, Leslie Dillingham, Maura Ellyn, William Ha'O, Susan Murakoshi, Kathy Paulo, David Rousseve, Muna Tseng, Jean Erdman

February 10–March 7, 1982 (15 performances)
THE COACH WITH THE SIX INSIDES adapted from James Joyce's "Finnegan's Wake" by Jean Erdman; Staged by Miss Erdman; Music, Teiji Ito; Decor, Dan Butt; Projections, Milton Howarth; Lighting, Kathryn Reid; Costumes, Gail Ryan; Stage Managers, Dyana Lee, Doug Gettel

Below: Randy Frazier, Michele Cannon, J. J. Cole, Elton Becket, Matthew Idason, John Redwood in "The Sun Gets Blue"
(Ken Howard Photo)

March 17–April 4, 1982
PUNCH WITH JUDY by Rosemary Foley; Director, Dana Coen; Music, John Yanelli; Set, Rob Hamilton; Masks/Puppets, Eric Bass; Lighting, Phil Monat; Costumes, Sue Ellen Rohrer; Stage Managers, Bo Metzler, Susan Baker. CAST: David Combs (Punch), Jeff Abbott (Law), Joel Bernstein (Penny), Julia McLaughlin (WWW), Kirtan Coan (Judy), Dana Mills (Work), Jeanne Cullen (Inscrutable Woman), Warren Sweeney (Doctor)

April 14–May 2, 1982
THE SUN GETS BLUE by William "Electric" Black; Choreography, Mr. Black; Director, Amie Brockway; Music, Paul Shapiro; Set/Lighting, Adrienne B. Brockway; Costumes, Karen Selby; Sound, Dyana Lee; Stage Managers, Richard Heeger, Theresa Marsh. CAST: Elton Beckett (T. J.), Michele Cannon (Sweet Dee), J. J. Cole (Cat), Randy Frazier (Nick), Matthew Idason (Wine), Carol London (Sister Howard), Theresa Marsh (Gail), Daniel Neusom (Sonny), John Henry Redwood (Iceman), Judy Thames (Momma Blue), Raymond Anthony Thomas (Fast Eddie)

Open Space Theatre Experiment

Tenth Season

Artistic Director, Lynn Michaels; Administrator, Harry Baum; Administrative Assistant, Iris Pelowitz, Donna Herman; Technical Directors, Rick Shannin, Ken Young; Press, Jeffrey Richards Associates.

OPEN SPACE THEATRE/MAIN STAGE

November 5–December 13, 1981 (24 performances)
SIDE STREET SCENES by Sam Henry Kass; Director, Peter Kass; Music/Lyrics, Stuart Bloom; Arrangements, Debbie Lapidus, Stuart Bloom; Set, Bob Wallace; Lighting, Gregory MacPherson; Costumes, Pearl Somner; Visuals, Phillip Brooke; Sound, Charles Wantman; Music Director, Debbie Lapidus; Visual Design, Charles Wantman; Phillip Brooke; Casting, Robert Kass; Wardrobe, Karla Barker; Stage Managers, Crystal Huntington, Amy Merz; CAST: Stuart Bloom (Max), Patricia Stern (Laurie), Michael Lombard (Ralph/Frank), Rochelle Parker (Phoebe/Rose), Peter Boruchowitz (Tusky), Max Mayer (Louie), Joie Gallo (Donna). A play with music in 2 acts and 10 scenes.

January 7–February 7, 1982 (21 performances)
WHEN WE DEAD AWAKEN by Henrik Ibsen; Translated by Rolf Fjelde; Director, Stephen Zuckerman; Set, James Fenhagen; Lighting, Richard Winkler; Costumes, Carol H. Beule; Music, Dan Erkkila; Sound, Carl Frano; Casting, Darlene Kaplan; Stage Managers, Crystal Huntington, Karla Barker, Margaret Catov, Amy Merz. CAST: Ken Costigan (Manager), Kim Hunter (Irene), Dana Cameron Keeler (Nun), Tom Klunis (Arnold Rubek), Anne Twomey (Maja Rubek), Nicholas Wyman (Ulfhejm). A play in three scenes, performed without intermission.

April 22–May 23, 1982 (20 performances)
THE MISUNDERSTANDING by Albert Camus; Translated by Stuart Gilbert; Director, Susan Einhorn; Set/Costumes, Frank J. Boros; Lighting, Richard Nelson; Sound, Phil Lee; Casting, Douglas Aibel; Stage Managers, Crystal Huntington, Gail Arthur. CAST: Paul R. Cox (Manservant), Jean DeBaer (Martha), Elizabeth Lawrence (Mother), Susan Merson (Maria), Dan Ziske (Jan). A drama in 3 acts performed without intermission. The action takes place in the public room and a bedroom of a small inn in Moravia, a province of Czechoslovakia, in the spring of 1945.

OPEN SPACE THEATRE/GARRET

October 14–November 1, 1981 (12 performances)
THE CLOUDBERRY FIELD by Karen Johnson; Director, Nancy Gabor; Set/Lights, Harry Baum; Costumes, Martha Hally; Production Assistant, Karla Barker; Stage Managers, Brian Chavanne, Debbie Friedman. CAST: Annette Hunt (Birgitta), James Johnston (Harvald). The action takes place in a shattered house in a war-torn country in the middle of a hot afternoon.

January 28–February 28, 1982 (20 performances)
THE PELICAN by August Strindberg; Translated by Arvid Paulson; Director, Rosemary Hay; Set/Lights, Robert Thayer; Costumes, Martha Hally; Cellist, Belden Randolph Merims; Stage Managers, Gail Arthur, Callee A. Frith. CAST: Helen-Jean Arthur (Mother), Florence Anglin (Margaret), Rudi Caporaso (Son), Robin Thomas (Son-in-law), Karla Barker (Daughter). Performed without intermission. The action takes place in the living room of a Stockholm apartment on a November evening of 1907.

March 4–28, 1982 (16 performances)
THE SEA ANCHOR by Ted (E. A.) Whitehead; Director, Alex Dmitriev; Set, Bob Phillips; Lights, Richard Dorfman; Costumes, Barbara Weiss; Dialect Coach, Geddeth Smith; Stage Manager, Maureen Palmer. CAST: Caroline Lagerfelt (Jean), John Pietrowski (Les), Peter Rogan (Andy), Amy Stoller (Sylvia). A drama in 3 acts performed with one intermission. The action takes place during a day and the following morning on a jetty in Dublin Bay.

Above: Tom Klunis, Kim Hunter, Anne Twomey in "When We Dead Awaken"

Pan Asian Repertory Theatre

Founder/Artistic Director, Tisa Chang; General Manager, Thomas M. Madden; Lighting, Edward R. F. Matthews; Press, Sam Rudy

SOHO REPERTORY THEATRE

August 6–23, 1981 (16 performances)
YELLOW IS MY FAVORITE COLOR by Edward Sakamoto; Director, Ron Nakahara; Costumes, Valerie Charles; Stage Manager, Viveca Yrisarry. CAST: Raul Aranas (Mino), Ellen Boggs (Shirley), Valerie Charles (Mary Jane), Lynette Chun (Madelyn), William P. Ogilvie (Freddie), Freda Foh Shen (Mama), Henry Yuk (Henry). A play in two acts.

28th STREET PLAYHOUSE

November 19–December 6, 1981 (16 performances)
BULLET HEADED BIRDS by Philip Kan Gotanda; Director, Tisa Chang; Set, Michael DeSousa; Costumes, Lydia Tanji; Sound, Lenore Bode; Musical Direction, Geoff Lee; Choreography, Ching Valdes; Stage Manager, Viveca Yrisarry. CAST: Raul Aranas (Quazimoto), Lynette Chun (Voodoo Mannequin), Jessica Hagedorn (Zelda/Kirin), Chris Odo (Suicide Shadow), Gedde Watanabe (Paul), Ching Valdes (Sensei). A play with music in three acts.

March 11–21, 1982 (12 performances)
ROHWER by Lionelle Hamanaka; Director, Ernest Abuba; Costumes, Stephanie Kerley; Choreography, Sachiyo Ito; Composer, Kuni Mikami; Fight Director, Peter Nels; Sound, Regge Life; Stage Manager, Eddas M. Bennett. CAST: Jody Long (Commentator), Ron Nakahara (Mas), Anne Miyamoto (Haruko), Helen Yng Wong (Reb), Arline Miyazaki (Suzuko), Bruce Hamilton (FBI/Edwards), Keith Brandwen (FBI/Parker), Donald Li (Nobu), Lynette Chun (Mrs. Hosaka), Thomas Ikeda (Akira), William P. Ogilvie (Taylor), Tom Matsusaka (Kenji), Valerie Charles (Doctor). A drama in 2 acts and 8 scenes with an epilogue. The action takes place in 1941.

March 14–April 4, 1982 (12 performances)
BEHIND ENEMY LINES by Rosanna Yamagiwa Alfaro; Director, Ron Nakahara; Set, Ronald Kajiwara; Costumes, Valerie Charles; Lighting, Viveca Yrisarry; Sound, Regge Life; Stage Manager, Allan B. Williams. CAST: Natsuko Ohma (Mine), Carol A. Honda (Fumiko), Keenan Shimizu (Mike), Thomas Ikeda (Kazuo), Michael G. Chin (Lenny), Ann Oshita (Amy), William P. Ogilvie (Charles), Soldiers: Parlan McGaw, Mel Gionson. A drama in three acts. The action takes place in California during WW2.

April 7–18, 1982 (12 performances)
STATION J by Richard France; Director, Tisa Chang; Set, Atsushi Moriyasu; Costumes, Eiko Yamaguchi; Lighting, Victor En Yu Tan; Fight Director, Peter Nels; Hairstylist, Christine Cooper; Dance Consultant, Sachiyo Ito; Slides, Corky Lee; Sound, Regge Life; Stage Manager, Eddas M. Bennett. CAST: James Jenner (Auctioneer/Commandant), Glenn Kubota (Taro), Ronald Yamamoto (Ken), William Kennedy (Interviewer/Officer), Alvin Lum (Chiyoji), Elizabeth Sung (Yuki), Lynette Chun (Emiko), Richard Voights (Candidate/Judge/Mayor), Keenan Shimizu (Nisei/Sgt.), Natsuko Ohama (Issei/Waitress), Peter Yoshida (Issei/House Capt.), Mari Scott (Mother/Nisei), Billy Rodriguez (Son/Newsboy), Mel D. Gionson (Kibei), Michael G. Chin (Kibei), Henry Yuk (Zootsuiter/Osaka Mayor), Donald Li (Zootsuiter/Sansei). A drama in 3 acts and 17 scenes with an epilogue. The action takes palce from May 1942 to 1968.

Phoenix Theatre

T. Edward Hambleton, Managing Director, Twenty-ninth Season
Artistic Director, Steven Robman; General Manager, Harold Sogard; Literary Manager, Anne Cattaneo; Casting, Bonnie G. Timmermann; Production Manager, Donna Lieberman; Production Consultant, Myles Warren; Props, Nina Sheffy; Wardrobe, Ronn Tombaugh; Press, Susan L. Schulman, Claudia McAllister, Sandi Kimmel

MARYMOUNT MANHATTAN THEATRE

Saturday, September 26–October 11, 1981 (16 performances)
The Phoenix Theatre by arrangement with Garth H. Drabinsky and Norman Kean presents:
MAGGIE AND PIERRE by Linda Griffiths; Director, Paul Thompson; Scenery, John Kasarda; Costumes, Denise Romano; Lighting, Jim Plaxton; Stage Managers, J. Thomas Vivian, Kathleen Marsters
CAST: Eric Peterson (Henry), Linda Griffiths (Margaret/Pierre)
A play in two acts. The action takes place in the recent past.

Monday, November 23–December 13, 1981 (20 performances)
AFTER THE PRIZE by Fay Weldon; Director, Steven Robman; Scenery, Adrianne Lobel; Costumes, Linda Fisher; Lighting, Arden Fingerhut; Fights Staged by B. H. Barry; Sound, Tom Gould; Wardrobe, Linda Schultz; Props, Nina Sheffy; Company Manager, Donna Lieberman; Stage Managers, J. Thomas Vivian, Stacey Fleischer
CAST: John Horton (Edwin), Veronica Castang (Wasp), Lois Markle (Bee), David McCallum (Brian)
A play in two acts. The action is set in England at the present time.

MARYMOUNT MANHATTAN THEATRE

Monday, December 28, 1981–January 17, 1982 (22 performances)
The Phoenix Theatre by arrangement with George W. George and Preen Productions presents:

KAUFMAN AT LARGE adapted by John Lithgow from the writings of George S. Kaufman; Directed by John Lithgow with Steven Robman; Scenery, Marjorie Bradley Kellogg; Costumes, Ann Roth; Lighting, Ronald M. Bundt; Sound, David Rapkin; Assistant Director, Bob Edgar; Stage Manager, J. Thomas Vivian
CAST: John Lithgow as George S. Kaufman
A theatre piece in two acts. The action takes place in Mr. Kaufman's bedroom/workroom in his townhouse on East 94th Street in New York City on August 21, 1936.

MARYMOUNT MANHATTAN THEATRE

Thursday, March 4–28, 1982 (30 performances)
WEEKENDS LIKE OTHER PEOPLE by David Blomquist; Director, Ulu Grosbard; Scenery, David Jenkins; Costumes, Jennifer von Mayrhauser; Lighting, Pat Collins; Sound, David Rapkin; Company Manager, Donna Lieberman; Stage Managers, J. Thomas Vivian, Stacey Fleischer; Press, Susan L. Schulman, Joel W. Dein, Mercedes Cordero
CAST: Rose Gregorio (Laurie), Kenneth McMillan (Dan)
The action takes place at the present time during autumn in a small apartment on the northwest side of Chicago.

Center: (L) Lynette Chun, Raul Aranas in "Bullet Headed Birds" *(Carol Rosegg Photo)* (R) Rose Gregorio, Kenneth McMillan in "Weekends Like Other People" *(Martha Swope Photo)*

Playwrights Horizons

Eleventh Season

Artistic Director, Andre Bishop; Managing Director, Paul Daniels; Development, Janet Stott; Musical Director, Ira Weitzman; Business Manager, Rory Vanderlick; Assistant to Mr. Bishop, Hillary Nelson; Assistant to Mr. Daniels, Kathi S. Levitan; Press, Bob Ullman

MAINSTAGE
October 16, 1981–February 21, 1982. (240 performances)
(Moved to Westside Arts Theatre February 24, 1982 and still playing May 31, 1982)

SISTER MARY IGNATIUS EXPLAINS IT ALL FOR YOU
and THE ACTOR'S NIGHTMARE

By Christopher Durang; Director, Jerry Zaks; Sets, Karen Schulz; Costumes, William Ivey Long; Lighting, Paul Gallo; Sound, Aural Fixation; Production Assistants, Lori Steinberg, Lon Scott; Props, Frank Molina; Technical Director, Bob Bertrand; Wardrobe, Daryl Kroken; Casting, John Lyons; Production Managers, William M. Camp, Rachel Chanoff

CAST

"The Actor's Nightmare"

George Spelvin	Jeff Brooks†1	Dame Ellen Terry	Mary Catherine Wright†3
Meg	Polly Draper†2	Henry Irving	Timothy Landfield
Sarah Siddons	Elizabeth Franz		

The action takes place on a stage.
Intermission
"Sister Mary Ignatius Explains It All For You"

Sister Mary Ignatius	Elizabeth Franz	Gary Sullavan	Timothy Landfield
Thomas	Mark Stefan	Philomena Rostovich	Mary Catherine Wright†3
Diane Symonds	Polly Draper†2	Aloysius Benheim	Jeff Brooks†1

The action takes place in a lecture hall.

† Succeeded by: 1. Christopher Durang during vacation, 2. Deborah Rush, Alice Playten, 3. Carol Mignini

Jeff Brooks, Carolyn Mignini, Elizabeth Franz (front) in "Actor's Nightmare"

Mark Stefan, Elizabeth Franz in "Sister Mary Ignatius ..."

Thursday, February 11, 1982 and still playing May 31, 1982. Moved April 27, 1982 to Astor Place Theatre. Playwrights Horizons (Andre Bishop, Artistic Director; Paul Daniels, Managing Director) presents:

THE DINING ROOM

By A. R. Gurney, Jr. Director, David Trainer; Set, Loren Sherman; Costumes, Deborah Shaw; Lighting, Frances Aronson; Business Manager, Rory Vanderlick; Press, Bob Ullman; Production Manager, William M. Camp; Casting, John Lyons; Technical Director, Bob Bertrand; Props, Carol Kalil, Nancy Rifkin; Wardrobe, Susan Gibney; Production Assistants, Tim Claussen, Alice Perlmutter

CAST

Lois de Banzie	John Shea†1
W. H. Macy	Pippa Pearthree†2
Ann McDonough	Remak Ramsay†3

A play performed with one intermission. The action takes place in a dining room—or rather, many dining rooms—over the course of many years.

† Succeeded by: 1. Richmond Hoxie, John Getz, 2. Patricia Wettig, 3. Charles Kimbrough

Remak Ramsay, Pippa Pearthree, W. H. Macy, Lois de Banzie, Ann McDonough, John Shea

MAINSTAGE

April 28–June 6, 1982 (44 performances)
(Moved June 22, 1982 to Douglas Fairbanks Theatre)
GENIUSES by Jonathan Reynolds; Director, Gerald Gutierrez; Set, Andrew Jackness; Lighting, James F. Ingalls; Costumes, Ann Emonts; Sound, Scott Lehrer; Light, B. H. Barry; Special Effects, Esquire Jauchem, Gregory Meeh; Assistant to Director, Jennifer McCray; Wardrobe, Karen Schionning; Props, Gabelle Aarons; Production Assistants, David Margolis Cady, Deborah Gavito; Makeup, Peg Shierholz; Technical Director, Bob Bertrand; Casting, John Lyons; Production Managers, William M. Camp, Rachel Chanoff; Press, Louise Ment
CAST: Michael Gross (Jocko Pyle) succeeded by Peter Evans, Joanne Camp (Skye Bullene), Thomas Ikeda (Winston Legazpi), David Rasche (Eugene Winter), Kurt Knudson (Bart Keely), David Garrison (Milo McGee McGarr). A comedy in three acts. The action takes place during May of the present time in a village 200 miles north of Manila in the Philippines.

Joanne Camp, David Rasche

Puerto Rican Traveling Theatre

Fifteenth Season
Miriam Colon Edgar, Executive Director

NEW YORK CITY PARKS

LOS JIBAROS PROGRESISTAS by Ramon Mendez Quinones; Director, Francisco Prado; Producer, Miriam Colon; Set, Daniel H. Ettinger; Costumes, Efraim Malave; Assistant to Director, Carmen Gutierrez; Music adapted by Gilberto Diaz. CAST: Freddy Valle (Cleto), Marta de la Cruz (Chepa), Miriam Cruz (Juaniya), David Crommett (Anton), Gilberto Diaz, Antonio Mondesire (Neighbors)

PUERTO RICAN TRAVELING THEATRE

January 27–February 21, 1982 (28 performances)
THE MAN AND THE FLY by Jose Ruibal; Translated by Gregory Rabassa; Director, Jack Gelber; Set, Andrew Jackness; Costumes, Nancy Thun; Lighting, John Tissot; Composer, Teiji Ito; Producer, Miriam Colon Edgar in association with the Sanctuary Theatre; Technical Director, Joel Howard; Production Assistant, Roger Kent Brechner; Props, Jon Ringbom; Wardrobe, Susan Kuss; Hairstylist, Eddie Grossman; Stage Manager, Susana Meyer; Press, Max Eisen, Maria Somma. CAST: Rip Torn (The Man in English), Norman Briski (The Man in Spanish), Lazaro Perez (The Double), David Crommett (Angel/Musician), Felipe Gorostiza (Devil/Musician). A drama in two acts. The action takes place at the present time in a cupola in an unidentified country.

March 10–April 4, 1982 (28 performances)
SHE, THAT ONE, HE AND THE OTHER by Jacobo Morales; Translated by Manuel Power Viscasillas; Director, Alba Oms; Set, Christina Weppner; Costumes, Maria Contessa; Lighting, John Tissot; Composer, Cornelia Post; Producer, Miriam Colon Edgar; Technical Director, Paul Klaeysen; Stage Managers, Charles Douglass, Candido Tirado; Press, Max Eisen, Maria Somma. CAST: Liz Torres (She), Shawn Elliott (He). Performed without intermission. The action takes place at the present time in a theatre.

April 21–May 16, 1982 (28 performances)
PAPER FLOWERS by Egon Wolff; Translated by Margaret Peden; Director, Victoria Espinosa; Producer, Miriam Colon Edgar; Set, Gary English; Lighting, John Tissot; Costumes/Stage Manager, Santiago Seijo; Props/Wardrobe, David Tineo; Sound, Billy Harper; Technical Director, Paul Klaeysen.
CAST: Gilda Miros (Eva), Ricardo Matamoros (The Hake). A play in 2 acts and 5 scenes. The action takes place at the present time in New York.

Lazaro Perez, Rip Torn in "The Man and the Fly"
(Peter Krupenye Photo)

Quaigh Theatre

Artistic Director, Will Lieberson; Managing Director, Isabella Schwartz; Adminstrative Director, Peggy Ward; Production Assistant, Dolores Lawrence; Sound, George Jacobs; Press, Max Eisen, Reva Cooper

June 5, 6, 7, 1981
DRAMATHON '81: continuous performances of 54 plays.

September 26–October 17, 1981 (20 performances)
FINAL HOURS by Harold Steinberg; Director, Dennis Rickbee; Set, Geoffrey Hall; Lights, Lisa Grossman; Stage Managers, Lysbeth Hopper, Marnie Cooper. CAST: Allison Brennan (Maggie), Joseph Jamrog (Whitney), Kricker James (Hank). A play in two acts with epilogue. The action takes place "a few years ago."

October 28–November 22, 1981 (20 performances)
NOTES OF AN UNFINISHED SPRING by Louis LaRusso II; Directed by Mr. LaRusso; Set/Stage Manager, Dennis LaRusso; Lighting/Costumes, Maureen Strutton. CAST: Frank Megna (Larry), Joe Pollard (Richie), Joyce Renee Korbin (Gracie), Frank Bongiorno (Nick), Wendy MacDonald (Beauty). A play in two acts. The action takes place in a loft along River Street in Hoboken, N.J.

January 26–February 14, 1982 (20 performances)
VATZLAV by Slawomir Mrozek; Translated by Ralph Manheim; Director, Will Lieberson; Set, Geoffrey Hall; Costumes, Jessica Fasman; Lights, E. St. John Villard; Choreography, Isabella Schwartz, Kelly Schleigh; Music, Ken Ducore; Stage Managers, Adam Phillips, Fred Berg, Polly Humphreys.
CAST: Frank Dwyer (Vatzlav), Richard Spore (Mr. Bat), Gerry Lou (Mrs. Bat), Gary Klar (Bobbie), Dennis Lieberson (Quail), Robert Zukeman (Sassafras), Dickson Shaw (Genius), Rebecca Wells (Justine), Ernst Muller (Oedipus), Ron Berliner (Lackey/Guide), John Febbraro, Stephen Hepperle, Kerry Kollmar (Soldiers), Tony Page (Gen. Barbaro), Isabella Schwartz (Executioner), Dancers: Jill Albert, Kristin Norman, Diane Rodgers, Isabella Schwartz. A play in 2 acts and 77 scenes.

February 19–March 14, 1982 (20 performances)
SOME OF MY BEST FRIENDS ARE/THEIR OWN WORST ENEMIES by Laurence Blackmore; Director, Frank Biancamano; Set, Pip Biancamano; Lights, Paul Bartlett; Stage Managers, Len Stranger, Fred Berg, Mark Hamilton Taylor, Polly Humphreys. CAST: Mila Burnette (Belle Goldman/Madam), Sal Carollo (Eli Cohen/David/General), Terence Cartwright (Dr. Moses Aaron/Adviser/Michael), Understudies: Joyce Renee Korbin, Len Stanger

April 5–May 10, 1982 (29 performances)
LIVINGSTONE AND SECHELE by David Pownall; Director, Will Lieberson; Set, Geoffrey Hall; Costumes, Bob Horek; Lights, Paul Bartlett, Jacquelyn Clymore; Stage Managers, Fred Berg, Kathy LaCommare. CAST: Afema (Sechele), Mike Champagne (Livingstone), Prudence Wright Holmes (Mary), Esther Ryvlin (Mokokon). A drama in 3 acts. The action takes place in the settlement of the Kwena (Crocodile) tribe on the edge of the dried-up Kolobeng River in the Kalahari Desert in Southern Africa, during August of 1848 and on January 1, 1849.

Esther Ryvlin, Mike Champagne, Afemo Omilami in "Livingstone and Sechele"
(Anita Feldman-Shevett Photo)

New York Shakespeare Festival Public Theater

Producer, Joseph Papp; General Manager, Robert Kamlot; Company Manager, Mitzi Harder; Play Department, Gail Merrifield; Literary Manager, Lynn Holst; Casting, Rosemarie Tichler; Production Supervisor, Jason Steven Cohen; Production Manager, Andrew Mihok; Technical Director, Mervyn Haines, Jr.; Props, Joe Toland; Press, Merle Debuskey, Richard Kornberg, Ed Bullins, Dennis Thread, John Howlett, Bruce Sherwood

PUBLIC/OTHER STAGE

Thursday, June 18–July 12, 1981 (29 performances)

HOW IT ALL BEGAN by the cast: Edited by John Palmer; Director, Des McAnuff; Scenery, Heidi Landesman; Costumes, Leslie Calumet; Lighting, Fred Buchholz; Stage Managers, Mo Donley, Eddie Elias; Props, Chris Shriver, Steven Westfield; Wardrobe, Kate Loague; Technical Director, Richard Rose; A Dodger Theater Production

CAST: Benjamin Donenberg, Jessica Drake, Paula Fritz, Brian Hargrove, Mary Lynn Johnson, Val Kilmer, Linda Kozlowski, Liane Langland, Gregory Mortensen, Patrick O'Connell, Kim Staunton, Pamela M. White, Richard Ziman

An adaptation of the autobiography of former West German terrorist Michael "Bommi" Baumann in two parts.

PUBLIC/ANSPACHER THEATER

Thursday, July 16–December 20, 1981 (187 performances)

THE DANCE AND THE RAILROAD

By David Henry Hwang; Direction and Choreography, John Lone; Set, Karen Schulz; Lighting, Victor En Yu Tan; Costumes, Judy Dearing; Props, Randy Tyler; Wardrobe, Russell Duke; Stage Manager, Alice Jankowiak; Music, John Lone; Production Supervisor, Jason Steven Cohen

CAST

Lone...John Lone
Ma..Tzi Ma

A play in five scenes, performed without intermission. The action takes place in June of 1867 on a mountain top near the transcontinental railroad.

PUBLIC/OTHER STAGE

Tuesday, August 4–26, 1981 (13 performances)

THE LAUNDRY HOUR by Mark Linn-Baker, Lewis Black, William Peters, Paul Schierhorn; Director, William Peters; Composer/Musical Director, Paul Schierhorn; Choreography, Eric Elice; Lighting, Gerard P. Bourcier; Props, Carl Sturmer; Wardrobe, Judith Ann Chew; Production Supervisor, Jason Steven Cohen; Stage Manager, Evan Canary

CAST: Mark Linn-Baker, Lewis Black, Paul Schierhorn

PUBLIC/LuESTHER HALL

Tuesday, October 6–11, 1982 (7 performances and 30 previews)

DEXTER CREED by Michael Moriarty; Director, James Milton; Scenery and Lighting, John Gisondi; Costumes, Amanda J. Klein; Music, Michael Moriarty; Musical Arrangements, Louis Forestieri; Production Supervisor, Jason Steven Cohen; Props, Jane Hubbard; Wardrobe, Cathay Brackman; Stage Manager, Fredric H. Orner

CAST: Michael Moriarty (The Interpreter), Linda Kozlowski (Eris), Michael Freeley (Stefan Schweik), Michael Moriarty (Dexter Creed)

Performed without intermission.

PUBLIC/NEWMAN THEATER

Sunday, October 18–December 20, 1981 (87 performances)

FAMILY DEVOTIONS by David Henry Hwang; Director, Robert Allan Ackerman; Scenery, David Gropman; Lighting, Tom Skelton; Costumes, Willa Kim; Original Music, John Lone; Arranged and Performed by Lucia Hwong, Charlie Chin; Production Supervisor, Jason Steven Cohen; Wardrobe, Dawn Johnson; Hairstylist, Ray Iagnocco, Michael Heller; Props, John Masterson, Frances Smith; Assistant to Director, Franco Zavani; Stage Managers, Michael Chambers, Loretta Robertson

CAST: Victor Wong (Di-Gou), Jim Ishida (Wilbur), Jodi Long (Joanne), Lauren Tom (Jenny), Marc Hayashi (Chester), Tina Chen (Ama), June Kim (Popo), Michael Paul Chan (Robert), Helen Funai (Hannah), Understudies: June Angela, Hyung-In Choi, Lilah Kan, Fredric Mao, Keenan Shimizu

A play without intermission. The action takes place at the present time in the sunroom and backyard of a home in Bel Air, California.

PUBLIC/LuESTHER HALL

Sunday, December 13, 1981–February 28, 1982 (49 performances)

SPECIMEN DAYS by Meredith Monk; Direction and Music, Meredith Monk; Choreography, Meredith Monk, Gail Turner; Costumes and Decor, Yoshio Yabara; Lighting, Beverly Emmons; Film, Robert Withers; Production Supervisor, Jason Steven Cohen; Technical Director, Tony Giovanetti; Props, Martin Izquierdo, Chris van Scott; Assistant Director, Gail Turner; Stage Managers, Kayla Evans, Cathy Sonneborn; Sound, Michelle Hout; Wardrobe, Epp Kotkas

CAST: Cristobal Carambo, Robert Een, Ronnie Gilbert, Andrea Goodman, Paul Langland, Steve Lockwood, Meredith Monk, Nicky Paraiso, Margo Lee Sherman, Mary Shultz, Gail Turner, Mieke van Hoek, Pablo Vela

Performed without intermission.

Victor Wong, Tina Chen, June Kim in "Family Devotions" Above: John Lone, Tzi Ma in "The Dance and the Railroad" *(Martha Swope Photos)*

PUBLIC/MARTINSON HALL

Tuesday, December 22, 1981–January 31, 1982 (72 performances)
TWELVE DREAMS by James Lapine; Direction by Mr. Lapine; Scenery, Heidi Landesman; Costumes, William Ivey Long; Lighting, Frances Aronson; Music, Allen Shawn; Movement, Wesley Fata; Production Supervisor, Jason Steven Cohen; Projections, Wendell Harrington, Goran Billingskog; Wardrobe, Cathay Brackman; Hairstylist/Makeup, J. Roy Helland; Props, Jane Hubbard; Assistant to Director, Jeff Epstein; Stage Managers, Ginny Martino, Evan Canary
CAST: James Olson (Charles Hatrick), Olivia Laurel Mates (Emma Hatrick), Marcell Rosenblatt (Jenny), Stefan Schnabel (Professor), Thomas Hulce (Sanford Putnam), Carole Shelley (Dorothy Trowbridge), Valerie Mahaffey (Miss Banton), Stacey Glick (Rinday)
 A play in two acts. The action takes place in a university town in New England during the winter of 1936 and the spring of 1937. The play was inspired by a case study of Carl Jung's as recorded in the book "Man and His Symbols." Although the character of the Professor may suggest Jung, it in no way purports to be an accurate historical representation. All characters and events are fictional.

PUBLIC/OTHER STAGE

Sunday, January 17–February 28, 1982 (43 performances)
ZASTROZZI by George F. Walker; Director, Andrei Serban; Scenery and Costumes, Manuel Lutgenhorst; Lighting, Jennifer Tipton; Combat Staging, Larry Carpenter; Production Supervisor, Jason Steven Cohen; Hairstylist/Makeup, Antonio Belo; Wardrobe, Dawn Johnson, Judy Chew; Props, Ronald Gest; Production Assistant, Christine Sinclair; Director's Assistant, Page Burkholder; Stage Managers, Susan Green, Richard Jakiel
CAST: Andreas Katsulas (Bernardo), Jan Triska (Zastrozzi), Robert Langdon-Lloyd (Victor), Grzegorz Wagrowski (Verezzi), Judith Roberts (Matilda), Frances Conroy (Julia), Understudies: Dan Nutu (Zastrozzi), Christopher McCann (Victor/Verezzi), Lauren Kim (Julia/Matilda), John Capodice (Bernardo)
 A play performed without intermission. The action takes place during the 1890's in Europe, probably Italy.

PUBLIC/NEWMAN THEATER

Tuesday, February 9–March 7, 1982 (45 performances)
LULLABYE AND GOODNIGHT written, composed and directed by Elizabeth Swados; Scenery, David Jenkins; Lighting, Marcia Madeira; Costumes, Hilary Rosenfeld; Choreography, Ara Fitzgerald; Production Supervisor, Jason Steven Cohen; Hairstylists/Makeup, J. Roy Helland, Andrew Reese; Wardrobe, Cathay Brackman; Props, Anthony Papp, Frances Smith; Stage Managers, Jeff Lee, Sherry Cohen
CAST: Frances Asher (Retail), Gail Boggs (Velvet Puppy), Jesse Corti (Deputy), Jossie de Guzman (Lullabye), Ula Hedwig (Stiletto), Bruce Hubbard (Trojan), Larry Marshall (Snow), Olga M. Meredi (Saint), Tim Moore (Cody), Rudy Roberson (Chameleon), Understudies: Vicky Blumenthal, Clifford Lipson
MUSICAL NUMBERS: Prologue, Gentlemen of Leisure, Port Authority, I Am Sick of Love, When a Pimp Meets a Whore, Love Loves the Difficult Things, In the Life, The Moth and the Flame, Why We Do It, Wife Beating Song, You're My Favorite Lullabye, When Any Woman Makes a Running Issue Out of Her Flesh, Now You Are One of the Family, Turn Her Out, You Gave Me Love, Let the Day Perish When I Was Born, Keep Working, Deprogramming Song, Lies Lies Lies, Ladies Look at Yourselves, Don't You Ever Give It All Away, Man That Is Born of Woman, Sub-Babylon, Getting from Day to Day, Sweet Words, The Nightmare Was Me
 "A musical romance" in two acts.

PUBLIC/LuESTHER HALL

Tuesday, March 30–May 23, 1982 (62 performances)
THE HAGGADAH by Elizabeth Swados; Adapted and Directed by Miss Swados; Narration adapted from texts by Élie Wiesel; Lighting, Arden Fingerhut; Scenery/ Costumes/Puppetry/Masks by Julie Taymor; Production Supervisor, Jason Steven Cohen; Piano/Musical Director, Judith Fleisher; Vocal Director, Carolyn Dutton; Wardrobe, Cathay Brackman, Peter White; Hairstylist/Makeup, Andrew Reese; Props, Frances Smith; Stage Managers, Sherry Cohen, William E. Sheppard
CAST: Tichina Arnold, Anthony Asbury, Steven Bland, Rebecca Bondor, Craig Chang, Victor Cook, Jesse Corti, Sheila Dabney, Nina Dova, Ron Eichaker, Aramis Estevez, Sol Frieder, Tom Howe, Bruce Hubbard, Onni Johnson, Sally Kate, Esther Levy, Clifford Lipson, Eileen Malloy, William Marks, Larry Marshall, Olga Merediz, David Schechter, Ira Siff, Martha Wingate
 A Passover Cantata performed without intermission.

Carole Shelley, Olivia Laurel Mates, James Olson in "Twelve Dreams" *(Martha Swope Photo)*

Jan Triska in "Zastrozzi" *(Martha Swope Photo)*

Frances Asher, Ula Hedwig, Larry Marshall, Jossie de Guzman, Gail Boggs, Olga Merediz in "Lullabye and Goodnight" *(Martha Swope Photo)*

PUBLIC/ANSPACHER THEATER

Tuesday, April 6–May 16, 1982 (62 performances)
THREE ACTS OF RECOGNITION by Botho Strauss; Translated by Sophie Wilkins; Director, Richard Foreman; Scenery, Sally Jacobs; Lighting, F. Mitchell Dana; Costumes, Franne Lee; Paintings, Jeanne Hedstrom; Sound, Daniel M. Schreier; Production Supervisor, Jason Steven Cohen; Hairstylist/Makeup, Andrew Reese; Wardrobe, Dawn Johnson; Props, John Masterson; Assistant to Director, Denise Luccioni; Stage Managers, Michael Chambers, Anne King; General Manager, Robert Kamlot
CAST: William Atherton (Richard), Stephen Baccus (Klaus), Wade Barnes (Kiepert), Leonardo Cimino (Martin), James Cromwell (Felix), Carl Don (Guard), Sam Gray (Franz), Richard Jordan (Moritz), Joan MacIntosh (Suzanne), Kate Manheim (Ruth), Frank Maraden (Answald), Kathleen Masterson (Johanna), Christopher McCann (Peter), Ruth Nelson (Vivien), Bill Raymond (Lothar), Cristine Rose (Elfriede), Karen Young (Marlies)
UNDERSTUDIES: Eric Booth (Moritz/Peter/Felix), Norma Fire (Elfriede/Vivien/Suzanne), Patricia Hodges (Johanna/Marlies/Ruth), George Hosmer (Answald/Lothar/Richard), Moultrie Patten (Guard/Franz/Kiepert/Martin), Darrell Stern (Klaus)

A play in three acts. The action takes place in a museum at the opening of an exhibition of "Capitalist Realism."

PUBLIC/NEWMAN THEATER

Tuesday, April 13–May 16, 1982 (59 performances)
GOOSE AND TOMTOM by David Rabe; Director, John Pynchon Holms; Scenery and Costumes, Dean Tschetter; Lighting, Victor En Yu Tan; Production Supervisor, Jason Steven Cohen; Hairstylists, Andrew Reese, Alan J. Perna; Props, John Doyle; Wardrobe, Kim Druce; Stage Managers, John C. Forman, Sally J. Greenhut
CAST: Jerry Mayer (Tomtom), Frederick Neumann (Goose), Gale Garnett (Lorraine), Leslie Busa (Lulu), Will Patton (Bingo), Clarence Felder (The Man), Henchmen: Jesse Doran, Jack R. Marks, Brian Delate, Adam LeFevre, Peter Jolly, Understudies: Brian Delate (Man), Jesse Doran (Goose), Adam LeFevre (Bingo), Jack R. Marks (Tomtom), Ellen Spier (Lorraine/Lulu)

A comedy in two acts.

James Cromwell, William Atherton in "Three Acts of Recognition" *(Martha Swope Photo)*

PUBLIC/MARTINSON HALL

Tuesday, April 27–June 6, 1982 (62 performances)
ANTIGONE by Sophocles; New Translation by John Chioles; Director, Joseph Chaikin; Music, Richard Peaslee; Scenery and Costumes, Sally Jacobs; Lighting, Beverly Emmons; Production Supervisor, Jason Steven Cohen; Wardrobe, Timothy Buckley, Candace Gay Hibbard; Assistant to Director, Kate Lushington; Stage Managers, Ruth Kreshka, Jane Hubbard
CAST: Rosemary Quinn (Ismene), Lisa Banes (Antigone), George Lloyd (Chorus Leader), F. Murray Abraham (Creon), Roger Babb (Guard), Peter Francis-James (Haemon), Priscilla Smith (Teiresias), Jeffrey Bravin (Boy), Raymond Barry (Messenger), Shami Chaikin (Euridice), Chorus: B. Constance Barry, Hunt Cole, Ann Dunnigan, Richard Frisch, Ronnie Gilbert, Clark Morgan, Understudies: Raymond Barry (Creon), Sylvia Gassell (Chorus/Euridice), Annette Helde (Antigone), Hal Lehrman, Jr. (Messenger/Guard/Haemon), Virginia Ness (Ismene/Teiresias), Paul Richards (Chorus)

Performed without intermission.

PUBLIC/OTHER STAGE

Wednesday, May 12–23, 1982 (29 performances)
RED AND BLUE by Michael Hurson; Director, JoAnne Akalaitis; Scenery and Lighting, John Arnone; Sound, L. B. Dallas; Projections, Stephanie Rudolph; Production Consultant, B-St. John Schofield; Production Supervisor, Jason Steven Cohen; "Le Chemin de la Croix" by Marcel Dupre; Organist, Wolfram Gehring
CAST: Randy Danson (Blue), Earl Hindman (Red), James Hurdle (Voice)

Lisa Banes as Antigone *(Martha Swope Photo)*

Roundabout Theatre

ROUNDABOUT STAGE ONE

Tuesday, June 23–December 5, 1981 (185 performances)

MISALLIANCE

By George Bernard Shaw; Director, Stephen Porter; Set, Roger Mooney; Costumes, Jane Greenwood; Lighting, Ronald Wallace; Original Score, Philip Campanella; Stage Manager, Martha R. Jacobs.

CAST

John Tarleton, Jr	Rand Bridges	John Tarleton	Philip Bosco
Bentley Summerhays	Keith McDermott	Joseph Percival	Peter Coffield†2
Hypatia Tarleton	Jeanne Ruskin	Lina Szczepanowska	Patricia Elliott
Mrs. Tarleton	Patricia O'Connell	Gunner	Anthony Heald
Lord Summerhays	Fred Stuthman†1		

A comedy in two acts. The action takes place in John Tarleton's house in Hindhead, Surrey, on May 31, 1909.

† Succeeded by: 1. Ronald Drake, 2. Nigel Reed

ROUNDABOUT STAGE TWO

Tuesday, September 22, 1981–March 14, 1982 (197 performances)
PLAYING WITH FIRE by August Strindberg; Translated by Michael Meyer; Director, Gene Feist; Scenery, Roger Mooney; Costumes, A. Christina Giannini; Sound, Philip Campanella; Lighting, Marshall Spiller; Hairstylist, Charles Elsen; Stage Manager, Michael S. Mantel
CAST: Geoffrey Pierson (The Son), Giulia Pagano succeeded by Janet Zarish (The Daughter-in-law), Elizabeth Owens (The Mother), Dillon Evans (The Father), Janet Zarish (The Cousin), John Michalski (The Friend). Performed without an intermission. The action takes place in a seaside resort in Sweden on a summer morning towards the end of the last century. This play was dropped from the program on Feb. 7, 1982 after 70 performances.
MISS JULIE by August Strindberg; Translated by Michael Meyer; Director, Gene Feist
CAST: Alma Cuervo succeeded by Priscilla Smith (Christine, the cook), Stephen Schnetzer (Jean, the valet), Giulia Pagano succeeded by Janet Zarish (Miss Julie), Country Folk: Dillon Evans, Janet Zarish, Elizabeth Owens, John Michalski, Mickey Bessoir
The action takes place in the Count's kitchen on a midsummer night at the end of the last century. Performed without intermission.

ROUNDABOUT STAGE ONE

Tuesday, December 15–27, 1981 (16 performances)
A KURT WEILL CABARET: His Broadway and Berlin Songs. Performed by Martha Schlamme and Alvin Epstein with Steven Blier at the piano.
PROGRAM: Moritat, Barbara Song, Alabama Song, Herr Jakob Schmidt, Ballad of Sexual Slavery, Ballad of the Pimp and the Whore, Pirate Jenny, Kanonensong, Soldatenweib, Eating, That's Him, September Song, The Saga of Jenny, Bilboa Song, Sailor's Tango, Surabaya Johnny, The Life That We Lead

Tuesday, December 29, 1981–January 3, 1982 (8 performances)
MARTHA SCHLAMME: A Cabaret-Concert with either Steven Blier or Richard Bower at the piano. Performed with one intermission.

Tuesday, January 5–20, 1982 (19 performances)
DEAR LIAR by Jerome Kilty; Adapted from the correspondence of George Bernard Shaw and Mrs. Patrick Campbell; Directed by Mr. Kilty; Costumes, Deborah Dryden; Music, Sol Kaplan; Stage Manager, Howard Kolins.
CAST: Jerome Kilty (George Bernard Shaw), Katherine McGrath (Mrs. Patrick Campbell) Performed with one intermission. The action covers the years from 1899 to 1938.

Wednesday, February 24–March 21, 1982 (30 performances and 39 previews)
THE CARETAKER by Harold Pinter; Director, Anthony Page; Set, Roger Mooney; Lighting, Ronald Wallace; Costumes, A. Christina Giannini; Sound, Philip Campanella; Staged Fights, Fred Collins; Props, Mary O'Leary; Dialect Coach, Elizabeth Smith; Stage Manager, M. R. Jacobs CAST: Daniel Gerroll (Mick), Anthony Heald (Aston), F. Murray Abraham (Davies)
A drama in 3 acts and 8 scenes. The action takes place in a house in West London at the present time.

Daniel Gerroll, F. Murray Abraham, Anthony Heald in "The Caretaker"
Above: Patricia Elliott, Philip Bosco in "Misalliance"
(Martha Swope Photos)

THE TWELVE-POUND LOOK

By J. M. Barrie; Director, Stephen Porter; Setting, Roger Mooney; Costumes, Sarah G. Conly; Lighting, Walter Uhrman; Sound, Philip Campanella; Wigs/Hairstylist, Paul Huntley; Stage Manager, Michael S. Mantel

CAST

Sir Harry Sims	Lee Richardson	Kate	Sheila Allen
Lady Sims	Joyce Fideor	Tombes, a butler	James Higgins

The action takes place in the home of Sir Harry Sims in Mayfair, on a March afternoon in 1911.

with

THE BROWNING VERSION

by Terrence Rattigan

John Taplow	Bruce Wall	Dr. Frobisher	James Higgins
Frank Hunter	Edmond Genest	Peter Gilbert	Josh Clark
Millie Crocker-Harris	Sheila Allen	Mrs. Gilbert	Joyce Fideor
Andrew Crocker-Harris	Lee Richardson		

The action takes place in the sitting room of the Crocker-Harris's flat at a public school in the South of England on a day in July of 1947.

Bruce Wall, Lee Richardson, Edmond Genest, Sheila Allen in "The Browning Version" Right: Irene Worth, Constance Cummings (seated) in "The Chalk Garden"

THE CHALK GARDEN

By Enid Bagnold; Director, John Stix; Set, Roger Mooney; Lighting, Martin Aronstein; Costumes, Judith Dolan; Sound, Philip Campanella; Wigs/Hairstylist, Paul Huntley; Assistant to Director, Paul Booth; Stage Manager, M. R. Jacobs

CAST

Miss Madrigal	Irene Worth	Mrs. St. Maugham	Constance Cummings
Maitland	Donal Donnelly	Nurse	Eunice Anderson
Second Applicant	Eunice Anderson	Olivia	Elizabeth Owens
Laurel	Sallyanne Tackus	Judge	I. M. Hobson
Third Applicant	Betty Low	Standby	Betty Low

A play in three acts. The action takes place in a room in a manor house in Sussex, England in 1954.

St. Regis-Sheraton/King Cole Room

Executive Producer, Jerry Kravat; Producer, Harve Brosten; Musical Director, Grant Sturiale; Creative Consultant/Writer, Barry Harman; Lighting, Helen Anne Gatling; Press, Henry Luhrman Associates

June 1–September 12, 1981
THE SOUNDS OF RODGERS & HAMMERSTEIN PART II directed by Charles Repole; Assistant Musical Director, Wayne Abravanel; Stage Manager, Ed Oster; CAST: Susan Bigelow, Ron Holgate (succeeded by Kenneth Kantor), Martin Vidnovic, Laura Waterbury

September 14–January 16, 1982
THEY SAY IT'S WONDERFUL: A Salute to Irving Berlin; Directed and Staged by Billy Wilson; Musical Arrangements, Grant Sturiale, Billy Wilson; Fashions, Mary McFadden for Jack Mulqueen; Stage Manager, Ed Oster. CAST: Terry Burrell, Larry Kert (succeeded by Walter Willison), Andrea McArdle, Debbie Shapiro

January 18–April 3, 1982
CAN'T HELP SINGING: A Salute to Jerome Kern; Directed and Staged by Michael Lichtefeld; Musical Director, Keith Herrmann; Assistant to Director, Christina Stolberg; Stage Manager, Ed Oster. CAST: Judy Kaye, Armelia McQueen (succeeded by Terry Burrell), Ken Page (succeeded by Ira Hawkins), Cris Groenendaal (succeeded by Patrick Quinn)

April 5–June 26, 1982.
MORE OF LOESSER: Frank Loesser Revued; Conceived by Barry Harman, Grant Sturiale, Michael Lichtefeld; Directed and Staged, Michael Lichtefeld; Assistant Musical Director, Sand Lawn; Fashions, John Yang for Jack Mulqueen; Stage Manager, Ed Oster. CAST: Robert Morse, Lynne Thigpen, Liz Callaway, Regina O'Malley

Armelia McQueen, Ken Page, Judy Kaye in "Can't Help Singing"

Lisa Banes, Elizabeth McGovern in "My Sister in This House"
(Stephanie Saia Photo)

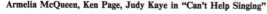

The Second Stage

Third Season
Artistic Directors, Robyn Goodman, Carole Rothman; Associate Director, Drew Farber; Press, Richard Kornberg

Thursday, November 5, 1981–January 3, 1982 (57 performances)
MY SISTER IN THIS HOUSE by Wendy Kesselman; Directors, Inverna Lockpez, Carole Rothman; Set, Jim Clayburgh; Lighting, Arden Fingerhut; Costumes, Susan Hilferty; Sound, Gary Harris; Hairstylist, Antonio Soddu; Production Supervisor, Kim Novick; Casting, Meg Simon/Fran Kumin; Stage Managers, Fredric H. Horner, Judith Ann Chew, Ami Rothschild; Props, Laura Toffler; Wardrobe, Jill Jones; Technical Director, Louis Berman
CAST: Lisa Banes (Christine), Elizabeth McGovern (Lea), Beverly May (Madam Danzard), Brenda Currin (Isabele)
A drama performed without intermission. The action takes place in LeMans, France during the early 1930's. It is based on an historical incident which occurred in Le Mans in 1933.

Sunday, January 31–February 14, 1982 (20 performances)
FLUX by Susan Miller; Director, Michael Kahn; Set and Costumes, Ernest Allen Smith; Lighting, William Armstrong; Sound, Gary Harris; Production Supervisor, Kim Novick; Casting, Meg Simon/-Fran Kumin; Technical Director, Louis Berman; Production Assistant, Michael Simon; Wardrobe, Cindy Flowers; Props, Robin Croteau; Stage Managers, Larry Spiegel, D. King Roger
CAST: Robyn Goodman (Jess), Michael Tucker (Sanelli), Jean DeBaer (Dina), Daryl Edwards (Bobby), Clare Timoney (Karen), Sam Robards (Saul), Kevin Bacon (Michael)
A comedy performed without intermission.

Sunday, April 11–21, 1982 (23 performances)
PASTORALE by Deborah Eisenberg; Director, Carole Rothman; Set, Heidi Landesman; Lighting, Frances Aronson; Costumes, Nan Cibula; Sound, Gary Harris; Production Supervisor, Kim Novick; Technical Director, Louis Berman; Casting, Simon and Kumin, Barbara Sacharow; Wardrobe, Rita Robbins; Stage Managers, James McConnell-Clark, Jr., Rebecca Pease, Robin Croteau
CAST: Judith Ivey (Melanie), Christine Estabrook (Rachel), Thomas Waites (Steve), Howard Renensland (Man), Elizabeth Austin (Edie), Jeffrey Fahey (John), Taylor Miller (Celia), Rebecca Pease (Woman), Coloradans: David B. Hunt, Bjorn Johnson, Paul Loughlin
A comedy performed without intermission.

Sunday, May 16–30, 1982 (20 performances and 4 previews)
THE WOODS by David Mamet; Directed by Mr. Mamet; Set, Marjorie Bradley Kellogg; Lighting, Pat Collins; Costumes, Clifford Capone; Fight Sequence, B. H. Barry; Production Supervisor, Kim Novick; Casting, Meg Simon/Fran Kumin; Assistant Director, Betsy Carpenter; Technical Director, Robert W. Mogel; Wardrobe, Rita Robbins; Stage Managers, Daniel Morris, Kate Hancock
CAST: Patti LuPone (Ruth), Peter Weller (Nick)
A drama in two acts and three scenes. The action takes place in early September on the porch of a summer house.

Soho Repertory Theatre

Seventh Season

Artistic Directors, Jerry Engelbach, Marlene Swartz; Technical Director, Lawrence P. Gorrell; Director, Carol Tanzman; Dramaturge, Victor Gluck; Stage Managers, Brian Chavanne, Deborah Friedman

November 12–December 20, 1981 (31 performances)
DARK RIDE written and directed by Len Jenkin; Set, John Arnone; Projections, Gerald Marks; Lighting, Bruce Porter; Costumes, David C. Woolard; Sound, Kathleen King; Stage Manager, Joanne McEntire; A Pequod Production. CAST: David Brisbin (Translator), Melissa Hurst (Margot), Bill Sadler (Jeweler), Will Patton (Thief), Betsy LaRoe (Waitress), Eric Loeb (General), Walter Hadler (Ed), Saun Ellis (Edna), Joanne Akalaitis (Mrs. Lammle), John Nesci (Zendavesta)

February 4–28, 1982 (20 performances)
NATHAN THE WISE by Gotthold Ephraim Lessing; Translation, Bayard Quincy Morgan; Director, Jerry Engelbach; Costumes, Steven L. Birnbaum; Set, Duke Durfee; Lighting, Rick Gray; Props, Leslie Johnson. CAST: Stan Lachow (Nathan), Nan Wilson (Daya), Karen Jones (Rachel), Pat Freni (Al), Grover Zucker (Templar), Time Winters (Brother Bonafides), John Genke (Sultan Saladin), Megan McCombs (Sittah), Pat Freni (Patriarch), Kai Ephron, Orlando Romero (Servants)

March 11–April 4, 1982 (20 performances)
SUBJECT TO FITS by Robert Montgomery; Music and Songs, Mr. Montgomery; Director, Barry Koron; Costumes, Mary L. Hayes; Set, Barry Axtell; Lighting, Susan A. White; Musical Director, Catherine Reid; Projections, William T. Ericsson; Assistant Director, Stephanie Silverman; Fight Director, Randy Kovitz. CAST: Victor Talmadge (Myshkin), Mitchell Carrey (Rogazhin), Robert Schlee (Lebedev), Diane Armistead (Mme. Yepanchin) succeeded by Laurie Franks, Alison Bevan (Aglaya), Scott Sparks (Ganya), Nicholas Saunders (Gen. Ivoglin), Jim Dachik (Ippolit), Jana Schneider (Natasha)

April 16–May 2, 1982 (12 performances)
THE GIRL WHO ATE CHICKEN BONES by Stan Kaplan; Music, David Hollister; Lyrics, Kaplan/Hollister; Director, Marlene Swartz; Musical Staging/Assistant Director, Joseph Holloway; Musical Director, John McMahon; Set/Costumes, Steven L. Birnbaum; Lighting, Mary Jo Dondlinger; Sound, Kathleen King. CAST: Jody Hiatt (Madeleine), Steve Sterner (Minstrel), Terry Kirwin (Little Prince), Lloyd David Hart (Big Prince), Marlea Evans (Queen), Roy Steinberg (Insurance Agent), Mary Eileen O'Donnell (Voice), James Mallory (Drayman), Elizabeth Bayer, Ryn Hodes (Persimmons)

May 7–23, 1982 (12 performances)
THREE AMERICAN ONE-ACT OPERAS presented by Soho Rep and Golden Fleece. **THE AUDIENCE** with music by Royce Dembo; Libretto, Glenn Miller; Director, Scott Clugstone. CAST: Lucy Sorlucco or Kathleen Silloway (Martha), David Nash Denham or Bob Riker (Raymond), David Saybrook or Mark Baur-Peters (Maestro). **MR. LION** with music and libretto by Linder Charlson; Director, Lou Rodgers. CAST: Kathleen Silloway or Barbara Norcia (Mom), David Nash Denham or Bob Riker (Dad), Mark Baur-Peters or David Saybrook (Adult Laddie), Lucy Sorlucco or Linda Denham (Young Laddie or Girl)

MIYAKO with music, libretto and direction by Lou Rodgers; Musical Director, John Klingberg; Set/Costumes, Fred Marchese; Lighting, David M. Shepherd; Stage Managers, Thomas Farrington, Catherine Dickerson. CAST: Del Green (Lady Izumi), Bob Riker/Michael Schilke (Akira), Mark Baur-Peters/David Saybrook (High Priest), Andrea Goodzeit/Lucy Sorlucco (Akai Oni), Michael Schilke/Ricki G. Ravitts (Midori Oni), Linda Denham/Andrea Goodzeit (Fumi), Barbara Norcia (Innkeeper), David Saybrook/Mark Baur-Peters (Gambler/Pusher), Kathleen Silloway (Geisha/Addict)

June 3–27, 1982 (20 performances)
BARBARIANS by Barrie Keeffe; Director, Peter Byrne; Set, Tarrant Smith; Costumes, Steven L. Birnbaum; Lighting, David N. Weiss; Assistant Director, Nina Stachenfeld; Stage Manager, Brian Chavanne. A trilogy composed of KILLING TIME, ABIDE WITH ME, IN THE CITY.
CAST: Greg Martyn (Jan), Kevin Spacey (Paul), Michael Wright (Louis)

Nan Wilson, Stan Lachow, Karen Jones in "Nathan the Wise"

Gregory Cooke, Laura Solow, Marshall Nalle in "The Overcoat"

Ten Ten Players

Second Season
Producing Directors, Gary F. Martin, Courtney Tucker; Managing Director, Philip Wentworth

February 19–March 7, 1982 (10 performances)
THE OVERCOAT by Nicolai Gogol; English Adaptation, Tom Lantner, Frank S. Torok; Director, Mathew Bulluck; Costumes, Kat Stroebel; Choreography, Dierdre Towers; Lighting/Technical Director, Dennis Drab; Sound, J. Bilbert Kaufman. CAST: John Baird (Gogol), Tom Aulino (Akaky), Laura Solow (Anna/Maria), Gregory Cooke (Ivan), Marshall Nalle (Arina), Peggy Bayer (Nena Yegorovna), J. Gilbert Kaufman (Stefan), Kim Ivan Motter (Sasha)

March 18–April 4, 1982 (12 performances)
BELL, BOOK AND CANDLE by John Van Druten; Director, Gary F. Martin; Set/Lighting, Dennis Drab; Costumes, Sharon DeRosa; Sound, J. Gilbert Kaufman; Stage Manager, Liz Thackston. CAST: Anne Newhall (Gillian), Tony Blake (Shepherd), Enid Blaymore (Miss Holroyd), Mike Rogers (Nicky), Jerry Beal (Sidney)

April 16–25, 1982 (6 performances)
SHEDDERS by Albert Obuchowski; Director, Frank Petrilli; Lighting, Dennis Drab; Costumes, Melissa Nichols-Meyers; Sound, Richard Valenzon, J. Gilbert Kaufman; Props, Debrah Heilig; Stage Manager, Ramona Spinelli. CAST: Betty Pia (Nora), Phoebe Burston (Elizabeth), Melissa Nichols-Meyers (Rebecca), Beth See (Amy), Barbara Halas (Orange), Laurance Greeley (Anvil), Michael Evan Davis (Mert), Frank Delia (Junior), Arnie Kelman (Page), Robert Nutt (Preacher), Charles Iorio (Asa), John A. Hamilton (Lester), Lucille Corri, J. Gilbert Kaufman (Tourists), Howard Fenn (Chris), Ed King (Kilton)

Theater for the New City

Twelfth Season

Artistic Directors, George Bartenieff, Crystal Field; Administrative Assistant, Linda Chapman; Development, Harvey Seifter; General Manager, Steven Miller

June 18–July 5, 1981 (12 performances)
DWELLING IN MILK and **CHAPEL ST. LIGHT** by Barry Marshall; Special Music, Linda Smukler; Two one-act plays with Michael Balcanof, George Gerdes, Chris McCann, Deirdre O'Connell, Susan Telcher, Judson Camp, Steven Lysohir, Brian McEleney, Steven Pace

August 8–September 20, 1981 (12 performances)
THE RESTAURANT OR YOUR GOOSE IS COOKED by Crystal Field, George Bartenieff and the company; Director, Miss Field; Music, Mark Hardwick; Set, Anthony Angel, Dolly Holmes, Seth Price; Masks/Props., Pamela Badyk, Joni Wong; Musical Director, Rob Felstein; Stage Managers, Steven Miller, Marshal Williams, Raphael Risemberg. CAST: Amber, Bruce Altman, Douglas Anderson, Alexander Bartenieff, Harlan Bebell, George Billeci, Martha Bowers, Luis Betancourt, Georgette Connell, Joseph C. Davies, John Detommaso, Christine Dubensky, Crystal Field, Lana Forrester, Greg Holtz, Fracaswell Hyman, Stephen Landsman, Arthur Lundquist, Margaret Miller, Vince Monzo, Sandra Nieves, Michael Ortiz, John Anderson Parker, Robert Rosario, Tracy Sherman, Laure Solet, Ray Stough, Melissa Thies

August 20–30, 1981 (8 performances)
RAGGED DICK by Paul Foster; Director, Lester Malizia; Choreography, Susan Rasmusson; Music Director, Kevin Wakefield Cristy. CAST: Robert Alan Morrow, Timothy Mathias, Anthony B. Asbury, Paul Malec, Joseph C. Davies, Cocoa, Linda Andrea Johnson, Jay Duchan, Auston Jetton, John Bertelsen, Todd Lewey, Stephe Rechner, Randy Long. A "midsummer revusical" in 2 acts.

October 1–18, 1981 (8 performances)
MY HEART IS IN YOUR SHOES written and directed by Yuri Belov; performed by The Clown Conspiracy: Yury Belov, Jan Greenfield, Joe Killian, John Grimaldi, Fred Yockers, Tanya Sadofyeva

October 22–November 8, 1981 (8 performances)
BLACK AND BLUES by Reinaldo Povod; Director, Patricia Contaxis; Set/Lights, Joni Wong; Costumes, Edmond Felix; Stage Manager, Manny Cavaco. CAST: Maria Pessino, Eric Kohner, Paul Ben-Victor, Drunell Gross.

November 5–22, 1981 (12 performances)
SELMA by Shami Chaikin; Director, Karen Ludwig; Set, Sally Jacobs; Music, Gorilla, My Love; Costumes, Mary Brecht; Lights, Beverly Emmons; Stage Manager, Kate Mennone. CAST: Suzanne Costallos, Jon Huberth, Harvey Perr, Gordana Rashovich, Alice Spivak

November 26–December 13, 1981 (12 performances)
RENT by Walter Corwin; Director, Carol Ilson; Set, Tracy Sherman; Costumes, Jill Anderson; Stage Manager, Kaethe Cherney. CAST: Julie Ariola, Robert Frink, Barry Einstein, Ray Iannicelli, Norman Kruger, Kaethe Cherney, Louise Hochberg, Steve Pezenik

December 24, 1981–January 10, 1982 (12 performacnes)
ZEKS by Maria A. Rasa: Director, Jonas Jurasas; Set/Costumes, Alex Okun; Composer, Alex Peskunov; Translation, A. Byla. CAST: Jeffrey Bingham, Robert Harper, Dane Knell, Timothy Lonsdale, Robert Lovitz, Karl Perry, Nicholas Saunders, Bill Smitrovich, Roy Steinberg, Susan Stevens, J. D. Swain, Michael Thompson, Martin Treat

December 24, 1981–January 10, 1982 (12 performances)
A VISIT by Maria Irene Fornes; Director, Ms. Fornes; Set/Lights, Donald Estman; Costumes, Gabriel Berry; Music, George Quincy; Musical Director, Mary L. Rodgers; Stage Managers, Steven Miller, Esteban Fernandez. CAST: Penelope Bodry, Joseph C. Davies, Richard DeDomenico, Candace Derra, Mary Beth Lerner, Eduardo Machado, Chris Tanner, Florence Tarlow

February 4–21, 1982 (12 performances)
LADY OF THE CASTLE with music and lyrics by Mira J. Spektor; Director/Book Adaptation, Andrea F. Balis; Based on play by Lea Goldberg; Musical Direction, Harry Fuchs; Set, Larry Steckman; Stage Manager, Debra Miller. CAST: Paul Ukena, John Sheets, Susan Phillips, Karen Merchant

February 25–March 14, 1982 (12 performances)
THE TENANT by Marshall Williams; Director, Anthony Major; Costumes, John Lakesmith; Lights, Tim Phillips. CAST: Myra Anderson, Leon Summers, Jr.

February 25–March 21, 1982 (16 performances)
THE BLONDE LEADING THE BLONDE by Stephen Holt; Director, John Albano; Set, Bobjack Callejo; Lights, Richard Currie; Stage Managers, Kate Mennone, Avishy Greenfield. CAST: Frederikke Meister, Alex Mustelier, Reety Holt, Stephen Holt, Lola Pashalinski, Crystal Field, Meryl Vladimer, Joel Marks, Florence Tarlow, Margaret Miller, Terry Nixon, Dayna Lee, Alexander Bartenieff, Frank Dudley, Lynn Oliver, Marilyn Roberts, Helen Hanft

April 1, 1982–
LETTERS TO BEN by Charles Choset; Director, Lisa Simon; Choreography, Sharon Kinney; Set/Lights, Joe Ray; Costumes, Don Sheffield; Musical Directors, Curtis Blaine, Russell Daisey; Stage Managers, Ana F. Pettit, Bill Livingston, Steven Miller. CAST: Carol Harris, Jamie Beth Nathan, Diane Irwin, Bebe Landis, Kenneth Cortland, John Gallogly, Michael Conant, Perry Stephens, Adrienne Doucette, Allen Hidalgo, Philip McKinley, Donna Trinkoff

April 1–18, 1982 (12 performances)
THE CROCK OF GOLD adapted and directed by Rina Elisha from the novel by James Stephens; Set, Douglas Player; Costumes, Lisa Keim; Lighting, Lisa Grossman; Choreography, James Sutton; Stage Manager, Carroll Cartwright III. CAST: Richard Spore, James Anthony, Charlotte Booker, Christina Swing, Margaret Meany, Omri Elisha, Ron Litman, Carolyn Murray, Maura Ellyn, Ralph Pezzullo, Godfrey Deeny, Whip Hubley, Barry Theiler

April 22–May 9, 1982 (12 performances)
RESTING PLACE by Donald Magulies; Director, Steven Reisner; Set, Lise Engel; Costumes, Brenda Colling; Lights, Rick Rogers; Stage Manager, Craig Brodie. CAST: Arthur French, Mady Kaplan, Tony Shultz

April 29–May 23, 1982 (20 performances)
THE DISPOSSESSED by Leonard Melfi; Director, Crystal Field; Set, Ron Kajiwara; Lights, Joanna Schielke; Costumes, Edmond Felix; Musical Director, Robert Felstein; Assistant Director, Esteban Fernandez; Stage Managers, Steven Miller, Paul Allman. CAST: Crystal Field, George Bartenieff, Alexander Bartenieff, Vira Colorado, Alexis Mylonas, Mary Adams, Leonard Melfi, Fred Engel, Kenneth Laron Johnson, Robert Rosario, H. S. Thies

April 29–May 23, 1982 (16 performances)
WHO DO YOU WANT, PIÈRE VIDAL? by Rochelle Owens; Director, Ernest Abuba; Composer, Kuni Mikami; Set, Mike Sullivan; Lights, Chaim Gitter, Edward R. F. Matthews; Stage Managers, Nikki Carlino, Arlene Roseman. CAST: Valerie Charles, Ron Nakahara

May 13–30, 1982 (12 performances)
CRAZY AS ZALOOM a one-man show by Paul Zaloom.

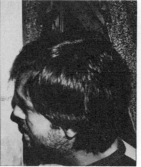

Steven Lysohir, Judson Camp, Steven Pace in "Chapel St. Light"
(Karel Steiner Photo)

Leonard Melfi, George Bartenieff, Crystal Field in
"The Dispossessed"

Theatre Off Park

Patricia Flynn Peate, Producing Director
Joanna Ward, Production Manager

February 3–27, 1982 (12 performances)
VONETTA SWEETWATER CARRIES ON . . . by Johnny Brandon; Director/Choreographer, Otis Sallid; Musical Direction/Vocal and Dance Arrangements, Thom Bridwell; Set, Bob Provenza; Costumes, Ellen Lee; Lighting, Stephen Shereff; Orchestrations, Zane Mark; Stage Manager, Carolyn Greer. Press, Keith Sherman; CAST: Catherine Campbell, Jim Cyrus, Adele Foster, Shelton Ray, Lynne Bell

March 26–April 10, 1982 (12 performances)
THE WIND THAT SHOOK THE BARLEY by Declan Burke-Kennedy; Director, Jamie Brown; Set, Gordon A. Juel; Costumes, Mary Hayes; Lighting, Daniel J. Farley; Stage Manager, Malcolm Ewen; Press, Keith Sherman. CAST: Jarlath Conroy, Denis O'Neill, Kathleen Roland, Mary Tierney

Catherine Campbell, Jim Cyrus, Lynne Bell in "Venetta Sweetwater Carries On"

Trinity Theatre

Fourth Season
Artistic Director, Wendy Kaufman; General Manager, Penelope Morgan; Casting, Susan Cella; Press, Fred Hoot, Ken Munzing

October 29–November 21, 1981 (13 performances)
CHILDREN OF DARKNESS by Edwin Justice Mayer; Director, Worth Howe; Set, Joe Mobilia; Lighting, Murphy Roberts; Costumes, Nancy Neilson; Stage Manager, Virginia Jones. CAST: Edward Conery, Ralph Gunderman, Gael Hammer, Alan Hemingway, Sean Hopkins, David Montee, Lloyd Pace, Bernie Tato, Nancy Trumbo

May 13–29, 1982 (12 performances)
SUFFRAGETTE! a musical with book by Josh Rubins, Andrew Cadiff, George Birnbaum; Music and Lyrics, Josh Rubins; Musical Director, Mary L. Rodgers; Choreographer, Lisa Brailoff; Set, Joe Mobilia; Lights, Alan P. Symonds; Costumes, Thomas McKinley; Production Supervisor, Clayton Phillips; Stage Managers, Floyd Meurrier, Jay C. Theriault; Production Coordinator, Dale Kaufman; Technical Director, Richard R. Jones. CAST: Alice Cannon, Kathleen Conry, Kimberly Farr, Mary Jane Hoffman, Rebecca Hoodwin, Jane Milne, Paula Parker, Chrisse Roccaro, Jennifer Smith, Jane Smulyan, Cynthia Sophiea, Dan Strickler

Right: Jane Milne, Alice Cannon, Kimberly Farr in "Suffragette"

Union Square Theatre

Sixth Season
July 1, 1981–June 30, 1982
Founder/Artistic Director, Evadne Giannini; Producing Director, Lee Pucklis; Associate to Directors, William E. Mack; Sets and Costumes, A. Christina Giannini; Lighting, Robert F. Strohmeier; Sound, Bruce Goldstein

THE LESSON by Eugene Ionesco; Director, Evadne Giannini; Sculpture, Francis Hines; Stage Manager, Duane Fletcher. CAST: Carol Stevenson, Rachel Ticotin, Don Perkins
HITTING TOWN by Stephen Poliakoff; Director, Evadne Giannini; Stage Manager, Duane Fletcher.
CAST: Gail Pepper, Gary McCleery, Victoria Bradbury
THE SCARECROW by Percy MacKaye; Artistic Co-Directors, Evadne Giannini, William E. Mack; Director, Brad Williams; Set, Rob Hamilton; Lighting, Frederick Buchholz; Puppets/Masks, Brad Williams; Music, Ray Leslee; Stage Manager, Ana F. Pettit. CAST: Fran Salisbury, Jay Raphael, Ken Natter, Judith Bliss, John Basil Giletto, Tom O'Leary, Lynn Hippen, Dan Johnson, Nancy Siegworth, Lowell Marin, Sterling Swann, Timothy Jenkins
THE CLOWNMAKER by Richard Crane. See Off-Broadway Calendar.

Sterling Swann, Judith Bliss, Timothy Jenkins and puppets in "The Scarecrow"

WPA Theatre

Kyle Renick, Producing Director   Fifth Season

Artistic Director, Howard Ashman; Resident Designer, Edward T. Gianfrancesco; Lighting, Craig Evans; General Manager, Michael Kartzmer; Casting, Darlene Kaplan; Technical Directors, Terry Ariano, Peter Brassard; Production Manager, Paul Mills Holmes; Administrative Assistant, Karen Gellman; Press, Fred Hoot, Ken Munzing

Thursday, October 15–November 8, 1981 (23 performances)
BIG APPLE MESSENGER by Shannon Keith Kelley; Director, Stephen Zuckerman; Set, Edward T. Gianfrancesco; Lighting, Phil Monat; Costumes, Mimi Maxmen; Production Assistant, Rick Soule; Stage Managers, Paul Mills Holmes, Betsy Nicholson
CAST: Merwin Goldsmith (Morty), Mark Soper (Fetch), Joseph Warren (Hooter), Michael Huddleston (Mitchell), Ken Costigan (Arlen), Gregory T. Daniel (Reginald), Kim Sullivan (Lydell), Rod Houts (Abramowitz), Emil Belasco (Enriquez), Edward Gallardo (Arturo), Dave Florek (Ben), Richard Zobel (Roland), Eddie Jones (Hal), Terrance Terry Ellis (Jerry)
A play in 2 acts and 5 scenes. The action takes place at the present time in the Big Apple Messenger Service office.

Tuesday, December 1–20, 1981 (20 performances)
GHOSTS OF THE LOYAL OAKS by Larry Ketron; Director, Amy Saltz; Setting, Edward T. Gianfrancesco; Lighting, Craig Evans; Costumes, Judy Dearing; Stage Manager, Paul Mills Holmes
CAST: Mary Elaine Monti (Esta), Loudon Wainwright III (Wylan), William Russ (Cooper), John Goodman (Davis), Linda Cook (Roxy)
A drama in two acts. The action takes place outside a town near the Tennessee-North Carolina border.

Tuesday, February 2–21, 1982 (20 performances)
THE WHALES OF AUGUST by David Berry; Director, William Ludel; Set, Edward T. Gianfrancesco; Costumes, David Murin; Lighting, Phil Monat; Wigs, Charles LoPresto; Production Assistants, Beth Kushnick, Tom Rutherford; Stage Managers, Paul Mills Holmes, Sarah Whitham
CAST: Bettie Endrizzi (Sarah Louise Logan Webber), Elizabeth Council (Elizabeth Mae Logan Strong), Vivienne Shub (Letitia Benson Doughty), Daniel Keyes (Joshua Brackett), George Lloyd (Nicholas Maranov)
A play in two acts. The action takes place during August of 1954 on an island off the coast of Maine.

Thursday, March 11–April 4, 1982 (28 performances)
WHAT WOULD JEANNE MOREAU DO? by Elinor Jones; Director, Stuart White; Setting, Terry Arlano; Lighting, Craig Evans; Costumes, Anne Watson; Props. Beth Anne Kushnick; Technical Director, Peter Brassard; Stage Manager, Paul Mills Holmes
CAST: Burke Pearson (Jerry Jennings), Lynn Milgrim (Cathy Bridges), James Hilbrandt (Carlos), Joaquim DeAlmeida (Mirko Knezevitch)
A play in two acts. The action takes place at the present time in New York City.

Thursday, May 6–June 6, 1982 (24 performances)
LITTLE SHOP OF HORRORS based on film by Roger Corman; Book/Lyrics/Direction, Howard Ashman; Music, Alan Menken; Musical Staging, Edie Cowan; Setting, Edward T. Gianfrancesco; Lighting, Craig Evans; Costumes, Sally Lesser; Puppets, Martin P. Robinson; Vocal Arrangements/Musical Supervision, Bob Billig; Instrumental Arrangements, Robby Merkin; Stage Managers, Paul Mills Holmes, Sarah Whitham
CAST: Leilani Jones (Chiffon), Jennifer Leigh Warren (Crystal), Sheila Kay Davis (Ronnette), Michael Vale (Mushnik), Ellen Greene (Audrey), Lee Wilkof (Seymour), Martin P. Robinson (Derelict), Franc Luz (Orin/Berstein/Snip/Luce/Everyone Else), Ron Taylor/Martin P. Robinson (Audrey II)

Top Right: Rod Houts, Mark Soper, Merwin Goldsmith in "Big Apple Messenger" Below: Lynn Milgrim, Joaquim de Almeida in "What Would Jeanne Moreau Do?" *(Chip Goebert Photos)*

Lee Wilkof, Ellen Greene in "Little Shop of Horrors" *(Peter Cunningham Photo)*

York Theatre Company

Janet Hayes Walker, Artistic Director   Thirteenth Season

CHURCH OF THE HEAVENLY REST
November 20–December 6, 1981 (16 performances)
THE PRIVATE EAR/THE PUBLIC EYE by Peter Shaffer; Director, William Cain; Set, James Morgan; Lighting, David Gotwald; Costumes, Konnie Kittrell Berner; Sound, Joseph D. Sukaskas; Technical Directors, Deborah Alix Martin, Sally Smith; Stage Managers, Molly Grose, Mark Rhodes. CAST: "The Private Ear": Paul Murray (Tchaik), Guy Louthan (Ted), Kristine Sutherland (Doreen) "The Public Eye": Timothy Hall (Julian), James Secrest (Charles), Diane Warren (Belinda)

January 21–31, 1982 (10 performances)
THE ENCHANTED by Jean Giraudoux; Adapted by Maurice Valency; Director, Janet Hayes Walker; Set, James Morgan; Lighting, David Gotwald; Costumes, Susan Sudert; Technical Directors, Sally Smith, Deborah Alix Martin; Stage Manager, Molly Grose. CAST: Kermit Brown, Ralph David Westfall, Susan Frazer, Tristine Schmuckler, Julia Kay, Amy Beatie, Carrie Drosnes, Heidi Hemingway Bendrat, Dyllan McGee, John Rainer, Brockman Seawell, I. Mary Carter, Denise Bouche, Arthur Hanket, Aaron Lusting, Ed Simone

March 19–April 10, 1982 (20 performances)
LOLA a musical with book and lyrics by Kenward Elmslie; Music, Claibe Richardson; Director, John Going; Choreography, David Holdgreiwe; Musical Director, David Bishop; Set, James Morgan; Lighting, David Gotwald; Costumes, William Schroder; Assistant Musical Director, Dean Johnson; Technical Directors, Deborah Alix Martin, Sally Smith; Musical Supervision, Bruce Pomahac. CAST: Gretchen Albrecht, Leigh Beery, Michael Brogan, Jack Dabdoub, Tom Flagg, John Foster, Joseph B. Giuffre, Kevin Gray, Marshall Hagins, Sean McGuirk, Bud Nease, Patrick Parker, Robert Stillman, Shaver Tillitt, Jane White

May 14–June 6, 1982 (20 performances)
110 IN THE SHADE directed by Fran Soeder; Book, N. Richard Nash; Based on his play "The Rainmaker"; Music, Harvey Schmidt; Lyrics, Tom Jones; Musical Direction, Gregory Martindale; Set, James Morgan; Lighting, Kirk Bookman; Costumes, Sydney Brooks; Technical Director, Sally Smith; Stage Managers, Molly Grose, Jean Davis, Mark Rhodes. CAST: Nan Burling, Jesse Cline, Scott Ellis, Ralph Gunderman, Rich Hebert, Linda Jacobs, Jane Jensen, Dyllan McGee, Don Murphy, Jan Pessano, Craig Shepherd, Luke Sickle, Belle Smith, Laurie Stephenson, Robert Stoeckle, Mark Zimmerman

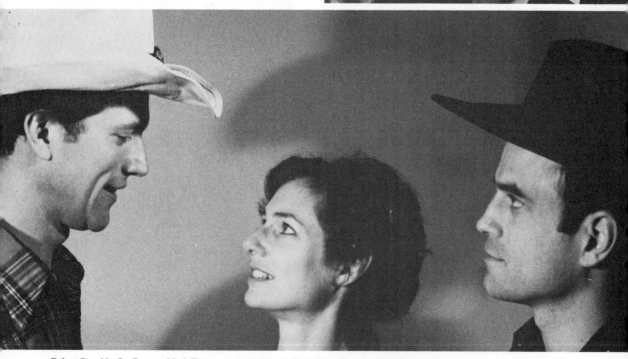

Robert Stoeckle, Jan Pessano, Mark Zimmerman in "110 in the Shade" Top: **Timothy Hall, Diane Warren in "Private Ear/Public Eye"** Center: **Gretchen Albrecht, Jane White, Leigh Beery in "Lola"**

OFF-BROADWAY PRODUCTIONS FROM PAST SEASONS
THAT PLAYED THROUGH THIS SEASON

THE FANTASTICKS

Book and Lyrics, Tom Jones; Suggested by Edmond Rostand's "Les Romanesques"; Music, Harvey Schmidt; Director, Word Baker; Original Musical Direction/Arrangements, Julian Stein; Designed by Ed Wittstein; Associate Producers, Sheldon Baron, Dorothy Olim, Robert Alan Gold; Assistant Producers, Bill Mills, Thad Noto; Production Assistant, John Krug; Original Cast Album by MGM Records; Presented by Lore Noto at the Sullivan Street Playhouse. Opened Tuesday, May 3, 1960.*

CAST

The Narrator/El Gallo	George Lee Andrews†1	The Old Actor	Robert Molnar†4
The Girl	Marty Morris†2	The Man Who Dies/Indian	James Cook†5
The Boy	Jeff Knight†3	The Mute	Alan Hemingway†6
The Boy's Father	Lore Noto	At the Piano	Norman Weiss
The Girl's Father	Byron Grant	At the Harp	Winifred Starks

UNDERSTUDIES: David Gebel (Narrator/Boy), Joan Wiest (Girl), Henry J. Quinn (Boy's Father)

MUSICAL NUMBERS: Try to Remember, Much More, Metaphor, Never Say No, It Depends on What You Pay, Soon It's Gonna Rain, Rape Ballet, Happy Ending, This Plum Is Too Ripe, I Can See It, Plant a Radish, Round and Round, They Were You
   A musical in two acts.

Press: Anthony Noto; *Stage Managers:* K. R. Williams, David Gebel

* Still playing May 31, 1982. For original production, see THEATRE WORLD Vol. 16.
† Succeeded by: 1. Lance Brodie, 2. Elizabeth Bruzzese, 3. Howard Paul Lawrence, 4. Bryan Hull, 5. Robert R. Oliver, 6 David Gebel

Robert Oliver, Bryan Hull in
"The Fantasticks"

Bruce Strickland, Carol Woods (L), Peggy
Alston, Frozine Jo Thomas in
"One Mo' Time"

ONE MO' TIME

Conceived and Directed by Vernel Bagneris; Musical Arrangements, Lars Edegran, Orange Kellin; Music Performed by The New Orleans Blue Serenaders; Costumes, Joann Clevenger; Setting, Elwin Charles Terrel II; Lighting, Joanna Schielke; Additional Staging, Dean Irby; Sound, Seltzer; Production Consultant, Pepsi Bethel; Wardrobe, Rhonda Stubbins, Jocelyn Eccles; Special Guest Trumpeter, Dick Vance; Presented by Art D'Lugoff, Burt D'Lugoff, Jerry Wexler in association with Shari Upbin at the Village Gate/Downstairs. Opened Monday, October 22, 1979.*

CAST

Bertha	Carol Woods	Papa Du	Bruce Strickland
Ma Reed	Frozine Jo Thomas	Theatre Owner	James "Red" Wilcher
Thelma	Peggy Alston		

UNDERSTUDIES: Maurice Felder (Papa Du), Gwen Shepherd (Big Bertha/Ma Reed), Val Eley (Thelma), Albert Poland (Theatre Owner)
   An evening of 1920's black vaudeville performed with one intermission. Bertha Williams and her touring company are in the Lyric Theatre in New Orleans, La., to perform.

General Manager: Albert Poland; *Company Manager:* Pamela Hare; *Press:* Solters/Roskin/Friedman, Milly Schoenbaum, Warren Knowlton, Kevin Patterson; *Stage Managers:* Duane Mazey, Frederick Tyson

* Still playing May 31, 1982. For original production, see THEATRE WORLD Vol. 36.

CLOUD 9

By Caryl Churchill; Director, Tommy Tune; Set, Lawrence Miller; Costumes, Michel Stuart, Gene London; Lighting, Marcia Madeira; Title Song/Incidental Music, Maury Yeston; Sound, Warren Hogan; Hairstylist, Ethyl Eichelberger, Michael Gottfried; Associate Producer, Mark Beigelman; General Management, Marilyn S. Miller, Berenice Weiler, Barbara Carrellas, Marshall Purdy; Casting, Mary Colquhoun; Wardrobe, Terrence Mintern; Technical Coordinator, Tom Shilhanek; Stage Managers, Murray Gitlin, Michael Morris, Barry Cullison, Steven Stahl; Press, Judy Jacksina, Glenna Freedman, Diane Tomlinson; Presented by Michel Stuart and Harvey J. Klaris in association with Michel Kleinman Productions at the Theatre De Lys (re-named Lucille Lortel Theatre). Opened Monday, May 18, 1981.*

CAST

ACT I
Clive	Jeffrey Jones†1
Betty	Zeljko Ivanek†2
Joshua	Don Amendolia†3
Edward	Concetta Tomei†4
Victoria	Herself
Maud	Veronica Castang†5
Ellen/Mrs. Saunders	E. Katherine Kerr†6
Harry Bagley	Nicolas Surovy

ACT II
Betty	E. Katherine Kerr†6
Edward	Jeffrey Jones†1
Victoria	Concetta Tomei†4
Martin	Nicholas Surovy
Lin	Veronica Castang†5
Cathy	Don Amendolia†3
Gerry	Zeljko Ivanek†2

UNDERSTUDIES: Michael Morris, Martin Shakar, Barry Cullison, Steve Stahl, Barbara Berg, Katherine Borowitz, Catherine Wold

A comedy in two acts. The action takes place in Africa in 1880 (Act I) and London in 1980 (Act II) . . . but for the characters it is only 25 years later.

* Still playing May 31, 1982. For original production, see THEATRE WORLD Vol. 37.

† Succeeded by: 1. Ivar Brogger, 2. Michael Jeter, John Pankow, 3. Michael Jeter, 4. Katherine Borowitz (on Tuesday and Wednesday) succeeded by Caroline Lagerfelt, 5. Barbara Berg during vacation, 6. Catherine Wolf, Cynthia Harris

E. Katherine Kerr, Jeffrey Jones

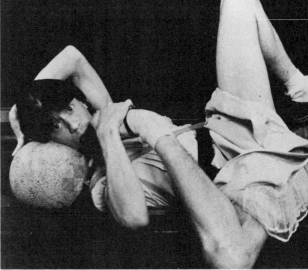

Jeffrey Jones, Zeljko Ivanek, Veronica Castang, E. Katherine Kerr, Nicolas Surovy Above: Michael Jeter

NATIONAL TOURING COMPANIES

ANNIE

Book, Thomas Meehan; Music, Charles Strouse; Lyrics, Martin Charnin; Director, Mr. Charnin; Choreography, Peter Gennaro; Sets, David Mitchell; Costumes, Theoni V. Aldredge; Lighting, Judy Rasmuson; Musical Direction, Glen Clugston; Dance Arrangements, Peter Howard; Orchestrations, Philip J. Lang; Producers, Mike Nichols, Irwin Meyer, Stephen R. Friedman, Lewis Allen, Peter Crane, Alvin Nederlander Associates, JFK Center, Icarus Productions; Stage Manager, Robert J. McNally III; Press, David Powers, Barbara Carroll; Company Manager, Morry Efron. Opened Thursday, March 23, 1978 at O'Keefe Center, Toronto, Canada, and closed Sept. 6, 1981 at JFK Center, Washington, D.C.

CAST

Annie	Louanne†1	Sandy	Himself
Oliver Warbucks	Norwood Smith†2	Bundles McCloskey/Ickes	Jim Brett
Miss Hannigan	Ruth Kobart	Dog Catcher/Bert Healy/Hull	James Todhill
Grace Farrell	Martha Whitehead	Dog Catcher/Jimmy Johnson/Guard	Edmond Dante
Rooster Hannigan	Michael Calkins	Lt. Ward/Justice Brandeis	Charles Cagle
FDR	Randall Robbins	Sophie/Cecile/Ronnie Boylan	Janet Yetka
Lily	Pamela Matteson†3	Drake	John Anania
July	Vicky Todd	Mrs. Pugh/Connie Boylan	Fern Radov
Tessie	Rachael Antill	Mrs. Greer/Page/Perkins	Lynne Winterseller†4
Pepper	Tammy Kauffman	Annette/Bonnie Boylan	Kerry Casserly
Duffy	Kia Joy Goodwin	Fred McCracken/Howe	John-Charles Kelly
Kate	Kim Davis		Ensemble Alternates: Neal Klein, Reby Howells
Molly	Danyle Heffernan		

MUSICAL NUMBERS: See Broadway Calendar, page 35. For original NY production, see THEATRE WORLD Vol. 33.

† Succeeded by: 1. Becky Snyder, 2. John Schuck for one week, 3. Linda Manning, 4. Terry Baughn

Louanne, Norwood Smith, Ruth Kobart

Kirsti Coombs, Jane Connell,
Reid Shelton

ANNIE

Musical Direction, Milton Greene; Company Manager, Don Joslyn; Assistant, Gregg Harlan; Stage Managers, Bryan Young, L. A. Lavin, Robert J. McNally, Janice Steele; Associate Conductor, Boyd D. Staplin; Props, George Green, Alan P. Price; Wardrobe, Adelaide Laurino, Robert Daily; Hairstylists, Jack Mei Ling, Lily Pon; Press, David Powers, Margie Korshak. For additional credits, see preceding listing. Opened Thursday, June 22, 1978 at the Curran Theatre, San Francisco, Ca., and still touring May 31, 1982.

CAST

Molly	Regina Meredith	Sophie/Mrs. Pugh/Perkins	Maralyn Nell
Pepper	Wendy Finnegan†1	Grace Farrell	Krista Neumann†7
Duffy	Jennifer Maillet†2	Drake	Chuck Bergman†8
July	Denise Meredith†3	Mrs. Greer/Connie Boylan	Sigrid Heath
Tessie	Arlene Kulis	Cecile/Bonnie Boylan	Janet Aldrich†9
Kate	Alyssa Jayne Milano†4	Annette/Ronnie Boylan	Kathryn Skatula†10
Annie	Kristi Coombs	Oliver Warbucks	Reid Shelton
Miss Hannigan	Jane Connell	Rooster Hannigan	Tom Offt†11
Bundles McCloskey/Ickes	Leslie Feagan	Lily	Maggy Gorrill†12
Dog Catcher/Fred McCracken/Guard	John LaMotta	Jimmy Johnson/Howe	Jon Rider†13
Dog Catcher/Bert Healy/Hull	Roy Hausen†5	FDR	Allan Wikman†14
Sandy	Buttercup	A Star to Be	Janet Aldrich†15
Lt. Ward/Morganthau/Brandeis	Edmund Gaynes		

MUSICAL NUMBERS: See Broadway Calendar, page 35. For original production see THEATRE WORLD Vol. 33.

† Succeeded by: 1. Alison Grambs, 2. Chris Noel, 3. Alyssa Jayne Milano, 4. Denise Meredith, 5. Charles Goff, 6. James Todkill, 7. Ann Peck, 8. David Wasson, 9. Janet Yetka, 10. Judith Bro, 11. Gary Beach, 12. Linda Manning, 13. Dick DeCareau, 14. Randall Robbins, 15. Janet Yetka

ANNIE

Musical Direction, Arthur Greene; Casting, Peter Cereghetti; Assistant to Management, J. Anthony Magner; Hairstylists, Richard Orton, David Dunn; Wardrobe, Frank Green; Props, Richard Sawyer, George Green, Jr.; Assistant Conductor, Richard Riccardi; Company Managers, Steven H. David, Ken Shelley; Stage Managers, David Clive, Janyce Ann Wagner, Chip Neufeld, Tory Alexander; Press, David Powers, Jim Kerber. For additional credits, see preceding listing. Opened Wednesday Oct. 3, 1979 at Dallas, Tx., State Fair Music Hall and still touring May 31, 1982.

CAST

Molly	Senta Moses†1	Sophie/Annette/Ronnie/Perkins	Ann Heinricher†7
Pepper	Deborah Webster†2	Grace Farrell	Lauren Mitchell†8
July	Kathleen Kollar†3	Drake/Morganthau	David Barron
Tessie	Sarah Navin†4	Mrs. Pugh/Page	Jill Harwood†9
Kate	Alyson Kirk†5	Mrs. Greer/Connie Boylan	Elizabeth Stiles
Annie	Bridget Walsh	Cecile/Bonnie Boylan	Barbara Richardson†10
Miss Hannigan	Kathleen Freeman	Oliver Warbucks	Harve Presnell†11
Bundles McCloskey/Ickes	Robert Calvert	Rooster Hannigan	Dennis Parlato†12
Jimmy Johnson/Howe	Travis DeCastro	Lily	Wendy Kimball
Dog Catcher/Healy/Honor Guard	Charles Goff†6	Duffy	Colleen Simon†13
Sandy	Moose	FDR	Jack Denton†14
Lt. Ward/McCracken/Hull/Brandeis	Ronald Highley		

MUSICAL NUMBERS: see Broadway Calendar, page 35.

† Succeeded by: 1. Monica Miller, 2. Jessica Smith, 3. Tara Carnes, 4. Melissa Kalfa, 5. Sharon Jordan, 6. Roy Hausen, 7. Liz Larsen, 8. Kathryn Boule, 9. Fern Radov, 10. Angelina Fiordellisi, 11. Rhodes Reason, 12. Jon Rider, 13. Maura Sullivan, 14. David Green.

ANNIE

Musical Direction, Janice Aubrey; Directed by Bryan Young; Based on original by Martin Charnin; Production Supervised by Mr. Charnin; Tour Director, Columbia Artists Theatrical Corp.; Company Manager, Jane Montgomery; Hairstylist, G. Lamara Jackson; Wardrobe, Lynn Cunningham, Jerry A. Wolf; Props, David Cunningham, Glen Cunningham; Assistant Conductor, James Simmons; Stage Managers, Patrick O'Leary, Naomi Wexler, Karl Lengel; Press, David Powers, Barbara Carroll; For additional credits, see preceding listing. For original Broadway production, see THEATRE WORLD Vol. 33. Opened Sept. 11, 1981 in Eisenhower Hall, West Point, NY, and still touring May 31, 1982.

CAST

Molly	Dee Hilligoss	Grace Farrell	Lynne Wintersteller
Pepper	Kimberly Mucci	Drake/Morganthau	Gary Holcombe
Tessie	Theresa Diane	Mrs. Greer/Star to Be/Bonnie/Perkins	Cathy Mundy
Kate	Jennifer Gottesman	Cecile/Connie Boylan	Nancy Holcombe
Annie	Mollie Hall	Annette/Ronnie Boylan	Jan Maxwell
Miss Hannigan	Ruth Williamson	Oliver Warbucks	Ron Holgate
Bundles McCloskey/Fred McCracken/Hull	Stanley Bojarski	Rooster Hannigan	William McClary
Dog Catcher/Bert Healy/Guard/Brandeis	Hal Maxwell	Lily	Ann Casey
Sandy	Roxanne	Sound Effects/Ickes	Robert Herrig
Lt. Ward/Jimmy Johnson/Howe	Erick Johnson	FDR	William Metzo
Sophie/Mrs. Pugh	Jill Harwood		

Ensemble Alternates: Scott Dainton, Linda Lipson, Karl Lengel

MUSICAL NUMBERS: See Broadway Calendar, page 35. For original Broadway production, see THEATRE WORLD Vol. 33.

Bridget Walsh, Rhodes Reason

Lynne Wintersteller, Ron Holgate, Mollie Hall (Annie)

BARNUM

Music Director, Robert Billig; Production Supervisors, Mary Porter Hall, Edward Kresley; Casting, Howard Feuer, Jeremy Ritzer; Hairstylists, Ted Azar, Christine Domenech, Ann Miles, Charles McMahon; Management Assistants, Michael Gill, Marsha Best; Wardrobe, Warren Morill, John Corbo; Props, William Pomeroy, Paul Everett; Edward Slaggert; Technical Supervisor, Peter Feller; General Manager, James Walsh; Company Manager, John Corkill; Stage Managers, Warren Crane, Kate Pollock, Steve Wappel; Press, David Powers, Barbara Carroll, Jon Essex; For additional credits, see Broadway Calendar, page . Opened Tuesday, May 12, 1981 at Saenger Performing Arts Center, New Orleans, La., and closed Aug. 22, 1981 in the Fisher Theatre, Detroit, Mi. For original Broadway production, see THEATRE WORLD Vol. 36.

CAST

Phineas Taylor Barnum	Stacy Keach	Baton Twirler	Darlene Cory
Chairy Barnum	Dee Hoty	White-faced Clown	Michael Oster
Ringmaster/James A. Bailey	Gabriel Barre	High Wire Lady	Andrea Wright
Chester Lyman	Melvin Roberts	Sherwood Stratton/Wilton	Richard Gervais
Joice Heth	Terri White	Tom Thumb	Bobby Lee
Amos Scudder	Andrew Hill Newman	Julius Goldschmidt/Humbert Morrissey	Steve Hall
Acrobat Extraordinaire	Malcolm Perry	Jenny Lind	Catherine Gaines
Lady Plate Balancer/Mrs. Stratton	Stephanie Nash	One-Man Band/Edgar Templeton	Paul Browne
Lady Bricklayer	K. Leslie	Lady Aerialist	Diane Abrams

STANDBYS AND UNDERSTUDIES: Jess Richards/ Steve Hall (Barnum), Linda Hohenfeld/Andrea Wright (Chairy/Jenny), K. Leslie (Joice), Richard Gervais (Ringmaster), Michael Oster (Tom Thumb), Bo Gerard (Lyman/Stratton/Goldschmidt/Morrisey), Gordon Weiss (Scudder/Wilton/Templeton), Swing: Betty Ann LaRusso, Leslie Wing, Bo Gerard, Gordon Weiss.

MUSICAL NUMBERS: There Is a Sucker Born Ev'ry Minute, Thank God I'm Old, The Colors of My Life, One Brick at a Time, Museum Song, I Like Your Style, Bigger Isn't Better, Love Makes Such Fools of Us All, Out There, Come Follow the Band, Black and White, Prince of Humbug, Join the Circus

A musical in two acts. The action takes place all over America and the major capitals of the world from 1835 through 1880.

BARNUM

Music Director, Ross Allen; General Management, James Walsh; Company Manager, John Corkill; Hairstylists, Ted Azar, Christine Domenech, Suzy Mezzareze, Charles McMahon; Wardrobe, Warren Morrill, John Corbo; Props, William Pomeroy, David Paterson; Stage Managers, Marc Schlackman, Bethe Ward, Steve Wappel, Leslie Wing; Press, David Powers, Barbara Carroll, Alan Eichler; Additional credits in Broadway Calendar, page . Opened Wednesday, Dec. 16, 1981 in Golden Gate Theatre, San Francisco, Ca., and closed Apr. 4, 1982 in Pantages Theatre, Los Angeles, Ca.

CAST

Phineas Taylor Barnum	Jim Dale	White-faced Clown	Derek Meader
Chairy Barnum	Glenn Close	Sherwood Stratton/One-Man Band	Charles Edward Hall
Ringmaster/Julius Goldschmidt/James A. Bailey	Terrence V. Mann		
		Mrs. Stratton	Barbara Nadel
Chester Lyman/Wilton	Bruce Robertson	Tom Thumb	Ray Roderick
Joice Heth	Terri White	Mrs. Wilson	Robbi Morgan
Amos Scudder/Edgar Templeton	Gordon Weiss	Susan B. Anthony	Betty LaRusso
Acrobat Extraordinaire	Malcolm Perry	Jenny Lind	Catherine Gaines
Lady Tightrope Walker	Catherine Carr	Humbert Morrissey	Bo Gerard
Baton Twirler	Darlene Cory	Pianists	Dennis Buck, Jack Mezzano
Chief Bricklayer	Skip Lackey		

Alternates: Donna Ingram, Don Johanson, Jim Ruttman, Leslie Wing

MUSICAL NUMBERS: See preceding listing. For original Broadway production, see THEATRE WORLD, Vol. 36.

Stacy Keach, Dee Hoty

Jim Dale (C)

THE BEST LITTLE WHOREHOUSE IN TEXAS

Book, Larry L. King, Peter Masterson; Music and Lyrics, Carol Hall; Directors, Peter Masterson, Tommy Tune; Choreographers, Tommy Tune, Thommie Walsh; Costumes, Ann Roth; Set, Lawrence Miller; Lighting, Beverly Emmons; Sound, Abe Jacob; Hairstylists, Lamara Jackson, Peter Bonsignore; Producers, Stevie Phillips, Universal Pictures, Bonnie Champion, Danny Kreitzberg; General Management, American Theatre Productions; Production Supervisor, Paul Phillips; Company Manager, Peter H. Russell; Musical Director, Guy Strobel; Wardrobe, Jerry A. Wolf; Stage Managers, Michael Frank, Grant Brown, Marian Reed; Press, Jeffrey Richards Associates, Fred Weterick; Opened Monday, Nov. 17, 1980 at Playhouse, Wilmington, De., closed June 27, 1982 in Opera House, Lexington, Ky. For original Broadway production, see THEATRE WORLD Vol. 35.

CAST

Edsel . . . . Ernie Reed†1
Girls . . . . Gena Scriva, Kristie Hannum,
                               Charmion Clark, Marcia Mitzman
Farmer/Melvin P. Thorpe/Chip Brewster Steven Earl-Edwards†2
Shy Kid/Soundman/Aggie 48/Photographer . . . . Joey Morris†3
Miss Wulla Jean/Doatsey Mae . . . . Marian Reed†4
Traveling Salesman/C. J. Scruggs . . . . Robert Weil†5
Slick Dude/Aggie 42 Specialty Dance . . . . Eric Aaron†6
Angel/Imogene Charlene . . . . Jenny Lee Wax
Shy . . . . Martha Gehman†7
Jewel . . . . Susan Baubian
Mona Stangley . . . . Francie Mendenhall†8
Her Girls: Linda Lou (Diane Pennington), Dawn (Gena Scriva), Ginger (Charmion Clark), Beatrice (Kristie Hannum), Ruby Rae (Marcia Mitzman), Eloise (Jane Matera)

MUSICAL NUMBERS: See Broadway Calendar, page 33.

† Succeeded by: 1. Jamie Hines, 2. Jason Byce, 3. Jonathan Relyea, 4. Jan Buttram, 5. James Cade, 6. Cecil Fulfer, 7. Patricia Roark, 8. Darleigh Miller, 9. Richard Reuter-Smith, 10. Ted Pritchard

Aggies: Stephen Terrell, Peter Wandel, Brian Sutherland, Guy Strobel, Vincent Vogt
Melvin Thorpe Singers: Jan Buttram, Marcia Mitzman, Stephen Terrell, Richard Reuter-Smith, Guy Strobel, Kristie Hannum, Peter Wandell, Jane Matera
Angelettes: Jane Matera, Diane Pennington, Marcia Mitzman, Kristie Hannum, Gena Scriva, Jenny Lee Wax
Choir: Susan Beaubian, Brian Sutherland, Jacqueline Lowe, Diane Pennington, Cecil Fulfer, Richard Reuter-Smith, Jane Matera, Stephen Terrell, Peter Wandel, Vincent Vogt
Leroy Sliney/Aggie 25/Ranger . . . . Alan Bruun†9
Dogettes . . . . Richard Reuter-Smith,
                 Vincent Vogt, Stephen Terrell, Guy Strobel
Sheriff Ed Earl Dodd . . . . Christopher Wynkoop
Mayor Rufus Poindexter/Senator Wingwoah . . Page Johnson†10

Christopher Wynkoop, Darleigh Miller

Angelettes Above: Susan Beaubian and Miss Mona's girls

CHILDREN OF A LESSER GOD

By Mark Medoff; Director, Gordon Davidson; Set, David Jenkins; Costumes, Nancy Potts; Lighting, Tharon Musser; Producers, Emanuel Azenberg, The Shubert Organization, Dasha Epstein, Ron Dante, William P. Wingate, Kenneth Brecher; General Managers, Jose Vega, Jane Robison, Linda Cohen; Wardrobe, G. Scarbough; Stage Managers, Mark Wright, Sally Greenhut, Robert Daniels, Scott Faris, Gary M. Zabinski, Charles Rosenow; Company Manager, L. Liberatore; Assistant Director, Richard Gershman; Press, Bill Evans, Harry Davies, Leslie Anderson-Lynch, Ellen Friedberg. Opened Friday, Nov. 21, 1980 at Parker Playhouse, Ft. Lauderdale, Fl., and closed Feb. 24, 1982 at the Colonial Theatre in Boston, Ma. For original Broadway production, see THEATRE WORLD Vol. 36.

CAST

Sarah Norman	Linda Bove†1	Mrs. Norman	Stanja Lowe
James Leeds	Peter Evans†2	Lydia	Nanci Kendall
Orin Dennis	Richard Kendall	Edna Klein	Deanna Dunagan†4
Mr. Franklin	Ken Letner†3		

STANDBYS AND UNDERSTUDIES: Jackie Roth Kinner (Sarah), Charles Rosenow (James), Camille Jeter (Lydia), Robert Daniels (Orin), Stratton Walling (Franklin), Jo Farwell (Mrs. Norman), Victoria Thatcher (Edna)
† Succeeded by: 1. Ella Mae Lentz, 2. James N. Stephens, 3. Gwil Richards, 4. Jo Farwell

CHILDREN OF A LESSER GOD

Presented by Marvin A. Krauss and Irving Siders; Re-staged by Jonathan Lee; Tour Direction, Columbia Artists Theatricals; Casting, Julie Hughes/Barry Moss; Wardrobe, Frederick N. Brown; Company Manager, Jerry Livengood; Stage Managers, Thomas P. Carr, Randy Buck, Kenneth Bridges; Press, Cheryl Sue Dolby/Merle Frimark, The Merlin Group Ltd.; Additional credits in preceding listing. Opened Monday, Aug. 31, 1981 at Hines Hall, Pittsburgh, Pa., and closed in Kansas City's Lyric Theatre on June 13, 1982.

CAST

Sarah Norman	Freda Norman	Mrs. Norman	Diane Martella
James Leeds	Philip Reeves	Lydia	Mary Beth Barber
Orin Dennis	Charles Jones	Edna Klein	Mimi Bensinger
Mr. Franklin	Herbert Duval		

UNDERSTUDIES: Rita Corey (Sarah), Rico Peterson (James), Katherine Wiberg (Lydia), Robin Bartholick (Orin), Mimi Bensinger (Mrs. Norman), Shannon Reeves (Edna), Kenneth Bridges (Franklin)
   A drama in two acts.

Ella Mae Lentz, James N. Stephens

Philip Reeves, Freda Norman *(Gerry Goodstein Photo)*

COLETTE

Book and Lyrics, Tom Jones; Music, Harvey Schmidt; Staged and Directed by Dennis Rosa; Choreography, Carl Jablonski; Costumes, Raoul Pene du Bois; Scenery, John Conklin; Lighting, Gilbert V. Hemsley, Jr.; Musical Direction/Vocal Arrangements, Larry Blank; Orchestrations, Larry Wilcox; Dance Music Arrangements, David Krane; Sound, John McClure; Hairstylist, Stephen LoVullo; Assistant Choreographer, Michon Peacock; Associate Producer, Frank Montalvo; General Manager, Alan Wasser; Presented by Harry Rigby, The Kennedy Center, The Denver Center and James M. Nederlander; Production Assistants, Steve Knox, Sebastien Esteban, Patrick D'Antonio; Assistant to Director, Peter Meyers; Wardrobe, Joy MacPherson-Ortiz; Props, Walter Murphy; Associate Conductor, Ken Collins; Casting, Terry Fay; Company Manager, Alexander Holt; Stage Managers, Robert Vandergriff, Dan Hild, Bill Braden; Press, Henry Luhrman, Bill Miller, Terry M. Lilly, Kevin P. McAnarney. Opened Tuesday, Feb. 9, 1982 at the Fifth Avenue Theatre, Seattle, Wash., and closed March 20, 1982 in the Auditorium Theatre, Denver, Colo.

CAST

Colette	Diana Rigg	Mme. Semiramis/Pauline	Mary Stout
Sido	Marta Eggerth	Nita	Jane Lanier
Willy	John Reardon	Writer	Michael Cone
Jacques	Robert Helpmann	Ida	Nancy Callman
Maurice	Martin Vidnovic	Boudou/Collaborator	Russell Leib
Henri de Jouvenal	Ron Raines	Master of Ceremonies/German Officer	Ralph Braun
Colette de Jouvenal	Rhoda Butler	Danielle	Dana Moore
Missy	Marti Stevens		

ENSEMBLE: Don Bernhardt, Ralph Braun, Carol Burt, Rhoda Butler, Nancy Callman, Arlene Columbo, Michael Cone, Ron Farrar, Jane Lanier, Valerie Lemon, Dana Moore, Daryl Murphy, Harry Lee Nordyke, Peggy Marten, David Scala, Carol Schuberg, Mary Stout, Ivan Torres, Joel Whittaker, Zachary Wilde, Swings: Lisa Guignard, Lester Holmes

UNDERSTUDIES: Nancy Callman (Colette/Missy), Ron Raines (Willy), Russell Leib (Jacques), Ralph Braun (Henri), Valerie Lemon (Sido), Bill Braden (Boudou/Collaborator)

MUSICAL NUMBERS: There's Another World, Come to Life, Do Not Hold On, Semiramis, Do It For Willy, Claudine, Two Claudines, Father of Claudine, Why Can't I Walk through the Door?, Music Hall, Dream of Egypt, I Miss You, La Vagabonde, Music Hall Scandal, Act One Ending, Act Two Opening, Curiosity, Riviera Nights, Oo-la-la, Something for the Summer, Something for the Winter, Madame Colette, Be My Lady, The Room Is Filled with You, Victory, Growing Older, Joy

A musical biography in 2 acts and 20 scenes, covering the 64 years in the life of the French writer Colette. The action takes place between 1890 and 1954.

DANCIN'

A "musical entertainment" conceived, directed and choreographed by Bob Fosse; Re-created by Gail Benedict; Scenery, Peter Larkin; Costumes, Willa Kim; Lighting, Jules Fisher; Sound, Abe Jacob; Musical Arrangements, Gordon Lowry Harrell; Orchestrations, Ralph Burns, Michael Gibson; Musical Director, Milton Setzer; Presented by Tom Mallow in association with James Janek; Stage Managers, Mark S. Krause, Ron Rudolph; Press, Max Eisen, Barbara Glenn, Irene Gandy. Opened Tuesday, July 29, 1980 in Performing Arts Center, Milwaukee, Ws., and still touring May 31, 1982. For original NY production, see THEATRE WORLD Vol. 34.

CAST

Jo-Ann Baldo, William H. Brown, Jr., Jim Corti, Germaine Edwards, Karen E. Fraction, Ramon Galindo, Tonda Hannum, Nancy Hess, Stella Hiatt, Allison Renee Manson, Daniel May, Michael Lafferty, Barbara McKinley, Lynne Patrick, Roumel Reaux, Willie Rosario, Linda Smith, Tomas Tofel

MUSICAL NUMBERS: See Broadway Calendar, page 39.

Center: (L) John Reardon, Diana Rigg in "Colette" (R) "Dancin' "

EVITA

Lyrics, Tim Rice; Music, Andrew Lloyd Webber; Director, Harold Prince; Choreography, Larry Fuller; General Manager, Howard Haines; Company Manager, David Wyler, Barbara Seinfeld; Casting, Joanna Merlin, John-David Wilder; Production Assistant, Wilfy Hausam; Hairstylist, Wayne Herndon, Richard Allen, Gary Stavens; Wardrobe, Dorothy Priest; Props, George Green, Jr., Henry Howes, Bruce Glaser; Associate Conductor, Robert Webb; Stage Managers, Robert Bennett, Donald Walters, Mark A. Lipschutz, Timothy Smith; Press, Mary Bryant, Violet Welles; For additional credits, see Broadway Calendar. Opened Sunday, Jan. 13, 1980 at Shubert Theatre, Los Angeles, Ca., and closed June 13, 1982 at Golden Gate Theatre in San Francisco, Ca. For original Broadway production, see THEATRE WORLD, Vol. 36

CAST

Eva	Loni Ackerman†1	Magaldi	Sal Mistretta†4
	Matinees:Derin Altay†2	Peron's Mistress	Kelli James
Peron	Jon Cypher†3		

PEOPLE OF ARGENTINA: Leslie Bisno, Pamela Blake, Mark Bradford, Richard Byron, David Cantor, Jonathan Curtsinger, Janie Dale, John Dorrin, Mary Ann Dunroe, Karen Elise-Brown, Ed Forsyth, Barry Gorbar, David Gold, Jill B. Gounder, Anna Marie Gutierrez, Mark Harryman, Barbara Hartman, Ed Kerrigan, Anita Morales, Doug Okerson, Iris Revson, David Romano, Wayne Scherzer, Bruce Senesac, Tara Sitser, Timothy Smith, Dan Tullis, Jr., Yvette Van Voorhees, Robert Vega, Brian Whitaker, Christina Wilcox, Karen Yarmat, Children: Laura Baker, Nancy Baker, K. Patrick O'Brien

UNDERSTUDIES: Iris Revson (Eva), Brian Whitaker (Peron), David Cantor (Che), Barry Gorbar (Magaldi), Mary Ann Dunroe (Mistress)

MUSICAL NUMBERS: see Broadway Calendar, page 40.

† Succeeded by: 1. Derin Altay, 2. Pamela Blake, 3. David Brummel, 4. Mark Syers

EVITA

Musical Supervisor, Paul Gemignani; Musical Director, Jack Gaughan; Production Assistants, Charles Christensen, Patrick Fitzpatrick; Hairstylists/Makeup, Richard Allen, Lake Watson; Wardrobe, Frank Marblo; Props, John Alfredo; Assistant Musical Director, Pam Drews; Stage Managers, Thomas M. Guerra, Christine Lawton, Jayne Turner; Press, Mary Bryant, Philip Rinaldi, Patsy Hunt; For additional credits, see Broadway Calendar. Opened Tuesday, Sept. 20, 1980 at the Shubert Theatre in Chicago, and still playing May 31, 1982. For original NY Production, see THEATRE WORLD Vol. 36.

CAST

Eva	Valerie Perri†1	Peron	Robb Alton
	Matinees:Joy Lober	Peron's Mistress	Cynthia Simpson†3
Che	John Herrera†2	Magaldi	Peter Marinos†4

PEOPLE OF ARGENTINA: Arminae Azarian, Riselle Bain, Dennis Callahan, Gregg Edelman, Michael Ehlers, John Eskola, Elaine Freedman, Paul Harman, James Harms, Lois Hayes, Didi Hitt, Rudy Hogenmiller, Michelle C. Kelly, Ken Land, Mark Lazore, James A. Linduska, Joy Lober, Michael Lofton, Charles Lubeck, Giselle Montanez, Susan Lubeck Oken, Candice Prior, Jeffory Robinson, William Ryall, Laura Soltis, Richard Stafford, Cheryl Stern, Bruce Taylor, Joanie Winter

UNDERSTUDIES: Riselle Bain (Eva), Paul Harman (Che/Peron), Rudy Hogenmiller (Magaldi), Susan Lubeck Oken (Mistress)

MUSICAL NUMBERS: See Broadway Calendar, page 40.

† Succeeded by: 1. Nancy Opel, 2. Anthony Crivello, R. Michael Baker, 3. Jamie Dawn Gangi, 4. David Annehl

Derin Altay, David Brummel, Scott Holmes

Robb Alton, Valerie Perri

EVITA

Musical Supervisor, Paul Gemignani; Musical Director, Kevin Farrell; Hairstylist/Makeup, Richard Allen, Dale E. Bronell; Wardrobe, Yvonne T. Stoney; Props, Fred Belosic, Mike Chickey; Assistant Musical Director, Tim Stella; Company Manager, Robert Ossenfort; Stage Managers, Frank Marino, Arturo E. Porazzi, Fredric Hanson; Press, Mary Bryant, Philip Rinaldi, Jon Essex; For additional credits, see Broadway Calendar. Opened in Masonic Temple, Detroit, Mi., Sunday, Feb. 28, 1982, and still touring May 31, 1982. For original Broadway production, see THEATRE WORLD Vol. 36.

CAST

Eva.................................... Florence Lacey
Matinees: Patricia Hemenway
Che................................... Tim Bowman
Peron................................. John Leslie Wolfe
Peron's Mistress...................... Patricia Ludd
Magaldi............................... Vincent Pirillo

PEOPLE OF ARGENTINA: Marianna Allen, R. Michael Baker, Scott Bodie, John McCool Bowers, Laurie Crochet, Mark Dovey, Diane Duncan, Lynn East, Mark East, Mark East IV, Donna Marie Elio, Kerry Finn, Joanna Glushak, Thomas Scott Gordon, Curtis Gregory, Michael Hansen, Patricia Hemenway, Ken Miller, Jeff Mooring, Marilu Morreale, Ron Rusthoven, Lynn Sterling, Robert Torres, Kathy Vestuto, Sam Viverito, Kenneth H. Waller, Don Wonder

UNDERSTUDIES: Donna Marie Elio (Eva), R. Michael Butler (Che), Ron Rusthoven (Peron), Scott Bodie (Magaldi), Marianna Allen (Mistress)

MUSICAL NUMBERS: See Broadway Calendar, page 40.

Tim Bowan, Florence Lacey in "Evita"

Paxton Whitehead, JoAnne Worley, Clive Revill, Pam Dawber, Andy Gibb, Barry Bostwick in "Pirates..."

THE PIRATES OF PENZANCE

By Gilbert and Sullivan; Director, Wilford Leach; Choreography, Graciela Daniele; Scenery, Bob Shaw, Wilford Leach; Costumes, Patricia McGourty; Lighting, Jennifer Tipton; Sound, Don Ketteler; Conductor, Vincent Fanuele; Hairstylist/Makeup, J. Roy Helland; Presented by Joseph Papp; Company Managers, Noel Gilmore, Debbie Hoy; Props, George Wagner; Wardrobe, Anne Kelleher; Stage Managers, R. Derek Swire, Howard Chitjian, Tom Ashworth; Production Supervisor, Jason Steven Cohen; General Managers, Robert Kamlot, Laurel Ann Wilson; Press, Merle Debuskey, John Howlett, Rick Miramontez. Opened June 10, 1981 at the Ahmanson Theatre, Los Angeles, and still touring May 31, 1982.

CAST

Pirate King........................... Barry Bostwick†1
Samuel, his lieutenant................ Jerry Scurlock†2
Frederic.............................. Andy Gibb†3
Ruth, a pirate maid................... Jo Anne Worley†4
The Sergeant.......................... Paxton Whitehead†10
Major-General Stanley................. Clive Revill†5
His Daughters:
Edith................................. Caroline Peyton†6
Kate.................................. Linden Waddell†7
Mabel................................. Pam Dawber†9
Isabel................................ Patti Cohenour†8
and Diane Benedict, Suzanne Buirgy, Pamela Cord, Erica Rose

PIRATES AND POLICE: Paul Ainsley, Jeffrey Bryan, James Caddell, Thom Fielder, Al Flannagan, Warren Kaplan, Wally Kurth, Michael Laughlin, Gary T. Ragland, Evans Ray, Patrick Richwood, Craig Schaefer, Jerome Stocco, Randy Stumpf, Louis Valenzi†11

UNDERSTUDIES: Paul Ainsley (Pirate King), Evans Ray (Samuel), Jerome Stocco (Frederic), Marsha Bagwell (Ruth), Suzanne Buirgy (Edith), Janene Lovullo (Kate), Jacqueline Trudeau (Isabel), Caroline Peyton (Mabel), Jerry Scurlock (Major-General), Paul Ainsley/Warren Kaplan (Sergeant), Swings: Jacqueline Trudeau, Tom Ashworth

MUSICAL NUMBERS: See Broadway Calendar, page 43.

† Succeeded by: 1. James Belushi, 2. Louis Valenzi, 3. Peter Noone, 4. Marsha Bagwell, 5. Leo Leyden, 6. Suzanne Buirgy, 7. Jacqueline Trudeau, 8. Janene Lovullo, 9. Caroline Peyton, 10. Paul Ainsley, 11. Larry French, Patrick Godfrey, Paul Hewitt, David McDaniel, Eugene Moose, Art Neill, Dean Regan, George Riddle, Thom Rogers, Tony Stokes

SEVEN BRIDES FOR SEVEN BROTHERS

Book, Lawrence Kasha, David Landay; Based on MGM film and "The Sobbin' Women" by Stephen Vincent Benet; Lyrics, Johnny Mercer; Music, Gene de Paul; New Songs, Al Kasha, Joel Hirschhorn; Director, Lawrence Kasha; Choreography and Musical Staging, Jerry Jackson; Sets and Lighting, Robert Randolph; Costumes, Robert Fletcher; Sound, Abe Jacob; Musical Director, Richard Parrinello; Orchestrations, Irwin Kostal; Dance Arrangements, Robert Webb; Associate Producers, Martin Gould, Bernard Hodes; Presented by Kaslan Productions; General Manager, Marvin A. Krauss, Gary Gunas, Eric Angelson, Steven C. Callahan; Company Manager, Drew Murphy; Assistant to Director, Daniel Knowles; Assistant to Producers, Donald Martocchio; Props, Charles Zuckerman, Gregory Martin; Wardrobe, Dolores Childers; Assistant Conductor, Jerry Sternbach; Hairstylists, Juan Rodriguez, Rick Burns; Stage Managers, Larry Dean, Polly Wood, Jack Ritschel; Press, David Powers, Barbara Carroll. Opened Monday, Dec. 21, 1981 in Fox Theatre, San Diego, Ca., and still touring May 31, 1982.

CAST

Gideon	Craig Peralta	Alice	Nancy Fox
Mrs. McClane	Jeanne Bates	Liza	Jan Mussetter
Ephraim	Jeffrey Reynolds	Martha	Laurel van der Linde
Daniel	Jeff Calhoun	Sarah	Linda Hoxit
Benjamin	D. Scot Davidge	Preacher	Jack Ritschel
Adam	David-James Carroll	Preacher's Wife	Jeanne Bates
Caleb	Lara Teeter	Mrs. Perkins	Katherine Somers
Frank	Michael Ragan	Jeb	Russell Giesenschlag
Mr. Bixby	Fred Curt	Carl	Don Steffy
Dorcas	Manette LaChance	Zeke	Kurtis Woodruff
Mr. Perkins	Gino Gaudio	Matt	Gary Moss
Milly	Debby Boone	Luke	James Horvath
Ruth	Sha Newman	Joel	Clark Sterling

TOWNSPEOPLE: Jeanne Bates, Cheryl Crandall, Fred Curt, Gino Gaudio, Russell Giesenschlag, James Horvath, Marylou Hume, Gary Moss, David Pavlosky, Jack Ritschel, Conley Schnaterbeck, Sam Singhaus, Katherine Somers, Don Steffy, Clark Sterling, Stephanie Stromer, Kurtis Woodruff

UNDERSTUDIES: Cheryl Crandall (Milly), Gino Gaudio (Adam), Russell Giesenschlag (Gideon), Gary Moss (Daniel), Don Steffy (Benjamin), Kurtis Woodruff (Frank), Clark Sterling (Ephraim), James Horvath (Caleb), Marylou Hume, Katherine Somers, Stephanie Stromer (Brides), David Pavlosky, Conley Schnaterbeck, Sam Singhaus (Suitors), Fred Curt (Preacher), Jack Ritschel (Bixby/Perkins), Katherine Somers (Mrs. McClane), Jeanne Bates (Mrs. Perkins), Alternates: Stephanie Stromer, Sam Singhaus

MUSICAL NUMBERS: Get a Wife, Bless Your Beautiful Bride, Wonderful Wonderful Day, I Married Seven Brothers, Goin' Courting, Social Dance, Love Never Goes Away, Sobbin' Women, A Woman Ought to Know Her Place, We Gotta Make It Through the Winter, It's Up to Us, Spring Dance, Glad That You Were Born, Wedding Dance

A musical in two acts. The action takes place in the Pacific Northwest in the 1850's.

Sha Newman, Lara Teeter, Manette LaChance, D. Scott Davidge, Jan Mussetter, Jeff Calhoun, Debby Boone, David-James Carroll, Laurel van der Linde, Jeffrey Reynolds, Linda Hoxit, Michael Ragan, Nancy Fox, Craig Peralta

SOPHISTICATED LADIES

Concept, Donald McKayle; Based on music of Duke Ellington; Director, Michael Smuin; Musical Staging/Choreography, Donald McKayle, Michael Smuin; Co-Choreographer/Tap, Henry LeTang; Associate Choreographer, Bruce Heath; Assistant Choreographer/Repiteur, Claudia Asbury; Assistant Choreographer, Mercedes Ellington; Production Supervisor, Martin Gold; Music under direction of Mercer Ellington; Settings, Tony Walton; Costumes, Willa Kim; Lighting, Jennifer Tipton; Sound, Otts Munderloh, Bernard Fox; Hairstylists, Danny Wintrode, Jeffrey Sacino, Marc Daniels; Orchestrations, Al Cohn; Music and Dance Arrangements, Lloyd Mayers; Vocal Arrangements, Malcolm Dodds, Lloyd Mayers; Musical Consultant/Additional Arrangements, Paul Chihara; Presented by Roger S. Berlind, Manheim Fox, Sondra Gilman, Burton L. Litwin and Louise Westergaard in association with Belwin Mills Corp. and Norzar Productions; Assistant Conductor, Carl Schroeder; Wardrobe, Mario Brera; Props, Paul Biega, Edward Schneck; General Management, Joseph P. Harris, Peter T. Kulok, Steven E. Goldstein, Ira Bernstein, Nancy Simmons; Managers, Kathleen Lowe, Bruce Klinger; Stage Managers, John H. Lowe III, Keith Stava, Parker Young; Press, Fred Nathan, Eileen McMahon, Anne S. Abrams, Judi Davidson, Tim Choy, Barbra Desatnik, Ellen Friedberg. Opened Wednesday, Jan. 27, 1982 at the Shubert Theatre, Los Angeles, Ca., and still touring May 31, 1982.

CAST

Gregory Hines, Paula Kelly, Dee Dee Bridgewater, Hinton Battle, Gregg Burge, Terri Klausner, Mark Fotopoulos, Loretta Giles, Leata Galloway, Wynonna Smith, Sophisticated Ladies and Gentlemen: Sheri Cowart, Sandra Asbury-Johnson, Jamilah Lucas, Wynona Smith, Michael Graham, Garry Q. Lewis, Lacy Darryl Phillips, Roger Spivy
UNDERSTUDIES: Hinton Battle/Gregg Burge (Mr. Hines), Lorraine Fields/Wynonna Smith (Miss Kelly), Leata Galloway (Miss Bridgewater), Garry Q. Lewis/Eugene Fleming (Mr. battle), Roger Spivy/Michael Graham (Mr. Burge), Sheri Cowart (Miss Klausner), Eugene Fleming (Mr. Fotopoulos), Leata Galloway/Terri Klausner (Miss Giles), Loretta Giles/Terri Klausner (Miss Galloway), Sophisticated Ladies and Gentlemen: Lorraine Fields, Casey Cole, Eugene Fleming, Steve Marder
MUSICAL NUMBERS: see Broadway Calendar, page 44.

Gregory Hines and the Sophisticated Ladies

Toni Kaye, Eddie Bracken, Mimi Hines, Luke Stallings
(front) in "Sugar Babies"

SUGAR BABIES

Presented by Gingerbread Productions; Conceived by Ralph G. Allen, Harry Rigby; Musical Director, Kay Cameron; Assistant Conductor, Mike Huffman; Wardrobe, Carolyn Suder; Props, Larry Berryman; Company Manager, Don Grilley; Stage Managers, Lesley Stewart, David Wahl, Ted Bouton; Press, A. Stephen Cucich; For additional credits, see Broadway Calendar, page 45. Opened Tuesday, Sept. 15, 1981 at the Macauley Center, Louisville, Ky., and closed at the Palace Theatre, Cincinnati, Oh., May 2, 1982.

CAST

Eddie Bracken	Jaye P. Morgan†
Jay Stuart	Phil Ford
Sam Kressen	Toni Kaye

GAIETY QUARTET: G. Brandon Allen, Dale Hensley, Luke Stallings, Frank Stancati, Richard Parman (Alternate)
SUGAR BABIES: Blake Atherton, Paula Joy Belis, Madonna Christian, Andrea Cohen, Debbie DiBiase, Carla Farnsworth, Mary Anne Fiordalisi, Sarah Elizabeth Grove, Anne Gunderson, Erin Lareau, Lina Manning, Terry Nelson, Leslie Stevens
SKITS AND MUSICAL NUMBERS: A Good Old Burlesque Show, Let Me Be Your Sugar Baby, Meet Me Round the Corner, Don't Blame Me, Broken Arms Hotel, Travelin', Scenes from Domestic Life, Feathered Fantasy, Monkey Business, Ellis Island Love Story, Little Red Schoolhouse, Orientale, World's Greatest Knife Thrower, Mickey and Dolly, Mme. Rentz and Her All-Female Ministrels, Candy Butcher, Girls and Garters, Court of Last Retort, In a Greek Garden, Presenting Mme. Alla Gazaza, Tropical Madness, Cautionary Tales, McHugh Medley, Michael Rollov and Blake, Old Glory.
† Succeeded by Mimi Hines

SWEENEY TODD

Music and Lyrics, Stephen Sondheim; Book, Hugh Wheeler; Based on a version of "Sweeney Todd" by Christopher Bond; Director, Harold Prince; Dance and Movement, Larry Fuller; Assistant to Director, Arthur Masella; Setting, Eugene Lee; Costumes, Franne Lee; Lighting, Ken Billington; Orchestrations, Jonathan Tunick; Musical Supervisor, Paul Gemignani; Musical Director, Randy Booth; Presented by Tom Mallow in association with James Janek; Production Assistants, Susan O'Brien, Brian Callanan; Associate Musical Director, Jeff Conrad; Hairstylist, Brent Dillon; Wardrobe, Linda Berry, Wendy Hubschman; Props, Robert Michael, Douglas Edwards; General Manager, James Janek; Assistants to Producers, Jay Brooks, Arthur Katz, George MacPherson, Jan Mallow; Company Manager, Daryl T. Dodson; Stage Managers, Luis Montero, Richard Warren Pugh; Press, Max Eisen, Maria Somma. Opened Monday, Feb. 22, 1982 in Playhouse Theatre, Wilmington, De., and closed July 17, 1982 in Royal Alexandra, Toronto, Canada. For original Broadway production, see THEATRE WORLD Vol. 35.

CAST

Anthony Hope........................... Spain Logue	The Beadle........................... Calvin Remsberg
Sweeney Todd........................... Ross Petty	Johanna .... Malanie Vaughan
Beggar Woman........................... Carolyn Marlow	Tobias Ragg............................... Steven Jacob
Mrs. Lovett............................... June Havoc	Pirelli............................... Richard Warren Pugh
Judge Turpin........................... Robert Ousley	Jonas Fogg............................... Michael Kalinyen

ENSEMBLE: Skip Harris, Mary Johansen, James Edward Justiss, Michael Kalinyen, Steven Kosinski, Duane Morris, Meredith Rawlins, Michael Rockne, Clark Sayre, Laury Tatz, Joyce Tomanec, Maryrose Wood, Swings: Edmund John Koury, Colleen McNamara
MUSICAL NUMBERS: The Ballad of Sweeney Todd, No Place Like London, The Barber and His Wife, Worst Pies in London, Poor Thing, My Friends, Green Finch and Linnet Bird, Ah Miss, Johanna, Pirelli's Miracle Elixir, The Contest, Wait, Kiss Me, Ladies in Their Sensitivities, Quartet, Pretty Women, Epiphany, A Little Priest, God That's Good, Not While I'm Around, Parlor Songs, City on Fire, Finale.

June Havoc, Ross Petty in "Sweeney Todd"   Richard Ryder, Dawn Wells in "They're Playing Our Song"

THEY'RE PLAYING OUR SONG

Book, Neil Simon; Music, Marvin Hamlisch; Lyrics, Carole Bayer Sager; Director, Philip Cusack; Musical Numbers Staged by Patricia Birch; Scenery and Projections, Douglas W. Schmidt; Costumes, Ann Roth; Lighting, Tharon Musser; Musical Director, Roger Neil; Music Supervisor, Fran Liebergall; Orchestrations, Larry Blank; Sound, Tom Morse; Presented by Tom Mallow in association with James Janek; Wigs/Hairstylist, David Brian Brown, Mary Lou Flaherty; Assistant Conductor, O. T. Myers; Wardrobe, Linda Berry; Props, Devon Query, Greg Gfell; General Manager, James Janek; Company Manager, Terence Erkkila; Stage Managers, Charles Collins, Harold Goldfaden, Roy Miller; Press, Max Eisen, Barbara Glenn. Opened Monday, Jan. 19, 1981 in the Playhouse, Wilmington, De. and still touring, May 31, 1982. For original Broadway production, see THEATRE WORLD, Vol. 35.

CAST

Vernon Gersch .... John Hammil†1	Voices of Vernon.. George-Paul Fortuna, Paul Mack, Roy Miller
Sonia Walsk............................... Lorna Luft†2	Voice of Phil, the engineer.............. George-Paul Fortuna
	Swings: Daniel Neiden, Deborah Graham

Voices of Sonia . Lynne Lamberis, Gail Oscar, Peggy A. Stamper
MUSICAL NUMBERS: Fallin', Workin' It Out, If He Really Knew Me, They're Playing Our Song, Right, Just for Tonight, When You're in My Arms, I Still Believe in Love, Fill in the Words
† Succeeded by: 1. Richard Ryder, 2. June Gable, Dawn Wells

PROFESSIONAL RESIDENT COMPANIES

(Failure to meet deadline necessitated omissions)

ACT: A Contemporary Theatre

Seattle, Washington   June 4, 1981–May 27, 1982   Seventeenth Season
Producing Director, Gregory A. Falls; Administrative Manager, Louise Campion Cummings; Production Manager/Technical Director, Phil Schermer; Music Director, Stan Keen; Stage Manager, Michael Weholt; Costumer, Julie James; Props, Nancy Provence, Renee D. Reilly; Production Assistants, Joan Kennedy, Debra Sanderson; Press, Michael Eagan, Jr.

GETTING OUT by Marsha Norman; Director, Gregory A. Falls; Set, Scott Weldin; Costumes, Nanrose Buchman; Lighting, Jody Briggs. **CAST:** Nesbitt Blaisdell, Elaine Bromka, Jeffrey Covell, Sheila Crofut, Daniel Daily, Cynthia Darlow, R. A. Farrell, David Hunter Koch, David Mong, Hersha Parady, Rod Pilloud, Laurel Watt, Maureen Kilmurry

BILLY BISHOP GOES TO WAR By John Gray and Eric Peterson; Director, Robert Loper; Set, Scott Weldin; Costumes, Nanrose Buchman; Lighting, Donna Grout. **CAST:** Tom Hill, David Colacci

NIGHT AND DAY by Tom Stoppard; Director, Robert Egan; Set, Bill Raoul; Costumes Nanrose Buchman; Lighting, Randall G. Chiarelli. **CAST:** John Aylward, William Cain, Katherine Ferrand, Neil Fitzpatrick (Guest Artist), William Jay, Christopher Marks, Ben Prager, Stephen Sneed, Maureen Kilmurry

LOOSE ENDS by Michael Weller; Director, Richard Edwards; Set, Shelley Henze Schermer; Costumes, Susan Min; Lighting, Phil Schermer. **CAST:** David Colacci, Heidi Helen Davis, R. A. Farrell, Maureen Kilmurry, Daniel Mahar, Allen Nause, Clare Nono, John Procaccino, Steven Rose, Diane Schenker, Christopher Wong

WHOSE LIFE IS IT ANYWAY? by Brian Clark; Director, Clayton Corzatte; Set, William Forrester; Costumes, Julie James; Lighting, Jody Briggs. **CAST:** Kenneth Campbell, Cameron Dokey, R. A. Farrell, Maureen Kilmurry, Jerry Harper, Zoaunne LeRoy, Robert Loper, Daniel Mahar, Allen Nause, Rod Pilloud, Jeffrey Prather, Sally Pritchard, Stephen Sneed, Nina Wishengrad

A CHRISTMAS CAROL by Charles Dickens; Adapted by Gregory A. Falls; Director, Eileen MacRae Murphy; Set, Shelley Henze Schermer; Costumes, Julie James; Lighting, Phil Schermer. **CAST:** Edward Baran, Daniel Daily, R. A. Farrell, Michael Flynn, John Gilbert, Suzy Hunt, Christopher Marks, Noah Marks, Diana McBaine, David Mong, Richard Riehle, Elizabeth Rukavina, Jane Ryan, Michael Santo, Bradley Stam, Amy Steltz, Nina Wishengrad

ALI BABA AND THE FORTY THIEVES written and directed by Gregory A. Falls; *World Premiere;* Set/Costumes, Shelley Henze Shermer; Lighting, Jody Briggs. Cast not submitted.

"5 × 5" by Rob Duisberg, Jean Burch Falls, John Engerman, Phil Shallat, Chad Henry, Hub Miller, D. J. Wilson, G. Jean Anderson; *World Premiere;* Director, Roberta Levitow; Musical Director, Bruce Sevy; Choreographer, Susan Glass Burdick; Set, Shelley Henze Schermer; Costumes, Julie James; Lighting, Donna Grout. **CAST:** Colleen Carpenter, David Hunter Koch, Karen Marra, Jayne Muirhead, Jonathan Simmons, Suzy Hunt (Understudy)

DA by Hugh Leonard; Director, Richard Edwards; Set, Karen Gjelsteen; Costumes, Julie James; Lighting, Jody Briggs. **CAST:** R. A. Farrell, James Hilbrandt, Kathryn Mesney, Ursula Meyer, Allen Nause, Bill O'Leary, Rick Tutor, Lyn Tyrrell

Cynthia Darlow in "Getting Out"

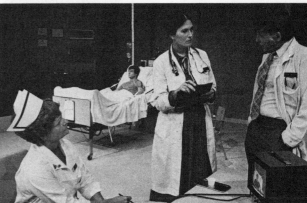

Zoaunne LeRoy, Kenneth Campbell, Maureen Kilmurry, Jerry Harper in "Whose Life Is It Anyway?" Above: Heidi Helen Davis, John Procaccino in "Loose Ends"

Actors Theatre of St. Paul

St. Paul, Minnesota   October 30, 1981–April 15, 1982
Artistic Director, Michael Andrew Miner; Managing Director, Jan Miner; Business Manager, Christopher Marquardt; Stage Directors,
Robert Mailand, Jeff Steitzer, Jim Cada, Jon Cranney, Michael Andrew Miner; Sets, James Guenther, Dick Leerhoff, Larry Kaushansky,
Chris Johnson, Don Yunker; Costumers, Michael L. Hanson, Jill Hamilton, Don Yunker, Arthur Ridley; Lighting, Chris Johnson, Michael
Vennerstrom, Don Yunker; Sound, Mark T. Nelson; Composer, Randall Davidson; Stage Managers, Steven Bishoff, Barbara A. Lutz; Press,
Fred Goudy

COMPANY: Barbara Kingsley, Louise Goetz, Sally Wingert, Spencer Beckwith, David Kwiat, Jim Cada, with *Guest Artists* Maria Rovang, Dianne Benjamin Hill, Ted Chase, Jane MacIver

PRODUCTIONS: Hedda Gabler, Absurd Person Singular, Waiting for the Parade, How I Got That Story, The Subject Was Roses, The Increased Difficulty of Concentration, Tartuffe, Old Explorers, John Barrymore: Confessions of an Actor

Barbara Kingsley as Hedda Gabler

James Hurdle, Cara Duff-MacCormick in "An Enemy of the People"
(Jim Lavrakas Photo)

Alaska Repertory Theatre

Anchorage/Fairbanks, Alaska   November 12, 1981–May 29, 1982   Sixth Season
Artistic Director, Robert J. Farley; Producing Director, Paul Brown; Managing Director, Mark Somers; Coordinator, Hugh F. Hall, Jr.;
Production Manager, Ben Taber; Stage Managers, Ann Mathews, Carol Chiavetta, James A. Woodward, Phyllis Schray; Press, Jane
Bradbury, Bobbie Winkel, Patricia Eckert

THE MAN WHO CAME TO DINNER by George S. Kaufman, Moss Hart; Director, John Going; Set, William Schroder; Costumes, James Berton Harris; Lighting, Spencer Mosse; Sound, Stephen Bennett. **CAST:** John Ahearn, James Aiken, William Arnold, Tom Bradley, Claire Wipperman, Albert Corbin, Ron Evans, Tom Flagg, June Gibbons, Sharon Harrison, Brian Keeler, Daren Kelly, Lynn Lentz, Maeve McGuire, Jonathan McMurtry, Monica Merryman, Moultri Patten, John Perkins, Marian Primont, Lori Putnam, Julian Rivers, Joan Ulmer, Ryal White, John Wylie, Kevin Craig, Derek Hansel, Ryan Pernela, Richard Piaskowski, Michael Rutherford, Paul Szopa, Ed Nolde

A CHRISTMAS CAROL by Charles Dickens; Director, Dan Sedgwick; Set, Jamie Greenleaf; Costumes, Nanrose Buchman; Lighting, James D. Sale; Sound, Stephen Bennett; Music Director, Mary Pat Graham; Choreography, Lisa Brailoff. **CAST:** Charles Antalosky, Brett Baker, Charles Berendt, Jill Bess, Tom Bradley, Lisa Brailoff, Daniel Church, A. D. Cover, Steve Crosby, Sasha Ensign, Harry Frazier, Sharon Harrison, Dana Hart, James Hotchkiss, Marta Lastufka, Craig Lee McIntosh, Joe Meek, Jane Moore, Lora Morrow, Perrin Morse, Virginia Patterson, Benjamin Ryken, Joan Shangold, Lynne Soffer, David Westgor, Adam Crenshaw

AN ENEMY OF THE PEOPLE by Henrik Ibsen; Director, Irene Lewis; Set, Hugh Landwehr; Costumes, Linda Fisher; Lighting, Pat Collins; Sound, Stephen Bennett. **CAST:** Brett Baker, Nesbitt Blaisdell, Albert Corbin, Cara Duff-MacCormick, Ron Frazier, Ben Gottlieb, Sharon Harrison, John Heginbotham, James Hurdle, Cynthia Judge, James McDonnell, Jack Murdock

THE HOT L BALTIMORE by Lanford Wilson; Director, Robert J. Farley; Set, Jamie Greenleaf; Costumes, Nanrose Buchman; Lights, Judy Rasmuson. **CAST:** Linda Atkinson, Marian Baer, Tom Bradley, Nora Chester, Damon DiPietro, Arthur Hammer, G. E. Jacobsen, Jack Murdock, Diedre Owens, Leon Parsons, Marina Posvar, Richard Riehle, Donn Ruddy, Joan Rue, Judith Tillman

FOOLS by Neil Simon; Director, Walton Jones; Set, Kevin Rupnik; Costumes, Dunya Ramicova; Lights, Lauren MacKenzie Miller; Choreography, Laurie Boyd; Sound, Stephen Bennett. **CAST:** Tom Bade, Bill Buell, Douglas Fisher, Harry Frazier, Virginia Hammer, J. R. Horne, James Maxwell, Elizabeth Norment, Mary Ed Porter, Richard Riehle, Robert Sieger

Alley Theatre

Houston, Texas   October 15, 1982–June 27, 1982   Thirty-fifth Season

Artistic Director, Pat Brown; Managing Director, Iris Siff; Business Manager, Bill Halbert; Production Manager, Bettye Fitzpatrick; Director of Design, Michael Olich; Resident Director, Beth Sanford; Sets, William Bloodgood, Edward Lipscomb, Michael Olich, Matthew Grant, John Bos; Costumes, John Carver Sullivan, Deborah M. Dryden, Michael Olich, Rosemary Ingham, Edward Lipscomb; Lighting, Francis Lynch, James Sale, Jonathan Duff; Stage Managers, Florine Pulley, Janice Heidke, Michael McEowen; Development, Brenda Dubay; Casting, George Anderson; Company Manager, Chuck Lutke; Press, Bob Feingold, John Eaton

CYRANO DE BERGERAC by Edmond Rostand; Translation, Brian Hooker; Director, B. H. Barry. **CAST:** Timothy Arrington, Milton Blankenship, Bob Burrus, Michael Butler, Michael Cunningham, Robert Graham, Lanny Green, Helen Halsey, J. Rorey Hayden, Brian Hinson, Veronica Kemp-Henson, Cynthia Lammel, Dan LaRocque, Gwendolyn Lewis, Jim McQueen, Stephen Markle, Terry Masters, Vernon Morris, Robin Moseley, Jean Proctor, Emily Riddle, Phil Schuster, Sandi Shackelford, Gram Slaton, Kathy Paul Warren, Dennis Wells

YOU KNOW AL HE'S A FUNNY GUY written and performed by Jerry Mayer; Director, John Pynchon Holms

THE RED BLUEGRASS WESTERN FLYER SHOW with Book and Lyrics by Conn Fleming; Music, Clint Ballard, Jr.; Director, Pat Brown; Choreography, Dennis J. Grimaldi; Musical Director, Jeff Waxman. **CAST:** Danny Alford, J. Brent Alford, Rob Babbitt, Neil Badders, Chalyce Blair, Milton Blankenship, Celia Braswell, Julie Challenger, Robert Donley, Bettye Fitzpatrick, Karen Garelick, Brian Hinson, Lynn Humphrey, Dan LaRocque, Jim McQueen, Nancy Miller, Sharon Montgomery, Colleen O'Kit, Brent Rogers, Sharon Shepley, Brandon Smith, Leann Sparacina, Walker Stevens

THE HOUSE OF BLUE LEAVES by John Guare; Director, Ivan Rider, Jr. **CAST:** Jay Bell, Robert Graham, Helen Halsey, J. Rorey Hayden, Veronica Kemp-Henson, Michael LaGue, Carol Locatell, Robin Moseley, Linda Selman, Cynthia Lammel, Charles Jackson

THE ELEPHANT MAN by Bernard Pomerance; Director, Beth Sanford; Music, Jan Cole. **CAST:** Danny Alford, Jay Bell, Jan Cole, Henry Dardenne, Lillian Evans, Robert Graham, Helen Halsey, Michael LaGue, Cynthia Lammel, Dan LaRocque, Vernon Morris, Robin Moseley, Gary Wynn

"AND IF THAT MOCKINGBIRD DON'T SING" by William M. Whitehead; Lyrics, Mr. Whitehead; Music, David Huffman, Howard Platt, Tony Swartz; Director, Neil Havens; Musical Director, Neil Havens. **CAST:** Charles Jackson, Veronica Kemp-Henson, Blue Deckert, James Belcher, Brandon Smith, Sharon Thomas-Montgomery, Jim McQueen, Billy Nowell, J. Shane McClure, Bob Burrus, Timothy Arrington, Milton Blankenship, Matthew Posey, Rodney Hudson, J. Rorey Hayden

PARADISE by Monty Philip Holamon; Director, Beth Sanford, **CAST:** Bettye Fitzpatrick, Michael LaGue, Robin Moseley, Bob Burrus, Helen Halsey *(World Premiere)*

WAY UPSTREAM by Alan Ayckbourn *(U.S. Premiere);* Director, Mr. Ayckbourn. **CAST:** Robin Bowerman, Carole Boyd, Robin Herford, Lavinia Bertram, Susan Uebel. Understudies: Jeni Giffen, John Skitt. (All members of England's Stephen Joseph Theatre in the Round Company)

ABSENT FRIENDS written and directed by Alan Ayckbourn; Performed by members of the Stephen Joseph Theatre in the Round Company from England. **CAST:** Graeme Eton, Lavinia Bertram, Robin Bowerman, Gillian Bevan, Robin Herford, Susan Uebel, Understudies: Jeni Giffen, John Skitt

THE WALL by Millard Lampell; Based on novel by John Hersey; Director, Pat Brown. **CAST:** Danny Alford, Timothy Arrington, Milton Blankenship, Bob Burrus, Steve Cassling, Henry Dardenne, Blue Deckert, Matt Duffin, Lillian Evans, Joe Finkelstein, Philip Fisher, Robert Graham, Bruce Hall, Helen Halsey, Michael LaGue, Cynthia Lammel, Dan LaRocque, Dede Lowe, J. Shane McClure, Robin Moseley, Sallie Weathers, Dennis Wells, James Belcher, J. Rorey Hayden, Alan Litsey, Cassie McCollum, Paris Peet, Matthew Posey, Scott Roser, Brenda Williams, Cary Winscott

HEIDI by Donald Antrim from the novel by Johanna Spyri; Original Music, Stephen Houtz; Director, John Vreeke; Choreography, Terry Masters. **CAST:** Cynthia Lammel, Sandi Shackelford, Tom Flynn, Scott Roser, Brenda Williams, J. Rorey Hayden, Steve Cassling, Henry Dardenne, Emily Riddle, Teresa Heck, Matthew Posey, Dede Lowe, James Belcher, Paris Peet

TALLEY'S FOLLY by Lansford Wilson; Director, Beth Sanford. **CAST:** Ron Rifkin, Holly Villaire

Graeme Eton, Carole Boyd, Robin Herford, Lavinia Bertram in "Way Upstream"   Lillian Evans, Bob Burrus in "The Wall"

Alliance Theatre Company

Atlanta, Georgia   October 21, 1981–May 23, 1982

Managing Director, Bernard Havard; Artistic Director, Fred Chappell; Associate Director, Charles Abbott; Administrative Director, Edith Love; Production Manager, Billings Lapierre; Sets, Mark Morton; Costumes, Thom Coates; Lighting, Michael Orris Watson; Musical Director, Michael Fauss; Stage Managers, Pat Waldorf, Gretchen Van Horne; Press, Mark Arnold

WHOSE LIFE IS IT ANYWAY? by Brian Clark. **CAST:** Linda Stephens, Jihad Babatunde, Terry Beaver, Marian Bolton, Tom Campbell, Alan Cook, Adrian Elder, Al Hamacher, Yetta Levitt, Denise Burse-Mickelbury, Jim Peck, Mary Nell Santacroce, David Wasman

BRIGADOON with Music by Frederick Loewe; Book/Lyrics, Alan J. Lerner. **CAST:** Mark Jacoby, Lynn Fitzpatrick, Amy Bailey, Jason Miles Benjamin, Brent Black, J. Mark Blihovde, Shellie Bransford, Sharon Caplan, Marc Clement, Alan Cook, Adrian Elder, Ken Ellis, Nancy Farrar, John Forrest Ferguson, Al Hamacher, Betsy Banks Harper, Charlie Hensley, Chris Kayser, Terri Kayser, Joseph Kelly, Stephanie Kornegay, Judy Langford, Suzanne Loebus, Robert Lund, Barbara Hancock Madden, Jan Maris, Megan McFarland, Bobby Minnear, Gordon Paddison, Peter D. Powlus, Dawn Ricker, Don Spalding, Jim Tillman, Denton Yockey

PRIVATE LIVES by Noel Coward. **CAST:** Brooks Baldwin, Lynn Fitzpatrick, Judith Robinson, Rob Roper, Chondra Wolle

LOOSE ENDS by Michael Weller. **CAST:** Jihad Babatunde, Jill Jane Clements, Marianne Hammock, Thomas C. Hammond, David Head, Charlie Hensley, Gordon Paddison, Ellen Ishino Rankart, Marshall Rosenblum, Jamey Sheridan, Sherry Steiner, Kent Stephens (Guest Director)

CABARET with Book by Jose Masteroff; Music, John Kander; Lyrics, Fred Ebb. **CAST:** Charles Abbott, Christina Allen, Brent Black, Daniel Bale, Shellie Bransford, Sharon Caplan, David Carr, Nancy Jane Clay, Ken Ellis, Lorna Erickson, Richard Fagan, Karen Hunt, Kurt Johnson, Jinny Kordek, Wayne Lancaster, Robert Lund, Byron L. Love, Jan Maris, Vonne Martin, Kay McClelland, Sean McGinty, Theresa Neer, Gordon Paddison, Ginny Parker, Woody Romoff, Lynn Safrit, Tambra Smith, Chick Durrett-Smith, Dennis Durrett-Smith, Don Spalding, Victoria Tabaka, Libby Whittemore

A MIDSUMMER NIGHT'S DREAM by William Shakespeare; **CAST:** Terry Beaver, Brent Black, Suzanne Calvert, Dave Carr, Marc Clement, John Courtney, Diane D'Aquila, Dennis Durrett-Smith, Rudolph A. Goldschmidt, Al Hamacher, Marianne Hammock, Betsy Banks Harper, Celine Havard, David Head, Charlie Hensley, Jody Howard, Scott Isert, Lisa Kriho, Eddie Lee, David McCann, MichaelJohn McGann, Jay McMillan, Gordon Paddison, Marshall Rosenblum, Lynn Safrit, Philip C. Sneed, Don Spalding, Bea Swanson, Chondra Wolle

BILLY BISHOP GOES TO WAR by John Gray and Eric Peterson. **CAST:** Robert Browning, Joe Collins

SONS AND FATHERS OF SONS by Ray Arahna *(WORLD PREMIERE)*. **CAST:** Jihad Babatunde, Jarrett Ellis-Beal, Rob Cleveland, Ernest L. Dixon, Kin Dixon, Veda S. Kimber, Denise Burse-Mickelbury, Rebecca Williams

A COUPLA WHITE CHICKS SITTING AROUND TALKING by John Ford Noonan. **CAST:** Nancy Jane Clay, Jan Maris

THE DIVINERS by Jim Leonard, Jr. **CAST:** Terry Beaver, Suzanne Calvert, Marc Clement, Rudolph A. Goldschmidt, Marianne Hammock, Betsy Banks Harper, David W. Head, Charlie Hensley, Eddie Lee, Bea Swanson, Chondra Wolle

DUNGEONS AND GRYPHONS by Linden Petersen. **CAST:** Abb Disckson, James Caden, Marianne Hammock, John McAdams, Jay McMillan, Wanda Strange, Peter Thomasson

SNEAKERS with Book by Judith Weinstein, Arnold Somers; Music, Elissa Shreiner; Lyrics, Sunnie Miller. **CAST:** Jennifer Cole, Stanton Cunningham, Melanie Hobbs, Roberta Illg, Larry Johnson, Dana Laughlin, B. J. McCroskey, Matt McCuen, Jay McMillan, Robbie McNeill, Will Montgomery, Richard Moore, Brian Porter, Robert Schultz, Tari Tamiroff, Kevin Vickery

Charles Abbott (C) in "Cabaret"

"A Midsummer Night's Dream"

American Conservatory Theatre

San Francisco, California   October 10, 1981–May 29, 1982   Sixteenth Season

General Director, William Ball; Executive Producer, James B. McKenzie; Executive Director, Edward Hastings; Conservatory Director, Allen Fletcher; General Manager, Benjamin Moore; Production Managers, John A. Woods, John Brown; Production Coordinator, James Sulanowski; Production Assistant, Eric Shortt; Stage Directors, William Ball, James Edmondson, Allen Fletcher, Edward Hastings, Elizabeth Huddle, Nagle Jackson, Laird Williamson, Michael Winters; Associate Directors, Eugene Barcone, John C. Fletcher, Janice Garcia-Hutchins, James Haire, Sarah Ream, Larry Russell; Musical Director, Richard Hindman; Composers, Larry D. Linger, Lee Hoiby; Lighting, Joseph Appelt, Mark Bosch, Dirk Epperson, James Sale, Duane Schuler; Sets and Costumes, Robert Blackman, Martha Burke, Michael Casey, Ralph Funicello, Richard Hay, Robert Morgan, Michael Olich, Richard Seger, Vicki Smith, Walter Watson; Sound, Randy Bobo, Alfred Tetzner; Stage Managers, James Haire, Eugene Barcone, James L. Burke, Cornelia Twitchell, Karen Van Zandt; Props, Oliver C. Olsen, David Nash, Eric Norton; Wardrobe, Donald Long-Hurst, Thea Heinz, Suzanne Raftery; Press, Marne Davis Kellogg, Johanna Kelly, Kirsten Mickelwait

COMPANY: Joseph Bird, Raye Birk, Mimi Carr, Barbara Dirickson, Peter Donat, Gina Ferrall, John C. Fletcher, Julia Fletcher, Janice Garcia-Hutchins, Lydia Hannibal, Thomas Harrison, Lawrence Hecht, John Noah Hertzler, Jill Hill, Elizabeth Huddle, John Hutton, Johanna Jackson, Jane Jones, Nicholas Kaledin, Richard Kuss, Anne Lawder, Dakin Matthews, William McKereghan, DeAnn Mears, Mark Murphey, Sharon Newman, Thomas Oglesby, Frank Ottiwell, William Paterson, Greg Patterson, Wendi Radford, Stacy Ray, Ray Reinhardt, Randall Richard, Frank Savino, Garland J. Simpson, Sally Smythe, Deborah Sussel, Sydney Walker, Marrian Walters, Isiah Whitlock, Jr., Bruce Williams, Robert Wortham-Krimmer, D. Paul Yeuell

PRODUCTIONS: Richard II by William Shakespeare, I Remember Mama by John Van Druten, The Three Sisters by Anton Chekhov, The Admirable Crichton by James M. Barrie, A Christmas Carol by Charles Dickens, *World Premiere* of Happy Landings by William Hamilton, Black Comedy by Peter Shaffer, The Browning Version by Terence Rattigan, Mourning Becomes Electra by Eugene O'Neill, Cat Among the Pigeons by Georges Feydeau, Another Part of the Forest by Lillian Hellman

Sally Smythe, Janice Garcia-Hutchins, Jill Hill in "The Admirable Crichton" Top Right: Julia Fletcher, Dakin Matthews, Thomas Oglesby in "Mourning Becomes Electra"

American Mime Theatre

New York, N.Y.   June 1, 1981–May 31, 1982
Founder/Director, Paul J. Curtis; Administrator, Jean Barbour; Counsel, Joel S. Charleston.

COMPANY: Jean Barbour, Charles Barney, Joseph Citta, Paul Curtis, Dale Fuller, Kevin Kaloostian, Erica Sarzin, Mr. Bones
REPERTOIRE: The Lovers, The Scarecrow, Dreams, Hurly-Burly, Evolution, Sludge, Six, The Unitaur

"The Lovers"

American Repertory Theatre

Cambridge, Massachusetts   Third Season

SGANARELLE an evening of Moliere farces directed by Andrei Serban; Translations, Albert Bermel; Music, Stephen Drury. **CAST:** John Bottoms, Francois de la Giroday, Thomas Derrah, Jeremy Geidt, Richard Grusin, Cherry Jones, Karen MacDonald, Jonathan Marks, Marianne Owen, Tony Shalhoub

ORLANDO by George Frideric Handel; Director, Peter Sellars; Music, Craig Smith. **CAST:** Robert Honeysucker, James Maddalena, Jeffrey Gall, Sanford Sylvan, Susan Larson, Sharon Baker, Jane Bryden, Janet Brown, Mary Kendrick Sego, Pamela Gore

THE JOURNEY OF THE FIFTH HORSE by Ronald Ribman; Director, Adrian Hall. **CAST:** Marianne Owen, Richard Grusin, Thomas Derrah, Francois de la Giroday, Cherry Jones, Tony Shalhoub, Karen MacDonald, Paul Benedict, Jonathan Marks, John Bottoms, Maja Hellmold, Jeremy Geidt, Shirley Wilber, Nicolette Webb

TRUE WEST by Sam Shepard; Director, David Wheeler. **CAST:** John Bottoms, Francois de la Giroday, Richard Grusin, Shirley Wilber

RUNDOWN by Robert Auletta *(World Premiere)*; Director, William Foeller; Sound, Stephen Drury. **CAST:** Stephen Rowe, Karen MacDonald, Marianne Owen, Tony Shalhoub, Thomas Derrah

GHOSTS by Henrik Ibsen; Adapted and Directed by Robert Brustein. **CAST:** Kathleen Widdoes, John Belucci, Alvin Epstein, Cherry Jones, Jeremy Geidt

ORCHIDS IN THE MOONLIGHT by Carlos Fuentes *(World Premiere)*; Director, Joann Green. **CAST:** Rosalind Cash, Ellen Holly, Frank Licato

Kathleen Widdoes, Alvin Epstein in "Ghosts"

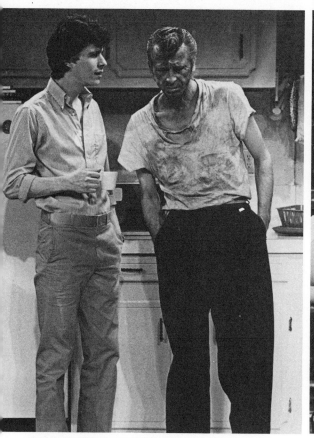

Francois de la Giroday, John Bottoms in "True West"

Karen MacDonald, Stephen Rowe in "Rundown"

125

American Theatre Arts

Hollywood, California   Fifth Season

Artistic Director, Don Eitner; Executive Director, John Terry Bell; Conservatory Director, Nancy Jeris; Production Director, Janice M. Christensen; Development/Marketing, Jim Bennett; Technical Director, Robert Smitherman; Lighting, Nancy Shaffer; Staff Assistant, Todd Durwood; Press, Sharon Mazer

COMPANY: David Abbott, Philip Abbott, Howard Adler, John Terry Bell, Pamela Bohnert, Mary Bomba, Gary Brockette, Lisa Carole, Freddye Chapman, Juanita Copeland, Oren Curtis, Joanne Dalsass, Earlene Davis, Rob Donohoe, Robert Dore, Nora Morgan Eckstein, Lou Fant, Betty Ferber, Lisa Figus, Chandler Garrison, Tanya George, Jeanne Hepple, Patricia Herd, Nancy Jeris, Richard Kendall, Carol Locatell, Justin Lord, John McKinney, Greg Michaels, Elaine Nalee, Kip Niven, George Parish, Mary Patton, Cathryn Perdue, Betty Ramey, Ray Roberts, Joseph Ruskin, Robert Sampson, Sara Shearer, Jayne Taini, Jeannie VanDam, Kay Worthington, Nora Denny, and *Guest Artists:* Irene Tedrow, Naomi Stevens, Don Starr, Emory Bass

PRODUCTIONS: Riverwind by John Jennings, Catsplay by Istvan Orkeny, After the Rain by John Bowen, Towards Zero by Agatha Christie, *U.S. Premiere* of The Times Table by Alan Ayckbourn, and *World Premieres* of Body to Light by Doraine Poretz, Embarcadero Fugue by Tom Strelich

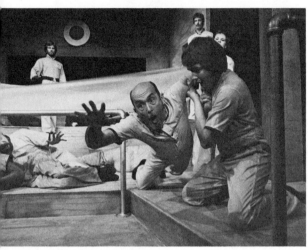

Freddye Chapman, John Terry Bell, Oren Curtis, Arlee Reed in "After the Rain"

Jim Metzler, Earlene Davis, Irene Tedrow in "Towards Zero"

Stephen McHattie, Stanley Anderson in "K2"
(Joan Marcus Photos)

Christine Estabrook, Robert W. Westenberg in "Major Barbara"

ARENA STAGE productions copy not submitted

Arizona Theatre Company

Tucson, Arizona November 5, 1981–June 6, 1982

Managing Director, David R. Hawkanson; Artistic Director, Gary Gisselman; Marketing/Press, Sharon Griggins; Development, Barbara R. Levy; Business Manager, Daphne L. Rudolph; Press, Kathy Frisch; Production Manager, Peter A. Davis; Technical Director, Steven B. Peterson; Costumes, Christopher Beesley; Stage Managers, David G. Larson, Nancy Thomas; Sets, Kent Dorsey, Jack Barkla, Peter A. Davis, Gene Davis Buck; Costumes, Christopher Beesley, Gene Davis Buck, Jack Barkla, Bobbi Culbert; Lighting, John B. Forbes, Don Darnutzer, Kent Dorsey, Steven B. Peterson; Sound, Bob Bish, Warren Hogan; Composer/Musical Director, Maida Libkin; Directors, Gary Gisselman, Michael Maggio, Jon Cranney, Lewis Whitlock (also choreographer).

THE RAINMAKER by N. Richard Nash. **CAST:** Paul C. Thomas, Tony DeBruno, Arnie Krauss, Jane Murray, John Cannon Nichols, Benjamin Stewart, Logan Pope

A CHRISTMAS CAROL by Charles Dickens. **CAST:** Carl Craig, Tony DeBruno, Bruno Fazzolare, Michael Goodsite, Claudine Gootter, June Grushka, Claire Harlan, Carla Howard, Henry Kendrick, Arnie Krauss, Diane Landis-Gifford, Mark Leonard, Ann Carlson Brown, David Marsh, Leonard Meenach, Penny Metropulos, Jane Murray, John Cannon Nichols, David Nevins, Hilary Quick, Philip Rosenberg, James Shafer, Benjamin Stewart, Paul C. Thomas

WAITING FOR GODOT by Samuel Beckett. **CAST:** Paul Ballantyne, Robert Ellenstein, Benjamin Stewart, Clifford Rakerk, Michael E. Goodsite

MISALLIANCE by George Bernard Shaw. **CAST:** Tim Halligan, Clifford Rakerd, Jane Murray, Patricia Fraser, Benjamin Stewart, Paul C. Thomas, John Cannon Nichols, Lynnie Greene, Tony DeBruno

AS YOU LIKE IT by William Shakespeare. **CAST:** Ann Carlson-Brown, Carl Craig, Kitty Carroll, Tony DeBruno, Mark DeMichele, Lynnie Greene, Tim Halligan, Roy Henderson, Larry Hines, Henry Kendrick, Arnie Krauss, Hugh McCracken, David Marsh, Leonard Meenach, Penny Metropulos, Jane Murray, Joseph Nassi, John Cannon Nichols, Clifford Rakerd, Mark Ruch, Benjamin Stewart, Paul C. Thomas

THE GIN GAME by D. L. Coburn. **CAST:** Robert Ellenstein, Patricia Fraser

TINTYPES by Mary Kyte with Mel Marvin and Gary Pearle. **CAST:** Ross Lehman, Benjamin Stewart, Nedra Dixon, Kitty Carroll, Penny Metropulos

Patricia Fraser, Robert Ellenstein in "The Gin Game" Top Right: Penny Metropulos, Nedra Dixon, Kitty Carroll (front), Ross Lehman, Benjamin Stewart in "Tintypes"

127

Asolo State Theater

Sarasota, Florida   Twenty-second Season

Executive Director, Richard G. Fallon; Managing Director, David S. Levenson; Artistic Director, Robert Strane; Artistic Adviser, Stuart Vaughan; Musical Director, John Franceschina; Manager, Thomas G. Veeder; Press, Edith N. Anson; Stage Directors, Neal Kenyon, Eberle Thomas, Bernard Engel, Jim Hoskins, Gregory Abels, Donald Madden, Thomas Gruenewald; Sets, Holmes Easley, William Barclay, John Ezell, Thomas Michael Cariello, Peter Dean Beck, Sam Bagarella; Costumes, Catherine King, Sally A. Kos, Paige Southard, Vicki S. Holden, Ellis Tillman; Lighting, Martin Petlock; Stage Managers, Stephanie Moss, John J. Toia, Dolly Meenan; Technical Director, Victor Meyrich

COMPANY:

February 19–September 6, 1981

Paula Dewey, Michele Franks, Davis Gaines, Mark Jacoby, Patricia Masters, Alan Brooks, Bernerd Engel, David S. Howard, James Hunt, Jeffrey Bryan King, Kathleen Klein, Philip LeStrange, Carolyn Ann Milay, Robert Murch, Bette Oliver, Barbara Redmond, Wesley Stevens, Eberle Thomas, Isa Thomas, Charles Bennison, Charles Cronk, Rob Ferguson, Jeanann Glassford, Marc H. Glick, Elizabeth Harrell, Michael Hodgson, Arthur Glen Hughes, Robert Kratky, Robin Llewellyn, Lowry Marshall, Peter Massey, Jon Michaelsen, Mark Rosenwinkel, Connie Rotunda, Elizabeth Streiff, Laurence Daggett, Ray Frewen, Leo Garcia, Richard Grubbs, Jay Keye, Graves Kiely, Philip Lombardo, Vicki March, Carol McCann, Mark Mikesell, Jane Rosinski, Sharon Taylor, Carlos Valdes-Dapena

February 18–September 5, 1982

Denise Bessette, Dion Chesse, Rob Ferguson, Mary Elizabeth Horowitz, David S. Howard, Douglas Jones, Paul Milikin, Robert Murch, Bette Oliver, Viveca Parker, Karl Redcoff, Wesley Stevens, Isa Thomas, Laurence Daggett, Ray Frewen, Leo Garcia, Richard Grubbs, Jay Keye, Graves Kiely, Philip Lombardo, Vici March, Carol McCann, Mark Mikesell, Jane Rosinski, Sharon Taylor, Carlos Valdes-Dapena, Kevin Brief, Dub Croft, Phillip Douglas, Suzanne Grodner, Kelley Hazen, Randy Hyten, Paul Kassel, Tom Kendall, Keith LaPan, Jerry Plourde, Brant Pope, Wendy Scharfman, Jane Smillie, Leslie J. Smith, Duncan Stephens, Lizbeth Trepel, Ellia English, P. J. Hoffman, Lance Roberts, Paul M. Elkin

PRODUCTIONS: The Song Is Kern!, The Three Musketeers by Eberle Thomas *(World Premiere)*, Picnic, Once in a Lifetime, A Midsummer Night's Dream, Mrs. Warren's Profession, The Show-Off, The All-Night Strut

Left: Wesley Stevens, Denise Bessette, Robert Murch, Mary Elizabeth Horowitz, Rob Ferguson, Douglas Jones in "A Midsummer Night's Dream" *(Gary Sweetman Photos)*

Robert Murch, Wesley Stevens, Paul Milikin, Karl Redcoff, Isa Thomas, Viveca Parker in "Mrs. Warren's Profession"

Barter Theatre

Abingdon/Fairfax, Virginia   June 3, 1981–May 22, 1982   Forty-ninth Season

Artistic Director/Producer, Rex Partington; Business Manager, Pearl Hayter; Press, Lou Flanigan; Associate Artistic Consultant, Owen Phillips; Directors, Rex Partington, Fred Chappell, Pamela Hunt, Lawrence Kornfeld, Ada Brown Mather, John Olon, Mark Sumner, George Touliatos; Sets, Daniel H. Ettinger, C. L. Hundley, John C. Larrance, Lynn Pecktal, Bob Phillips, David W. Weiss; Costumes, Nance Atkinson, C. L. Hundley, Sigrid Insull, Judianna Makovsky, Mary Jane McCarty; Lighting, Christopher H. Shaw; Musical Director, Marvin Jones; Stage Managers, Debra Acquavella, Don Buschmann, Champe Leary

DULCY by George S. Kaufman, Marc Connelly; with Mary Benson, Mike Chapagne, Carolyn Clark, Byron Grant, James Hilbrandt, Ray Hill, Daniel Oreskes, Con Roche, Carol Schultz, Richard Tabor, Gerald Walling

ON GOLDEN POND by Ernest Thompson; with Mike Champagne, Spencer Cox, Harry Ellerbe, Marion Hunter, Patricia Place, Gerald Walling, Ross Bickell, Travis Fine, Cleo Holladay, Philip Locker

ARMS AND THE MAN by George Bernard Shaw; with Mike Champagne, Barbara Durchy, Edward Gero, Del Green, George Hosmer, Carolyn Olga Kruse, Robert Thames, Gerald Walling

DEATHTRAP by Ira Levin; with Eunice Anderson, Ross Bickell, Mike Champagne, Edward Gero, Cleo Holladay, Craig Kuehl

TALLEY'S FOLLY by Lanford Wilson; with Katie Grant, Eugene Troobnick

OH, COWARD! by Noel Coward; Devised by Roderick Cook; with Suzanne Dawson, Larry Hansen, Richard Kevlin-Bell

GALLOWS HUMOR by Jack Richardson; with Ray Hill, Craig Kuehl, Carol Schultz

TWO BY FIVE by John Kander and Fred Ebb; Conceived by Seth Glassman; with Susan Edwards, Larry Hansen, Karl Heist, Marion Hunter, Marvin Jones

THE CORN IS GREEN by Emlyn Williams; with Charles Beatty, Ross Bickell, Robert Bornarth, Marlene Bryan, Sarah Buxton, Allison Davis, Dean Dietrich, Kathy Fleig, Catherine Flye, Edward Gero, Mary Hamill, Cleo Holladay, Craig Kuehl, Mark Miller, Charles Muckle, Elizabeth Todd, Jeff Wallace

THE HEIRESS by Ruth and Augustus Goetz; with Ross Bickell, Libby Hisey, Cleo Holladay, Olivia Negron, Dixie Partington, Tony Partington, Rex Partington, Patricia Place, Piper Smith

LOVE'S LABOUR'S LOST by William Shakespeare; with Lee Alexander, Arthur Barsamian, Jack L. Davis, Ethan Kane Dufault, Barbara Durchy, Edward Gero, Carolyn Olga Kruse, Paula Mann, Anderson Matthews, Geoffrey Reid, Armin Shimerman, Victor Slezak, Judy Soffian, Kitty Swink, Richard Tabor, Zeke Zaccaro

Byron Grant, Carolyn Clark, Mary Benson, Carol Schultz in "Dulcy"
Above: Harry Ellerbe, Patricia Place in "On Golden Pond"
(John Cornelius Photos)

Body Politic Theatre

Chicago, Illinois

Artistic Director, James O'Reilly; Managing Director, Sharon Phillips; Marketing Director, John Stillwell; Business Manager, Gretchen Althen; Literary Manager, Terry McCabe; Stage Manager, Nels Anderson, Tony Norrenbrock, Jeffery Bauer, Chris Phillips; Costumes, Virgil Johnson, Kerry Fleming, Nan Zabriskie, Elizabeth Passman; Lighting, Rita Pietraszek, Gary Heitz, Chris Phillips; Directors, James O'Reilly, Tom Mula, Susan Dafoe, Pauline Brailsford

COMPANY: Names not submitted

PRODUCTIONS: Twelfth Night by William Shakespeare, The Seahorse by Edward J. Moore, Holding Patterns by Jeffrey Sweet *(World Premiere)*, The Petrified Forest by Robert E. Sherwood, Taming of the Shrew by William Shakespeare, Eve by Larry Fineberg, Confusions by Alan Ayckbourn, Translations by Brian Friel

Top Right: A. J. Morey, Lucy Childs in "The Petrified Forest"
Below: Bob Keenan, Peg Small in "Eve" *(Jennifer Girard Photos)*

Caldwell Playhouse

Boca Raton, Florida   July 14, 1981–May 1, 1982   Second Season

Artistic/Managing Director, Michael Hall; Sets, Frank Bennett; Costumes, Bridget Bartlett; Lighting, Jas Myers, Joyce Fleming; Scenic Artist, Marion Kolsby; Stage Manager, Linda Van Horn; Manager/Press, Patricia Burdett

VANITIES by Jack Heifner; with Viki Boyle, Susan Hatfield, Patricia Nesbit

THE ELEPHANT MAN by Bernard Pomerance; with Louis Tyrell, Peter Haig, Barbara Bradshaw, Joseph H. Reed, Susan Hatfield, Miller Lide, Dennis Bateman

THE WALTZ OF THE TOREADORS by Jean Anouilh; with Curry Worsham, Barbara Bradshaw, Ronald Wendschuh, Sue Vos, Wayne Lee Michaels, Peter Haig, Linda Marie Boni, Angela Lloyd, Erin Brady

THE HEIRESS by Ruth and Augustus Goetz; with Barbara Bradshaw, Ronald Wendschuh, Robert Walsh, Rica Martens, Erin Brady, Wayne Lee Michaels, Mary Lowry, Ann Sams, Angela Lloyd

FIVE FINGER EXERCISE by Peter Shaffer; with Sann Sams, J. C. Hoyt, Wayne Lee Michaels, Julian Barnes, Ellen Adamson

ABSENCE OF A CELLO by Ira Wallach; with Michael Coerver, Deirdre Owens, Ruby Payne, Will Osborne, Conni Atkins, John Everson, Cynthia Judge

Barbara Bradshaw, Robert Walsh, Ronald Wendschuh in "The Heiress"

Ann Sams, Wayne Lee Michaels in "Five Finger Exercise"

Capital Repertory Company

Albany, New York

Producing Directors, Bruce Bouchard, Peter H. Clough; General Manager, Martha E. Gottlieb; Press, Pamela Sawchuk Associates; Technical Director, David Yergan; Stage Manager, Karen Wiltshire

TABLE MANNERS by Alan Ayckbourn; Director, Michael J. Hume; Set, Dale F. Jordan; Lighting, Lary Opitz; Costumes, Lloyd Waiwaiole; Props, Susan B. Smyth; **CAST:** Kate Kelly, Mary E. Baird, Richard Zobel, Michael Arkin, James Goodwin Rice, Kit Flanagan

A STREETCAR NAMED DESIRE by Tennessee Williams; Director, Louis Schaefer; Set, Robert Thayer; Lighting, Mark DiQuinzio; Costumes, Cinthia Waas; Sound, George L. Toman; **CAST:** Michael J. Hume, Richard Zobel, Michael Arkin, Kim Ameen, Mary E. Baird, Sofia Landon, James Goodwin Rice, Stephen Hytner, Pat Titterton, Charles Losacco

FEATHERS by Jeanne Darnell *(World Premiere);* Director, Susan Lehman; Set, Ray Recht; Costumes, Lloyd Waiwaiole; Props, Susan B. Smyth. **CAST:** Chris Weatherhead, Kate Kelly, Louis Schaefer, James Goodwin Rice, Richard Zobel, Stephen A. Hytner

FRANKENSTEIN an adaptation of Mary Shelley's novel by Oakley Hall III and Kathleen Masterson; Director, Peter H. Clough; Design, Dale F. Jordan, Leslie Taylor; Original Music, George Andoniadis. **CAST:** Kate Kelly, Shaw Purnell, James Goodwin Rice, Mary E. Baird, Richard Gambe, Michael Arkin, Michael J. Hume, Leonard Tucker, Pat Titterton, John Patrick McEneny, Richard Council

Above: (L) Sofia Landon, Kim Ameen in "A Streetcar Named Desire" (R) James Goodwin Rice, Chris Weatherhead in "Feathers"
(Skip Dickstein Photos)

Center Stage

Baltimore, Maryland   September 18, 1981–June 13, 1982   Third Season

Artistic Director, Stanley Wojewodski, Jr.; Managing Director, Peter W. Culman; Associate Artistic Director, Jackson Phippin; Dramaturg, Warren McIsaac; Technical Directors, Jeff Muskovin, David York; Costumer, Lesley Skannal; Sound, George O'Brien; Props, Rich Goodwin; Press, Sally Livingston

A LESSON FROM ALOES by Athol Fugard; Director, Jackson Phippin; with James Hurdle, Beth Dixon, Charles Henry Patterson
MUCH ADO ABOUT NOTHING by William Shakespeare; Director, Stanley Wojewodski, Jr. **CAST:** Emery Battis, Scott Waara, Tana Hicken, Frank Savage, Peter Vogt, John Wojda, Terrance O'Quinn, Castulo Guerra, Wendel Meldrum, Catherine Ann Christainson, Pamela Pascoe, Steve Hofvendahl, William Duff-Griffin, Lance Davis, William Preston, Bill Chappelle, Michael Nostrand, Daniel Szelag, Edith Kauffman
THE AMEN CORNER by James Baldwin; Director, Walter Dallas. **CAST:** Frances Foster, Deloris Gaskins, Gwen Shepherd, Leila Danette, Lizan Mitchell, Jeffery V. Thompson, Peter Wise, Bill Cobbs, Valencia Emanuel, Vacountess E. Payne, Verna Lee Day, Kevin Brown, Natalie E. Carter, Kay L. Lawal, Eleanor Lawrence, Joan Thompson, Carolyn Marcus, Lloyd M. Marcus, Lisa Denise Nesbitt, Lee Pittman, Marvin T. Sampson, Grafton Gray

THE WORKROOM by Jean Claude Grumberg; Adapted by Daniel A. Stein, Sara O'Connor; Director, Stanley Wojewodski, Jr. **CAST:** Barbara Spiegel, Nancy Donohue, June Squibb, Pamela Pascoe, Rosemary Knower, Susan Sharkey, Larry Block, Thomas Kopache, William Jensen, Kevin O'Rourke, Max Gulack, Julian Fleisher
TERRA NOVA by Ted Tally; Director, Stanley Wojewodski, Jr. **CAST:** Brian Murray, J. Kenneth Campbell, Beth Dixon, Lance Davis, Peter Burnell, James Harper, Patrick Clear
SAVAGES by Christopher Hampton. **CAST:** George Morfogen, Stanja Lowe, Joaquim De Almeida, Malcolm Stewart, Nesbitt Blaisdell, Tom Todoroff, John Henry Cox, Graham Beckel

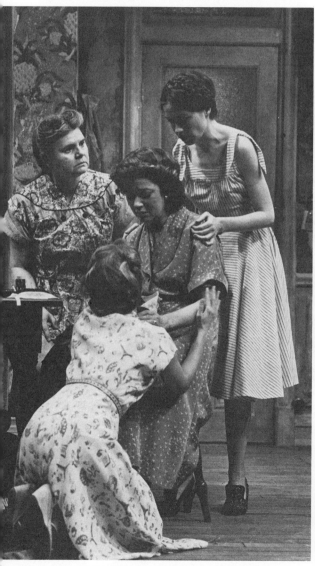

June Squibb, Susan Sharkey, Nancy Donohue, Pamela Pascoe (kneeling) in "The Workroom"

Frances Foster in "The Amen Corner" Above: James Harper, Brian Murray, Lance Davis in "Terra Nova"

131

Center Theatre Group/ Ahmanson Theatre

Los Angeles, California   September 25, 1981–May 29, 1982   Fifteenth Season
Artistic Director, Robert Fryer; Managing Director, Michael Grossman; Associate Artistic Director, James H. Hansen; Press, Rupert Allan, Stone Associates, Michelle McGrath; Production Administrator, Ralph Beaumont; Technical Director, Robert Routolo

THE LITTLE FOXES by Lillian Hellman; Director, Austin Pendleton; Set, Andrew Jackness; Costumes, Florence Klotz; Lighting, Paul Gallo; Hairstylist, Patrik D. Moreton; Presented by Zev Bufman with Donald C. Carter and Jon Cutler; Music Adapted by Stanley Silverman; General Management, Theatre Now; Stage Manager, Patrick Horrigan. **CAST:** Novella Nelson (Addie), Joe Seneca (Cal), Maureen Stapleton (Birdie), Nicolas Coster (Oscar), William Youmans (Leo), Elizabeth Taylor (Regina), Humbert Allen Astredo (Marshall), Robert Lansing (Benjamin), Ann Talman (Alexandra), J. D. Cannon (Horace). Understudies: Tom Klunis (Horace/Oscar/Marshall), Richard Hayes (Leo), Louise Stubbs (Addie), Hugh L. Hurd (Cal), Wendy Rosenberg (Alexandra), Carol Teitel (Birdie/Regina)

MORNING'S AT SEVEN by Paul Osborn; Director, Vivian Matalon; Set, William Ritman; Costumes, Linda Fisher; Lighting, Richard Nelson; Associate Director, Marnel Sumner; Production Supervisor, Roger Franklin; Presented by Elizabeth I. McCann, Nelle Nugent, Ray Larsen; Company Manager, Johanna Pool; Stage Manager, Robert Bruce Holley. **CAST:** Maurice Copeland (Theodore), Teresa Wright (Cora), Elizabeth Wilson (Aaronetta), Kate Reid (Ida), King Donovan (Carl), Robert Moberly (Homer), Elizabeth Hartman (Myrtle), Maureen O'Sullivan (Esther), Russell Nype (David). Understudies: Lawrence C. Lott (Homer), Martha Miller (Aaronetta/Myrtle), Bob Carroll (David/Theodore/Carl), Harriet Rogers (Ida/Cora), Peg Osborne (Esther)

ANOTHER PART OF THE FOREST by Lillian Hellman; Director, George Schaefer; Set, Douglas W. Schmidt; Costumes, Noel Taylor; Lighting, Martin Aronstein; Music, Conrad Susa; Production Administrator, Ralph Beaumont; Stage Managers, Robert Borod, Patrick Watkins, Joe Cappelli. **CAST:** Tovah Feldshuh (Regina), Laurence Guittard (John), Dorothy McGuire (Lavinia), Virginia Capers (Coralee), Richard Dysart (Marcus), David Dukes (Benjamin), Dino Shorte (Jacob), Wiley Harker (Simon), Edward Edwards (Oscar), Barbara Whinnery (Birdie), Jack Fletcher (Harold), Barry Cutler (Gilbert), Patricia McCormack (Laurette). Understudies: Elizabeth Hoffman (Lavinia), Ross Evans (Marcus/Penniman/Isham), Vaughn Armstrong (Benjamin/John), Claire Malis (Regina), Minnie Lindsey (Coralee), Jessica Nelson (Laurette/Birdie), Alvin Ross (Oscar), Joe Cappelli (Gilbert/John), Richard Penn (Jacob)

THE HASTY HEART by John Patrick; Director, Martin Speer; Presented by Center Theatre Group/Ahmanson Theatre, Franklin R. Levy, Leslie Moonves in association with the Catalina Production Group; Set, A. Clark Duncan; Costumes, Madeline Ann Graneto; Lights, Paul Gallo; Stage Managers, Robert L. Borod, Russell Werthman, Joe Cappelli. **CAST:** Ron Kapra (Orderly), Kurt Russell (Yank), John Corey (Digger), Rob Monroe (Kiwi), Jessie Lawrence Ferguson (Blossom), Will Nye (Tommy), Lisa Eichhorn (Margaret), Michael Evans (Colonel), Gregory Harrison (Lachlen). Understudies: Vaughn Armstrong, Claire Malis, Ron Kapra, Beau Billingslea, Joe Cappelli, Daniel Grace

Kate Reid, Elizabeth Wilson, Teresa Wright, Maureen O'Sullivan in "Morning's at 7" Above: Maureen Stapleton, Elizabeth Taylor in "The Little Foxes"

David Dukes, Dorothy McGuire, Richard Dysart, Tovah Feldshuh in "Another Part of the Forest" Above: Gregory Harrison, Kurt Russell, Lisa Eichhorn in "The Hasty Heart"

Cincinnati Playhouse

Cincinnati, Ohio   October 6, 1981–June 27, 1982

Producing Director, Michael Murray; Managing Director, Baylor Landrum; Directors, Michael Murray, Ron Lagomarsino, Woodie King, Jr., George Bunt, James Milton, Michael Hankins, Josephine R. Abady, Thomas Bullard, Donald MacKechnie, Worth Gardner; Musical Directors, Skip Hartshirn, Boyd Staplin; Choreographer, George Bunt; Fight Director, David S. Leong; Sets, Lowell Detweiler, David Ariosa, Robert D. Soule, Paul Shortt, Karl Eigsti, Alan Kimmel, John Jensen; Lights, William Mintzer, Jay Depenbrock, Victor En Yu Tan, Barry Arnold, Neil Peter Jampolis, Spencer Mosse, Amy Merrell; Costumes, Caley Summers, Rebecca Senske, Kurt Wilhelm, Elizabeth Covey, Ann Firestone; Stage Managers, Patricia Ann Speelman, G. Rober Abell, Peter Muste; Press, Jerri Roberts

BORN YESTERDAY with Jack Collard, Bob Cunningham, Venida Evans, John Hardy, Hugh Hodgin, Tony Hoty, Linda Lee Johnson, Monica Mathis, Samuel Maupin, David O. Petersen, Douglas Rees, Riki Tye, David Upson, Mary Jane Wells, Rax Xifo
HOME with Carl Crudup, Nadyne C. Spratt, Elizabeth Van Dyke
PETER PAN with John Beran, Terry Brown, Scott Campbell, George Cavey, Kevin Clark, Rob Cunningham, Owen Franc, Susan Glaze, Jeff Gurley, Tripp Hanson, Bill Hedge, Jack Hoffmann, Joshua Kaplan, Joe Kovacs, Howard Krakovsky, Linda Kay Leonard, Todd Louiso, Mark Lowry, Linda Madama, Donald Mark, Carolann Mary, James Moore, Jan Neuberger, Daniel O'Grady, Richard Perry, Sarah Simon, Reisa Sperling, Claudia Stefany, Susan Stroman, Ginger Timberlake
A LIFE IN THE THEATRE with Josh Clark, John Wylie
BETRAYAL with Laura Copland, James Harper, Eberle Thomas, Thomas Walker
A COUPLA WHITE CHICKS SITTING AROUND TALKING with Peggy Cosgrave, Cynthia Crumlish
MACBETH with Gerry Bamman, Sarah Bradley, George Cavey, Tony Darnell-Davis, Patrick Scott Downey, Edwin Dundon, Tracy Griswold, John Hardy, Tana Hicken, Hugh Hodgin, Gillian Jordan, Delroy Lindo, Todd Louiso, John D. McNally, Donald MacKechnie, John Milligan, Christine Parks, Robert Pescovitz, Richard Pruitt, Douglas Rees, Carla Roberts, Adrian Sparks, Thomas Walker, Marcia Weiland
A LESSON FROM ALOES with Leonard Jackson, Tanny McDonald, Eugene Troobnick
TEN LITTLE INDIANS with Julian Barnes, Darryl Croxton, Shelly Desai, Ellen Fiske, Roger Forbes, Cynthia Mason, Monica Mathis, John Milligan, Jonathan Moore, Harsh Nayyar, Richard Pruitt
TALLEY'S FOLLY with Steven Gilborn, Lynn Ritchie

James Harper, Laura Copland in "Betrayal" Above: Cynthia Crumlish, Peggy Cosgrave in "A Coupla White Chicks ..."
(Sandy Underwood Photos)

Josh Clark, John Wylie in "A Life in the Theatre" Above: Leonard Jackson, Eugene Troobnick in "A Lesson from Aloes"
(Sandy Underwood Photos)

Clarence Brown Company

Knoxville, Tennessee   February 12–July 3, 1982

Artistic Director, Wandalie Henshaw; General Manager, Margaret Forrester; Sets, Robert Cothran; Costumes, Marianne Custer, Bill Black; Lighting, L. J. DeCuir; Technical Director, Robert Field; Stage Managers, Bashie English, Chris Deatherage; Press, Robert Hutchens

MEDEA by Euripides; Freely adapted by Robinson Jeffers; Director, Robert Whitehead; Set, Ben Edwards; Costumes, Jane Greenwood; Lighting, Martin Aronstein; Music/Sounds, David Amram; Stage Managers, Mitchell Erickson, Stephen A. Nasuta. **CAST:** Judith Anderson, Peter Brandon, Zoe Caldwell, Lucien Douglas, Emily King, Amy Lovell, Don McHenry, Jessica Moran, Rosemary Murphy, Stephen Nasuta, Harriet Nichols, Brian Pruitt, Trey Reynolds, Ralph Roberts, Mitchell Ryan, Paul Sparer
TWO GENTLEMEN OF VERONA by William Shakespeare; Director, Jeffrey Huberman; Set, Robert Cothran; Costumes, Bill Black; Lighting, Chris Kaseta; Sound, Keith Cornelius; Stage Managers, Chris Deatherage, Hugh Sinclair. **CAST:** Paul V. Ames, Barbara Callander, Robertson Carricart, Arthur Hanket, Robert Hutchens, Leonard Kelly-Young, Ellen McLain, Lisa Norman-Leigh, Hugh Sinclair, Jim Stubbs
THE MIKADO by Gilbert and Sullivan; Director, Wandalie Henshaw; Set, Robert Cothran; Costumes, Marianne Custer; Lighting, L. J. DeCuir; Music, Timothy Duncan, Douglas Barber; Choreography, Cynthia Robertson; Stage Managers, Chris Deatherage, Bashie English. **CAST:** James Berry, Jeffery Brocklin, Thomas Brooks, Maurice Brown, Jane Burke, Jeffrey Wayne Davies, John Holleman, Erik Johanson, Ellen McLain, Katherine Newlon, Claire Padien, Michael Wayne Robinson, Joanna Seaton, Joan Susswein, Robert Trenthan, Jocylyn Wilkes, K. C. Wilson

Zoe Caldwell, Brian Pruitt, Trey Reynolds (her children), Mitchell Ryan
in "Medea"

The Cricket Theatre

Minneapolis, Minnesota   October 14, 1981–June 5, 1982

Artistic Director, Lou Salerni; Managing Director, Cynthia Mayeda; Development, Sara Burstein; Associate Director, Sean Michael Dowse; Marketing, Pamela Hendrick; Technical Director, Bob Davis; Literary Manager, John Orlock; Stage Managers, Brian Rehr, Lawrence S. Wechsler; Guest Artists, Vera Polovko-Mednikov (Costume and Set Designer), Michael Vennerstrom, Lisa Johnson (Lighting), Jerry R. Williams (Set and Costume Designer), James Berton Harris (Costumes), Lawrence Fried, Bill Breidenbach (Sound)

THE GIN GAME by D. L. Coburn; with Warren Frost, Patricia Fraser
TINTYPES by Mary Kyte with Mel Marvin and Gary Pearle; Director/Choreographer, Lewis Whitlock; Musical Director, Anita Ruth. **CAST:** Richard K. Allison, Christopher Bloch, Susan Long, Molly Sue McDonald, Louise Robinson, Christopher Drobny
BETRAYAL by Harold Pinter; with Camille Gifford, Allen Hamilton, James J. Lawless, Stephen D'Ambrose
CHILDE BYRON by Romulus Linney; Director, Steve Pearson. **CAST:** Robert Mailand, Allison Giglio, Janet Burrows, James Harris, Stephen D'Ambrose, Carole Kastigar, Chris Forth, John Newcome
TRUE WEST by Sam Shepard; Costumes, Colin Tugwell. **CAST:** Stephen D'Ambrose, Robert Breuler, James J. Lawless, Naomi Hatfield
DEAR RUTH by Norman Krasna; Director, Robert Moss. **CAST:** Nancy Bagshaw, Carole Kastigar, Wendy Lawless, James J. Lawless, Louise Goetz, Craig Benson, James Harris, Mary Sue Larkin, John Newcome, Lawrence S. Wechsler

Top Right: Camille Gifford, James J. Lawless, Allen Hamilton in "Betrayal" Below: Naomi Hatfield, Robert Breuler, Stephen D'Ambrose in "True West" *(Pat Boemer Photos)*

Cleveland Play House

Cleveland, Ohio   September 16, 1981–May 9, 1982   Sixty-sixth Season

Director, Richard Oberlin; Acting Associate Director, Kenneth Albers; General Manager, Janet Wade; Business Manager, Nelson Isekeit; Dramaturg, Peter Sander; Production Manager, James Irwin; Sets, Richard Gould; Press, Edwin P. Rapport; Administrative Assistants, Sheila Ann Heyman, Pat Messer; Directors, Kenneth Albers, Paul Lee, Evie McElroy, Richard Oberlin, William Rhys, David Connell, Judith Haskell, Harper Jane McAdoo, Ed Stern, Dennis Zacek; Designers, Richard Gould, James Irwin, Estelle Painter, Gary Eckhart, Wayne Merritt, Colleen Muscha; Costumes, Estelle Painter; Music Director, David Gooding; Props, Jamie Reich; Stage Managers, Anthony Berg, Deborah A. Gosney, Richard Oberlin, Michael Stanley

COMPANY: Mary Adams-Smith, Kenneth Albers, Norm Berman, Sharon Bicknell, Allan Byrne, Gregory M. Del Torto, Paul A. Floriano, Richard Halverson, James P. Kisicki, Joe D. Lauck, Allen Leatherman, Paul Lee, Morgan Lund, Evie McElroy, Judy Nevits, Richard Oberlin, Carolyn Reed, William Rhys, James Richards, Gary Smith, Wayne S. Turney, Cassandra Wolfe, and *Guest Artists:* Catherine Albers, Ken Armour, Cliff Bemis, Kenneth W. Daugherty, Elisabeth Farwell, Ralph Gunderman, Providence Hollander, Theresa Piteo, Alden Redgrave, Dudley Swetland, Maggie Thatcher, Yvetta

PRODUCTIONS: The Flying Karamazov Brothers, Tintypes by Mary Kyte with Mel Marvin and Gary Pearle, Translations by Brian Friel, Daughters by John Morgan Evans, A Christmas Carol adapted from Charles Dickens by Doris Baizley, Sherlock Holmes and the Curse of the Sign of Four by Dennis Rosa, Romeo and Juliet by William Shakespeare, Betrayal by Harold Pinter, Pantomime by Derek Walcott, Talley's Folly by Lanford Wilson, Cole devised by Alan Strachan and Benny Green, Chekhov in Yalta by John Driver and Jeffrey Haddow, and *American Premiere* of Trespassers Will Be Prosecuted by Peter Kenna.

Yvetta, Wayne S. Turney, Theresa Piteo, Sharon Bicknell, Cliff Bemis in "Tintypes" Above: (L) "Chekhov in Yalta" (R) "Cole"
(Mike Edwards Photos)

135

Dallas Theater Center

Dallas, Texas   October 13, 1981–August 14, 1982

Artistic Directors, Paul Baker, Mary Sue Jones; General Manager, Albert Milano; Marketing, Andrew Gaupp; Development, Lou Ann Bower; Press, Sarah Birge; Administrative Coordinator, Sharon Benge;

COMPANY: Yoichi Aoki, Sally Askins, Virgil Beavers, Randy Bonifay, Hanna Cusick, Judith Davis, Cheryl Denson, Robert Duffy, John Figlmiller, Robyn Flatt, Andrew Gaupp, Martha Goodman, Tim Green, Tim Haynes, Russell Henderson, John Henson, Allen Hibbard, Kaki Hopkins, Mary Lou Hoyle, Pamela Hurst, Mary Sue Jones, Deborah A. Kinghorn, Jeffrey Kinghorn, Elly Lindsay, John Logan, Ronni Lopez, Peter Lynch, Kim Marvin, Ryland Merkey, Norma Moore, Randy Moore, Paul Munger, Bryant J. Reynolds, Mary Rohde, Synthia Rogers, Michael Scudday, Glenn Allen Smith, Louise Mosley Smith, Ann Stephens, Randolph Tallman, Lynn Trammell, Dennis Vincent, Lee Wheatley, Ronald Wilcox, Nancy Munger

GUEST ARTISTS: Joan Vail Thorne, Richard Dow, Roger DeKoven, David Pursley, Anton Rodgers, Cliff Osmond, Warren Hammack, Jo Livingston, Walter Learning, Eric Hause
PRODUCTIONS: War and Peace, Tintypes, A Christmas Carol, Of Mice and Men, Tartuffe, Black Coffee, The Gin Game, and *World Premieres* of Under Distant Skies by Jeffrey Kinghorn, Pigeons on the Walk by Andrew Johns, The Wisteria Bush by Jo Vander Voort, Beowulf—Nocturnal Solstice by Jim Marvin

Below: Cliff Osmond, Warren Hammack, Ryland Merkey in "Of Mice and Men" Left: Synthia Rogers, Victor Bravo, Norma Moore, Richard Dow in "War and Peace" *(Linda Blase Photos)*

Delaware Theatre Company

Wilmington, Delaware   October 7, 1981–March 20, 1982   Third Season

Artistic Director, Cleveland Morris; Managing Director, Raymond Bonnard; Associate Director, Peter DeLaurier; Development, D'Arcy Webb; Business Manager, Ray Barto; Stage Manager, Linda Harris; Technical Director, Howard P. Beals, Jr.; Sets, Howard Beals, Cleveland Morris, Thomas Schraeder, Dennis M. Size; Lighting, Rachel Budin, Harry Sangmeister, Thomas Schraeder, Dennis M. Size; Costumes, Teri Beals, Kenneth M. Yount; Sound, Alan Gardner

THE MISANTHROPE by Moliere; Director, Cleveland Morris; with Peter Aylward, David Baffone, Anne Eder, James Jenner, James Kassees, Paula Mann, Iliff McMahan, Paul Moriella, Robert Moyer, Ceal Phelan, Frank Vignola.
THE INNOCENTS by William Archibald; Director, Cleveland Morris; with Lori Bellamy, Holly Cordes, James Kassees, Michael Manning, Ceal Phelan, Nannette Rickert.
A CHRISTMAS CAROL by Charles Dickens; Adapted and Directed by Peter DeLaurier; with Bob Barto, Lori Bellamy, Charles Conway, Anne Eder, David Hopson, Rhiannon Howell, John Janney, Michael Petro, Ceal Phelan, David Pichette, Tom Szymanski, James Zvanut

GEMINI by Albert Innaurato; Director, Frank Girardeau; with Marvin Gendelman, John Basil Giletto, Shirley Green, Felisa Kazen, Jack Koenig, Tim Quinn, Vicki Shelton
THE CRIME ON GOAT ISLAND by Ugo Betti; Director, Richard Hardin; with Jude Ciccolella, Madeleine LeRoux, Joanne Munisteri, Ceal Phelan, Mike Zalatoris
PEG O' MY HEART by J. Hartley Manners; Director, Cleveland Morris; with Nora Baetz, Kathleen Claypool, Catherine Curran, Peter DeLaurier, John Kirman, Anthony Newfield, Nicholas Olcott, Fred Royal, Gabrielle Sinclair

Above: (L) Paul Morella, Peter Aylward, Paul Mann, Iliff McMahon in "The Misanthrope" (R) Ceal Phelan, Mike Zalatoris in "The Crime on Goat Island" *(Richard Carter Photos)*

136

Denver Center Theatre Company

Denver, Colorado   December 4, 1981–May 8, 1982   Third Season

Artistic Director, Edward Payson Call; Managing Director, Gully Stanford; Production Manager, Danny Ionazzi; Assistant to Mr. Call, Dan Hiester; Business Manager, Madeline Kwok-Dodd; Company Manager, Jayne Gall-Newcomb; Literary Manager, Larry Eilenberg; Sets/Costumes, Lowell Detweiler, Thomas A. Walsh, Michael Stauffer, John David Ridge, Christina Haatainen, Ursula Belden, Elizabeth P. Palmer; Lighting, Allen Lee Hughes, Duane Schuler, Robert Jared, Danny Ionazzi; Music/Sound, Bruce Odland, Bill Ballou, Lin Esser, Herb Pilhofer, Barbara Damashek; Choreography, Lynda Hatfield, John Broome; Stage Managers, Ron Durbian, D. Wayne Hughes, Megan Miller-Shields, Jane Page, Stanford Paris, Pamela J. Young; Press, Ken Miller, Mary Nelson, Barbara Lindstrom, Eleanor Glover; Directors, Edward Payson Call, Richard Russell Ramos, Michael Lessac, Mark Cuddy, Larry Arrick, George Touliatos

COMPANY: Gregory Abels, Gregg Almquist, Duane Black, Debra Brickhaus, Kathryn Cain, Jeannie Carson, Maury Cooper, Shelley Crandall, Ted Denious, Jeff Dinmore, Lewis H. Dunlap, Derek Edward-Evans, Karen Erickson, Lin Esser, Ken Fenwich, Mark Fuller, Julian Gamble, Kathryn Gray, Leslie Hicks, Jetta Hines, Mary Gail Horan, Richard Hoyt-Miller, Maureen Kane, Christopher Kendall, Jason Kenny, David Kristin, Tim LaBoria, Raymond Lang, Tara Loewenstern, Joseph McDonald, Michael Mancuso, Gary Mazzu, Bill McCutcheon, Biff McGuire, Gary Montgomery, Randall Montgomery, Lisa Mounteer, Margery Murray, John H. Napierala, James Newcomb, Caitlin O'Connell, Pamela O'Conner, Michael Parker, Larry Pine, Bruce C. Purcell, Tyson Douglas Rand, Jeffrey Reese, Brenda Brock Rogers, Mercedes Ruehl, David Sage, Keith Ashley Sellon, Jeremy Shamos, Stan C. Soto, Teig Stanley, Susan-Joan Stefan, Theodore Stevens, Bret Torbeck, David Trim, W. Francis Walters, Jerry Webb, Jonathan Wilhoft, Gene Wilkins, Dave Wright, Vince Zaffiro

PRODUCTIONS: Androcles and the Lion by George Bernard Shaw, Tartuffe by Moliere (Richard Wilbur translation), An Enemy of the People by Henrik Ibsen, The World of Sam Shepard/Suicide in B Flat by Sam Shepard, Much Ado About Nothing by William Shakespeare, Antigone by Jean Anouilh, Yanks 3 Detroit 0 Top of the Seventh by Jonathan Reynolds, What the Babe Said by Martin Halpern

WORLD PREMIERES:

A BALLAD OF COLORADO by Frank X. Hogan, Julian Gamble, Bettiann Panvini, Jose Payo; Music/Lyrics, Jose Payo, Chuck Wilcox, Stephen Jimenez; Director, Mark Cuddy. **CAST:** Duane Black, Ann Ducati, Julian Gamble, Leslie Hicks, Jose Payo, Chuck Wilcox

BUCKHORN EXCHANGES by Craig Volk; Director by Peter Hackett. **CAST:** Vince Zaffiro, Charles M. Burke, Jeff Dinmore, Karen Erickson, Paula Eschweiler, Richard Maynard, Randall Montgomery, Roz Brown

QUILTERS by Molly Newman, Barbara Damashek; Music/Lyrics/Direction, Miss Damashek. **CAST:** Marjorie Berman, Shelley Crandall, Judy Leavell, Mallory Maxwell, Carol Strawn, Sandy Walper, Carolyn Odell

DENVER MESSIAH by Frank X. Hogan; Director, Walter Schoen. **CAST:** Craig Stout, Margery Murray, Duane Black, David Trim, Stephen Mendillo, Jason Kenny, David Ode

Mark Fuller, Duane Black, Bruce Purcell in "The World of Sam Shepard"
Top Right: Bill McCutcheon, John Napierala in "Androcles and the Lion"

Mercedes Ruehl, Larry Pine in "Much Ado About Nothing"

Detroit Repertory Theatre

Detroit, Michigan   November 5, 1981–June 27, 1982

Artistic Director, Bruce E. Millan; Executive Director, Robert Williams; Administrative Assistant, Anne Saunders; Business Manager, Barbara J. Busby; Development, Dee Andrus; Chairman of the Board, Dorothy Brown; Sets, Bruce E. Millan, Patrick Czeski; Lighting, Marylynn Kacir, Jeff Shabazz, Dick Smith; Costumes, Bernadine Vida Darrell, Anna Kriistine Flones-Czeski, Anne Saunders; Stage Manager, Dee Andrus

A LESSON FROM ALOES by Athol Fugard; Director, Bruce E. Millan; with William Boswell, Barbara Busby, Robert Williams
THE CAPTIVITY OF PIXIE SHEDMAN by Romulus Linney; Director, Barbara Busby; with James Budd, Ruth Palmer, Robert Rucker, William Boswell, Willie Hodge, Charlotte Nelson
AN ENEMY OF THE PEOPLE by Henrik Ibsen; Translated by Rolf Fjelde; Director, Dee Andrus; with Von Washington, Monika Ziegler, Monica Deeter, Aleta Marshall, Aaron Ford, William Boswell, Mack Palmer, Todd M. Hissong, Robert Williams, Bruce Economou, Paul E. Scheier, James Budd, Milfordean Luster, Theola O'Neal, Al Joseph, LeDene Barron, Shadolph Johnson, Mark Murri, Roy Hunes, P. De Lois Clinkscales
BYRON'S GHOST by Paul Simpson; Director, Bruce E. Millan; *World Premiere.* CAST: Robert Williams (Byron), Paul Scheier (Johnny), Phyllis Counts (Ghost)

East West Players

Los Angeles, California   July 16, 1981–May 16, 1982

Artistic Director, Mako; Administrator, Janet Mitsui; Assistant to Mako, Alberto Isaac; Assistant Administrator, Joyce Yamashita; Producers, Jim Ishida, Dione Young; Press, Emily Kuroda, Betty Muramoto; Directors, Mako, Alberto Isaac, Shizuko Hoshi, Saburo; Sets/Costumes, Mako, Terry Tam Soon, Rae Creevey, Rodney Kageyama, Fred Chuang, Terrence Tam Soon; Lighting, Rae Creevey, G. Shizuko Herrera; Stage Managers, Jay Koiwai, Merv Maruyama, Josie Pepito, Jack Clemons, Lorna McClellan, Benjamin Lum

THE LIFE OF THE LAND by Ed Sakamoto; with Dian Kobayashi, Patti Yasutake, Sala Iwamatsu, Jim Ishida, Clyde Kusatsu, Ken Mochizuki, Shizuko Hoshi, Jerry Tondo, Dom Magwili, Jane Mandy, Vladimir Velasco, Keone Young

STATION J by Richard France; with Mako, Keone Young, Glen Chin, Merv Maruyama, Jerry Tondo, Shizuko Hoshi, Leigh Kim, Kim Miyori, Richard Narita, Thomas Bellin, Jack Clemons, Charles Davis, Susan Haruye Ioka, Dian Kobayashi, Jay Koiwai, Bill Lee, Deborah Nishimura, Don Paul, Doreen Remo, Woody Romine, Saachiko, Ellen Wakamatsu, Edmund Balin, Rae Creevey, Michael Fox, Richard France, Edward Lamel, Ryan McDonald, Jim Nolan, Jack B. Sowards, David White

CHRISTMAS IN CAMP by Mako, Dom Magwili; Musical Direction, Glen Chin; with Deborah Nishimura, Rodney Kageyama, Merv Maruyama, Dom Magwili, Susan Haruye Ioka, Betty Muramoto, Dian Kobayashi, Saachiko, Patty Toy, Benjamin Lum, Jeannie Inouye, Bill Lee, Rob Narita, J. Kawaii, Alberto Isaac, Jack Clemons, Mimosa Iwamatsu, Sala Iwamatsu, Shizuko Hoshi, Emily Kuroda, Jenny Nagatani, Myra Shindo, James Young
OOFTY-GOOFTY by Frank Chin; with Jerry Tondo, Patty Yasutake, Saachiko Magwili, Rodney Kageyama, Bill Lee, Jack Clemons, Keone Young, Ben Lum, Patty Toy, Jim Ishida, Alberto Isaac, Dom Magwili, Leigh Kim, Doug Yasuda, Ellen Wakamatsu, Jenny Nagatani
"12-1-A" by Wakako Yamauchi; with Nobu McCarthy, Ellen Wakamatsu, James Saito, Dian Kobayashi, Doug Yasuda, Haunani Minn, Benjamin Lum, Glen Chin, Rodney Kageyama, Tim Dang, Jenny Nagatani, Bill Lee
WIND DANCES by Diane Aoki; with Kim Miyori, Sala Iwamatsu, Don Sato, June Kim, Keone Young, Jay Koiwai, James Saito, Tom Donaldson, Pat Rand

Center: (L) Barbara Busby, William Boswell, Robert Williams in "A Lesson from Aloes" (R) Shizuko Hoshi, Mako (standing), Kim Miyori in "Station J" *(Chris Komuro Photo)* Above: Paul E. Scheier, Phyllis Counts, Robert Williams in "Byron's Ghost"

Folger Theatre Group

Washington, D. C.   September 29, 1981–July 11, 1982   Twelfth Season

Artistic Producer, John Neville-Andrews; General Manager, Mary Ann deBarbieri; Production Manager, Elizabeth Hamilton; Stage Manager, Kevin Kinley; Press, Mary Charbonnet; Sets/Costumes, Hugh Lester, Bary Allen Odom, Kay Haskell, Russell Metheny, Lewis Folden; Lighting, Hugh Lester, Robby Monk, Richard Winkler; Composer, William Penn

JULIUS CAESAR by William Shakespeare; Director, Louis W. Scheeder; with Jim Beard, Ralph Cosham, David Cromwell, Franchelle Stewart Dorn, Earle Edgerton, Michael Gabel, Carlos Juan Gonzalez, Lewis Grenville, Terry Hinz, Floyd King, Paul Norwood, Gerry Paone, David Sage, Peter Webster, Dylan Baker, Chip Bolcik, David Brazda, Robert Brock, Mark Donahue, John Gibson, Jack Hrkach, Peter Linden, Leonard Martinoli, Tim O'Hare, Paul Preston, David Wano, Stephen Zazanis, Eric Zengota

THE ROVER by Aphra Behn; Director/Adapter, Michael Diamond; Music, William Bly; Choreography, Virginia Freeman; Fights, Chip Bolcik; with Dylan Baker, Jim Beard, Robert Brock, Lucinda Jenney, Peter Linden, Celeste Morrow, Rebecca Nelson, Tim O'Hare, Lorraine Pollack, William Pullman, Howard Lee Sherman, Sherry Skinker, John Thomas Waite, David Wano, Karen Wells, Jack Wetherall, Jerry Whidon

THE TEMPEST by William Shakespeare; Director, Roger Hendricks Simon; Composer/Music Director, John Webber; with Paul Anderson, Dylan Baker, Jim Beard, Chip Bolcik, David Cromwell, Herb Davis, Terry Hinz, Liane Langland, Michael Nostrand, Tim O'Hare, Gregory Roberts, Charles Turner, Joseph Wiseman, Thomas Allen, Tracy Flint, Ann Gelston, Skip Guidry, Felisa Kazen, Maureen McGinnis, Kim Merrill, Celeste Morrow, Kathleen Weber

THE COMEDY OF ERRORS by William Shakespeare; Director, John Neville-Andrews; with Jim Beard, Ralph Cosham, David Cromwell, Lance Davis, Terry Hinz, Stuart Lerch, Stephen Mottram, Paul Norwood, Ruth Pritchard, Timothy Rice, Cecelia Riddett, Gregory Roberts, Anne Stone, Diana Van Fossen, Margaret Winn, Craig Paul Wroe, David Brazda, Maureen McGinnis, Celeste Morrow, Kathleen Weber

Right: Jack Wetherall, Lucinda Jenney in "The Rover"
(Joan Marcus Photos)

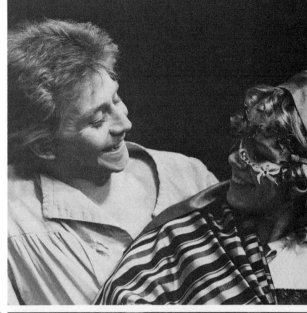

Gregory Roberts, David Cromwell in "Comedy of Errors"

David Cromwell, Ralph Cosham in "Julius Caesar"

GeVa Theatre

Rochester, N.Y.   October 31, 1981–April 18, 1982

Producing Director, Gideon Y. Schein; General Manager, Timothy C. Norland; Marketing/Development, Ellen Klein; Literary Director, Bruce E. Rodgers; Technical Director/Production Coordinator, Michael Powers; Props, Nick Fici; Costumes, Pamela Scofield, Karen Matthews, Ellen Kozak; Sets, Richard M. Isackes, Jeremy Conway, Susan Hilferty, Richard Hoover, Gary Baugh, John Jensen; Lighting, Sid Bennett, Ann Wrightson, John Gisondi, Rachel Budin; Scenic Artist, Cynthia Sweetland; Stage Managers, Nicholas Dunn, Catherine Norberg; Press, Cherrie Barbour

THE PASSION OF DRACULA by Bob Hall, David Richmond; Director, Gideon Y. Schein; with Peter Murphy, Alan Zampese, Arn Weiner, Alice White, Kermit Brown, Curt Karibalis, Sophie Schwab, Fritz Sperberg, Francisco Prado, Michelle Hagwell, Sydney Ann Snyder, Lara H. Wilder
PANTOMIME by Derek Walcott; Director, Ben Levit; with John Swindells, Basil Wallace
SHE STOOPS TO CONQUER by Oliver Goldsmith; Director, Beth Dixon; with Alan Zampese, Mark Arnott, John Scanlon, Nick Stannard, Matthew Kimbrough, Robert Gossett, Patricia Kilgarriff, J. Smith-Cameron, Radha Delamarter, Darcy Eckers, Bruce Castler, Lonny Salzman, David Sell

HOW I GOT THAT STORY by Amlin Gray; Director, Steven Katz; with Joe Morton, Richard Zobel
ARTICHOKE by Joanna M. Glass; Director, Sharon Ott; with Moultrie Patten, Alexander Reed, Gisela Caldwell, Robert Baines, Edward Cannan, Joan Shangold, Tom Blair
CONSTANCE AND THE MUSICIAN (*World Premiere*) with Book and Lyrics by Caroline Kava; Music, Mel Marvin; Director, Gideon Y. Schein; Musical Director, Guy Strobel; Musical Staging, Theodore Pappas; with Marilyn Caskey, Guy Strobel, Mary Jay, Margaret Lamee, Peter Boynton, Charles Michael Wright, Ray Gill

Francisco Prado in "The Passion of Dracula"

Goodman Theatre

Chicago, Illinois   October 2, 1981–July 2, 1982

Artistic Director, Gregory Mosher; Managing Director, Roche Schulfer; Associate Directors, David Mamet, Richard Nelson, Jennifer Tipton; Assistant to Mr. Mosher, Sandra Grand; Business Manager, Barbara Janowitz; Literary Manager, Peregrine Whittlesey; Development, Marie O'Connor; Press, Carol Ball, Barbara Fordney, Susan D. Levine, Suzanne Plunkett, Patricia Cox, Larry Sloan; Production Manager, Philip Eickhoff; Stage Managers, Joseph Drummond, Chuck Henry, Melinda Degucz, Marsha Gitkind, Tom Biscotto; Scenic Artist, Bill Bartelt; Props, James Swank; Wardrobe, Rosalie Piazza; Sound, Michael Schweppe; Sets/Costumes, William Ivey Long, Joseph Nieminski, James Edmund Brady, David Gropman, Michael Merritt, Christa Scholtz, Karen Schulz, Michael H. Yeargan, Dunya Ramicova, Philip Eickhoff, Marsha Kowal; Lighting, Jennifer Tipton, F. Mitchell Dana, Rachel Budin, James F. Ingalls, Rita Pietraszek

THE FRONT PAGE by Ben Hecht, Charles MacArthur; Director, Michael Maggio; with John E. Mohrlein, Roger Mueller, Guy Barile, Jack Wallace, Gary Houston, Ted Raymond, Rob Riley, Jerry Tullos, Vince Viverito, W. H. Macy, Colin Stinton, Kevin Dunn, Dennis Kennedy, William Munchow, Robert Thompson, David E. Chadderdon, Robert Clites, J. Michael Gerrity, Frank Miley, Jo Ann Cameron, Kathy Joosten, Bonnie Sue Arp, Barbara E. Rogertson, Marji Bank, Jonathan Joosten, Robert Neuhaus

A CHRISTMAS CAROL by Charles Dickens; Adapted by Barbara Field; Director, Tony Mockus; Choreography, Gus Giordano; with Robert Thompson, William J. Norris, Robert Scogin, Roger Mueller, John Ostrander, Laurence Russo, Ralph Concepcion, Tony Lincoln, Tim Halligan, Del Close, Belinda Bremner, Heather Gray, Geoffrey Herden, Elizabeth Perkins, Aaron Kramer, Richard Gilbert-Hill

PANTOMIME by Derek Walcott; Director, Gregory Mosher; with Brian Murray, Roscoe Lee Browne

LAKEBOAT by David Mamet; Director, Gregory Mosher; with Ron Dean, Rob Knepper, Bruce Jarchow, Mike Nussbaum, Robert Scogin, Dennis Kennedy, Jack Wallace, Nathan Davis

WELCOME TO OUR LIVING ROOM featuring the Flying Karamazov Brothers and Avner the Eccentric.

A HOUSE NOT MEANT TO STAND by Tennessee Williams; Director, Andre Ernotte; with Frank Hamilton, Peg Murray, Scotty Bloch, Scott Jaeck, Les Podewell, Cynthia Baker, Brooks Gardner, Nathan Davis, Jeremy Sisto, Meadow Sisto, Jamie Wild

SGANARELL, AN EVENING OF MOLIERE FARCES featuring the American Repertory Theatre (see page   )

KUKLA AND OLLIE LIVE! with Burr Tillstrom

THE WOOLGATHERER by William Mastrosimone; Director, Sandra Grand; with Jack Wallace, Emilie Borg

EDMOND *(World Premiere)* by David Mamet; Director, Gregory Mosher; with Paul Butler, Rick Cluchey, Joyce Hazard, Laura Innes, Bruce Jarchow, Linda Kimbrough, Marge Kotlisky, Ernest Perry, Jr., Jose Santana, Colin Stinton, Jack Wallace

Colin Stinton, Ernest Perry, Jr., Jose Santana in "Edmond"

Frank Hamilton, Peg Murray in "A House Is Not Meant to Stand"

Roscoe Lee Browne, Brian Murray in "Panto"

Hartman Theatre

Stamford, Connecticut   September 24, 1981–April 25, 1982   Seventh Season

Artistic Director, Edwin Sherin; Executive Director, Harris Goldman; General Manager, Todd Haimes; Assistant to Mr. Sherin, Judy Richfield; Assistant to Mr. Goldman, Brandy Browning; Development, Donna Gillroy; Marketing, Joyce A. Schreiber; Press, Carole C. Cortese, Gregg Feistman; Production Supervisor, David N. Feight; Props, Kathleen Iacobacci; Wardrobe, Patricia Wehman

HEDDA GABLER by Henrik Ibsen; Translation, Eva LeGallienne; Director, Edwin Sherin; Set, Marjorie Bradley Kellogg; Costumes, Nancy Potts, Lighting, Marcia Madeira; Stage Managers, Amy Pell, Susanne Jul. **CAST:** Jan Miner, Leigh Curran, Edward Herrmann, Jane Alexander, Pamela Payton-Wright, Lee Richardson, David Selby

CATHOLICS by Brian Moore; Director, Tom Kerr; Scenery/Costumes, Robert Fletcher; Lighting, Bill Williams, David Gauthier; Stage Managers, Hope Chillington, Michael Kohlmann. **CAST:** Michael Higgins, Alan Scarfe, Maurice Good, Edward Greenhalgh, Deryck Hazel, William Forrest MacDonald, Gannon McHale, Russell J. Roberts, Des Smiley, Lee Taylor

THE MILLIONAIRESS by George Bernard Shaw; Director, Jerome Kilty; Set, James Leonard Joy; Costumes, Jane Greenwood; Lighting, John McLain; Musical Arrangements, Richard Jameson Bell; Fights, W. A. Finlay; Stage Managers, Pamela Singer, Amy Schecter. **CAST:** Tammy Grimes, Richard Council, Jerry-Allan Jones, Katherine McGrath, Lee Richardson, Ken Ruta, Paul Sparer

NIGHT MUST FALL by Emlyn Williams; Director, Edwin Sherin; Set, Richard M. Isackes; Costumes, Ann Wallace; Lighting, Sid Bennett; Stage Managers, Robert I. Cohen, Susanne Jul. **CAST:** Leta Anderson, Toni Darnay, Mary Fogarty, Samuel Maupin, Richard Merrell, Jan Miner, Jeanne Ruskin, Bill Sadler

THE MAGISTRATE by Arthur Wing Pinero; Director, Edward Hastings; Set, Don Beaman; Costumes, David Murin; Lighting, Roger L. Meeker; Stage Managers, Robert G. Adams, Michael Kohlmann. **CAST:** Ivar Brogger, John Cullum, Mary Donnet, George Ede, Sean Griffin, Brian Hargrove, Jessi K. Jones, Jerome Kilty, Katherine McGrath, Fredi Olster, Armin Shimerman

MAHALIA by Don Evans (Book/Lyrics) and John Lewis (Music); Director, Gerald Freedman; Choreography, Talley Beatty; Set, Robin Wagner; Sound, Jack Shearing; Costumes, Judy Dearing; Casting, Olaiya; Lighting, John McLain; Vocal Arrangements, Choral Direction, Brenda Saunders-Hampden; Musical Supervision, Joyce Brown; Produced in association with J. Lloyd Grant, Lucy Kroll, Richard Bell. **CAST:** Nat Adderley, Danny Miller Beard, Fran Bennett, Keith David, Michael Edward-Stevens, Ebony Joann, Esther Marrow, Tucker Smallwood, Michelle Weeks, Curtis Worthy, Jr., Doug Eskew, Yolanda Graves, Milt Grayson, Assata Hazell, Denise Yvette Howell, Alde Lewis, Jr., Edwina Lewis, Jenifer Lewis, L. Craig Moore, Nat Morris

Right: Jerome Kilty, John Cullum in "The Magistrate" **Above:**
Tammy Grimes, Lee Richardson, Katherine McGrath
in "The Millionairess"

Esther Marrow in "Mahalia"

David Selby, Pamela Payton-Wright, Jane Alexander in "Hedda Gabler"

Long Wharf Theatre

New Haven, Connecticut   October 13, 1981–June 27, 1982   Seventeenth Season

Artistic Director, Arvin Brown; Executive Director, M. Edgar Rosenblum; Press, Jill McGuire, Rosalind Heinz; Stage Directors, Arvin Brown, John Tillinger, Nancy Meckler, John Dillon, Kenneth Frankel, William Ludel, Harris Yulin; Sets, Hugh Landwehr, Marjorie Bradley Kellogg, David Jenkins, Laura Maurer, Steven Rubin, John Jensen; Costumes, Bill Walker, Carol Oditz, Linda Fisher, Rachel Kurland, Ann Roth; Lighting, Geoffrey T. Cunningham, Judy Rasmuson, Ronald Wallace, Jamie Gallagher; Stage Managers, Robin Kevrick, Anne Keefe, James Harker, Christopher Greene; General Manager, John K. Conte.

THIS STORY OF YOURS (*American Premiere*) by John Hopkins; with John McMartin (John Johnson), Joyce Ebert (Maureen Johnson), John Seitz (Capt. Cartwright), J. T. Walsh, John Spencer (Kenneth Baxter), Ray Horvath (Jessard), Paul F. Ugalde, Robert Caserta (Officers)

A DAY IN THE DEATH OF JOE EGG by Peter Nichols; with Richard Dreyfuss, Stockard Channing, Tenney Walsh, Christina Pickles, John Tillinger, Margaret Hilton

A VIEW FROM THE BRIDGE by Arthur Miller; with Stephen Mendillo, John Shepard, William Swetland, Tony LoBianco, Saundra Santiago, Cathryn Damon, Alan Feinstein, Robert Caserta, James Hayden, Ramon Ramos, James Vitale, George C. Rieger, Jeanette Lemire Marcucci, Richard Pizzini, Steven Villano, Mal Goering

THE WORKROOM (*L'Atelier*) by Jean-Claude Grumberg; Translation, Tom Kepinski; with Tanya Berezin, Marcia Jean Kurtz, Barbara Sohmers, Jane Cronin, Eve Bennett Gordon, Christine Estabrook, Gerald Hiken, David Strathairn, Rick Pizzini, Steve Villano, Stephen Mendillo, Joseph Leon, David Lurie

LAKEBOAT by David Mamet; with Ed O'Neill, David Marshall Grant, Walter Atamaniuk, Clarence Felder, Larry Shue, Ralph Byers, Dominic Chianese, John Spencer

THE DOCTOR'S DILEMMA by George Bernard Shaw; with Shirley Bryan, John Jellison, Harris Yulin, Emery Battis, Robert Pastene, Rex Robbins, Richard Woods, Richard Ramos, Ellen Parker, John Glover, John Shepard, Johanna Leister

THE CARMONE BROTHERS ITALIAN FOOD PRODUCTS CORP'S ANNUAL PASTA PAGEANT (*World Premiere*) by Tom Griffin; with Robert Harper (Doober), Gretchen Corbett (Roxanne), Jeffrey DeMunn (Slimy), John Spencer (Artie), Sloane Shelton (Walter)

ETHAN FROME by Edith Wharton; Dramatized by Owen Davis, Donald Davis; with Frances Conroy, Jon DeVries, Robert Burns, Valerie Mahaffey, Emery Battis, Edward Earle, Curtis Borg, Susan O'Sullivan, Peter Michael Goetz, William Barry, John D'Amico, David Hartman, Andrea Iovino, Graceanne Malloy, Andrea Riskin, Jack Rushen, Nicolette Vannais

THE FRONT PAGE by Ben Hecht, Charles MacArthur; with Alice Beardsley, Severn Darden, Bruce Davison, Jake Dengel, Brian Dennehy, John Doolittle, Cara Duff-MacCormick, Pierre Epstein, Mary Fogarty, Dorothea Hammond, Baxter Harris, Bernie McInerney, Michael Medeiros, Dick O'Neill, Stephen Pearlman, Rand Bridges, Lois Smith, William Swetland, James Tolkan, Max Wright, John Basinger, Jasper Burr, John D'Amico, Robert Koon, Ronald P. Lonicki, Timothy Smyth, James Vitale

Stockard Channing, Richard Dreyfuss in "A Day in the Death of Joe Egg"
Top Right: Joyce Ebert, John McMartin in "This Story of Yours"

Brian Dennehy, Bruce Davison in "The Front Page" Above: Larry Shu
David Marshall Grant in "Lakeboat"

Los Angeles Actors' Theatre

Los Angeles, California   June 1, 1981–May 31, 1982

Producing Director, Bill Bushnell; Producer, Diane White; Managing Director, Alan Mandell; Operations Manager, Stephen Richards; Press, Leif Bentsen, Rickey Momii; Administrative Assistant, M'Lisa MacLaren; Associate Producer, Adam Leipzig; Production Manager, John York; Sets/Costumes, Barbara Ling, Michele Jo Blanche, Tom Clover, Steve Lavino, Naila Aladdin, Russell Pyle, Steven Ralph, John York, Jane Greenwood; Lighting, Edward P. Layton, Charles Schuman, Steve Lavino, Barbara Ling, Pat Kelly, Joe Morrissey; Sound, Sandy Berry; Stage Managers, Beth Petersen, Alexander Rubinstein, Paul Backer, Melvin Weiss, S. Ann Ng, William Robert, Thomas Curby, Elaine Jewell, Steve DeSanctis, Charles Schuman, John York, Jean Sportelli, Michael Schmalz, Sylvia Klein, David Russell

FESTIVAL OF ONE-ACTS: The Interview by Joseph Cardinale, Vagaries by Silas Jones, Junkfood by Willard Manus, Chug by Ken Jenkins, On a Cold Frosty Morning by Joseph Scott Kierland, Carrier by Paul Benjamin, Tap Dancing and Bruce Lee Kicks by Miguel Pinero, Blood Engine by Paul Minx, City Park by Sean Michael Rice, The Former One-on-One Basketball Champion by Israel Horovitz, Girlfriends by Veronica Reed, Conversations with a Despised Character by Friedrich Durrenmatt

A TRAVELLING JEWISH THEATRE by Naomi Newman Pollack, Albert Greenberg, Corey Fisher; director, Miss Pollack; with Corey Fisher, Albert Greenberg

WE WON'T PAY! WE WON'T PAY! translated from the Italian and directed by R. G. Davis; with Marilyn Coleman, Art Evans, Rosie Lee Hooks, Roger Robinson, Joe Spano

NEVIS MOUNTAIN DEW by Steve Carter; Director, Edmund J. Cambridge; with Graham Brown, Lee Chamberlin, Marguerite De-Lain, Norma Donaldson, David Downing, Danny Glover, Sidney Hibbert, Lincoln Kilpatrick, Carl Lumbly, Janet MacLachlan, Tony Ralph-Wilson, Roxy Roker, Esther Rolle, Carl Weathers, Charles Weldon, Myrna White, Hal Williams

PARK YOUR CAR IN THE HARVARD YARD by Israel Horovitz; Director, Bill Bushnell; with Barbara Babcock, Stefan Gierasch, Rocky

THESE MEN by Mayo Simon; Director, Bill Bushnell; with Lisa Persky, Kelly Jean Peters, Patti Johns, Grace Woodard, Sally Kirkland

THREE BY BECKETT: (Rockaby, Ohio Impromptu, Footfalls) by Samuel Beckett; Director, Alan Mandell; with Martin Beck, Alan Mandell, Beatrice Manley, Bea Silvern

FACES OF LOVE by Carol Teitel; Director, Bruce Franchini; with Carol Teitel

MARTHA ROSE AND THE MINERS by Jamie and Sheila Ellis; Director, Al Rossi with Pendleton Brown, Colleen Fitzpatrick, Sean Michael Kelly, John Lansing, Jay T. Loudenback, Lee Lucas, Teck Murdock, Katie Sagal, Billy Valentine

TWO BY SOUTH: (Rattlesnake in a Cooler/Precious Blood) by Frank South; Director, Robert Altman; with Leo Burmester, Danny Darst, Cliff DeYoung, Alfre Woodard

Betty Bennett, Richard S. Bailey Photos

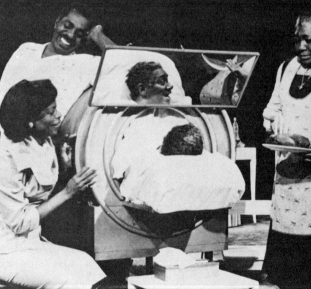

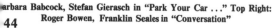
Barbara Babcock, Stefan Gierasch in "Park Your Car ..." Top Right: Roger Bowen, Franklin Seales in "Conversation"

Lincoln Kilpatrick, Roxie Roker, Graham Brown, Esther Rolle in "Nevis Mt. Dew" Above: "City Park"

44

McCarter Theatre Company

Princeton, N.J.   September 30, 1981–April 10, 1982

Artistic Director, Nagle Jackson; Managing Director, Alison Harris; Associate Artistic Director, Robert Lanchester; Production Manager, Rafe Scheinblum; Business Manager, C. G. Brian Thomas; Development, Gary C. Porto; Press, Linda S. Kinsey; Stage Managers, Trey Altemose, Jacque Desnoyers, Francis X. Kuhn, Cynthia J. Tillotson; Designers, Lowell Achziger, Nanzi Adzima, Frances Aronson, Daniel Boylen, Elizabeth Covey, F. Mitchell Dana, Desmond Heeley, John Jenson, Brian Martin, Sean Murphy, Giorgos Patsas, Marc B. Weiss

JUST BETWEEN OURSELVES (*U. S. Premiere*) by Alan Ayckbourn; with Herb Foster (Dennis), Peggy Cowles (Vera), Robert Lanchester (Neil), Joan White (Marjorie), Jill Tanner (Pam)
THE NIGHT OF THE IGUANA by Tennessee Williams; with Kelly Bishop, Clifford Fetters, Kevin Tighe, Ann Adams, Karl Light, Barbara Riffe, Greg Thornton, Darrie Lawrence, Penelope Reed, Rebecca Nibley, Jay Doyle, Gerald Lancaster
A CHRISTMAS CAROL by Charles Dickens; Adapted by Hagle Jackson; with Herb Foster, Robert Lanchester, Greg Thornton, Gerald Lancaster, John Mansfield, Jay Doyle, Penelope Reed, Lawrence Holofcener, Bruce Somerville, Rebecca Nibley
KEYSTONE by Lance Mulcahy, John McKellar, Dion McGregor; with John Sloman, Randy Graff, Mark Martino, Keith Curran, Valerie Beaman, Karen Giombetti, Douglas Walker, Thomas Lee Sinclair, Gina Buntz, Tommy Breslin
THE OVERLAND ROOMS by Richard Hobson; with Anne Sheldon, Greg Thornton, Susan Jordan, Karl Light, Zivia Flomenhaft
IPHIGENIA AT AULIS by Euripides; with Tom Klunis, William Denis, Neil Vipond, Robert Lanchester, Holly Barron, Monique Fowler, Drew Keil, Tom Hewitt, Ann Adams, Annie Combs, Venida Evans, Laura Gardner, Sharita Hunt, Leona Johnson, Cheryl Yvonne Jones, Sagan Lewis, Susan Kay Logan, Diana Van Fossen
ARMS AND THE MAN by George Bernard Shaw; with Gordana Rashovich, Margaret Hilton, Penelope Reed, Bruce Somerville, Robin Chadwick, Jay Doyle, Greg Thornton

Robert I. Faulkner, Cliff Moore Photos

Leona Johnson and chorus in "Iphigenia in Aulis"

Gordana Rashovich in "Arms and the Man"

Randy Graff, Karen Ciombetti, Kim Morgan, Valerie Beaman in "Ke stone" Above: Peggy Cowles, Herb Foster in "Just Between Ourselve

Meadow Brook Theatre

Rochester, Michigan   October 8, 1981–May 16, 1982

Artistic/General Director, Terence Kilburn; Assistant to Mr. Kilburn/Tour Director, Frank F. Bollinger; Production Manager, John Walker; Technical Director, Barry Griffith; Sound, Kim Kaufman, Thomas Hansen; Directors, Terence Kilburn, Arif Hasnain, John Ulmer, Charles Nolte; Sets, Peter-William Hicks, Barry Griffith, C. Lance Brockman; Lighting, Barry Griffith, Reid G. Johnson, Larry A. Reed, Deatra Smith; Stage Managers, Terry W. Carpenter, Thomas D. Spence; Scenic Artists, Deatra Smith, Rebecca Castle; Costume Coordinator, Mary Lynn Crum; Wardrobe, Jill Patterson; Props, Mary Chmelko; Marketing, Kevin Gilmartin

OTHELLO with Andrew Barnicle, Richard Bradshaw, Lou Brockway, Clayton Corbin, Donald W. Dailey, Andrew Dunn, George Gitto, Zdzislawa Gumul, Richard Jamieson, Nancy Linehan, Yolanda Lloyd, Phillip Locker, Carl Schurr, Peter Van Wagner, Dennis Wrosch

ON GOLDEN POND with Spencer Cox, Harry Ellerbe, Nancy Linehan, Phillip Locker, Carl Schurr, Anne Shropshire

HAY FEVER with Jeanne Arnold, Andrew Barnicle, Sara Morrison, Mary Cutler, George Gitto, Fredi Olster, Carl Schurr, Beth Taylor

A VIEW FROM THE BRIDGE with Andrew Barnicle, Richard Bradshaw, Stephen Daley, Henry Ferrentino, Gretchen Lord, David Regal, Victor Slezak, Colleen Smith-Wallnau

END OF RAMADAN (*World Premiere*) with Mary Benson, Barbara Berge, Jody Broad, Randall Forte, Mary Pat Gleason, Jillian Lindig, Wil Love, Carl Schurr, Anne Shropshire

A MAN FOR ALL SEASONS with Andrew Barnicle, Richard Bradshaw, Booth Coleman, A. D. Cover, Donald W. Dailey, Andrew Dunn, Donald Ewer, Zdzislawa Gumul, Jillian Lindig, Phillip Locker, Wil Love, Sara Morrison, David Regal, Carl Schurr

WAIT UNTIL DARK with Grace Aiello, Andrew Barnicle, Bethany Carpenter, Richard Bradshaw, Donald W. Dailey, Peter-William Hicks, Trueman Kelley, John LaGioia, Phillip Locker, Wil Love

CHAPTER TWO with Fran Brill, Jane Lowry, David Regal, Paul Vincent

Fran Brill, Paul Vincent in "Chapter Two" Above: "A Man for All Seasons" Top Right: Clayton Corbin, Yolanda Lloyd in "Othello"

Mary Pat Gleason, Carl Schurr, Barbara Berge, Mary Benson, Jillian Lindig, Anne Shropshire in "End of Ramadan" Above: Beth Taylor, Jeanne Arnold, Andrew Barnicle in "Hay Fever"

Merrimack Regional Theatre

Lowell, Massachusetts   October 30, 1981–May 9, 1982   Third Season
Artistic Director, Mark Kaufman; Managing Director, Patricia A. Littrell; Press, Christine Eyre; Costumiers, Karl Wendelin, Carol Kunz; Props, Margaret Keefe; Stage Managers, Thomas Clewell, Patricia Frey; Directors, Mark Kaufman, Nora Hussey, Ted Davis, Arif Hasnain; Sets, Michael Anania, David "Sparky" Lockner, Jim Steere, Edward Cesaitis, Patricia Woodbrige; Lighting, David "Sparky" Lockner

THE MIRACLE WORKER by William Gibson; with Peter Bos, Gardenia Cole, Edmund Davys, Sara Feeney, Richards Ford, Emily Hacker, Mary Lowry, Rica Martens, Vance Mizelle, Anissa Parekh, Maryann Plunkett, Brian Smiar, Dawna Sugarman
THE LION IN WINTER by James Goldman; with Edmund Davys, Richards Ford, Dolores Kenan, Jim Oyster, Paul Penfield, Maryann Plunkett, David Zoffoli
TWO FOR THE SEESAW by William Gibson; with Lynda Robinson, Michael Young
THE PRICE by Arthur Miller; with Jerry Gershman, Nancy Linehan, Terrence Markovich, Jim Oyster
THE GIN GAME by D. L. Coburn; with Jerry Gershman, Anne Shropshire
THE MOUSETRAP by Agatha Christie; with Lynn Bowman, Susan Campbell, Edmund Davys, De French, Jerry Gershman, Terrence Markovich, Jim Oyster, Robert Rutland

Right: De French, Jim Oyster in "The Mousetrap"

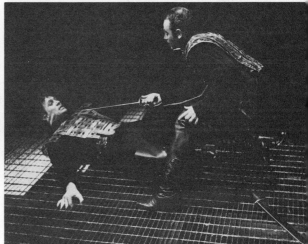

Milwaukee Repertory Theater

Milwaukee, Wisconsin   September 11, 1981–May 23, 1982
Artistic Director, John Dillon; Managing Director, Sara O'Connor; Business Manager, Peggy Haessler Rose; Directors, Sharon Ott, Rene Buch, Braham Burray, Robert Goodman, Nick Faust; Playwrights, Amlin Gray, Larry Shue, Andrew Johns, Kermit Frazier; Production Manager, Gregory S. Murphy; Stage Managers, Robert Goodman, Robin Rumpf, Stephen Howe, Cassandra McFatridge; Sets, Laura Maurer, Tim Thomas, Christopher M. Idoine, Bil Mikulewicz, Elmon Webb, Virginia Dancy; Costumes, Elizabeth Covey, Joy Barrett Densmore, Linda Fisher, Ellen M. Kozak, Colleen Muscha, Carol Oditz; Lighting, Rachel Budin, Dawn Chiang, Arden Fingerhut, Dan Kotlowitz, Spencer Mosse, Ben White; Props, Sandy Struth; Music Director, Edmund Assaly; Composers, Larry Delinger, Mark Van Hecke; Wardrobe, Carol Jean Horaitis; Development, Susan Medak, Cheryl Jones; Press, Phil Orkin

COMPANY: Rhonda Aldrich, Pat Bowie, Ritch Brinkley, Alan Brooks, Dorothy Brooks, Jim Butchart, L. Scott Caldwell, Erma Campbell, Montgomery Davis, Sheila Dabney, Gregory T. Daniel, Ellen Dolan, Razz Jenkins, Dilys Hamlett, Eric Hill, Kurt Knudson, Marge Kotlisky, Ellen Lauren, William Leach, Delroy Lindo, Daniel Mooney, Paul Meacham, W. Alan Nebelthau, Michael Patterson, James Pickering, Rose Pickering, Larry Shue, Sam Singleton, Jonathan Smoots, Daniel Stein, Susan Stevens, Henry Strozier, Robert Michael Tomlinson, Charmaine Underheim, Victor Raider-Wexler, Jane Gabbert-Wilson

PRODUCTIONS: Fridays by Andrew Johns, Boesman and Lena by Athol Fugard, Born Yesterday by Garson Kanin, Secret Injury Secret Revenge by Calderon de la Barca, Dinah Washington Is Dead by Kermit Frazier, *American Premieres* of Have You Anything to Declare? by M. A. Hennequin and P. Veber, The Fall Guy by Linda Aronson, At Fifty She Discovered the Sea by Denise Chalem translated by Sara O'Connor, *World Premieres* of Kingdom Come by Amlin Gray, Countertalk/Today's Special by Andrew Johns, Wenceslas Square by Larry Shue

Above: (L) "Kingdom Come" (R) Eric Hill, James Pickering in "Secret Injury, Secret Revenge"

Missouri Repertory Theatre

Kansas City, Missouri   July 9, 1981–April 11, 1982

Producing Director, Patricia McIlrath; Business Manager, Daniel P. Baker; Business Manager, Diana Coles; Marketing, Marilyn Kiene; Press, Rendall Himes; Development, Andyla Widders; Dramaturg, Felicia Hardison Londre; Production Manager, Ronald Schaeffer; Technical Director, Douglas C. Taylor; Directors, James Assad, Francis Cullinen, Norris Houghton, Patricia McIlrath, Cedric Messine, Albert Pertalion, John Reich; Sets, Harry Feiner, John Ezell, Carolyn L. Ross, Howard Jones; Costumes, Vincent Scassellati, Michele Bechtold, Mariann Verheyen, John Carver Sullivan, Douglas E. Enderle; Lighting, Susan A. White, Joseph Appelt, Ruth E. Ludwick, Keri Muri; Sound, Bruce Richardson, Jeannie Wilkerson, Tristan Wilson, Tom Mardikes; Stage Managers, Joyce McBroom, Terrence Dwyer, Beverly Shatto

COMPANY: Zachary Alexander, Peter Bakely, Ellen Baker, Jim Birdsall, Deborah Bremer, Janet Brooks, Bryan Burch-Worch, Carolgene Burd, Brenda G. Burnette, Montie F. Chambers, James Robert Daniels, John L. Dennis, Cynthia Dozier, Jo Anna Evans, Frances Farah-Giron, Darla Germeroth, Sharon K. Grosshart, Richard Gustin, Richard Halverson, Kevin Paul Hofeditz, Barbara Houston, Jennifer Lynne Houston, Jeannine Hutchings, Rosemary John, Tony Johnson, Robert Lewis Karlin, Kristina Kemper, Gerry Kinerk, John Kreipe, George M. Kuhn, Bruce Lecuru, Faith E. Luther, Jane MacPherson, Jane McDonald, Patti McGill, Mary Anne Moll, Laura Moore, Edith Owen, Woody Owen, Mike Parker, Steven Passer, Aleksandr Peterson, Rebekah Presson, Juliet Randall, Cynthia M. Rendlen, Jacquelyn Riggs, Mark Robbins, Elizabeth Ross, Danny Schaeffer, Laura Schaeffer, David Schuster, Susan K. Selvey, Katie Sinnett, Peg Small, Tom Small, Raymond E. Smith, Kent Stout, Mark Torchia, Melanie Tossell, Kathleen Vinlove, Graham Wallace, Patricia Hamarstrom Williams

Peter Aylward, Lynn Annitra Barnett, Glynis Brooks, Kay Christ, Walter Coppage, Rosanna E. Coppedge, Cain DeVore, Glenna Forde, Robert Graham, Paul Fielding Gray, Craig Handel, Susie Hills, Melissa Judd, Mark A. Klemetsrud, Vickie S. Little, John O'Byrne, David Olds, Jeff Olson, Brian Peebles, Vernon Quinzy, Jay E. Raphael, Bruce Roach, Becca Ross, Elizabeth C. Rubino, Laura Schaeffer, David Schramm, Josh Shelton, R. L. Smith, Mark Titus, Ronetta Wallman, Susan Warren, Alice White

PRODUCTIONS: Three Sisters by Anton Chekhov, Talley's Folly by Lanford Wilson, Picninc by William Inge, The Good Person of Szechwan by Bertolt Brecht, The Royal Family by G. S. Kaufman, Edna Ferber; Loose Ends by Michael Weller, Macbeth by William Shakespeare, and World Premiere of Crown of Thorns by Wendy MacLaughlin

Jeannine Hutchings, David Schuster in "Talley's Folly"

Alice White in "Macbeth"

Glenna Forde, Mark Robbins in "Crown of Thorns"

Nassau Repertory Theatre

Hempstead/New Hyde Park, N.Y. October 22, 1981–May 30, 1982

Artistic Director, Clinton J. Atkinson; Managing Director, Kenneth E. Hahn; Production Coordinator, Sally Cohen; Technical Director, John Pender; Stage Manager, J. Barry Lewis; Lighting, John Hickey; Props, Shirley Lerner; Wardrobe, Felicia Hittner; Development, Ruby L. Balter; Press, Vivian Lawrence; Director, Clinton J. Atkinson; Sets, Jack Stewart, Gerard P. Bourcier, Andrew Earl Jones, James Singelis, Daniel H. Ettinger; Costumes, Otis Gustafson, Debra Stein, Fran Rosenthal, Margie Peterson; Musical Director, Benny Key

PRIVATE LIVES By Noel Coward; with Laura Copland, Philip Le Strange, Laura Perrotta, Ross Petty, Renee Dutton
THE ECCENTRICITIES OF A NIGHTINGALE by Tennessee Williams; with Pamela Burrell, Ronald Willoughby, Robert Riley, Mona Stiles, Georgia Southcotte, Lee Sloan, Roberta Platt, Laura Castro, Brian Manning, William Kalmenson
THE FANTASTICKS by Tom Jones and Harvey Schmidt; with Tom Hafner, Ann-Ngaire Martin, David Cameron Anderson, P. J. Barry, Buck Hobbs, Peter Bartlett, Lee Sloan, Michael Heintz, Ava B. Tulchin
FLIRTATIONS (Liebelei) by Arthur Schnitzler; Adapted by C. J. Atkinson, A. S. Wensinger, Susanne Mrozik *(World Premiere)* with Robert Riley, John Abajian, Mary Munger, Tania Myren, David Cohen, Nancy-Elizabeth Kammer, Patrick Beatey
OVERRULED and **VILLAGE WOOING** by George Bernard Shaw; with Susan Browning, Harry Bennett, Roger Middleton, Joleen Fodor, Samuel Maupin, Jacqueline Bellamy
SPIDER'S WEB by Agatha Christie; with John High, William Lawrence, Richard Stack, Caroline Lagerfelt, Blaise Bulfair, Mary Pat Gleason, George E. Wolf, Peter Gatto, David Cohen, Ian Stuart, David Logan Rankin

Right: Peter Bartlett, David Cameron Anderson, Lee Sloan in "The Fantasticks"

Susan Browning, Harry Bennett in "Overruled"

Pamela Burrell, Robert Riley in "The Eccentricities of a Nightingale"

New Playwrights' Theatre

Washington, D. C.   October 21, 1981–June 13, 1982

Founder/Artistic Director, Harry M. Bagdasian; Managing Director, Todd Bethel; Literery Manager, Lloyd Rose; Production Manager, Tom Moseman; Technical Director, James S. Katen; Press, Diane S. Nahabedian; Development, Deborah Spence Schiro; Assistant to Mr. Bethel, Michael A. Shoop; Directors, Harry M. Bagdasian, Ken Bloom, Fred Zirm, John E. Jacobsen, Jay Beckner, James Nicola; Sets, Wally Coberg, Russell Metheny, Wally Coberg, Lewis Folden; Costumes, Liz Bass, Henry Carter Shaffer, Mary Ann Powell, Maryclare Gromet, B. Belino; Lighting, Richard Moore, Jim Albert Hobbs, James S. Katen; Stage Managers, Alan S. Eisen, Pat Cochran, Valerie Greenhouse

NIGHTMARE with Book/Music/Lyrics by Tim Grundmann; Choreography, Anne Reynolds Day; with Fredric Stewart, Juli Cooper, Tanis Roach, Dan Curry, Jan Frederick Shiffman, Anthony "Chip" Brienza, Barbara Rappaport, Amelia Esten

EULOGY by Diane Ney; with Nick Mathwick, Kathleen Weber, Ernie Meier

PHALLACIES by John Nassivera; with Eric Zengota, Nick Olcott, T. G. Finkbinder, Lynnie Raybuck, Jim Fyfe, Hank Jackelen, Susan Cassidy *(World Premiere)*

THE LIVES OF THE GREAT COMPOSERS by Tim Grundmann *World Premiere;* with Bari Biern, Jim Humphrey, Steven LeBlanc, Tanis Roach, Scott Sedar

JESSE'S LAND by Ernest Joselovitz; with Barbara Rappaport, Alessandro Cima, Robert Sloane, Cary Ann Spear, Michael Heitzman

FESTIVAL OF ONE-ACT PLAYS: The Tangled Snarl by John Rustan and Frank Semerano; with William deRham, Dale Stein, Debra Macut, David Stevens, Nick Olcott, Dominic Ambrose, Tony Schiro. Never Say Never by Tobey Chappell; with Susan Goldstein, Hank Jackelen. The Finer Points of the Situation by Peter Perhonis; with Barri Boudreaux, Seymour M. Horowitz, Buzz Roddy, Ernie Meier, Deborah Seidel.

Right: Dale Stein, William deRham, Debra Macut in "The Tangled Snarl"

Tanis Roach, Scott Sedar in "The Lives of the Great Composers"

Amelia Estin, Jan Frederick Shiffman, Barbara Rappaport, Anthony Brienza in "Nightmare!"

North Light Repertory

Evanston, Illinois   September 16, 1981–June 27, 1982   Seventh Season

Artistic Director, Eric Steiner; Managing Director, Jeffrey Bentley; Associate Artistic Director, Mary F. Monroe; Business Manager, Richard Schnackenberg; Marketing, Eileen Gill; Press, Ellie Meindl; Technical Coordinator, Teri McClure; Stage Manager, John P. Kenny III

THE GIN GAME by D. L. Coburn; Director, Michael Hankins; Set/Lighting, Jeremy Conway; Costumes, Kate Bergh. **CAST:** Fern Persons, Luke Sickle

PLYMOUTH ROCK ISN'T PINK by William Hamilton; Director, Eric Steiner; Set, Gary Baugh; Costumes, Kate Bergh; Lighting, Dawn Hollingsworth; with Ellen Crawford, Susan Dafoe, Mike Genovese, Ann McDonough, Jack McLaughlin-Gray, Greg Vinkler

THE GLASS MENAGERIE by Tennessee Williams; Director, Eric Steiner; Set, Jeremy Conway; Lighting, Rita Pietraszek; Costumes, Jessica Hahn; with Glenne Headly, Tom Irwin, Terry Kinney, Peg Murray

THE REAR COLUMN by Simon Gray; Director, John Malkovich; Set/Costumes/Lighting, Michael Merritt; Stage Managers, John P. Kenny III, Mary Kenny; with Kenny Foster, Joe Van Slyke, James Sudik, Roger Mueller, Rick Snyder, Peter Syvertsen, Billie Neil, Michael Tezla

LES BELLES SOEURS by Michel Tremblay; Translated by John Van Burek, Bill Glassco; Director, Eric Steiner; Set, Nels Anderson, Costumes, Kate Bergh; Lighting, Dawn Hollingsworth; Associate Director, Mary F. Monroe; Stage Manager, Mary Murphy-Kenny; with Marji Bank, Mary Ellen Falk, Sheila Megan McTavish, Fern Persons, Jo Ann Cameron, Allison Giglio, Ann Goldman, Joyce O'Brien, Gail Silver, Anne Edwards, Caitlin Hart, Jane MacIver, Elizabeth Perkins, Lora Staley

EMLYN WILLIMAS AS CHARLES DICKENS

THE PROMISE by Aleksei Arbuzov; Translation, Ariadne Nicolaeff; Director, Gus Kaikkonen; Set, Bob Barnett; Costumes, Kate Bergh; Lighting, Stuart Duke; Stage Manager, Mary Murphy-Kenny; with Jonathan Fuller, Barbara E. Robertson, James W. Sudik

SATELLITE SEASON: Shirley Basin by Jack Gilhooley, Matinee Idyll and Play It Again, Mr. Goodbar by Dean Corrin, High Rolling by Robert Lutz. Cast and credits not submitted.

Greg Vinkler, Mike Genovese, Jack McLaughlin-Gray in "Plymouth Rock Isn't Pink"

Fern Persons in "Les Belles Soeurs"

Terry Kinney in "The Glass Menagerie"

Pennsylvania Stage Company

Allentown, Pennsylvania   September 30, 1981–May 9, 1982

Producing Director, Gregory S. Hurst; Managing Director, Jeff Gordon; Stage Directors, Susan Kerner, Steve Rothman, Gregory S. Hurst, Thomas Gruenewald, Sue Lawless; Sets, Raymond C. Recht, Kevin Wiley, Paul Wonsek, Ursula Belden, Curtis Dretsch; Costumes, Thomas Keller, Mary-Anne Aston, Elizabeth Palmer, Ken Yount, Colleen Muscha; Lights, Betsy Adams, Curtis Dretsch, Mark Hendren; State Managers, James Tinsley, Peter S. Del Vecho; Press, Sharon P. Bernstein

DEATHTRAP by Ira Levin; with Michael Connolly, Annie Murray, Jamie Sheridan, Jacqueline Bertrand, Lee Moore

THE GIN GAME by D. L. Coburn; with Norma Ransom, Arthur Peterson

THE PRICE by Arthur Miller; with Gerald Richards, Lynn Cohen, David Hurst, John Ramsey

TWO GENTLEMEN OF VERONA by William Shakespeare; with Joe Morton, Ron Siebert, Reg E. Cathey, Maggie Baird, Catherine Haun, Stan Lachow, John Coughlan, Patricia Kalember, James Lally, Dietrich Snelling, Sam Guncler, Donn Giammarco, Liz Silon

SONG OF MYSELF (World Premiere) conceived by Gregory S. Hurst; Book, Gayle Stahlhuth and Mr. Hurst; Lyrics, Gayle Stahlhuth; Music, Arthur Harris; Director, Gregory S. Hurst; Choreography, Rodney Griffin; Musical Direction/Vocal Arrangements, Paul Trueblood; with Walter Charles, Whitney Webster, Regina Davis, Peggy Atkinson, Frank Kopyc, David Green, Kevin Marcum, Russell Leib, Lucinda Hitchcock-Cone, Robin Hansen, Catherine Haun, John Coughlan, Donn Giammarco, Cameron Smith, Rick Emery, Joanna Glushak

NURSE JANE GOES TO HAWAII (American Premiere) by Allan Stratton; Director, Sue Lawless; with Georgia Engel, Jennifer Bassey, Brandon Maggart, Ronn Carroll, Catherine Haun, Jeff Dreisbach, Liz Otto

Right: Jamey Sheridan, Michael Connolly in "Deathtrap"

Arthur Peterson, Norma Ransom in "The Gin Game"

Reg E. Cathey, Joe Morton in "Two Gentlemen of Verona"

Philadelphia Drama Guild

Philadelphia, Pennsylvania   October 15, 1981–May 9, 1982

Artistic/Managing Director, Gregory Poggi; Marketing/Press, Mary Bensel; Business Manager, Timothy Brennan; Development/Planning, Tom Sherman; Sets, Patricia Woodbridge, Christopher Nowak, Eldon Elder, John Conklin; Costumes, Linda Fisher, Ernest Allen Smith, Frankie Fehr, Patricia Adshead, Susan Tsu, Jennifer von Mayrhauser; Stage Managers, Pat DeRousie, Melissa Logan, Joe Watson; Lighting, Jane Reisman, Ann Wrightsman, F. Mitchell Dana, Pat Collins

OF MICE AND MEN by John Steinbeck; Director, Kurt Reis; with Kent Broadhurst, Mike Starr, George Hall, Walter Flanagan, Gordon Clapp, Diane Lasko, Nesbitt Blaisdell, J. Winston Carroll, Joe Aufiery, Carl Gordon

GEMINI by Albert Innaurato; Director, Jerry Zaks; with Ron Fassler, Janice Fuller, Joseph Adams, Lynn Johnson, Larry Singer, John LaGioia, Cordelia Biddle

DEAR DADDY *(World Premiere)* by Denis Cannan; Director, William Woodman; with Joseph Maher (Bernard), Jo Henderson (Mary), Ellen Parker (Gillian), Jack Gilpin (Billy), John Leighton (Frank), Robert Burns (Charles), Jessica Drake (Gwen,) Pauline Flanagan (Delia)

SERVANT OF TWO MASTERS by Carlo Goldoni; New Version by Tom Cone; Director, Andre Ernotte; with May Quigley, Munson Hicks, Joe Palmieri, Steve Massa, Joel Kramer, Denny Dillon, Michael McCormick, Carole Monferdini, Tom Offt, Peter Marinos, Robert Lovitz

THE CONTEST by Shirley Lauro; Director, Jerry Zaks; with Estelle Omens, Melanie Wells, George Axler, Mimi Cozzens, Hy Anzell, Marnie Cooper, Georgia Southcotte, Heidi Dunham, A. J. Jones

Right: Joseph Maher, Pauline Flanagan in "Dear Daddy"

Kent Broadhurst, Mike Starr in "Of Mice and Men"

Melanie Wells, Estelle Omens in "The Contest"

Players State Theatre

Coconut Grove, Florida   October 9, 1981–April 25, 1982   Fifth Season
Artistic/Producing Director, David Robert Kanter; Managing Director, G. David Black; General Manager, Barry J. W. Steinman; Planning, Alan Yaffe; Press, Susan Westfall; Sets, Marsha Hardy, Ron Foundaw, Kenneth N. Kurtz, David Trimble; Costumes, Claire Gatrell, Barbara A. Bell, Maria Marrero, Barbara Forbes, Jill Young Zuckerman; Lighting, Michael Newton-Brown, Kenneth N. Kurtz, David Martin Jacques, Pat Simmons, James Riley; Sound, J. W. Snyder, Ken Libutti; Stage Managers, Rafael V. Blanco, Jan Crean, Debbie Ann Thompson, Lee Geisel

DA by Hugh Leonard; Director, David Robert Kanter; with Barbara Bernoudy, Donald Ewer, Bill Hindman, Bruce MacVittie, Virginia Mattis, Kelly Pino, William Pitts, Paul Vincent
OEDIPUS REX by Sophocles; Adapted and Directed by Charles Nolte; with Richard Allen, John Archie, Robert Colston, Ray Forchion, Peter Francis-James, Mel Johnson, Jr., Barbara Montgomery, Claudia Robinson, Clarence Thomas, Samuel E. Wright, Kokuma Adisa Ensemble Dancers
A CHRISTMAS CAROL by Charles Dickens; Adapted by David Robert Kanter; with Ellen Adamson, Harold Bergman, Tom Buckland, Norma Davids, Donald Ewer, Gregory Gilbert, Anne Gilliam, Thom Haneline, Robert Holtzman, Geoffrey Infeld, Heidi Kanter, Karin Kanter, Kevin Kiley, Kathleen Deegan Lee, George McCulloch, Raul Melo, Kelly Pino, Joseph Reed, Eileen Russell, Ronald Shelley, Alan Sills, Glenn Swan
THE SUMMER PEOPLE by Charles Nolte; Director, Mr. Nolte; with Ellen Adamson, Booth Colman, Norma Davids, Greg Gilbert, Thom Haneline, Joseph Jamrog, Susan Jenkins, Jane Lowry, George McCulloch, Virginia Mattis, Kelly Pino, Cyd Quilling, Paul Vincent
A MOON FOR THE MISBEGOTTEN by Eugene O'Neill; Director, Lou Salerni; Robert Donley, Peter Galman, Robert Gaston, Lisa McMillan, Fred Thompson
TALLEY'S FOLLY by Lanford Wilson; Director, James Riley; with Jeff David, Linda Stephens
BLACK COFFEE by Agatha Christie; Director, David Robert Kanter; with Mary Benson, Harold Bergman, Tom Buckland, Philip Church, Tim Crowther, Max Howard, Ron Johnston, Kathleen Klein, Dana Kyle, Philip LeStrange, Ronald Shelley, Fred Thompson, Stephen Van Benschoten

Harold Bergman in "A Christmas Carol"

"Oedipus Rex" Above: "The Summer People"   Linda Stephens, Jeff David in "Talley's Folly"

Playmakers Repertory Company

Chapel Hill, N. C.   September 1981–April 1982
Director, David Rotenberg; Managing Director, Edgar Marston; Development, Priscilla Bratcher; Costumes, Bobbi Owen; Lighting, Norman Coates; Stage Manager, Kimberly Francis Kearsley

COMPANY: Patricia Barnett, Gregory Boyd, Russell Graves, Joy Javits, Ann Shepherd, Hamilton Gillett, Paul Miles, Richard Larry Pait, Emile Trimble, and *Guest Artists:* Gordon Ferguson, Gerald Unks, Peter J. Saputo, Carol A. Klevay, Ivar Brogger, Wanda Bimson, Edward Cannan, Matthew Lewis, Edward Binns, Jimm Larson, Edwin J. McDonough, Eunice Anderson, John Tyson, Linda Lee Johnson, Dan Desmond, Henry Hoffman, Pirie Macdonald, Carole Lockwood, Paul Schierhorn, J. Smith Cameron, John Rainer, Maxine Taylor-Morris
PRODUCTIONS: The Front Page, Betrayal, The Glass Menagerie, Angel Street, Twelfth Night, and *World Premiere* of Mobile Hymn

Right: Henry Hoffman, Linda Lee Johnson in "Angel Street"
(Gary Davis Photos)

Center Left: Ann Shepherd, Emile Trimble, Gregory Boyd, Ivar Brogger in "The Front Page"

Hamilton Gillett, Jill Larson in "The Glass Menagerie"   Carole Lockwood, Pirie MacDonald in "Mobile Hymn"

Portland Stage Company

Portland, Maine   November 6, 1981–March 20, 1982

Producing Director, Barbara Rosoff; Business Manager, Patricia Egan; Development, Lindsay Hancock; Sets, John Doepp, Leslie Taylor; Costumes, Rachel Kurland, Heidi Hollmann, Ellen McCartney, Leslie Taylor; Lighting, Gregg Marriner, Dale Jordan, Arden Fingerhut

THE GLASS MENAGERIE by Tennessee Williams; Director, Patricia Carmichael; with Anna Minot, Faith Catlin, Derek Hoxby, John Griesemer

PRIVATE LIVES by Noel Coward; Director, Edward Herrmann; with Chris Weatherhead, Alexander Spencer, Lezlie Dalton, Michael J. Hume, Andrea Standar

THE SEA HORSE by Edward J. Moore; Director, Gordon Edelstein; with Eric Conger, Judith Drake

ALTERATIONS *(World Premiere)* by Leigh Curran; Director, Barbara Rosoff; with Jean DeBaer, Mimi Weddell, Kate Purwin, David Rosenbaum, Joanne Camp

THE DEATH OF A MINER *(World Premiere)* by Paul Cizmar; Director, Barbara Rosoff; with Mary McDonnell, Cotter Smith, Sarah Jessica Parker (Succeeded by Margaret MacLeod), Kristin Jolliff, Dave Florek, John Griesemer, Shaw Purnell, Ritch Brinkley, Douglas Gower, Steven Loring

Right: Alexander Spencer, Chris Weatherhead in "Private Lives"
(Dean Abramson Photos)

Cotter Smith, Mary McDonnell, John Griesemer, Kristin Jolliff, Dave Florek in "The Death of a Miner"

Seattle Repertory Theatre

Seattle, Washington   October 28, 1981–May 16, 1982

Artistic Director, Daniel Sullivan; Producing Director, Peter Donnelly; Associate Artistic Director, Robert Egan; Business Manager, Marene Wilkinson; Press, Marta Mellinger, Marnie Andrews; Marketing, Jerry Sando; Technical Director, Robert Scales; Production Manager, Vito Zingarelli; Wardrobe, Sally Roberts; Sets/Costumes, Robert Dahlstrom, Robert Blackman, Kurt Wilhelm, John Kasarda, Laura Crow, Robert Wojewodski, Ralph Funicello; Lighting, Richard Nelson, Spencer Mosse, James F. Ingalls, Robert Dahlstrom; Stage Managers, Joel Grynheim, Marc Rush, Bonnie Ernst.

ANOTHER PART OF THE FOREST by Lillian Hellman; Director, Edward Hastings; with Kate Mulgrew, Mark Jenkins, Kim Hunter, Tamu Gray, John Kelloff, Keith Carradine, William Hall, Jr., Paul Hostetler, John Procaccino, Donna Snow, Robert Loper, Edward Sampson, Libby Boone

TWO GENTLEMEN OF VERONA by William Shakespeare; Director, Daniel Sullivan; Music, Ken Benshoof; Fight Choreography, David Boushey; with Clayton Corzatte, Byron Jennings, John Christopher Jones, Ted D'Arms, John Aylward, Glenn Mazen, R. Hamilton Wright, John Procaccino, Edward Sampson, Nora McLellan, Katherine Ferrand, Eve Roberts, Susan Ludlow, David Boushey, Scott Honeywell, Lachlan Macleay, Jean Sherrard, Gayle Bellows, Christina Burz, Susan Wands, Brian Faker, Donald Matt

AWAKE AND SING by Clifford Odets; Director, Robert Loper; with William Myers, Eve Roberts, Lou Hettler, Eva Charney, Michael Albert Mantel, John Procaccino, Mark Jenkins, John Hallow, Peter Silbert

BEDROOM FARCE by Alan Ayckbourn; Director, Daniel Sullivan; with Clayton Corzatte, Susan Ludlow, Ted D'Arms, Megan Cole, Laurence Ballard, Christine Healy, Michael Santo, Nora McLellan

SAVAGES by Christopher Hampton; Director, Robert Egan; Sound, Michael Holton; Music, Daniel Birnbaum; with Derek Ralston, Mark Jenkins, Megan Cole, Joseph Siravo, Glenn Mazen, Muni Zano, Ted D'Arms, John Kauffman, Michael Santo, William P. Ontiveros, Muni Zano, Nina Esquerdo, Lee Ann Fujii, Donald Matt, Lani Okimoto, Eduardo Zuniga

MAJOR BARBARA by George Bernard Shaw; Director, Daniel Sullivan; with Nathan Haas, Eve Roberts, William Crossett, Kate Mulgrew, Diana Stagner, Ray Dooley, Daniel Daily, Bernard Behrens, Susan Ludlow, Laurence Ballard, Nina Wishengrad, Derek Ralston, John Procaccino, Marjorie Nelson, Roderick Aird, Mark McConnell

John Kellogg, Kate Mulgrew in "Another Part of the Forest" Above: Muni Zano, Mark Jenkins in "Savages"

Bernard Behrens in "Major Barbara" Above: John Hallow, Lou Hetler, Eve Roberts in "Awake and Sing"

South Coast Repertory

Costa Mesa, California   September 15, 1981–July 3, 1982

Artistic Directors, David Emmes, Martin Benson; General Manager, Tom Spray; Marketing, Paula Bond; Press, John Mouledoux, Michael Bigelow Dixon; Literary Manager, Jerry Patch; Technical Director, Leo Collin; Props, Michael Beech; Wardrobe, Nancy J. Hamann; Stage Managers, Linda L. Kimball, Julie Haber, Bonnie Lorenger; Directors, John Allison, Martin Benson, David Emmes, Richard Gershman, John-David Keller, Paul Rudd, Lee Shallat; Sets, Michael Devine, Mark Donnelly, Cliff Faulkner, Ralph Funicello, Keith Hein, Steve Lavino, Lisette Thomas; Lighting, Tom Ruzika, Cameron Harvey, Paulie Jenkins, Donna Ruzika, Susan Tuohy; Costumes, Nanrose Buchman, Barbara Cox, Merrily Ann Murray, Dwight Richard Odle, Tom Rasmussen, Skipper Skeoch, Charles Tomlinson

AH, WILDERNESS! by Eugene O'Neill; with Irene Arranga, K Callan, Robert Cornthwaite, Richard Doyle, Mark Dressler, James Gallery, Anne Gerety, Pamela Hastain, Mark Herrier, Jack Holland, Art Koustik, Anni Long, Martha McFarland, Joe McNeely, Sam Helfrich, Richard Stanley

LOOSE ENDS by Michael Weller; with Paul Rudd, Marnie Mosiman, Anni Long, Robert Crow, Michael MacRae, Lois Foraker, Don Tuche, Patti Yasutake, Howard Shangraw, John-David Keller, Ron Boussom

A CHRISTMAS CAROL by Charles Dickens; Adapted by Jerry Patch; with Hal Landon, Jr., John Ellington, Noreen Hennessy, Michelle Wallen, Dan Guzman, Michelle Young, Charlie Cummins, Richard Doyle, Ron Michaelson, Don Tuche, Dennis Palmieri, Candice Copeland, Linda Woods, Art Koustik, Martha McFarland, Howard Shangraw, Patti Wojcik, Robert Crow, Wayne Alexander, Bryan Rasmussen, Darcy Nuber, Jason Schnieder

THE PLAY'S THE THING by Ferenc Molnar; Adapted by P. G. Wodehouse; with Jonathan Farwell, Michael Keenan, Nicholas Walker, John-David Keller, Linda Thorson, Robert Machray, John Ellington, Robert Crow, Bryan Rasmussen

HENRY IV PART I by William Shakespeare; with Wayne Grace, David Chemel, Bryan Rasmussen, John-David Keller, Robert Machray, George Woods, David Darlow, Hugh Reilly, Anni Long, Michael H. Winckler, Kathryn Johnson, Kay E. Kuter, Richard Doyle, Keith Fowler, Thomas Hill, Ron Boussom, Don Tuche, Nathan Adler, Martha McFarland, Gary Cowl, Robert Crow, Mark Daukas, James Fisk, Rick Hill, Mark McDonough, David Messenger, Jon Sidoli, Steve Vermeulen, Steve Workman

DA by Hugh Leonard; with Dean Santoro, Ron Boussom, Thomas Toner, Katherine MacGregor, John Greenleaf, William Glover, Patti Johns, Margaret Muse

TINTYPES by Mary Kyte, Mel Marvin and Gary Pearle; with Jonelle Allen, Stanley Grover, Ken Jennings, Angelina Reaux, Susan Watson, John Ellington

TRUE WEST by Sam Shepard; with Ed Harris, John Ashton, Richard Doyle, Iris Korn

BODIES by James Saunders; with Christina Pickles, Tandy Cronyn, Matthew Faison, Lawrence Pressman

BLOOD KNOT by Athol Fugard; with Tom Bower, Sydney Hibbert

COMING ATTRACTIONS by Ted Talley; Music, Jack Feldman; Lyrics, Bruce Sussman, Jack Feldman; with Richard Doyle, Howard Shangraw, Diane dePriest, John Ellington, Art Koustik, Anni Long, Don Tuche

THE MAN WHO COULD SEE THROUGH TIME by Terri Wagener; with Charles Lanyer, Linda Purl

Thomas Toner, Dean Santoro in "Da" Top Right: "Tintypes"

Anni Long, Ron Roussom, Marni Mosiman, Paul Rudd in "Loose Ends" Above: David Chemel, David Darlow in "Henry IV Part I"

158

Stagewest

West Springfield, Massachusetts   October 22, 1981–May 1, 1982

Producing Director, Stephen E. Hays; Managing Director, Robert Rosenbaum; Development, Sheldon Wolf; Production Manager, Ken Denison; Press, Tara K. Becker; Marketing, Kate Farrell; Technical Director, Joseph Long; Costumer, Jan Morrison; Administrative Assistant, Julie Monohan; Props, Carroll Ann Simon; Sets/Costumes, Jeffrey Struckman, Frank J. Boros, Elizabeth Covey, Joseph Long, Leslie Miller, Anne Thaxter Watson, Deborah Shaw, Wally Coberg, Jeffrey Fiala; Lighting, Paul J. Horton, Bonnie Ann Brown, Barry Arnold; Sound, Paul J. Horton, Karen Reed; Stage Managers, Kaz J. Reed, Ken Denison, Juliet O. Campbell

TERRA NOVA by Ted Tally; Director, Harold Scott; with Curt Dawson, Adrian Sparks, Tania Myren, Doug Jones, Eric Conger, Gary Armagnac, Gregory Mortensen
TALLEY'S FOLLY by Lanford Wilson; Director, Stephen E. Hays; with Erika Petersen, Eugene Troobnick
TINTYPES by Mary Kyte, Mel Marvin and Gary Pearle; Director, Wayne Bryan; with Sal Biagini, Richert Easley, Carol Lugenbeal, Ursuline Kairson, Robin Taylor
HELLO AND GOODBYE by Athol Fugard; Director, Donald Hicken; with Tana Hicken, Richard Pilcher
DEAD WRONG *(World Premiere)* by Nick Hall; Director, Richard Gershman; with Curt Dawson, Judith McConnell, Glenn Scherer, Richard Zavaglia, James DeMarse
ARTICHOKE by Joanna M. Glass; Director, Timothy Near; with Lewis Arlt, Gary Armagnac, Bernard Frawley, Holly Hunter, David O. Petersen, Lisabeth Shean, Henry Thomas
YOU NEVER CAN TELL by George Bernard Shaw; Director, Stephen E. Hays; with Kenneth Mesroll, Cindy Rosenthal, Kate Farrell, Christopher Stafford Nelson, Mary Fogarty, Nancy Boykin, Bernard Frawley, Henry Thomas, David O. Petersen, Tom Grenon, David Pursley, Bernadette Williams

Right: Kenneth Meseroll, Kate Farrell, Bernard Frawley in "You Never Can Tell"

Erika Petersen, Eugene Troobnick in "Talley's Folly"

Curt Dawson, Judith McConnell in "Dead Wrong"

Studio Arena Theatre

Buffalo, New York   September 25, 1981–May 16, 1982   Seventeenth Season
Artistic Director, David Frank; Managing Director, Barry Hoffman; Executive Assistant, Carol A. Kolis; Dramaturg, Kathryn Long; Technical Director/Production Coordinator, Brett Thomas; Wardrobe, Gail Evans; Props, Lois Griffing; Marketing/Press, Richard Goldsmith; Press, Blossom Cohan; Sound, Rick Menke; Sets, Wally Coberg, Grady Larkins, Paul Wonsek, Quentin Thomas, John Arnone, David Woolard; Lighting, Robby Monk, Paul Wonsek, Quentin Thomas; Costumes, Lewis D. Rampino, Bill Walker, Robert Morgan, Janice I. Lines, Andrew Blackwood Marlay

WHOSE LIFE IS IT ANYWAY? by Brian Clark; Director, David Frank; with Munson Hicks, Patricia Kilgarriff, Madeleine Potter, Ascanio Sharpe, Shaine Marinson, Dale Helward, Deborah Taylor, Stephen Tobolowsky, Moultrie Patten, Robert Darnell, David Fendrick, Gerald Finnegan, Derek Campbell, Carla Williams

THE MISS FIRECRACKER CONTEST by Beth Henley; Director, Davey Marlin-Jones; with Kathryn Grody, K. T. Baumann, Donna Davis, Stephen Tobolowsky, Robert Darnell, Cam Kornman

DEATHTRAP by Ira Levin; Director, David Frank; with Stephen Gilborn, Margery Shaw, Andrew Davis, Mickey Hartnett, Robert Darnell

TARTUFFE by Moliere; Director, David Frank; with Elizabeth Hiller, William Kiehl, Holly Barron, Charles Shaw-Robinson, Cindy Rosenthal, Hall Hunsinger, Donald Gantry, Robert Darnell, Lisa Goodman, David Fendrick, David Hyde-Lamb, Amy Hoffman

DERELICT *(World Premiere)* by Robert Schenkkan; Director, A. J. Antoon; with Evan Handler, Robert Darnell, Everett Ensley, Sharon Laughlin, Gerald Halter, Eugene Key, Dan Oreskes, Ronald O. J. Parson, Robert J. Paul, Tod Wheeler, Fritz Sperberg, William Cain

OF MICE AND MEN by John Steinbeck; Director, Geoffrey Sherman; with Don Perkins, Michael Brennan Starr, William Preston, Walter Flanagan, Eric Uhler, Pamela Lewis, Robert Darnell, John Tormey, John T. Dolphin, Stephen Henderson

RHINO FAT FROM RED DOG NOTES!?! by Patrick Desmond, David Marlin-Jones, and Studio Arena Theatre Company; Director, Davey Marlin-Jones; with K. T. Baumann, Lucinda Hitchcock Cone, Robert Darnell, Alison Fraser, Mickey Hartnett, Stephen Henderson, Eugene Key, Don Perkins, Sharon Schlarth, Carl Schurr, Richard Seer, Robert Spencer

Right: Ronald O. J. Parsons, Robert Darnell, Evan Handler, Tod Wheeler, Eugene Key, Everett Easley, Robert J. Paul in "Derelict" Above: Holly Baron, Robert Darnell in "Tartuffe"

William Preston, Astro Mutt, Don Perkins, Michael Brennan Starr in "Of Mice and Men"

"Rhino Fat From Red Dog Notes!?!"

160

Syracuse Stage

Syracuse, N.Y.   October 30, 1981–May 23, 1982   Ninth Season

Producing Director, Arthur Storch; Managing Director, James A. Clark; Business Manager, Betty Starr; Development, Shirley Lockwood; Press, Jenifer Breyer; Marketing, Barbara Beckos; Dramaturg, Tom Walsh; Production Manager, Bob Davidson; Technical Director, Donald R. Fassinger; Sound, David A. Schnirman; Props, Diann Fay; Costumer, Anne Shanto; Scenic Artist, Susan Lanham; Sets/Costumers, Charles Cosler, David Toser, Hal Tine, Nanzi Adzima, James Berton Harris, James Tilton, Anne Shanto, John Doepp, Charles Cosler; Lighting, Charles Cosler, Judy Rasmuson, Robert F. Strohmeier, Paul Mathiesen, Michael Newton-Brown; Stage Manager, Cynthia Poulson

BETRAYAL by Harold Pinter; Director, Terry Schreiber; with Lynn Milgrim, Richard Greene, Edmond Genest, Sam Goldsman
A CHRISTMAS CAROL by Charles Dickens; Director, Stephen Willems; Choreography, Linda Sabo; Music Direction, Brent Wagner; with Gary L. Hass, Gerard Moses, Daniel Krempel, David Greenham, David Lowenstein, Michael Haight, Alan Brasington, Mike Champagne, Richard Peterson, David Tabor, Kensyn Crouch, Gerardine Clark, Robert Jackson, Kristin Brady, Emily Goodpaster, Susan Keill, Robert Eller, Courtney Woodard, Christopher Doane, Fred Lopez, Michael Eller, Curt Karibalis, Joseph Eller, Sarah Felder, Dawn Vanessa Brown, Bill Molesky, Joseph Muzikar, Joyce Krempel, Kit LeFever, Elizabeth Fried, Mike Sweeney, Nick Corley, Tom Fay, Bethany Bloomer
THE MERCHANT OF VENICE by William Shakespeare; Director, Ken Jenkins; with Yusef Bulos, David Tabor, Mike Champagne, Joseph Muzikar, Peter-Francis James, John Seidman, Erika Peterson, Freda Foh Shen, Gary Armagnac, Robert Jackson, Richard Peterson, Kensyn Crouch, Yolanda Lloyd, Curt Karibalis, Daniel S. Krempel, Kensyn Crouch, Bill Molesky, William Herndon, Kathryn Baird, Aaron Sorkin, Nick Corley, Susan Goldsman, David Lowenstein, Corrine Mandell, Rachel Potash, Barbara Baptiste, Christopher Doane, Emily Goodpaster
TWICE AROUND THE PARK (World Premiere) by Murray Schisgal; Director, Arthur Storch; with Anne Jackson, Eli Wallach
TALLEY'S FOLLY by Lanford Wilson; Director, John Ulmer; with David Rosenbaum, Ellen Barry
K2 by Patrick Meyers; Director, Terry Schreiber; Music, Herman Chessid; with Michael Tolaydo, Jay Patterson

Right: Richard Greene, Lynn Milgrim in "Betrayal" Above: Alan Brasington as Scrooge in "A Christmas Carol"

Eli Wallach, Anne Jackson in "Twice Around the Park"

Michael Tolaydo, Jay Patterson in "K2"

161

Theatre By The Sea

Portsmouth, New Hampshire   September 25, 1981–June 6, 1982   Eighteenth Season
Producing Director, Jon Kimbell; Executive Director, Karl Gevecker; Business Manager, Lois Woodbury; Press, David James; Technical Director, Paul Eldridge; Stage Directors, Jon Kimball, Peter Bennett, Kent Paul, B. Rodney Marriott; Sets, Jack Doepp, Kathie Iannicelli, Laryy Fulton, Joan Brancale; Costumes, Kathie Iannicelli, Eliza Pietsch Chugg; Lighting, Bruce K. Morriss; Sound, Chuck London, Bruce K. Morriss; Stage Manager, John L. Becker

THE MOUSETRAP by Agatha Christie; with Allan Carlsen, Tom Celli, Nancy Walton Fenn, Nancy Nichols, K. Lype O'Dell, Michael Rothhaar, Robert Rutland, Stephanie Voss
THE RAINMAKER by N. Richard Nash; with Allan Carlsen, Tom Celli, Terrence Markovich, K. Lype O'Dell, Peter Reardon, Michael Rothhaar, Stephanie Voss
CHARLEY'S AUNT by Brandon Thomas; with Allan Carlsen, James Carruthers, Tom Celli, Terrence Markovich, K. Lype O'Dell, Michael Rothhaar, Ginny Russell, Maxine Taylor-Morris, Linda Smythe, Stephanie Voss
ABSURD PERSON SINGULAR by Alan Ayckbourn; with Tom Celli, K. Lype O'Dell, Maxine Taylor-Morris, Michael Rothhaar, Ginny Russell, Stephanie Voss
A STREETCAR NAMED DESIRE by Tennessee Williams; with Michael Beirne, James Carruthers, Tom Celli, Frank Girardeau, Marjorie Johnson, Mary Carol Johnson, Dale Merchant, Monica Merryman, Ken Olin, Stephanie Voss, Patricia Wettig
K2 by Patrick Meyers; with Timothy Shelton, Danton Stone
MAN OF LA MANCHA with Book by Dale Wasserman; Lyrics, Joe Darion; Music, Mitch Leigh; Choreographer, Antony Devecchi; Musical Director, John Spalla; with Nancy Callman, Tom Celli, Kymberly Dawson, Jason Edwards, Steven Greenberg, Lauri Landry, Helen Masloff, Hector Mercado, Bill Nolte, David Perry, Loyd Sannes, Jack Sevier, Richard Stillman, Edmond Varrato, Stefan Windroth

Right: Danton Stone, Timothy Shelton in "K2"

Monica Merryman, Ken Olin in "A Streetcar Named Desire"

Allan Carlsen, Stephanie Voss in "The Rainmaker"

162

Theater Center

Philadelphia, Pennsylvania   July 18, 1981–June 20, 1982

Artistic Director, Albert Benzwie; Business Manager, Lorraine Bittner; Managing Director, Judith Panetta; Sets/Costumes, Gardner Robinson, Robert Hubbard, Laurel Odhner, Michael Matthews, Helen Henry, George Storm, Christin Graham-Markunas, Cat Hebert, Phyllis Priester, Judith Panetta, Linda Maylish; Lighting, George Storm, Robin Miller, John Bitterman, Liz Flax; Press, Lorraine Bittner, Sallie Gross; Stage Managers, Kenneth Starrett, Karlo Dudley, Madeline Slisky, Robin Miller, Martha Chaseman

WALK TOGETHER CHILDREN conceived, directed and performed by Vinie Burrows

THE SLAVE by Amiri Baraka; Director, Andre Jones; with Bruce Robinson, Karen St. Pierre, Laurence Rapp

SIZWE BANSI IS DEAD by Athol Fugard, John Kani and Winston Ntshona; Director, Robert Hubbard; with Robert Hubbard, Lionel Ford

AMEN CORNER by James Baldwin; Director, Robert Hightower, with Doris LaVeice Beatty, Odessa Griffin, Judith Harris, Belle McKinney, Jo Ann B. Ford, Vaughn Dwight Morrison, Eric Hightower, Thom Wilkins, Geraldine White, Altris Shirdan, Rosemond Wilmer, Marian Davis, Mary Caul, Yvonne Taylor, Yvette Taylor, Anthony Cooper, Janice Jenkins

GOGOL by Nikolai Gogol; Adapted and Directed by Cat Hebert; with A. E. Westover, Jackie Osisek, Susannah Harris, Vic Diamond, Sandra Smith, Timothy A. Judson, Fawn Baron, David Adam Baker, Stephen J. Stone, Susan Wainer, Beverly Alfano, Rose Scavullo, Barbara Eiswerth, Cat Hebert

THE BLOOD KNOT by Athol Fugard; Robert Hubbard; with Christopher G. Markunas, Lionel Ford

World Premieres:

THE TENOR'S SUITE by Joseph Summer; Director, Lea Jorgensen; Choreography, Donald T. Lunsford II; with Eileen Bendersky, Donald T. Lunsford II, Noel Espiritu Velasco, Barbara Noska, Reid A. Westergaard, Emanuel Meli, Bruce Robinson

SYMPHONY PASTORALE by J. Robert Barnett; Director, Judith Panetta; with Camilla Lindan, Susan Kurowski, Frank Holton, Timothy Cox, Edward Gavin

GETTING UP AND GETTING DRESSED by Ann Morrissett Davidon; Director, Albert Benzwie; with Jane Marie Glodek, Taylor Zimmerman, Mary Jane Slavin, Anthony Cassidy, Christopher G. Markunas, Walt Vail

BEIN' HERE TONIGHT by Sharita Hunt, Doris Mezler, Veronika Nowag, Barbara Walden, Stanley Walden; Music/Lyrics, Stanley Walden; Director, Veronika Nowag; Musical Direction, Gary Rusnak; Choreography, Chico Garcia; with Miriam Hamilton, Jeanne Fisher, Jane Marie Glodek, Alexander Toussaint, Lawrence Bender

THE PERSECUTION OF CITIZEN VASILYCH by Bill Hollenbach; Director, Judith Panetta; with Joe Torrisi, Frank Holton, John McKevitt, Al Wright, Doug Wild, Geneva Wiggins-Collins, Richard Houser, Dean Dogherty, Martha Chaseman

EL SALVADOR by Judith Gleason; Director, Judith Panetta; with Mary Adams, Aswad Cambugi, Lisa Evans, Laurence H. Geller, Susan Kurowski, Eita Long, Russel Mahrt, Gabriel Rivas, Lionel Ford

Joe Torrisi, Frank Holton in "The Persecution of Citizen Vasilych" Top Right: Aswad Cambugi, Russell Mahrt in "El Salvadore" Below: "Bein' Here Tonight"

Theatre Three

Dallas, Texas   October 6, 1981–August 21, 1982   Twentieth Season
Founding Director, Norma Young; Executive Producer/Director, Jac Alder; Associate Directors, Charles Howard, Laurence O'Dwyer; Assistant to Producer, Shannon McNear; Technical Director, Daniel Perry; Sets/Costumes, Charles Howard, Patty Greer McGarity, Beverly Nachimson, Jac Alder, Julie Dale; Lighting, Shari Melde, Peter Metz; Stage Managers, Jimmy Mullen, Charles Howard, Peter Channell, Keith Allgeier, Wendye Clarendon, Jac Alder, Deborah Brooks

WORKING based on book by Studs Terkel; Adapted by Stephen Schwartz; Director, Jac Alder; Choreography, Laura Cash; Musical Director, Terry Dobson; with Doug Ahders, Keith Allgeier, Kristina Baker, Jerry Chapa, Sa'mi Chester, Wendye Clarendon, Cynthia Dorn, Leslie Evans, Bryan Foster, Anna Heins, Philip Hernandez, Paul Lazar, Victoria Levesque, Norman Meullen, Connie Nelson, John Rainone, Gary Schenk, Holly Schenk, Norma Young

THE GONDOLIERS by Gilbert and Sullivan; Direction/Choreography, Jack Eddleman; with Jac Alder, Keith Allgeier, Judy Blue, Jim Caruso, Peter Channell, Carol Cleaver, Cathy Cummings, Julie Dale, Gary Daniel, Eleanor Eby, Hector Garcia, Karon High, Hillary Hight, Dana Jackson, Wendy Jackson, Stephen Kean, Paul Lazar, Victoria LeVesque, Kevin Ligon, Jeffrey Marler, Haley McLane, David Pucek, Greg Pugh, Carolyn Whitaker

EMLYN WILLIAMS AS CHARLES DICKENS (one-man show)

EDEN COURT by Murphy Guyer; Director, Laurence O'Dwyer; with Sharon Bunn, Jeanne Campise, Ron Jackson, Thurman Moss

MARK TWAIN TONIGHT! with Hal Holbrook in a one-man performance.

SPLENDID REBELS by Ernest Joselovitz; Director, Charles Howard; with Jac Alder, Keith Allgeier, Rodger Boyce, Hugh Feagin, Sard Fleeker, Anna Heins, Jim Ivey, Paul Lazar, Jeff Marler, Norman Neullen, Jack Robinson, Cliff Stephens, Gary Taggart, Steve Turner, Mary Lee York, Norma Young, Thomas Zinn

DESIGN FOR LIVING by Noel Coward; Director, Laurence O'Dwyer; with Keith Allgeier, Wendye Clarendon, Sally Cole, Dwain Fail, Niki Flacks, Paul Lazar, Jimmy Mullen, Laurel Nelson, Gary Taggart, Michael van Dalsem

CLOSE OF PLAY by Simon Gray (cast not submitted)

Right: Paul Lazar, Laurence O'Dwyer, Amy Mills in "The Physician in spite of Himself"

Gary Daniel, Jeffrey Marler, Kevin Ligon, Jack Eddleman in "The Gondoliers"

Trinity Square Repertory Company

Providence, Rhode Island   June 12, 1981–June 6, 1982   Nineteenth Season

Director, Adrian Hall; Managing Director, E. Timothy Langan; Assistant to Mr. Hall, Marion Simon; General Manager, Michael Ducharme; Musical Director, Richard Dumming; Press, Scotti DiDonato; Sets, Eugene Lee, Robert D. Soule; Lighting, John F. Custer; Costumes, William Lane; Stage Directors, Adrian Hall, Philip Minor, David Wheeler, Suzanne Shepherd, George Martin, Melanie Jones, Peter Gerety; Choreographer, Sharon Jenkins; Stage Managers, Maureen F. Gibson, Rebecca Linn

COMPANY: Barbara Blossom, Dan Butler, Vince Ceglie, Timothy Crowe, Richard Dumming, Timothy Daly, Maurice Dolbier, Richard Ferrone, Monique Fowler, Peter Gerety, Tom Griffin, Ed Hall, Richard Jenkins, Keith Jochim, David C. Jones, Melanie Jones, Richard Kavanaugh, David Kenneth, Richard Kneeland, Howard London, George Martin, Ruth Maynard, Derek Meader, Betty Moore, Nancy Nichols, Barbara Orson, Ford Rainey, Anne Scurria, April Shawhan, Patricia Thomas, Amy Van Nostrand, Daniel Von Bargen

Guest Artists: Cynthia Carle, Margot Dionne, Michele Fraioli, Robin Grove, Conrad McLaren, Margaret Phillips, Marran Smith

PRODUCTIONS: Of Mice and Men, Buried Child, L'Atelier, The Gin Game, A Lesson from Aloes, A Flea in Her Ear, A Christmas Carol, Dead Souls, Talley's Folly, The Elephant Man, True West, 5th of July, and "The Hothouse" by Harold Pinter

April Shawhan, Richard Kavanaugh, Ed Hall in "A Lesson from Aloes"
Above: "Dead Souls"

Richard Jenkins, Keith Jochim in "True West" Above: Timothy Daly, Betty Moore in "5th of July"

165

Tyrone Guthrie Theater

Minneapolis, Minnesota   June 5, 1981–April 10, 1982   Nineteenth Season

Artistic Director, Liviu Ciulei; Managing Director, Donald Schoenbaum; Associate Artistic Director, Garland Wright; Dramaturg, Richard Nelson; Sets, Liviu Ciulei, Richard Foreman, Karl Eigsti, John Lee Beatty, James Guenther, Jack Barkla, John Arnone, Santo Loquasto, Marsha L. Weist-Hines; Costumes, Jack Edwards, Patricia Zipprodt, Marjorie Slaiman, Jennifer von Mayrhauser, Jared Aswegan, Kurt Wilhelm, Santo Loquasto, James Guenther, Marsha L. Weist-Hines; Lighting, Duane Schuler, Richard Riddell, Dennis Parichy, Paul Scharfenberger, Karlis Ozols, Craig Miller, Jennifer Tipton; Stage Managers, Bill Gregg, Sharon Ewald, Diane DiVita, Charles Ottie, Megan Miller-Shields; Press, Dennis Behl

COMPANY: C. B. Anderson, Fred Applegate, Chuck Bailey, Hillary Bailey, Marshall Borden, Alexandra Borrie, Roy Brocksmith, Catherine Burns, Elizabeth Bussey, Michael Butler, Johann Carlo, Jody Catlin, Oliver Cliff, Joel Colodner, Frances Conroy, Katherine Cortez, Richard Cox, Hume Cronyn, Stephen D'Ambrose, Robert Dorfman, James Eckhouse, Jonathan Fuller, Boyd Gaines, Francois de la Giroday, Brad Hall, Sara Hennessy, Richard Hilger, Maren Hinderlie, Richard Howard, Val Kilmer, Paul Laakso, John Lewin, Patti LuPone, Donald Madden, J. Patrick Martin, James McKeel, Peter McRobbie, Fred Melamed, Betty Miller, Isabell Monk, Robert Nadir, William Newman, Kristine Nielsen, Peggy O'Connell, Richard Ooms, Laurence Overmire, Suzanne Petri, Adam Redfield, Carol Rosenfeld, Clive Rosengren, Eliot Ross, Martin Ruben, Ken Ruta, Hayden Saunier, Peggy Schoditsch, John Seitz, William Simington, Mim Solberg, Melodie Somers, Dale Soules, Cherie Sprosty, Henry Stram, John E. Straub, Jessica Tandy, Peter Thoemke, Jan Triska, William Verderber, Keliher Walsh, David Warrilow, Binky Wood, Alan Woodward, Ray Xifo

PRODUCTIONS: THE TEMPEST by William Shakespeare and directed by Liviu Ciulei, DON JUAN by Moliere and directed by Richard Foreman, OUR TOWN by Thornton Wilder and directed by Alan Schneider, A CHRISTMAS CAROL by Charles Dickens and directed by Jon Cranney, CANDIDE by Voltaire and directed by Garland Wright, AS YOU LIKE IT by William Shakespeare and directed by Liviu Ciulei, *World Premieres* of FOXFIRE by Susan Cooper and Hume Cronyn directed by Marshall W. Mason, EVE OF RETIREMENT by Thomas Bernhard, ELI by Nelly Sachs and directed by Garland Wright

Bruce Goldstein Photos
Right: Boyd Gaines, Frances Conroy in "The Tempest"

Betty Miller, Donald Madden, Catherine Burns (seated) in "Eve of Retirement"

Hume Cronyn, Jessica Tandy in "Foxfire"

166

Virginia Museum Theatre

Richmond, Virginia   September 25, 1981–April 24, 1982   Twenty-seventh Season

Artistic Director, Tom Markus; Managing Director, Ira Schlosser; Associate Artistic Director, Terry Burgler; Audience Services, Anne E. Conable; Business Manager, Edward W. Rucker; Company Manager, Phil Crosby; Press, Dave Griffith, Don Dale; Sets/Costumes, Charles Caldwell, Bronwyn Jones Caldwell, C. Jane Epperson, Thomas W. Hammond, Tom Targownik, Carol H. Beule, Julie D. Keen, Joseph A. Varga; Lighting, Richard Moore, Lynne M. Hartman; Sound, Margi Heiple; Stage Managers, Doug Flinchum, Andy Wiesnet

COUNT DRACULA by Ted Tiller; Director, Tom Markus; with Kensyn Crouch, William Denis, Maury Erickson, Margery Murray, Daniel Robbins, Jean Sincere, Peter Umbras, Robert Walsh
MOVE *(World Premiere)* by Margaret Mitchell Dukore; Director, Tom Markus; with Donald Gantry, Marilyn McIntyre, Elizabeth Perry
TINTYPES by Mary Kyte, Mel Marvin and Gary Pearle; Director/Choreographer, Darwin Knight; Musical Director, Robert J. Bruyr; with Wendy-Jo Belcher (succeeded by Ann Hodapp), Randy Brenner, Catherine Gaines, Olivia Virgil Harper, James LeVaggi
A CHRISTMAS CAROL by Charles Dickens; Adapted by Tom Markus; Director, Terry Burgler; with Bev Appleton, Susan Brandner, Marylouise Burke, Donald Christopher, Lucien Douglas, Jeff Q. Erickson, Maury Erickson, Nathan Fairman, Robert Foley, Jeffrey Fuquay, Tracy O'Neil Heffernan, Daniel Timothy Johnson, Anne Lynn, Margaret Reed, Daniel Robbins, Emily Skinner, Walter Williamson, John Winn III, Nan Wray
NEVER THE TWAIN *(American Premiere)* by Bertolt Brecht, Rudyard Kipling; Compiled by John Willett; Music by Weill, Eisler, Dessau, Cobb, Dalby, Druce; Additional Music/Musical Director, Raphael Crystal; Director, Wal Cherry; with Gary Brubach, Ted Pejovich, Ian Stuart, Henrietta Valor
TALLEY'S FOLLY by Lanford Wilson; Director, Terry Burgler; with Nancy Boykin, David Rosenbaum
THE FATHER by August Strindberg; Adaptor/Director, Tom Markus; with Charles T. Baxter, Terry Burgler, Donald Christopher, Warren Kelley, Christine Mitchell, Jane Moore, Walter Rhodes, Anne Sheldon
JUST ACROSS THE BORDER *(World Premiere)* by Robert Potter; Director, Tom Markus; with Francisco Prado, Anne Sheldon, Sherry Skinker, Geddeth Smith
CANDIDE by Hugh Wheeler, Leonard Bernstein, Richard Wilbur, Stephen Sondheim, John LaTouche; Director/Choreographer, Darwin Knight; Musical Director, Mark Goodman; with Bev Appleton, Jerry Bradley, Elizabeth Cade, Leslie Harrington, Maj-Lis Jalkio, Richard Kinter, Johanna Lawrence, John McNamara, Leilani Mickey, Stephen Schmidt, Todd Taylor, Valerie Toth, Jan van der Swaagh, Barbara Walsh
MACBETH ABRIDGED adapted and directed by Terry Burgler; with Kathleen Bishop, Jerry Bradley, Jonathan Epstein

Top Right: David Rosenbaum, Nancy Boykin in "Talley's Folly"

James LeVaggi, Catherine Gaines, Randy Brenner, Olivia Virgil Harper,
Wendy-Jo Belcher in "Tintypes"

Ted Pejovich, Gary Brubach in "Never the Twain"

167

Virginia Stage Company

Norfolk, Virginia   November 1, 1981–May 22, 1982   Third Season

Producing Director, Robert Tolan; General Manager, Randy Adams; Development, Patricia Rhodes; Marketing/Press, Lane Marshall; Business Manager, Charles W. Joyce, Assistant to Mr. Tolan, Janet Stanford; Production Manager, Joe Ragey; Costumes/Sets, Joe Ragey, Carrie Curtis, Duke Durfee, Ann Wallace, James Morgan, Anne-Marie Wright; Lighting, Joe Ragey, Bonnie Ann Brown, Ted Bartenstein; Stage Managers, J. P. Elins, Sarah Cornelia

THE GIN GAME directed by Robert Tolan; with Margaret Thomson, Samy Gray

A CHRISTMAS CAROL directed by Michael Hankins; with Michael Connolly, Davis Hall, Mara Scottwood, Mitchell Thomas, Thomas Carson, Peter Murphy, Art Kempf, Jay Oney, Robert Bullington, Margaret Thomson, Nancy Allen, Brandon Boyce, Fritz Bronner, Terri Hain, Deborah Hale, Jay Lockamy, Peter Lockamy, Richard Marlow, Bruce Marvin, David Paterson, Sara Seidman, Amy Sigmund, Bonnie Thomas

THERESE directed by Stephen Willems; with Margaret Thomson, Davis Hall, Wanda Bimson, James Goodwin Rice, Thomas Carson, Deborah Hale, Peter Murphy

STRIDER directed by Lynne Gannaway; Musical Director, John Clifton; Associate Director, Gerard Brentte; with Gary Gage, Richard Bowne, Tracey Carnes, Igors Gavon, John Newton, Jann Paxton, Elizabeth Bracken, Rob Bullington, Jay Oney, Sara Seidman, Bonnie E. Thomas, Terri Hain, Deborah Hale, Deborah Stern, Edward Conery, Fritz Bronner, David Lively, John Clifton, Dennis Hribar, Robert Cross, Peter Dimitrov

CHARLEY'S AUNT directed by Michael Hankins; with John Newton, Gary Gage, Richard Bowne, Robert Bullington, Edward Conery, David Lively, I. Mary Carter, Terri Hain, Deborah Hale, Janet Stanford

GEMINI directed by Robert Tolan; with Dominic Guastaferro, Robin Tate, I. Mary Carter, Michael Cone, Fritz Bronner, Bonnie Thomas, Deborah Stern

WORLD PREMIERES of **LEAVINGS** by Michael Richey; Director, Robert Tolan; with Mara Scott-Wood (Euna), Art Kempf (Ellert), Nancy Allen (Willie), Peter Murphy (Cye), Margaret Thomson (Emma), Thomas Carson (Doc), Davis Hall (Beau), Jay Oney (Hap), Fritz Bronner, Robert Bullington, Jay Lockamy (Deputies).

WHATEVER BECAME OF LOVE? by Ed Meyerson; Director, Stephen Willems; with Jay Oney (Lt. Galloway), Wanda Bimson (Gioia), Margaret Thomson (Francesca), Peter Murphy (Alberto), Davis Hall (Cosmo), Mara Scott-Wood (Bettina), James Goodwin Rice (Marco)

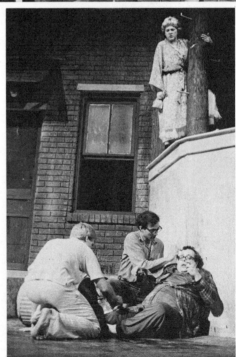

Edward Conery, John Newton in "Strider" Top Right: Wanda Bimson, Jay Oney in "Whatever Became of Love?"

I. Mary Carter in "Gemini" Above: Margaret Thomson, Sam Gray in "The Gin Game"

Whole Theater Company

Montclair, New Jersey   October 1981–April 1982

Producing Director, Arnold Mittelman; Artistic Director, Olympia Dukakis; Education Director, Judith Delgado; General Manager, Robert Alpaugh; Marketing, Helen Stein; Assistant Producing Director, Lynn Peyser

COMPANY: Maggie Abeckerly, Apollo Dukakis, Louis Zorich, Olympia Dukakis, Arnold Mittelman, Judith Delgado, and *Guest Artists:* Austin Pendleton, Jose Ferrer

PRODUCTIONS: Kurt Weill Cabaret, Marat/Sade, and *Premieres* of "USO Show" and "Off Broadway." (No other details submitted)

Jessica Allen, Jim McDonnell in "Off-Broadway"
Above: Judith Delgado in "Marat/Sade"

Katina Commings, Olympia Dukakis, Apollo Dukakis in "The Cherry Orchard" Above: Sandy Laufer, David Brummel in "Cole"

169

Yale Repertory Theatre

New Haven, Connecticut   October 6, 1981–May 22, 1982   Sixteenth Season

Artistic Director, Lloyd Richards; Managing Director, Edward A. Martenson; Literary Managers, Michael Cadden, Barbara Davenport, Joel Schecter; Production Coordinator, Bronislaw J. Sammler; Press, J. Ellen Gainor, Rosalind Heinz, Ellen Russell, Robert Wildman, Catherine M. Wilson; Sets, Ming Cho Lee, Michael H. Yeargan, Alison Ford, Douglas O. Stein, Ricardo Morin, Andrew Rubenoff, Jane Clark, Joel Fontaine, Tony Straiges; Costumes, Dunya Ramicova, Sheila McLamb, Gene K. Lakin, Quina Fonseca, Wing Lee, Catherine Zuber, Jane Greenwood; Lighting, Jennifer Tipton, David Noling, Timothy J. Hunter, William B. Warfel, Stephen Strawbridge; Stage Managers, Frank S. Torok, Neal Ann Stephens, Patrice Thomas, Dana Graham, Poco Smith, Judy Martel, Shannon J. Sumpter

UNCLE VANYA by Anton Chekhov; Director, Lloyd Richards; with Glenn Close, Ricky L. Grove, Georgine Hall, William Mesnik, Ruth Nelson, Melissa Smith, William Swetland, Lee Wallace, Harris Yulin

MRS. WARREN'S PROFESSION by George Bernard Shaw; Director, Stephen Porter; with Barbara Baxley, Robert Brown, Thomas A. Carlin, Richard Clarke, Frances McDormand, Richard Woods

RIP VAN WINKLE OR "THE WORKS" *(World Premiere)* by Richard Nelson; Director, David Jones; with Seth Allen, Gerry Bamman, Zakiah Barksdale, Dan Desmond, Charles S. Dutton, Laura Esterman, Michael Grodenchik, John E. Harnagel, Baxter Harris, Richard Jamieson, Jane Kaczmarek, Warren David Keith, Stephen Lang, Kaiulani Lee, John Lloyd, Becky London, Kevin McClarnon, Patricia McGuire, Frank Maraden, Vic Polizos, Alan Rosenberg, Steven Ryan, Mary Van Dyke, Jon Walker

BEEF, NO CHICKEN by Derek Walcott; Director, Walton Jones; with Angela Bassett, Herb Downer, Charles S. Dutton, Keith Grant, D. A. Green, Michael C. Knight, Elly Koslo, William Kux, Gilbert Lewis, Mary Louise, Norman Matlock, Barbara Montgomery, Leon Morenzie, Clark Morgan, Sullivan Walker

FLASH FLOODS by Dare Clubb; Director, Dennis Scott; with Kim Beaty, Ricky Grove, Cecilia Rubino, Vytautas Ruginis, John Seitz

GOING OVER by Stuart Browns; Director, Jim Peskin; with Gary Basaraba, Paddy Croft, James Greene, Jon Krupp, John Lloyd, William Mesnik

THE MAN WHO COULD SEE THROUGH TIME by Terri Wagener; Director, David Hammond; with Jane Kaczmarek, Theodore Sorel

MASTER HAROLD. . . . AND THE BOYS *(World Premiere)* by Athol Fugard; Director, Mr. Fugard; with Zeljko Ivanek, Danny Glover, Zakes Mokae

JOHNNY BULL by Kathleen Betsko; *(World Premiere);* Director, Lloyd Richards; with Rikki Borge, Kevin Geer, Anna Levine, Jamie Schmitt, Suzanne Shepherd

LOVE'S LABOUR'S LOST by William Shakepeare; Director, Mladen Kiselov; with Daniel Benzali, Robert Brown, Kate Burton, Christian Clemenson, Keith Grant, Gordon Gray, David Alan Grier, Jane Kaczmarek, Warren David Keith, Jon Krupp, John Lloyd, Becky London, William Mesnik, Cecelia Rubino, Vytautas Ruginis, Melissa Smith, Scott Rickey Wheeler

Gerry Goodstein/Kirsten Beck Photos
Right: Suzanne Shepherd, Anna Levine in "Johnny Bull" Above: Lee Wallace, Glenn Close in "Uncle Vanya"

David Alan Grier, Jane Kaczmarek in "Love's Labour's Lost"

Barbara Baxley, Frances McDormand in "Mrs. Warren's Profession"

ANNUAL SHAKESPEARE FESTIVALS

Alabama Shakespeare Festival

Anniston, Alabama   July 9–August 23, 1981   Tenth Season

Artistic Director, Martin L. Platt; Executive Producer, Josephine E. Ayers; Managing Director, Michael Maso; Sets, Michael Stauffer, Tom Tutino; Costumes, Lynne C. Emmert, Susan A. Cox; Lighting, Lauren M. Miller; Composer/Musical Director Philip Rosenberg; Musical Director, Michael Fauss; Technical Directors, Jeff McKay, Charles J. Kilian, Jr.; Props, Susan Weiss, Susan Skeen; Wardrobe, Caren Carr; Guest Directors, Jay Broad, Judith Haskell; Choreographer, Louise Crofton; Fencing, James Donadio, Bruce Cromer; Stage Managers, Dan Sedgwick, Gretchen Van Horne, Pamela Guion, Rod Harter, Michael Oliver; Business Manager, Charles D. Hudson; Company Manager, Alexine Saunders; Press, Patricia S. Lavender, Bernice Harrison

COMPANY: Charles Antalosky, Karen Bauder, Lisa Brailoff, Cathy Brewer-Moore, Kermit Brown, Robert Browning, Beaumont Bruestle, Evelyn Carol Case, Bruce C. Collier, James T. Cotten, A. D. Cover, Bruce Cromer, James Donadio, Shannon Eubanks, Deborah Fezelle, Donna Haley, Arthur Hanket, Jacob Harran, Byron Hays, Bill Jenkins, John-Frederick Jones, Judy Langford, Michael K. Lippert, Ed Marona, Hunter May, Sean Mims, Timothy Mooney, Catherine Moore, David Nava, Douglas R. Nielsen, William Preston, Richard Ruskell, Steven Sutherland, Robert C. (R.C.) Torri, Mark Varian, Richard Voigrs, Tom Whyte, Linda C. Yerina
PRODUCTIONS: A Midsummer Night's Dream by William Shakespeare, Henry IV Part I by William Shakespeare, Much Ado About Nothing, by William Shakespeare, The Servant of Two Masters by Carlo Goldoni adapted by Tom Cone, Oh, Coward! devised by Roderick Cook from the works of Noel Coward

Right: Robert Browning, Cathy Brewer-Moore, Robert C. Torri in "Oh, Coward!" *(Carmel Modica Photo)*

John-Frederick Jones in "Henry IV Part I" *(Michael Doege Photos)*

James Donadio, Shannon Eubanks in "Much Ado About Nothing"

171

American Players Theatre

Spring Green, Wisconsin   July 17–October 4, 1981   Second Season
Artistic Director, Randall Duk Kim; Managing Director, Charles J. Bright; General Manager, Daniel F. Kearns; Literary Director, Anne Occhiogrosso; Development, Karen Johnson; Press, Jean Louise Sassor, Kathleen L. Winters; Costumes/Sets, Kathleen Blake, Bud Hill, Sam Kirkpatrick; Lighting, John B. Forbes, Elizabeth Green; Stage Managers, Marcia Orbison, Mik Derks; Combat/Fight Choreographer, David Cecsarini; Production Assistant, Sandra Rowe, Reigel Ernst, Colleen D. Lewis; Wardrobe, Carolyn Plemitscher; Production Manager, Bill DuPuy; Props, David Ellertson, Harlan Ferstl; Technical Director, Robert Wood

COMPANY: John Aden, Paul Bentzen, David Cecsarini, Dean Dobberfuhl, Lee Elmer Ernst, Geoffrey Ewing, Winnie Geweke, Margaret Goergen-Rood, Steven Helmeke, James Hulin, Jeffrey Lowell Jackson, Bertina Johnson, Terry Kerr, Peter Kettler, Randall Duk Kim, Steven Kozelka, Rita Litton, Howard Lucas, Marie Mathay, W. Alan Nebelthau, James Phipps, William Schlaht, Jonathan Smoots, Dana Snodgrass, Theodore Swetz

PRODUCTIONS: The Comedy of Errors by William Shakespeare; Director, Anne Occhiogrosso; King John by William Shakespeare; Directors, Anne Occhiogrosso, Mik Derks: The Two Gentlemen of Verona by William Shakespeare; Directors, Anne Occhiogrosso, Mik Derks; A Midsummer Night's Dream by William Shakespeare; Directed by Anne Occhiogrosso, Mik Derks; Titus Andronicus by William Shakespeare; Directors, Anne Occhiogrosso, Mik Derks; Music Director, Douglas Brown; Composer, Clyde Thompson

Right: "A Midsummer Night's Dream"

Theodore Swetz, Randall Duk Kim in "Two Gentlemen of Verona"

Howard Lucas, Margaret Goergen-Rood in "The Comedy of Errors"

172

American Shakespeare Theatre

Stratford, Connecticut   July 7–September 5, 1981

Artistic Director, Peter Coe; Executive Director, Richard E. Bader; Business Manager, Charles Parker; Marketing/Press, Richard Pheneger; Development, Barbara Sirois; Marketing/Press, Tom Holehan; Press, Anne Montarro; Company Manager, Robert Sheftic; Props, Mario Fedeli; Sound, John Tassinaro; Wardrobe, Millie Patria; Stage Managers, Stephen Nasuta, Dianne Trulock; Assistant to Mr. Coe, Elliott Woodruff; Vocal Coach, Brendan Barry; Fight Director, Randy Kovitz; Production Assistant, Neil Einleger; Set and Costumes, Robert Fletcher; Lighting, Marc B. Weiss; Hairstylist, Patrick D. Moreton; Fight Director, B. H. Barry

HENRY V by William Shakespeare; Director, Peter Coe; with Christopher Plummer (Henry V), Kelsey Grammer (Gloucester), Randy Kovitz (Bedford), Robert Strattel (Exeter), Donald Symington (Westmoreland), Paul Craig (Archbishop), Kelsey Grammer (Cambridge), Pirie MacDonald (Scroop), Randy Kovitz (Grey), Richard Dix (Erpingham), Roy Dotrice (Fluellen), Paul Craig (Gower), Pirie MacDonald (Jamy), Armin Shimerman (MacMorris), Raymond Skipp (Williams/Bardolph), Norman Allen (Bates/Nym), Graeme Campbell (Pistol), Peter James (Boy), Aideen O'Kelly (Hostess/Isabel), Edward Atienza (Charles VI), Stephen Nesbitt (Dauphin), Peter Alzado (Montjoy), Douglas Stender (Orleans), John Peter Linton (Delabreth), Armin Shimerman (LeFer), Isabelle Rosier (Katherine), Ruby Holbrook (Alice), Attendants: Albert Malafronte, Kim Bemis, Ellen Newman, Robert Ousley, David Pendleton, Bern Sundstedt, Jeff Dolan, Stephen Rust
OTHELLO by William Shakespeare; Director, Peter Coe; with James Earl Jones (Othello), Christopher Plummer (Iago), Shannon John (Desdemona), Kelsey Grammer (Cassio), Aideen O'Kelly (Emilia), Geoanne Sosa (Bianca), Graeme Campbell (Roderigo), Robert Burr (Duke of Venice/Governor of Cyprus), David Sabin (Brabantio), Richard Dix (Gratiano), Raymond Skipp (Lodovico), Kim Bemis (Herald), Robert Ousley, Harry Murphy, Stephen Nesbitt (Senators/Gentlemen of Cyprus), Ellen Newman, Bern Sundstedt (Servants), David Garfield, Jeff Schwartz (Soldiers)

Right: Christopher Plummer, James Earl Jones in "Othello"

Roy Dotrice, Christopher Plummer in "Henry V"

Christopher Plummer as Henry V

173

Camden Shakespeare Company

July 3–September 6, 1981   Fourth Season

Artistic Director, Kirk Wolfinger; Managing Director, Mary Rindfleisch; Technical Director, Vincent Boucher; Costumes, Ellen McCartney; Press, Alexa Fogel, Katrinka Wilder; Props, Thomas Harty; Composer/Musical Director, Ruth McClure, Throop Wilder; Production Assistants, Ellen Clark, Meghan Cox, Deborah Martin

COMPANY: Julian Bailey, Richard Boddy, Dwight Burtis, Linda Cushing, Susanne Egli, Kevin Gardner, Ron Canada, Casey Kizziah, Robert Martini, Kenneth Metivier, Gregg Ostrin, Victoria Pearson, Michael Perea, Joyce Sozen, Jean Tafler, Karen Wells, Stephen White

PRODUCTIONS: HAMLET by William Shakespeare, directed by William Kelly; THE IMPORTANCE OF BEING EARNEST by Oscar Wilde, directed by Casey Kizziah; OTHELLO by William Shakespeare, directed by John Hertzler

Casey Kizziah as Hamlet

Victoria Pearson, Julian Bailey in "The Importance of Being Earnest"

Champlain Shakespeare Festival

Burlington, Vermont   July 8–August 22, 1981   Twenty-third Season

Producer-Director, Judith W. B. Williams; Business Manager/Associate Producer, Heidi Racht; Scenery, Bob Barnett; Lighting, Richard L. Dean; Costumes, Rachel Ronsley, Muriel Stockdale; Stage Designer, W. M. Schenk; Fight Choreographer, Eli Simon; Choreographer, Pam Wessels; Press, Rosemarie F. Eldridge; Music Directors, David Hall, Barbara Fretheim; Stage Manager, Robert Lovell

COMPANY: Bob Barnett, Jon Beaupre, David Cohen, Steven Culp, Richard L. Dean, Rosemarie F. Eldridge, Gretchen Feeser, Barbara Fretheim, London Green, David Hall, Lisa A. Hennessy, Veronique Hovde, Donna Kalil, Amy London, Robert Lovell, Ted McAdams, Eric Menyuk, Donna Miller, Kelly C. Morgan, Michael Nee, Sam Pierson, Heidi Racht, Rachel Ronsley, David Schraffenberger, Ian D. Shupeck, W. M. Schenk, Eli Simon, Cynthia Smith, Muriel Stockdale, Rebecca Sullivan, Pamela Wessels, Beth Wiemann
PRODUCTIONS: ROMEO AND JULIET by William Shakespeare, directed by Judith W. B. Williams; THE MERRY WIVES OF WINDSOR by William Shakespeare, directed by Jon Beaupre; ROSENCRANTZ AND GUILDENSTERN ARE DEAD by Tom Stoppard, directed by Michael Nee; SPOON RIVER ANTHOLOGY

Ted McAdams in "Rosencrantz and Guildenstern Are Dead"

Chris Merrill in "The Merry Wives of Windsor"

Colorado Shakespeare Festival

Boulder, Colorado   July 17–August 21, 1981   Twenty-fourth Season

Producing Director, Daniel S. P. Yang; Production Manager, C. V. Bennett; Special Consultant, Martin Jenkins; Lighting, Richard Devin; Sound, Shirley Grubb; Voice Coach, Bonnie Raphael; Technical Director, Stancil Campbell; Makeup, Jean Bolte; Special Projects, Fiona Mary Galbraith; Hairstylist, David Cushing; Assistant Directors, Debra S. Farmer, Mac Groves, Carolyn Burns Harper, Janet L. Kalas, Kimberley Stone; Combat Master, Charles Wilcox; Press, Nan Pirnack, Roger Mark Bullock, Tom Weston; Costumes, Jeannie Davidson; Sets, Norvid Jenkins Roos

COMPANY: Dan Bedard, David S. Brauer, Peter Crook, James Drevescraft, Lou Estes, Christopher Burritt Freeman, Megan Gallagher, Gary Glasgow, Clare-Marie Guthrie, David O. Harum, Jason Kenny, Randy Stephen Kleffner, Barry Kramer, Richard Olas Malmberg, Michael Mancusq, David Manis, Lynn Mathis, Randall McBride, Kirk McCrea, Tom Mitchell, Duncan T. Osborne, Margaret Reed, Tom Rowan, Andrea S. Rutledge, Samuel Sandoe, David H. Shortridge, Tom Sadler, Laurel White, Charles Wilcox, Will York, and Paul Barchilon, Jeanne Bonnet, Julius Dahne, John Moore, Michael Urbanski, Ian Wilcox, Jason Y. Nottingham
PRODUCTIONS: THE TAMING OF THE SHREW directed by Tom Markus, JULIUS CAESAR directed by Martin Cobin, ALL'S ALL'S WELL THAT ENDS WELL directed by Michael Kahn

Below: Samuel Sandoe, Tom Mitchell, Will York, Laurel White in "Julius Caesar" (Left) "The Taming of the Shrew"

David O. Harum, Margaret Reed in "Taming of the Shrew"

Megan Gallagher, Peter Crook in "All's Well That Ends Well"

Dallas Shakespeare Festival

Dallas, Texas   July 10–November 7, 1981   Tenth Season

Founder/Producer, Robert Glenn; Artistic Director, Kenneth Frankel; Managing Director, John Houchin; Business Manager, Phillip Glenn; Tour Manager, Douglas Parker; Press, Robin Carbone, JoAnn Holt; Production Manager, Richard Sodders; Technical Director, Thomas V. Korder; Sets, James Wolk; Costumes, Susan Rheaume, Patricia Paine; Lighting, John Gisondi; Sound, Jerry Worden; Props, R. E. Waldorf, Jr.; Music, Tom Fay, David Barton; Choreography, Anne Marie Kuehling; Fight Direction, B. H. Barry; Stage Managers, Anne Marie Kuehling, Francis X. Kuhn

ROMEO AND JULIET by William Shakespeare; Director, Kenneth Frankel; with William Barry, Dennis Boutsikaris, Jon DeVries, Kathryn Dowling, Gini Ellett, Julian Gamble, Kenton Holden, Mark Hougland, L. R. Hults, Kim Matthew Ker, Conrad McMillan, Norma Moore, Randy Moore, Paul Mullins, Douglas Parker, Carter Reardon, William Converse-Roberts, Jack Robinson, Gary Sloan, Annie Stafford, Robert Whiteley, Michael Bennett, Glenda Greenwood, David W. Hoover, Jeri Leer, Ginger Lewis, Jill Moore, Eileen Nixon, Chip Washabaugh

AS YOU LIKE IT by William Shakespeare; Directors, Harris Yulan, Max Margulis; with William Barry, Michael Bennett, Dennis Boutsikaris, Jon DeVries, Kathryn Dowling, Julian Gamble, Kenton Holden, L. R. Hults, Lyle Kanouse, Kim Matthew Ker, Norma Moore, Randy Moore, Douglas Parker, Carter Reardon, William Converse-Roberts, Jack Robinson, Gary Sloan, Annie Stafford, Jim Townsend, Sigourney Weaver, Gini Ellet, Mark Hougland, Jeri Leer, Ginger Lewis, Conrad McMillan, Jill Moore, Paul Mullins, Chip Washabaugh, Robert Whiteley

KEMP'S JIG compiled by Chris Harris and John David; Director, Mr. David; Performed by Mr. Harris

THE HOLLOW CROWN devised by John Barton; Director, Robert Glenn; with Michael Dendy, Martha Gaylord, Robert Glenn, Stephen Kean, William Keck

Right: Kathryn Dowling, Dennis Boutsikaris in "Romeo and Juliet"

Norma Moore, Sigourney Weaver, Randy Moore in "As You Like It"

Great Lakes Shakespeare Festival

Lakewood, Ohio   July 1–September 26, 1981   Twentieth Season

Artistic Director, Vincent Dowling; General Manager, Mary Bill; Marketing/Press, Shirley Clark; Business Manager, Richard Parker; Development, Rita C. Boker; Guest Directors, Dorothy Silver, Edward Stern; Voice Coach, Robert Neff Williams; Sets, John Ezell; Costumes, Mary-Anne Aston, Estelle Painter, Lewis Rampino, Kurt Wilhelm; Lighting, Kirk Bookman; Technical Director, John Sadler; Wardrobe, Mileta Foster; Props, Mary K. Stone; Dramaturg, Peter Manos; Stage Managers, Olwen O'Herlihy, Jane Page, Robert Mingus; Press, Anne Bill

COMPANY: Kenneth Albers, Tom Blair, Madylon Branstetter, John Q. Bruce, Bairbre Dowling, Robert Elliott, Larry Gates, John Greenleaf, Michael Haney, Bernard Kates, Bruce Matley, Michael-John McGann, Sarah Nall, Beatrice O'Donnell, Holmes Osborne, Clive Rosengren, Maggie Thatcher, Michael Thompson, Dan Westbrook

PRODUCTIONS: The Matchmaker, King Lear, A Doll's House, Much Ado About Nothing, Streetsongs (One-woman show by Geraldine Fitzgerald), My Lady Luck (One-man show by Vincent Dowling)

Below: Maggie Thatcher in "A Doll's House" Left: Vincent Dowling in "My Lady Luck"

MichaelJohn McGann, Larry Gates in "King Lear"

Beatrice O'Donnell, Bernard Kates, Bairbre Dowling in "The Matchmaker"

178

National Shakespeare Festival

San Diego, California   June 9–October 4, 1981   Thirty-second Season

Executive Producer, Craig Noel; Artistic Director, Jack O'Brien; Managing Director, Thomas R. Hall; Directors, Jack O'Brien, Craig Noel, Edward Berkeley, Gerald Freedman; Dramaturge, Diana Maddox; Sets, Sam Kirkpatrick, Mark Donnelly, Steven Rubin, Richard Seger; Costumes, Robert Morgan, Sam Kirkpatrick, Deborah Dryden, Steven Rubin; Lighting, Gilbert V. Hemsley, Jr., Kent Dorsey, Donald Darnutzer; Sound, Roger Gans, David Hoyt; Composer, Conrad Susa; Stage Managers, Peter Hackett, Douglas Pagliotti, John Light; Press, Bill Eaton

COMPANY: Lisa Banes, G. W. Bailey, Edward Feimforth, Kim Bennett, Arnie Burton, Barbara Bosch, Richard E. Cary, Susan Chapman, Kevin Conroy, Tandy Cronyn, David Dukes, Tovah Feldshuh, Leslie Geraci, John Glover, Tom Henschel, Dan La-Rocque, David McCullough, Joe McNeely, Michael Lueders, Jonathan McMurtry, Katherine McGrath, Phil Meyer, Jonathan Miller, Lisa Mounteer, Wendi Radford, Ron Randell, Reno Roop, Richard Rossi, Alan Schack, Madolyn Smith, David Ogden Stiers, Kristoffer Tabori, Bill Walters, Norman Welsh, G. Wood

PRODUCTIONS: King Lear directed by Jack O'Brien, Much Ado About Nothing directed by Edward Berkeley, Measure for Measure directed by Gerald Freedman, The Country Wife directed by Jack O'Brien, Dear Liar directed by Craig Noel

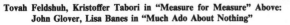

Tovah Feldshuh, Kristoffer Tabori in "Measure for Measure" Above: John Glover, Lisa Banes in "Much Ado About Nothing"

G Wood, Tovah Feldshuh in "The Country Wife" Above: Norman Welsh, Tandy Cronyn in "Dear Liar"

New Jersey Shakespeare Festival

Madison, New Jersey   June 23–December 13, 1981   Seventeenth Season
Artistic Director, Paul Barry; Producing Director, Ellen Barry; Musical Director, Deborah Martin; Press, Debra Waxman; Business Manager, Donna M. Gearhardt; Development, Deidre Jacobson; Administrative Assistant, Lynne Holley; Sets, Peter Harrison; Costumes, Erica Hollmann, Alice S. Hughes; Lighting, Richard Dorfman; Stage Manager, Jon P. Ogden

COMPANY: Bob Ari, Curtis Armstrong, Ellen Barry, Paul Barry, Patrick Beatey, Denise Bessette, Victoria Boothby, Peter Burnell, Faith Catlin, Casey Childs, Richard Davidson, Clarence Felder, Kenneth Gray, Mary Hara, David S. Howard, Susanne Marley, Ronald Martell, Stephen McNaughton, Laura Mirsky, Geddeth Smith, Eric Tavaris, Scott Walters, Chris Weatherhead

Carol Appleyard, Christine Medea Arnold, Scott Barton, Faith E. Baum, Sharon Laurel Bernson, Claudia Black, Kim Boehm, John Boyle, Mahala Buckingham, Ellen Bush, Brenda Lynn Bynum, Pamela D. Chabora, Jim Clifton, Amy Beth Cohn, Michael Faber Connolly, Lisa Edelstein, Margaret Emory, Susan Michel Garrett, Dave Gearino, Judy Ann Gregory, Aimee Halperin, Dina Hampton, Carol Ann Hanlon, Christie R. House, Richard Hugendubler, Donnamarie Hyderkhan, Barbara C. Inglehart, Warren Kelder, Emily King, Robert A. Klein, Jeff Kramer, George Kupczak, Steve Loring, Marion Mackliss, Corrine Mandell, Christiane McCloskey, Kathleen McGovern, Russell Merbeth, Stephen Minor, Mark Monaco, William Morino, Rodman Neumann, Bill Nickerson, Patricia Noone, Jorge Ortoll, David Pacht, Daria Maria Pampaloni, Pat Kallo Phillips, John Pietrowski, Amy Potozkin, Robert E. Quinn, Richard Randall, Maryann Rozsas Ronksley, Alison Rosenzweig, Ken Scherer, Marion Solomon, Marla Speer, Elizabeth Speir, Alan Sporing, Robert Starkand, Alex Stuhl, Robert Suttile, Nancy Travis, Alan Turnball, Elizabeth J. Vessels, Anne Vitti, Maria Wallace, Scott Winters, Mark Woodbridge

PRODUCTIONS: ROMEO AND JULIET by William Shakespeare; CYMBELINE by William Shakespeare, TARTUFFE by Moliere; DA by Hugh Leonard—all directed by Paul Barry; THE ENTERTAINER by John Osborne, directed by Ronald Martell; VANITIES by Jack Heifner, directed by Alex Dmitriev

Paul Barry in "The Entertainer" Above: Kenneth Gray, David S. Howard in "Da"

Peter Burnell, Chris Weatherhead in "Cymbeline" Above: Scott Walters, Denise Bessette in "Romeo and Juliet"

New York Shakespeare Festival

Delacorte Theatre   Joseph Papp, Producer   Twenty-sixth Season   Friday, June 26–July 26, 1981 (26 performances)

THE TEMPEST by William Shakespeare; Director, Lee Breuer with Ruth Maleczech; Scenic Consultant, David Mitchell; Costumes, Carol Oditz; Lighting, Spencer Mosse; Hairstylist/Makeup, J. Roy Helland; Choreography, Marion D'Cruz; Contact Improvisation, Steven Paxton; Gamelon Music, Barbara Benary; Samba Music, Nana Vasconcelos; Magic, Jack Adams; Production Supervisor, Jason Steven Cohen; General Manager, Robert Kamlot; Company Manager, Mitzi Harder; Press, Merle Debuskey, Richard Kornberg, Ed Bullins; Stage Managers, Michael Chambers, Susan Green; Production Assistant, Chris Sinclair; Technical Director, David Lawson; Props, Pat Robertson; Wardrobe, Dawn Johnson
CAST: Raul Julia (Prospero), Jessica Nelson (Miranda), Clove Galilee (Young Miranda), Ariel: Craig Chang, Aramis Estevez, Michael Pearlman, Lute Ramblin', Ken Seymour, Iwatora, Eric Elice, Leo Holder, Esai Morales, Terry O'Reilly, and David Sotolongo, Barry Miller (Caliban), David Marshall Grant (Ferdinand), Joseph Costa (Alonso), Steven Keats (Antonio), Carl Lumbly (Francisco), Frederick Neumann (Gonzalo), Bill Raymond (Sebastian), Stephen Rowe (Adrian), Lola Pashalinski (Trinculo), Louis Zorich (Stephano), Maya Pallu Hedstrom-O'Reily (Iris), Panda Weiss (Ceres), Clove Galilee (Juno)
Performed in two acts.

Friday, July 31–September 6, 1981 (39 performances)
HENRY IV PART ONE by William Shakespeare; Director, Des McAnuff; Scenery, Stuart Wurtzel; Costumes, Patricia McGourty; Lighting, Richard Nelson; Music, Richard Peaslee; Hairstylist/Makeup, J. Roy Helland; Fight Sequences, B. H. Barry; Production Supervisor, Jason Steven Cohen; General Manager, Robert Kamlot; Production Assistant, Stacy Tarter; Stage Managers, Sherman Warner, Wendy Chapin
CAST: Philip Craig (Prologue/Carrier/Peto), Stephen Markle (Henry IV), Raphael Sbarge (John of Lancaster), Rex Robbins (Earl of Westmoreland), John Goodman (Sir Walter Blunt), John Vickery (Henry Prince of Wales), Kenneth McMillan (Falstaff), John Bottom (Bardolph), Philip Casnoff (Poins), Ralph Drischell (Thomas Percy), Clement Fowler (Northumberland), Mandy Patinkin (Henry Percy), Matthew Gottlieb (Carrier/Gadshill), Larry Block (Gadshill), Margaret Whitton (Lady Percy), Val Kilmer (Servant to Hotspur), Richard Ziman (Francis), Robert Westenberg (Vintner/Sir Richard Vernon), Beulah Garrick (Mistress Quickly), Peter Rogan (Sheriff), Todd Waring (Edmund Mortimer), Max Wright (Owen Glendower), Susan Berman (Lady Mortimer), Ralph Byers (Earl of Douglas), George Lloyd (Archbishop of York), Benjamin Donenberg (Sir Michael), Kevin Spacey (Messenger), and Christopher Colt, Brian Delate, Henry Ferree, Paula Fritz, Gerald Gilmore, Brian Hargrove, Mary Johnson, Linda Kozlowski, Conal O'Brien, Rick Parks, David Price, Rich Rand, Jack Stehlin
Performed with one intermission. The action takes place in England and Wales.

Raul Julia (R) and Top Right with Clove Galilee, Jessica Nelson in "The Tempest"

Kenneth McMillan, John Vickery, also above with Rex Robbins in "Henry IV Part I"

Oregon Shakespeare Festival

Ashland, Oregon   February 24–October 31, 1981   Forty-sixth Season

Artistic Director, Jerry Turner; Executive Director, William W. Patton; President of the Board, Stephen W. Ryder; Composer/Music Director, Todd Barton; Costumes, Jeannie Davidson, Deborah M. Dryden; Lighting, Robert Peterson, Richard Riddell; Sets, William Bloodgood, Richard L. Hay, Jesse Hollis; Production Manager, Pat Patton; Technical Directors, Tom Knapp, Eric Shortt; Wardrobes, Lynn M. Ramey; Props, Paul-James Martin; Sound, Kimberley Jean Barry, Gary J. Carr; Stage Managers, Peter W. Allen, Kirk Boyd, David W. Brock, Mary Steinmetz, K. Wynne West; General Manager, Paul E. Nicholson; Press, Margaret Rubin, Hilary Tate

COMPANY: Linda Alper, Denis Arndt, James Avery, Wayne Ballantyne, Traber Burns, James Carpenter, Phyllis Courtney, Philip Davidson, Stuart Duckworth, Paul Duke, James Edmondson, Richard Elmore, Larry Friedlander, Bill Geisslinger, Bruce Gooch, Annette Helde, J. Wesley Huston, Barry Kraft, Anne Krill, Shirley Patton, Jeanne Paulsen, Lawrence Paulsen, Richard Poe, Samuel Pond, Richard Riehle, Patricia Slover, Joan Stuart-Morris, Kirk Thornton, Joseph Vincent, Cal Winn, Jeffrey Woolf, Kathy Brady,
PRODUCTIONS: Twelfth Night by William Shakespeare, directed by Pat Patton; Two Gentlemen of Verona by William Shakespeare, directed by David Ostwald; Henry IV Part I by William Shakespeare, directed by James Edmondson; Death of a Salesman by Arthur Miller, directed by Robert Loper; 'Tis Pity She's a Whore by John Ford, directed by Jerry Turner; Wild Oats by John O'Keeffe, directed by Jerry Turner; Othello by William Shakespeare, directed by Sanford Robbins; Artichoke by Joanna M. Glass, directed by Joy Carlin; The Birthday Party by Harold Pinter, directed by Andrew J. Traister; The Island by Athol Fugard, John Kani and Winston Nrshona, directed by Luther James

Right: Sam Pond, Joan Stuart-Morris in "Twelfth Night"

Annette Helde, Joyce Harris in "Othello"

Joan Stuart-Morris, Stuart Duckworth in " 'Tis Pity She's a Whore"

Shakespeare & Company

Lenox, Massachusetts   July 8–September 6, 1981   Fourth Season

Artistic Director, Tina Packer; Associate Director, Dennis Krausnick; Movement, John Broome, Susan Dibble; Fights/Tumbling, B. H. Barry; Business Manager, Ann Olson; Assistant to Miss Packer, Bernadette Colbert; Development, Tim Salvner, Jayne Gall; Sets/Technical Director, Bill Ballou; Costumes, Kiki Smith; Props, Louise Reinke; Wardrobe, Susan Becker; Stage Managers, J. P. Elins, Dawn Darfus; Press, Judy Salsbury, Sue Osthoff; Music, Bruce Odland; Choreography, John Broome

COMPANY: Zoe Alexander, Bill Ballou, B. H. Barry, John Broome, Kaia Calhoun, David Coffin, Gregory Uel Cole, Kevin Coleman, Merry Conway, Dawn Darfus, J. P. Elins, John Hadden, Gregory Johnson, Dennis Krausnick, Michael Lamothe, Kristin Linklater, Judianna Lunseth, Paul Massie, Virginia Ness, James Newcomb, Bruce Odland, Tim Saukiavicus, Rocco Sisto, Kiki Smith, Robert Bristol, Kimberly Burroughs, Elizabeth Dennehy, Angelica R. Dewey, Laura Ernst, Alexandra Rambusch, Roderick Spencer, Courtenay Bernard Vance, George Williams, Susan Becker, Diane Lambert, Louise Reinke

PRODUCTIONS: Twelfth Night by William Shakespeare, directed by Tina Packer; As You Like It by William Shakespeare, directed by Tina Packer

Right: Tim Saukiavicus, Gregory Uel Cole in "As You Like It"

Rocco Sisto, Kevin Coleman, Paul Massie in "Twelfth Night"

Stratford Festival of Canada

Stratford, Ontario   June 15–October 31, 1981   Twenty-ninth Season

Artistic Director, John Hirsch; Producer, Muriel Sherrin; General Manager, Gary Thomas; Music Director, Berthold Carriere; Literary Manager, Michal Schonberg; Production Managers, Peter Roberts, Dwight Griffin; Technical Directors, Kent McKay, Gie Roberts; Press, Anne Selby, Elaine Lomenzo; Marketing, John Uren; Company Manager, Ron Francis; Music Administrator, Arthur Lang; Stage Managers, Nora Polley, Vincent Berns, Michael Benoit, Laurie Freeman, Thomas Montvila, Margaret Palmer, Renee Schouten, Michael Shamata; Directors, Brian Bedford, Peter Dews, Jean Gascon, Derek Goldby, Leon Major; Designers, Susan Benson, Molly Harris Campbell, John Ferguson, Desmond Heeley, Astrid Janson, Murray Laufer, John Pennoyer, Phillip Silver, David Walker; Lighting, Harry Frehner, David F. Segal, Michael J. Whitfield; Composers, Berthold Carriere, Gabriel Charpentier, Alan Laing, Norman Symonds

COMPANY: Jan Austin, Shaun Austin-Olsen, Kenneth Baker, Scott Baker, Barrie Baldaro, Diana Barrington, Rodger Barton, Stephen Beamish, Rod Beattie, Brian Bedford, Anthony Bekenn, Mervyn Blake, Peter Boretski, Arthur Brand, Michael Burgess, George Buza, Len Cariou, Barbara Chilcott, Patrick Christopher, David Clark, Janet Coates, Wendy Creed, Stephen Cross, Richard Curnock, Keene Curtis, Ian Deakin, Daniel Delabbio, Elise Dewsberry, Keith Dinicol, Margot Dionne, Eric Donkin, Terence Durrant, Desmond Ellis, Colm Feore, Sharry Flett, Colin Fox, Pat Galloway, Paul Gatchell, Dennis Goodwin, Lewis Gordon, Lynne Griffin, Jeffrey Guyton, Mary Haney, Ron Hastings, Max Helpmann, Jeremy Henson, Peter Hutt, William Hutt, Scott Hylands, Deborah Jarvis, John Jarvis, Debora Joy, Eric Keenleyside, Patricia Kern, Avo Kittask, David Langton, Leo Leyden, Arthur Lightbourn, Anne Linden, Richard March, Ted Marshall, Paul Massel, Loreena McKennitt, James McLean, Peter Messaline, Dale Mieske, Richard Monette, Elizabeth Murphy, Barney O'Sullivan, Kenneth Pearl, Nicholas Pennell, Kenneth Pogue, Miles Potter, Paul Punyi, Pamela Redfern, Fiona Reid, Mary Rutherford, Ronn Sarosiak, Alexis Smith, Scott Smith, Gerald Smuin, Reid Spencer, Heather Suttie, Katherine Terrell, Marcia Tratt, Walter Villa, Peggy Watson, Dale Wendel, Lynn West, Tim Whelan, Jim White, Sandy Winsby, Karen Wood, Susan Wright

PRODUCTIONS: William Shakespeare's The Taming of the Shrew, The Comedy of Errors, and Coriolanus; Moliere's The Misanthrope translated by Richard Wilbur; H.M.S. Pinafore by Gilbert and Sullivan; The Rivals by Richard Brinsley Sheridan; The Visit by Friedrich Durrenmatt, adapted by Maurice Valency; Wild Oats by John O'Keeffe

Right: Alexis Smith, William Hutt in "The Visit"

Len Cariou, Sharry Flett in "Taming of the Shrew"

Len Cariou, Lynne Griffin in "Coriolanus"

International Theatre Festival

Baltimore, Maryland   Al Kraizer, Artistic Director; Seymour Krawitz, Press   First Year   June 6–27, 1981

HABIMAH NATIONAL THEATRE OF ISRAEL presents A SIMPLE TALE by S. Y. Agnon; Adapted by S. Nitzan, J. Goren; Director, Yossi Ysraely; Music, Y. Mar-Chayim. **CAST:** Lia Keonig, Eliezer, Yung, Moshe Becker, Ethel Kovinska, Nachum Buchman, Sandra Sade, Yael Perl, Shlomo Bar-Shauit, Israel Rubin-tiek, Eli Gorstein, Talia Lubran, Amiran Attis, Alex Peleg, Tuvia Tavi, Samuel Hudes, Miko Lazarowitz

TEATRE DE LA CLACA of Barcelona, Spain, presents ANTOLOGIA with Joan Baixas, Teresa Calafell, Pep Santacana, Marta Cera, Oscar Olavaria

ELS JOGLARS of Barcelona, Spain, present LAETIUS directed by Albert Boadella; Assistant, D. Caminal; Technicians, Jordi Cano, Jordi Costa, Montse Prat. **CAST:** Ana Barderi, Jose Fernandez, Carmen Periano, Domingo Reixach, Antoni Valero

THE MOVING PICTURE MIME SHOW of London, England, presents THE SEVEN SAMURAI AND OTHER STORIES with Toby Sedgwick, Paul Filipiak, David Gaines

ACTORS THEATRE of Louisville, Kentucky (Jon Jory, Producing Director) presents EXTREMITIES by William Mastrosimone; Director, John Bettenbender. **CAST:** Ellen Barber, Danton Stone, . eggity Price, Kathy Bates

MAMAKO AND COMPANY of Tokyo, Japan, presents PIERRETTE; Director, Mamako Yoneyama; Lighting, Noboru Iizuka; Sound, Coreyafu Fufao; with Mamako Yoneyama, Seigo Hiraga, Ikuo Fujii, Katsue Suzuki, Keiko Ito, Yashiko Hattori

THE ABBEY THEATRE of Dublin, Ireland, presents SHADOW OF A GUNMAN by Sean O'Casey; with Desmond Cave, Donal McCann, Eileen Colgan, Jim Sheridan

NATIONAL THEATRE OF GREAT BRITAIN, London, England, presents THE BROWNING VERSION by Terrence Rattigan on a double bill with HARLEQUINADE by Mr. Rattigan; both directed by Michael Rudman (No other details submitted)

Right: Peggity Price, Ellen Barber, Kathy Bates in "Extremities"
Below: Mamako and company in "Pierrette" Top: Desmond Cave, Donald McCann, Maire O'Neill in "Shadow of a Gunman"

Alec McCowen, Geraldine McEwan in "Harlequinade"   El Joglars in "Laetius"

PULITZER PRIZE PRODUCTIONS

1918–Why Marry?, **1919**–No award, **1920**–Beyond the Horizon, **1921**–Miss Lulu Bett, **1922**–Anna Christie, **1923**–Icebound, **1924**–Hell-Bent fer Heaven, **1925**–They Knew What They Wanted, **1926**–Craig's Wife, **1927**–In Abraham's Bosom, **1928**–Strange Interlude, **1929**–Street Scene, **1930**–The Green Pastures, **1931**–Alison's House, **1932**–Of Thee I Sing, **1933**–Both Your Houses, **1934**–Men in White, **1935**–The Old Maid, **1936**–Idiot's Delight, **1937**–You Can't Take It with You, **1938**–Our Town, **1939**–Abe Lincoln in Illinois, **1940**–The Time of Your Life, **1941**–There Shall Be No Night, **1942**–No award, **1943**–The Skin of Our Teeth, **1944**–No award, **1945**–Harvey, **1946**–State of the Union, **1947**–No award, **1948**–A Streetcar Named Desire, **1949**–Death of a Salesman, **1950**–South Pacific, **1951**–No award, **1952**–The Shrike, **1953**–Picnic, **1954**–The Teahouse of the August Moon, **1955**–Cat on a Hot Tin Roof, **1956**–The Diary of Anne Frank, **1957**–Long Day's Journey into Night, **1958**–Look Homeward, Angel, **1959**–J. B., **1960**–Fiorello!, **1961**–All the Way Home, **1962**–How to Succeed in Business without Really Trying, **1963**–No award, **1964**–No award, **1965**–The Subject Was Roses, **1966**–No award, **1967**–A Delicate Balance, **1968**–No award, **1969**–The Great White Hope, **1970**–No Place to Be Somebody, **1971**–The Effect of Gamma Rays on Man-in-the-Moon Marigolds, **1972**–No award, **1973**–That Championship Season, **1974**–No award, **1975**–Seascape, **1976**–A Chorus Line, **1977**–The Shadow Box, **1978**–The Gin Game, **1979**–Buried Child, **1980**–Talley's Folly, **1981**–Crimes of the Heart, **1982**–A Soldier's Play

NEW YORK DRAMA CRITICS CIRCLE AWARDS

1936–Winterset, **1937**–High Tor, **1938**–Of Mice and Men, Shadow and Substance, **1939**–The White Steed, **1940**–The Time of Your Life, **1941**–Watch on the Rhine, The Corn is Green, **1942**–Blithe Spirit, **1943**–The Patriots, **1944**–Jacobowsky and the Colonel, **1945**–The Glass Menagerie, **1946**–Carousel, **1947**–All My Sons, No Exit, Brigadoon, **1948**–A Streetcar Named Desire, The Winslow Boy, **1949**–Death of a Salesman, The Madwoman of Chaillot, South Pacific, **1950**–The Member of the Wedding, The Cocktail Party, The Consul, **1951**–Darkness at Noon, The Lady's Not for Burning, Guys and Dolls, **1952**–I Am a Camera, Venus Observed, Pal Joey, **1953**–Picnic, The Love of Four Colonels, Wonderful Town, **1954**–Teahouse of the August Moon, Ondine, The Golden Apple, **1955**–Cat on a Hot Tin Roof, Witness for the Prosecution, The Saint of Bleecker Street, **1956**–The Diary of Anne Frank, Tiger at the Gates, My Fair Lady, **1957**–Long Day's Journey into Night, The Waltz of the Toreadors, The Most Happy Fella, **1958**–Look Homeward Angel, Look Back in Anger, The Music Man, **1959**–A Raisin in the Sun, The Visit, La Plume de Ma Tante, **1960**–Toys in the Attic, Five Finger Exercise, Fiorello!, **1961**–All the Way Home, A Taste of Honey, Carnival, **1962**–Night of the Iguana, A Man for All Seasons, How to Succeed in Business without Really Trying, **1963**–Who's Afraid of Virginia Woolf?, **1964**–Luther, Hello, Dolly!, **1965**–The Subject Was Roses, Fiddler on the Roof, **1966**–The Persecution and Assassination of Marat as Performed by the Inmates of the Asylum of Charenton under the Direction of the Marquis de Sade, Man of La Mancha, **1967**–The Homecoming, Cabaret, **1968**–Rosencrantz and Guildenstern Are Dead, Your Own Thing, **1969**–The Great White Hope, 1776, **1970**–The Effect of Gamma Rays on Man-in-the-Moon Marigolds, Borstal Boy, Company, **1971**–Home, Follies, The House of Blue Leaves, **1972**–That Championship Season, Two Gentlemen of Verona, **1973**–The Hot l Baltimore, The Changing Room, A Little Night Music, **1974**–The Contractor, Short Eyes, Candide, **1975**–Equus, The Taking of Miss Janie, A Chorus Line, **1976**–Travesties, Streamers, Pacific Overtures, **1977**–Otherwise Engaged, American Buffalo, Annie, **1978**–Da, Ain't Misbehavin', **1979**–The Elephant Man, Sweeney Todd, **1980**–Talley's Folly, Evita, Betrayal, **1981**–Crimes of the Heart, A Lesson from Aloes, Special Citations to Lena Horne, "The Pirates of Penzance, **1982**–The Life and Adventures of Nicholas Nickleby, A Soldier's Play, (no musical honored)

AMERICAN THEATRE WING
ANTOINETTE PERRY (TONY) AWARD PRODUCTIONS

1948–Mister Roberts, **1949**–Death of a Salesman, Kiss Me, Kate, **1950**–The Cocktail Party, South Pacific, **1951**–The Rose Tattoo, Guys and Dolls, **1952**–The Fourposter, The King and I, **1953**–The Crucible, Wonderful Town, **1954**–The Teahouse of the August Moon, Kismet, **1955**–The Desperate Hours, The Pajama Game, **1956**–The Diary of Anne Frank, Damn Yankees, **1957**–Long Day's Journey into Night, My Fair Lady, **1958**–Sunrise at Campobello, The Music Man, **1959**–J. B., Redhead, **1960**–The Miracle Worker, Fiorello! tied with The Sound of Music, **1961**–Becket, Bye Bye Birdie, **1962**–A Man for All Seasons, How to Succeed in Business without Really Trying, **1963**–Who's Afraid of Virginia Woolf?, A Funny Thing Happened on the Way to the Forum, **1964**–Luther, Hello, Dolly!, **1965**–The Subject Was Roses, Fiddler on the Roof, **1966**–The Persecution and Assassination of Marat as Performed by the Inmates of the Asylum of Charenton under the Direction of the Marquis de Sade, Man of La Mancha, **1967**–The Homecoming, Cabaret, **1968**–Rosencrantz and Guildenstern Are Dead, Hallelujah Baby!, **1969**–The Great White Hope, 1776, **1970**–Borstal Boy, Applause, **1971**–Sleuth, Company, **1972**–Sticks and Bones, Two Gentlemen of Verona, **1973**–That Championship Season, A Little Night Music, **1974**–The River Niger, Raisin, **1975**–Equus, The Wiz, **1976**–Travesties, A Chorus Line, **1977**–The Shadow Box, Annie, **1978**–Da, Ain't Misbehavin', Dracula, **1979**–The Elephant Man, Sweeney Todd, **1980**–Children of a Lesser God, Evita, Morning's at Seven, **1981**–Amadeus, 42nd Street, The Pirates of Penzance, **1982**–The Life and Adventures of Nicholas Nickleby, Nine, Othello

1982 THEATRE WORLD AWARD WINNERS

KAREN AKERS
of "Nine"

DANNY GLOVER
of "Master Harold . . . and the Boys"

DAVID ALAN GRIER
of "The First"

LAURIE BEECHMAN
of "Joseph and the Amazing Technicolor Dreamcoat"

JENNIFER HOLLIDAY
of "Dreamgirls"

ANTHONY HEALD
of "Misalliance"

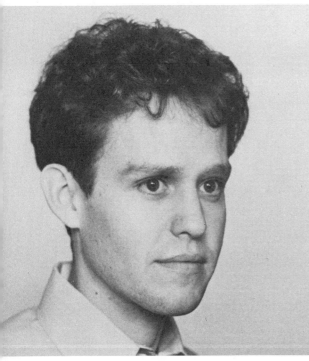

PETER MacNICOL
of "Crimes of the Heart"

LIZBETH MACKAY
of "Crimes of the Heart"

ELIZABETH McGOVERN
of "My Sister In This House"

MICHAEL O'KEEFE
of "Mass Appeal"

JAMES WIDDOES
of "Is There Life After High School?"

ANN MORRISON
of "Merrily We Roll Along"

Theatre World Awards, Thursday, June 3, 1982. Top: Peggy Cass, Robert Morse, Lesley Ann Warren, Ken Page, Tovah Feldshuh, Cliff Robertson; Patricia Elliott, Betty Comden; Orson Bean, Bambi Linn, Lonny Price, Lucie Arnaz, James Woods. Below: Ken Page, Jennifer Holliday, Ann Morrison, Elizabeth McGovern, Laurie Beechman, Robert Morse, James Widdoes, Bambi Linn. Third Row: Karen Akers, Danny Glover, Betty Comden, Cliff Robertson, Lizbeth Mackay, Peter MacNicol, Lesley Ann Warren. Bottom Row: Lucie Arnaz, Anthony Heald, Michael O'Keefe, James Woods, David Alan Grier, Tovah Feldshuh

J. M. Viade, Van Williams Photos

190

Top: Marianne Tatum, Liliane Montevecchi; Cliff Robertson, Barry Grove, Lynne Meadow, Clive Barnes; John McMartin, William Atherton. Below: Dina Merrill, Cliff Robertson, Jacqueline Brookes; Christopher Walken, Marian Seldes; Leonard Harris, Peggy Cass, Lee Roy Reams. Third Row: Patricia Elliott, Anthony Heald; Bo Rucker, Sheila Anderson; Juliette Koka, Armelia McQueen. Bottom: Brian Mitchell, Karen Akers; Joan Bennett, Harry Marinsky (designer of awards); Tovah Feldshuh, Michael Higgins, Milo O'Shea

J. M. Viade, Van Williams Photos

191

David Birney

Bonnie Franklin

Clifton Davis

Anita Gillette

John Raitt

Melba Moore

PREVIOUS THEATRE WORLD AWARD WINNERS

1944–45: Betty Comden, Richard Davis, Richard Hart, Judy Holliday Charles Lang, Bambi Linn, John Lund, Donald Murphy, Nancy Noland, Margaret Phillips, John Raitt

1945–46: Barbara Bel Geddes, Marlon Brando, Bill Callahan, Wendell Corey, Paul Douglas, Mary James, Burt Lancaster, Patricia Marshall, Beatrice Pearson

1946–47: Keith Andes, Marion Bell, Peter Cookson, Ann Crowley, Ellen Hanley, John Jordan, George Keane, Dorothea MacFarland, James Mitchell, Patricia Neal, David Wayne

1947–48 Valerie Bettis, Edward Bryce, Whitfield Connor, Mark Dawson, June Lockhart, Estelle Loring, Peggy Maley, Ralph Meeker, Meg Mundy, Douglass Watson, James Whitmore, Patrice Wymore

1948–49 Tod Andrews, Doe Avedon, Jean Carson, Carol Channing, Richard Derr, Julie Harris, Mary McCarty, Allyn Ann McLerie, Cameron Mitchell, Gene Nelson, Byron Palmer, Bob Scheerer

1949–50: Nancy Andrews, Phil Arthur, Barbara Brady, Lydia Clarke, Priscilla Gillette, Don Hanmer, Marcia Henderson, Charlton Heston, Rick Jason, Grace Kelly, Charles Nolte, Roger Price

1950–51: Barbara Ashley, Isabel Bigley, Martin Brooks, Richard Burton, Pat Crowley, James Daly, Cloris Leachman, Russell Nype, Jack Palance, William Smothers, Maureen Stapleton, Marcia Van Dyke, Eli Wallach

1951–52 Tony Bavaar, Patricia Benoit, Peter Conlow, Virginia de Luce, Ronny Graham, Audrey Hepburn, Diana Herbert, Conrad Janis, Dick Kallman, Charles Proctor, Eric Sinclair, Kim Stanley, Marian Winters, Helen Wood

1952–53: Edie Adams, Rosemary Harris, Eileen Heckart, Peter Kelley, John Kerr, Richard Kiley, Gloria Marlowe, Penelope Munday, Paul Newman, Sheree North, Geraldine Page, John Stewart, Ray Stricklyn, Gwen Verdon

1953–54: Orsen Bean, Harry Belafonte, James Dean, Joan Diener, Ben Gazzara, Carol Haney, Jonathan Lucas, Kay Medford, Scott Merrill, Elizabeth Montgomery, Leo Penn, Eva Marie Saint

1954–55: Julie Andrews, Jacqueline Brookes, Shirl Conway, Barbara Cook, David Daniels, Mary Fickett, Page Johnson, Loretta Leversee, Jack Lord, Dennis Patrick, Anthony Perkins, Christopher Plummer

1955–56: Diane Cilento, Dick Davalos, Anthony Franciosa, Andy Griffith, Laurence Harvey, David Hedison, Earle Hyman, Susan Johnson, John Michael King, Jayne Mansfield, Sara Marshall, Gaby Rodgers, Susan Strasberg, Fritz Weaver

1956–57: Peggy Cass, Sydney Chaplin, Sylvia Daneel, Bradford Dillman, Peter Donat, George Grizzard, Carol Lynley, Peter Palmer, Jason Robards, Cliff Robertson, Pippa Scott, Inga Swenson

1957–58: Anne Bancroft, Warren Berlinger, Colleen Dewhurst, Richard Easton, Tim Everett, Eddie Hodges, Joan Hovis, Carol Lawrence, Jacqueline McKeever, Wynne Miller, Robert Morse, George C. Scott

1958–59: Lou Antonio, Ina Balin, Richard Cross, Tammy Grimes, Larry Hagman, Dolores Hart, Roger Mollien, France Nuyen, Susan Oliver, Ben Piazza, Paul Roebling, William Shatner, Pat Suzuki, Rip Torn

1959–60: Warren Beatty, Eileen Brennan, Carol Burnett, Patty Duke, Jane Fonda, Anita Gillette, Elisa Loti, Donald Madden, George Maharis, John McMartin Lauri Peters, Dick Van Dyke

1960–61: Joyce Bulifant, Dennis Cooney, Sandy Dennis, Nancy Dussault, Robert Goulet, Joan Hackett, June Harding, Ron Husmann, James MacArthur, Bruce Yarnell

1961–62: Elizabeth Ashley, Keith Baxter, Peter Fonda, Don Galloway, Sean Garrison, Barbara Harris, James Earl Jones, Janet Margolin, Karen Morrow, Robert Redford, John Stride, Brenda Vaccaro

1962–63: Alan Arkin, Stuart Damon, Melinda Dillon, Robert Drivas, Bob Gentry, Dorothy Loudon, Brandon Maggart, Julienne Marie, Liza Minnelli, Estelle Parsons, Diana Sands, Swen Swenson

1963–64: Alan Alda, Gloria Bleezarde, Imelda De Martin, Claude Giraud, Ketty Lester, Barbara Loden, Lawrence Pressman, Gilbert Price, Philip Proctor, John Tracy, Jennifer West

1964–65: Carolyn Coates, Joyce Jillson, Linda Lavin, Luba Lisa, Michael O'Sullivan, Joanna Pettet, Beah Richards, Jaime Sanchez, Victor Spinetti, Nicolas Surovy, Robert Walker, Clarence Williams III

1965–66: Zoe Caldwell, David Carradine, John Cullum, John Davidson, Faye Dunaway, Gloria Foster, Robert Hooks, Jerry Lanning, Richard Mulligan, April Shawhan, Sandra Smith, Lesley Ann Warren

1966–67: Bonnie Bedelia, Richard Benjamin, Dustin Hoffman, Terry Kiser, Reva Rose, Robert Salvio, Sheila Smith, Connie Stevens, Pamela Tiffin, Leslie Uggams, Jon Voight, Christopher Walken

1967–68: David Birney, Pamela Burrell, Jordan Christopher, Jack Crowder (Thalmus Rasulala), Sandy Duncan, Julie Gregg, Stephen Joyce, Bernadette Peters, Alice Playten, Michael Rupert, Brenda Smiley, Russ Thacker

1968–69: Jane Alexander, David Cryer, Blythe Danner, Ed Evanko, Ken Howard, Lauren Jones, Ron Leibman, Marian Mercer, Jill O'Hara, Ron O'Neal, Al Pacino, Marlene Warfield

1969–70: Susan Browning, Donny Burks, Catherine Burns, Len Cariou, Bonnie Franklin, David Holliday, Katharine Houghton, Melba Moore, David Rounds, Lewis J. Stadlen, Kristoffer Tabori, Fredricka Weber

1970–71: Clifton Davis, Michael Douglas, Julie Garfield, Martha Henry, James Naughton, Tricia O'Neil, Kipp Osborne, Roger Rathburn, Ayn Ruymen, Jennifer Salt, Joan Van Ark, Walter Willison

1971–72: Jonelle Allen, Maureen Anderman, William Atherton, Richard Backus, Adrienne Barbeau, Cara Duff-MacCormick, Robert Foxworth, Elaine Joyce, Jess Richards, Ben Vereen, Beatrice Winde, James Woods

1972–73: D'Jamin Bartlett, Patricia Elliott, James Farentino, Brian Farrell, Victor Garber, Kelly Garrett, Mari Gorman, Laurence Guittard, Trish Hawkins, Monte Markham, John Rubinstein, Jennifer Warren, Alexander H. Cohen (Special Award)

1973–74: Mark Baker, Maureen Brennan, Ralph Carter, Thom Christopher, John Driver, Conchata Ferrell, Ernestine Jackson, Michael Moriarty, Joe Morton, Ann Reinking, Janie Sell, Mary Woronov, Sammy Cahn (Special Award)

1974–75: Peter Burnell, Zan Charisse, Lola Falana, Peter Firth, Dorian Harewood, Joel Higgins, Marcia McClain, Linda Miller, Marti Rolph, John Sheridan, Scott Stevensen, Donna Theodore, Equity Library Theatre (Special Award)

1975–76: Danny Aeillo, Christine Andreas, Dixie Carter, Tovah Feldshuh, Chip Garnett, Richard Kelton, Vivian Reed, Charles Repole, Virginia Seidel, Daniel Seltzer, John V. Shea, Meryl Streep, A Chorus Line (Special Award)

1976–77: Trazana Beverley, Michael Cristofer, Joe Fields, Joanna Gleason, Cecilia Hart, John Heard, Gloria Hodes, Juliette Koka, Andrea McArdle, Ken Page, Jonathan Pryce, Chick Vennera, Eva LeGallienne (Special Award)

1977–78 Vasili Bogazianos, Nell Carter, Carlin Glynn, Christopher Goutman, William Hurt, Judy Kaye, Florence Lacy, Armelia McQueen, Gordana Rashovich, Bo Rucker, Richard Seer, Colin Stinton, Joseph Papp (Special Award)

1978–79: Philip Anglim, Lucie Arnaz, Gregory Hines, Ken Jennings, Michael Jeter, Laurie Kennedy, Susan Kingsley, Christine Lahti, Edward James Olmos, Kathleen Quinlan, Sarah Rice, Max Wright, Marshall W. Mason (Special Award)

1979–80: Maxwell Caulfield, Leslie Denniston, Boyd Gaines, Richard Gere, Harry Groener, Stephen James, Susan Kellermann, Dinah Manoff, Lonny Price, Marianne Tatum, Anne Twomey, Dianne Wiest, Mickey Rooney (Special Award)

1980–81: Brian Backer, Lisa Banes, Meg Bussert, Michael Allan Davis, Giancarlo Esposito, Daniel Gerroll, Phyllis Hyman, Cynthia Nixon, Amanda Plummer, Adam Redfield, Wanda Richert, Rex Smith, Elizabeth Taylor (Special Award)

1981–82: Karen Akers, Laurie Beechman, Danny Glover, David Alan Grier, Jennifer Holliday, Anthony Heald, Lizbeth Mackay, Peter MacNicol, Elizabeth McGovern, Ann Morrison, Michael O'Keefe, James Widdoes, Manhattan Theatre Club (Special Award)

BIOGRAPHICAL DATA ON THIS SEASON'S CASTS

AARON, ERIC. Born Oct. 27, 1954 in Eugene, Or. Attended UOr., Portand State U. Debut OB 1978 in "Can-Can," Bdwy 1981 in "The Best Little Whorehouse in Texas."

ABRAHAM, F. MURRAY. Born Oct. 24, 1939 in Pittsburgh, PA. Attended UTex. OB bow 1967 in "The Fantasticks," followed by "An Opening in the Trees," "Fourteenth Dictator," "Young Abe Lincoln," "Tonight in Living Color," "Adaptation," "Survival of St. Joan," "The Dog Ran Away," "Fables," "Richard III," "Little Murders," "Scuba Duba," "Where Has Tommy Flowers Gone?," "Miracle Play," "Blessing," "Sexual Perversity in Chicago," "Landscape of the Body," "The Master and Margarita," "Biting the Apple," "The Seagull," "The Caretaker," "Antigone," Bdwy in "The Man in the Glass Booth" (1968), "6 Rms Riv Vu," "Bad Habits," "Legend," "Teibele and Her Demon."

ABUBA, ERNEST. Born Aug. 25, 1947 in Honolulu, HI. Attended Southwestern Col. Bdwy debut 1976 in "Pacific Overtures," followed by "Loose Ends," OB in "Sunrise," "Monkey Music," "Station J."

ACKERMAN, LONI. Born Apr. 10, 1949 in NYC. Attended New School. Bdwy debut 1968 in "George M.!," followed by "No, No Nanette," "So Long 174th Street," "Magic Show," "Evita," OB in "Dames at Sea," "Starting Here Starting Now."

ACKROYD, DAVID. Born May 30, 1940 in Orange, NJ. Graduate Bucknell, Yale, Bdwy debut 1971 in "Unlikely Heroes," followed by "Full Circle," "Hamlet," "Hide and Seek," "Children of a Lesser God," OB in "Isadora Duncan Sleeps with the Russian Navy."

ADAMS, BROOKE. Born in NYC in 1949. Attended Dalton Sch. Debut 1974 OB in "The Petrified Forest," followed by "Split," "Key Exchange."

ADAMS, POLLY. Born in Nashville, Tn. Graduate Stanford U, Columbia U. Bdwy debut 1976 in "Zalmen, or the Madness of God," followed OB in "Ord-way Ames-gay."

ADLER, BRUCE. Born Nov, 27, 1944 in NYC. Attended NYU. Debut 1957 OB in "It's a Funny World," followed by "Hard to Be a Jew," "Big Winner," Bdwy in "A Teaspoon Every 4 Hours" (1971), "Oklahoma!" (1979), "Oh, Brother!"

AHEARN, DAN. Born Aug. 7, 1948 in Washington, DC. Attended, Carnegie Mellon. Debut OB 1981 in "Woyzek," followed by "Brontosaurus Rex."

AKERS, KAREN. Born Oct. 13, 1945 in NYC. Hunter College grad. Bdwy debut 1982 in "Nine" for which she received a Theatre World Award.

ALDERFER, ERIC. Born Nov. 14, 1954 in Springfield, Oh. Attended Wheaton Col., UCin. Debut 1979 OB in "Mary," Bdwy 1981 in "My Fair Lady."

ALEX, MARILYN. Born Oct. 30, 1930 in Hollywood, Ca. Attended RADA. Bdwy debut 1981 in "Deathtrap," OB in "Invitation to a March."

ALEXANDER, JASON. Born Sept. 23, 1959 in Irvington, NJ. Attended Boston U. Bdwy bow 1981 in "Merrily We Roll Along."

ALEXIS, ALVIN. Born July 5 in NYC. Debut 1976 OB in "In the Wine Time," followed by "Rear Column," "Class Enemy," "Zooman and the Sign."

ALICE, MARY. Born Dec. 3, 1941 in Indianola, MS. Debut OB 1967 in "Trials of Brother Jero," followed by "The Strong Breed," "Duplex," "Thoughts," "Miss Julie," "House Party," "Terraces," "Heaven and Hell's apartment," "In the Deepest Part of Sleep," "Cockfight," "Julius Caesar," "Nongogo," "Second Thoughts," "Spell #7," "Zooman and The Sign," "Glasshouse," Bdwy 1971 in "No Place to be Somebody."

ALLEN, BEAU. Born Mar. 2, 1950 in Wilmington, DE. Graduate Tufts U. Bdwy debut 1972 in "Jesus Christ Superstar," followed by "Two Gentlemen of Verona," "Best Little Whorehouse in Texas."

ALLEN, DAVE. Born July 6, 1936 in Dublin, Ireland. Bdwy debut 1981 in "An Evening with Dave Allen."

ALLEN, DEBBIE (aka Deborah) Born Jan. 16, 1950 in Houston, Tx. Graduate Howard U. Debut 1972 OB in "Ti-Jean and His Brothers," followed by "Anna Lucasta," "Louis," Bdwy in "Raisin" (1973), "Ain't Misbehavin'," "West Side Story."

ALLEN, SHEILA. Born Oct. 22, 1932 in Chard, Somerset, Eng. RADA Graduate. Debut with Royal Shakespeare Co's 1975 season at BAM. With BAM Theatre Co. in "Winter's Tale," "The Barbarians," "The Wedding," "A Midsummer Night's Dream," "The Wild Duck," "Oedipus the King," "Vikings," OB in "The Browning Version."

ALLISON, MICHAEL. Born in London; attended Lausanne U, RADA. Bdwy bow 1960 in "My Fair Lady," (also 1981 revival), followed by "Hostile Witness," "Come Live With Me," "Coco," "Angel Street," OB in "The Importance of Being Earnest," "Staircase."

ALLMON, CLINTON. Born June 13, 1941 in Monahans, Tx. Graduate OkStateU. Bdwy debut 1969 in "Indians," followed by "The Best Little Whorehouse in Texas," OB in "Bluebird," "Khaki Blue," "One Sunday Afternoon."

ALTAY, DERIN, Born Nov. 10, 1954 in Chicago, IL. Attended Goodman School, AmCons. Broadway debut 1981 in "Evita."

ALTMAN, JANE. Born Sept. 7 in Philadelphia, Pa. Graduate Temple U. Debut OB in "The Importance of Being Earnest," followed by "Taming of the Shrew," "Candida," "A Doll's House," "Magda," "The Three Musketeers," "And So to Bed," "Saints," "I Take These Women."

ALTMAN, NANCY ADDISON. Born March 21, 1950 in NYC. Attended Fisher Col., NYU. Debut OB 1975 in "Clarence," Bdwy 1981 in "A Talent for Murder."

ALYSON, EYDIE. Born Aug. 28, 1955 in Chicago, Il. Graduate UIll. Bdwy debut 1981 in "Fiddler on the Roof."

AMENDOLIA, DON. Born Feb. 1, 1945 in Woodbury, NJ. Attended Glassboro State Col., AADA. Debut 1966 OB in "Until the Monkey Comes," followed by "Park," "Cloud 9."

ANDERMAN, MAUREEN. Born Oct. 26, 1946 in Detroit, MI. Graduate UMich. Bdwy debut 1970 in "Othello," followed by "Moonchildren" for which she received a Theatre World Award, "An Evening with Richard Nixon ...," "The Last of Mrs. Lincoln," "Seascape," "Who's Afraid of Virginia Woolf," "A History of the American Film," "The Lady from Dubuque," "The Man Who Came to Dinner," "Einstein and the Polar Bear," OB in "Hamlet," "Elusive Angel," "Out of Our Father's House," "Sunday Runners," "Macbeth."

ANDERSON, JUDITH. Born in Adelaide, Aust., Feb. 10, 1898. Bdwy debut 1923 in "Peter Weston," followed by "Cobra," "The Dove," "Strange Interlude," "As You Desire Me," "Firebird," "The Mask and the Face," "Come of Age," "The Old Maid," "Family Portrait," "Hamlet," "Macbeth," "The Three Sisters," "Medea" (1947/1982), "Tower Beyond Tragedy," "John Brown's Body," "In the Summer House," "Chalk Garden," "Comes a Day," "Elizabeth the Queen," and as Hamlet in 1971.

ANDREAS, CHRISTINE. Born July 4, 1951 in Camden, NJ. Bdwy debut 1975 in "Angel Street," followed by "My Fair Lady" for which she received a Theatre World Award, "Oklahoma" (1979). OB in "Disgustingly Rich," "Rhapsody in Gershwin," "Alex Wilder: Clues to a Life."

ANDREWS, GEORGE LEE. Born Oct. 13, 1942 in Milwaukee, Wi. Debut OB 1970 in "Jacques Brel Is Alive," followed by "Starting Here Starting Now," "Vamps and Rideouts," Bdwy in "A Little Night Music" (1973), "On the 20th Century."

ANDROS, DOUGLAS. Born Nov. 27 in NYC. Attended NYU. Debut 1958 OB in "Good Woman of Setzuan," followed by "Last of the Red Hot Lovers," "Smoking Pistols," "This Side of Paradise," "Most Happy Fella," "Piaf—A Remembrance," "Happy Sunset Inc."

ANGLIM, PHILIP. Born Feb. 11, 1953 in San Francisco, CA. Yale graduate. Debut OB and Bdwy 1979 in "The Elephant Man" for which he received a Theatre World Award, followed by "Macbeth," OB in "Judgment," "Welded."

ANTHONY, FRAN. Born July 18, in Brooklyn, NY. Graduate Queens Col. Debut OB 1953 in "Climate of Eden," followed by "Pappa Is Home," "Summer Brave," "The Warriors Husband," "Kind Lady," "House Music."

ARANAS, RAUL. Born Oct. 1, 1947 in Manila, Phil. Pace U. grad. Debut 1976 OB in "Savages," followed by "Yellow Is My Favorite Color," "49," "Bullet Headed Birds," Bdwy 1978 in "Loose Ends."

ARDAO, DAVID. Born July 24, 1951 in Brooklyn, NY. Graduate Rutgers U. Bdwy debut 1981 in "Joseph and the Amazing Technicolor Dreamcoat."

ARELL, SHERRY H. Born Aug. 4, 1950 in Quincy, Ma. Attended Stage I Drama Workshop. Debut 1982 OB in "One Night Stand."

ARGETSINGER, GETCHIE. Born Oct. 29, 1947 in Youngstown, Oh. Attended St. Bonaventure U., UGrenoble. Debut OB 1981 in "Italian Straw Hat."

ARLT, LEWIS. Born Dec. 5, 1949 in Kingston, NY. Graduate Carnegie Tech. Bdwy debut 1975 in "Murder Among Friends," followed by "Piaf," OB in "War and Peace," "The Interview," "Applause" (ELT), "House Across the Street."

ARMAGNAC, GARY. Born Aug. 17, 1952 in New Jersey. Iona Col. grad. Debut 1981 OB in "A Taste of Honey."

ARNOLD, VICTOR. Born July 1, 1936 in Herkimer, NY. Graduate NYU. OB in "Shadows of Heroes," "Merchant of Venice," "3X3," "Eyes," "Fortune and Men's Eyes," "Time for Bed, Take Me to Bed," "Emperor of Late Night Radio," "Macbeth," "Sign in Sidney Brustein's Window," "Cacciatore," "Maiden Stakes," "My Prince My King," Bdwy in "The Deputy" (1964), "Malcolm," "We Bombed in New Haven," "Fun City."

ARNOTT, MARK. Born June 15, 1950 in Chicago, Il. Graduate Dartmouth Col. Debut OB 1981 in "Hunchback of Notre Dame," followed by "Buddies."

ARONSON, JONATHAN. Born June 17, 1953 in Miami, FL. Attended Dade Col. AMDA. Bdwy debut 1979 in "Whoopee!" followed by "Sugar Babies," "Five O'Clock Girl," "Little Johnny Jones," OB in "Tip-Toes."

ARTHUR, CAROL. Born Aug. 4, 1935 in Hackensack, NJ. Attended AMDA. Bdwy debut 1964 in "High Spirits," followed by "Once Upon a Mattress," "Kicks and Co." "Oh, What a Lovely War!," "On the Town," "I Can Get It for You Wholesale," "Music Man.","Woman of the Year."

ARTHUR, HELEN-JEAN. Born Nov. 2, 1933 in Chicago, IL. Graduate Beloit Col. Debut 1957 OB in "Othello," followed by "Twelve Pound Look," "Streets of New York," "Vera with Kate," "Declasse," "Teach Me How to Cry," Bdwy in "Send Me No Flowers," "Moon Beseiged," "Look Back in Anger."

ASHER, DAVID. Born June 3, 1953 in Cleveland, Oh. Graduate Stanford, Yale. Debut OB 1974 in "The Proposition," Bdwy in "Most Happy Fella" (1979), "Joseph and the Amazing Technicolor Dreamcoat."

ASHLEY, ELIZABETH. Born Aug. 30, 1939 in Ocala, Fl. Attended Neighborhood Playhouse. Bdwy debut 1959 in "The Highest Tree," followed by "Take Her, She's Mine" for which she received a Theatre World Award, "Barefoot in the Park," "Ring Round the Bathtub," "Cat on a Hot Tin Roof," "The Skin of Our Teeth," "Legend," "Caesar and Cleopatra," "Hide and Seek," "Agnes of God."

ASHLEY, MARY ELLEN. Born June 11, 1938 in Long Island City, NY. Graduate Queens Col. Bdwy debut 1943 in "Innocent Voyage," followed by "By Appointment Only," "Annie Get Your Gun," "Yentl," OB in "Carousel," "Polly," "Panama Hattie," "Soft Touch," "Suddenly the Music Starts," "The Facts of Death.", "A Drifter, the Grifter and Heather McBride."

ASKEW, TIMOTHY. Born Sept. 19, 1951 in Atlanta, GA. Graduate Emory U. Debut 1978 OB in "The Devil's Disciple," followed by "Jimmy the Veteran," "Redback," "Cityscapes 3."

ASSANTE, ARMAND. Born Oct. 4, 1949 in NYC. Attended AADA. Debut 1971 OB in "Lake of the Woods," followed by "Yankees 3 Detroit 0," "Rubbers," "Boccacio," Bdwy in "Comedians," "Romeo and Juliet," "Kingdoms."

ASTREDO, HUMBERT ALLEN. Born in San Francisco, CA. Attended SFU. Debut 1967 OB in "Arms and the Man," followed by "Fragments," "Murderous Angels," "Beach Children," "End of Summer," "Knuckle," "Grand Magic," "Big and Little," "The Jail Diary of Albie Sachs," Bdwy in "Les Blancs," "An Evening with Richard Nixon....," "The Little Foxes."

ATHERTON, WILLIAM. Born July 30, 1947 in Orange, CT. Graduate Carnegie Tech. Debut 1971 OB in "House of Blue Leaves," followed by "The Basic Training of Pavlo Hummel," "Suggs" for which he received a Theatre World Award, "Rich and Famous," "The Passing Game," "Three Acts of Recognition," Bdwy in "The Sign in Sidney Brustein's Window" (1972), "Happy New Year," "The American Clock."

ATKINSON, PEGGY. Born Oct. 1, 1943 in Brooklyn, NY. Attended Ithaca Col. Bdwy debut 1967 in "Fiddler on the Roof," followed by "Two Gentlemen of Verona," OB in "Boccaccio," "The Faggot," "One Free Smile," "One Cent Plain," "Hostage.", "Bags."

AUMONT, JEAN-PIERRE. Born Jan. 5, 1913 in Paris. Attended Ntl. Sch. of Dramatic Art. Bdwy debut 1942 in "Rose Burke," followed by "My Name Is Aquilon," "Heavenly Twins," "Second String," "Tovarich," "Camino Real" (LC), "Murderous Angels" (OB)," "Days in the Trees," "A Talent for Murder."

AUSTIN, ELIZABETH (formerly Beth) Born May 23, 1952 in Philadelphia, PA. Graduate Point Park Col., Pittsburgh Playhouse. Debut 1977 OB in "Wonderful Town," followed by "The Prevalence of Mrs. Seal," "Engaged," "Pastoral," "Head over Heels," "A Drifter, the Grifter and Heather McBride," Bdwy 1977 in "Sly Fox," followed by "Whoopee," "Onward Victoria."

AVERA, TOM. Born Feb. 21, 1923 in Rocky Mount, NC. UNC grad. Bdwy debut 1944 in "One Touch of Venus," followed by "Carousel," "Oklahoma!," "Lo and Behold," "Marathon 33," "On the Town," "Best Little Whorehouse in Texas," "Woman of the Year."

AYR, MICHAEL. Born Sept. 8, 1953 in Great Falls, MT. Graduate SMU. Debut 1976 OB in "Mrs. Murray's Farm," followed by "The Farm," "Ulysses in Traction," "Lulu" "Cabin 12," "Stargazing," "The Deserter," "Hamlet," "Mary Stuart," "Save Grand Central," "The Beaver Coat," "Richard II," "Great Grandson of Jedediah Kohler," Bdwy 1980 in "Hide and Seek," "Piaf."

AZITO, TONY. Born July 18, 1948 in NYC. Attended Juilliard. Debut 1971 OB in "Red, White and Black," followed by "Players Project," "Secrets of the Citizens Correction Committee," "Threepenny Opera," Bdwy 1977 in "Happy End," followed by "Pirates of Penzance."

BABATUNDE, OBBA. Born in Jamaica, NY. Attended Brooklyn Col. Debut OB 1970 in "The Secret Place," followed by "Guys and Dolls," "On Toby Time," "The Breakout," "Scottsborough Boys," "Showdown Time," "Dream on Monkey Mt.," "Sheba," Bdwy in "Timbuktu," "Reggae," "It's So Nice to Be Civilized.", "Dreamgirls."

BACALL, LAUREN. Born Sept. 16, 1924 in NYC. Attended AADA. Bdwy debut 1942 in "Johnny 2 X 4," followed by "Goodbye Charlie," "Cactus Flower," "Applause," "Woman of the Year."

BACCUS, STEPHEN. Born Nov. 25, 1969 in Miami Beach, Fl. Attended NYU. Debut 1982 OB in "The House Across the Street," followed by "Three Acts of Recognition."

BACKER, BRIAN. Born Dec. 5, 1956 in NYC. Attended Neighborhood Playhouse. Bdwy debut 1981 in "The Floating Light Bulb" for which he received a Theatre World Award.

BACKUS, RICHARD. Born Mar. 28, 1945 in Goffstown, NH. Harvard graduate. Bdwy debut 1971 in "Butterflies Are Free," followed by "Promenade, All!" for which he received a Theatre World Award, "Ah, Wilderness!," "Camelot" (1981), OB in "Studs Edsel," "Gimme Shelter," "Sorrows of Stephen," "Missing Persons."

BACON, KEVIN. Born July 8, 1958 in Philadelphia, PA. Debut 1978 OB in "Getting Out," followed by "Glad Tidings," "Album," "Flux," "Poor Little Lambs."

BADOLATO, DEAN. Born June 6, 1952 in Chicago, IL. Attended UIll. Bdwy debut 1978 in "A Chorus Line," followed by "Pirates of Penzance."

BAER, MARIAN. Born Aug. 18, 1926 in Sedalia, Mo. Graduate AADA. Debut 1958 OB in "The Night Is My Enemy," followed by "The Glass Menagerie," "Ugly Duckling," "A Delicate Balance," "A Month in the Country," "King John," Bdwy 1981 in "My Fair Lady."

BAFF, REGINA. Born Mar. 31, 1949 in The Bronx, NY. Attended Western Reserve, Hunter Col. Debut 1969 OB in "The Brownstone Urge," followed by "Patrick Henry Lake Liquors," "The Cherry Orchard," "Domino Courts," Bdwy in "Story Theatre," "Metamorphosis," "Veronica's Room," "West Side Waltz."

BAGDEN, RONALD. Born Dec. 26, 1953 in Philadelphia, PA. Graduate Temple U., RADA. Debut OB 1977 in "Oedipus Rex," followed by "Oh! What A Lovely War!," Bdwy 1980 in "Amadeus."

BAILEY, DENNIS. Born Apr. 12, 1953 in Grosse Point Woods, MI. UDetroit graduate. Debut 1977 OB in "House of Blue Leaves," followed by "Wonderland," "Head over Heels," Bdwy 1978 in "Gemini."

BAILEY, JANET. Born Sept. 8, 1952 in Los Angeles, Ca. Graduate CalStateU. Debut 1979 OB in "Lovers and Other Strangers," followed by "Ah, Wilderness!," "Look Homeward, Angel," "Chamber Music," "La Ronde."

BAILEY, LARRY G. Born Oct. 5, 1947 in York, Pa. Graduate York Col. Bdwy debut 1974 in "Jumpers," followed by "A Chorus Line," "The Little Prince and the Aviator." followed by "Clownmaker."

BAKER, BLANCHE. (nee Brocho Freyda Garf) Dec. 20, 1956 in NYC. Attended Wellesley Col. Bdwy debut 1981 in "Lolita," followed by "Poor Little Lambs" (OB).

BAKER, MARK. Born Oct. 2, 1946 in Cumberland, MD. Attended Wittenberg U., Carnegie-Mellon U., Neighborhood Playhouse, AADA. Bdwy debut 1972 in "Via Galactica," followed by "Candide" for which he received a Theatre World Award, "Habeas Corpus," OB in "Love Me, Love My Children," "A Midsummer Night's Dream," "From Rodgers and Hart with Love," "Edgar Allan."

BALLARD, KAY. Born Nov. 20, 1926 in Cleveland, Oh. Debut 1954 OB in "The Golden Apple," followed by "Cole Porter Revisited," Bdwy in "Carnival," "The Beast in Me," "Royal Flush," "Molly," "Pirates of Penzance."

BALOU, BUDDY. Born in 1953 in Seattle, WA. Joined American Ballet Theatre in 1970, rising to soloist. Joined Dancers in 1977; "A Chorus Line" in 1980.

BANCROFT, ANNE. Born Sept. 15, 1931 in NYC. Attended AADA. Bdwy debut 1958 in "Two for the Seesaw" for which she received a Theatre World Award, followed by "The Devils," "The Little Foxes" (1967), "A Cry of Players," "Golda," "Duet for One."

BANES, LISA. Born July 9, 1955 in Chagrin Falls, OH. Juilliard grad. Debut OB 1980 in "Elizabeth I," followed by "A Call from the East," "Look Back in Anger" for which she received a Theatre World Award., "My Sister in This House," "Antigone."

BARANSKI, CHRISTINE. Born May 2, 1952 in Buffalo, NY. Graduate Juilliard Sch. Debut OB 1978 in "One Crack Out," followed by "Says I Says He," "The Trouble with Europe," "Coming Attractions," "Operation Midnight Climax," "Sally and Marsha," Bdwy 1980 in "Hide and Seek."

BARBOUR, THOMAS. Born July 25, 1921 in NYC. Graduate Princeton, Harvard. Bdwy debut 1968 in "Portrait of a Queen," followed by "Great White Hope," "Scratch," "The Lincoln Mask," "Kingdoms," OB in "Twelfth Night," "Merchant of Venice," "Admirable Bashful," "The Lady's Not for Burning," "The Enchanted," "Antony and Cleopatra," "The Saintliness of Margery Kemp," "Dr. Willy Nilly," "Under the Sycamore Tree," "Epitaph for George Dillon," "Thracian Horses," "Old Glory," "Sjt. Musgrave's Dance," "Nestless Bird," "The Seagull," "Wayside Motor Inn," "Arthur," "The Grinding Machine," "Mr. Simian," "The Sorrows of Frederick," "The Terrorists," "Dark Ages."

BARON, EVALYN. Born Apr. 21, 1948 in Atlanta, GA. Graduate Northwestern, UMinn. Debut OB 1979 in "Scrambled Feet," followed by "Hijinks," "I Can't Keep Running in Place," "Jerry's Girls," Bdwy 1980 in "Fearless Frank."

BARRE, GABRIEL. Born Aug. 26, 1957 in Brattleboro, Vt. Graduate AADA. Debut 1977 OB in "Jabberwock," followed by "T.N.T."

BARRETT, BRENT. Born Feb. 28, 1957 in Quinter, Ks. Graduate Carnegie-Mellon U. Bdwy debut 1980 in "West Side Story," OB in "March of the Falsettos."

BARRETT, LESLIE. Born Oct. 30, 1919 in NYC. Bdwy bow 1936 in "But for the Grace of God," followed by "Enemy of the People," "Dead End," "Sundown," "There's Always a Breeze," "Primrose Path," "Stroke of 8," "Horse Fever," "Good Neighbor," "All in Favor," "Counsellor-at-Law," "Deadfall," "Rhinoceros," "The Investigation," "Slapstick Tragedy," "What Did We Do Wrong," "The Dresser," OB in "Hamp," "The Contractor," "Play Me Zoltan," "Savages," "The Dragon," "Trial of Dmitri Karamazov," "Purple Dust," "My Old Friends," "Romeo and Juliet."

BARROWS, DIANA. Born Jan. 23, 1966 in NYC. Bdwy debut 1975 in "Cat on a Hot Tin Roof," followed by "Panama Hattie" (ELT), "Annie."

BARRY, B. CONSTANCE. Born Apr. 29, 1913 in NYC. Attended Hofstra, New School. Debut 1974 OB in "Blue Heaven," followed by "Dark of the Moon," "Native Son," "Passing Time," "All the Way Home" (ELT), "Naomi Court," "Antigone."

BARRY, RAYMOND J. Born Mar. 14, 1939 in Hempstead, NY. Graduate Brown U. Debut 1963 OB in "Man Is Man," followed by "Penguin Touquet," Bdwy 1975 in "The Leaf People," "Hunting Scenes."

BARTENIEFF, GEORGE. Born Jan. 24, 1933 in Berlin, Ger. Bdwy bow 1947 in "The Whole World Over," followed by "Venus Is," "All's Well That Ends Well," "Quotations from Chairman Mao Tse-Tung," "The Death of Bessie Smith," "Cop-Out," "Room Service," "Unlikely Heroes," OB in "Walking to Waldheim," "Memorandum," "The Increased Difficulty of Concentration," "Trelawny of the Wells," "Charley Chestnut Rides the IRT," "Radio (Wisdom): Sophia Part I," "Images of the Dead," "Dead End Kids.", "The Blonde Leading the Blonde," "The Dispossessed."

BARTLETT, D'JAMIN. Born May 21 in NYC. Attended AADA. Bdwy debut 1973 in "A Little Night Music" for which she received a Theatre World Award, OB in "The Glorious Age," "Boccacio," "2 by 5," "Lulu," "Alex Wilder: Clues to Life."

BARTLETT, LISABETH. Born Feb. 28, 1956 in Denver, Co. Graduate Northwestern U. Bdwy debut 1971 in "The Dresser."

BARTLETT, ROBIN. Born Apr. 22, 1951 in NYC. Graduate Boston U. Bdwy debut 1975 in "Yentl," followed by "The World of Sholem Aleichem," OB in "Agamemnon," "Fathers and Sons," "No End of Blame."

BARTON, FRED. Born Oct. 20, 1958 in Camden, NJ. Graduate Harvard. Debut 1982 OB in "Forbidden Broadway."

BASESCU, ELINOR. Born Mar. 5, 1927 in Trenton, NJ. Graduate Oberlin Col. Bdwy debut 1950 in "Detective Story," OB in "Sands of the Negev," "The Second Mrs. Tanqueray," "Meegan's Game," "Teach Me How to Cry."

BASSETT, STEVE. Born June 25, 1952 in Escondido, CA. Graduate Juilliard. Bdwy debut 1979 in "Deathtrap," OB in "Spring Awakening," "Booth."

BATES, KATHY. Born June 18, 1948 in Memphis, Tn. Graduate S. Methodist U. Debut 1976 OB in "Vanities," followed by "The Art of Dining," Bdwy in "Goodbye Fidel" (1980), "5th of July," "Come Back to the 5 & Dime, Jimmy Dean."

BATTAGLIA, RICHARD. Born June 8, 1955 in Philadelphia, PA. Attended Temple U. Debut OB 1982 in "Meegan's Game."

BATTISTA, LLOYD. Born May 14, 1937 in Cleveland, Oh. Graduate Carnegie Tech. Bdwy debut 1966 in "Those That Play the Clowns," followed by "The Homecoming," OB in "The Flame and the Rose," "Murder in the Cathedral," "The Miser," "Gorky," "Sexual Perversity in Chicago," "King of Schnorrers," "Francis," "The Keymaker."

BATTLE, HINTON. Born Nov. 29, 1956 in Neubraecke, Ger. Joined Dance Theatre of Harlem. Bdwy debut 1975 in "The Wiz," followed by "Dancin'," "Sophisticated Ladies."

BAUM, SUSAN J. Born July 12, 1950 in Miami, Fl. Graduate UFl. Has appeared OB in "The Children's Hour," "Holy Ghosts," "Hay Fever," "Doctor in the House," "Trifles," "Arms and the Man," "Uncle Vanya," "Hedda Gabler," "Close Enough for Jazz."

BAVAN, YOLANDE. Born June 1, 1942 in Ceylon. Attended UColombo. Debut 1964 OB in "A Midsummer Night's Dream," followed by "Jonah," "House of Flowers," "Salvation," "Tarot," "Back Bog Beast Bait," "Leaves of Grass," "The End of the War," Bdwy in "Heathen," "Snow White."

BEACH, GARY. Born Oct. 10, 1947 in Alexandria, VA. Graduate NCSch. of Arts. Bdwy bow 1971 in "1776," followed by "Something's Afoot," "Moony Shapiro Songbook," "Annie," OB in "Smile, Smile, Smile," "What's a Nice Country Like You. . . .," "Ionescapade," "By Strouse."

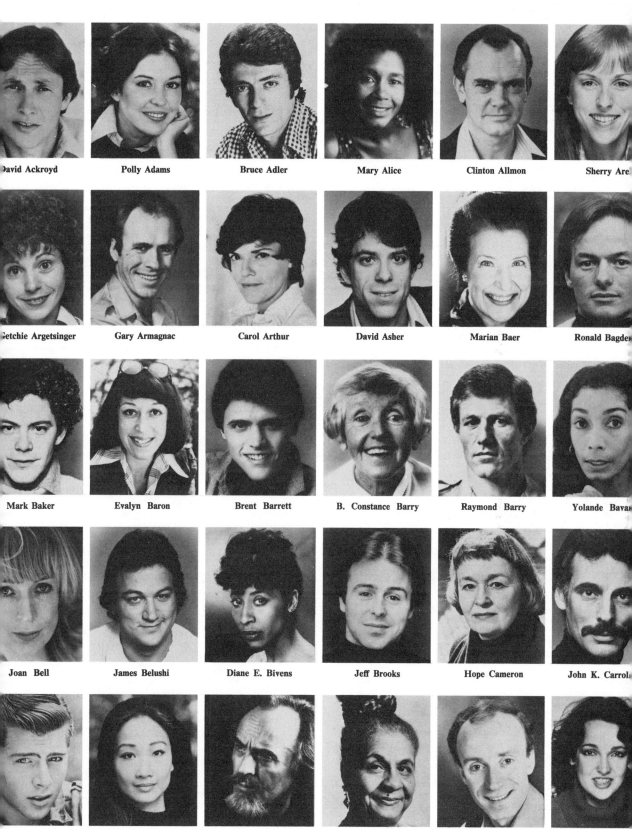

David Ackroyd

Polly Adams

Bruce Adler

Mary Alice

Clinton Allmon

Sherry Are

Getchie Argetsinger

Gary Armagnac

Carol Arthur

David Asher

Marian Baer

Ronald Bagden

Mark Baker

Evalyn Baron

Brent Barrett

B. Constance Barry

Raymond Barry

Yolande Bava

Joan Bell

James Belushi

Diane E. Bivens

Jeff Brooks

Hope Cameron

John K. Carrol

Maxwell Caulfield

Tina Chen

Renato Cibelli

Leila Danette

Rick DeFilipps

Karla DeVito

BEACHNER, LOUIS. Born June 9, 1923 in Jersey City, NJ. Bdwy bow 1942 in "Junior Miss," followed by "No Time for Sergeants," "Georgy," "The Changing Room," "National Health," "Where's Charley?," OB in "Time to Burn," "The Hostage," "Savages," "The Overcoat."

BEAN, ORSON. Born July 22, 1928 in Burlington, VT. Bdwy bow 1953 in "Men of Distinction," followed by "John Murray Anderson's Almanac" for which he received a Theatre World Award, "Will Success Spoil Rock Hunter?," "Nature's Way," "Mister Roberts" (CC), "Subways Are for Sleeping," "Say, Darling" (CC), "Never Too Late," "I Was Dancing," "Ilya Darling," OB in "Home Movies," "A Round with Ring," "Make Someone Happy," "I'm Getting My Act Together.", "40 Deuce."

BEAN, REATHEL. Born Aug. 24, 1942 in Missouri. Graduate Drake U. OB in "America Hurrah," "San Francisco's Burning," "The Love Cure," "Henry IV," "In Circles," "Peace," "Journey of Snow White," "Wanted," "The Faggot," "Lovers," "Not Back with the Elephants," "The Art of Coarse Acting," "The Trip Back Down."

BEECHMAN, LAURIE. Born Apr. 4, 1954 in Philadelphia, Pa. Attended NYU. Bdwy debut 1977 in "Annie," followed by "Pirates of Penzance," "Joseph and the Amazing Technicolor Dreamcoat" for which she received a Theatre World Award.

BEERS, FRANCINE. Born Nov. 26 in NYC. Attended Hunter Col., CCNY, HB Studio. Debut 1962 OB in "King of the Whole Damned World," followed by "Kiss Mama," "Monopoly," "Cakes with Wine," Bdwy in "Cafe Crown," "6 Rms Riv Vu," "The American Clock.", "Curse of an Aching Heart."

BEERY, LEIGH. Born March 20 in Minneapolis, Mn. Attended McPhail School. Debut 1965 OB in "Leonard Bernstein's Theatre Songs," followed by "Pic-a-Number," "Oklahoma!" (LC), "Lola," Bdwy 1963 in "Cyrano."

BEHREN, RICHARD. Born Mar. 18, 1952 in St. Louis, Mo. Graduate Southeast MoU. Debut 1980 OB in "War Play," followed by "La Ronde."

BELASCO, EMIL. Born Sept. 11, 1921 in Utuado, PR. Attended Pasadena Playhouse, RADA. Debut OB 1948 in "Are You Mr. Sherensky?," followed by "Big Apple Messenger," Bdwy in "6 Rms Riv Vu" (1973), "Plaza Suite."

BELL, JOAN. Born Feb. 1, 1935 in Bombay, Ind. Studied at Sylvia Bryant Sch. Bdwy debut 1963 in "Something More," followed by "Applause," "Chicago," "Woman of the Year."

BELL, VANESSA. Born Mar. 20, 1957 in Toledo, OH. Graduate OhU. Bdwy debut 1981 in "Bring Back Birdie," followed by "El Bravo!," "Dreamgirls."

BELUSHI, JAMES A. Born June 15, 1954 in Chicago, Il. Graduate S.Ill.U. Bdwy debut 1982 in "Pirates of Penzance."

BEMIS, KIM. Born Jan. 3, 1954 in St. Paul, Mn. Graduate Colorado Col. Debut 1979 OB in "A Dream Play," Bdwy 1982 in "Othello."

BENJAMIN, ALLAN. Born March 19, 1949 in Brooklyn, NY. Graduate UDenver, UCopenhagen. DebuT OB 1982 in "A Trinity."

BENJAMIN, P. J. Born Sept. 2, 1951 in Chicago, IL. Attended Loyola U., Columbia. Bdwy debut 1973 in "Pajama Game," followed by "Pippin," "Sarava," "Charlie and Algernon," "Sophisticated Ladies."

BENSON, ROBBY. Born Jan. 21, 1956 in Dallas, Tx. Attended AADA. Bdwy bow 1969 in "Zelda," followed by "The Rothschilds," "Pirates of Penzance."

BERENSON, STEPHEN. Born Mar. 29, 1953 in NYC. Graduate Drake U. Debut 1978 OB in "Dead End," followed by "Men in White," "The Butterfingers Angel," "Close Enough for Jazz."

BEREZIN, TANYA. Born Mar. 25, 1941 in Philadelphia, PA. Attended Boston U. Debut OB 1967 in "The Sandcastle," followed by "Three Sisters," "Great Nebula in Orion," "him," "Amazing Activity of Charlie Contrare," "Battle of Angels," "Mound Builders," "Serenading Louie," "My Life," "Brontosaurus," "Glorious Morning," "Mary Stuart," "The Beaver Coat.", Bdwy 1981 in "5th of July."

BERGER, STEPHEN. Born May 16, 1954 in Philadelphia, Pa. Attended UCin. Bdwy debut 1982 in "Little Me."

BERKSON, SUSAN. Born Apr. 10 in Michigan City, In. Graduate UMinn. Debut OB 1981 in "What the Hell, Nell," followed by "The Prince and the Pauper," "Winds of Change" and "Nymph Errant."

BERMAN, DONALD F. Born Jan. 23, 1954 in NYC. Graduate USyracuse. Debut 1977 OB in "Savages," followed by "Dona Rosita," "The Lady or the Tiger," "The Overcoat."

BERNARDI, HERSCHEL. Born in NYC in 1923. Began career at 3. Credits include "The World of Sholom Aleichem," "Fiddler on the Roof," "Bajour," "Zorba," "The Goodbye People," and 1981 revival of "Fiddler on the Roof."

BERNER, GARY. Born in Mt. Kisco, NY. Attended Hampshire Col., Brandeis U. Debut 1979 OB in "Minnesota Moon," followed by "The Runner Stumbles," "Richard II," "The Great Grandson of Jedediah Kohler."

BESSETTE, MIMI. Born Jan. 15, 1956 in Midland, Mi. Graduate TCU, RADA. Debut 1978 OB in "The Gift of the Magi," Bdwy 1981 in "The Best Little Whorehouse in Texas."

BEVERLEY, TRAZANA. Born Aug. 9, 1945 in Baltimore, Md. Graduate NYU. Debut 1969 OB in "Rules for Running Trains," followed by "Les Femmes Noires," "Geronimo," "Antigone," "The Brothers," Bdwy in "My Sister, My Sister," "For Colored Girls Who have Considered Suicide . . ." for which she received a Theatre World Award.

BIGGS, CASEY. Born Apr. 4, 1955 in Toledo, Oh. Attended Juilliard. Debut 1981 OB in "Il Campiello," followed by "Twelfth Night," "The Country Wife."

BILLINGTON, LEE. Born July 15, 1932 in Madison, Wi. Attended UWisc. Bdwy debut 1969 in "But Seriously," OB in "Dance of Death," "3 by O'Neill," "Our Town," "Capt. Brassbound's Conversion," "Henry VIII," "Boy with a Cart," "Epicoene," "The Homecoming," "Paterson," "Windmills."

BILLONE, JOSEPH. Born Mar. 24, 1953 in Greenwich, Ct. Graduate UCt., NYU. Debut 1978 OB in "Gay Divorce," Bdwy 1981 in "My Fair Lady."

BIRNEY, REED. Born Sept. 11, 1954 in Alexandria, Va. Attended Boston U. Bdwy debut 1977 in "Gemini," OB in "The Master and Margarita," "Bella Figura."

BITTNER, JACK. Born in Omaha, Ne. Graduate UNeb. Has appeared OB in "Nathan the Wise," "Land of Fame," "Beggar's Holiday," "Rip Van Winkle," "Dear Oscar," "What Every Woman Knows," "By Bernstein," "The Philanderer," Bdwy in "Harold and Maude" (1980), "Little Johnny Jones."

BIVENS, DIANE E. Born June 19, 1948 in NYC. Attended NYU. Debut OB 1972 in "Ti-Jean and His Brothers," followed by "Canterbury Tales," "For Colored Girls. . . .," "The Mighty Gents," Bdwy 1974 in "My Sister, My Sister."

BLACK, KAREN. Born July 1, 1942 in Park Ridge, Il. Attended Northwestern. Debut 1962 OB in "We're Civilized," Bdwy 1965 in "Playroom," followed by "Keep It in the Family," "Come Back to the 5 & Dime, Jimmy Dean."

BLAIR, PAMELA. Born Dec. 5, 1949 in Arlington, VT. Attended Ntl. Acad. of Ballet. Made Bdwy debut in 1972 in "Promises, Promises," followed by "Sugar," "Seesaw," "Of Mice and Men," "Wild and Wonderful," "A Chorus Line," "The Best Little Whorehouse in Texas," "King of Hearts," OB in "Ballad of Boris K.," "Split," "Real Life Funnies.", "Double Feature."

BLAKE, TIFFANY. Born July 3, 1971 in Fresh Meadows, NY. Bdwy debut 1980 in "Annie."

BLEVINS, MICHAEL. Born Sept. 2, 1960 in Orlando, Fl. Attended UNC, NYU. Bdwy debut 1981 in "Bring Back Birdie," followed by "Little Me," OB in "Time Pieces," "Bags."

BLOCH, SCOTTY. Born Jan. 28 in New Rochelle, NY. Attended AADA. Debut 1945 OB in "Craig's Wife," followed by "Lemon Sky," "Battering Ram," "Richard III," "In Celebration," "An Act of Kindness," "The Price," "Grace," Bdwy in "Children of a Lesser God."

BLOCK, LARRY. Born Oct. 30, 1942 in NYC. Graduate URI. Bdwy bow 1966 in "Hail Scrawdyke," followed by "La Turista," OB in "Eh?," "Fingernails Blue as Flowers," "Comedy of Errors," "Coming Attractions.", "Henry IV Part 2," "Feuhrer Bunker" "Manhattan Love Songs."

BLOUNT, HELON. Born Jan. 15 in Big Spring, TX. Graduate UTx. Bdwy debut 1956 in "Most Happy Fella," followed by "How to Succeed in Business . . .," "Do I Hear a Waltz?" "Fig Leaves Are Falling," "Follies," "Very Good Eddie," "Musical Chairs," "Woman of the Year," OB in "Fly Blackbird," "Riverwind," "My Wife and I," "Curley McDimple," "A Quarter for the Ladies Room," "Snapshot."

BLUM, MARK. Born May 14, 1950 in Newark, NJ. Graduate UPa., UMinn. Debut 1976 OB in "The Cherry Orchard." followed by "Green Julia," "Say Goodnight, Gracie," "Table Settings.", "Key Exchange."

BLUMENFELD, ROBERT. Born Feb. 26, 1943 in NYC. Graduate Rutgers, Columbia. Bdwy debut 1970 in "Othello," OB in "The Fall and Redemption of Man," "Tempest," "The Dybbuk," "Count Dracula," "Nature and Purpose of the Universe," "House Music," "The Keymaker."

BODIN, DUANE. Born Dec. 31, 1932 in Duluth, MN. Bdwy debut 1961 in "Bye Bye Birdie," followed by "La Plume de Ma Tante," "Here's Love" "Fiddler on the Roof," "1776," "Sweeney Todd.", "El Bravo."

BOGARDUS, STEPHEN. Born Mar. 11, 1954 in Norfolk, VA. Princeton graduate. Bdwy debut 1980 in "West Side Story," OB in "March of the Falsettos."

BOGGS, GAIL. Born Aug. 10, 1951 in Glen Ridge, NJ. Attended AADA. Debut 1971 OB in "Iphigenia," followed by "Ti-Jean and His Brothers," "Lullabye and Goodnight," Bdwy 1972 in "Mother Earth."

BOND, SUDIE. Born July 13, 1928 in Louisville, Ky. Attended Rollins Col. OB in "Summer and Smoke," "Tovarich," "American Dream," "Sandbox," "Endgame," "Theatre of the Absurd," "Home Movies," "Softly Consider the Nearness," "Memorandum," "Local Stigmatic," "Billy," "New York! New York!," "The Cherry Orchard," "Albee Directs Albee," "Dance for Me Simeon," Bdwy in "Waltz of the Toreadors," "Auntie Mame," "The Egg," "Harold," "My Mother, My Father and Me," "Impossible Years," "Keep It in the Family," "Quotations from Chrmn. Mao Tse-Tung," "American Dream," "Forty Carats," "Hay Fever," "Grease," "Come Back to the 5 & Dime, Jimmy Dean."

BOOCKVOR, STEVEN. Born Nov. 18, 1942 in NYC. Attended Queens Col., Juilliard. Bdwy debut 1966 in "Anya," followed by "A Time for Singing," "Cabaret," "Mardi Gras," "Jimmy," "Billy," "The Rothschilds," "Follies," "Over Here," "The Lieutenant," "Musical Jubilee," "Annie," "Working," "The First."

BORN, LYNNE P. Born Aug. 6, 1956 in Richmond, Va. Attended Northwestern U. Debut 1982 OB in "Catholic School Girls."

BOSCO, PHILIP. Born Sept. 26, 1930 in Jersey City, NJ. Graduate Catholic U. Credits: "Auntie Mame," "Rape of the Belt," "Ticket of Leave Man" (OB), "Donnybrook," "Man for All Seasons," "Mrs. Warren's Profession," with LCRep in "The Alchemist," "East Wind," "Galileo," "St. Joan," "Tiger at the Gate," "Cyrano," "King Lear," "A Great Career," "In the Matter of J. Robert Oppenheimer," "The Miser," "The Time of Your Life," "Camino Real," "Operation Sidewinder," "Amphitryon," "Enemy of the People," "Playboy of the Western World," "Good Woman of Setzuan," "Antigone," "Mary Stuart," "Narrow Road to the Deep North," "The Crucible," "Twelfth Night," "Enemies," "Plough and the Stars," "Merchant of Venice," and "A Streetcar Named Desire," "Henry V," "Threepenny Opera," "Streamers," "Stages," "St. Joan," "The Biko Inquest," "Man and Superman," "Whose Life Is It Anyway," "Major Barbara," "A Month in the Country," "Bacchae," "Hedda Gabler," "Don Juan in Hell," "Inadmissible Evidence.", "Eminent Domain.", "Misalliance."

BOTTOMS, JOSEPH. Born in 1954 in Santa Barbara, Ca. Bdwy debut 1981 in "5th of July."

BOTTOMS, TIMOTHY. Born Aug. 30, 1951 in Santa Barbara, Ca. Bdwy debut 1981 in "5th of July."

BOUCHER, GLORIA. Born Dec. 17, 1954 in Muskegon, Mi. Attended AADA, AMDA. Debut OB 1982 in "Street Scene."

BOUDREAU, ROBIN. Born Nov. 7, in Pittsburgh, PA. Graduate NYU. Bdwy debut 1981 in "Pirates of Penzance."

BOULE, KATHRYN. Born Dec. 27 in Washington, DC. Graduate UMd Debut 1977 OB in "Fiorello!," followed by "Ten Little Indians," Bdwy 1980 in "Annie."

BOULEY, FRANK. Born May 6, 1928 in Spokane, Wa. Attended UWash, AmThWing. Bdwy debut 1954 in "Peter Pan," followed by "Damn Yankees," "Camelot," "Cabaret," "The Yearling," "Hot Spot," "Mr. President," "Carmelina," "Mack and Mabel," "Baker Street," "Lolita," "Passion of Josef D.," "My Fair Lady," OB 1977 in "The Fantasticks."

BOURNEUF, STEPHEN. Born Nov. 24, 1957 in St. Louis, Mo. Graduate St. Louis U. Bdwy debut 1981 in "Broadway Follies," followed by "Oh, Brother!"

BOUTSIKARIS, DENNIS. Born Dec. 21, 1952 in Newark, NJ. Graduate Hampshire Col. Debut 1975 OB in "Another Language," followed by "Funeral March for a One-Man Band," "All's Well That Ends Well," "A Day in the Life of the Czar," Bdwy in "Filumena," "Bent.", "Amadeus."

BOVA, JOSEPH. Born May 25 in Cleveland, OH. Graduate Northwestern U. Debut 1959 OB in "On the Town," followed by "Once upon a Mattress," "House of Blue Leaves," "Comedy," "The Beauty Part," "Taming of the Shrew," "Richard III," "Comedy of Errors," "Invitation to a Beheading," "Merry Wives of Windsor," "Henry V," "Streamers," Bdwy in "Rape of the Belt," "Irma La Douce," "Hot Spot," "The Chinese," "American Millionaire," "St. Joan," "42nd Street."

BOVASSO, JULIE. Born Aug. 1, 1930 in Brooklyn, NY. Attended CCNY. Bdwy in "Monique," "Minor Miracle," "Gloria and Esperanza," OB in "Naked," "The Maids," "The Lesson," "The Typewriter," "Screens," "Henry IV Part I."

BOWERS, JEANIE. Born Apr. 18, 1953 in Greenville, Oh. Graduate IndU., Miami U. Bdwy debut 1982 in "Nine."

BOWMAN, REGIS. Born Aug. 22, 1935 in Butler, Pa. Graduate WVaU. Debut 1980 OB in "Room Service," followed by "T.N.T."

BOYD, TOM. Born Oct. 1 in Hamilton, Ont., Can. Bdwy debut 1962 in "How to Succeed in Business. . . .," followed by "Walking Happy," "Irene," "Sugar Babies."

BOYDEN, PETER. Born July 19, 1945 in Leominster, Ma. Graduate St. Anselm Col., Smith Col. Debut OB in "One Flew over the Cuckoo's Nest," followed by "Nice Girls," "Claw," "Berkeley Square," "Pericles," "Pig!," "Smart Alek," "Booth," Bdwy in "Whoopee!" (1979.)

BOYLE, ROBERT. Born Mar. 28, 1950 in Patton, PA. Graduate Carnegie-Mellon U. Debut 1980 OB in "Merton of the Movies" followed by "Pericles," "King of Hearts," "What a Life!"

BOYLE, VIKI. Born May 3, 1952 in Ellwood City, Pa. Graduate WVaU. Debut 1982 OB in "Two".

BOYS, KENNETH. Born June 19, 1960 in Seaford, De. Attended UDel. Debut OB 1976 in "Apple Pie," followed by "The Madman and the Nun," "T.N.T."

BOZYK, REIZL (ROSE). Born May 13, 1914 in Poland. Star of many Yiddish productions before 1966 Bdwy debut in "Let's Sing Yiddish," followed by "Sing, Israel, Sing," "Mirele Efros," OB in "Light, Lively and Yiddish," "Rebecca, the Rabbi's Daughter," "Wish Me Mazel-Tov.", "Roumanian Wedding."

BRACKEN, EDDIE. Born Feb. 7, 1920 in Astoria, NY. Bdwy bow 1931 in "The Man on Stilts," followed by "The Lady Refuses," "Life's Too Short," "Iron Men," "Brother Ray," "What a Life!," "Too Many Girls," "Seven Year Itch," "Teahouse of the August Moon," "Shinbone Alley," "Beg, Borrow or Steal," "The Odd Couple," "You Know I Can't Hear You . . .," "Hello, Dolly!" (1978), "Damn Yankees" (JB).

BRAMI, JAK. Born Oct. 2, 1943 in The Bronx, NY. Attended UBridgeport. Debut 1982 OB in "Street Scene."

BRAND, GIBBEY. Born May 20, 1946 in NYC. Ithaca Col. graduate. Debut 1977 OB in "The Castaways," followed by "The Music Man" (JB), "Real Life Funnies.", Bdwy in "Little Me" (1981.)

BRANDON, PETER. Born July 11, 1926 in Berlin, GER. Attended Neighborhood Playhouse. Bdwy debut 1950 in "Cry of the Peacock," followed by "Come of Age," "Tovarich," "Ondine," "The Young and the Beautiful," "Hidden River," "Infernal Machine," "A Man for All Seasons," "The Investigation," "An Evening with the Poet-Senator" (OB), "Medea."

BRASINGTON, ALAN. Born in Monticello, NY. Attended RADA. Bdwy debut 1968 in "Pantagleize," followed by "The Misanthrope," "Cock-a-Doodle Dandy," "Hamlet," "Patriot for Me," "Shakespeare's Cabaret," OB in "Sterling Silver," "Charlotte Sweet.

BRENNAN, MAUREEN. Born Oct. 11, 1952 in Washington, DC. Attended UCin. Bdwy debut 1974 in "Candide" for which she received a Theatre World Award, followed by "Going Up," "Knickerbocker Holiday," "Little Johnny Jones," OB in "Shakespeare's Cabaret."

BRENNAN, MIKE. Born Feb. 4, 1948 in NYC. Fordham U. Graduate. Debut 1973 OB in "Arms and the Man," followed by "Gay Divorce," "Blues for Mr. Charlie," "Scenes from La Vie de Boheme," "Italian Straw Hat."

BRENNAN, TOM. Born Apr. 16, 1926 in Cleveland, OH. Graduate Oberlin, Western Reserve. Debut 1958 OB in "Synge Trilogy," followed by "Between Two Thieves," "Easter," "All in Love," "Under Milkwood," "An Evening with James Purdy," "Golden Six," "Pullman Car Hiawatha," "Are You Now or Have You . . .," "Diary of Anne Frank," "Milk of Paradise," "Trancendental Love," "The Beaver Coat," "The Overcoat."

BRIDGES, RAND. Born Jan. 10 in Chicago, Il. Attended Pfeiffer Col., Trinity U. Bdwy debut 1979 in "Dracula," followed by "Major Barbara," "Macbeth" (1982), OB in "Misalliance."

BRILL, FRAN. Born Sept. 30, in PA. Attended Boston U. Bdwy debut 1969 in "Red, White and Maddox," OB in "What Every Woman Knows," "Scribes," "Naked," "Look Back in Anger," "Knuckle," "Routed."

BRODERICK, DIANA. Born July 15 in NYC. Attended NYU. Bdwy debut 1979 in "The Best Little Whorehouse in Texas."

BRODERICK, MATTHEW. Born in 1963 in NYC. Debut OB 1981 in "Torch Song Trilogy."

BROGGER, IVAR. Born Jan. 10, 1947 in St. Paul, MN. Graduate UMn. Debut 1979 OB in "In the Jungle of Cities," followed by "Collected Works of Billy the Kid." "Magic Time," "Cloud 9," Bdwy 1981 in "Macbeth."

BROMKA, ELAINE. Born Jan. 6 in Rochester, NY. Smith Col. graduate. Debut 1975 OB in "The Dybbuk," followed by "Naked," "Museum," "The Son," "Inadmissible Evidence," Bdwy 1982 in "Macbeth."

BROOKES, JACQUELINE. Born July 24, 1930 in Montclair, NJ. Graduate UIowa, RADA. Bdwy debut 1955 in "Tiger at the Gates," followed by "Watercolor," "Abelard and Heloise," OB in "The Cretan Woman" for which she received a Theatre World Award, "The Clandestine Marriage," "Measure for Measure," "Duchess of Malfi," "Ivanov," "Six Characters in Search of an Author," "An Evening's Frost," "Come Slowly, Eden," "The Increased Difficulty of Concentration," "The Persians," "Sunday Dinner," "House of Blue Leaves," "A Meeting by the River," "Owners," "Hallelujah," "Dream of a Blacklisted Actor," "Knuckle," "Mama Sang the Blues," "Buried Child," "On Mt. Chimorazo," "Winter Dancers," "Hamlet," "Old Flames," "The Diviners," "Richard II."

BROOKS, JEFF. Born Apr. 7, 1950 in Vancouver, Can. Attended Portland State U. Debut 1976 OB in "Titanic," followed by "Fat Chances," "The Nature and Purpose of the Universe," "Actor's Nightmare," "Sister Mary Ignatius Explains It All," Bdwy (1978) in "A History of the American Film."

BROWN, KERMIT. Born Feb. 3, 1937 in Asheville, NC. Graduate Duke U. With APA in "War and Peace," "Judith," "Man and Superman," "The Show-Off," "Pantagleize," "The Cherry Orchard," OB in "The Millionairess," "Things," "Lulu," "Heartbreak House," "Glad Tidings," "Anyone Can Whistle," "Facade," "The Arcata Promise."

BROWNE, ROSCOE LEE. Born in 1925 in Woodbury, NJ. Attended Lincoln U, Columbia; Debut OB in "Julius Caesar," followed by "Taming of the Shrew," "Titus Andronicus," "Romeo and Juliet," "Othello," "Aria da Capo," "The Blacks," "Brecht on Brecht," "King Lear," "Winter's Tale," "The Empty Room," "Hell Is Other People," "Benito Cereno," "Troilus and Cressida," "Danton's Death," "Volpone," "Dream on Monkey Mountain," "Behind the Broken Words," Bdwy in "General Seeger" (1962), "Tiger, Tiger Burning Bright," "Ballad of the Sad Cafe," "A Hand Is on the Gate."

BRUCE, SHELLEY. Born May 5, 1965 in Passaic, NJ. Debut OB 1975 in "The Children's Mass," Bdwy 1977 in "Annie."

BRUMMEL, DAVID. Born Nov. 1, 1942 in Brooklyn, NY. Bdwy debut 1973 in "The Pajama Game," followed by "Music Is," "Oklahoma!," OB in "Cole Porter," "The Fantasticks."

BRUNEAU, RALPH. Born Sept. 22, 1952 in Phoenix, AZ. Graduate UNotre Dame. Debut 1974 OB in "The Fantasticks," followed by "Saints," "Suddenly the Music Starts," "On a Clear Day You Can See Forever," "King of the Schnorrers," "The Buddy System," "Chantecler."

BRUNNER, HOWARD. Born Aug. 20, 1940 in Atlanta, GA. Attended Pasadena Playhouse, Actors Inst. Bdwy debut 1980 in "Children of a Lesser God."

BRUNO, JEAN. Born Dec. 7, 1926 in Brooklyn, NY. Attended Hofstra Col. Bdwy debut 1960 in "Beg, Borrow or Steal," followed by "Midgie Purvis," "Music Man," "Family Affair," "Minnie's Boys," "The Lincoln Mask," "Lorelei," OB in "All That Fall," "Hector," "Hotel Paradiso," "Pidgeons in the Park" "Ergo," "Trelawny of the Wells," "Song for the First of May," "The Hairy Ape."

BRYAN, KENNETH. Born July 30, 1953 in New Jersey. Graduate IndU. Bdwy debut 1981 in "Joseph and the Amazing Technicolor Dreamcoat."

BRYANT, DAVID. Born May 26, 1936 in Nashville, TN. Attended TnStateU. Bdwy debut 1972 in "Don't Play Us Cheap," followed by "Bubbling Brown Sugar," "Amadeus."

BRYGGMAN, LARRY. Born Dec. 21, 1938 in Concord, Ca. Attended CCSF, AmThWing. Debut 1962 OB in "A Pair of Pairs" followed by "Live Like Pigs," "Stop, You're Killing Me," "Mod Donna," "Waiting for Godot," "Ballymurphy," "Marco Polo Sings a Solo," "Brownsville, Raid," "Two Small Bodies," "Museum," "Winter Dancers," "The Resurrection of Lady Lester," Bdwy in "Ulysses in Nighttown," "Checking Out," "Basic Training of Pavlo Hummel," "Richard III."

BRYNE, BARBARA. Born in London, Eng. Attended RADA. NY Debut OB 1981 in "Entertaining Mr. Sloane."

BUELL, BILL. Born Sept. 21, 1952 in Paipai, Taiwan. Attended Portland State. Debut 1972 OB in "Crazy Now," followed by "Declassee," Bdwy (1979) in "Once a Catholic," "The First.

BUFFALOE, KATHARINE. Born Nov. 7, 1953 in Greenville, SC. Graduate NC School of Arts. Bdwy debut 1981 in "Copperfield," followed by "Joseph and the Amazing Technicolor Dreamcoat."

BUKA, DONALD. Born Dec. 18, 1921 in Cleveland, Oh. Attended Carnegie Tech. Has appeared in "Twelfth Night," "The Corn Is Green," "Bright Boy," "Helen Goes to Troy," "Sophie," "Live Life Again," "Those That Play the Clowns," "Major Barbara," OB in "Heritage," "In the Matter of J. Robert Oppenheimer."

BULOFF, JOSEPH. Born Dec. 6, 1907 in Wilno, Lith. Bdwy debut 1936 in "Don't Look Now," followed by "Call Me Ziggy," "To Quito and Back," "The Man from Cairo," "Morning Star," "Spring Again," "My Sister Eileen," "Oklahoma!," "The Whole World Over," "Once More with Feeling," "Fifth Season," "Moonbirds," "The Wall," OB in "Yoshkie Musikant," "The Price," "Chekhov Sketchbook," "The Price."

BURCH, SHELLY. Born Mar. 19, 1960 in Tucson, AZ. Attended Carnegie-Mellon U. Bdwy debut 1978 in "Stop the World I Want to Get Off," followed by "Annie," "Nine."

BURGE, GREGG. Born 1959 in NYC. Graduate Juilliard. Bdwy debut 1975 in "The Wiz," followed by "Sophisticated Ladies."

BURKE, ROBERT. Born July 25, 1948 in Portland, ME. Graduate Boston Col. Debut 1975 OB in "Prof. George," followed by "Shortchanged Review," "The Arbor," "Slab Boys," "Gardenia."

BURKHARDT, GERRY. Born June 14, 1946 in Houston, TX. Attended Lon Morris Col. Bdwy debut 1968 in "Her First Roman," followed by "The Best Little Whorehouse in Texas."

BURKHART, JENIFER. Born Feb. 1, 1957 in Baltimore, Md. Graduate Towson State U. Debut 1982 OB in "Street Scene."

BURR, ROBERT. Born in Jersey City, NJ. Attended Colgate U. Has appeared in "The Cradle Will Rock," "Mr. Roberts," "Romeo and Juliet," "Picnic," "The Lovers," "Anniversary Waltz," "Top Man," "Remains to Be Seen," "The Wall," "Andersonville Trial," "A Shot in the Dark," "Man for All Seasons," "Luther," "Hamlet," "Bajour," "White Devil," "Royal Hunt of the Sun," "Dinner at 8," "King John," "Henry VI," "Love-Suicide at Schofield Barracks," "Wild and Wonderful," "Look Back in Anger" (OB), "The Philadelphia Story," "Othello."

BURSKY, JAY. Born Mar. 27, 1954 in Cleveland, OH. Graduate Indiana U. OB and Bdwy debut 1978 in "The Best Little Whorehouse in Texas."

BURSTYN, MIKE. (Formerly Burstein) Born July 1, 1945 in The Bronx, NY. Bdwy debut 1968 in "The Megilla of Itzik Manger," followed by "Inquest," "Wedding in Shtetl" (OB), "Barnum."

BUSSERT, MEG. Born Oct. 21, 1949 in Chicago, IL. Attended UIll, HB Studio Bdwy debut 1980 in "The Music Man" for which she received a Theatre World Award, followed by "Brigadoon," "Camelot," "New Moon," "Lola" (OB)

BUTLER, BRUCE. Born March 11, 1954 in Clanton, NC. Graduate NC Central U. Debut 1982 OB in "Street Scene."

BUTTRAM, JAN. Born June 19, 1946 in Clarkesville, TX. Graduate NTex-State. Debut 1974 OB in "Fashion," followed by "Startup," Bdwy 1978 in "The Best Little Whorehouse in Texas."

BYERS, CATHERINE. Born Oct. 7 in Sioux City, IA. Graduate UIa, LAMDA. Bdwy debut 1971 in "The Philanthropist," followed by "Don't Call Back," "Equus," OB in "Petrified Forest," "All My Sons," "Murder in the Cathedral," "Grace," "The Fuehrer Bunker."

BYRNE, MARTHA. Born Dec. 23, 1969 in Ridgewood, NJ. Bdwy debut 1980 in "Annie."

BYRON, JOHN. Born Jan. 5, 1920 in St. Paul, Mn. Debut 1973 OB in "Venus Observed," followed by "The Hostage," "Leave It to Jane," "Put Them Out to Pasture," "Oh, Dad, Poor Dad . . ."

CADY, DAVID. Born Nov. 21, 1960 in NYC. Attended NYU. Debut 1979 OB in "The City Suite," Bdwy 1981 in "Merrily We Roll Along."

CAHILL, JAMES. Born May 31, 1940 in Brooklyn, NY. Bdwy debut 1967 in "Marat/-deSade," followed by "Break a Leg," OB in "The Hostage," "The Alchemist," "Johnny Johnson," "Peer Gynt," "Timon of Athens," "An Evening for Merlin Finch," "The Disintegration of James Cherry," "Crimes of Passion," "Rain," "Screens," "Total Eclipse," "Entertaining Mr. Sloane," "Hamlet," "Othello," "The Trouble with Europe," "Lydie Breeze," "Don Juan."

CAHN, LARRY. Born Dec. 19, 1955 in Nassau, NY. Graduate Northwestern U. Bdwy debut 1980 in "The Music Man," OB in "Susan B!"

CALDER, JEFFREY. Born Oct. 30, 1952 in Sutton, Ne. Graduate NeWesleyanU, UNColo. Bdwy debut 1981 in "My Fair Lady."

CALDWELL, ZOE. Born Sept. 14, 1933 in Melbourne, Aust. Attended Methodist Ladies Col. Bdwy debut 1965 in "The Devils," followed by "Slapstick Tragedy" for which she received a Theatre World Award, "The Prime of Miss Jean Brodie," "The Creation of the World and Other Business," "Medea" (1982), OB in "Colette," "Dance of Death," "Long Day's Journey into Night."

CALEB, JOHN. Born July 8, 1959 in Mexico City, Mx. Bdwy debut 1981 in "My Fair Lady."

CAMERON, HOPE. Born Feb. 21, 1920 in Hartford, Ct. Attended AADA. Bdwy debut 1947 in "All My Sons," followed by "Death of a Salesman," OB in "The Strindberg Brothers," "The Last Days of Lincoln," "Grace."

CAMERON, NANCY. Born March 26, 1949 in Hartford, Ct. Attended Central State Col., Hartford Cons. Debut 1982 in ELT's "Street Scene."

CAMP, JOANNE. Born Apr. 4, 1951 in Atlanta, Ga. Graduate FlaAtlanticU, GeoWashU. Debut 1981 OB in "The Dry Martini," followed by "Geniuses."

CAMPBELL, MARILYN. Born March 16, 1948 in Seattle, Wa. Attended MichStateU, EMichU. Debut 1981 OB in "My Own Stranger."

CAMPBELL, PETER. Born July 9, 1952 in New Jersey. Attended CalInstofArts, Webber Douglas Academy. Debut 1981 OB in "Split."

CANNON, ALICE. Born June 25 in Rochester, NY. Graduate Cornell U. Debut 1962 OB in "The Fantasticks," followed by "Silent Night Lonely Night," "By Bernstein," "Man with a Load of Mischief," "All in Love," "Sufragette," Bdwy in "Fiddler on the Roof" (1965), "Johnny Johnson," "Education of Hyman Kaplan," "Company."

CARBERRY, JOSEPH. Born May 5, 1948 in NYC. Attended Lawrence U., Brandeis U. Debut 1974 OB in "Short Eyes," followed by "Leaving Home," "Nesting," "Gloves."

CAREY, DAVID. Born Nov. 16, 1945 in Brookline, MA. Graduate Boston U, Ohio U. Debut 1969 OB in "Oh, what a Wedding," followed by "Let's Sing Yiddish," "Dad Get Married," "Light, Lively and Yiddish," "Wedding in Shtetl," "Big Winna," "Rebecca, the Rabbi's Daughter," "Wish Me Mazel-Tov," "Roumanian Wedding."

CARIOU, LEN. Born Sept. 30, 1939 in Winnipeg, Can. Bdwy debut 1968 in "House of Atreus," followed by "Henry V" and "Applause" for which he received a Theatre World Award, "Night Watch," "A Little Night Music," "Cold Storage," "Sweeney Todd," OB in "A Sorrow Beyond Dreams," "Up from Paradise."

CARLE, CYNTHIA. Born March 4, 1951 in Hollywood, Ca. Graduate Carnegie-Mellon U. Bdwy debut 1978 in "The Crucifer of Blood," followed by "Piaf," "Is There Life after High School?"

CARLIN, THOMAS A. Born Dec. 10, 1928 in Chicago, IL. Attended Loyola U. Catholic U. Credits include "Time Limit!," "Holiday for Lovers," "Man in the Dog Suit," "A Cook for Mr. General," "Great Day in the Morning," "A Thousand Clowns," "The Deputy," "Players," OB in "Thieves Carnival" "Brecht on Brecht," "Summer," "Wonderland," "Solitude 40."

CARPENTER, CARLETON. Born July 10, 1926 in Bennington, VT. Attended Northwestern U. Bdwy bow 1944 in "Bright Boy," followed by "Career Angel," "Three to Make Ready," "Magic Touch," "John Murray Anderson's Almanac," "Hotel Paradiso," "Box of Watercolors," "Hello Dolly!," OB in "Stage Affair," "Boys in the Band," "Dylan," "Greatest Fairy Story Ever Told," "Good Old Fashioned Revue," "Miss Stanwyck Is Still in Hiding," "Rocky Road," "Something for the Boys."

CARR, CATHERINE. Born May 25, 1956 in Ironton, MO. Graduate Oberlin Col., NYU. Bdwy debut 1980 in "Barnum."

CARROLL, DANNY. Born May 30, 1940 in Maspeth, NY. Bdwy bow in 1957 in "The Music Man," followed by "Flora the Red Menace," "Funny Girl," "George M!," "Billy," "Ballroom," "42nd Street," OB in "Boys from Syracuse," "Babes in the Woods."

CARROLL, DAVID-JAMES. Born July 30, 1950 in Rockville, Centre, NY. Graduate Dartmouth Col. Debut 1975 OB in "A Matter of Time," followed by "Joseph and the Amazing Technicolor Dreamcoat," Bdwy in "Rodgers and Hart" (1975), "Where's Charley?", "Oh, Brother!"

CARROLL, JOHN K. Born in NYC; graduate Boston Col. Bdwy debut 1978 in "Man and Superman," followed by "A Taste of Honey."

CARRUBBA, PHILIP. Born May 3, 1951 in San Francisco, Ca. Graduate SFStateU. Bdwy debut 1981 in "Joseph and the Amazing Technicolor Dreamcoat."

CARSON, THOMAS LEE. Born May 27, 1939 in Iowa City, 10. Graduate UIo. Debut 1981 OB in "The Feuhrer Bunker," followed by "The Broken Pitcher."

CARTER, ROSANNA. Born Sept. 20 in Rolle Town, Bahamas. Attended NEC Workshop. OB in "Lament of Rasta Fari," "Burghers of Callais," "Scottsboro Boys," "Les Femmes Noires," "Killings on the Last Line," Bdwy 1980 in "The American Clock" followed by "Inacent Black," "Who Loves the Dancer."

CARUSO, BARBARA. Born in East Orange. NJ. Graduate Douglass Col., RADA. Debut 1969 OB in "The Millionairess," followed by "Picture of Dorian Gray," "Wars of the Roses," "Chez Nous," "Ride a Cock Horse," "Inadmissible Evidence," "Ned and Jack," Bdwy in "Night of the Iguana (1976)."

CARVER, MARY. Born May 3, 1924 in Los Angeles, CA. Graduate USC. Debut 1950 OB in "Bury the Dead," followed by "Rhinoceros," "Life of Galileo," Bdwy in "Out West of 8th," "Low and Behold," "The Shadow Box," "5th of July."

CARYL, JEANNE. (formerly Caryl Tenney and Carol Jeanne) Born July 11 In Thatcher, AZ. Bdwy debut 1968 in "I'm Solomon," followed by "Two by Two," "Desert Song," "Carmelina," "Snow White," "Camelot" ('80).

CASHIN, TOM. Born Oct. 9, 1953 in Brooklyn, NY. Attended Hunter Col. Bdwy debut 1978 in "The Best Little Whorehouse in Texas."

CASS, PEGGY. Born May 21, 1926 in Boston, Ma. Attended Wyndham Sch. Credits include "Touch and Go," "Live Wire," "Bernardine," "Othello," "Henry V," "Auntie Mame" for which she received a Theatre World Award, "A Thurber Carnival," "Children from Their Games," "Don't Drink the Water," "Front Page" (1969), "Plaza Suite," "Once a Catholic," "42nd Street," OB in "Phoenix '55," "Are You Now or Have You Ever Been."

CASSIDY, PATRICK. Born Jan. 4, 1961 in Los Angeles, Ca. Bdwy debut 1982 in "Pirates of Penzance."

CASSIDY, TIM. Born March 22, 1952 in Alliance, OH. Attended UCincinnati. Bdwy debut 1974 in "Good News," followed by "A Chorus Line."

CASTANG, VERONICA. Born Apr. 22 in London, Eng. Attended Sorbonne. Bdwy debut 1946 in "How's the World Treating You?," followed by "The National Health," "Whose Life Is It Anyway?," OB in "The Trigon," "Sjt. Musgrave's Dance," "Saved," "Water Hens," "Self-Accusation," "Kaspar," "Ionescapade," "Statements after and Arrest under the Immorality Act," "Ride a Cock Horse," "Banana Box," "Bonjour La Bonjour," "A Call from the East," "Close of Play," "Cloud 9," "After the Prize."

CASTANOS, LUZ. Born July 15, 1935 in NYC. Graduate CUNY. Debut OB 1959 in "Last Visit," followed by "Eternal Sabbath," "Finis for Oscar Wilde," "Young and Fair," "La Dama Duende," "A Media Luz Los Tres," "Yerma."

CAULFIELD, MAXWELL. Born Nov. 23, 1959 in Glasgow, Scot. Debut OB 1979 in "Class Enemy" for which he received a Theatre World Award, followed by "Crimes and Dreams," "Entertaining Mr. Sloane."

CHAIKIN, SHAMI. Born Apr. 21, 1931 in NYC. Debut 1966 OB in "America Hurrah," followed by "Serpent," "Terminal," "Mutation Show," "Viet Rock," "Mystery Play," "Electra," "The Dybbuk," "Endgame," "Bag Lady," "The Haggadah," "Antigone."

CHALFANT, KATHLEEN. Born Jan. 14, 1945 in San Francisco, CA. Graduate Stanford U: Bdwy debut 1975 in "Dance with Me," followed by OB "Jules Feiffer's Hold Me," "Killings on the Last Line," "The Boor."

CHAMPAGNE, MICHAEL. Born Apr. 10, 1947 in New Bedford, MA. Graduate SMU, MSU. Debut 1975 OB in "The Lieutenant," followed by "Alinsky," "The Hostage," "Livingstone and Sechele."

CHANDLER, JEFFREY ALAN. Born Sept. 9 in Durham, NC. Graduate Carnegie-Mellon. Bdwy debut 1972 in "Elizabeth I," followed by "The Dresser," OB in "The People vs Ranchman," "Your Own Thing," "Penguin Touquet."

CHAPIN, MILES. Born Dec. 6, 1954 in NYC. Attended HB Studio. Debut 1974 OB in "Joan of Lorraine," followed by "Two Rooms," "Poor Little Lambs," Bdwy 1975 in "Summer Brave."

CHAPMAN, GARY. Born Apr. 20, 1953 in Brooklyn, NY. Attended CalifInstof Arts. Bdwy debut 1979 in "Dancin'," followed by "Sophisticated Ladies."

CHAPMAN, ROGER. Born Jan. 1, 1947 in Cheverly, Md. Rollins Col. graduate. Debut 1976 OB in "Who Killed Richard Corey?," followed by "My Life," "Hamlet," "Innocent Thoughts, Harmless Intentions," "Richard II," "The Great Grandson of Jedediah Kohler," "Threads."

CHARNEY, DEBORAH. (aka Didi) Born Aug. 1, 1951 in NYC. Graduate Carleton Col. Debut 1976 OB in "Heartbreak House," followed by "Twelfth Night," "My Life," "Romeo and Juliet," "The Chronicle of Jane," "Lysistrata."

CHARNEY, EVA. Born June 7 in Brooklyn, NY. Graduate Douglass Coll., Boston U. Debut 1977 OB in "NYC Street Show," followed by "The Wanderers," "Caligula," "I Can't Keep Running . . .," "Battle of the Giants," "American Heroes," Bdwy 1977 in "Hair."

CHEN, TINA. Born Nov. 2 in Chung King, China. Graduate Brown U. Debut 1972 OB in "A Maid's Tragedy," followed by "Family Devotions," Bdwy in "The King and I," "Rashomon."

CHER (nee Cherilyn Sarkisian) Born May 20, 1946 in El Centro, Ca. Bdwy debut 1982 in "Come Back to the 5 & Dime, Jimmy Dean."

CHIANESE, DOMINIC. Born Feb. 24, 1932 in NYC. Graduate Brooklyn Col. Debut 1952 OB with American Savoyards, followed by "Winterset," "Jacques Brel Is Alive . . .," "Ballad for a Firing Squad," "City Scene," "End of the War," "Passione," "Midsummer Night's Dream," "Recruiting Officer," "The Wild Duck," "Oedipus the King," "Hunting Scenes," "Operation Midnight Climax," "Rosario and the Gypsies," "Bella Figura," Bdwy in "Oliver," "Scratch," "The Water Engine," "Richard III."

CHOATE, TIM. Born Oct. 11, 1954 in Dallas Tx. Graduate UTx. Bdwy debut 1979 in 'Da,' followed by "Crimes of the Heart," OB in "Young Bucks."

CHRIS, MARILYN. Born May 19 in NYC. Appeared in "The Office," "Birthday Party," "7 Descents of Myrtle," "Lenny," OB in "Nobody Hears a Broken Drum," "Fame," "Juda Applause," "Junebug Graduates Tonight," "Man Is Man," "In the Jungle of Cities," "Good Soldier Schweik," "The Tempest," "Ride a Black Horse," "Screens," "Kaddish," "Lady from the Sea," "Bread," "Leaving Home," "Curtains," "Elephants."

CHRISTOPHERSON, INDIRA STEFANIANNE. Born Dec. 6 in San Francisco, CA. Attended San Francisco State Col/San Mateo. Debut 1979 OB in "The Umbrellas of Cherbourg," followed by "Harry Ruby's Songs My Mother Never Sang."

CIBELLI, RENATO. Born Sept. 28, 1915 in The Bronx, NY. Attended RADA. Bdwy debut 1956 in "Happy Hunting," followed by "Milk and Honey," "Happiest Girl in the World," "Man of La Mancha" (original and 1977), "Macbeth."

CITERA, TOMMY. Born Jan. 8, 1964 in Brooklyn, NY. Debut 1981 OB in "Forty-Deuce."

CLAIRE, LUDI. Born Apr. 15 in Indiana. Attended Ecole Intl. Appeared in "The Small Hours," "Gramercy Ghost," "Tower Beyond Tragedy," "Venus Observed," "Someone Waiting," "Legend of Lovers," "Silk Stockings," "First Gentleman," "Country Wife," "Duel of Angels," "Hamlet," "Prisoner of Second Avenue," "West Side Waltz."

CLARK, CHERYL. Born Dec. 7, 1950 in Boston, MA. Attended Ind. U., NYU. Bdwy debut 1972 in "Pippin," followed by "Chicago," "A Chorus Line."

CLARK, JOSH. Born Aug. 16, 1955 in Bethesda, MD. Attended NCSch. of Arts. Debut 1976 OB in "The Old Glory," followed by "Molly," "Just a Little Bit Less Than Normal," "Rear Column," "The Browning Version," Bdwy in "The Man Who Came to Dinner" (1980).

CLARK, PHILLIP. Born Aug. 12, 1941 in San Diego, CA. Attended USCal. Bdwy debut 1966 in "We Have Always Lived in the Castle," followed by "5th of July," OB in "The Boys in the Band."

CLARKE, CAITLIN. Born May 3, 1952 in Pittsburgh, Pa. Graduate Mt. Holyoke Col., Yale. Debut 1981 OB in "No End of Blame."

CLEMENT, MARIS. Born July 11, 1950 in Philadelphia, PA. Graduate Rollins Col. Debut 1976 OB in "Noel and Cole," Bdwy in "On the 20th Century," "Copperfield," "Little Me."

CLEMENTE, RENE. Born July 2, 1950 in El Paso, TX. Graduate WestTxStateU. Bdwy debut 1977 in "A Chorus Line."

CLOSE, GLENN. Born Mar. 19, 1947 in Greenwich, CT. Graduate William & Mary Col. Bdwy debut 1974 with Phoenix Co. in "Love for Love," "Member of the Wedding," and "Rules of the Game," followed by "Rex," "Crucifer of Blood," "Barnum," OB in "The Crazy Locomotive," "Uncommon Women and Others," "Wine Untouched," "The Winter Dancers."

COCO, JAMES. Born Mar. 21, 1930 in NYC. Debut 1956 OB in "Salome," followed by "Moon in the Yellow River," "Squat Betty/The Sponge Room," "That 5 A.M. Jazz," "Lovey," "The Basement," "Fragments," "Witness," "Next," "Monsters (The Transfiguration of Benno Blimpie)," Bdwy in "Hotel Paradiso," "Everybody Loves Opal," "Passage to India," "Arturo Ui," "The Devils," "Man of LaMancha," "The Astrakan Coat," "Here's Where I Belong," "Last of the Red Hot Lovers," "Wally's Cafe," "Little Me."

COFFIELD, PETER. Born July 17, 1945 in Evanston, IL. Graduate Northwestern, U.Mich. Bdwy in "The Misanthrope," "Cock-a-Doodle Dandy," "Hamlet," "Abelard and Heloise," "Vivat! Vivat Regina!," "Merchant of Venice," "Tartuffe," "The Man Who Came to Dinner," OB in "Misalliance."

COFFIN, FREDERICK. Born Jan. 16, 1943 in Detroit, Mi. Graduate UMich. Debut 1971 OB in "Basic Training of Pavlo Hummel," followed by "Much Ado About Nothing," "King Lear," "As You Like It," "Boom Boom Room," "Merry Wives of Windsor," "Secret Service," "Boy Meets Girl," "Hot Grog," "God Bless You, Mr. Rosewater," "Children of Darkness," Bdwy 1975 in "We Interrupt This Program."

COHEN, ANDREA. Born June 24, 1958 in St. Louis, Mo. Attended Ntl. Academy of Arts. Debut 1981 OB in "Anything Goes."

COHEN, LYNN. Born Aug. 10 in Kansas City, MO. Graduate NorthwesternU. Debut 1979 OB in "Don Juan Comes Back from the Wars," followed by "Getting Out," "The Arbor," "The Cat and the Canary," "Suddenly Last Summer," "Chinese Viewing Pavilion."

COLBERT, CLAUDETTE. Born Sept. 13, 1903 in Paris. Bdwy debut 1925 in "Wild Westcotts," followed by "Ghost Train," "Kiss in a Taxi," "The Barker," "Mulberry Bush," "LaGringa," "Tin Pan Alley," "Dynamo," "See Naples and Die," "Janus," "The Marriage-Go-Round," "Jake, Julia and Uncle Joe," "Irregular Verb to Love," "The Kingfisher," "A Talent for Murder."

COLBY, CHRISTINE. Born Feb. 27 in Cincinnati, OH. Attended UCincinnati. Bdwy debut 1978 in "Dancin'."

COLE, KAY. Born Jan. 13, 1948 in Miami, FL. Bdwy debut 1961 in "Bye Bye Birdie," followed by "Stop the World I Want to Get Off," "Roar of the Greasepaint . . .," "Hair," "Jesus Christ Superstar," "Words and Music," "Chorus Line," OB in "The Cradle Will Rock," "Two If By Sea," "Rainbow," "White Nights," "Sgt. Pepper's Lonely Hearts Club Band."

COLES, ZAIDA. Born Sept. 10, 1933 in Lynchburg, Va. Credits include OB's "The Father," "Pins and Needles," "Life and Times of J. Walter Smintheus," "The Cherry Orchard," "Bayou Legend," "Divine Comedy," "Second Thoughts," "Keyboard," Bdwy in "Weekend," "Zelda."

COLITTI, RIK. Born Feb. 1, 1934 in NYC. Graduate USCal. Debut 1961 OB in "Montserrat," followed by "One Flew over the Cuckoo's Nest," "Gandhi," "The Queen and the Rebels," "Threepenny Opera," Bdwy in "The Ritz," "Macbeth" (1982).

COLL, IVONNE. Born Nov. 4, in Fajardo, PR. Attended UPR, LACC, HB Studio. Debut 1980 OB in "Spain 1980," followed by "Animals," "Wonderful Ice Cream Suit," Bdwy 1980 in "Goodbye Fidel."

COLLAMORE, JEROME. Born Sept. 25, 1891 in Boston, MA. Debut 1918 with Washington Square Players in "Salome," and subsequently in, among others, "Christopher Bean," "Hamlet," "Romeo and Juliet," "Kind Lady," "Androcles and the Lion," "George Washington Slept Here," "The Would-Be Gentleman," "Cheri," "Abraham Cochran," "That Hat," Bam Co.'s "New York Idea," "Trouping Since 1912," "The Dresser."

COLLINGS, LEE. Born Oct. 30, 1935 in Kingsbury, In. Attended Goodman Theatre. Debut 1982 OB in "Six O'Clock Boys."

COLLINS, BILL. Born Mar. 27, 1935 in Santa Monica, Ca. UCLA graduate. Debut 1961 OB in "King of the Dark Chamber," followed by "Lost in the Stars," "Days of the Dancing," "Tenth Man," "School for Wives," Bdwy in "The Desert Song" (1973).

COLLINS, JOHNNIE III. Born Aug. 27, 1946 in Greenville, NC. Graduate Wake Forest U. Debut 1982 OB in "The Six O'Clock Boys."

COLLINS, PAUL. Born July 25, 1937 in London, Eng. Attended LACC. OB in "Say Nothing," "Cambridge Circus," "The Devils," "Rear Column," "Jail Diary of Albie Sachs," "The Fuehrer Bunker," Bdwy in "The Royal Hunt of the Sun," "A Minor Adjustment," "A Meeting by the River," "Eminent Domain."

COLORADO, VIRA. Born July 6 in Blue Island, Il. Debut 1971 OB in "The Screens," followed by "Women Behind Bars," "The Three Sisters," "The Petrified Forest," "Puerto Rican Obituary," "The Dispossessed."

COMBS, DAVID. Born June 10, 1949 in Reno, Nv. Graduate UNv, Wayne State U. Bdwy debut 1975 in "Equus," OB in "The Passion of Dracula," "Punch with Judy."

CONNOLLY, JOHN P. Born Sept. 1, 1950 in Philadelphia, Pa. Temple U. graduate. Debut 1973 OB in "Paradise Lost," followed by "The Wizard of Oz," "Fighting Bob."

CONROY, FRANCES. Born in 1953 in Monroe, GA. Attended Dickinson Col., Juilliard, Neighborhood Playhouse. Debut 1978 OB with the Acting Co. in "Mother Courage," "King Lear," "The Other Hand," followed by "All's Well That Ends Well," "Othello," "Sorrows of Stephen," "Girls Girls Girls," "Zastrozzi," Bdwy 1980 in "The Lady from Dubuque."

CONROY, JARLATH. Born Sept. 30, 1944 in Galway, IR. Attended RADA. Bdwy debut 1976 in "Comedians," followed by "The Elephant Man," "Macbeth," OB in "Translations," "The Wind That Shook the Barley," "Gardenia."

CONRY, KATHLEEN. Born Nov. 15, 1947 in Cleveland, Oh. Bdwy debut 1968 in "George M!," followed by "No, No Nanette," OB in "The Sign in Sidney Brustein's Window," "Suffragette."

COOK, JILL. Born Feb. 25, 1954 in Plainfield, NJ. Bdwy debut 1971 in "On the Town," followed by "So Long, 174th Street," "Dancin'," "Best Little Whorehouse in Texas," "Perfectly Frank," OB in "Carnival," "Potholes."

COOK, LINDA. Born June 8 in Lubbock, Tx. Attended Auburn U. Debut 1974 OB in "The Wager," followed by "Hole in the Wall," "Shadow of a Gunman," "Be My Father," "Ghosts of the Loyal Oaks."

COOK, RODERICK. Born 1932 in London. Attended Cambridge U. Bdwy debut 1961 in "Kean," followed by "Roar Like a Dove," "The Girl Who Came to Supper," "Noel Coward's Sweet Potato," "The Man Who Came to Dinner," "Woman of the Year," OB in "A Scent of Flowers," "Oh, Coward!"

COOPER, JED. Born Jan. 6, 1955 in NYC. Graduate UMich., Neighborhood Playhouse. Bdwy debut 1977 in "Vieux Carre," OB in "Scenes from La Vie de Boheme."

COOPER, MARILYN. Born Dec. 14, 1936 in NYC. Attended NYU. Appeared in "Mr Wonderful," "West Side Story," "Brigadoon," "Gypsy," "I Can Get It for You Wholesale," "Hallelujah Baby!," "Golden Rainbow," "Mame," "A Teaspoon Every 4 Hours," "Two by Two," "On the Town," "Ballroom," "Woman of the Year," OB in "The Mad Show," "Look Me Up."

COOPER, ROY. Born Jan. 22, 1930 in London, Eng. Bdwy debut 1968 in "The Prime Of Miss Jean Brodie," followed by "Canterbury Tales," "St. Joan," OB in "A Month in the Country," "Mary Stuart," "Henry IV Part I."

COPELAND, JOAN. Born June 1, 1922 in NYC. Attended Brooklyn Col., AADA. Debut 1945 OB in "Romeo and Juliet," followed by "Othello," "Conversation Piece," "Delightful Season," "End of Summer," "The American Clock," Bdwy in "Sundown Beach," "Detective Story," "Not for Children," "Hatful of Fire," "Something More," "The Price," "Two by Two," "Pal Joey," "Checking Out," "The American Clock."

CORFMAN, CARIS. Born May 18, 1955 in Boston, MA. Graduate FlaStateU, Yale. Debut 1978 OB in "Wings," Bdwy 1980 in "Amadeus."

CORREIA, DON. Born Aug. 28, 1951 in San Jose, Ca. Attended San Jose State U. Bdwy debut 1980 in "A Chorus Line," followed by "Perfectly Frank," "Little Me," "Sophisticated Ladies."

CORREN, DONALD. Born June 5, 1952 in Stockton, Ca. Attended Juilliard. Bdwy debut 1980 in "A Day in Hollywood/A Night in the Ukraine," followed by "Tomfoolery" (OB).

CORTEZ, KATHERINE. Born Sept. 28, 1950 in Detroit, Mi. Graduate UNC. Debut 1979 OB in "The Dark at the Top of the Stairs," followed by "Corners," "Confluence," "The Great Grandson of Jedediah Kohler."

COSTA, JOSEPH. Born June 8, 1946 in Ithaca, NY. Graduate Gettysburg Col., Yale. Debut 1978 OB in "The Show-Off" followed by "The Tempest."

COSTALLOS, SUZANNE. Born Apr. 3, 1953 in NYC. Attended NYU, Boston Consv., Juilliard. Debut OB 1977 in "Play and Other Plays by Beckett," followed by "Elizabeth I," "The White Devil," "Hunting Scenes from Lower Bavaria," "Selma."

COSTIGAN, KEN. Born Apr. 1, 1934 in NYC. Graduate Fordham U., Yale U. Debut 1960 OB in "Borak," followed by "King of the Dark Chamber," "The Hostage," "Next Time I'll Sing to You," "Curley McDimple," "The Runner Stumbles," "Peg o' My Heart," "The Show-Off," "Midsummer Night's Dream," "Diary of Anne Frank," "Knuckle Sandwich," "Seminary Murder," "Declassee," "Big Apple Messenger," "When We Dead Awaken," Bdwy 1962 in "Gideon."

COURTENAY, TOM. Born Feb. 25, 1937 in Hull, Eng. RADA graduate. Bdwy debut 1977 in "Otherwise Engaged," followed by "The Dresser."

COWAN, EDIE. Born Apr. 14 in NYC. Graduate Butler U. Bdwy debut 1964 in "Funny Girl," followed by "Sherry," "Annie."

COX, CATHERINE. Born Dec. 13, 1950 in Toledo, OH. Wittenberg U. graduate. Bdwy debut 1976 in "Music Is," followed by "Whoopee!," "Oklahoma!," "Shakespeare's Cabaret," "Barnum," OB in "By Strouse."

COX, PAUL R. Born Sept. 17, 1926 in Chicago, Il. Brooklyn Col., NYU graduate. Debut 1982 OB in "The Misunderstanding."

COX, RICHARD. Born May 6, 1948 in NYC. Yale graduate. Debut 1970 OB in "Saved," followed by "Fuga," "Moonchildren," "Alice in Concert," "Richard II," "Fishing," Bdwy in "The Sign in Sidney Brustein's Window," "Platinum."

CRABTREE, DON. Born Aug. 21, 1928 in Borger, TX. Attended Actors Studio. Bdwy bow 1959 in "Destry Rides Again," followed by "Happiest Girl in the World," "Family Affair," "Unsinkable Molly Brown," "Sophie," "110 in the Shade," "Golden Boy," "Pousse Cafe," "Mahagonny (OB), "The Best Little Whorehouse in Texas," "42nd Street."

CRAIG, DONALD. Born Aug. 14, 1941 in Abilene, TX. Graduate Hardin-Simmons Col., UTex. Debut 1975 OB in "Do I Hear a Waltz?," (ELT) Bdwy 1977 in "Annie."

CRAIN, STEPHEN . Born Oct. 3, 1952 in Tokyo, Japan. MIT graduate. Bdwy debut 1979 in "Oklahoma!," followed by "The First."

CRAWFORD, ELLEN. Born Apr. 29, 1951 in Dayton, Oh. Carnegie Tech graduate. Bdwy debut 1982 in "Do Black Patent Leather Shoes Really Reflect Up?"

CRISTOFER, MICHAEL. Born Jan. 22, 1945 in Trenton, NY. Attended Catholic U. Debut 1977 OB in "The Cherry Orchard" for which he received a Theatre World Award, followed by "Conjuring an Event," "Chinchilla," "No End of Blame."

CRISWELL, KIM. Born July 19, 1957 in Hampton, Va. Graduate UCin. Bdwy debut 1981 in "The First," followed by "Nine."

CRIVELLO, ANTHONY. Born Aug. 2, 1955 in Milwaukee, Wi. Bdwy debut 1982 in "Evita."

CRIVELLO, MARY LOU. Born July 22, 1954 in Brooklyn, NY. Attended New School. Debut 1978 OB in "The Coolest Cat in Town," followed by "Boy Meets Swan," "T.N.T.," "Seesaw."

CROFOOT, LEONARD JOHN. Born Sept. 20, 1948 in Utica, NY. Bdwy debut 1968 in "The Happy Time," followed by "Come Summer," "Gigi," "Barnum," OB in "Circus," "Joseph and the Amazing Technicolor Dreamcoat."

CRONIN, JANE. Born Apr. 4, 1936 in Boston, MA. Attended Boston U. Bdwy debut 1965 in "Postmark Zero," OB in "Bald Soprano," "One Flew over the Cuckoo's Nest," "Hot l Baltimore," "The Gathering," "Catsplay," "The Violano Virtuoso," "Afternoons in Vegas," "The Frequency," "A Month in the Country," "The Trading Post," "Booth."

CROTHERS, JOEL. Born Jan. 28, 1941 in Cincinnati, Oh. Harvard graduate. Bdwy debut 1953 in "The Remarkable Mr. Pennypacker," followed by "A Case of Libel," "Barefoot in the Park," "The Jockey Club Stakes," OB in "Easter," "The Office Murders," "Torch Song Trilogy."

CROUSE, LINDSAY. Born May 12, 1948 in NYC. Radcliffe graduate. Bdwy debut 1972 in "Much Ado About Nothing," OB in "The Foursome," "Fishing," "Long Day's Journey into Night," "Total Recall," "Father's Day," "Hamlet," "Reunion," "Twelfth Night," "Childe Byron," "Richard II."

CRYER, DAVID. Born Mar. 8, 1936 in Evanston, IL. Attended DePauw U. OB in "The Fantasticks," "Streets of New YOrk," "Now is the Time for All Good Men," "Whispers on the Wind," "The Making of Americans," "Portfolio Revue," Bdwy in "110 in the Shade," "Come Summer" for which he received a Theatre World Award, "1776" "Ari," "Leonard Bernstein's Mass," "Desert Song," "Evita."

CUERVO, ALMA. Born Aug. 13, in Tampa, FL. Graduate Tulane U., Yale U. Debut 1977 OB in "Uncommon Women and Others," followed by "A Foot in the Door," "Put Them All Together," "Isn't It Romantic," "Miss Julie," Bdwy in "Once in a Lifetime," "Bedroom Farce," "Censored Scenes from King Kong," "Is There Life after High School?"

CULLEN, JEANNE. Born Dec. 21, 1951 in Passaic, NY. Graduate UConn. Debut 1982 OB in "Lysistrata," followed by "Punch with Judy."

CULLITON, JOSEPH. Born Jan. 25, 1948 in Boston, Ma. Attended CalStateU. Debut 1982 OB in "Francis."

CULLUM, JOHN. Born Mar. 2, 1930 in Knoxville, TN. Graduate U. Tenn. Bdwy bow 1960 in "Camelot," followed by "Infidel Caesar," "The Rehearsal," "Hamlet," "On a Clear Day You Can See Forever" for which he received a Theatre World Award," "Man of LaMancha," "1776," "Vivat! Vivat Regina!," "Shenandoah," "Kings," "The Trip Back Down," "On the 20th Century," "Deathtrap," OB in "Three Hand Reel," "The Elizabethans," "Carousel," "In the Voodoo Parlor of Marie Leveau," "The King and I" (JB), "Whistler."

CUMMINGS, CONSTANCE. Born May 15, 1910 in Seattle, Wa. Bdwy debut 1928 in "Treasure Girl," followed by "The Little Show," "This Man's Town," "June Moon," "Accent on Youth," "Young Madame Conti," "Madame Bovary," "If I Were You," "One-Man Show," "The Rape of the Belt," "Hamlet" (1969), "Wings," "The Chalk Garden" (OB).

CUNNINGHAM, JOHN. Born June 22, 1932 in Auburn, NY. Graduate of Yale and Dartmouth. OB in "Love Me Little," "Pimpernel," "The Fantasticks," "Love and Let Love," "The Bone Room," "Dancing in the Dark," "Father's Day," "Snapshot," "Head over Heels," Bdwy in "Hot Spot," "Zorba," "Company," "1776," "Rose."

CURRY, CHRISTOPHER. Born Oct. 22, 1948 in Grand Rapids, Mi. Graduate UMich Debut 1974 OB in "When You Comin' Back, Red Ryder?," followed by "The Cherry Orchard," "Spelling Bee," "Ballymurphy," "Isadora Duncan Sleeps with the Russian Navy," "The Promise," "Mecca," "Soul of the White Ant," "Strange Snow," Bdwy in "The Crucifer of Blood."

CURTIS, KEENE. Born Feb. 15, 1925 in Salt Lake City, UT. Graduate UUtah. Bdwy bow 1949 in "Shop at Sly Corner," with APA in "School for Scandal," "The Tavern," "Anatole," "Scapin," "Right You Are," "Importance of Being Earnest," "Twelfth Night," "King Lear," "Seagull," "Lower Depths," "Man and Superman," "Judith," "War and Peace," "You Can't Take It With You," "Pantagleize," "Cherry Orchard," "Misanthrope," "Cocktail Party," "Cock-a-Doodle Dandy," and "Hamlet," "A Patriot for Me," "The Rothschilds," "Night Watch," "Via Galactica," "Annie," "Division Street," OB in "Colette," "Ride across Lake Constance."

DABDOUB, JACK. Born Feb. 5 in New Orleans, LA. Graduate Tulane U. OB in "What's Up," "Time for the Gentle People," "The Peddler," "The Dodo Bird," "Annie Get Your Gun," "Lola," Bdwy in "Paint Your Wagon," (1952), "My Darlin' Aida," "Happy Hunting," "Hot Spot," "Camelot," "Baker St.," "Anya," "Her First Roman," "Coco," "Man of LaMancha," "Brigadoon" ('80).

DALE, JIM. Born in 1936 in Rothwell, Eng. Debut 1974 OB with Young Vic Co. in "Taming of the Shrew," followed by "Scapino" that moved to Bdwy, "Barnum."

DALEY, DONNA. Born June 2, 1952 in Providence, RI. Graduate UBridgeport. Debut 198[illegible] OB in "A Coupla White Chicks Sitting Around Talking." followed by "Hamster of Happiness."

DALY, CAROLINE. Born Jan. 10, 1968 in NYC. Bdwy debut 1980 in "Annie."

DANEK, MICHAEL. Born May 5, 1955 in Oxford, PA. Graduate Columbia Col. Bdwy debut 1978 "Hello, Dolly!" followed by "A Chorus Line," "Copperfield," "Woman of The Year," OB in "Big Bad Burlesque," "Dreams."

DANETTE, LEILA. Born Aug. 23, 1909 in Jacksonville, Fl. Graduate Morgan State Col. UMd. Bdwy debut 1968 in "The Great White Hope," OB in "Don't Let It Go to Your Head," "Amen Corner," "The Long Black Block," "The Brothers."

DANIAS, STARR. Born March 18, 1949 in NYC. Performed with Joffrey Ballet before OB debut 1981 in "El Bravo."

DANSON, RANDY. Born Apr. 30, 1950 in Plainfield, NJ. Graduate Carnegie Mellon. Debut 1978 OB in "Gimme Shelter," followed by "Big and Little," "The Winter Dancers," "Time Steps," "Casualties," "Red and Blue," "The Resurrection of Lady Lester."

DANTUONO, MICHAEL. Born July 30, 1942 in Providence, RI. Debut 1974 OB in "How to Get Rid of It," followed by "Maggie Flynn," "Charlotte Sweet," Bdwy 1977 in "Caesar and Cleopatra," "Can-Can" ('81).

DARLING, CANDY. Born March 6, 1954 in Toronto, Can. Bdwy debut 1976 in "Very Good Eddie," followed by "Censored Scenes from King Kong," "Whoopee," "Dreamgirls."

DARNAY, TONI. Born Aug. 11 in Chicago, IL. Attended Northwestern U. Debut 1942 OB in "Name Your Poison," followed by "When the Bough Breaks," "Nocturne in Daylight," "The Gold Watch," "Possibilities," "Dead Giveaway," "The Sound of Music" (JB), Bdwy in "Sadie Thompson" ('44), "Affair of Honor," "Life with Father," "The Women," "Molly," "The Heiress," "Vieux Carre."

DAVIDSON, JACK. Born July 17, 1936 in Worcester, MA. Graduate Boston U. Debut 196[illegible] OB in "Moon for the Misbegotten," followed by "Big and Little," "The Battle of Angels," "Midsummer Night's Dream," "Hot l Baltimore," "A Tribute to Lili Lamont," "Ulysses in Traction," "Lulu," "Hey, Rube," "In the Recovery Lounge," "The Runner Stumbles," "Winter Signs," "Hamlet," "Mary Stuart," "Ruby Ruby Sam Sam," "The Diviners," "Marching to Georgia," "Hunting Scenes from Lower Bavaria," "Richard II," "The Great Grandson of Jedediah Kohler," Bdwy in "Capt. Brassbound's Conversion" (1972), "Anna Christie."

DAVIDSON, RICHARD M. Born May 10, 1940 in Hamilton, Ont., Can. Graduate UToronto, LAMDA. Debut 1978 OB in "The Beasts," followed by "The Bacchae," "The Broken Pitcher," Bdwy in "The Survivor" ('81).

DAVIS, BRUCE ANTHONY. Born Mar. 4, 1959 in Dayton, OH. Attended Juilliard. Bdwy debut 1979 in "Dancin'."

DAVIS, CLAYTON. Born May 18, 1948 in Pensacola, Fl. Graduate FlStateU, Princeton. Debut 1978 OB in "Oklahoma!," followed by "Oh, Johnny."

DAVIS, MICHAEL ALLEN. Born Aug. 23, 1953 in San Francisco, CA. Attended Clown Col. Bdwy debut 1981 in "Broadway Follies" for which he received a Theatre World Award followed by "Sugar Babies."

DAVIS, SUSAN. Born Apr. 27, 1960 in Tulsa, OK. Debut 1980 OB in "And Other Songs," followed by "El Bravo," Bdwy 1980 in "Barnum."

DAWSON, MARGARET. Born Sept. 22, 1927 in NYC. Rutgers U. graduate. Debut 1980 OB in "The Devil's Disciple."

DeALMEIDA, JOAQUIN. Born March 15, 1957 in Portugal. Attended Lisbon Consv. Has appeared OB in "The Marriage Proposal," "The Sign in Sidney Brustein's Window," "A Christmas Carol," "Talk to Me Like Rain," "What Would Jeanne Moreau Do?"

DEAN, JACQUE. Born Jan. 21 in Washington, DC. Attended UMd. Debut 1961 OB in "Little Mary Sunshine," followed by "Gorky," "Mata Hari," "Ruby Ruby Sam Sam," "The Heiress," Bdwy in "The Student Gypsy" (1963), "Lolita My Love," "Coco," "Dear World," "I'm Solomon," "Drat! The Cat!," "I Had a Ball."

de BANZIE, LOIS. Born May 4 in Glasgow, Scot. Bdwy debut 1966 in "Elizabeth the Queen," followed by "Da," "Morning's at 7," OB in "Little Murders," "Mary Stuart," "People Are Living There," "Ride Across Lake Constance," "The Divorce of Judy and Jane," "What the Butler Saw," "Man and Superman," "The Judas Applause," "The Dining Room."

DeFILIPPS, RICK. Born Apr. 16, 1950 in Binghamton, NY. Attended AMDA. Debut 1976 OB in "Panama Hattie," followed by "Wonderful Town," "Beowulf," "Nymph Errant."

DeFRANK, ROBERT. Born Nov. 29, 1945 in Baltimore, MD. Graduate Towson State, Essex Community Col. Debut 1977 OB in "The Crazy Locomotive," followed by "The Taming of the Shrew." "The Madman and the Nun," "We Won't Pay," "Variations on a Theme.," "The Good Parts."

Roy Doliner

Mary Anne Dorward

Craig Dudley

Mercedes Ellington

Terrance Terry Ellis

Barbara Erwin

Charlotte Fairchild

Paul Farin

Fannie Flagg

Luther Fontaine

Gloria Foster

Paul Fouquet

Peter Francis-James

Alison Fraser

Morgan Freeman

Catherine Fries

Rick Friesen

Mary Gaeble

Jane Galloway

Chamaco Garcia

Julie Garfield

Chip Garnett

Gale Garnett

Peter Gatto

Igors Gavon

Maggy Gorrill

Robert Gossett

Maria Guida

Baxter Harris

Cynthia Harris

DE LA PENA, GEORGE. Born in NYC in 1956. Performed with American Ballet Theatre before Bdwy debut 1981 in "Woman of the Year."

DELBERT, ROBERT. Born Dec. 28, 1946 in Poinsitt, Ak. Graduate UMo. Bdwy debut 1969 in "Penny Wars," OB in "The Trial of Denmark Vesey," "Linty Lucy."

DeMATTIS, RAY. Born June 1, 1945 in New Haven, Ct. Graduate Catholic U. Bdwy debut 1974 in "Grease," OB in "El Bravo!"

DEMPSEY, JEROME. Born Mar. 1. 1929 in St. Paul, MN. Toledo U graduate. Bdwy bow 1959 in "West Side Story," followed by "The Deputy," "Spofford," "Room Service," "Love Suicide at Schofield Barracks," "Dracula," OB in "Cry of Players," "Year Boston Won the Pennant," "The Crucible," "Justice Box," "Trelawny of the Wells," "The Old Glory," "Six Characters in Search of an Author," "Threepenny Opera," "Johnny on the Spot," "The Barbarians," "He and She," "Midsummer Night's Dream," "The Recruiting Officer," "Oedipus the King," "The Wild Duck," "The Fuehrer Bunker," "Entertaining Mr. Sloane," "Clownmaker."

DENGEL, JAKE. Born June 19, 1933 in Oshkosh, WI. Graduate Northwestern U. Debut OB in "The Fantasticks," followed by "Red Eye of Love," "Fortuna," "Abe Lincoln in Illinois," "Dr. Faustus," "An Evening with Garcia Lorca," "Shrinking Bride," "Where Do We Go from Here?," "Woyzeck," "Endgame," "Measure for Measure," "Ulysses in Traction," "Twelfth Night," "The Beaver Coat," "Great Grandson of Jedediah Kohler," Bdwy in "Royal Hunt of the Sun," "Cock-a-Doodle Dandy," "Hamlet," "The Changing Room."

DENNIS, SANDY. Born Apr. 27, 1937 in Hastings, Ne. Bdwy debut 1957 in "The Dark at the Top of the Stairs," followed by "Burning Bright" (OB), "Face of a Hero," "The Complaisant Lover," "A Thousand Clowns" for which she received a Theatre World Award, "Any Wednesday," "Daphne in Cottage D," "How the Other Half Loves," "Let Me Hear You Smile," "Absurd Person Singular," "Same Time Next Year," "Supporting Cast," "Come Back to the 5 & Dime, Jimmy Dean."

DERRA, CANDACE. Born Jan. 4 in Chicago, Il. Graduate UCLA. Debut 1980 OB in "The Ladder," followed by "Valentine," "Two by One," "A Visit."

DESAI, SHELLY. Born Dec. 3, 1935 in Bombay, India. Graduate OkStateU. Debut 1968 OB in "The Indian Wants the Bronx," followed by "Babu," "Wonderful Year," "Jungle of Cities," "Gandhi," "Savages," "Cuchulain," "Hamlet," "Merchant of Venice," Bdwy 1981 in "A Talent for Murder."

DEVINE, LORETTA. Born Aug. 21 in Houston, Tx. Graduate UHouston, Brandeis U. Bdwy debut 1977 in "Hair," followed by "A Broadway Musical," "Dreamgirls," OB in "Godsong," "Lion and the Jewel," "Karma," "The Blacks," "Mahalia."

DeVITO, KARLA. Born in 1953 in Oak Lawn, IL. Attended Loyola U. Debut 1974 OB in "El Grande de Coca Cola," followed by "Jubilee," "Midsummer Night's Dream," Bdwy 1981 in "The Pirates of Penzance."

DEVLIN, JAY. Born May 8, 1929 in Ft. Dodge, IA. OB in "The Mad Show," "Little Murders," "Unfair to Goliath," "Ballymurphy," "Front Page," "Fasnacht Day," Bdwy 1978 in "King of Hearts."

DILLON, MIA. Born July 9, 1955 in Colorado Springs, CO. Graduate Penn State U. Bdwy debut 1977 in "Equus," followed by "Da," "Once a Catholic," "Crimes of the Heart," OB in "The Crucible," "Summer," "Waiting for the Parade," "Crimes of the Heart," "Fables for Friends," "Scenes from La Vie de Boheme."

DISHY, BOB. Born in Brooklyn; graduate Syracuse U. Bdwy debut 1955 in "Damn Yankees," followed by "Can-Can," "Flora the Red Menace," "Something Different," "The Goodbye People," "A Way of Life," "Creation of the World and Other Business," "American Millionaire," "Sly Fox," "Murder at the Howard Johnson's," "Grownups," OB in "Chic," "When the Owl Screams," "Wrecking Ball," "By Jupiter," "The Unknown Soldier and His Wife."

DIXON, MacINTYRE. Born Dec. 22, 1931 in Everett, Ma. Graduate Emerson Col. Bdwy debut 1965 in "Xmas in Las Vegas," followed by "Cop-Out," "Story Theatre," "Metamorphosis," "Twigs," "Over Here!," "Once in a Lifetime," OB in "Quare Fellow," "Plays for Bleecker St.," "Stewed Prunes," "Cat's Pajamas," "Three Sisters," "3 X 3," "Second City," "Mad Show," "Meow!," "Lotta," "Rubbers," "Conjuring an Event," "His Majesty the Devil," "Tomfoolery."

DODSON, COLLEEN. Born June 29, 1954 in Chicago, Il. Graduate UIl. Debut 1981 OB in "The Matinee Kids," Bdwy 1982 in "Nine."

DOLINER, ROY. Born June 27, 1954 in Boston, Ma. Attended Tufts U. Debut 1977 OB in "Don't Cry Child, Your Father's an American," followed by "Zwi Kanar Show," "Big Bad Burlesque," "Lysistrata."

DOLLASE, DAVID J. Born July 28, 1955 in North Plainfield, NJ. Graduate UKy., AMDA. Debut 1982 OB in "Street Scene" (ELT).

DON, CARL. Born Dec. 15, 1916 in Vitebsk, Russia. Attended Western Reserve U. Bdwy debut 1954 in "Anastasia," followed by "Romanoff and Juliet," "Dear Me, the Sky Is Falling," "The Relapse," "The Tenth Man," "Zalmen," "Wings," OB in "Richard III," "Twelfth Night," "Winterset," "Arms and the Man," "Between Two Thieves," "He Who Gets Slapped," "Jacobowsky and the Colonel," "Carnival," "The Possessed," "Three Acts of Recognition."

DONHOWE, GWYDA. Born Oct. 20, 1933 in Oak Park, Il. Attended Drake U., Goodman Theatre. Bdwy debut 1957 in "Separate Tables," followed by "Half a Sixpence," "Flip Side," "Paris Is Out," "Applause," "The Show-Off," "War and Peace," "Right You Are," "You Can't Take It with You," "Shadow Box," "A Broadway Musical," OB in "Philosophy in the Boudoir," "Rondelay," "How Far Is It to Babylon?," "Head over Heels."

DONNELLY, DONAL. Born July 6, 1931 in Bradford, Eng. Bdwy debut 1966 in "Philadelphia, Here I Come," followed by "A Day in the Death of Joe Egg," "Sleuth," "The Faith Healer," "The Elephant Man," OB in "My Astonishing Self," "The Chalk Garden."

DONNELLY, JAMIE. Bdwy debut 1965 in "Flora the Red Menace," followed by "George M!," "Rodgers and Hart," "Rocky Horror Show," OB in "You're a Good Man, Charlie Brown," "Little Mother."

DORWARD, MARY ANNE. Born June 29, 1958 in Berkeley, Ca. Graduate UBerkeley. Debut 1982 OB in "T.N.T."

DOSSEY, MARALYN. Born July 31, 1944 in Peoria, Il. Attended UIowa, UMn. Bdwy debut 1977 in "Gemini," OB in "Lysistrata."

DOUGLAS, LUCIEN. (formerly Lucien Zabielski) Born Aug. 5, 1949 in Torrington, Ct. Graduate UCt., RADA. Debut 1972 OB in "Hope Is the Thing with Feathers," followed by "Naked," "Under Milk Wood," "The Tempest," "Candida," Bdwy 1982 in "Medea."

DOVEY, MARK. Born Jan. 13, 1954 in Vancouver, Can. Attended UBritish Columbia. Bdwy debut 1980 in "A Chorus Line," followed by "The Little Prince and the Aviator."

DOW, ALEXIS. Born Apr. 22, 1973 in Woburn, Ma. Debut 1982 OB in "Hollywood Snapshots."

DRAKE, DONNA. Born May 21, 1953 in Columbia, SC. Attended USC, Columbia. Bdwy debut 1975 in "A Chorus Line," followed by "It's So Nice to Be Civilized," "1940's Radio Hour," "Woman of the Year," "Sophisticated Ladies."

DRISCHELL, RALPH. Born Nov. 26, 1927 in Baldwin, NY. Attended Carnegie-Tech. Bdwy debut in "Rhinoceros," "All in Good Time," "Rosencrantz and Guildenstern Are Dead," "The Visit," "Chemin de Fer," "Ah, Wilderness," "Stages," "The American Clock," "The Survivor," OB in "Playboy of the Western World," "The Crucible," "The Balcony," "Time of Vengeance," "Barroom Monks," "Portrait of the Artist," "Abe Lincoln in Illinois," "The Caretaker," "A Slight Ache," "The Room," "The Year Boston Won the Pennant," "The Time of Your Life," "Camino Real," "Operation Sidewinder," "Beggar on Horseback," "Threepenny Opera," "Henry IV Part II."

DRIVER, JOHN. Born Jan 16, 1947 in Erie, PA. Graduate Smith Col., Northwestern U. Debut OB 1972 in "One Flew over the Cuckoo's Nest," followed by "Scrambled Feet," Bdwy in "Grease," (1973), "Over Here" for which he received a Theatre World Award.

DRUMMOND, ALICE. Born May 21, 1929 in Pawtucket, RI. Attended Pembroke Col. Bdwy debut 1963 in "Ballad of the Sad Cafe," followed by "Malcolm" "The Chinese," "Thieves," "Summer Brave," "Some of My Best Friends," OB in "Royal Gambit," "Go Show Me a Dragon," "Sweet of You to Say So," "Gallows Humor," "American Dream," "Giants' Dance," "Carpenters," "Charles Abbot & Son," "God Says There Is No Peter Ott," "Enter a Free Man," "Memory of Two Mondays," "Secret Service," "Boy Meets Girl," "Savages," "Killings on the Last Line," "Knuckle," "Wonderland."

DUDLEY, CRAIG, Born Jan, 22, 1945 in Sheepshead Bay, NY. Graduate AADA, AmTh-Wing. Debut 1970 OB in "Macbeth," followed by "Zou," "Othello," "War and Peace."

DUFOUR, VAL. Born Feb. 5, 1928 in New Orleans, La. Attended LSU. Credits include "The Grass Harp," "Frankie and Johnny," "Elektra," "Abie's Irish Rose" (1954), "Three by Pirandello" (OB).

DUKAKIS, OLYMPIA. Born in Lowell, Ma. Debut 1960 OB in "The Breaking Wall," followed by "Nourish the Beast," "Curse of the Starving Class," "Snow Orchid," Bdwy in "The Aspern Papers" (1962), "Abraham Cochrane," "Who's Who in Hell."

DUNAWAY, FAYE. Born Jan. 14, 1941 in Tallahassee, Fl. Attended UFl., Boston U. Bdwy debut 1962 in "A Man for All Seasons," followed by "The Curse of an Aching Heart," OB in "After the Fall," "But For Whom Charlie," "Tartuffe," "Hogan's Goat" for which she received a Theatre World Award.

DUNDAS, JENNIFER. Born Jan. 14, 1971 in Boston, Ma. Bdwy debut 1981 in "Grownups."

DWYER, FRANK. Born Feb. 1, 1945 in Kansas City, MO. Graduate NYU, SUNY. Debut 1970 OB in "Moby Dick," followed by "Hamlet," "Bacchai," "Streetcar Named Desire," "Darkness at Noon," "Vatzlav."

EASTON, SAMUELE. (formerly Eskind) Born Dec. 14 in Tennessee. Graduate San Jose State U. Debut 1980 OB in "Towards Zero," followed by "Bravo", "Lysistrata."

eda-YOUNG, BARBARA. Born Jan 30, 1945 in Detroit, MI. Bdwy debut 1968 in "Lovers and Other Strangers," OB in "The Hawk," LCRep's "The Time of Your Life," "Camino Real," "Operation Sidewinder," "Kool Aid" and "A Streetcar Named Desire," "The Gathering," "The Terrorists," "Drinks before Dinner," "Shout Across the River," "After Stardrive," "Birdbath," "Crossing the Crab Nebula," "Maiden Stakes."

EDDON, RICHARD. Born Feb. 13, 1956 in Toronto, Can. Attended AADA. Debut 1981 OB in "Entertaining Mr. Sloane."

EDE, GEORGE, Born Dec. 22, 1931 in San Francisco, CA. Bdwy debut 1969 in "A Flea in Her Ear," followed by "Three Sisters," "The Changing Room," "The Visit," "Chemin de Fer," "Holiday," "Love for Love," "Rules of the Game" "Member of the Wedding," "Lady from the Sea," "A Touch of the Poet," "Philadelphia Story," OB in "The Philanderer," "The American Clock," "The Broken Pitcher," "No End of Blame."

EDEIKEN, LOUISE. Born June 23, 1956 in Philadelphia, Pa. Graduate GeoWashU. Bdwy debut 1982 in "Nine."

EDENFIELD, DENNIS. Born July 23, 1946 in New Orleans, LA. Debut 1970 OB in "The Evil That Men Do," followed by "I Have Always Believed in Ghosts," "Nevertheless They Laugh," Bdwy in "Irene" ('73), "A Chorus Line,"

EDWARDS, BRANDT. Born Mar. 22, 1947 in Holly Springs, MS. Graduate UMiss. NY debut off and on Bdwy 1975 in "A Chorus Line."

EDWARDS, NAZIG. Born Feb. 2, 1952 in Philadelphia, Pa. Debut 1981 OB in "Oh, Johnny!"

EILBER, JANET. Born July 27, 1951 in Detroit, Mi. Attended Juilliard and danced with Martha Graham Co. Bdwy debut 1980 in "Dancin'," followed by "Swing," "The Little Prince and the Aviator."

ELEY, STEPHANIE. Born Nov. 3, 1951 in Hominy, Ok. Graduate NCSch of Arts. Bdwy debut 1981 in "Dreamgirls."

ELIC, JOSEP. Born Mar. 21, 1921 in Butte, Mt. Attended UWis. Debut OB in "Threepenny Opera," followed by "Don Juan in Hell," "Leave It to Jane," "Comic Strip," "Coriolanus," "Too Much Johnson," "Stag Movie," "Rise and Fall of Burlesque," "Big Bad Burlesque," "Hollywood Hotel," Bdwy in "Hamlet," "Baptiste," "West Side Story," "Sign in Sidney Brustein's Window," "Kelly."

ELIO, DONNA MARIE. Born Oct. 30, 1962 in Paterson, NJ. Bdwy debut 1974 in "Gypsy," followed by "Merrily We Roll Along."

ELLIN, DAVID. Born Jan. 10, 1925 in Montreal, Can. Attended AADA. Bdwy in "Swan Song," "West Side Story," "Education of Hyman Kaplan," "Light, Lively and Yiddish," OB in "Trees Die Standing," "Mirele Efros," "End of All Things Natural," "Yoshe Kalb," "Fiddler on the Roof" (JB), "Rebecca, the Rabbi's Daughter," "Wish Me Mazel-Tov.", "Roumanian Wedding."

ELLINGTON, MERCEDES. Born Feb. 9, 1949 in NYC. Juilliard graduate. Bdwy debut 1970 in "No, No, Nanette," followed by "The Grand Tour," "Happy New Year," "Black Broadway," OB in "Around the World" (JB), "An Evening of Jerome Kern," "Sophisticated Ladies."

ELLIOTT, ALICE. Born Aug. 22, 1950 in Durham, NC. Graduate Carnegie-Mellon, Goodman Theatre. Debut 1972 OB in "In the Time of Harry Harass," followed by "American Gothics," "Bus Stop," "As You Like It," "King of Hearts."

ELLIOTT, PATRICIA. Born July 21, 1942 in Gunnison, CO. Graduate U. Colo., London Academy. Debut with LCRep 1968 in "King Lear," and "A Cry of Players," followed OB in "Henry V," "The Persians," "A Doll's House," "Hedda Gabler," "In case of Accident," "Water Hen," "Polly," "But Not for Me," "By Bernstein," "Prince of Homburg," "Artichokes," "Wine Untouched," "Misalliance," Bdwy bow 1973 in "A Little Night Music" for which she received a Theatre World Award, followed by "The Shadow Box," "Tartuffe," "13 Rue de L'Amour," "The Elephant Man."

ELLIS, SCOTT. Born Apr. 19, 1957 in Washington, DC. Attended Goodman Theatre. Bdwy debut in "Grease," followed by "Musical Chairs," OB in "Mrs. Dally Has a Lover," "Hijinks.," "110 in the Shade."

ELLIS, TERRANCE TERRY. Born Sept. 20, 1957 in Chicago, Il. Graduate UIl. Debut 1980 OB in "Zooman and the Sign," followed by "Who Loves the Dancer," "Big Apple Messenger."

ELSTON, ROBERT. Born May 29, 1934 in NYC. Graduate Hunter Col., CCNY. Bdwy debut 1958 in "Maybe Tuesday," followed by "Tall Story," "Golden Fleecing," "Spoon River Anthology," "You Know I Can't Hear You When. . . ," "Vivat! Vivat Regina!," OB in "Undercover Man," "Conditioned Reflex," "Archy and Mehitabel," "Notes from the Underground.," "After Many a Summer."

EMMETT, ROBERT. Born Sept. 28, 1921 in Monterey, Ca. Attended UCal., Neighborhood Playhouse. Credits include "Peer Gynt" (1951), "Two on the Aisle," "Mid-Summer," "Madam, Will You Walk," "Comes the Happy Hour."

ENSSLEN, DICK. Born Dec. 19, 1926 in Reading, PA. Attended MTA. Bdwy debut 1964 in "Anyone Can Whistle," followed by "Bajour," "Education of Hyman Kaplan," "Canterbury Tales," "Desert Song." "I Remember Mama," "Annie."

EPSTEIN, ALVIN. Born May 14, 1925 in NYC. Attended Queens Col., Decroux School of Mime. Appeared on Bdwy with Marcel Marceau, and in "King Lear," "Waiting for Godot," "From A to Z," "No Strings," "The Passion of Josef D.," "Postmark Zero," "A Kurt Weill Cabaret," OB in "Purple Dust," "Pictures in a Hallway," "Clerambard," "Endgame," "Whores, Wares and Tin Pan Alley," "A Place without Doors," "Crossing Niagara."

ERWIN, BARBARA. Born June 30, 1937 in Boston, MA. Debut 1973 OB in "The Secret Life of Walter Mitty," followed by "Broadway," Bdwy in "Annie," "Ballroom," "Animals."

ESKENAS, LINDA. Born Sept. 11, 1950 in Boston, Ma. Attended Boston U, Neighborhood Playhouse. Debut 1965 OB in "A View from the Bridge," followed by "Electra," "A Doll's House," "Ondine," "Moon," "Balm for Gilead," "Importance of Being Earnest," "Medea," "Willy and Sahara," Bdwy 1974 in "American Millionaire."

ESPOSITO, GIANCARLO. Born Apr. 26, 1958 in Copenhagen, Den. Bdwy debut 1968 in "Maggie Flynn," followed by "The Me Nobody Knows," "Lost in the Stars," "Seesaw," "Merrily We Roll Along," OB in "Zooman and the Sign," for which he received a Theatre World Award, "Keyboard," "Who Loves the Dancer."

ESTEY, SUELLEN. Born Nov. 21 in Mason City. IA. Graduate Stephens Col., Northwestern U. Debut 1970 OB in "Some Other Time," followed by "June Moon," "Buy Bonds Buster," "Smile, Smile, Smile," "Carousel," "The Lullaby of Broadway," "I Can't Keep Running," Bdwy 1972 in "The Selling of the President," followed by "Barnum."

EVANS, DILLON. Born Jan. 2, 1921 in London, Eng. Attended RADA. Bdwy debut 1950 in "The Lady's Not for Burning," followed by "School for Scandal," "Hamlet," "Ivanov," "Vivat! Vivat Regina!," "Jockey Club Stakes," "Dracula," OB in "Druid's Rest," "Rondelay," "Little Foxes," "Playing with Fire."

EVANS PETER. Born May 27, 1950 in Englewood, NJ. Graduate Yale, London Central School of Speech. Debut OB 1975 in "Life Class," followed by "Streamers," "A Life in the Theatre," "Don Juan Comes Back from the War," "The American Clock," "Geniuses," Bdwy in "Night and Day" (1979)., "Children of a Lesser God."

EVERETT, TOM. Born Oct. 21, 1948 in Oregon. Graduate NYU, LAMDA. Debut 1972 OB in "Elizabeth I," followed by "Boccaccio," "Hosanna," "A Midsummer Night's Dream," "A Life in the Theatre," "Winning Isn't Everthing," "Rockaway Boulevard," "Dance for Me Simeon," "Sleep Beauty," "Philistines," Bdwy 1976 in "Habeas Corpus."

EVERHART, REX. Born June 13, 1920 in Watseka, Il. Graduate UMo, NYU. Bdwy bow 1955 in "No Time for Sergeants," followed by "Tall Story," "Moonbirds," "Tenderloin," "A Matter of Position," "Rainy Day in Newark," "Skyscraper," "How Now Dow Jones," "1776," "The Iceman Cometh," "Chicago," "Working," "Woman of the Year."

EVERS, BRIAN. Born Feb. 14, 1942 in Miami, Fl. Graduate Capital U, UMiami. Debut 1979 OB in "How's the House?," followed by "Details of the 16th Frame," "Divine Fire."

FABER, RON. Born Feb. 16, 1933 in Milwaukee, WI. Graduate Marquette U. Debut OB 1959 in "An Enemy of the People," followed by "The Exception and the Rule," "America, Hurrah," "Ubu Cocu," "Terminal," "They Put Handcuffs on Flowers," "Dr. Selavy's Magic Theatre," "Troilus and Cressida," "The Beauty Part," "Woyzeck," "St. Joan of the Stockyards," "Jungle of Cities," "Scenes from Everyday Life," "Mary Stuart," "3 by Pirandello," Bdwy in "Medea" (1973), "First Monday in October."

FAIRCHILD, CHARLOTTE. Born June 3, 1930 in Dayton, Oh. Attended Western Reserv U, Cleveland Play House. Bdwy debut 1957 in "Damn Yankees," followed by "Fiorello," "Mr. President," "Mame," "All the Girls Came Out to Play," "42nd Street," OB in "Penny Friend," "O Coward!"

FALZONE, PAUL. Born May 18, 1947 in St. Louis, Mo. Attended AADA. Debut 1978 OB in "International Stud," Bdwy 1982 in "Macbeth."

FANCY, RICHARD. Born Aug. 2, 1943 in Evanston, IL. Attended LAMDA Debut 1973 OB in "The Creeps," followed by "Kind Lady," "Rites of Passage.," "A Limb of Snow," "The Meeting."

FARIN, PAUL. Born July 1, 1947 in NYC. Graduate St. Michael's, Catholic U. Debut 1980 OB in "Elizabeth and Essex" followed by "The Evangelist."

FARR, KIMBERLY. Born Oct. 16, 1948 in Chicago, Il. Graduate UCLA. Bdwy debut 1972 in "Mother Earth," followed by "The Lady from the Sea," "Going Up," "Happy New Year," OB in "More Than You Deserve," "The S. S. Benchley," "At Sea with Benchley," "Suffragette."

FARRAR, MARTHA. Born Apr. 22, 1928 in Buffalo, NY. Graduate Smith Col. Bdwy debut 1953 in "A Pin to See the Peepshow," OB in "The Cretan Woman," "Easter," "Half-Life.," "Touched."

FAWCETT, ALLEN. Born in 1947 in Schenectady, NY. Bdwy debut 1982 in "Joseph and the Amazing Technicolor Dreamcoat."

FEARL, CLIFFORD. Born in NYC; Columbia graduate. Bdwy debut 1950 in "Flahooley," followed by "3 Wishes for Jamie," "Two's Company," "Kismet," "Happy Hunting," "Oh, Captain," "Redhead," "Let It Ride," "110 in the Shade," "Ben Franklin in Paris," "Mame," "La Plume de Ma Tante," "Dear World," "Jimmy," "My Fair Lady," "The Music Man" (JB), "My Fair Lady" (1981)

FELDER, CLARENCE. Born Sept. 2, 1938 in St. Matthew, SC. Debut 1964 OB in "The Room," followed by "Are You Now or Have You Ever Been," "Claw," "Henry V," "Winter Dancers," "Goose and Tomtom," Bdwy in "Red, White and Maddox," "Love for Love," "Rules of the Game," "Golden Boy," "A Memory of Two Mondays," "They Knew What They Wanted."

FERRY, DAVID. Born Sept. 6, 1951 in Owen Sound, Can Attended Memorial U. Newfoundland. Bdwy debut 1980 in "A Life," OB in "A Tale Told."

FETTEN, JENNIFER. Born May 14, 1969 in Shirley, NY. Bdwy debut 1981 in "The Little Prince and the Aviator."

FIEDLER, JOHN. Born Feb. 3, 1925 in Plateville, Wi. Attended Neighborhood Playhouse. OB in "The Seagull," "Sing Me No Lullaby," "The Terrible Swift Sword," "The Raspberry Picker," Bdwy in "One Eye Closed," "Howie," "Raisin in the Sun," "Harold," "The Odd Couple," "Our Town."

FIERSTEIN, HARVEY. Born June 6, 1954 in Brooklyn, NY. Graduate Pratt Inst. Debut 1971 OB in "Pork," followed by "International Stud," "Fugue in a Nursery," Bdwy 1982 in "Torch Song Trilogy."

FINKEL, FYVUSH. Born Oct. 9, 1922 in Brooklyn, NY. Bdwy debut 1970 in "Fiddler on the Roof" (also 1981 revival), OB in "Gorky."

FISKE, ELLEN. Born May 1 in Paterson, NY. Graduate Wilmington Col., Ohio U. Debut 1974 OB in "Arms and the Man," followed by "La Ronde," "Art of Coarse Acting," Bdwy in "The Royal Family."

FITCH, ROBERT. Born Apr. 29, 1934 in Santa Cruz, CA. Attended USanta Clara. Bdwy debut 1961 in "Tenderloin," followed by "Do Re Me," "My Fair Lady," "The Girl Who Came to Supper," "Flora the Red Menace," "Baker Street," "Sherry," "Mack and Mabel," "Henry Sweet Henry," "Mame," "Promises Promises," "Coco," "Lorelei," "Annie," "Do Black Patent Leather Shoes Really Reflect UP?," OB in "Lend an Ear," "Half-Past Wednesday," "Anything Goes," "Crystal Heart," "Broadway Dandies," "One Cent Plain," "Sweet Thighs of New England Women."

FITZGERALD, FERN. Born Jan 7, 1947 in Valley Stream, NY. Bdwy debut 1976 in "Chicago," followed by "A Chorus Line."

FITZPATRICK, JIM. Born Nov. 26, 1950 in Omaha, NE. Attended UNeb. Debut 1977 OB in "Arsenic and Old Lace" (ELT), followed by "Merton of the Movies" (ELT), "Oh, Boy!", "Time and the Conways," "Street Scene."

FLAGG, FANNIE. Born Sept. 21, 1944 in Birmingham, AL. Attended Pittsburgh Playhouse. Debut 1963 OB in "Just for Opening," followed by "Patio/Porch," "Come Back to the 5 & Dime, Jimmy Dean," Bdwy 1980 in "The Best Little Whorehouse in Texas."

FLAGG, TOM. Born Mar. 30, 1949 in Canton, OH. Attended Kent State U., AADA. Debut 1975 OB in "The Fantasticks," followed by "Give Me Liberty," "The Subject Was Roses," "Lola," Bdwy in "Legend," "Shenandoah," "Players."

FLANAGAN, PAULINE. Born June 29, 1925 in Sligo, Ire. Debut 1958 OB in "Ulysses in Nighttown," followed by "Pictures in the Hallway," "Later," "Antigone," "The Crucible," "The Plough and the Stars," "Summer," "Close of Play," Bdwy in "God and Kate Murphy," "The Living Room," "The Innocents," "The Father," "Medea."

FLEISCHMAN, MARK. Born Nov. 25, 1935 in Detroit, MI. Attended UMi. Bdwy debut 1955 in "Tonight in Samarkand," followed by "A Distant Bell," "The Royal Family," "The World of Sholom Aleichem," OB In "What Every Woman Knows," "Lute Song," "The Beautiful People," "Big Fish, Little fish," "Incident at Vichy."

FLOREK, DAVE. Born May 19, 1953 in Dearborn, MI. Graduate Eastern MiU. Debut 1976 OB in "The Collection," followed by "Richard III," "Much Ado about Nothing," "Young Bucks," "Big Apple Messenger," "Death of a Miner," Bdwy 1980 in "Nuts."

FONTAINE, LUTHER. Born Apr. 14, 1947 in Kansas City, Ks. Graduate UMo, NYU. Bdwy debut 1973 in "Two Gentlemen of Verona," followed by "Timbuktu," "The First," OB in "All Night Strut," "Feeling Good," "Dream on Monkey Mountain," "Bojangles."

FORD, BARRY. Born Mar. 27, 1933 in Oakland, CA. Graduate CaStateU. Debut 1972 OB in "Ruddigore," followed by "The Devil's Disciple," "Nymph Errant."

FORD, CLEBERT, Born Jan 29, 1932 in Brooklyn, NY. Graduate CCNY, Boston U. Bdwy debut 1960 in "The Cool World," followed by "Les Blancs," "Ain't Supposed to Die a Natural Death," "Via Galactica," "Bubbling Brown Sugar," "The Last Minstrel Show," OB in "Romeo and Juliet," "Antony and Cleopatra," "Ti-Jean and His Brothers," "The Blacks," "Ballad for Bimshire," "Daddy," "Gilbeau," "Coriolanus," "Before the Flood," "The Lion and the Jewel," "Branches from the Same Tree," "Dreams Deferred."

FORD, RUTH. Born July 7, 1915 in Hazelhurst, Ms. Bdwy debut 1938 in "Shoemaker's Holiday," followed by "Danton's Death," "Swingin' the Dream," "No Exit," "This Time Tomorrow," "Clutterbuck," "House of Bernarda Alba," "Island of Goats," "Requiem for a Nun," "The Milk Train Doesn't Stop Here Anymore," "Grass Harp," "Harold and Maude," OB in "Glass Slipper," "Miss Julie," "Madame de Sade," "A Breeze from the Gulf," "Confluence."

FORREST, PAUL. Born July 2, 1923 in Philadelphia, Pa. Graduate UPa., Temple U. Bdwy debut 1969 in "Jimmy," followed by "The First."

FOSTER, FRANCES. Born June 11 in Yonkers, NY. Bdwy debut 1955 in "The Western Trees," followed by "Nobody Loves an Albatross," "Raisin in the Sun," "The River Niger," "First Breeze of Summer," OB in "Take a Giant Step," "Edge of the City," "Tammy and the Doctor," "The Crucible," "Happy Ending," "Day of Absence," "An Evening of One Acts," "Man Better Man," "Brotherhood," "Akokawe," "Rosalee Pritchett," "Sty of the Blind Pig," "Ballet Behind the Bridge," "Good Woman of Setzuan" (LC), "Behold! Cometh the Vanderkellans," "Orrin," "Boesman and Lena," "Do Lord Remember Me," "Nevis Mountain Dew," "Daughters of the Mock," "Big City Blues," "Zooman and the Sign," "Sleep Beauty."

FOSTER, GLORIA. Born Nov. 15, 1936 in Chicago, IL. Attended IllState U. Goodman Th. Debut 1963 OB in "In White America," followed by "Medea" for which she received a Theatre World Award, "Yerma," "A Hand Is on the Gate," "Black Visions," "The Cherry Orchard," "Agamemnon," "Coriolanus," "Mother Courage," "A Long Day's Journey into Night," "Trespassing."

FOSTER, HORACE, JR. Born Aug. 22 in NYC. Debut 1958 OB in "The Egg and I," followed by "Railroad Bill."

FOUQUET, PAUL. Born Oct. 13, 1954 in Rochester, NY. Graduate UDayton. Debut 1982 OB in "Divine Fire."

FOWLER, CLEMENT. Born Dec. 27, 1924 in Detroit, Mi. Graduate Wayne State U. Bdwy debut 1951 in "Legend of Lovers," followed by "The Cold Wind and the Warm," "Fragile Fox," "The Sunshine Boys," "Hamlet (1964), OB in "The Eagle Has Two Heads," "House Music."

FRANCIS-JAMES, PETER. Born Sept. 16, 1956 in Chicago, Il. Graduate RADA. Debut 1979 OB in "Julius Caesar," followed by "Long Day's Journey into Night," "Antigone."

FRANK, RICHARD. Born Jan. 4, 1954 in Boston, Ma. Graduate UMich. Debut 1978 OB in "Spring Awakening," followed by "Salt Lake City Skyline," Bdwy 1981 in "The Dresser."

FRANKFATHER, WILLIAM. Born Aug. 4, 1944 in Kermit, TX. Graduate NMexStateU, Stanford U. Bdwy debut 1980 in "Children of a Lesser God."

FRANZ, ELIZABETH, Born June 18, 1941 in Akron, OH. Attended AADA. Debut 1965 OB in "In White America," followed by "One Night Stands of a Noisy Passenger," "The Real Inspector Hound," "Augusta," "Yesterday Is Over," "Actor's Nightmare," "Sister Mary Ignatius Explains It All," Bdwy in "Rosencrantz and Guildenstern Are Dead," "The Cherry Orchard."

FRANZ, JOY. Born in 1944 in Modesto, CA. Graduate UMo. Debut 1969 OB in "Of Thee I Sing," followed by "Jacques Brel Is Alive. . . ." "Out of This World," "Curtains," "I Can't Keep Running in Place," "Tomfoolery," Bdwy in "Sweet Charity," "Lysistrata," "A Little Night Music," "Pippin," "Musical Chairs."

FRASER, ALISON. Born July 8, 1955 in Natick, MA. Attended Carnegie-Mellon U., Boston Consv. Debut 1979 OB in "In Trousers," followed by "March of the Falsettos."

FRATANTONI, DIANE. Born Mar. 29, 1956 in Wilmington, DE. Bdwy debut 1979 in "A Chorus Line."

FREEMAN, MORGAN. Born June 1, 1937 in Memphis, TN. Attended LACC. Bdwy bow 1967 in "Hello, Dolly!" followed by "The Mighty Gents," OB in "Ostrich Feathers," "Niggerlovers," "Exhibition," "Black Visions," "Cockfight," "White Pelicans," "Julius Caesar," "Coriolanus," "Mother Courage," "The Connection," "The World of Ben Caldwell."

FRELICH, PHYLLIS. Born Feb. 29, 1944 in NDakota. Graduate Gallaudet Col. Bdwy debut 1970 in Ntl. Theatre of the Deaf's "Songs from Milkwood," followed by "Children of a Lesser God," OB in "Poets from the Inside."

FRENCH, ARTHUR. Born in NYC. Attended Brooklyn Col. Debut 1962 OB in "Raisin' Hell in the Sun," followed by "Ballad of Bimshire," "Day of Absence," "Happy Ending," "Jonah," "Black Girl," "Ceremonies in Dark Old Men," "An Evening of One Acts," "Man Better Man," "Brotherhood," "Perry's Mission," "Rosalee Pritchett," "Moonlight Arms," "Dark Tower," "Brownsville Raid," "Nevis Mt. Dew," "Julius Caesar," "Friends," "Court of Miracles," Bdwy in "Ain't Supposed to Die a Natural Death," "The Iceman Cometh," "All God's Chillun Got Wings," "The Resurrection of Lady Lester."

FRENCH, VALERIE. Born in London, Eng. Bdwy debut 1965 in "Inadmissible Evidence," followed by "Help Stamp Out Marriage," "Mother Lover," "Children, Children," OB in "Tea Party," "Trelawny of the Wells," "Studs Edsel," "Henry V," "John Gabriel Borkman," "Fallen Angels," "A Taste of Honey."

FRIEDMAN, PETER. Born Apr. 24, 1949 in NYC. Debut 1971 OB in "James Joyce Memorial Liquid Theatre," followed by "Big and Little," "A Soldier's Play," Bdwy in "The Visit," "Chemin de Fer," "Love for Love," Rules of the Game," "Piaf!"

FRIES, CATHERINE. Born Oct. 7, 1961 in Hollywood, Ca. Attended USCal. Bdwy debut 1982 in "Do Black Patent Leather Shoes Really Reflect Up?"

FRIESEN, RICK. Born Nov. 29, 1943 in Minneapolis, Mn. Graduate UKan. Debut 1972 OB in "Mystery Play," followed by "Chantecler," Bdwy 1976 in "Fiddler on the Roof."

GABLE, JUNE. Born June 5, 1945 in NYC. Carnegie Tech graduate. OB in "Macbird," "Jacques Brel Is Alive and Well. . . ." "A Day in the Life of Just About Everyone," "Mod Donna," "Wanted," "Lady Audley's Secret," "Comedy of Errors," "Chinchilla," "Star Treatment," "Coming Attractions," Bdwy in "Candide" (1974), "The Ritz."

GAEBLER, MARY. Born May 4, 1951 in Davenport, IA. Graduate UWi., Oxford U. Bdwy debut 1980 in "The Music Man," OB in "Sea-Dream."

GAINES, BOYD. Born May 11, 1953 in Atlanta, GA. Juilliard graduate. Debut 1978 OB in "Spring Awakening," followed by "A Month in the Country" for which he received a Theatre World Award, BAM Theatre Co.'s "Winter's Tale," "The Barbarians," and "Johnny On a Spot," "Vikings.'

GALBRAITH, PHILIP. Born Dec. 12, 1950 in Toronto, Can. Graduate UWindsor. Debut 1982 OB in "Nymph Errant."

GALE, DAVID. Born Oct. 2, 1936 in England. Debut 1958 OB in "Elizabeth the Queen," followed by "Othello," "White Devil," "Baal," "What Do They Know about Love Uptown?," "Joe Egg," "The Trial," "Buy the Bi and Bye," "Dumbwaiter," "The Dodge Boys," "Biko Inquest," "Orpheus Descending," "The Price," Bdwy in "Of Mice and Men" (1974), "Sweet Bird of Youth."

GALLAGHER, HELEN. Born in 1926 in Brooklyn, NY. Bdwy debut 1947 in "Seven Lively Arts," followed by "Mr Strauss Goes to Boston," "Billion Dollar Baby," "Brigadoon," "High Button Shoes," "Touch and Go," "Make a Wish," "Pal Joey," "Guys and Dolls," "Finian's Rainbow," "Oklahoma!," "Pajama Game," "Bus Stop," "Portofino," "Sweet Charity," "Mame," "Cry for Us All," "No, No, Nanette," "A Broadway Musical," "Sugar Babies," OB in "Hothouse," "Tickles by Tucholsky," "The Misanthrope," "I Can't Keep Running in Place."

GALLOGLY, JOHN. Born Aug. 23, 1952 in Providence, RI. Attended UNotre Dame. Debut OB 1975 in "Gorky," followed by "The Gathering," "The Meehans," "Letters to Ben," Bdwy in "Runaways," "The Utter Glory of Morrissey Hall," "A Stitch in Time."

GALLOWAY, JANE. Born Feb. 27, 1950 in St. Louis, Mo. Attended Webster Col. Debut 1976 OB in "Vanities," followed by "Domino Courts," "Comanche Cafe," Bdwy debut 1982 in "Little Johnny Jones."

GANTRY, DONALD. Born June 11, 1936 in Philadelphia, Pa. Attended Temple U. Bdwy debut 1961 in "One More River," followed by "Ah, Wilderness," OB in "The Iceman Cometh," "Children of Darkness," "Here Come the Clowns," "Seven at Dawn," "Long Day's Journey into Night," "Enclave," "Bags."

GARBER, VICTOR. Born Mar. 16, 1949 in London, Can. Debut 1973 OB in "Ghosts" for which he received a Theatre World Award, followed by "Joe's Opera," "Cracks," Bdwy in "Tartuffe," "Deathtrap," "Sweeney Todd," "They're Playing Our Song," "Little Me."

GARCIA, CHAMACO. Born May 14, 1938 in Havana, Cuba. Debut 1981 OB in "El Bravo!"

GARDNER, KATHRYN. Born June 23, 1958 in Lorain, Oh. Graduate UCin. Debut 1981 OB in "Seesaw."

GARDNER, LAURA. Born Mar. 17, 1951 in Flushing, NY. Graduate Boston U., Rutgers U. Debut 1979 OB in "The Office Murders," followed by "Welded."

GAREE, RYON C. Born Dec. 31, 1950 in Merrillville, In. Graduate SUNY/Binghamton. Debut 1976 OB in "Fiorello!," followed by "Lysistrata," Bdwy 1977 in "Equus."

GARFIELD, JULIE. Born Jan. 10, 1946 in Los Angeles, CA. Attended UWi., Neighborhood Playhouse. Debut 1969 OB in "Honest-to-God Schnozzola," followed by "East Lynne," "The Sea," "Uncle Vanya" for which she received a Theatre World Award," "Me and Molly," "Chekhov Sketchbook," "Rosario and the Gypsies," "Occupations," Bdwy in "The Good Doctor," "Death of a Salesman," "The Merchant."

GARLAND, GEOFF. Born June 10, 1932 in Warrington, Eng. OB in "The Hostage," "Trelawny of the Wells," "Timon of Athens," "Waiting for Godot," "Billy Liar," Bdwy in "Hamlet," "Imaginary Invalid," "Touch of the Poet," "Tonight at 8:30," "Front Page," "Capt. Brassbound's Conversion," "Cyrano," "My Fat Friend," "Sly Fox," "The Dresser."

GARNETT, CHIP. Born May 8, 1953 in New Kensington, PA. Attended IndU. Debut 1973 OB in "Inner City," followed by "Rhapsody in Gershwin," Bdwy in "Candide," "Bubbling Brown Sugar" for which he received a Theatre World Award, "The Little Prince and the Aviator."

GARNETT, GALE. Born July 23 In Auckland, NZ. Debut 1959 OB in "Jack," followed by "Sisters of Mercy," "Greatest Fairy Story Ever Told," "Cracks," "Ladyhouse Blues," "My Sister's Keeper," "Goose and Tomtom," Bdwy in "The World of Suzie Wong," "Ulysses in Nighttown."

GARRETT, BETTY. Born May 23, 1919 in St. Joseph, Mo. Credits include "Of V We Sing," "Let Freedom Ring," "Something for the Boys," "Jackpot," "Laffing Room Only," "Call Me Mister," "Bells Are Ringing," "Beg, Borrow or Steal," "Spoon River Anthology," "A Girl Could Get Lucky," "Supporting Cast."

GARRICK, BEULAH. Born Jun 12, 1921 in Nottingham, Eng. Bdwy debut 1959 in "Shadow and Substance," followed by "Auntie Mame," "Juno," "Little Moon of Alban," "High Spirits," "The Hostage," "Funny Girl," "Lovers," "Abelard and Heloise," "Ulysses in Nightown," "Copperfield," OB in "Little Boxes," "Berkeley Square," "Fallen Angels," "Henry IV Part II."

GARRIPOLI, MARY. Born Mar. 15, 1956 in NJ. Graduate Ramapo Col. Debut 1978 OB in "Pins and Needles," followed by "T.N.T.," Bdwy in "The Utter Glory of Morrissey Hall," (1979), "Peter Pan."

GARRISON, DAVID. Born June 30, 1952 in Long Branch, NJ. Graduate Boston U. Debut OB in "Joseph and the Amazing Technicolor Dreamcoat," followed by "Living at Home," "Geniuses," Bdwy in "A History of the American Film," "A Day in Hollywood/A Night in the Ukraine," "Pirates of Penzance."

GATTO, PETER. Born Jan. 24, 1946 in Brooklyn, NY. Graduate Bklyn Col., Neighborhood Playhouse. Debut 1970 OB in "Edward II," followed by "Bus Riley's Back in Town," "Volpone," "Sacraments," "Chiaroscuro," "Heroes."

GAVON, IGORS. Born Nov. 14, 1937 in Latvia. Bdwy bow 1961 in "Carnival," followed by "Hello Dolly!," "Marat/deSade," "Billy," "Sugar," "Mack and Mabel," "Musical Jubilee," "Strider," OB in "Your Own Thing," "Promenade," "Exchange," "Nevertheless They Laugh," "Polly," "The Boss," "Biography: A Game," "Murder in the Cathedral."

GECKS, NICHOLAS. Born Jan. 9, 1952 in Penang, Malaysia. Graduate UEast Anglia, London Central School of Speech. Bdwy debut 1981 in "Nicholas Nickleby."

GEFFNER, DEBORAH. Born Aug 26, 1952 in Pittsburgh, PA. Attended Juilliard, HB Studio. Debut 1978 OB in "Tenderloin," Bdwy in "Pal Joey," "A Chorus Line."

GELKE, BECKY. Born Feb. 17, 1953 in Ft. Knox, KY. Graduate Western Ky.U. Debut 1978 OB and Bdwy in "The Best Little Whorehouse in Texas."

GENEST, EDMOND. Born Oct. 27, 1943 in Boston, MA. Attended Suffolk U. Debut 1972 OB in "The Real Inspector Hound," "The Browning Version," Bdwy in "Dirty Linen/New-Found-Land," "Whose Life Is It Anyway?" "Onward Victoria."

GENTLES, AVRIL. Born Apr. 2, 1929 in Upper Montclair, NJ. Graduate UNC. Bdwy debut 1955 in "The Great Sebastians," followed by "Nude with Violin," "Present Laughter," "My Mother, My Father and Me," "Jimmy Shine," "Grin and Bare It," "Lysistrata," "Texas Trilogy," OB in "Dinny and the Witches," "The Wives," "Now Is the Time," "Man with a Load of Mischief," "Shay," "Winter's Tale," "Johnny on a Spot," "The Barbarians," "The Wedding," "Nymph Errant."

GERACI, FRANK. Born Sept. 8, 1939 in Brooklyn, NY. Attended Yale, HB Studio. Debut 1961 OB in "Color of Darkness," followed by "Mr. Grossman," "Balm in Gilead," "The Fantasticks," "Tom Paine," "End of All Things Natural," "Union Street," "Uncle Vanya," "Success Story," "Hughie," Bdwy in "Love and Suicide at Schofield Barracks."

GERETY, PETER. Born May 17, 1940 in Providence, RI. Attended URI, Boston U. Debut 1964 OB in "In the Summer House," followed by "Othello," "Baal," Bdwy 1982 in "The Hothouse."

GERROLL, DANIEL. Born Oct. 16, 1951 in London, Eng. Attended Central Sch. of Speech. Debut 1980 OB in "The Slab Boys," followed by "Knuckle" and "Translations" for which he received a Theatre World Award, "The Caretaker," "Scenes from La Vie de Boheme."

GERSHENSON, SUE ANNE. Born Feb. 18, 1953 in Chicago, Il. Attended IndU. Debut 1976 OB in "Panama Hattie," followed by "Carnival," "Street Scene."

GETTY, ESTELLE. Born July 25, 1923 in NYC. Attended New School. Debut 1971 OB in "The Divorce of Judy and Jane," followed by "Widows and Children First," "Table Settings," "Demolition of Hannah Fay," "Never Too Old," "A Box of Tears," "Hidden Corners," "I Don't Know Why I'm Screaming," "Under the Bridge There's a Lonely Place," "Light Up the Sky," "Pocketful of Posies," "Fits and Starts," Bdwy 1982 in "Torch Song Trilogy."

GIANNINI, CHERYL. Born June 15 in Monessen. PA. Bdwy debut, 1980 in "The Suicide," followed by "Grownups."

GILBERT, ALAN. Born Mar. 4, 1949 in Seneca, Ks. Graduate USyracuse. Debut 1972 OB in "No Strings," followed by "Follies," Bdwy in "My Fair Lady" (1981), "The Little Prince and the Aviator."

GILBERT, RONNIE. Born Sept. 7 in NYC. Bdwy debut 1968 in "The Man in the Glass Booth," OB in "America Hurrah," "Hector the Herioc," "Hot Buttered Roll," "Viet Rock," "Tourists and Refugees," "Antigone," "Trespassing."

GILBORN, STEVEN. Born in New Rochelle, NY. Graduate Swarthmore Col., Stanford U. Bdwy debut 1973 in "Creeps," followed by "The Basic Training of Pavlo Hummel," "Tartuffe," OB in "Rosmersholm," "Henry V," "Measure for Measure," "Ashes," "The Dybbuk," "Museum," "Shadow of a Gunman," "The Middle Ages."

GILETTO, JOHN BASIL. Born Sept. 27, 1950 in Philadelphia, Pa. Graduate Temple U. Debut 1977 OB in "Dance on a Country Grave," followed by "Innocent Thoughts, Harmless Intentions," "The Bacchae," "The Halls Where Fatima Once Stood," "The Scarecrow."

GILFORD, JACK. Born July 25, 1907 in NYC. Bdwy debut 1940 in "Meet the People," followed by "They Should Have Stood in Bed," "Count Me In," "The Live Wire," "Alive and Kicking," "Once Over Lightly," "Diary of Anne Frank," "Romanoff and Juliet," "The Tenth Man," "A Funny Thing Happened on the Way to the Forum," "Cabaret," "3 Men on a Horse," "No, No Nanette," "The Sunshine Boys," "Sly Fox," "Supporting Cast," "The World of Sholom Aleichem."

GILL, TERI. Born July 16, 1954 in Long Island City, NY. Graduate USIU. Bdwy debut 1976 in "Going Up," followed by "Evita," OB in "Allegro."

GILLETTE, ANITA. Born Aug. 16, 1938 in Baltimore, MD. Debut 1960 OB in "Russell Patterson's Sketchbook" for which she received a Theatre World Award, followed by "Rich and Famous," Bdwy in "Carnival," "All American," "Mr. President," "Guys and Dolls," "Don't Drink the Water," "Cabaret," "Jimmy," "Chapter Two," "They're Playing Our Song."

GILPIN, JACK. Born May 31, 1951 in Boyce, VA. Harvard graduate Debut 1976 OB in "Goodbye and Keep Cold," followed by "Shay," "The Soft Touch," "Beyond Therapy," "The Lady or the Tiger," "The Middle Ages," Bdwy in "Lunch Hour" ('80).

GINTER, LINDSEY. Born Dec. 13, 1950 in Alameda, CA. Attended UPacific. Debut 1980 OB in "Hamlet," followed by "Mary Stuart," "A Tale Told," Bdwy in "5th of July."

GIOMBETTI, KAREN. Born May 24, 1955 in Scranton, PA. Graduate NYU. Bdwy debut 1978 in "Stop the World, I Want to Get Off," followed by "The Most Happy Fella," "Woman of the Year."

GIONSON, MEL. Born Feb. 23, 1954 in Honolulu, Hi. Graduate UHi. Debut 1979 OB in "Richard II," followed by "Sunrise," "Monkey Music," "Behind Enemy Lines," "Station J."

GIRARDEAU, FRANK. Born Oct. 19, 1942 in Beaumont. TX. Attended Rider Col., HB Studio. Debut 1972 OB in "22 Years," followed by "The Solider," "Hughie," "An American Story," "El Hermano," "Dumping Ground."

GLASS, JERALYN. Born Dec. 7, 1958 in Encino, Ca. Attended USC, USCLA. Bdwy debut 1981 in "My Fair Lady."

GLEASON, PAUL. Born May 4, 1941 in Miami, Fl. Graduate FlStateU. Debut 1973 OB in "One Flew Over the Cuckoo's Nest," followed by "Economic Necessity," "Niagara Falls," "Alfred the Great," "Violano Virtuoso," "Roads to Home."

GLOVER, DANNY. Born July 22, 1947 in San Francisco, Ca. Attended SFStateCol. Debut 1980 OB in "The Bloodknot," followed by "Master Harold . . . and the boys" for which he received a Theatre World Award.

GLOVER, JOHN. Born Aug. 7, 1944 in Kingston, NY. Attended Towson State Col. Debut 1969 OB in "A Scent of Flowers," followed by "Government Inspector," "Rebel Women," "Treats," "Booth," Bdwy in "The Selling of the President," "Great God Brown," "Don Juan," "The Visit," "Chemin de Fer," "Holiday," "The Importance of Being Earnest," "Frankenstein."

GLYNN, CARLIN. Born Feb. 19, 1940 in Cleveland, OH. Attended Sophie Newcomb Col., Actors Studio. Debut 1959 OB in "Waltz of the Toreadors," followed by "Cassatt," Bdwy 1978 in "The Best Little Whorehouse in Texas" for which she received a Theatre World Award.

GODFREY, JOE. Born Feb. 27, 1946 in Boston, Ma. Graduate Lehigh U. Debut 1974 OB in "Up in the Air Boys," followed by "Rabbit Ears," "Preacherman," "Two."

GOLD, JULIANNE. Born June 18, 1960 in Rochester, MN. Attended CaStateU. Bdwy debut 1980 in "Children of a Lesser God!"

GOLD, RUSSELL. Born Oct. 23, 1917 in New Britain, CT. Attended Pasadena Playhouse, AmThWing. Bdwy debut 1948 in "Harvey," followed by "Romeo and Juliet," "Point of No Return," "Dear Charles," "Little Foxes," "Amadeus," OB in "Royal Gambit," "The Prodigal," "Rendezvous at Senlis," "Place for Chance," "Corruption in the Palace of Justice," "Winterset."

GOLDSMITH, MERWIN. Born Aug. 7, 1937 in Detroit, MI. Graduate UCLA, Old Vic. Bdwy debut 1970 in "Minnie's Boys," followed by "The Visit," "Chemin de Fer," "Rex," "Dirty Linen," "The 1940's Radio Show," OB in "Hamlet as a Happening," "Chickencoop Chinaman," "Wanted," "Comedy," "Rubbers," "Yankees 3, Detroit 0," "Trelawny of the Wells," "Chinchilla," "Real Life Funnies," "Big Apple Messenger."

GOLDSTEIN, LESLIE. Born Jan. 22, 1940 in Newark, NJ. Graduate Newark Col. Debut 1976 OB in "Men in White," followed by "Native Bird," "Antigone," "The Lover," "Middle of the Night," "Second Avenue Rag," "Darkness at Noon," "Happy Sunset Inc.," Bdwy 1979 in "Meeting by the River."

GOODMAN, GERRY. Born Apr. 30, 1955 in New Rochelle, NY. Graduate SUNY/Purchase. Debut 1982 OB in "Teach Me How to Cry" (ELT).

GOODMAN, JOHN. Born June 20, 1952 in St. Louis, MO. Graduate Southwest MoStateU. Debut 1978 OB in "A Midsummer Night's Dream," followed by "The Chisholm Trail," "Henry IV Part II," "Ghosts of the Loyal Oaks."

GOODMAN, ROBYN. Born Aug. 24, 1947 in NYC. Graduate Brandeis U. Debut 1973 OB in "When You Comin' Back, Red Ryder?" followed by "Richard III," "Museum," "Bits and Pieces," "Fishing," "Flux."

GORDON, CARL. Born Jan 20, 1932 in Richmond, VA. Bdwy 1966 in "The Great White Hope," followed by "Ain't Supposed to Die a Natural Death," OB in "Day of Absence," "Happy Ending," "The Strong Breed," "Trials of Brother Jero," "Kongi's Harvest," "Welcome to Black River," "Shark," "Orrin and Sugar Mouth," "A Love Play," "The Great MacDaddy," "In an Upstate Motel," "Zooman and the Sign."

GORDON, LEE. Born July 7, 1968 in Ft. Worth, Tx. Bdwy debut 1982 in "The Little Prince and the Aviator."

GORRILL, MAGGY. Born Feb. 19, 1952 in Long Island City, NY. Attended Barnard Col. Debut 1975 OB in "Diamond Studs," followed by "Bags," Bdwy in "Dr Jazz," "A Broadway Musical," "Peter Pan."

GOSSETT, ROBERT. Born Mar. 3, 1954 in The Bronx, NY. Attended AADA. Debut 1973 OB in "One Flew over the Cuckoo's Nest," followed by "The Amen Corner," "Weep Not for Me," "Colored People's Time."

GOTTLEIB, MATTHEW. Born Apr. 6, 1951 in Ann Arbor, MI. Graduate CalnstofArts. Debut 1980 OB in "Friend of the Family," followed by "Henry IV Part 2."

GOTTSCHALL, RUTH. Born Apr. 14, 1957 in Wilmington, De. Bdwy debut 1981 in "The Best Little Whorehouse in Texas."

GOULD, ELLEN. Born Dec. 30, 1950 in Worcester, MA. Graduate Brandeis U,NYU. Debut 1979 OB in "Confessions of a Reformed Romantic," followed by "Gewandter Songs," "Three Irish No Plays," "Yeats Trio," "Heat of Reentry," Bdwy in "Macbeth" ('81).

GOULD, GORDON. Born May 4, 1930 in Chicago, IL. Yale graduate. With APA in "Man and Superman," "War and Peace," "Judith," "Lower Depths," "Right You Are," "Scapin," "Impromptu at Versailles," "You Can't Take It With You," "The Hostage," "The Tavern," "A Midsummer Night's Dream," "Merchant of Venice," "Richard II," "Much Ado About Nothing," "Wild Duck," "The Show-Off," and "Pantagleize," "Strider," Bdwy in "Freedom of the City," "Amadeus."

GOULD, HAROLD. Born Dec. 10, 1923 in Schenectady, NY. Graduate SUNY, Cornell. Debut 1969 OB in "The Increased Difficulty of Concentration," followed by "Amphitryon," "House of Blue Leaves," "Touching Bottom," Bdwy in "Fools," (1981), "Grownups."

GOUTMAN, CHRISTOPHER. Born Dec. 19, 1952 in Bryn Mawr, Pa. Graduate Haverford Col., Carnegie-Mellon U. Debut 1978 OB in "The Promise" for which he received a Theatre World Award, followed by "Grand Magic," "The Skirmishers."

GOZ, HARRY. Born June 23, 1932 in St. Louis, MO. Attended St. Louis Inst. Debut 1957 in "Utopia Limited," followed by "Bajour," "Fiddler on the Roof," "Two by Two," "Prisoner of Second Avenue," OB in "To Bury a Cousin," "Ferocious Kisses."

GRAAE, JASON. Born May 15, 1958 in Chicago, IL. Graduate Cincinnati Consv. Debut 1981 OB in "Godspell," Bdwy 1982 in "Do Black Patent Leather Shoes Really Reflect Up?"

GRADL, CHRISTINE. Born June 29, 1960 in St. Louis, Mo. Attended Kent State U. Bdwy debut 1982 in "Do Black Patent Leather Shoes Really Reflect Up?"

GRAFF, RANDY. Born May 23, 1955 in Brooklyn, NY. Graduate Wagner Col. Debut 1978 OB in "Pins and Needles," followed by "Station Joy," Bdwy in "Sarava," "Grease."

GRAHAM, DONNA. Born Sept. 28, 1964 in Philadelphia, PA. Bdwy debut 1977 in "Annie."

GRAMMIS, ADAM. Born Dec. 8, 1947 in Allentown, PA. Graduate Kutztown State Col. Bdwy debut 1971 in "Wild and Wonderful," followed by "Shirley MacLaine Show," "A Chorus LIne," OB in "Dance Continuum," "Joseph and the Amazing Technicolor Dreamcoat."

GRANGER, FARLEY. Born July 1, 1928 in San Jose, CA. Bdwy debut 1959 in "First Impressions," followed by "The Warm Peninsula," "Advise and Consent," CC's "The King and I" and "Brigadoon," "The Seagull," "The Crucible," "Deathtrap," OB in "The Carefree Tree," "A Month in the Country."

GRANT, DAVID MARSHALL. Born June 21, 1955 in New Haven, CT. Attended ConnCol., Yale. Debut OB 1978 in "Sganarelle," followed by "Table Settings," "The Tempest," Bdwy in "Bent" ('79), "The Survivor."

GRANT, EVA. Born Nov. 1, 1961 in NYC. Bdwy debut 1970 in "The Grass Harp," OB in "Nymph Errant."

GRAY, SAM. Born July 18, 1923 in Chicago, Il. Graduate Columbia U. Bdwy debut 1955 in "Deadfall," followed by "Six Fingers in a Five Finger Glove," "Saturday, Sunday, Monday," "Golda," OB in "Ascent of F-6," "Family Portrait," "One Tiger on a Hill," "Shadow of Heroes," "The Recruiting Officer," "The Wild Duck," "Jungle of Cities," "3 Acts of Recognition."

GREEN, PETER. Born Dec. 16, 1955 in NYC. Graduate SUNY/Purchase. Debut 1979 OB in "The City Suite," followed by "Badgers."

GREEN, TERRY F. Born April 28 in NYC. Graduate Lehman Col. Debut 1982 OB in "The Trip Back Down."

GREENE, ELLEN. Born Feb. 22 in NYC. Attended Ryder Col. Debut 1973 in "Rachel Lily Rosenbloom," followed OB by "In the Boom Boom Room," "Threepenny Opera," "The Nature and Purpose of the Universe," "Teeth 'n' Smiles," "The Sorrows of Stephen," "Disrobing the Bride," "The Little Shop of Horrors," Bdwy 1981 in "The Little Prince and the Aviator."

GREENE, JAMES. Born Dec. 1, 1926 in Lawrence, MA. Graduate Emerson Col. OB in "The Iceman Cometh," "American Gothic," "The King and the Duke," "The Hostage," "Plays for Bleecker Street," "Moon in the Yellow River," "Misalliance," "Government Inspector," "Baba Goya," LCRep 2 years, "You Can't Take It With You," "School for Scandal," "Wild Duck," "Right You Are," "The Show-Off," "Pantagleize," "Festival of Short Plays," "Nourish the Beast," "One Crack Out," "Artichoke," "Othello," "Salt Lake City Skyline," "Summer," "The Rope Dancers," "Frugal Repast," "Bella Figura," "The Freak," Bdwy in "Romeo and Juliet," "Girl on the Via Flaminia," "Compulsion," "Inherit the Wind," "Shadow of a Gunman," "Andersonville Trial," "Night Life," "School for Wives," "Ring Round the Bathtub," "Great God Brown," "Don Juan."

GREENE, MARTY. Born June 19, 1909 in Brooklyn, NY. Bdwy bow 1940 in "Summer Night," followed by "Night Music," "Golden Boy," "Enter Laughing," "Out West of Eighth," OB in "God Bless You, Harold Fineberg," "Threepenny Opera," "Whose Little Boy Are You?," "The Wonderful Ice Cream Suit."

GREENHOUSE, MARTHA. Born June 14 in Omaha, Ne. Attended Hunter Col., Theatre Wing. Bdwy debut 1942 in "Sons and Soldiers," followed by "Dear Me, the Sky Is Falling," "Family Way," "Woman Is My Idea," "Summer Brave," OB in "Clerambard," "Our Town," "3 by Ferlinghetti," "No Strings," "Cackle," "Philistines."

GREGORIO, ROSE. Born in Chicago, Il. Graduate Northwestern, Yale. Debut 1962 OB in "The Days and Nights of Beebee Fenstermaker," followed by "Kiss Mama," "The Balcony," "Bivouac at Lucca," "Journey to the Day," "Diary of Anne Frank," "Weekends Like Other People," Bdwy in "The Owl and the Pussycat," "Daphne in Cottage D," "Jimmy Shine," "The Cuban Thing," "The Shadow Box."

GREGORY, MICHAEL SCOTT. Born Mar. 13, 1962 in Ft. Lauderdale, Fl. Attended Atlantic Foundation for Performing Arts. Bdwy bow 1981 in "Sophisticated Ladies."

GRIER, DAVID ALAN. Born June 30, 1955 in Detroit, Mi. Graduate UMich., Yale. Bdwy debut 1981 in "The First" for which he received a Theatre World Award, OB in "A Soldier's Play."

GRIESEMER, JOHN. Born Dec. 5, 1947 in Elizabeth, NJ. Graduate Dickinson Col., URI. Debut 1981 OB in "Turnbuckle," followed by "Death of a Miner."

GRIFFIN, SEAN G. Born Oct. 14, 1942 in Limerick, Ire. Graduate Notre Dame, UKan. Bdwy debut 1974 in "The National Health," followed by "Poor Murderer" "Ah, Wilderness!," "Ned and Jack."

GRIFFITH, KRISTIN. Born Sept. 7, 1953 in Odessa, TX. Juilliard graduate. Bdwy debut 1976 in "A Texas Trilogy," OB in "Rib Cage," "Character Lines," "3 Friends/2 Rooms," "A Month in the Country," "Fables for Friends," "The Trading Post," "Marching to Georgia," "American Garage."

GRIMES, TAMMY. Born Jan. 30, 1934 in Lynn, MA. Attended Stephens Col., Neighborhood Playhouse. Debut 1956 OB in "The Littlest Revue," followed by "Clerambard," "Molly," "Trick," "Are You Now or Have You Ever Been," "Father's Day," "A Month in the Country," Bdwy in "Look After Lulu" (1959) for which she received a Theatre World Award, "The Unsinkable Molly Brown," "Rattle of a Simple Man," "High Spirit," "The Only Game in town" "Private Lives," "Musical Jubilee," "California Suite," "Tartuffe," "42nd Street."

GRODY, SVETLANA McLEE. Born Sept. 22, 1929 in Hollywood, Ca. Bdwy debut 1953 in "Me and Juliet," followed by "Damn Yankees," "Ziegfeld Follies," "Happy Hunting," "My Fair Lady," "Wonderful Town," "Foxy," "My Fair Lady" (1981), OB in "The Boys from Syracuse."

GROENENDAAL, CRIS. Born Feb. 17, 1948 in Erie, PA. Attended Allegheny Col., Exeter (Eng) U, HB Studio. Bdwy debut 1979 in "Sweeney Todd," OB in "Francis."

GROENER, HARRY. Born Sept. 10, 1951 in Augsburg. Ger. Graduate UWash. Bdwy debut 1979 in "Oklahoma!" for which he received a Theatre World Award, followed by "Oh, Brother!," "Is There Life after HIgh School," OB in "Beside the Seaside."

GROLLMAN, ELAINE. Born Oct. 22, 1928 in The Bronx, NY. Debut 1974 OB in "Yentl the Yeshiva Boy," followed by "Kaddish," "The Water Hen," "Millions of Miles," "Come Back, Little Sheba," "Biography: A Game," "House Music," Bdwy in "Yentl."

GROSS, GENE. Born Feb. 17, 1920 in NYC. Debut 1957 OB in "Career," followed by "Cannibals," "After Many a Summer," Bdwy in "Handful of Fire," "J.B.," "The Passion of Josef D."

GROSS, MICHAEL. Born in 1947 in Chicago, IL. UIll and Yale graduate. Debut 1978 OB in "Sganarelle," followed by "Othello," "Endgame," "The Wild Duck," "Oedipus the King," "Put Them All Together," "No End of Blame," "Geniuses," Bdwy in "Bent." ('79), "The Philadelphia Story."

GUARDINO, HARRY. Born Dec. 23, 1925 in NYC. Credits include "End as a Man," "A Hatful of Rain," "Natural Affection," "Anyone Can Whistle," "The Rose Tattoo" ('66), "The Seven Descents of Myrtle," "Woman of the Year."

GUIDA, MARIA. Born May 1, 1953 in Jackson Heights, NY. Graduate NYU. Debut 1972 OB in "Bread and Roses," followed by "Fallen Angels," "Impromptu," "Dutchman," "Pirates of Penzance," Bdwy in "King of Hearts," "Pirates of Penzance."

GUNDERSON, STEVE. Born June 9, 1957 in San Diego, Ca. Attended SDStateU. Debut 1982 OB in "Street Scene."

GUNTON, BOB. Born Nov. 15, 1945 in Santa Monica, CA. Attended UCal. Debut 1971 OB in "Who Am I?," followed by "The Kid," "Desperate Hours," "Tip-Toes," "How I Got That Story," Bdwy in "Happy End" (1977), "Working," "King of Hearts," "Evita."

GURNEY, RACHEL. Born March 5 in England. Debut 1977 OB in "You Never Can Tell," followed by "Heartbreak House," Bdwy in "Major Barbara" (1980), "The Dresser."

GUSKIN, HAROLD. Born May 25, 1941 in Brooklyn, NY. Graduate Rutgers U, Ind. U. Debut 1980 OB in "Second Avenue Rag," followed by "Grand Street," "Crazy for You Revue."

GWILLIM, JACK. Born Dec. 15, 1915 in Canterbury, Eng. Attended Central School. Bdwy debut 1956 in "Macbeth," followed by "Romeo and Juliet," "Richard II," "Troilus and Cressida," "Laurette," "Ari," "Lost in the Stars," "The Iceman Cometh," "The Constant Wife," "Romeo and Juliet" ('77), "My Fair Lady" ('81), OB in "The Farm."

HADARY, JONATHAN. Born Oct. 11, 1948 in Chicago, IL. Attended Tufts U. Debut 1974 OB in "White Nights," followed by "El Grande de Coca-Cola," "Songs from Pins and Needles," "God Bless You, Mr. Rosewater," "Pushing 30," "Scrambled Feet," "Coming Attractions," "Tomfoolery," Bdwy 1977 in "Gemini" (also OB).

HALL, GEORGE. Born Nov. 19, 1916 in Toronto. Can. Attended Neighborhood Playhouse. Bdwy bow 1946 in "Call Me Mister," followed by "Lend an Ear," "Touch and Go," "Live Wire," "The Boy Friend," "There's a Girl in My Soup," "An Evening with Richard Nixon . . .," "We Interrupt This Program," "Man and Superman," "Bent," OB in "The Balcony," "Ernest in Love," "A Round with Ring," "Family Pieces," "Carousel," "The Case Against Roberta Guardino," "Marry Me! Marry Me!" "Arms and the Man," "The Old Glory," "Dancing for the Kaiser," "Casualties," "The Seagull," "A Stitch in Time," "Mary Stuart," "No End of Blame."

HALL, STEVE. Born June 4, 1958 in Washington, DC. Attended NCSchool of Arts. Bdwy debut 1981 in "Marlowe," OB in "T.N.T."

HALLETT, JACK. Born Nov. 7, 1948 in Philadelphia, Pa. Attended AADA. Debut 1972 OB in "Servant of Two Masters," Bdwy in "The 1940's Radio Show," "The First."

HANAN, STEPHEN. Born Jan. 7, 1947 in Washington, DC. Graduate Harvard, LAMDA. Debut 1978 OB in "All's Well That Ends Well," followed by "Taming of the Shrew," Bdwy 1981 in "Pirates of Penzance."

HANDLER, EVAN. Born Jan. 10, 1961 in NYC. Attended Juilliard. Debut 1979 OB in "Biography: A Game," followed by "Strider," Bdwy in "Solomon's Child."

HANKET, ARTHUR. Born June 23, 1954 in Virginia. Graduate UVa., FLStateU. Debut 1979 OB in "Cuchculain Cycle."

HANKS, BARBARA. Born Sept. 1, 1951 in Salt Lake City, UT. Debut 1978 OB in "Gay Divorce," Bdwy 1979 in "Sugar Babies."

HARALDSON, MARIAN. born Sept. 5, 1933 in Northwood, ND. Graduate St. Olaf Col. Bdwy debut 1959 in "First Impressions," followed by "The Unsinkable Molly Brown," "Mr. President," "Girl Who Came to Supper," "Merry Widow," "Walking Happy," "Dear World," "No, No, Nanette," "Lorelei," "Woman of the Year," OB in "Peace."

HARDING, JAN LESLIE. Born 1956 in Cambridge, MA. Graduate Boston U. Debut 1980 OB in "Album," followed by "Sunday Picnic," "Buddies."

HARDWICK, MARK. Born Apr. 18, 1954 in Carthage, Tx. Graduate SMU. Bdwy debut 1982 in "Pump Boys & Dinettes."

HARMAN, PAUL. Born July 29, 1952 in Mineola, NY. Graduate Tufts U. Bdwy debut 1980 in "It's So Nice to Be Civilized," OB in "City Suite."

HARNEY, BEN. Born Aug. 29, 1952 in Brooklyn, NY. Bdwy debut 1971 in "Purlie," followed by "Pajama Game," "Tree-monisha," "Pippin," "Dreamgirls," OB in "Don't Bother Me I Can't Cope," "The Derby," "The More You Get."

HARPER, CHARLES THOMAS. Born Mar. 29, 1949 in Carthage, NY. Graduate Webster Col. Debut 1975 OB in "Down by the River . . .," followed by "Holy Ghosts," "Hamlet," "Mary Stuart," "Twelfth Night," "The Beaver Coat," "Richard II," "Great Grandson of Jedediah Kohler," "Applause" (ELT).

HARPER, ROBERT. Born May 19, 1951 in NYC. Graduate Rutgers U. Bdwy debut 1978 in "Once in a Lifetime," followed by "Inspector General," "The American Clock," "Zeks."

HARPER, RON. Born Jan. 12, 1936 in Turtle Creek, Pa. Princeton graduate. Debut OB 1955 in "3 by Dylan Thomas," followed by "A Palm Tree in a Rose Garden," "Meegan's Game," Bdwy in "Sweet Bird of Youth," "Night Circus," "6 Rms Riv Vu."

HARRINGTON, DELPHI. Born Aug. 26 in Chicago, IL. Northwestern U. graduate. Debut 1960 OB in "Country Scandal," followed by "Moon for the Misbegotten," "Baker's Dozen" "The Zykovs," "Character Lines," "Richie," "American Garage," Bdwy in "Thieves," "Everything in the Garden," "Romeo and Juliet," Chapter 2"

HARRINGTON, DON. Born June 27, 1944 in Washington, DC. Graduate American U. Debut 1978 OB in "All's Well That Ends Well," followed by "A Midsummer Night's Dream," "Street Scene."

HARRIS, BAXTER. Born Nov. 18, 1940 in Columbus, Ks. Attended UKan. Debut 1967 OB in "America Hurrah," followed by "The Reckoning," "Wicked Women Revue," "More Than You Deserve," "Pericles," "him," "Battle of Angels," "Down by the River," "Selma," "Ferocious Kisses."

HARRIS, CYNTHIA. Born in NYC. Graduate Smith Col. Bdwy debut 1963 in "Natural Affection," followed by "Any Wednesday," "Best Laid Plans," "Company," OB in "The Premise," "3 by Wilder," "America Hurrah," "White House Murder Case," "Mystery Play," "Bad Habits," "Merry Wives of Windsor," "Beauty Part," "Jules Feiffer's Hold Me," "Second Avenue Rag," "Cloud 9."

HARRIS, STEVEN MICHAEL. (formerly Steven Michael) Born Aug. 31, 1957 in Fall River, MA. Attended Pasadena City Col., Clown Col. Bdwy debut 1980 in "Barnum."

HARRISON, REX. Born Mar. 5, 1908 in Huyten, Eng. Attended Liverpool Col. Bdwy debut 1936 in "Sweet Aloes," followed by "Anne of a Thousand Days," "Bell, Book and Candle," "Venus Observed," "Love of Four Colonels," "My Fair Lady" (1956/1981), "Fighting Cock," "Emperor Henry IV," "In Praise of Love," "Caesar and Cleopatra," "The Kingfisher."

HART, CECILIA. Born June 6 in Cheyenne, Wy. Graduate Emerson Col. Debut 1974 OB in "Macbeth," followed by "Emperor of Late Night Radio," "The Good Parts," Bdwy in "The Heiress" (1976), "Othello" (1982).

| Paul E. Hart | Nancy Heikin | Peter Heuchling | Ryn Hodes | Rudy Hornish | Anna Horsfor |

| Holly Hunter | Robert Hyman | Jane Ives | Stephen James | Marilyn Johnson | Page Johnso |

| Eddie Jones | Leilani Jones | Robert Joy | Nancy Kawalek | Robert Kellett | Laurie Kenne |

| Pamela Khoury | Kurt Knudson | Ronna Kress | Gary Lahti | Ann Lange | Tom Lantzy |

| Adam LeFevre | Marcia Lewis | Miller Lide | Jodi Long | Edward Love | Marcella Lowe |

HART, PAUL E. Born July 20, 1939 in Lawrence, Ma. Graudate Merrimack Col. Debut 1977 OB in "Turandot," followed by "Darkness at Noon," "Light Shines in the Darkness," Bdwy 1981 in "Fiddler on the Roof."

HARUM, EIVIND. Born May 24, 1944 in Stavanger, Norway, Attended Utah State U. Credits include "Sophie," "Foxy," "Baker Street," "West Side Story" ('68), "A Chorus Line," "Woman of the Year."

HATTAN, MARK. Born Mar. 21, 1952 in Portland, Or. Graduate UVa. Debut 1975 OB in "Our Father," followed by "Maggie Flynn," "Ferocious Kisses."

HAWKINS, TRISH. Born Oct. 30, 1945 in Hartford, CT. Attended Radcliffe, Neighborhood Playhouse. Debut OB 1970 in "Oh! Calcutta!" followed by "Iphigenia," "The Hot l Baltimore" for which she received a Theatre World Award, "him," "Come Back, Little Sheba," "Battle of Angels," "Mound Builders," "The Farm," "Ulysses in Traction," "Lulu," "Hogan's Folly," "Twelfth Night," "A Tale Told," "Great Grandson of Jedediah Kohler," Bdwy 1977 in "Some of My Best Friends," "Talley's Folly" (1979).

HAYNES, TIGER. Born Dec. 13, 1907 in St. Croix, VI. Bdwy bow 1956 in "New Faces," followed by "Finian's Rainbow," "Fade Out—Fade In," "The Pajama Game," "The Wiz," "A Broadway Musical," "Comin' Uptown," OB in "Turns," "Bags," "Louis."

HAYS, REX. Born June 17, 1946 in Hollywood, CA. Graduate San Jose State U., Brandeis U. Bdwy debut 1975 in "Dance With Me," followed by "Angel," "King of Hearts," "Evita," "Onward Victoria," "Woman of the Year."

HEALD, ANTHONY. Born Aug. 25, 1944 in New Rochelle, NY. Graduate MiStateU. Debut 1980 OB in "The Glass Menagerie," followed by "Misalliance" for which he received a Theatre World Award, "The Caretaker."

HEARN, GEORGE. Born June 18, 1934 in St. Louis, MO. Graduate Southwestern Col. OB in "Macbeth," "Antony and Cleopatra," "As You Like It," "Richard III," "Merry Wives of Windsor," "Midsummer Night's Dream," "Hamlet," "Horseman, Pass By," Bdwy in "A Time for Singing," "The Changing Room," "An Almost Perfect Person," "I Remember Mama," "Watch on the Rhine," "Sweeney Todd."

HEATH, GORDON. Born Sept. 20, 1918 in NYC. Attended CCNY. Bdwy debut 1945 in "Deep Are the Roots," OB in "Oedipus," "Endgame," "Sounds of a Triangle," "Kohlhass," "Child of the Sun."

HEATH. D. MICHAEL. Born Sept. 22, 1953 in Cincinnati, Oh. Graduate UCin. Bdwy debut 1979 in "The Most Happy Fella," OB in "Chantecler," "Street Scene."

HEFLIN, MARTA. Born Mar. 29, 1945 in Washington, DC. Attended Northwestern, Carnegie Tech. Debut 1967 in "Life with Father" (CC), followed by "Jesus Christ Superstar," "Come BAck to the 5 & Dime, Jimmy Dean," OB in "Salvation," "Soon," "Wedding of Iphigenia," "The Broken Pitcher."

HEIKIN, NANCY. Born Nov. 28, 1948 in Philadelphia, PA. Graduate Sarah Lawrence Col. Bdwy debut 1981 in "The Pirates of Penzance."

HEINS, BARRY. Born Dec. 5, 1956 in El Paso, Tx. Juilliard graduate. Debut 1978 OB in "Spring Awakening," followed by "Twelfth Night," "The Country Wife."

HEIT, SALLY-JANE. Born Oct. 8, 1938 in NYC. Graduate Hunter Col. Bdwy debut 1979 in "Ballroom," followed by "The World of Sholom Aleichem," OB in "Amidst the Gladiolas."

HEMINGWAY, ALAN. Born Sept. 2, 1951 in Salt Lake City, Ut. Graduate Portland State U. Debut 1978 OB in "The Fantasticks," followed by "The Passion of Alice," "Children of Darkness."

HEMSLEY, WINSTON DeWITT. Born May 21, 1947 in Brooklyn, NY. Bdwy debut 1965 in "Golden Boy," followed by "A Joyful Noise," "Hallelujah, Baby," "Hello Dolly!," "Rockabye Hamlet," "A Chorus Line," "Eubie!," OB in "Buy Bonds Buster."

HENDERSON, JO. Born in Buffalo, NY. Attended WMiU. OB in "Camille," "Little Foxes," "An Evening with Merlin Finch," "29th Century Tar," "A Scent of Flowers," "Revival," "Dandelion Wine," "My Life," "Ladyhouse Blues," "Fallen Angels," "Waiting for the Parade," "Threads," "Bella Figura," Bdwy 1981 in "Rose."

HENIG, ANDI. Born May 6 in Washington, DC. Attended Yale U. Debut 1978 OB in "One and One," followed by "Kind Lady" (ELT).

HENRITZE, BETTE. Born May 3 in Betsy Layne, Ky. Graduate UTenn. OB in "Lion in Love," "Abe Lincoln in Illinois," "Othello," "Baal," "Long Christmas Dinner," "Queens of France," "Rimers of Eldritch," "Displaced Person," "Acquisition," "Crime of Passion," "Happiness Cage," "Henry VI," "Richard III," "Older People," "Lotta," "Catsplay," "A Month in the Country," Bdwy in "Jenny Kissed Me" (1948), "Pictures in the Hallway," "Giants, Sons of Giants," "Ballad of the Sad Cafe," "The White House," "Dr. Cook's Garden," "Here's Where I Belong," "Much Ado about Nothing," "Over Here," "Angel Street," "Man and Superman," "Macbeth" (1981).

HEPBURN, KATHARINE. Born Nov. 9, 1909 in Hartford, Ct. Graduate Bryn Mawr. Bdwy debut 1928 in "Night Hostess," followed by "These Days," "A Month in the Country," "Art and Mrs. Bottle," "Warrior's Husband," "The Lake," "Philadelphia Story," "Without Love," "As You Like It," "The Millionairess," "Coco," "A Matter of Gravity," "West Side Waltz."

HERRMANN, EDWARD. Born July 21, 1943 in Washington, DC. Graduate Bucknell U., LAMDA. Debut 1970 OB in "The Basic Training of Pavlo Hummel," followed by "Midsummer Night's Dream," "Gardenia," Bdwy in "Moonchildren" ('72), "Mrs. Warren's Profession," "Philadelphia Story."

HEUCHLING, PETER. Born May 26, 1953 in Evanston, Il. Graduate UMiami. Debut 1974 OB in "Oh Lady, Lady!," Bdwy in "The Best Little Whorehouse in Texas" (1980), "Do Black Patent Leather Shoes Really Reflect Up?"

HEYMAN, BARTON. Born Jan. 24, 1937 in Washington, DC. Attended UCLA. Bdwy debut 1969 in "Indians," followed by "Trial of the Catonsville 9," "A Talent for Murder," OB in "A Midsummer Night's Dream," "Sleep," "Phantasmagoria Historia," "Enclave," "Henry V."

HICKS, LOIS DIANE. Born Sept. 3, 1940 in Brooklyn, NY attended. NYCC, AADA. Debut 1979 OB in "On A Clear Day You Can See Forever," followed by "Yank in Beverly Hills," "The Rose Dancers," "Marching to Georgia," "The Heiress," "Divine Fire."

HIGGINS, JAMES. Born June 1, 1932 in Worksop, Eng. Graduate Cambridge U., Yale Debut 1963 OB in "The Magistrate," followed by "Stevie," "The Winslow Boy," "Grace," "The Browning Version," Bdwy in "The Zulu and the Zayda," "Whose Life Is It Anyway?

HIGGINS, MICHAEL. Born Jan. 20, 1926 in Brooklyn, NY. Attended AmThWing. Bdwy bow 1946 in "Antigone," followed by "Our Lan'," "Romeo and Juliet," "The Crucible," "The Lark," "Equus," "Whose Life Is It Anyway?," OB in "White Devil," "Carefree Tree," "Easter," "The Queen and the Rebels," "Sally, George and Martha," "L'Été," "Uncle Vanya," "The Iceman Cometh," "Molly," "Artichoke," "Reunion," "Chieftans," "A Tale Told," "Richard II."

HILBRANDT, JAMES. Born Aug. 13, 1934 in Valley Stream, NY. Graduate Rochester Inst of Tech. Debut 1967 OB in "Gorilla Queen," followed by "A Boy Named Dog," "Horse Opera," "Patrick Henry Lake Liquors," "Bus Stop," "Are You Now . . .," "Picnic," "As You Like It," "Get Out!," "What Would Jeanne Moreau Do?"

HILL, ROSE. Born May 6, 1914 in London. Attended Guildhall School. Bdwy debut 198 in "Nicholas Nickleby."

HILLNER, JOHN. Born Nov. 5, 1952 in Evanston, IL. Graudate Dension U. Debut 197 OB in "Essential Shepard," followed by Bdwy in "They're Playing Our Song," "Little Me."

HILTON, RICHARD. Born June 25, 1950 in Kalamazoo, Mi. Graduate WMichU. Debut 1981 OB in "Feiffer's People," followed by Bdwy (1982) in "Joseph and the Amazing Technicolor Dreamcoat."

HINES, GREGORY. Born Feb. 14, 1946 in NYC. Bdwy debut 1954 in "The Girl in Pink Tights," followed by "Eubie!" for which he received a Theatre World Award, "Comin Uptown," "Black Broadway," "Sophisticated Ladies."

HINES, MAURICE. Born in 1944 in NYC. Bdwy debut 1954 in "The Girl in Pink Tights," followed by "Eubie!," "Guys and Dolls," "Bring Back Birdie," "Sophisticated Ladies."

HINES, PATRICK. Born Mar. 17, 1930 in Burkesville, TX. Graduate TexU. Debut OB in "Duchess of Malfi," followed by "Lysistrata," "Peer Gynt," "Henry IV," "Richard III," "Ho Grog," BAM's "A Winter's Tale," "Johnny on a Spot," "Barbarians," "The Wedding" Bdwy in "The Great God Brown," "Passage to India," "The Devils," "Cyrano," "The Iceman Cometh," "A Texas Trilogy," "Caesar and Cleopatra," "Amadeus."

HODAPP, ANN. Born May 6, 1946 in Louisville, KY. Attended NYU. Debut 1968 OB in "You're a Good Man, Charlie Brown," followed by "A Round with Ring," "House of Leather," "Shoestring Revue," "God Bless Coney," "What's a Nice Country Like You . . .," "Oh, Lady! Lady!," "Housewives Cantata," "A Day in the Port Authority," "A Little Wine with Lunch," "Fiorello!," "Everybody's Gettin' Into the Act," Bdwy 1980 in "Fearless Frank."

HODES, RYN. Born Dec. 28, 1956 in NYC. Graduate NYU. Debut 1979 OB in "Mirandolina," followed by "Boy Meets Swan," "A Collier's Friday Night," "Suicide in B Flat."

HOFFMAN, MARY JANE. Born Jan. 16, 1952 in Ogden, Ut. Attended Weber State Col. Debut 1976 OB in "Apple Tree," "Dark of the Moon," "Suffragette."

HOFFMAN, PHILIP. Born May 12, 1954 in Chicago, Il. Graduate UIl. Bdwy debut 1981 in "The Moony Shapiro Songbook," followed by "Is There Life after High School?"

HOGAN, JONATHAN. Born June 13, 1951 in Chicago, IL. Graduate Goodman Theatre. Debut OB 1972 in "The Hot l Baltimore," followed by "Mound Builders," "Harry Outside," "Cabin 12," "5th of July," "Glorious Morning," "Innocent Thoughts, Harmless Intentions," "Sunday Runners," "Threads," Bdwy in "Comedians" (1976), "Otherwise Engaged," "5th of July."

HOLBROOK, RUBY. Born Aug. 28, 1930 in St. John's, Nfld. Attended Denison U. Debut 1963 OB in "Abe Lincoln in Illinois," followed by "Hamlet," "James Joyce's Dubliners," "Measure for Measure," "The Farm," "Do You Still Believe the Rumor?," Bdwy 1979 in "Da," "5th of July."

HOLLIDAY, JENNIFER. Born Oct. 19, 1960 in Houston, Tx. Bdwy debut 1980 in "Your Arms Too Short to Box with God," followed by "Dreamgirls" for which she received a Theatre World Award.

HOLMES, GEORGE. Born June 3, 1935 in London, Eng. Graduate ULondon. Debut 1978 OB in "The Changeling," followed by "Love From a Stranger," "The Hollow," "The Story of the Gadsbys," "Bravo!," "Design for Murder."

HOLMES, PRUDENCE WRIGHT. Born in Boston, Ma. Attended Carnegie Tech. Debut 1971 OB in "Godspell," followed by "Polly," "The Crazy Locomotive," "Dona Rosita," "Livingstone and Sechele," Bdwy 1977 in "Happy End."

HOLTON, MARY C. Born May 23, 1959 in Havelock, NC. Bdwy debut 1982 in "Little Me."

HOMAN, JAMES. Born Apr. 26 in Kenosha, WI. Graduate UWi. Bdwy debut 1978 in "Hello, Dolly!," followed by "The Five O'Clock Girl," "Little Johnny Jones."

HOOVER, PAUL. Born June 20, 1945 in Rockford, IL. Graduate Pikeville Col., Pittsburgh Sem. Debut 1980 OB in "Kind Lady."

HOPE, STEPHEN. Born Jan. 23, 1957 in Savannah, Ga. Attended ULouisville, CinConsv. Bdwy debut 1982 in "Joseph and the Amazing Technicolor Dreamcoat."

HORNISH, RUDY. Born Jan. 26, 1938 in Orange, NJ. Graduate UNotre Dame, Seton Hall U. Bdwy debut 1974 in "Fame," followed by "Richard III," OB in "Musical Merchant of Venice," "Philistines."

HORSFORD, ANNA. Born Mar. 6, 1947 in NYC. Attended Inter-American U. Debut 1969 in "Black Quartet," followed by "Perfect Party," "Les Femmes Noires," "Ladies in Waiting," "Sweet Talk," "In the Well of the House," "Coriolanus," "Peep," Bdwy 1976 in "For Colored Girls Who Have Considered Suicide . . ."

HOSBEIN, JAMES. Born Sept. 24, 1946 in Benton Harbor, Mi. Graduate UMich. Debut 1972 OB in "Dear Oscar," followed by "Darrel and Carol and Kenny and Jenny," Bdwy 1977 in "Annie."

HOUTS, ROD. Born Dec. 15, 1906 in Warrensburg, MO. Graduate UMo., NYU, Goodman Theatre. Bdwy debut 1932 in "Lucrece," OB in "Gallery Gods," "The Miracle Worker," "Early Dark," "The Dybbuk," "A Far Country," "Three Sisters," "Exhausting the Possibilities," "The Freak," "Big Apple Messenger."

HOXIE, RICHMOND. Born July 21, 1946 in NYC. Graduate Dartmouth Col., LAMDA. Debut 1975 OB in "Shaw for an Evening," followed by "The Family," "Justice," "Landscape with Waitress," "3 from the Marathon," "The Slab Boys," "Vivien," "Operation Midnight Climax," "The Dining Room."

HOYT, J. C. Born Mar. 6, 1944 in Mankato, Mn. Graduate UMn. Debut 1975 OB in "Heathen Piper," followed by "La Ronde," "Two Genetlemen of Verona."

HUDSON, CHARLES. Born Mar. 29, 1931 in Thorpsprings, TX. Attended AADA, AmThWing. Bdwy bow 1951 in "Billy Budd," followed OB in "Streets of New York," "Summer of Daisy Miller," "Great Scot!," "Any Resemblance to Persons Living or Dead," "Kaboom," "Antiques," "Funny Thing Happened on the Way to the Forum," "Ten Little Indians."

HUGHES, LAURA. Born Jan. 28, 1959 in NYC. Graduate Neighborhood Playhouse. Debut 1980 OB in "The Diviners," followed by "A Tale Told."

HUGHES, TRESA. Born Sept. 17, 1929 in Washington, DC. Attended Wayne U. Appeared OB in "Electra," "The Crucible," "Hogan's Goat," "Party on Greenwich Avenue," "Fragments," "Passing Through from Exotic Places," "Beggar on Horseback," "Early Morning," "The Old Ones," "Holy Places," "Awake and Sing," Bdwy in "Miracle Worker," "Devil's Advocate," "Dear Me, The Sky Is Falling," "Last Analysis," "Spofford," "Man in the Glass Booth," "Prisoner of Second Avenue," "Tribute."

HULCE, THOMAS. Born Dec. 6, 1953 in Plymouth, Mi. Graduate NCSch. of Arts. Bdwy debut 1975 in "Equus," followed by OB "A Memory of Two Mondays," "Julius Caesar, "Twelve Dreams."

HUNT, LINDA. Born Apr. 2, 1945 in Morristown, NJ. Attended Goodman Th. Debut 1975 OB in "Down by the River...," followed by "The Tennis Game," "Metamorphosis in Miniature," Bdwy in "Ah, Wilderness!" (1975).

HUNTER, HOLLY. Born Mar. 20, 1958 in Atlanta, Ga. Graduate Carnegie-Mellon U. Debut 1981 OB in "Battery," Bdwy 1982 in "Crimes of the Heart."

HUNTER, KIM. Born Nov. 12, 1922 in Detroit, MI. Attended Actors Studio. Debut 1947 in "A Streetcar Named Desire," followed by "Darkness at Noon," "The Chase," "The Children's Hour," "The Tender Trap," "Write Me a Murder," "Weekend," "Penny Wars," "The Women," "To Grandmother's House We Go," OB in "Come Slowly, Eden," "All Is Bright," "The Cherry Orchard," "When We Dead Awaken."

HURST, MELISSA. Born June 8, 1955 in Cleveland, Oh. Graduate NYU. Debut 1981 OB in "Dark Ride."

HURT, MARY BETH. Born in 1948 in Marshalltown, Ia. Attended UIa, NYU. Debut 1972 OB in "More Than You Deserve," followed by "As You Like It," "Trelawny of the Wells," "The Cherry Orchard," "Love for Love," "Member of the Wedding," "Boy Meets Girl," "Secret Service," "Father's Day," Bdwy 1981 in "Crimes of the Heart."

HURT, TOM. Born Feb. 25, 1945 in Staten Island, NY. Attended Old Dominion U., AMDA. Debut 1977 OB in "Creditors," followed by "The Seagull," "Miss Julie," "Heritage," "Edgar Allen," "The Importance of Being Earnest."

HURT, WILLIAM. Born Mar. 20, 1950 in Washington, DC. Graduate Tufts U., Juilliard. Debut 1976 OB in "Henry V," followed by "My Life," "Ulysses in Traction," "Lulu," "5th of July," "The Runner Stumbles." He received a 1978 Theatre World Award for his performances with Circle Repertory Theatre, followed by "Hamlet," "Mary Stuart," "Childe Byron," "The Diviners," "Richard II," "The Great Grandson of Jedediah Kohler."

HUTTON, BILL. Born Aug. 5, 1950 in Evansville, In. Graduate UEvansville. Debut 1979 OB in "Festival," Bdwy 1982 in "Joseph and the Amazing Technicolor Dreamcoat."

HYAMS, PAUL. Born Feb. 14, 1959 in Paris, France. Attended HB Studio. Bdwy debut 1981 in "Merrily We Roll Along."

HYDE-WHITE, ALEX. Born Jan. 30 in London, Eng. Attended Georgetown U. Bdwy debut 1981 in "Kingdoms."

HYMAN, EARLE, Born Oct. 11, 1926 in Rocky Mount, NC. Attended New School, Theatre Wing. Bdwy debut 1943 in "Run, Little Chillun," followed by "Anna Lucasta," "Climate of Eden," "Merchant of Venice," "Othello," "Julius Caesar," "The Tempest," "No Time for Sergeants," "Mr. Johnson" for which he received a Theatre World Award, "St. Joan," "Hamlet," "Waiting for Godot," "Duchess of Malfi," "Les Blancs," "The Lady from Dubuque," OB in "The White Rose and the Red," "Worlds of Shakespeare," "Jonah," "Life and Times of J. Walter Smintheus," "Orrin," "Cherry Orchard," "House Party." "Carnival Dreams," "Agamemnon," "Othello," "Julius Caesar," "Coriolanus," "Remembrance," "Long Day's Journey into Night," "Sleep Beauty."

HYMAN, PHYLLIS. Born July 6, 1941 in Philadelphia, PA. Attended Morris Jr. Col. Bdwy debut 1981 in "Sophisticated Ladies" for which she received a Theatre World Award.

HYMAN, ROBERT. Born Nov. 10, 1956 in Boston, Ma. Graduate Stanford U. Bdwy debut 1982 in "Joseph and the Amazing Technicolor Dreamcoat."

INGE, MATTHEW. Born May 29, 1950 in Fitchburg, Ma. Attended Boston U, Harvard. Bdwy debut 1976 in "Fiddler on the Roof," followed by "A Chorus Line."

INNERARITY, MEMRIE. Born Feb. 11, 1945 in Columbus, Ms. Attended USMs. Debut 1976 OB in "The Club," followed by "The Heebie Jeebies."

IRVING, GEORGE S. Born Nov. 1, 1922 in Springfield, MA. Attended Leland Powers Sch. Bdwy bow 1943 in "Oklahoma!," followed by "Call Me Mister," "Along 5th Ave.," "Two's Company," "Me and Juliet," "Can-Can," "Shinbone Alley," "Bells Are Ringing," "The Good Soup," "Tovarich," "A Murderer Among Us," "Alfie," "Anya," "Galileo," "4 on a Garden" "An Evening with Richard Nixon," "Irene," "Who's Who in Hell," "All Over Town," "So Long 174th St," "Once in a Lifetime," "I Remember Mama," "Copperfield, "Pirates of Penzance," OB in "Up Eden."

IVANEK, ZELJKO. Born Aug. 15, 1957 in Ljubljana, Yugo. Graduate Yale U., LAMDA. Bdwy debut 1981 in "The Survivor," followed OB by "Cloud 9."

IVES, JANE. Born Nov. 6, 1949 in NYC. Attended Ct. Col. Debut 1981 OB in "Murder in the Cathedral," followed by "Street Scene."

IVEY, DANA. Born Aug. 12, 1941 in Atlanta, GA. Graduate Rollins Col., LAMDA. Bdwy debut 1981 in "Macbeth" (LC), OB in "A Call from the East," "Vivien," "Dumping Ground," "Pastorale," "Two Small Bodies."

JABLONS, KAREN. Born July 19, 1951 in Trenton, NJ. Juilliard graduate. Debut 1969 OB in "The Student Prince," followed by "Sound of Music," "Funny Girl," "Boys from Syracuse," "Sterling Silver," "People in Show Business Make Long Goodbyes," "In Trousers," Bdwy in "Ari," "Two Gentlemen of Verona," "Lorelei," "Where's Charley?," "A Chorus Line."

JACKSON, CHELLI. Born Jan. 29, 1956 in North Hills, Pa. Graduate Elizabethtown Col. Debut 1981 OB in "Seesaw."

JACKSON, ERNESTINE. Born Sept. 18 in Corpus Christi, TX. Graduate Del Mar Col., Juilliard. Debut 1966 in "Show Boat" (LC), followed by "Finian's Rainbow," "Hello, Dolly!," "Applause," "Jesus Christ Superstar," "Tricks," "Raisin" for which she received a Theatre World Award, "Guys and Dolls," "Bacchae," OB in "Louis."

JACOB, STEVEN. Born May 11, 1959 in Lynne, Ma. Graduate NYU. Debut 1981 OB in "Florodora," Bdwy 1981 in "Merrily We Roll Along."

JACOBS, RUSTY. Born July 10, 1967 in NYC. Debut OB in 1979 in "Tripletale," followed by "Glory! Hallelujah!" "What a Life!" Bdwy 1979 in "Peter Pan."

JACOBSON, JOANNE. Born Dec. 19, 1937 in Cambridge, MA. Graduate Barnard Col. Debut 1958 OB in "Don't Destroy Me," followed by "Naomi Court," "Summertree."

JAKETIC, GARY. Born Apr. 24, 1953 in Cleveland, OH. Attended Carnegie-Mellon U. Bdwy debut 1980 in "Camelot," OB in "Chantecler."

JAMES, CLIFTON. Born May 29, 1921 in Spokane, Wa. Attended OreU., Actors Studio. Has appeared in "The Time of Your Life" (CC), "The Cave Dwellers," "Great Day in the Morning," "Andorra," "And Things That Go Bump in the Night," "The Trial of Lee Harvey Oswald," "Shadow Box," OB in "The Coop," "American Buffalo."

JAMES, JESSICA. Born Oct. 31, 1933 in Los Angeles, CA. Attended USC. Bdwy debut 1970 in "Company," followed by "Gemini," "Little Me," OB in "Nourish the Beast," "Hothouse," "Loss of Innocence," "Rebirth Celebration of the Human Race," "Silver Bee," "Gemini."

JAMES, STEPHEN. Born Feb. 2, 1952 in Mt. Vernon, OH. Princeton graduate. Debut 1977 OB in "Castaways," followed by "Greed Pond," Bdwy in "The 1940's Radio Hour" for which he received a Theatre World Award," "A Day in Hollywood/A Night in the Ukraine."

JAMES, WILLIAM. Born Apr. 29 in Jersey City, NJ. Graduate NJ State Teachers Col. Bdwy bow 1962 in "Camelot," followed by "Maggie Flynn," "Coco," "My Fair Lady" (CC & 1976), "Where's Charley?" (CC), "She Loves Me," "Camelot" ('81), OB in "Anything Goes," "Smith," "The Music Man" (JB).

JAMISON, JUDITH. Born in 1944 in Philadelphia, Pa. Debut with AmBalletTh 1965, and danced with Alvin Ailey company before Bdwy bow (1981) in "Sophisticated Ladies."

JAMROG, JOSEPH. Born Dec. 21, 1932 in Flushing, NY. Graduate CCNY. Debut 1970 OB in "Nobody Hears a Broken Drum," followed by "Tango," "And Whose Little Boy Are You?," "When You Comin' Back, Red Ryder?," "Drums at Yale," "The Boy Friend," "Love Death Plays," "Too Much Johnson," "A Stitch in Time," "Pantagleize," "Final Hours."

JAROSLOW, RUTH. Born May 22 in Brooklyn, NY. Attended HB Studio. Debut 1964 OB in "That 5 A.M. Jazz," followed by "Jonah," Bdwy in "Mame," "Fiddler on the Roof" (1964/'77/'81), "The Ritz."

JAY, DON. Born in Calif. Bdwy debut 1965 in "The Zulu and the Zayda," followed by "Hello, Dolly!," "Two Gentlemen of Verona," "Raisin," OB in "On-the Lock-In," "Louis!"

JAY, MARY. Born Dec. 23, 1939 in Brooklyn, NY. Graduate UMe, AmThWing. Debut 1962 OB in "Little Mary Sunshine," followed by "Toys in the Attic," "Telecast," "Sananda Sez," "Soul of the White Ant," Bdwy in "The Student Gypsy," "Candida" (1981).

JAY-ALEXANDER, RICHARD. Born May 24, 1953 in Syracuse, NY. Graduated S.IllU. Debut 1975 OB in "Boy Meets Boy," Bdwy 1979 in "Zoot Suit," followed by "Amadeus."

JECKO, TIMOTHY. Born Jan. 24, 1938 in Washington, DC. Yale Graduate. Bdwy debut 1980 in "Annie."

JENNER, JAMES. Born Mar. 5, 1953 in Houston, TX. Attended UTx, LAMDA. Debut 1980 OB in "Kind Lady," followed by "Station J."

JENNEY, LUCINDA. Born Apr. 23, in Long Island City, NY. Graduate Sarah Lawrence Col. Debut OB 1981 in "Death Takes a Holiday," Bdwy 1981 in "Gemini."

JENNINGS, CHRISTINE. Born Nov. 19, 1947 in Bayonne, NJ. Attended Jersey City State Col. Debut 1981 OB in "Spoon River Anthology."

JENNINGS, KEN. Born Oct. 10, 1947 in Jersey City, NJ. Graduate St. Peter's Col. Bdwy Debut 1975 in "All God's Chillun Got Wings," followed by "Sweeney Todd" for which he received a Theatre World Award.

JETER, MICHAEL. Born Aug. 26, 1952 in Lawrenceburg, TN. Graduate Memphis State U. Bdwy debut 1978 in "Once in a Lifetime," OB in "The Master and Margarita," "G. R. Point" for which he received a Theatre World Award, "Alice in Concert," "El Bravo," "Cloud 9."

JOCHIM, KEITH. Born Jan. 26, 1942 in Chicago, IL. Graduate KsU. UMi. Debut 1968 OB in "Macbird," followed by "America Hurrah," "Salt Lake City Skyline," "El Bravo!" Bdwy 1981 in "Frankenstein."

JOHNSON, DANIEL T. Born Aug. 13, 1947 in Michigan. Graduate Western Michigan, UOre. OB in "Romeo and Juliet," "The Scarecrow," "Meetings with Ben Franklin," "Edward II."

JOHNSON, MARILYN J. Born Sept. 15, 1938 in Cleveland, Oh. Attended Fenn Col. Debut 1970 OB in "Billy Noname," Bdwy 1981 in "The Best Little Whorehouse in Texas."

JOHNSON, PAGE, Born Aug. 25, 1930 in Welch, WV. Graduate Ithaca Col. Bdwy bow in 1951 in "Romeo and Juliet," followed by "Electra," "Oedipus," "Camino Real," "In April Once" for which he received a Theatre World Award, "Red Roses for Me," "The Lovers," "Equus," OB in "The Enchanted," "Guitar," "4 in 1," "Journey of the Fifth Horse," APA's "School for Scandal," "The Tavern," and "The Seagull," "Odd Couple," "Boys In The Band," "Medea," "Deathtrap," "Best Little Whorehouse in Texas."

JOHNSON, TINA. Born Oct. 27, 1951 in Wharton, TX, Graduate North Tx. State U. Debut 1979 OB in "Festival," Bdwy in "The Best Little Whorehouse in Texas."

JOHNSTON, AUDRE. Born July 22, 1939 in Chicago. Attended Northwestern U. Debut 1962 OB in "Half Past Wednesday," followed by "The Elizabethans," "Bags," Bdwy in "Company," "Fame."

JOHNSTON, J. J. Born Oct. 24, 1933 in Chicago, Il. Debut 1981 OB in "American Buffalo."

JONES, BAMBI. Born Apr. 14, 1961 in NYC. Debut 1969 OB in "An Evening of One Acts," followed by "Forty-Deuce!" "She Loves Me."

JONES, EDDIE. Born in Washington, PA. Debut 1960 OB in "Dead End," followed by "Curse of the Starving Class," "The Ruffian on the Stair," "An Act of Kindness," "Big Apple Messenger," "The Skirmishers," "Maiden Stakes," "The Freak," Bdwy in "That Championship Season" ('74), "Devour the Snow."

JONES, GORDON G. Born Nov. 1, 1941 in Urania, LA. Graduate LaTech., UAr. Debut OB 1980 in "Room Service," followed by "The Front Page," "Caine Mutiny Court Martial," "Panhandle," "Caveat Emptor," "Progress," "Italian Straw Hat."

JONES, JAMES EARL. Born Jan. 17, 1931 in Arkabutla, MS. Graduate MiU. OB in "The Pretender," "The Blacks," "Clandestine on the Morning Line," "The Apple," "Midsummer Night's Dream," "Moon on a Rainbow Shawl" for which he received a Theatre World Award, "P.S. 193," "Last Minstrel," "Love Nest," "Bloodknot," "Othello," "Baal," "Danton's Death," "Boesman and Lena," "Hamlet," "Cherry Orchard," Bdwy in "The Egghead," "Sunrise at Campobello," "The Cool World," "A Hand Is on the Gate," "The Great White Hope," "Les Blancs," "King Lear," "The Iceman Cometh," "Of Mice and Men," "Paul Robeson," "Lesson from Aloes," "Othello."

JONES, JEFFREY. Born Sept. 28, 1947 in Buffalo, NY. Graduate Lawrence U., LAMDA. Debut 1973 OB in "Lotta," followed by "The Tempest," "Trelawny of the Wells," "Secret Service," "Boy Meets Girl," "Scribes," "Cloud 9."

JONES, JEN. Born Mar. 23, 1927 in Salt Lake City, UT. Attended UUt. Debut 1960 OB in "Drums Under the Window," followed by "Long Voyage Home," "Diff'rent," "Creditors," "Look at Any Man," "I Knock at the Door," "Pictures in the Hallway," "Grab Bag," "Bo Bo," "Oh, Dad, Poor Dad..," Bdwy in "Dr. Cook's Garden," "But Seriously," "Eccentricities of a Nightingale," "Music Man" ('80).

JONES, LEILANI. Born May 14, 1957 in Honolulu, Hi, Graduate UHi. Debut 1981 OB in "El Bravo!", followed by "The Little Shop of Horrors."

JORDAN, RICHARD. Born July 19, 1938 in NYC. Attended Harvard U. Bdwy bow 1961 in "Take Her, She's Mine," followed by "Bicycle Ride to Nevada," "War and Peace," "Generation," "A Patriot for Me," OB in "Judith," "All's Well That Ends Well," "Trial of the Catonsville 9," "Three Acts of Recognition."

JOY, ROBERT. Born Aug. 17, 1951 in Montreal, Can. Graduate Nfd. Memorial U., Oxford U. Debut 1978 OB in "The Diary of Anne Frank," followed by "Fables for Friends," "Lydie Breeze," "Sister Mary Ignatius Explains It All," "Actor's Nightmare."

JOYCE, JOE. Born Nov. 22, 1957 in Pittsburgh, Pa. Graduate Boston U. Debut 1981 OB in "Close Enough for Jazz," followed by "Oh, Johnny!"

JUDD, ROBERT. Born Aug. 3, 1927 in NYC. Debut 1972 OB in "Don't Let It Go To Your Head," followed by "Black Visions," "Sweet Enemy," "The Lion Is a Soul Brother," "Welfare," "Zooman and the Sign," Bdwy in "Watch on the Rhine" (1980).

JUDE, PATRICK, Born Feb. 25, 1951 in Jersey City, NJ. Bdwy debut 1972 in "Jesus Christ Superstar," followed by 1977 revival, "Got Tu Go Disco," "Charlie and Algernon," "Marlowe," OB in "The Haggadah."

JULIA, RAUL. Born Mar. 9, 1940 in San Juan, PR. Graduate UPR. OB in "Macbeth," "Titus Andronicus," "Theatre in the Streets," "Life Is a Dream," "Blood Wedding," "Ox Cart," "No Exit," "Memorandum," "Frank Gagliano's City Scene," "Your Own Thing," "Persians," "Castro Complex," "Pinkville," "Hamlet," "King Lear," "As You Like It," "Emperor of Late Night Radio," "Threepenny Opera," "The Cherry Orchard," "Taming of the Shrew," "Othello," "The Tempest," Bdwy in "The Cuban Thing," "Indians," "Two Gentlemen of Verona," "Via Galactica," "Where's Charley?," "Dracula," "Betrayal," "Nine."

KABLE, LISA. Born Nov. 9, 1969 in NYC. Debut 1982 OB in "Best All Round"

KALEMBER, PATRICIA. Born Dec. 30, 1956 in Schenectady, NY. Graduate InU. Debut 1981 OB in "The Butler Did It," followed by "Sheepskin."

KAMMER, NANCY-ELIZABETH. Born Mar. 27, 1953 in Valdosta, Ga. Attended NYU. Debut 1977 OB in "Carnival," followed by "Turnbuckle," "My Own Stranger."

KAN, LILAH. Born Sept. 4, 1931 in Chicago, Il. Attended UCBerkeley, NYU. Debut 1974 OB in "Year of the Dragon," followed by "Pursuit of Happiness," "G.R. Point," "Primary English Class," "The Blind Young Man," "Paper Angels."

KANE, JOHN. Born Aug. 29, 1920 in Davenport, Ia. Attended St. Ambrose Col. Bdwy debut 1944 in "Three's a Family," followed by "Marcus in the High Grass," "Ding Dong Bell," "Uncle Willie," "The Visit," OB in "Hooray! It's a Glorious Day," "Ludwig."

KANSAS, JERI. Born Mar. 10, 1955 in Jersey City. NJ. Debut 1978 OB in "Gay Divorce," Bdwy 1979 in "Sugar Babies," followed by "42nd Street."

KANTOR, KENNETH. Born Apr. 6, 1949 in The Bronx, NY. Graduate SUNY, Boston U. Debut 1974 OB in "Zorba." followed by "Kiss Me, Kate," "A Little Night Music," "Buried Treasure," Bdwy in "The Grand Tour," "Brigadoon" ('80).

KARFO, ROBIN. Born Oct. 14 in NYC. Attended Lehman Col., NYU. Debut 1981 OB in "And I Ain't Finished Yet," followed by "Scenes from La Vie de Boheme."

KARNILOVA, MARIA. Born Aug. 3, 1920 in Hartford, Ct. Bdwy debut 1938 in "Stars in Your Eyes," followed by "Call Me Mister," "High Button Shoes," "Two's Company," "Hollywood Pinafore," "Beggar's Opera," "Gypsy," "Miss Liberty," "Out of This World," "Bravo Giovanni," "Fiddler on the Roof" (1964 & 1981), "Zorba," "Gigi," "God's Favorite," "Bring Back Birdie," OB in "Kaleidoscope."

KARR, PATTI. Born July 10 in St. Paul, Mn. Attended TCU. Bdwy debut 1953 in "Maggie," followed by "Carnival in Flanders," "Pipe Dream," "Bells Are Ringing," "New Girl in Town," "Body Beautiful," "Bye Bye Birdie," "New Faces of 1962," "Come on Strong," "Look to the Lilies," "Different Times," "Lysistrata," "Seesaw," "Irene," "Pippin," "A Broadway Musical," "Got Tu Go Disco," "Musical Chairs," OB in "A Month of Sundays," "Up Eden," "Snapshot," "Housewives Cantata," "Something for the Boys," "Baseball Wives."

KARRAKER, HUGH. Born May 16, 1948 in NYC. Graduate UCt., Guildhall School. Debut 1982 OB in "One Night Stand."

KATSULAS, ANDREAS. Born May 18, 1946 in St. Louis, Mo. Graduate St. Louis U, IndU. Debut 1982 OB in "Zastrozzi."

KAUFMAN, MICHAEL. Born July 28, 1950 in Washington, DC. Graduate UWi. Debut 1978 OB in "Hooters," followed by "First Thirty," "Warriors from a Long Childhood," "Scenes from La Vie de Boheme," Bdwy 1980 in "Gemini."

KAVANAUGH, RICHARD. Born in 1943 in NYC. Bdwy debut 1977 in "Dracula," followed by "Hothouse."

KAWALEK, NANCY. Born Feb. 25, 1956 in Brooklyn, NY. Graduate Northwestern U. Bdwy debut 1979 in "Strider," OB in "Success Story," "What a Life!"

KAYE, JUDY. Born Oct. 11, 1948 in Phoenix, AZ. Attended UCLA, Ariz. State U. Bdwy debut 1977 in "Grease," followed by "On the 20th Century" for which she received a Theatre World Award, "Moony Shapiro Songbook," "Oh, Brother!"

KAYE, LILA. Born Nov. 7, 1932 in Longon, Eng. Bdwy debut 1981 in "Nicholas Nickleby."

KAYE, TONI. BornAug. 26, 1946 in Chicago, IL. Bdwy debut 1979 in "Sugar Babies."

KEAGY, GRACE. Born Dec. 16 in Youngstown, OH. Attended New Eng. Consv. Debut 1974 OB in "Call Me Madam," Bdwy in "Goodtime Charley," "The Grand Tour," "Carmelina," "I Remember Mama," "Musical Chairs," "Woman of the Year."

KEARNEY, LYNN. Born Apr. 9, 1951 in Chicago, IL. Graduate NYU. Bdwy debut 1978 in "Annie," OB in "Captive Audiences."

KELLETT, ROBERT. Born Aug. 29, 1955 in Minneapolis, Mn. Attended UIl., Goodman Theatre. Debut 1981 in "Oh, Johnny!"

KELLIN, MIKE. Born Apr. 26, 1922 in Hartford, Ct. Attended Trinity Col., Yale. Bdwy bow 1949 in "At War with the Army," followed by "Bird Cage," "Stalag 17," "The Emperor's Clothes," "The Time of Your Life," "Pipe Dreams," "Who Was That Lady?," "God and Kate Murphy," "Ankles Aweigh," "Rhinoceros," "Odd Couple," "Mother Courage," OB in "Taming of the Shrew," "Diary of a Scoundrel," "Purple Dust," "Tevya and His Daughters," "Winkelberg," "Winterset," "Joan of Lorraine," "Bread," "American Buffalo," "Duck Variations," "Are You Now . . .," "Q.E.D."

KELLY, K. C. Born Nov. 12, 1952 in Baraboo, WI. Attended UWisc. Debut 1976 OB in "The Chicken Ranch," "Last of the Knucklemen," "Young Bucks," followed by Bdwy in "Romeo and Juliet," (1977), "The Best Little Whorehouse in Texas."

KENNEDY, CAROLYN. Born Mar. 18, 1955 in NYC. Graduate UIll. Debut 1980 in "Nell," followed by "Taken in Marriage."

KENNEDY, LAURIE. Born Feb. 14, 1948 in Hollywood, CA. Graduate Sarah Lawrence Col. Debut 1974 OB in "End of Summer," followed by "A Day in the Death of Joe Egg," "Ladyhouse Blues," "He and She," "The Recruiting Officer," "Isn't it Romantic," Bdwy in "Man and Superman," (1978) for which she received a Theatre World Award, "Major Barbara."

KENNEDY, TARA. Born Aug. 8, 1971 in Yonkers, NY. Bdwy debut 1979 in "I Remember Mama," followed by "Annie."

KENYON, LAURA. Born Nov. 23, 1948 in Chicago, Il. Attended USCal. Debut 1970 OB in "Peace," followed by "Carnival," "Dementos," "The Trojan Women," Bdwy in "Man of La Mancha" (1971), "On the Town," "Nine."

KEPROS, NICHOLAS. Born Nov. 8, 1932 in Salt Lake City, UT. Graduate UUt., RADA. Debut 1958 OB in "The Golden Six," followed by "Wars of Roses," "Julius Caesar," "Hamlet," "Henry IV," "She Stoops to Conquer," "Peer Gynt," "Octaroon," "Endicott and the Red Cross," "The Judas Applause," "Irish Hebrew Lesson," "Judgement at Havana," "The Millionairess," "Androcles and the Lion," "The Redemptor," "Othello," Bdwy "St. Joan" (1968), "Amadeus."

KERNER, NORBERTO, Born July 19, 1929 in Valparaiso, Chile. Attended Piscator Workshop, Goodman Theatre. Debut 1971 OB in "Yerma," followed by "I Took Panama," "The F. M. Sale," "My Old Friends," Sharon Shashanovah," "The Blood Wedding," "Crisp."

KERNS, LINDA. Born June 2, 1953 in Columbus, Oh. Attended Temple U, AADA. Debut 1981 OB in "Crisp," Bdwy 1982 in "Nine."

KERT, LARRY. Born Dec. 5, 1934 in Los Angeles, CA. Attended LACC. Bdwy bow 1953 in "John Murray Anderson's Almanac," followed by "Ziegfeld Follies," "Mr. Wonderful," "Walk Tall," "Look, Ma, I'm Dancin'," "Tickets Please," "West Side Story," "A Family Affair," "Breakfast at Tiffany's," "Cabaret," "La Strada," "Company," "Two Gentlemen of Verona," "Music! Music!" "Musical Jubilee," "Side by Side by Sondheim," OB in "Changes," "From Rodgers and Hart with Love," "They Say It's Wonderful."

KEY, TOM. Born July 6, 1950 in Birmingham, Al. Graduate UTenn. Debut 1981 OB in "Cotton Patch Gospel."

KEYES, DANIEL. Born Mar. 6, 1914 in Concord, MA. Attended Harvard. Bdwy debut 1954 in "Remarkable Mr. Pennypacker," followed by "Bus Stop," "Only in America," "Christine," "First Love," "Take Her, She's Mine," "Baker Street," "Dinner at 8," "I Never Sang for My Father," "Wrong Way Light Bulb," "A Place for Polly," "Scratch," "Rainbow Jones," "Angel," "Passione," OB in "Our Town," "Epitaph for George Dillon," "Plays for Bleecker St.," "Hooray! It's a Glorious Day!," "Six Characters in Search of an Author," "Sjt. Musgrave's Dance," "Arms and the Man," "Mourning Becomes Electra," "Salty Dog Saga," "Hot l Baltimore," "Artichoke," "Whales of August."

KEYLOUN, MARK. Born Oct. 20, 1955 in Brooklyn, NY. Attended Georgetown U. Debut 1980 OB in "Monsieur Amilcar," followed by "Forty Deuce."

KHOURY, PAMELA. Born May 17, 1954 in Beirut, Lebanon. Graduate UTx. Bdwy debut 1980 in "West Side Story," followed by "Oh, Brother!"

KILLMER, NANCY. Born Dec. 16, 1936 in Homewood, IL. Graduate Northwestern U. Bdwy debut 1969 in "Coco," followed by "Goodtime Charley," "So Long, 174th Street," "A Little Night Music," "Sweeney Todd," OB in "Exiles," "Mrs. Murray's Farm," "Pillars of Society," "Threads," "A Tale Told."

KIMBROUGH, CHARLES. Born May 23, 1936 in St. Paul, Mn. Graduate IndU, Yale. Bdwy bow 1969 in "Cop-Out," followed by "Company," "Love for Love," "Rules of the Game" "Candide," "Mr. Happiness," "Same Time, Next Year," OB in "All in Love," "Struts and Frets," "Troilus and Cressida," "Secret Service," "Boy Meets Girl," "Drinks Before Dinner," "The Dining Room."

KING, GINNY. Born May 12, 1957 in Atlanta, GA. attended NCSch. of Arts. Bdwy debut 1980 in "42nd Street."

KINGSLEY, PETER. Born Aug. 14, 1945 in Mexico City, MX. Graduate Hamilton Col., LAMDA. Debut 1974 OB in "The Beauty Part," followed by "Purification," "Moliere in Spite of Himself," "Old Man Joseph and His Family," Bdwy 1980 in "Amadeus."

KIRSCH, CAROLYN. Born May 24, 1942 in Shreveport, LA. Bdwy debut 1963 in "How to Succeed. . . ," followed by "Folies Bergere," "La Grosse Valise," "Skyscraper," "Breakfast at Tiffany's," "Sweet Charity," "Hallelujah, Baby!," "Dear World," "Promises, Promises," "Coco," "Ulysses in Nighttown," "A Chorus Line," OB in "Silk Stockings," "Telecast."

KIRSCH, GARY. Born July 14, 1953 in Buffalo, NY. Graduate SUNY/Fredonia. Debut 1980 OB in "Annie Get Your Gun," Bdwy 1981 in "The Five O'Clock Girl," followed by "Little Johnny Jones."

KLEIN, SALLY. Born Jan. 21 in Toledo, Oh. Graduate UAz. Bdwy Debut 1981 in "Merrily We Roll Along," followed by "Agnes of God."

KLIBAN, KEN. Born July 26, 1943 in Norwalk, CT. Graduate UMiami, NYU. Bdwy debut 1967 in "War and Peace," followed OB in "Puppy Dog Tails," "Istanbul," "Persians," "Home," "Elizabeth the Queen," "Judith," "Man and Superman," "Boom Boom Room," "Ulysses in Traction," "Lulu," "The Beaver Coat," "Troilus and Cressida," "Richard II," "Great Grandson of Jedediah Kohler."

KLUNIS, TOM. Born in San Francisco, CA. Bdwy debut 1961 in "Gideon," followed by "The Devils," "Henry V," "Romeo and Juliet," "St. Joan." "Hide and Seek," "Bacchae," OB in "The Immoralist," "Hamlet," "Arms and the Man," "Potting Shed," "Measure for Measure," "Romeo and Juliet," "The Balcony," "Our Town," "Man Who Never Died," "God is My Ram," "Rise Marlow," "Iphigenia in Aulis," "Still Life," "The Master and Margarita," "As You Like it," "The Winter Dancers," "When We Dead Awaken."

KMECK, GEORGE. Born Aug. 4, 1949 in Jersey City, NJ. Attended Glassboro State Col. Bdwy debut 1981 in "Pirates of Penzance."

KNELL, DANE. Born Sept. 27, 1932 in Winthrop, MA. Bdwy debut 1952 in "See the Jaguar," OB in "Ulster," "Moon Dances," "Court of Miracles, "Gas Station," "Zeks."

KNIGHT, LILY. Born Nov. 30, 1956 in Baltimore, MD. Graduate NYU. Debut 1980 OB in "After the Revolution," followed by the "The Wonder Years."

KNUDSON, KURT. Born Sept. 7, 1936 in Fargo, ND. Attended NDState U, UMiami. Debut1976 OB in "The Cherry Orchard," followed by "Geniuses," Bdwy 1982 in "Curse of an Aching Heart."

KOBART, RUTH. Born Aug. 24, 1924 in Des Moines, Ia. Graduate Chicago Cons., Hunter Col. Bdwy debut 1955 in "Pipe Dream," followed by "Maria Golovin," "How to Succeed in Business..," "A Funny Thing Happened on the Way to the Forum," "Oklahoma!" (CC), "A Flea in Her Ear," "Three Sisters," "Annie."

KOLBA, MICHAEL. Born Oct. 1, 1947 in Moorhead, Mn. Graduate Moorhead U, UHawaii. Debut 1976 OB in "The Cherry Orchard," followed by "Measure for Measure," "The Balcony," "The Further Inquiry."

KOPYC, FRANK. Born Aug. 6, 1948 in Troy, NY. Graduate Yankton Col. Debut 1973 OB in "Pop," followed by "Fiorello!," "El Bravo!," Bdwy in "Sweeney Todd."

KOREY, ALEXANDRA. Born May 14 in Brooklyn, NY. Graduate Columbia U. Debut 1976 OB in "Fiorello!" followed by "Annie Get Your Gun," "Jerry's Girls," Bdwy in "Hello, Dolly!" (1978).

KOVITZ, RANDY. Born Sept 28, 1955 in Arlington, VA. Graduate Carnegie-Mellon. Debut 1981 in "Macbeth" (LC), followed by "Othello" (1982).

KRESS, RONNA. Born Dec. 29, 1959 in Pittsburgh, Pa. Graduate Boston U. Debut 1982 OB in "Twelfth Night," followed by "The Country Wife."

KUREK, ANNETTE. Born Feb. 6, 1950 in Chicago, IL. Graduate UWi. Debut 1976 OB in "The Hairy Ape," followed by "Isadora Duncan Sleeps with the Russian Navy," "Word of Mouth," "Coming Attractions," "The Fuehrer Bunker," "Cowboy Mouth."

KUSHNER, JAMES. Born Dec. 10, 1968 in NYC. Debut 1981 OB in "March of the Falsettos."

LAGERFELT, CAROLYN. Born Sept 23 in Paris. Graduate AADA. Bdwy debut 1971 in "The Philanthropist," followed by "4 on a Garden," "Jockey Club Stakes," "The Constant Wife," "Otherwise Engaged," "Betrayal," OB in "Look Back in Anger," "Close of Play," "Sea Anchor."

LAHTI, CHRISTINE. Born Apr. 4, 1950 in Detroit, MI. Graduate UMich., HB Studio. Debut 1979 OB in "The Woods" for which she received a Theatre World Award, Bdwy 1980 in "Loose Ends," followed by "Division Street," "Scenes and Revelations."

LAHTI, GARY. Born June 22, 1952 in Albany, NY. Graduate SUNY/Albany, UMn. Debut 1978 OB in "Murder in Santa Cruz," followed by "Split."

LAMB, KAREN. Born in Providence, RI, Oct. 26, 1951. Graduate San Jose U. Debut 1982 OB in "Lysistrata."

LANCE, RORY. Born Apr. 10, 1954 in Brooklyn, NY. Graduate Brooklyn Col. Debut 1978 OB in "She Stoops to Conquer," followed by "Twelfth Night," "The Seagull," "The Miser," "Uncle Vanya," "Don Juan."

LANDAU, VIVIEN. (formerly Tisa Barone) Born Jan. 31 in NYC. Graduate CCNY. Debut 1958 OB in "Clerambard," followed by "Once in a Lifetime," "The Golden Six," "Death Takes a Holiday," "Invitation to a March."

LANDFIELD, TIMOTHY. Born Aug. 22, 1950 in Palo Alto, Ca. Graduate Hampshire Col. Bdwy debut 1977 in "Tartuffe," followed by "Crucifer of Blood," OB in "Actor's Nightmare," "Sister Mary Ignatius Explains It all."

LANG, CHARLEY, Born Oct. 24, 1955 in Passaic, NJ. Graduate Catholic U. Bdwy debut 1978 in "Da," followed by "Once a Catholic," OB in "Young Bucks."

LANG, STEPHEN. Born July 11, 1952 in NYC. Graduate Swarthmore Col. Debut 1975 OB in "Hamlet," followed by "Henry V," "Shadow of a Gunman," "A Winter's Tale," "Johnny on a Spot," "Barbarians," "Ah, Men," "Clownmaker," Bdwy 1977 in "St. Joan."

LANGE, ANN. Born June 24, 1953 in Pipestone, MN. Attended Carnegie-Mellon U. Debut 1979 OB in "Rat's Nest," followed by "Hunting Scenes from Lower Bavaria," Bdwy 1981 in "The Survivor."

LANGE, HOPE. Born Nov. 28, 1933 in Redding Ridge, Ct. Attended Reed Col. Bdwy debut 1943 in "The Patriots," followed by "The Hot Corner," "Same Time, Next Year," "Supporting Cast."

LANGELLA, FRANK. Born Jan. 1, 1940 in Bayonne, NJ. Graduate Syracuse U. Debut 1963 OB in "The Immoralist," followed by "The Old Glory," "Good Day," "White Devil," "Yerma," "Iphigenia in Aulis," "A Cry of Players," "Prince of Homburg," Bdwy in "Seascape," "Dracula," "Amadeus."

LANGLAND, LIANE. Born May 11, 1957 in Denver, Co. Graduate Juilliard. Debut 1981 OB in "How It all Began," Bdwy in "A Talent for Murder" (1981).

LANSBURY, ANGELA. Born Oct, 16, 1925 in London, Eng. Bdwy debut 1957 in "Hotel Paradiso," followed by "A Taste of Honey," "Anyone Can Whistle," "Mame," "Dear World," "Gypsy," "The King and I" (1978), "Sweeney Todd."

LANTZY, TOM. Born May 27, 1951 in Spangler, Pa. Graduate SUNY/Buffalo, FlaStateU. Debut 1977 OB in "Streets of Gold," followed by "The Jumping Place," "The Beast," "Chanticler," Bdwy in "Oh! Calcutta!" (1978).

LARKIN, EDITH. Born Jan. 31, 1921 in NYC. Attended Vassar. Bdwy debut 1940 in "The Male Animal," followed by "5th of July," OB in "Plaza Suite," "The Miracle Worker," "Let's Get a Divorce."

LARSEN, LIZ. Born Jan. 16, 1959 in Philadelphia, Pa. Attended Hofstra U, SUNY/Purchase. Bdwy debut 1981 in "Fiddler on the Roof."

LARSON, JILL. Born Oct. 7, 1947 in Minneapolis, Mn. Graduate Hunter Col. Debut 1980 OB in "These Men," followed by "Peep," "Serious Bizness," Bdwy in "Romantic Comedy" ('80).

LATHAN, BOBBI JO. Born Oct. 5, 1951 in Dallas, TX. Graduate N Tex State U. Bdwy debut 1979 in "The Best Little Whorehouse in Texas."

LATHEN, JANICE. Born Aug. 27 in Winner, SD. Graduate St. Benedict Col. Debut 1980 OB in "These Men," followed by "Playboy of the Western World," "Glory Hallelujah!," "Philistines."

LAUDICINO, DINO. Born Dec. 22, 1939 in Brooklyn, NY. Bdwy bow 1960 in "Christine," followed by "Rosencrantz and Guildenstern Are Dead," "Indians," "Scratch," "The Innocents," "Animals," OB in "King of the Dark Chamber," "Dollar," "Occupations."

LAURENCE, JAMES. Born June 2, 1949 in Passaic, NJ. Graduate Wm. Patterson Col. Debut 1980 OB in "Billy Irish," followed by "Domino Court," "Dustoff."

LAURIA, DAN. Born Apr. 12, 1947 in Brooklyn, NY. Graduate SConnState, UConn. Debut 1978 OB in "Game Plan," followed by "All My Sons," "Marlon Brando Sat Here," "Home of the Brave," "Collective Portraits," "Dustoff," "Niagara Falls."

LAWRENCE, ELIZABETH. Born Sept. 6, 1922 in Huntington, WVa. Graduate UMich, Yeshiva U. Bdwy debut 1954 in "The Rainmaker," followed by "All the Way Home," "Look Homeward, Angel," "A Matter of Gravity," OB in "The Misunderstanding."

LAYMAN, TERRY. Born Jan. 12, 1948 in Charlotte, NC. Graduate Wake Forest U. Debut 1980 OB in "Room Service," followed by "In the Matter of J. Robert Oppenheimer," "Ferocious Kisses."

LEAGUE, JANET. Born Oct. 13 in Chicago, Il. Attended Goodman Th. Debut 1969 OB in "To Be Young, Gifted and Black," followed by "Tiger at the Gates," "The Screens," "Mrs. Snow," "Please Don't Cry and Say No," "Banana Box," "The Brothers," Bdwy in "First Breeze of Summer" (1975), "For Colored Girls Who Have Considered Suicide . . ."

LEARY, DAVID. Born Aug 8, 1939 in Brooklyn, NY. Attended CCNY. Debut 1969 OB in "Shoot Anything That Moves," followed by "Macbeth," "The Plough and the Stars," "Emigres," Bdwy in "The National Health," "Da," "The Lady from Dubuque," "Piaf."

LEDERER, SUZANNE. Born Sept. 29, 1948 in Great Neck, NY. Graduate Hofstra U. Bdwy debut 1974 in "The National Health," followed by "Ah, Wilderness!," "Days in the Trees," "Amadeus," OB in "Treats."

LEE, ANDREA. Born Apr. 6, 1957 in Ohio. Attended Interlochen Arts Acad. Debut 1980 OB in "Oh, Boy!" followed by "A Funny Thing Happened on the Way to the Forum," "Nymph Errant."

LEE, BRYARLY. Born May 16, 1935 in Westerly, RI. Has appeared OB in "Maiden Voyage," "The Sea Gull," "Soft Shoulders," "My Prince My King."

LEE, JERRY. Born Jan. 23, 1946 in Oak Ridge, Tn. Attended E.MichU. Debut 1974 OB in "The Gospel According to Mark Twain," followed by "Ruby's Place," "Midsummer," "An Awfully Big Adventure," "The Conversion," "She Loves Me," "The Overcoat."

LEE, KAIULANI. Born Feb. 28, 1950 in Princeton, NJ. Attended American U. Bdwy debut 1975 in "Kennedy's Children," followed by "Macbeth," OB in "Ballad of the Sad Cafe," "Museum," "Safe House," "Othello," "Strange Snow."

LeFEVRE, ADAM. Born Aug. 11, 1950 in Albany, NY. Graduate Williams Col., UIa. Debut OB 1981 in "Turnbuckle," followed by "Badgers," "Goose and Tomtom."

LEFFERT, JOEL. Born Dec. 8, 1951 in NYC. Graduate Brown U. Debut 1976 OB in "Orphee," followed by "Heroes," "The Last Burning," "Relatively Speaking," "The Bachelor," "Scaramouche," "Macbeth," "Don Juan in Hell," "Village Wooing."

LEIBMAN, RON. Born Oct. 11, 1937 in NYC. Attended Ohio Wesleyan, Actors Studio. Bdwy debut 1963 in "Dear Me, the Sky Is Falling," followed by "Bicycle Ride to Nevada," "The Deputy," "We Bombed in New Haven" for which he received a Theatre World Award, "Cop-Out," "I Ought to Be in Pictures," OB in "The Academy," "John Brown's Body," "Scapin," "The Premise," "Legend of Lovers," "Dead End," "Poker Session," "Transfers," "Room Service," "Love Two," "Rich and Famous," "Children of Darkness."

LeMASSENA, WILLIAM. Born May 23, 1916 in Glen Ridge, NJ. Attended NYU. Bdwy bow 1940 in "Taming of the Shrew," followed by "There Shall Be No Night," "The Pirate," "Hamlet," "Call Me Mister," "Inside U.S.A.," "I Know My Love," "Dream Girl," "Nina," "Ondine," "Fallen Angels," "Redhead," "Conquering Hero," "Beauty Part," "Come Summer," "Grin and Bare It," "All over Town," "A Texas Trilogy," "Deathtrap," OB in "The Coop," "Brigadoon," "Life with Father," "F. Jasmine Addams," "The Dodge Boys."

LENCH, KATHERINE. Born Dec. 3, 1956 in Los Angeles, Ca. Debut 1982 OB in "Oh, Johnny!"

LeROY, KEN. Born Aug. 17, 1927 in Detroit, Mi. Attended Neighborhood Playhouse. Bdwy in "The American Way," "Morning Star," "Anne of England," "Oklahoma," "Carousel," "Brigadoon," "Call Me Madam," "Pajama Game," "West Side Story," "Fiddler on The Roof."

LEVINE, RICHARD S. Born July 16, 1954 in Boston, Ma. Graduate Juilliard. Debut 1978 OB in "Family Business," followed by "Magic Time," Bdwy in "Dracula."

LEVITT, JUDY. Born Sept. 17, 1945 in Detroit, Mi. Graduate UKan. Debut 1977 OB in "Twelfth Night," followed by "La Ronde."

LEWIS, JENIFER. Born Jan. 25, 1957 in St. Louis, MO. Graduate Webster College. Bdwy debut 1979 in "Eubie," followed by "Comin' Uptown," OB in "Sister Aimee," "El Bravo!"

LEWIS, MARCIA. Born Aug. 18, 1938 in Melrose, Ma. Attended UCin. OB in "Impudent Wolf," "Who's, Who, Baby?," "God Bless Coney," "Let Yourself Go," Bdwy in "The Time of Your Life," "Hello, Dolly!," "Annie."

LEWIS, R. J. Born July 30, 1955 in Morristown, NJ. Attended AADA. Bdwy debut 1981 in "Barnum."

LEWIS, TIMOTHY. Born June 28, 1947 in Chicago, Il. Attended UWs., Juilliard. Debut 1973 OB in "Waiting for Lefty," followed by "Lemon Sky," "Ten Little Indians," "The Comrades," "The Prophets."

LIDE, MILLER. Born Aug. 10, 1935 in Columbia, SC. Graduate USC, AmThWing. Debut 1961 OB in "Three Modern Japanese Plays," followed by "Trial at Rouen," "Street Scene," "Joan of Arc at the Stake," "The Heiress," Bdwy in "Ivanov," "Halfway Up the Tree," "Who's Who in Hell," "We Interrupt This Program," "The Royal Family."

LINAHAN, DONALD. Born Feb. 22, 1936 in Uniontown, Pa. Graduate William & Mary Col. Bdwy debut 1975 in "All God's Chillun Got Wings," followed by "Days in the Trees," "Kingdoms," OB in "Cracks."

LIND, JANE. Born Nov. 6, 1950 in Hump Back Bay, Perryville, AK. Attended NYU. Debut 1981 OB in "Black Elk Lives," followed by "49."

LIPPIN, RENEE. Born July 26, 1946 in NYC. Graduate Adelphi U. Debut 1970 OB in "The Way It Is," Bdwy in "Fun City," "The Inspector General," "The World of Sholom Aleichem."

LIPSON, CLIFFORD. Born Feb. 10, 1947 in Providence, RI. Attended Neighborhood Playhouse, AMDA. Bdwy bow 1970 in "Hair," OB in "Great Scot!," "Hooray, It's a Glorious Day," "The Indian Wants the Bronx," "Salvation," "Shaft of Love," "Lullabye and Goodnight."

LIPSON, PAUL. Born Dec. 23, 1913 in Brooklyn, NY. Attended Ohio State U., AmThWing. Bdwy bow 1942 in "Lily of the Valley," followed by "Heads or Tails," "Detective Story," "Remains to Be Seen," "Carnival in Flanders," "I've Got Sixpence," "The Vamp," "Bells Are Ringing," "Fiorello," "Sound of Music," "Fiddler on the Roof" (1964/1976/1981), OB in "Deep Six Briefcase," "The Inn at Lydda," "Golden Boy."

LISTMAN, RYAN. Born Dec. 30, 1939 in Newark, NJ. With LC Rep in "St. Joan," "Tiger at the Gates" and "Cyrano de Bergerac," OB in "Utopia," "Until the Monkey Comes," "Fortune and Men's Eyes," "Spiro Who?," "Blueberry Mountain," "A Midsummer Night's Dream," "Divine Fire."

LITHGOW, JOHN. Born Oct. 19, 1945 in Rochester, NY. Graduate Harvard U. Bdwy debut 1973 in "The Changing Room," followed by "My Fat Friend," "Comedians," "Anna Christie," "Once in a Lifetime," "Spokesong," "Bedroom Farce," "Division Street," "Beyond Therapy," OB in "Hamlet," "Trelawny of the Wells," "A Memory of Two Mondays," "Secret Service," "Boy Meets Girl," "Salt Lake City Skyline," "Kaufman at Large."

LITTLE, CLEAVON. Born June 1, 1939 in Chickasha, OK. Attended San Diego State U, AADA. Debut 1967 in "MacBird," followed by "Hamlet," "Someone's Coming Hungry," "Ofay Watcher," "Scuba Duba," "Narrow Road to the Deep North," "Great MacDaddy," "Joseph and the Amazing Technicolor Dreamcoat," "Resurrection of Lady Lester," "Keyboard," Bdwy in "Jimmy Shine," "Purlie," "All over Town," "The Poison Tree."

LLOYD, GOERGE. Born in Richmond, VA. Attended Carnegie Tech. Bdwy bow 1937 in "Julius Caesar," followed by "Shoemaker's Holiday," "The Fabulous Invalid," "One for the Money," "Hand in Glove," OB in "Glory! Hallelujah!," "Mary Stuart," "Henry IV Part II," "What the Butler Saw," "Whales of August," "Chinese Viewing Pavilion," "Antigone."

LO, RANDON. Born June 12, 1949 in Oakland, Ca. Graduate UCalBerkeley. Bdwy debut 1978 in "Stop the World, I Want to Get Off," followed by "Joseph and the Amazing Technicolor Dreamcoat."

LOCANTE, SAM. Born Sept. 12, 1918 in Kenosha, Wi. Graduate UWi. Bdwy bow 1955 in "Anniversary Waltz," followed by "Hidden Stranger," "Moonbirds," OB in "The Beaver Coat," "The Soldier," "Virgin Producers," "Game Plan," "The Time of Your Life," "Stone Killers," "Happy Anniversary," "Middle of the Night," "The Wrong Man," "The Relics," "3 by Pirandello."

LODGE, LILY. Born in 1934 in NYC. Graduate Wellesley Col., RADA. Debut 1954 OB in "Easter," followed by "The Music Crept by Me," "Ladies at the Alamo," "Crab Quadrille," "Choices," "After You've Gone," Bdwy in "Cyrano de Bergerac" (1955), "What Every Woman Knows," "The Wisteria Trees," "The Good Soup."

LOEWENSTERN, TARA. Born Nov. 11, 1951 in Los Angeles, Ca. Attended SMU, UTx, RADA. Debut 1977 OB in "The Crucible," followed by "Progress," Bdwy in "Macbeth" (1982).

LOMBARD, MICHAEL. Born Aug. 8, 1934 in Brooklyn, NY. Graduate Brooklyn Col, Boston U. OB in "King Lear," "Merchant of Venice," "Cages," "Pinter Plays," "LaTurista," "Elizabeth the Queen," "Room Service," "Mert and Phil," "Side Street Scenes," Bdwy in "Poor Bitos" (1964), "The Devils," "Gingerbread Lady," "Bad Habits," "Otherwise Engaged."

LONDON, HOWARD. Born Oct. 19, 1927 in NYC. Graduate Pasadena Playhouse. Debut 1958 OB in "The Trip to Bountiful," followed by "Orpheus Descending," "A Journey with Strangers," "The Mousetrap," Bdwy in "The Hothouse" (1982).

LONG, JODI. Born in NYC. graduate SUNY/Purchase. Bdwy debut 1963 in "Nowhere to Go but Up," followed by "Loose Ends," "Bacchae," OB in "Fathers and Sons," "Family Devotions," "Rohwer."

LOOZE, KAREN. Born Feb. 19, 1938 in Chicago, Il. Graduate IndU. Debut 1964 OB in "Streets of New York," followed by "The Wide Open Cage," "Grace."

LOPEZ, PRISCILLA. Born Feb. 26, 1948 in The Bronx, NY. Bdwy debut 1966 in "Breakfast at Tiffany's," followed by "Henry, Sweet Henry," "Lysistrata," "Company," "Her First Roman," "The Boy Friend," "Pippin," "A Chorus Line," "A Day in Hollywood/A Night in the Ukraine," OB in "What's a Nice Country Like You. . . .," "Key Exchange."

LOUD, DAVID. Born Nov. 28, 1961 in Cincinnati, Oh. Attended Yale U. Bdwy debut 1981 in "Merrily We Roll Along."

LOUDON, DOROTHY. Born Sept. 17, 1933 in Boston, MA. Attended Emerson Col., Syracuse U. Debut 1961 OB in "World of Jules Feiffer," Bdwy 1963 in "Nowhere to Go but Up," for which she received a Theatre World Award, followed by "Noel Coward's Sweet Potato," "Fig Leaves Are Falling," "Three Men on a Horse," "The Women," "Annie," "Ballroom," "West Side Waltz."

LOVELACE, CINDIE. Born Aug. 31, 1958 in Baltimore, Md. Graduate Boston U., Neighborhood Playhouse, LAMDA. Debut 1980 OB in "Forget the Alamo," Followed by "Long Day's Journey into Night," "Irish Coffee," "Teach Me How to Cry."

LOVETT, MARJORIE. Born Oct. 4, 1932 in Long Branch, NJ. Debut 1975 OB in "Another Language," Bdwy in "Einstein and the Polar Bear" (1981).

LOVING, LISA. Born Oct. 16, 1953 in Evanston, Il. Graduate UMd. Debut 1976 OB in "A Christmas Carol," followed by "Hunger Artist," "Flying Doctor," "The Fox," "Divine Fire."

LOW, MAGGIE. Born Apr. 23, 1957 in Nyack, NY. Debut 1982 OB in "Catholic School Girls."

LOWERY, MARCELLA. Born Apr. 27, 1945 in Jamaica, NY. Graduate Hunter Col. Debut 1967 OB in "Day of Absence," followed by "American Pastoral," "Ballet Behind the Bridge," "Jamimma," "A Recent Killing," "Miracle Play," "Welcome to Black River," "Anna Lucasta," "Baseball Wives," "Louis," Bdwy in "A Member of the Wedding" ('75), "Lolita."

LUBAR, CYNTHIA (aka Cindy) Born Apr. 16, 1954 in White Plains, NY. OB in "Life and Times of Sigmund Freud," "Deafman Glance," "Overture to Ka Mountain," "Ka Mountain and Gardenia Terrace," "Cyndi," "Life and Times of Joseph Stalin," "119 Comments," Bdwy 1975 in "A Letter for Queen Victoria."

LUCAS, CRAIG. Born April 30, 1951 in Atlanta, GA. Graduate Boston U. Debut 1974 OB in "Carousel" followed by "Marry Me a Little," "Alec Wilder: Clues to a Life," Bdwy in "Shenandoah" (1975), "Rex," "On the 20th Century," "Sweeney Todd."

LUCAS, J. FRANK. Born in Houston, TX. Graduate TCU. Debut 1943 OB in "A Man's House," followed by "Coriolanus," "Edward II," "Trip to Bountiful," "Orpheus Descending," "Guitar," "Marcus in the High Grass," "Chocolates," "To Bury a Cousin," "One World at a Time," Bdwy in "Bad Habits," "The Best Little Whorehouse in Texas."

LUCAS, RONN. Born Feb. 2, 1954 in Hico, Tx. Attended UTx. Bdwy debut 1981 in "Sugar Babies."

LUCAS, ROXIE. Born Aug. 25, 1951 in Memphis, Tn. Attended UHouston. Bdwy debut 1981 in "The Best Little Whorehouse in Texas."

LUGENBEAL, CAROL. Born July 14, 1952 in Detroit, MI. Graduate U.S. International U. Bdwy debut 1974 in "Where's Charley?" followed by "On the 20th Century," "Evita."

LUM, ALVIN. Born May 28, 1931 in Honolulu, HI. Attended UHi. Debut 1969 OB in "In the Bar of a Tokyo Hotel," followed by "Pursuit of Happiness," "Monkey Music," "Flowers and Household Gods," "Station J," Bdwy in "Lovely Ladies, Kind Gentlemen," "Two Gentlemen of Verona."

LUNA, BARBARA. Born Mar. 2 in NYC. Bdwy debut 1951 in "The King and I," followed by "West Side Story" (LC), "A Chorus Line."

LuPONE, PATTI. Born Apr. 21, 1949 in Northport, NY. Juilliard graduate. Debut 1972 OB in "School for Scandal," followed by "Women Beware Women," "Next Time I'll Sing to You," "Beggar's Opera," "Scapin," "Robber Bridegroom," "Edward II," "The Woods," Bdwy in "The Water Engine" (1978), "Working," "Evita."

LuPONE, ROBERT. Born July 29, 1956 in Brooklyn, NY. Juilliard graduate. Bdwy debut 1970 in "Minnie's Boys," followed by "Jesus Christ Superstar," "The Rothschilds," "Magic Show," "A Chorus Line," "St. Joan," OB in "Charlie Was Here," "Twelfth Night," "In Connecticut," "Snow Orchid."

LUTE, DENISE. Born Aug. 2, 1954 in NYC. Attended HB Studio. Debut 1975 OB in "Harry Outside," followed by "Green Fields," "Peep," "My Prince My King."

LUZ, FRANC. (aka as Frank C.) Born Dec. 22 in Cambridge, Ma. Attended NMxStateU. Debut 1974 O B in "The Rivals," followed by "Fiorello!," "The Little Shop of Horrors," Bdwy 1979 in "Whoopee!"

LYNCH, SUSAN. Born Dec. 11, 1949 in Seattle, Wa. Graduate Mills Col. Debut 1981 OB in "The Midnight Visitor."

LYND, BETTY. Born in Los Angeles, CA. Debut 1968 OB in "Rondelay," followed by "Love Me, Love My Children," Bdwy in "The Skin of Our Teeth" (1975), "A Chorus Line."

LYNDECK, EDMUND. Born Oct. 4, 1925 in Baton Rouge, LA. Graduate Montclair State Col., Fordham U. Bdwy debut 1969 in "1776," followed by "Sweeney Todd," "The King and I" (JB), "Mandragola," "A Safe Place," "Amoureuse," "Piaf: A Remembrance," "Children of Darkness."

LYNG, NORA MAE. Born Jan. 27, 1951 in Jersey City, NJ. Bdwy 1981 OB in "Anything Goes.'

MacINTOSH, JOAN E. Born Nov. 25, 1945 in NJ. Graduate Beaver Col., NYU. Debut OB 1969 in "Dionysus in '69" followed by "Makbeth," "Tooth of Crime," "Mother Courage," "Marilyn Project," "Seneca's Oedipus," "St. Joan of the Stockyards," "Wonderland in Concert," "Dispatches," "Endgame," "Killings on the Last Line," "Request Concert," "3 Acts of Recognition."

MACKAY, LIZBETH. Born March 7 in Buffalo, NY. Graduate Adelphi U., Yale. Bdwy debut 1981 in "Crimes of the Heart" for which she received a Theatre World Award.

MACKLIN, ALBERT. Born Nov. 18, 1958 in Los Angeles, Ca. Graduate StanfordU. Debut 1981 OB in "Ten Little Indians," followed by "Poor Little Lambs."

MACNAUGHTON, ROBERT. Born Dec. 19, 1966 in NYC. Debut 1980 OB in "The Diviners."

MacNICOL, PETER. Born April 10 in Dallas, Tx. Attended UMn. Bdwy debut 1981 in "Crimes of the Heart" for which he received a Theatre World Award.

 Joan MacIntosh

 Mark Manley

 Amelia Marshall

 John Martinuzzi

 Paige Massman

 Tom Matsusak

 Michael McBride

 Tanny McDonald

 Don McHenry

 Leilani Mickey

 Tod Miller

 Deborah Moldo

 Mary Elaine Monti

 Nat Morris

 Stephanie Murphy

 Bud Nease

 Mary Ann Niles

 Mustafa Noo

 Don Nute

 Jill O'Hara

 Gene O'Neill

 Paula Parker

 Richard Patrick-Warner

Tonya Pinki

 Marian Primont

Brian Quinn

 Paula Raflo

 Jess Richards

 Marilyn Roberts

 Casper Roos

213

MACY, W. H. Born Mar. 13, 1950 in Miami, FL. Graduate Goddard Col. Debut 1980 OB in "The Man in 605," followed by "Twelfth Night," "The Beaver Coat," "A Call from the East," "Sittin'," "Shoeshine," "The Dining Room."

MADDEN, SHARON. Born July 8, 1947 in St. Louis, MO. Debut 1975 OB in "Battle of Angels," followed by "The Hot 1 Baltimore," "Who Killed Richard Cory?," "Mrs. Murray's Farm," "The Passing of Corky Brewster," "Brontosaurus," "Ulysses in Traction," "Lulu," "In the Recovery Lounge," "In Connecticut," "Thymus Vulgaris."

MAGNUSON, MERILEE. Born June 11, 1951 in Tacoma, Wa. Attended UCal/Irvine. Bdwy debut 1973 in "Gigi," followed by "Irene," "The Best Little Whorehouse in Texas." OB in "Dancing in the Dark."

MAHAFFEY, VALERIE. Born June 16, 1953 in Sumatra, Indonesia. Graduate UTx. Debut 1975 OB in "Father Uxbridge Wants to Marry,," followed by "Bus Stop," "Black Tuesday," "Scenes and Revelations," (also Bdwy), "Twelve Dreams," "Translations," Bdwy in "Rex," "Dracula," "Fearless Frank."

MAHONE, JUANITA M. Born Sept. 12, 1952 in Boston, MA. Graduate Boston U. Debut 1975 OB in "Don't Bother Me, I Can't Cope," followed by "Birdland," "The Verandah," "Face of Love," "The Sun Always Shines for the Cool," "Antigone," "Single Room Occupancy," "Colored People's Time."

MAILLARD, CAROL LYNN. Born Mar. 4, 1951 in Philadelphia, PA. Graduate Catholic U. Debut 1977 OB in "The Great MacDaddy," followed by "It's So Nice To Be Civilized," "A Photograph," "Under Fire," "Zooman and the Sign," Bdwy in "Eubie!" (1979), "It's So Nice to Be Civilized."

MAIS, MICHELE. Born July 30, 1954 in NYC. Graduate CCNY. Debut 1975 OB in "Godspell," followed by "Othello," "Superspy," "Yesterday Continued," "We'll Be Right Back," "Que Ubo?," "El Bravo!," Bdwy 1979 in "Zoot Suit."

MANLEY, MARK. Born July 10, 1954 in Newark NJ. Attended Jersey City State Col. Debut 1979 OB in "Mary," Bdwy in "Fiddler on the Roof" (1981).

MANN, PJ. Born Apr. 9, 1953 in Pasadena, CA. Bdwy debut 1976 in "Home Sweet Homer," followed by "A Chorus Line," "Dancin'."

MANTELL, BERNARD. Born Nov. 21, 1953 in Brooklyn, NY. Graduate Carnegie-Mellon U. Debut 1980 OB in "Pushcart Peddlers," followed by "Little Malcolm," "Richard II," "Merchant of Venice," "Don Juan."

MARADEN, FRANK. Born Aug. 9, 1944 in Norfolk, VA. Graduate UMn., MichStateU. Debut 1980 OB with BAM Theatre Co. in "A Winter's Tale," "Johnny on a Spot," "Barbarians" "The Wedding," "Midsummer Night's Dream," "The Recruiting Officer," "The Wild Duck," "Jungle of Cities," "Three Acts of Recognition."

MARCH, ELLEN. Born Aug. 18, 1948 in Brooklyn, NY. Graduate AMDA. Debut 1967 OB in "Pins and Needles," followed by "I Can't Keep Running in Place," Bdwy in "Grease," "Once in a Lifetime," "The Floating Light Bulb."

MARCH, WILLIAM. Born Apr. 3, 1951 in St. Paul, MN. Graduate NYU. Debut 1975 OB in "The Gift of the Magi," followed by "Heart's Desire," "He, She, Shaw."

MARCUS, DANIEL. Born May 26, 1955 in Redwood City, CA. Graduate Boston U. Bdwy debut 1981 in "The Pirates of Penzance."

MARGOLIS, MARK. Born Nov. 26, 1939 in Malta. Attended Temple U. Bdwy debut 1962 in "Infidel Caesar," followed by "The World of Sholom Aleichem," OB in "Second Avenue Rag."

MARGULIES, DAVID. Born Feb. 19, 1937 in NYC. Graduate CCNY. Debut 1958 OB in "Golden Six," followed by "Six Characters in Search of an Author," "Tragical Historie of Dr. Faustus," "Tango," "Little Murders," "Seven Days of Mourning," "Last Analysis," "An Evening with the Poet Senator," "Kid Champion," "The Man with the Flower in His Mouth," "Old Tune," Bdwy in "The Iceman Cometh (1973), "Zalmen or the Madness of God," "Comedians," "Break a Leg," "West Side Waltz."

MARIE, JULIENNE. Born in 1943 in Toledo, OH. Attended Juilliard. Has appeared in "The King and I," "Whoop-Up," "Gypsy," "Foxy," "Do I Hear a Waltz?," "Ballroom," "Charlie and Algernon," OB in "The Boys from Syracuse" for which she received a Theatre World Award, "Othello," "Comedy of Errors," "Trojan Women," "Damn Yankees" (JB).

MARINOS, PETER. born Oct. 2, 1951 in Pontiac, MI. Graduate MiStateU. Bdwy debut 1976 in "Chicago," followed by "Evita."

MARKS, JACK R. Born Feb. 28, 1935 in Brooklyn, NY. Debut 1975 OB in "Hamlet," followed by "A Midsummer Night's Dream," "Getting Out," "Basic Training of Pavlo Hummel," "We Bombed in New Haven," "Angel Street," "Birthday Party," "Tarzan and Boy," "Goose and Tomtom."

MARKS, KENNETH. born Feb. 17, 1954 in Harwick, PA. Graduate UPa, Lehigh U. Debut 1978 OB in "Clara Bow Loves Gary Cooper," followed by "Canadian Gothic," "Time and the Conways," "Savoury Meringue."

MARR, RICHARD. Born May 12, 1928 in Baltimore, Md. Graduate UPa. Bdwy in "Baker Street," "How to Succeed . . .," "Here's Where I Belong," "Coco," "The Constant Wife," "So Long, 174th St.," OB in "Sappho," "Pilgrim's Progress," "Pimpernel," "Witness," "Antiquities," "Two by Tennessee," "King of Hearts," "What a Life!"

MARSHALL, AMELIA. Born Apr. 2, 1958 in Albany, Ga. Graduate UTx. Debut 1982 OB in "Applause" (ELT).

MARSHALL, LARRY. born Apr. 3, 1944 in Spartanburg, SC. Attended Fordham U., New Eng. Cons. Bdwy debut in "Hair," followed by "Two Gentlemen of Verona," "A Midsummer Night's Dream," "Rockabye Hamlet," "Porgy and Bess," "A Broadway Musical," "Comin' Uptown," "Oh, Brother!," OB in "Spell #7," "Jus' Like Livin'," "The Haggadah," "Lullabye and Goodnight."

MARSHALL, NORMAN THOMAS. Born Apr. 28, 1939 in Richmond, Va. Attended UVa, Hunter Col., CCNY. Debut 1966 OB in "Gorilla Queen," followed by "Boy on the Straight-back Chair," "Charlie Was Here and Now He's Gone," "The Rapists," "Home/Work," "The Broken Pitcher."

MARTIN, GEORGE. Born Aug. 15, 1929 in NYC. Bdwy debut 1970 in "Wilson in the Promise Land," followed by "The Hothouse."

MARTIN, JOYCE. Born Mar. 8, 1949 in St. Paul, Mn. Attended UMn. Bdwy debut 1976 in "Fiddler on the Roof" followed by 1981 revival.

MARTIN, LEILA. Born Aug. 22, 1932 in NYC. Bdwy debut 1944 in "Peepshow," followed by "Two on the Aisle," "Wish You Were Here," "Guys and Dolls," "Best House in Naples," "Henry, Sweet Henry," "The Wall," "Visit to a Small Planet," "The Rothschilds," "42nd Street," OB in "Ernest in Love," "Beggar's Opera,' "King of the U.S.," "Philemon," "Jerry's Girls."

MARTIN, LUCY. Born Feb. 8, 1942 in NYC. Graduate Sweet Briar Col. Debut 1962 OB in "Electra," followed by "Happy as Larry," "The Trojan Women," "Iphigenia in Aulis," Bdwy in "Shelter" (1973), "Children of a Lesser God."

MARTIN, MILLICENT. Born June 8, 1934 in Romford, Eng. Attended Italia Conti Sch. Bdwy debut 1954 in "The Boy Friend," followed by "Side by Side by Sondheim," "King of Hearts," "42nd Street."

MARTIN, VIRGINIA. Born Dec. 2, 1932 in Chattanooga, Tn. Attended AmThWing. Appeared on Bdwy in "South Pacific," "Pajama Game," "Ankles Aweigh," "New Faces of 1956," "How to Succeed . . .," "Little Me," "Carmelina," OB in "Buy Bonds Buster," "Joseph and the Amazing Technicolor Dreamcoat," "Sing Melancholy Baby," "Something for the Boys."

MARTIN, W. T. Born Jan. 17, 1947 in Providence, RI. Attended Lafayette Col. Debut 1972 OB in "The Basic Training of Pavlo Hummel," followed by "Ghosts," "The Caretaker," "Are You Now or Have You Ever Been," "Fairy Tales of New York," "We Won't Pay," "Black Elk Lives," "The End of War."

MARTINO, MARK. Born Aug. 26, 1953 in Indianapolis, In. Graduate Wm. and Mary Col. Bdwy debut 1981 in "Broadway Follies," followed by "Oh, Brother!"

MARTINUZZI, JOHN. Born Sept. 29 in Chicago, Il. Attended LAMDA. Bdwy debut 1981 in "Kingdoms," OB in "The Quality of Mercy," "Streamers," "The Sorrows of Stephen."

MASSMAN, PAIGE. Born Oct. 13, 1946. Graduate Webster Col., Purdue U. Debut 1976 OB in "The Boys from Syracuse," Bdwy 1981 in "Woman of the Year."

MASTERS, BEN. Born May 6, 1947 in Corvallis, Or. Graduate UOr. Debut 1970 OB in "Boys in the Band," followed by "What the Butler Saw," "The Cherry Orchard," "Key Exchange," Bdwy in "Capt. Brassbound's Conversion."

MASTRANTONIO, MARY E. Born Nov. 17, 1958 in Chicago, IL. Attended UIl. Bdwy debut 1980 in "West Side Story," followed by "Copperfield," "Oh, Brother!"

MATSUSAKA, TOM. Born Aug. 8 in Wahiawa, Hi. Graduate MiStateU. Bdwy bow 1968 in "Mame," followed by "Ride the Winds," "Pacific Overtures," OB in "Agamemnon," "Chu Chem," "Jungle of Cities," "Santa Anita '42," "Extenuating Circumstances," "Rohwer."

MAXWELL, ROBERTA. Born in Canada. Debut 1968 OB in "Two Gentlemen of Verona," followed by "A Whistle in the Dark," "Slag," "The Plough and the Stars," "Merchant of Venice," "Ashes," "Mary Stuart," "Lydie Breeze," Bdwy in "The Prime of Miss Jean Brodie," "Henry V," "House of Atreus," "The Resistible Rise of Arturo Ui," "Othello," "Hay Fever," "There's One in Every Marriage," "Equus," "The Merchant."

MAY, BEVERLY. Born Aug. 11, 1927 in East Wellington, BD, Can. Graduate Yale U. Debut 1976 OB in "Female Transport," followed by "Bonjour, La, Bonjour," "My Sister in This House," Bdwy 1977 in "Equus," followed by "Once in a Lifetime," "Whose Life Is It Anyway?," "Rose," "Curse of an Aching Heart."

MAY, WINSTON. Born Feb. 3, 1937 in Mammoth Spring, Ar. Graduate ArStateU, AmThWing. Debut 1967 OB in "The Man Who Washed His Hands," followed by "King Lear," "Candida," "Trumpets and Drums," "Otho the Great," "Uncle Vanya," "Servant of Two Masters," "The Play's the Thing," "Autumn Garden," "Madmen," "Villager."

MAYER, JERRY. Born May 12, 1941 in NYC. Graduate NYU. Debut 1968 OB in "Alice in Wonderland," followed by "L'Ete," "Marouf," "Trelawny of the Wells," "King of the Schnorrers," "Mother Courage," "You Know Al," "Goose and Tomtom," Bdwy in "Much Ado about Nothing" (1972).

MAYO, ANNETTE. Born Sept. 14, 1953 in Jersey City, NJ. Graduate Jersey City State Col. Debut 1982 OB in "A Trinity."

MAZUMDAR, MAXIM. Born Jan. 27, 1953 in Bombay, India. Graduate Loyola Col., McGill U. Debut 1981 OB in "Oscar Remembered."

McARDLE, ANDREA. Born Nov. 5, 1963 in Philadelphia, Pa. Bdwy debut 1977 in "Annie" for which she received a Theatre World Award, OB in "They Say It's Wonderful."

McBRIDE, MICHAEL. Born Sept. 2, 1953 in Madison, Wi. Attended Catholic U. Bdwy debut 1982 in "Deathtrap."

McCALL, NANCY. Born Jan. 12, 1948 in Atlanta, Ga. Graduate Northwestern U. Debut 1975 OB in "Godspell," followed by "Heebie Jeebies," Bdwy 1982 in "Nine."

McCALLUM, DAVID. Born Sept. 19, 1933 in Scotland. Attended Chapman Col. Bdwy debut 1968 in "The Flip Side," followed by "California Suite," OB in "After the Prize."

McCANN, CHRISTOPHER. Born Sept. 29, 1952 in NYC. Graduate NYU. Debut 1975 OB in "The Measures Taken," followed by "Ghosts," "Woyzzeck," "St. Joan of the Stockyards," "Buried Child," "Dwelling in Milk," "Tongues," "3 Acts of Recognition."

McCARTY, MICHAEL. Born Sept. 7, 1946 in Evansville, IN. Graduate InU., MiStateU. Debut 1976 OB in "Fiorello!," Bdwy in "Dirty Linens," "King of Hearts," "Amadeus."

McCAULEY, WILLIAM. Born Nov. 20, 1947 in Wayne, PA. Graduate Northwestern U., Goodman Th. Bdwy debut 1974 in "Saturday, Sunday, Monday," OB in "Captive Audiences," "Everybody's Gettin' into the Act."

McCLARNON, KEVIN. Born Aug. 25, 1952 in Greenfield, IN. Graduate Butler U, LAMDA. Debut 1977 OB in "The Homecoming," followed by "Heaven's Gate," "A Winter's Tale," "Johnny on a Spot," "The Wedding," "Between Daylight and Boonville," "Macbeth" (LC)., "Clownmaker."

McCRACKEN, JEFF. Born Sept. 12, 1952 in Chicago, Il. Debut 1981 OB in "In Connecticut," followed by "Am I Blue," "Thymus Vulgaris," "Confluence."

McCRANE, PAUL. Born Jan. 19, 1961 in Philadelphia, Pa. Debut 1977 OB in "Landscape of the Body," followed by "Dispatches," "Split," "Hunting Scenes," "Crossing Niagara," Bdwy in "Runaways," "Curse of an Aching Heart."

McDERMOTT, KEITH. Born in Houston, TX. Attended LAMDA. Bdwy debut 1976 in "Equus," followed by "A Meeting by the River," "Harold and Maude," OB in "Heat of Re-entry," "Misalliance."

MEMEL, STEVEN. Born Aug. 5, 1956 in Los Angeles, Ca. Graduate UCLA. Debut 1979 OB in "Modigliani," followed by "The Haggadah," "Two Precious Maidens Ridiculed," "Chantecler."

McDONALD, TANNY. Born Feb. 13, 1939 in Princeton, IN. Graduate Vassar Col. Debut OB with Am. Savoyards, followed by "All in Love," "To Broadway with Love," "Carrick-nabauna," "Beggar's Opera," "Brand," "Goodbye, Dan Bailey," "Total Eclipse," "Gorky," "Don Juan Comes Back from the War," "Vera with Kate," "Francis," Bdwy in "Fiddler on the Roof," "Come Summer," "The Lincoln Mask," "Clothes for a Summer Hotel."

McDONNELL, MARY. Born in 1952 in Ithaca, NY. Graduate SUNY Fredonia . Debut OB 1978 in "Buried Child," followed by "Letters Home," "Still Life," "Death of a Miner."

McDONOUGH, ANN. Born in Portland, ME. Graduate Towson State. Debut 1975 OB in "Trelawny of the Wells," followed by "Secret Service," "Boy Meets Girl," "Scribes," "Uncommon Women," "City Sugar," "Fables for Friends," "The Dining Room."

McDONOUGH, STEPHEN. Born Oct. 27, 1958 in Brooklyn, NY. Graduate SUNY/Potsdam. Debut 1981 OB in "The Fantasticks," followed by "Teach Me How to Cry."

McFARLAND, ROBERT. Born May 7, 1931 in Omaha, Ne. Graduate UMi, Columbia U. Debut 1978 OB in "The Taming of the Shrew," followed by "When the War Was Over," "Divine Fire," "Ten Little Indians," "The Male Animal," "Comedy of Errors."

McGOVERN, ELIZABETH. Born July 18, 1961 in Evanston, Il. Attended Juilliard. Debut 1981 OB in "To Be Young, Gifted and Black," followed by "Hotel Play," "My Sister in This House" for which she received a Theatre World Award.

McGOVERN, MAUREEN. Born July 27, 1949 in Youngstown, Oh. Bdwy debut 1981 in "Pirates of Penzance."

McGREGOR-STEWART, KATE. Born Oct. 4, 1944 in Buffalo, NY. Graduate Beaver Col, Yale U. Bdwy debut 1975 in "Travesties," followed by "A History of the American Film," OB in "Titanic," "Vienna Notes," "Beyond Therapy" (also Bdwy).

McGUIRE, MITCHELL. Born Dec. 26, 1936 in Chicago, Il. Attended Goodman Th., Santa Monica City Col. OB in "The Rapists," "Go, Go, God Is Dead," "Waiting for Lefty," "The Bond," "Guns of Carrar," "Oh! Calcutta!," "New York! New York!," "What a Life!"

McGUIRK, SEAN. Born Mar. 12, 1952 in Boston, Ma. Graduate UMa., AADA. Debut 1982 OB in "Applause," followed by "Lola."

McHENRY, DON. Born Feb. 25 in Paterson, NJ. Attended Rutgers U. Bdwy bow 1938 in "Don't Throw Glass Houses," followed by "Medea" (1947/1982), "Tower Beyond Tragedy," "The Crucible," "Fanny," "Destry Rides Again," "Tovarich," "Elizabeth the Queen," "King Lear," "Cry of Players," "Vivat! Vivat Regina!," OB in "Hamlet," "Conflict of Interest."

McINERNEY, BERNIE. Born Dec. 4, 1936 in Wilmington, DE. Graduate UDel., Catholic U. Bdwy debut 1972 in "That Championship Season," followed by "Curse of an Aching Heart," OB in "Life of Galileo," "Losing Time," "3 Friends," "The American Clock," "Father Dreams."

McINTYRE, MARILYN. Born May 23, 1949 in Erie, PA. Graduate PennState, NCSch. of Arts. Debut 1977 OB in "The Perfect Mollusc," followed by "Measure for Measure," "The Promise," "Action," Bdwy in "Gemini" (1980), "Scenes and Revelations."

McKINSEY, BEVERLEE. Born Aug. 9 in Oklahoma. Graduate UOk. Debut 1962 OB in "P.S. 193," followed by "Love Nest," "Dutchman," "Mert and Phil," "After Many a Summer," Bdwy in "Who's Afraid of Virginia Woolf?" "Barefoot in the Park."

McKITTERICK, TOM. Born Jan. 23 in Cleveland, Oh. Graduate Amherst. Debut 1978 OB in "Fathers and Sons," followed by "Say Goodnight, Gracie," "Salt Lake City Skyline," "Leavin' Cheyenne."

McLAIN, ELLEN. Born Dec. 1, 1952 in Silver Springs, Md. Graduate New Eng. Consv. Bdwy debut 1981 in "My Fair Lady."

McMARTIN, JOHN. Born in Warsaw, In. Attended Columbia U. Debut 1959 OB in "Little Mary Sunshine" for which he received a Theatre World Award, followed by "Too Much Johnson," "The Misanthrope," Bdwy in "Conquering Hero," "Blood, Sweat and Stanley Poole," "Children from Their Games," "Rainy Day in Newark," "Sweet Charity," "Follies," "Great God Brown," "Don Juan," "The Visit," "Chemin de Fer," "Love for Love," "Rules of the Game," "Happy New Year," "Solomon's Child."

McMILLAN, KENNETH. Born July 2, 1934 in Brooklyn, NY. Bdwy debut 1970 in "Borstal Boy," followed by "American Buffalo," OB in "Red Eye of Love," "King of the Whole Damn World," "Little Mary Sunshine," "Babes in the Wood," "Moonchildren," "Merry Wives of Windsor," "Where Do We Go from Here?," "Kid Champion," "Streamers," "Henry IV Part II," "Weekends Like Other People."

McNAUGHTON, STEPHEN. (Formerly Steve Scott) Born Oct. 11, 1949 in Denver, CO. Graduate UDenver, Debut 1971 OB in "The Drunkard," followed by "Summer Brave," "Monsters," "Chase a Rainbow," "Two on the Isles," Bdwy in "The Ritz" (1976), "Shenandoah," "Cheaters," "Da," "Best Little Whorehouse in Texas," "Joseph and the Amazing Technicolor Dreamcoat."

McRAE, CALVIN. Born Feb. 14, 1955 in Toronto, Can. Attended London Guildhall. Bdwy debut 1971 in "Anne of Green Gables," followed by "Music Man," "A Broadway Musical," "Going Up," "A Chorus Line," "Sophisticated Ladies."

McROBBIE, PETER. Born Jan. 31, 1943 in Hawick, Scot. Yale graduate. Debut 1976 OB in "The Wobblies," followed by "The Devil's Disciple," Bdwy in "Whose Life Is It Anyway?" (1979), "Macbeth" (1981).

MEACHAM, PAUL. Born Aug. 5, 1939 in Memphis, Tn. Graduate UTn, MiStateU. Debut 1973 OB in "Twelfth Night," followed by "The Homecoming," "The Tempest," "Moby Dick," "The Crucible," "The Passion of Dracula," "Fighting Bob."

MEADOWS, NANCY. Born July 11, 1953 in Glen Rock, NJ. Debut 1979 OB in "Mary," followed by "Nymph Errant."

MEDEIROS, MICHAEL. Born Sept. 15, 1949 in San Francisco, Ca. Attended UHi. Debut 1977 OB in "Museum," followed by "Stray Vessels," "A New World," "Split."

MEEK, JOE. Born Nov. 10, 1944 in Bremerton, Wa. Attended UWa. Debut 1981 OB in "Two Gentlemen of Verona," followed by "Edward II."

MELOCHE, KATHERINE. Born June 1, 1952 in Detroit, Mi. Bdwy debut 1976 in "Grease," followed by "Dancin'," OB in "Street Scene."

MEREDITH, LEE. Born Oct. 22, 1947 in River Edge, NJ. Graduate AADA. Bdwy debut 1969 in "A Teaspoon Every 4 Hours," followed by "The Sunshine Boys," "Once in a Lifetime," "Musical Chairs," OB in "Hollywood Hotel."

MERKIN, LEWIS. Born Dec. 18, 1955 in Philadelphia, PA. Attended CalStateU. Bdwy debut 1980 in "Children of a Lesser God."

MERLIN, JOANNA. Born July 15 in Chicago, IL. Attended UCLA. Debut 1958 OB in "The Breaking Wall," followed by "Six Characters in Search of an Author," "Rules of the Game," "A Thistle in My Bed," "Canadian Gothic/American Modern," Bdwy in "Becket," (1961), "A Far Country," "Fiddler on the Roof," "Shelter," "Uncle Vanya," "The Survivor," "Solomon's Child."

MERLINGTON, LAURAL. Born Oct. 22, 1953 in Lansing, Mi. Attended Eastern MiU. Debut 1982 OB in "The Chinese Viewing Pavilion."

MERSON, SUSAN. Born Apr. 25, 1950 in Detroit, Mi. Graduate Boston U. Bdwy debut 1974 in "Saturday Sunday Monday," followed by "Children of a Lesser God," OB in "Vanities," "Loves of Shirley Abramovitz," "Reflections of a China Doll," "Delmore," "The Misunderstanding."

MERYL, CYNTHIA. Born Sept. 25, 1950 in NYC. Graduate InU. Bdwy debut 1976 in "My Fair Lady," followed by "Nine," OB in "Before Sundown," "The Canticle," "The Pirate," "Dames at Sea," "Gay Divorce," "Sterling Silver," "Anything Goes."

METTE, NANCY. Born Jan. 22, 1955 in Pennsylvania. Graduate NCSch. of Arts. Debut 1982 OB in "The Good Parts."

MICHALSKI, JOHN. Born June 7, 1948 in Hammond, In. Juilliard graduate. Bdwy debut 1973 in "Beggar's Opera," followed by "Measure for Measure," "Herzl," "Gorey Stories," OB in "Hamlet," "Much Ado About Nothing," "Playing with Fire."

MICHELLE, ANNETTE. Born Sept. 29, 1956 in Buffalo, NY. Debut 1979 OB in "Fantasy Children," Bdwy in "Five O'Clock Girl," "Little Johnny Jones."

MICKEY, LEILANI. Born Jan. 18, 1955 in Honolulu, Hi. Juilliard graduate. Debut 1981 OB in "Everybody's Gettin' into the Act."

MILES, ROSS. Born in Poughkeepsie, NY. Bdwy debut 1962 in "Little Me," followed by "Baker Street," "Pickwick," "Darling of the Day," "Mame," "Jumpers," "Goodtime Charley," "Chicago," "Dancin'."

MILGRIM, LYNN. Born Mar. 17, 1944 in Philadelphia, PA. Graduate Swarthmore Col., Harvard U. Debut 1969 OB in "Frank Gagliano's City Scene," followed by "Crimes of Passion," "Macbeth," "Charley's Aunt," "The Real Inspector Hound," "Rib Cage," "Museum," "Bits and Pieces," "What Would Jeanne Moreau Do?," Bdwy in "Otherwise Engaged," "Bedroom Farce."

MILLER, ANN. Born Apr. 12, 1923 in Chireno, TX. Bdwy debut 1940 in "George White's Scandals," followed by "Mame," "Sugar Babies."

MILLER, BETTY. Born Mar. 27, 1925 in Boston, Ma. Attended UCLA. OB in "Summer and Smoke," "Cradle Song," "La Ronde," "Plays for Bleecker St.," "Desire under the Elms," "The Balcony," "The Power and the Glory," "Beaux Stratagem," "Gandhi," "Girl on the Via Flaminia," "Hamlet," Bdwy in "You Can't Take It With You," "Right You Are," "The Wild Duck," "The Cherry Orchard," "A Touch of the Poet," "Eminent Domain."

MILLER, COURT. Born Jan. 29, 1952 in Norwalk, Ct. Debut 1980 OB in "Elizabeth and Essex," followed by "Welded," Bdwy in "The First," "Torch Song Trilogy."

MILLER, DARLEIGH. Born May 28, 1955 in Seymour, IN. Graduate Ball State U. Bdwy debut 1980 in "The Music Man," followed by "Copperfield," OB in "Something for the Boys."

MILLER, FRED. Born Sept. 17, 1922 in Oklahoma City, Ok. Graduate Carnegie Tech. Bdwy debut 1955 in "Inherit the Wind," followed by "Take Me Along," "Oliver!," "The King and I," OB in "The Three Sisters," "The General," "Hamp," "Ten Little Indians."

MILLER, GREGORY. Born Oct. 2, 1954 in Cincinnati, OH. Graduate UMi. Debut 1978 OB in "The Vampire and the Dentist," followed by "The Passion of Alice," "Black People's Party," Bdwy 1981 in "Inacent Black."

MILLER, RUTH. Born June 25 in Chicago, Il. Graduate UChicago, Western Reserve. Debut 1980 OB in "Not Like Him," Bdwy 1982 in "Come Back to the 5 & Dime, Jimmy Dean."

MILLER, TOD. Born Sept. 15, 1944 in Quincy, Il. Attended Pasadena Playhouse. Bdwy bow 1967 in "Mame," followed by "Here's Where I Belong," "Cabaret," "Canterbury Tales," OB in "Stag Movie," "Hoofers."

MILLER, VALERIE-JEAN. Born Aug. 22, 1950 in Miami Beach, FL. Bdwy debut 1978 in "Dancin'."

MILLIGAN, TUCK (aka Jacob) Born Mar. 25, 1949 in Kansas City, Mo. Graduate UKC. Bdwy debut 1976 in "Equus," followed by "Crucifer of Blood," OB in "Beowulf," "Everybody's Gettin' into the Act."

MISTRETTA, SAL. Born Jan. 9, 1945 in Brooklyn, NY. Ithaca Col. graduate Bdwy debut 1976 in "Something's Afoot," followed by "On the 20th Century," "Evita."

MIYAMOTO, ANNE. Born in Honolulu, Hi. Graduate UHi., NYU. Debut 1962 OB in "Yanks Are Coming," followed by "And the Soul Shall Dance," "Roshwer," Bdwy in "The Basic Training of Pavlo Hummel" (1977).

MOLDOW, DEBORAH. Born Dec. 18, 1948 in NYC. Graduate Sarah Lawrence Col. Debut 1958 OB in "The Enchanted," followed by "The Power and the Glory," "The Pursuit of Happiness," "Romance Is," "Street Scene."

MOLNAR, ROBERT. Born June 22, 1927 in Cincinnati, OH. Attended OhNorthernU, UCin, CinConsv. of Music. Debut 1958 OB in "Hamlet of Stepney Green," followed by "Boys from Syracuse," Bdwy in "Camelot" (1980/1981).

MONSON, LEX. Born Mar. 11, 1926 in Grindstone, Pa. Attaended DePaul U, UDetroit. Debut 1961 OB in "The Blacks," followed by "Pericles," "Macbeth," "See How They Run," "Telemachus Clay," "Keyboard," "Oh My Mother Passed Away," "The Confession Stone," "Linty Lucy," Bdwy in "Moby Dick," "Trumpets of the Lord," "Watch on the Rhine."

MONTEITH, JOHN. Born Nov. 1, 1948 in Philadelphia, Pa. Graduate Boston U. Debut 1973 OB in "The Proposition," followed by "See America First," "Ferocious Kisses," Bdwy 1979 in "Monteith and Rand."

MONTI, MARY ELAINE. Born Sept. 18, 1948 in Waterbury, Ct. Debut 1974 OB in "Macbeth," followed by "Heat," "Kid Champion," "Gogol," "Flux," "Domino Court," "Cracks," "Split," "Ghosts of the Loyal Oaks," "Scenes from La Vie de Boheme."

MOONEY, DEBRA. Born in Aberdeen, SD. Graduate Auburn, UMinn. Debut 1975 OB in "Battle of Angels," followed by "The Farm," "Summer and Smoke," "Stargazing," "Childe Byron," "Wonderland," Bdwy 1978 in "Chapter 2," followed by "Talley's Folly."

MOOR, BILL. Born July 13, 1931 in Toledo, Oh. Attended Northwestern, Dennison U. Bdwy debut 1964 in "Blues for Mr. Charlie," followed by "Great God Brown," "Don Juan," "The Visit," "Chemin de Fer," "Holiday," "P.S. Your Cat Is Dead," "Night of the Tribades," "Water Engine," OB in "Dandy Dick," "Love Nest," "Days and Nights of Beebee Fenstermaker," "The Collection," "The Owl Answers," "Long Christmas Dinner," "Fortune and Men's Eyes," "King lear," "Cry of Players," "Boys in the Band," "Alive and Well in Argentina," "Rosmersholm,' "The Biko Inquest," "A Winter's Tale," "Johnny on a Spot," "Barbarians," "The Burging," "Potsdam Quartet."

MOORE, CHARLOTTE. Born July 7, 1939 in Herrin, IL. Attended Smith Col. Bdwy debut 1972 in "The Great God Brown," followed by "Don Juan," "The Visit," "Chemin de Fer," "Holiday," "Love for Love," "A Member of the Wedding," "Morning's at 7," OB in "Out of Our Father's House," "A Lovely Sunday for Creve Couer," "Summer," "Beside the Seaside."

MOORE, JUDITH. Born Feb. 12, 1944 in Princeton, WVa. Graduate IndU, Concord Col. Debut 1971 OB in "The Drunkard," followed by "Ten by Six," "Boys from Syracuse," "The Evangelist."

MOORE, MAUREEN. Born Aug. 12, 1951 in Wallingford, Ct. Bdwy debut 1974 in "Gypsy," followed by "Do Black Patent Leather Shoes Really Reflect Up?," OB in "Unsung Cole," "By Strouse."

MOORE, PETER. Born Jan. 27, 1956 in Minneapolis, Mn. Graduate PaStateU. Debut 1980 OB in "Cop-Out," followed by "Isolde of White Hands," "A Cry of Players," "The Rover," "Dancers on My Ceiling."

MORANZ, JANNET. (formerly Horsley) Born Oct. 13, 1954 in Los Angeles, CA. Attended CaStateU. Bdwy debut 1980 in "A Chorus Line."

MORATH, KATHY. (aka Kathryn) Born Mar. 23, 1955 in Colorado Springs, CO. Graduate Brown U. Debut 1980 OB in "The Fantasticks," followed by "Dulcy," "Snapshot," "Alice in Concert," "A Little Night Music," Bdwy in "Pirates of Penzance" (1982).

MORDEN, ROGER. Born Mar. 21, 1939 in Iowa City, IA. Graduate Coe Col., Neighborhood Playhouse. Debut 1964 OB in "Old Glory," followed by "3 by Ferlinghetti," "Big Broadcast," "The Incognita," "Bravo!," "Dead Giveaway," Bdwy in "Man of La Mancha."

MORDENTE, LISA. Born 1958 in NYC. Bdwy debut 1978 in "Platinum," followed by "Marlowe."

MORFOGEN, GEORGE. Born Mar. 30, 1933 in NYC. Graduate Brown U., Yale. Debut 1957 OB in "Trial of D. Karamazov," followed by "Christmas Oratorio," "Othello," "Good Soldier Schweik," "Cave Dwellers," "Once in a Lifetime," "Total Eclipse," "Ice Age," "Prince of Homburg," "Biography: A Game," Bdwy in "The Fun Couple," "Kingdoms."

MORIARTY, MICHAEL. Born Apr. 5, 1941 in Detroit, Mi. Graduate Dartmouth, LAMDA. Debut 1963 OB in "Antony and Cleopatra," followed by "Peanut Butter and Jelly," "Long Day's Journey into Night," "Henry V," "Alfred the Great," "Our Father's Failing," "G. R. Point," "Love's Labour's Lost," "Dexter Creed," Bdwy in "Trial of the Catonsville 9," "Find Your Way Home" for which he received a Theatre World Award, "Richard III."

MORITZ, MARC. Born Feb. 4, 1956 in Cleveland, Oh. Graduate Kent State U. Debut 1978 OB in "Androcles and the Lion," followed by "House of Blue Leaves," "Total Eclipse," Bdwy 1981 in "Merrily We Roll Along."

MORRIS, GARRETT. Born Feb. 1, 1944 in New Orleans, La. Graduate Dillard U. Debut 1960 OB in "Bible Salesman," followed by "Slave Ship," "Transfers," "Operation Sidewinder," "In New England Winter," "Basic Training of Pavlo Hummel," "What the Winesellers Buy," "The World of Ben Caldwell," Bdwy in "Porgy and Bess," "Hallelujah, Baby," "I'm Solomon," "The Great White Hope," "Ain't Supposed to Die a Natural Death."

MORRIS, NAT. Born Mar. 13, 1951 in Richmond, Va. Attended Howard U. Bdwy debut 1972 in "Hair," followed by "Jesus Christ Superstar," "Dude," OB in "The More You Get," "Children of the Sun."

MORRISEY, BOB. Born Aug. 15, 1946 in Somerville, MA. Attended UWi. Debut 1974 OB in "Ionescapade," followed by "Company," "Anything Goes," "Philistines," Bdwy 1981 in "The First."

MORRISON, ANN. Born Apr. 9, 1956 in Sioux City, Ia. Attended Boston Cons., Columbia U. Debut 1980 OB in "Dream Time," followed by Bdwy 1981 in "Merrily We Roll Along" for which she received a Theatre World Award.

MORSE, ROBERT. Born May 18, 1931 in Newton, Ma. Bdwy debut 1955 in "The Matchmaker" followed by "Say, Darling," for which he received a Theatre World Award, "Take Me Along," "How to Succeed in Business . . .," "Sugar," "So Long, 174th St.," OB in "More of Loesser."

MORSE, TIMOTHY W. (aka Tim) Born June 4, 1960 in Newport, RI. Graduate NYU. Debut 1982 OB in "Richard II," followed by "Great Grandson of Jedediah Kohler."

MORTENSEN, GREGORY. Born Sept. 21, 1955 in San Jose, Ca. Graduate San Jose State U. Bdwy debut 1982 in "Macbeth."

MORTON, JOE. Born Oct. 18, 1947 in NYC. Attended Hofstra U. Debut 1968 OB in "A Month of Sundays," followed by "Salvation," "Charlie Was Here and Now He's Gone," "G. R. Point," "Crazy Horse," "A Winter's Tale" "Johnny on a Spot," "Midsummer Night's Dream," "The Recruiting Officer," "Oedipus the King," "The Wild Duck," Bdwy in "Hair," "Two Gentlemen of Verona," "Tricks," "Raisin" for which he received a Theatre World Award, "Oh, Brother!"

MOYER, ROBERT. Born Nov. 1 in Baltimore Md. Graduate New Eng. Col. Bdwy debut 1981 in "The Best Little Whorehouse in Texas."

MUENZ, RICHARD. Born in Hartford, CT., in 1948. Attended Eastern Baptist College. Bdwy debut 1976 in "1600 Pennsylvania Avenue," followed by 'The Most Happy Fella," "Camelot."

MURNEY, CHRISTOPHER. Born July 20, 1943 in Narragansett, RI. Graduate URI, PaStateU. Bdwy debut 1973 in "Tricks" followed by "Mack and Mabel," OB in "As You Like It," "Holeville," "The Lady or the Tiger."

MURPHY, STEPHANIE. Born Feb. 2 in NYC. Graduate Smith Col. Debut 1981 OB in "Badgers," followed by "Buddies."

MURRAY, BRIAN. Born Oct. 9, 1939 in Johannesburg, S.A. Debut 1964 OB in "The Knack," followed by "King Lear," "Ashes," "The Jail Diary of Albie Sachs," "A Winter's Tale," "Barbarians," "The Purging," "Midsummer Night's Dream," "The Recruiting Officer," "The Arcata Promise," Bdwy in "All in Good Time," "Rosencrantz and Guildenstern Are Dead," "Sleuth," "Da."

MURRAY, MARY GORDON. Born Nov. 13, 1953 in Ridgewood, NJ. Attended Ramapo Col, Juilliard. Bdwy debut 1976 in "The Robber Bridegroom," followed by "Grease," "I Love My Wife," "Little Me."

MYERS, SHERI. Born Oct. 27, 1953 in Schenectady, NY. Graduate Ohio Wesleyan. Debut 1982 OB in "French Gray."

NAKAHARA, RON. Born July 20, 1947 in Honolulu, HI. Attended UHI, Tenri U. Debut 1981 OB in "Danton's Death," followed by "Flowers and Household Gods," "A Few Good Men," "Rohwer."

NASTASI, FRANK. Born Jan. 7, 1923 in Detroit, MI. Graduate Wayne U, NYU. Bdwy debut 1963 in "Lorenzo," followed by "Avanti," OB in "Bonds of Interest," "One Day More," "Nathan the Wise," "The Chief Things," "Cindy," "Escurial," "The Shrinking Bride," "Macbird," "Cakes with the Wine," "Metropolitan Madness," "Rockaway Boulevard," "Scenes from La Vie de Boheme," "Agamemnon," "Happy Sunset Inc."

NEASE, BUD. Born Oct. 22, 1953 in Los Angeles, Ca. Graduate USCsl. Debut 1980 OB in "Annie Get Your Gun," followed by "Lola."

NEGRO, MARY-JOAN. Born Nov. 9, 1948 in Brooklyn, NY. Debut 1972 OB in "The Hostage," followed by "Lower Depths," "Women Beware Women," "Ladyhouse Blues," "The Promise," "Modigliani," "Children of Darkness," Bdwy in "Three Sisters," "Measure for Measure," "Beggar's Opera," "Wings," "Scenes and Revelations."

NELSON, MARK. Born Sept. 26, 1955 in Hackensack, NJ. Graduate Princeton U. Debut 1977 OB in "The Dybbuk," followed by "Green Fields," "The Keymaker," Bdwy 1981 in "Amadeus."

NELSON, P. J. Born Nov. 17, 1952 in NYC. Attended Manhattan Sch. of Music. Bdwy debut 1978 in "Hello, Dolly!," followed by "The Music Man," OB in "Something for the Boys."

NELSON, RUTH. Born Aug. 2, 1905 in Saginaw, MI. Attended AmThLab. Bdwy debut 1931 in "House of Connolly," and other Group Theatre productions, and in "The Grass Harp," "Solitaire," "To Grandmother's House We Go," OB in "Collette," "Scenes from the Everyday Life," "3 Acts of Recognition."

NESBITT, CATHLEEN. Born Nov. 24, 1889 in Cheshire, Eng. Attended Victoria Col. Bdwy debut 1911 in "Well of the Saints," followed by "Justice," "Hush," "Such is Life," "Magic," "Garden of Paradise," "General Post," "Saving Grace," "Diversion," "Cocktail Party," "Gigi," "Sabrina Fair," "Portrait of a Lady," "Anastasia," "My Fair Lady" (1956 & 1981), "The Sleeping Prince," "Second String," "Romulus," "Uncle Vanya."

NEUMAN, JOAN. Born Oct. 4, 1926 in NYC. Graduate NYU. Debut 1964 OB in "A Woman of No Importance," followed by "Arsenic and Old Lace," "Camino Real," "All the King's Men," "Happy Sunset Inc."

NEWCASTLE, PATRICIA. Born Mar. 17, 1924 in NYC. Attended Academia Dante Alighieri. Debut 1977 OB in "Price of Genius," followed by "Mother Love," "Tropical Madness," "Taken in Marriage."

NEWMAN, ELLEN. Born Sept. 5, 1950 in NYC. Attended San Diego State U., London Central School. Debut 1972 OB in "Right You Are," followed by "Benya the King," LCRep's "Merchant of Venice," "Streetcar Named Desire," "The Importance of Being Earnest," "A Midsummer Night's Dream," Bdwy in "Othello" (1982).

NEWMAN, PHYLLIS. Born Mar. 19, 1935 in Jersey City, NJ. Attended Western Reserve U. Bdwy debut 1953 in "Wish You Were Here," followed by "Bells Are Ringing," "First Impressions," "Subways Are for Sleeping," "The Apple Tree," "On the Town," "Prisoner of Second Avenue," "Madwoman of Central Park West," OB in "I Feel Wonderful," "Make Someone Happy," "I'm Getting My Act Together," "Vamps and Rideouts."

NEWMAN, WILLIAM. Born June 15, 1934 in Chicago, IL. Graduate UWa., Columbia. Debut 1972 OB in "Beggar's Opera," followed by "Are You Now," "Conflict of Interest," "Mr. Runaway," "Uncle Vanya," "One Act Play Festival," "Routed," Bdwy in "Over Here," "Rocky Horror Show," "Strangers."

NEWTON, JOHN. Born Nov. 2, 1925 in Grand Junction, CO. UWash. graduate. Debut 1951 OB in "Othello," followed by "As You Like It," "Candida," "Candaules Commissioner," "Sextet," LCRep's "The Crucible" and "A Streetcar Named Desire," "The Rivals," "The Subject Was Roses," "The Brass Ring," "Hadrian VII," "The Best Little Whorehouse in Texas." Bdwy in "Weekend," "First Monday in October."

NICHOLS, ROBERT. Born July 20, 1924 in Oakland, CA. Attended Coll. of Pacific, RADA. Debut 1978 OB in "Are You Now or Have You Ever Been," followed by "Heartbreak House," Bdwy in "Man and Superman," "The Man Who Came to Dinner," "Einstein and the Polar Bear."

NIEHENKE, WALTER. Born Sept. 8, 1950 in Philadelphia, PA. Attended Temple U. Debut OB 1977 in "The Confidence Man," Bdwy 1981 in "Pirates of Penzance."

NILES, MARY ANN. Born May 2, in NYC. Attended Miss Finchley's Ballet Acad. Bdwy debut in "Girl from Nantucket," followed by "Dance Me A Song," "Call Me Mister," "Make Mine Manhattan," "La Plume de Ma Tante," "Carnival," "Flora the Red Menace," "Sweet Charity," "George M!," "No, No, Nanette," "Irene," "Ballroom," OB in "The Boys from Syracuse," CC's "Wonderful Town" and "Carnival."

NILES, RICHARD. Born May 19, 1946 in NYC. Graduate NYU. Debut 1969 OB in "Sourball," followed by "Innocent Thoughts, Harmless Intentions," "Elephants," Bdwy in "And Miss Reardon Drinks a Little," "Don't Call Back."

NIXON, CYNTHIA. Born Apr. 9, 1966 in NYC. Debut 1980 in "The Philadelphia Story" (LC) for which she received a Theatre World Award, OB in "Lydie Breeze."

NIXON, JAMES E. Born Oct. 12, 1957 in Jersey City, NJ. Attended Kean Col. Debut 1982 OB in "The Six O'Clock Boys."

NOAH, JOSEPH. Born Sept. 24, 1946 in Buffalo, NY. Graduate SUNY/Buffalo. Debut 1981 OB in "Unfettered Letters."

NOONAN, TOM. Born Apr. 12, 1951 in Greenwich, CT. Yale graduate. Debut 1978 OB in "Buried Child," followed by "The Invitational," "Farmyard," "The Breakers."

NOONE, PETER. Born Nov. 6, 1947 in Manchester, Eng. Attended St. Bene's Col. Bdwy debut 1982 in "Pirates of Penzance."

NOOR, MUSTAFA. Born Dec. 30, 1950 in Johore, Malaysia. Graduate NYU. Debut 1980 OB in "Sunrise," followed by "Fly Blackbird," "Double Dutch."

NORMENT, ELIZABETH. Born Dec. 31, 1952 in Washington, DC. Graduate Cornell U., Yale. Debut 1978 OB in "Sganarelle," followed by "No End of Blame."

NORTH, RUTH ANN. Born in Ada, Ok. Graduate UOk. Debut 1967 OB in "Where People Gather," followed by "The Heiress," "Divine Fire."

NOURI, MICHAEL. Born Dec. 9, 1945 in Washington, DC. Debut 1964 OB in "The Crucible," followed by "Booth," Bdwy 1968 in "40 Carats."

NUTE, DON. Born Mar. 13, in Connellsville, PA. Attended Denver U. Debut OB 1965 in "The Trojan Women" followed by "Boys in the Band," "Mad Theatre for Madmen," "The Eleventh Dynasty," "About Time," "The Urban Crisis," "Christmas Rappings," "The Life of a Man," "A Look at the Fifties."

O'BRIEN, CONAL. Born July 18 in Teaneck, NJ. Graduate Carnegie-Mellon U. Debut 1981 in "Macbeth" (LC). OB in "Henry IV Part 2."

O'BRIEN, DEVON. Born Jan. 8, 1958 in Norwalk, Ct. Graduate Brown U. Debut 1981 OB in "Peep."

O'BRIEN, MARCIA. Born Mar. 17, 1934 in Indiana. Graduate IndU. Bdwy debut 1970 in "Man of La Mancha," followed by "Evita," OB in "Now Is the Time for All Good Men," "House Party."

O'CONNELL, PATRICIA. Born May 17 in NYC. Attended AmThWing. Debut 1958 OB in "The Saintliness of Margery Kemp," followed by "Time Limit," "An Evening's Frost," "Mrs. Snow," "Electric Ice," "Survival of St. Joan," "Rain," "Rapists," "Who Killed Richard Cory?," "Misalliance," Bdwy in "Criss-Crossing," "Summer Brave," "Break a Leg," "The Man Who Came to Dinner."

O'CONNELL, PATRICK. Born July 7, 1957 in Norwalk, Ct. Juilliard graduate. Debut 1982 OB in "Twelfth Night," "The Country Wife."

O'CONNOR, KEVIN. Born May 7 in Honolulu, HI. Attended UHi., Neighborhood Playhouse. Debut 1964 OB in "Up to Thursday," followed by "Six from La Mama," "Rimers of Eldritch," "Tom Paine," "Boy on the Straightback Chair," "Dear Janet Rosenberg," "Eyes of Chalk," "Alive and Well in Argentina," "Duet," "Trio," "The Contractor," "Kool Aid," "The Frequency," "Chucky's Hunch," "Birdbath," "The Breakers," "Crossing the Crab Nebula," Bdwy in "Gloria and Esperanza," "The Morning after Optimism," "Figures in the Sand," "Devour the Snow," "The Lady from Dubuque."

O'HALLORAN, BRIAN. Born May 20, 1952 in San Jose, Ca. Graduate Principia Col., RADA. Bdwy debut 1977 in "Caesar and Cleopatra," OB in "Shay," "Strawberry Fields," "Lysistrata."

O'HARA, JILL. Born Aug. 23, 1947 in Warren, Pa. Attended Edinburgh State Teachers Col. Bdwy debut 1968 in "George M!," followed by "Promises Promises" for which she received a Theatre World Award, OB in "Hang Down Your Head and Die," "Hair," "Master Builder," "Alfred the Great," "Wayside Motor Inn," "I Can't Keep Running in Place."

O'KARMA, ALEXANDRA. Born Sept. 28, 1948 in Cincinnati, OH. Graduate Swarthmore Col. Debut 1976 OB in "A Month in the Country," followed by "Warbeck," "A Flea in Her Ear," "Knitters in the Sun," "The Beethoven," "Clownmaker."

O'KEEFE, MICHAEL. Born Apr. 24, 1955 in Westchester, NY. Attended NYU. Debut 1974 OB in "The Killdeer," Bdwy 1981 in "5th of July," followed by "Mass Appeal" for which he received a Theatre World Award.

O'KELLY, AIDEEN. Born in Dalkey, Ire. Member of Dublin's Abbey Theatre. Bdwy debut 1980 in "A Life," followed by "Othello."

OLIVER, LYNN. Born Sept. 18 in San Antonio, TX. Graduate UTx, UHouston. Debut 1970 OB in "Oh! Calcutta!," followed by "In the Boom Boom Room," "Redhead," "Blood," "Two Noble Kinsmen," "Curtains," "The Blonde Leading the Blonde."

OLIVER, ROCHELLE. Born Apr. 15, 1937 in NYC. Attended Brooklyn Col. Bdwy debut 1960 in "Toys in the Attic," followed by "Harold," "Who's Afraid of Virginia Woolf?," "Happily Never After," OB in "Brothers Karamazov," "Jack Knife," "Vincent," "Stop, You're Killing Me," "Enclave," "Bits and Pieces," "Roads to Home."

OLSON, JAMES. Born Oct. 8, 1930 in Evanston, Il. Attended Northwestern, Actors Studio. Bdwy bow 1955 in "The Young and the Beautiful, followed by "The Sin of Pat Muldoon," "J. B.," "The Chinese Prime Minister," "Three Sisters," "Slapstick Tragedy," "Of Love Remembered," OB in "Twelve Dreams."

O'NEAL, PATRICK. Born Sept. 26, 1927 in Ocala, Fl. Graduate UFl., Neighborhood Playhouse. Bdwy bow 1961 in "A Far Country," followed by "The Night of the Iguana," OB in "Children of Darkness."

O'NEILL, GENE. Born Apr. 7, 1951 in Philadelphia, PA. Graduate Loyola U. Bdwy debut 1976 in "Poison Tree," followed by "Best Little Whorehouse in Texas," OB in "Afternoons in Vegas," "The Slab Boys,", "No End of Blame."

ORBACH, JERRY. Born Oct. 20, 1935 in NYC. Attended Northwestern U. Bdwy debut 1961 in "Carnival," followed by "Guys and Dolls," "Carousel," "Annie Get Your Gun," "The Natural Look," "Promises Promises," "6 Rms Riv Vu," "Chicago," "42nd Street," OB in "Threepenny Opera," "The Fantasticks," "The Cradle Will Rock," "Scuba Duba."

O'SHEA, MILO. Born June 2, 1926 in Dublin, Ire. Bdwy debut 1968 in "Staircase," followed by "Dear World," "Mrs. Warren's Profession" (LC), "Comedians," "A Touch of the Poet," OB in "Waiting for Godot," "Mass Appeal." (also Bdwy).

OUSLEY, ROBERT. Born July 21, 1946 in Waco, Tx. Debut 1975 OB in "Give Me Liberty," Bdwy in "Sweeney Todd" (1979), "Othello" (1982).

OWENS, ELIZABETH. Born Feb. 26, 1938 in NYC. Attended New School, Neighborhood Playhouse. Debut 1955 OB in "Dr. Faustus Lights the Lights," followed by "Chit Chat on a Rat," "The Miser," "The Father," "Importance of Being Earnest," "Candida," "Trumpets and Drums," "Oedipus," "Macbeth," "Uncle Vanya," "Misalliance," "Master Builder," "American Gothics," "The Play's the Thing," "The Rivals," "Death Story," "The Rehearsal," "Dance on a Country Grave," "Othello," "Little Eyolf," "The Winslow Boy," "Playing with Fire," "The Chalk Garden," Bdwy in "The Lovers," "Not Now Darling," "The Play's the Thing."

PACINO, AL. Born Apr. 25, 1940 in NYC. Attended Actors Studio. Bdwy bow 1969 in "Does a Tiger Wear a Necktie?" for which he received a Theatre World Award, followed by "The Basic Training of Pavlo Hummel," "Richard III," OB in "Why Is a Crooked Letter," "Peace Creeps," "The Indian Wants the Bronx," "Local Stigmatic," "Camino Real" (LC), "Jungle of Cities," "American Buffalo."

PAGANO, GIULIA. Born July 8, 1948 in NYC. Attended AADA. Debut 1977 OB in "The Passion of Dracula," followed by "Heartbreak House," "The Winslow Boy," "Miss Julie," "Playing with Fire," Bdwy in "Medea" (1982).

PAGE, EVELYN. Born in Fremont, Ne. Attended UNe. Debut 1958 OB in "The Boy Friend," followed by "Brothers," "Two," Bdwy in "Plain and Fancy" (1956), "Mr. Wonderful," "Little Me," "On a Clear Day You Can See Forever," "Canterbury Tales."

PAGE, GERALDINE. Born Nov. 22, 1924 in Kirksville, Mo. Attended Goodman Th. Debut 1945 OB in "Seven Mirrors," followed by "Yerma," "Summer and Smoke," "Macbeth," "Look Away," "The Stronger," Bdwy 1953 in "Midsummer" for which she received a Theatre World Award, "The Immoralist," "The Rainmaker," "Innkeepers," "Separate Tables," "Sweet Bird of Youth," "Strange Interlude," "Three Sisters," "P.S. I Love You," "The Great Indoors," "White Lies," "Black Comedy," "The Little Foxes," "Angela," "Absurd Person Singular," "Clothes for a Summer Hotel," "Agnes of God."

PAGE, KEN. Born Jan. 20., 1954 in St. Louis, Mo. Attended Fontbonne Col. Bdwy debut 1976 in "Guys and Dolls" for which he received a Theatre World Award, followed by "Ain't Misbehavin'," OB in "Louis," "Can't Help Singing."

PAISNER, DINA. Born in Brooklyn, NY. Bdwy debut 1963 in "Andorra," OB in "The Cretan Woman," "Pullman Car Hiawatha," "Lysistrata," "If 5 Years Pass," "Troubled Waters," "Sap of Life," "Cave at Machpelah," "Threepenny Opera," "Montserrat," "Gandhi," "Blood Wedding," "The Trial of Dr. Beck," "Amidst the Gladiolas."

PALMIERI, JOSEPH. Born Aug. 1, 1939 in Brooklyn, NY. Attended Catholic U. OB in "Cyrano de Bergerac," "Butter and Egg Man," "Boys in the Band," "Beggar's Opera," "The Family," "The Crazy Locomotive," "Umbrellas of Cherbourg," "Amidst the Gladiolas," Bdwy in "Lysistrata," "Candide."

PARKER, ANDY. Born June 29, 1953 in Austin, Tx. Graduate UTx. Bdwy debut 1979 in "A New York Summer," followed by "The Best Little Whorehouse in Texas."

PARKER, PAULA. Born Aug. 14, 1950 in Chicago, Il. Graduate S.Ill.U. Debut 1971 OB in "The Debate," followed by "Maggie Flynn," "Metropolitan Madness," "Suffragette."

PARKER, ROCHELLE, Born Feb. 26, 1940 in Brooklyn, NY. Attended Neighborhood Playhouse. Bdwy debut 1980 in "The Survivor," OB in "Five Points," "Sheepskin," "Side Street Scenes," "Ruby and Pearl."

PARRIS, STEVE. Born in Athens, Greece. Graduate CCNY. Debut 1964 OB in "The Comforter," followed by "Consider the Lilies," "A Christmas Carol," "The Man with the Flower in His Mouth," "King David and His Wives," "3 by Pirandello," "Nymph Errant."

PARRY, WILLIAM. Born Oct. 7, 1947 in Steubenville, OH. Graduate Mt. Union Col. Bdwy debut 1971 in "Jesus Christ Superstar," followed by "Rockabye Hamlet," "The Leaf People," "Camelot" (1980/1981), OB in "Sgt. Pepper's Lonely Hearts Club Band," "The Conjuror," "Noah," "The Misanthrope," "Joseph and the Amazing Technicolor Dreamcoat," "Agamemnon," "The Coolest Cat in Town," "Dispatches," "The Derby."

PARSONS, ESTELLE. Born Nov. 20, 1927 in Lynn, MA. Attended Boston U, Actors Studio. Bdwy debut 1956 in "Happy Hunting," followed by "Whoop-Up!," "Beg, Borrow or Steal," "Mother Courage," "Ready When You Are, C.B.," "Malcolm," "The 7 Descents of Myrtle," "And Miss Reardon Drinks a Little," "The Norman Conquests," "Ladies at the Alamo," "Miss Margarida's Way," "Pirates of Penzance," OB in "Demi-Dozen," "Pieces of 8," "Threepenny Opera," "Automobile Graveyard," "Mrs. Dally Has a Lover" for which she received a Theatre World Award, "Next Time I'll Sing to You," "Come to the Palace of Sin," "In the Summer House," "Monopoly," "The East Wind," "Galileo," "Peer Gynt," "Mahagonny," "People Are Living There," "Barbary Shore," "Oh Glorious Tintinnabulation," "Mert and Paul," "Elizabeth and Essex," "Dialogue for Lovers.", "New Moon in Concert."

PARVIN, DOUGLAS. Born Jan. 12, 1972 in Princeton, NJ. Debut 1981 OB in "King of Hearts."

PATRICK-WARNER, RICHARD. Born May 14, 1951 in Berkeley, Ca. Graduate Providence Col., Catholic U. Debut 1980 OB in "Vikings," followed by "The Freak."

PATTON, LUCILLE. Born in NYC; attended Neighborhood Playhouse. Bdwy debut 1946 in "A Winter's Tale," followed by "Topaze," "Arms and the Man," "Joy to the World," "All You Need Is One Good Break," "Fifth Season," "Heavenly Twins," "Rhinoceros," "Marathon '33," "The Last Analysis," "Dinner at 8," "La Strada," "Unlikely Heroes," "Love Suicide at Schofield Barracks," OB in "Ulysses in Nighttown," "Failures," "Three Sisters," "Yes, Yes, No, No," "Tango," "Mme. de Sade," "Apple Pie," "Follies," "Yesterday Is Over," "My Prince My King."

PEARSON, PAULETTA. Born Sept. 28 in NC. Attended NCSch. of Arts, NTxStateU. Bdwy debut 1977 in "Jesus Christ Superstar," followed by "Shakespeare's Cabaret," OB in "Jule Styne Revue," "Sweet Main Street," "Ethel Waters Story," "Helen of Troy," "Frimbo.", "Jerry's Girls," "Children of the Sun," "Vamps and Rideouts."

PEARSON, SCOTT. Born Dec. 13, 1941 in Milwaukee, WI. Attended Valparaiso U, UWisc. Bdwy debut 1966 in "A Joyful Noise," followed by "Promises, Promises," "A Chorus Line."

PEARTHREE, PIPPA. Born Sept. 23, 1956 in Baltimore, MD. Attended NYU, Bdwy debut 1977 in "Grease," followed by "Whose Life Is It Anyway?," OB in "American Days," "Hunting Scenes from Lower Bavaria," "And I Ain't Finished Yet," "The Dining Room."

PELIKAN, LISA. Born July 12 in Paris, France. Attended Juilliard. Debut 1975 OB in "Spring's Awakening," followed by "An Elephant in the House," "The American Clock," "The Diviners," "The Midnight Visitor," Bdwy in "Romeo and Juliet" (1977).

PEN, POLLY. Born Mar. 11, 1954 in Chicago, Il. Graduate Ithaca Col. Debut 1978 OB in "The Taming of the Shrew," followed by "The Gilded Cage," "Charlotte Sweet," Bdwy in "The Utter Glory of Morrissey Hall."

PENDLETON, AUSTIN. Born Mar. 27, 1940 in Warren, Oh. Attended Yale. Debut 1962 OB in "Oh, Dad, Poor Dad . . .," followed by "The Last Sweet Day's of Isaac," "Three Sisters," "Say Goodnight, Gracie," "The Office Murders," "Up from Paradise," "The Overcoat," Bdwy in "Fiddler on the Roof," "Hail Scrawdyke," "The Little Foxes," "American Millionaire," "The Runner Stumbles."

PENDLETON, WYMAN. Born Apr. 18, 1916 in Providence, R.I. Graduate Brown U. Bdwy in "Tiny Alice," "Malcolm," "Quotations from Chairman Mao Tse-Tung," "Happy Days," "Henry V," "Othello," "There's One in Every Marriage," "Cat on a Hot Tin Roof," "Scenes and Revelations," OB in "Gallows Humor," "American Dream," "Zoo Story," "Corruption in the Palace of Justice," "Giant's Dance," "Child Buyer," "Happy Days," "Butter and Egg Man," "Othello," "Albee Directs Albee," "Dance for Me Simeon," "Mary Stuart," "The Collyer Brothers at Home," "Period Piece."

PENZNER, SEYMOUR. Born July 29, 1915 in Yonkers, NY. Attended CCNY. OB in "Crystal Heart," "Guitar," "Paterson," "The Possessed," "Philistines," Bdwy in "Oklahoma!," "Finian's Rainbow," "Call Me Madam," "Paint Your Wagon," "Can-Can," "Kean," "Baker Street," "Man of La Mancha."

PEREZ, LAZARO. Born Dec. 17, 1945 in Havana, Cuba. Bdwy debut 1969 in "Does a Tiger Wear a Necktie?," followed by "Animals," OB in "Romeo and Juliet," "12 Angry Men," "Wonderful Years," "Alive," "G. R. Point," "Primary English Class," "The Man and the Fly."

PERKINS, PATTI. Born July 9 in New Haven, CT. Attended AMDA. Debut 1972 OB in "The Contrast," followed by "Fashion," "Tuscaloosa's Calling Me. . .," "Patch Patch," "Shakespeare's Cabaret," "Maybe I'm Doing It Wrong," "Bdwy in "All Over Town," (1974), "Shakespeare's Cabaret."

PERLEY, WILLIAM. Born Nov. 24, 1942 in NYC. Graduate UFl. Debut 1975 OB in "Tenderloin," followed by "Housewives Cantata," "Count of Monte Cristo," Bdwy in "Vieux Carre" (1977).

PERRI, PAUL. Born Nov. 6, 1953 in New Haven, CT. Attended Elmira Col., UMe, Juilliard. Debut 1979 OB in "Say Goodnight, Gracie," followed by "Henry VI," "Agamemnon," "Julius Caesar," "Waiting for Godot," Bdwy in "Bacchae.", "Macbeth."

PESATURO, GEORGE. Born July 29, 1949 in Winthrop, MA. Graduate Manhattan Col. Bdwy debut 1976 in "A Chorus Line," OB in "The Music Man" (JB).

PESCOW, DONNA. Born Mar. 24, 1954 in Brooklyn, NY. Attended AADA. Debut 1974 OB in "Poor Old Fool," followed by "Friends of the Family," "Body Bags."

PESSAGNO, RICK (aka Richard) Born June 27, 1957 in Philadelphia, Pa. Bdwy debut 1979 in "Whoopee," followed by "Sophisticated Ladies," OB in "Tip-Toes."

PESSANO, JAN. Born Aug. 10, 1944 in San Jose, Ca. Graduate Fresno State Col. Debut 1976 OB in "She Loves Me," followed by "The Grass Harp," "Rogues to Riches," "110 in the Shade."

PETERS, BERNADETTE. Born Feb. 28, 1948 in Jamaica, NY. Bdwy debut 1967 in "Girl in the Freudian Slip," followed by "Johnny No-Trump," "George M!" for which she received a Theatre World Award, "La Strada," "On the Town," "Mack and Mabel," OB in "Curley McDimple," "Penny Friend," "Most Happy Fella," "Dames at Sea," "Nevertheless They Laugh," "Sally and Marsha."

PETERSON, LENKA. Born Oct. 16, 1925 in Omaha, NE. Attended UIowa. Bdwy debut 1946 in "Bathsheba," followed by "Harvest of Years," "Sundown Beach," "Young and Fair," "The Grass Harp," "The Girls of Summer," "The Time of Your Life," "Look Homeward, Angel," "All the Way Home," "Nuts," OB in "Mrs. Minter," "American Night Cry," "Leaving Home," "The Brass Ring," "Father Dreams," "El Bravo!"

PFISTER, DENNIS. Born Sept. 27, 1951 in Detroit, Mi. Bdwy debut 1980 in "Romeo and Juliet," OB in "Two Gentlemen of Verona."

PHERSON, ROB. Born Nov. 9, 1950 in Phoenix, Az. Graduate UAz. Debut 1976 OB in "The Mousetrap," followed by "Arms and the Man," "Ghosts."

PHILLIPS, PETER. Born Dec. 7, 1949 in Darby, Pa. Graduate Dartmouth, RADA. Debut 1976 OB in Henry V," followed by "The Cherry Orchard," "Total Eclipse," "Catsplay," "Warriors from a Long Childhood," "A Winter's Tale," "Johnny on a Spot," "Barbarians," Bdwy in "Equus" (1977) followed by "Macbeth" (1982).

PIERCE, HARVEY. Born June 24, 1917 in NYC. Graduate NYU. OB credits include "The Gentle People," "Native Son," "The Country Girl," "Men in White," "To Bury a Cousin," "Time of the Cuckoo," "Doctor's Office Disco."

PIERSON, GEOFFREY. Born June 16, 1949 in Chicago, IL. Graduate Fordham U, Yale U. Debut 1978 OB in "Wings," followed by "Playing with Fire," Bdwy 1980 in "Tricks of the Trade."

PIETROPINTO, ANGELA. Born Feb. 5, in NYC. Graduate NYU. OB credits include "Henry IV," "Alice in Wonderland," "Endgame," "Our Late Night," "The Sea Gull," "Jinxs Bridge," "The Mandrake," "Marie and Bruce," "Green Card Blues," "3 by Pirandello," "The Broken Pitcher," Bdwy 1980 in "The Suicide."

PIETROWSKI, JOHN. Born Mar. 30, 1958 in Trenton, NJ. Graduate NorthwesternU. Debut 1982 OB in "The Sea Anchor."

PINCHOT, BRONSON. Born May 20, 1959 in NYC. Graduate Yale. Debut 1982 OB in "Poor Little Lambs."

PINERO, JOHN. Born Jan. 31, 1945 in Brooklyn, NY. Attended HB Studio. Debut 1976 OB in "Where Is My Little Gloria," followed by "The Web," "A Yank in Beverly Hills," "A Few Good Men."

PINHASIK, HOWARD. Born June 5, 1953 in Chicago, IL. Attended OhU. Debut 1978 OB in "Allegro," followed by "Marya," "The Meehans," "Street Scene."

PINKINS, TONYA. Born May 30, 1962 in Chicago, Il. Attended Carnegie-Mellon U. Bdwy debut 1981 in "Merrily We Roll Along," OB in "Five Points."

PLANK, SCOTT. Born Nov. 11, 1958 in Washington, DC. Attended NCSch of Arts. Bdwy debut 1981 in "Dreamgirls."

PLAYTEN, ALICE. Born Aug. 38, 1947 in NYC. Attended NYU. Bdwy debut 1960 in "Gypsy" followed by "Oliver," "Hello, Dolly!," "Henry Sweet Henry," for which she received a Theatre World Award, "George M!," OB in "Promenade," "The Last Sweet Days of Isaac," "National Lampoon's Lemmings," "Valentine's Day'," "Pirates of Penzance," "Up from Paradise," "A Visit," "Sister Mary Ignatius Explains It All," "An Actor's Nightmare."

PLUMMER, AMANDA. Born Mar. 23, 1957 in NYC. Attended Middlebury Col., Neighborhood Playhouse. Debut 1979 OB in "Artichoke," followed by "A Month in the Country," "A Taste of Honey" for which she received a Theatre World Award, "Alice in Concert," "A Stitch in Time," Bdwy in "A Taste of Honey," "Agnes of God."

PLUMMER, CHRISTOPHER. Born Dec. 13, 1929 in Toronto, Can. Bdwy debut 1954 in "Starcross Story," followed by "Home Is the Hero," "The Dark Is Light Enough" for which he received a Theatre World Award, "Medea," "The Lark," "Night of the Auk," "J.B.," "Arturo Ui," "Royal Hunt of the Sun," "Cyrano," "The Good Doctor," "Othello," OB in "Drinks Before Dinner."

POGREBIN, ABBY. Born May 17, 1965 in NYC. Bdwy debut 1981 in "Merrily We Roll Along."

POLITO, JON. Born Dec. 29, 1950 in Philadelphia, Pa. Graduate Villanova U. Debut 1976 OB in "The Transfiguration of Benno Blimpie," followed by "Gemini," "New Jerusalem," "Emigres," "A Winter's Tale," "Johnny on a Spot," "Barbarians," "The Wedding," Bdwy in "American Buffalo" (1977), "Curse of an Aching Heart."

PONAZECKI, JOE. Born Jan. 7, 1934 in Rochester, NY. Attended Rochester U, Columbia U. Bdwy debut 1959 in "Much Ado About Nothing," followed by "Send Me No Flowers," "A Call on Kuprin," "Take Her, She's Mine," "Fiddler on the Roof," "Xmas in Las Vegas," "3 Bags Full," "Love in E-Flat," "90 Day Mistress," "Harvey," "Trial of the Catonsville 9," "The Country Girl," "Freedom of the City," "Summer Brave," "Music Is," "The Little Foxes," OB in "The Dragon," "Museeka," "Witness," "All Is Bright," "The Dog Ran Away," "Dream of a Blacklisted Actor," "Innocent Pleasures," "The Dark at the Top of the Stairs," "36," "After the Revolution," "The Raspberry Picker."

POOLE, ROY. Born Mar. 31, 1924 in San Bernardino, Ca. Graduate Stanford U. Bdwy debut 1950 in "Now I Lay Me Down to Sleep," followed by "St. Joan," "The Bad Seed," "I Knock at the Door," "Long Day's Journey into Night," "Face of a Hero," "Moby Dick," "Poor Bitos," "1776," "Scratch," "Once a Catholic," OB in "27 Wagons Full of Cotton," "A Memory of Two Mondays," "Secret Service," "Boy Meets Girl," "Villager."

PREDOVIC, DENNIS. Born Sept. 14, 1950 in Cleveland, Oh. Attended OhU. Debut 1973 OB in "Broadway," followed by "Romanov," "King of Hearts."

PREMICE, JOSEPHINE. Born July 21, 1926 in Brooklyn, NY. Graduate Columbia, Cornell U. Bdwy debut 1945 in "Blue Holiday," followed by Caribbean Carnival," "Mr. Johnson," "Jamaica," "A Hand Is on the Gate," "Bubbling Brown Sugar," OB in "House of Flowers," "Cherry Orchard," "American Night Cry," "The Brothers."

PRESCOTT, KEN. Born Dec. 28, 1945 in Omaha, Ne. Attended Omaha U, UUtah. Bdwy debut 1971 in "No, No Nanette," followed by "That's Entertainment," "Follies," "Lorelei," "42nd Street."

PRESNELL, HARVE. Born Sept. 14, 1933 in Modesto, CA. Attended USCa. Bdwy bow 1960 in "The Unsinkable Molly Brown," followed by "Carousel," "Annie Get Your Gun" (JB), "Annie."

PRESTIA, VINCENZO. Born July 30, 1942 in Reggio, Italy. Bdwy debut 1981 in "Camelot."

PRICE, LONNY. Born Mar. 9, 1959 in NYC. Attended Juilliard. Debut 1979 OB in "Class Enemy" for which he received a Theatre World Award, Bdwy 1980 in "The Survivor," followed by "Merrily We Roll Along," "Master Harold and the boys."

PRIMONT, MARIAN. Born Oct. 2, 1913 in NYC. Graduate NYU. Debut 1957 OB in "Richard III," followed by "The Anatomist," "Come Share My House," "Dona Rosita," "Killings on the Last Line," "Hijinks," "Good Help Is Hard to Find," Bdwy 1961 in "All the Way Home."

PRITCHETT, LIZABETH. Born Mar. 12, 1920 in Dallas, Tx. Attended SMU. Bdwy debut 1959 in "Happy Town," followed by "Sound of Music," "Maria Golovin," "The Yearling," "A Funny Thing Happened on the Way . . .," OB in "Cindy," "The Real Inspector Hound," "The Karl Marx Play," "Show Boat" (JB), "Umbrellas of Cherbourg," "Italian Straw Hat."

PROVENZA, SAL. Born Sept. 21, 1946 in Brooklyn, NY. Attended Bklyn Col., Juilliard. Debut 1980 OB in "The Fantasticks," Bdwy 1981 in "Oh, Brother!"

PRUETT, EDDIE. Born July 21, 1951 in Terre Haute, IN. Attended Austin Peay Col. Bdwy debut 1979 in "Sugar Babies."

PRUNCZIK, KAREN. Born July 21, 1957 in Pittsburgh, PA. Attended Pittsburgh Playhouse. Bdwy debut 1980 in "42nd Street."

PULLIAM, ZELDA. Born Oct. 18 in Chicago, IL. Attended Roosevelt U. Bdwy debut 1969 in "Hello, Dolly!," followed by "Purlie," 'Raisin,' "Pippin," "Dancin'," OB in "Croesus and the Witch."

PURDHAM, DAVID. Born June 3, 1951 in San Antonio, TX. Graduate UMd., UWa. Bdwy 1980 OB in "Journey's End," Bdwy 1981 in "Piaf," followed by "The Little Prince and the Aviator."

QUINN, BRIAN. Born Aug. 12, 1955 in Chicago, Il. Graduate Purdue U. Bdwy debut 1981 in "Copperfield," followed by "Little Me."

RACHELLE, BERNIE. Born Oct. 7, 1939 in NYC. Graduate Yeshiva U, Hunter Col. OB in "Winterset," "Golden Boy," "Street Scene," "World of Sholom Aleichem," "The Diary of Anne Frank," "Electra," "Nighthawks," "House Party," "Dancing in NY," "Metropolitan Madness," "Incident at Vichy," "Meegan'sGame."

RADIGAN, MICHAEL. Born May 2, 1949 in Springfield, IL. Graduate Springfield Col., Goodman Theatre. Bdwy debut 1974 in "Music! Music!" (CC), followed by "Sugar Babies," OB in "Broadway Dandies," "Beowulf."

RAFLO, PAULA. Born Sept. 2, 1951 in Brooklyn, NY. Graduate SUNY/Stonybrook. Debut 1978 OB in "Latinos," followed by "The Good Woman of Setzuan."

RAIKEN, LAWRENCE. Born Feb. 5, 1949 in Long Island, NY. Graduate Wm. & Mary Col., UNC. Debut 1979 OB in "Wake Up, It's Time to Go to Bed," Bdwy 1981 in "Woman of the Year."

RAKOV, THERESA. Born Sept. 6, 1952 in Clarkson, NY. Graduate SUNY/Fredonia. Bdwy "Romance Is," "Lady of the Castle."

RAMOS, RICHARD RUSSELL. Born Aug. 23, 1941 in Seattle, WA. Graduate UMn. Bdwy debut 1968 in "House of Atreus," followed by "Arturo Ui," OB in "Adaptation" "Screens" "Lotta," "The Tempest," "A Midsummer Night's Dream," "Gorky," "The Seagull," "Entertaining Mr. Sloane."

RAMSAY, REMAK. Born Feb. 2, 1937 in Baltimore, MD. Graduate Princeton U. Debut 1964 OB in "Hang Down Your Head and Die," followed by "The Real Inspector Hound," "Landscape of the Body," "All's Well That Ends Well" (CP), "Rear Column," "The Winslow Boy," "The Dining Room," Bdwy in "Half a Sixpence," "Sheep on the Runway," "Lovely Ladies, Kind Gentlemen," "On the Town," "Jumpers," "Private Lives," "Dirty Linen," "Every Good Boy Deserves Favor," (LC), "Save Grand Central."

RAMSEL, GENA. Born Feb. 19, 1959 in El Reno, OK. Graduate SMU. Bdwy debut 1974 in "Lorelei," followed by "The Best Little Whorehouse in Texas," "Come Back to the 5 & Dime, Jimmy Dean," OB in "Joe Masiell Not at the Palace."

RANDOLPH, BILL. Born Oct. 11, 1953 in Detroit, MI. Attended Allen Hancock Col., SUNY Purchase. Bdwy debut 1978 in "Gemini," OB in "Holy Places," "Young Bucks," "Teach Me How to Cry."

RASCHE, DAVID. Born Aug. 7, 1944 in St. Louis, MO. Graduate Elmhurst Col., U. Chicago. Debut 1976 OB in "John," followed by "Snow White," "Isadora Duncan Sleeps with the Russian Navy," "End of the War," "A Sermon," "Routed," "Geniuses," Bdwy in "Shadow Box" (1977), "Loose Ends," "Lunch Hour."

RASHOVICH, GORDANA. Born Sept. 18 in Chicago, Il. Graduate Roosevelt U, RADA. Debut 1977 OB in "Fefu and Her Friends" for which she received a Theatre World Award, followed by "Selma."

REAMS, LEE ROY. Born Aug. 23, 1942 in Covington, KY. Graduate U. Cinn. Cons. Bdwy debut 1966 in "Sweet Charity," followed by "Oklahoma!" (LC), "Applause," "Lorelei," "Show Boat" (JB), "Hello Dolly!" (1978), "42nd Street," OB in "Sterling Silver," "Potholes."

REARDON, JOHN. Born Apr. 8, 1930 in NYC. Attended Rollins Col. Bdwy debut 1954 in "The Saint of Bleecker Street," followed by "New Faces of 1956," "Song of Norway," "Do Re Mi," "New Moon in Concert."

REBHORN, JAMES. Born Sept. 1, 1948 in Philadelphia, Pa. Graduate Wittenberg U, Columbia U. Debut 1972 OB in "Blue Boys," followed by "Are You Now or Have You Ever Been," "Trouble with Europe," "Othello," "Hunchback of Notre Dame," "Period of Adjustment," "The Freak."

REDFIELD, ADAM. Born Nov. 4, 1959 in NYC. Attended NYU. Debut 1977 OB in "Hamlet," followed by "Androcles and the Lion," "Twelfth Night," "Reflected Glory," "Movin' Up," "The Unicorn," Bdwy 1980 in "A Life" for which he received a Theatre World Award.

REED, GAVIN. Born June 3, 1935 in Liverpool, Eng. Attended RADA. Debut 1974 OB in "The Taming of the Shrew," followed by "French without Tears," "Potsdam Quartet," Bdwy in "Scapino" (1974), "Some of My Best Friends."

REES, ROGER. Born May 5, 1944 in Wales. Graduate Slade School of Fine Art. Bdwy debut 1975 in "London Assurance," followed by "Nicholas Nickleby" (1981).

REILLY, LUKE. Born Apr. 3, 1949 in NYC. Graduate SUNY. Bdwy debut 1977 in "Vieux Carre," OB in "Particular Friendships."

REINGOLD, JACKIE. Born Mar. 13, 1959 in NYC. Graduate Oberlin Col. Debut 1978 OB in "A Wrinkle in Time," followed by "Marat/Sade," "Unfettered Letters."

REINHARDSEN, DAVID. Born Jan. 13, 1949 in NYC. Graduate Westminster Col. Bdwy debut 1976 in "Zalmen, or the Madness of God," OB in "Altar Boys," "Extenuating Circumstances."

REINKING, ANN. Born Nov. 10, 1949 in Seattle, WA. Attended Joffrey Sch., HB Studio. Bdwy debut 1969 in "Cabaret," followed by "Coco," "Pippin," "Over Here" for which she received a Theatre World Award, "Goodtime Charley," "A Chorus Line," "Chicago," "Dancin'."

REY, ANTONIA. Born Oct. 12, 1927 in Havana, Cuba. Graduate Havana U. Bdwy debut 1964 in "Bajour," followed by "Mike Downstairs," "Engagement Baby," "The Ritz," OB in "Yerma," "Fiesta in Madrid," "Camino Real" (LC), "Back Bog Beast Bait," "Rain," "42 Seconds from Broadway," "Streetcar Named Desire" (LC), "Poets from the Inside," "Blood Wedding," "Missing Persons.", "Crisp."

RICE, SARAH. Born Mar. 5, 1955 in Okinawa. Attended AzStateU. Debut 1974 OB in "The Fantasticks," followed by "The Enchantress," Bdwy 1979 in "Sweeney Todd" for which she received a Theatre World Award.

RICH, JAMES. Born Apr. 29, 1955 in Boston, Ma. Attended Boston U. Debut 1975 OB in "Let My People Come," followed by "Livin' Dolls," Bdwy in "Hair" (1977), "The Best Little Whorehouse in Texas," "Joseph and the Amazing Technicolor Dreamcoat."

RICHARDS, JEAN. Born in NYC. Attended Yale. Debut 1969 OB in "The Man with the Flower in His Mouth," followed by "Madwoman of Chaillot," "Poor Old Simon."

RICHARDS, JESS. Born Jan. 23, 1943 in Seattle, WA. Attended UWash. Bdwy debut 1966 in "Walking Happy," followed by "South Pacific" (LC), "Blood Red Roses," "Two by Two," "On the Town" for which he received a Theatre World Award, "Mack and Mabel," "Musical Chairs," "A Reel American Hero," "Barnum," OB in "One for the Money," "Lovesong," "A Musical Evening with Josh Logan," "The Lullaby of Broadway," "All Night Strut!", "Station Joy."

RICHARDS, TOG. Born Oct. 23, 1940 in Madison, Wi. Attended UWi. Bdwy in "Fiddler on the Roof" (1976/1981).

RICHIE, CHUCK. Born Apr. 2, 1947 in Lakewood, Oh. Graduate Denison U, LAMDA. Debut 1973 OB in "The Taming of the Shrew," followed by "Starmites," "Jubilee," "Romeo and Juliet," "Rhinegold," "Elektra," "Pericles," "Good Woman of Setzuan."

RICHERT, WANDA. Born Apr. 18, 1958 in Chicago, IL. Bdwy debut 1980 in "42nd Street" for which she received a Theatre World Award.

RILEY, LARRY. Born June 21, 1952 in Memphis, TN. Graduate Memphis State U. Bdwy debut 1978 in "A Broadway Musical," followed by "I Love My Wife," "Night and Day," "Shakespeare's Cabaret," OB in "Street Songs," "Amerika," "Plane Down," "Sidewalkin'," "Frimbo," "A Soldier's Play," "Maybe I'm Doing It Wrong."

RINEHART, ELAINE. Born Aug. 16, 1952 in San Antonio, TX. Graduate NC Sch of Arts. Debut 1975 OB in "Tenderloin," followed by "Native Son," Bdwy in "The Best Little Whorehouse in Texas."

RINGHAM, NANCY. Born Nov. 16, 1954 in Minneapolis, Mn. Graduate St. Olaf Col., Oxford U. Bdwy debut 1954 in "My Fair Lady" (also 1981), OB in "That Jones Boy."

RISLEY, ANN. Born Sept. 30, 1949 in Madison, Wi. Graduate UWi. Bdwy debut 1982 in "Come Back to the 5 & Dime, Jimmy Dean."

ROBBINS, REX. Born in Pierre, SD. Bdwy debut 1964 in "One Flew over the Cuckoo's Nest," followed by "Scratch," "The Changing Room," "Gypsy," "Comedians," "An Almost Perfect Person," "Richard III," OB in "Servant of Two Masters," "The Alchemist," "Arms and the Man," "Boys in the Band," "A Memory of Two Mondays," "They Knew What They Wanted," "Secret Service," "Boy Meets Girl," "Three Sisters," "The Play's the Thing," "Julius Caesar," "Henry IV Parts 1 and 2."

ROBERTS, MARILYN. Born Oct. 30, 1939 in San Francisco, Ca. Graduate SFStateCol. Debut 1963 OB in "Telemachus Clay," followed by "The Maids," "The Class," "Gabriella," "Tom Paine," "Futz," "Candaules Commissioner," "Persia," "Masque of St. George and the Dragon," "Split Lip," "Mert and Phil," "The Blonde Leading the Blonde."

ROBERTS, RALPH. Born Aug. 17 in Salisbury, NC. Attended UNC. Bdwy debut 1948 in "Angel Street," followed by "4 Chekhov Comedies," "S. S. Glencairn," "Madwoman of Chaillot," "Witness for the Prosecution," "The Lark," "Bells Are Ringing," "The Milk Train Doesn't Stop Here Anymore," "Love Suicide at Schofield Barracks," "A Texas Trilogy," "Medea," OB in "Siamese Connections," "Fishing."

ROBERTS, TONY. Born Oct. 22, 1939 in NYC. Graduate Northwestern U. Bdwy bow 1962 in "Something about a Soldier," followed by "Take Her, She's Mine," "Last Analysis," "Never Too Late," "Barefoot in the Park," "Don't Drink the Water," "How Now, Dow Jones," "Play It Again, Sam," "Promises, Promises," "Sugar," "Absurd Person Singular," "Murder at the Howard Johnson's," "They're Playing our Song," OB in "The Cradle Will Rock," "Losing Time," "The Good Parts,"

ROBERTSON, LILLIE. Born Sept. 5, 1953 in Houston, TX. Graduate Carnegie-Mellon U. Debut 1979 OB in "The Guardsman," followed by "Casualties," "The Chinese Viewing Pavilion."

ROCKAFELLOW, MARILYN. Born Jan. 22, 1939 in Middletown, NJ. Graduate Rutgers U. Debut 1976 OB in "La Ronde," followed by "The Art of Dining," "One Act Play Festival," "Open Admissions," Bdwy 1980 in "Clothes for a Summer Hotel."

RODGERS, ENID. Born Apr. 29, 1924 in London, Eng. Attended Royal Col. Debut 1969 OB in "Sourball," followed by "Getting Married," "Bird with Silver Feathers," "Nymph Errant," Bdwy in "Jockey Club Stakes (1973), "Crown Matrimonial."

ROGAN, PETER. Born May 11, 1939 in County Leitrim, Ire. Bdwy debut 1966 in "Philadelphia, Here I Come," OB in "The Kitchen," "Nobody Hears a Broken Drum," "Picture of Dorian Gray," "Macbeth," "Sjt. Musgrave's Dance," "Stephen D.," "People Are Living There," "The Plough and the Stars," "Look Back in Anger," "Sea Anchor."

ROGERS, GIL. Born Feb. 4, 1934 in Lexington, KY. Attended Harvard. OB in "The Ivory Branch," "Vanity of Nothing," "Warrior's Husband," "Hell Bent fer Heaven," "Gods of Lightning," "Pictures in the Hallway," "Rose," "Memory Bank," "A Recent Killing," "Birth," "Come Back, Little Sheba," "Life of Galileo," "Remembrance," "Mecca," Bdwy in "The Great White Hope," "The Best Little Whorehouse in Texas."

ROGERS, PAUL. Born Mar. 22, 1917 in Plympton, Eng. Attended Chekhov Th.Sch. Bdwy debut 1956 (with Old Vic) in "Macbeth," "Romeo and Juliet," "Troilus and Cressida," "Richard II," followed by "Photo Finish," "The Homecoming," "Here's Where I Belong," "Sleuth," "The Dresser."

ROLFING, TOM. Born Sept. 6, 1949 in Cedar Rapids, Ia. Graduate Carnegie Tech. Debut 1973 OB in "Godspell," followed by "Chantecler," "Francis," "What a Life!," Bdwy in "Godspell," "Equus," "Little Johnny Jones."

ROONEY, MICKEY. Born Sept. 23, 1920 in Brooklyn, NY. As a child, appeared in vaudeville with his parents Joe Yule and Nell Brown. Bdwy debut 1979 in "Sugar Babies," for which he received a Special Theatre World Award.

ROOS, CASPER. Born Mar. 21, 1925 in The Bronx, NY. Attended Manhattan School of Music. Bdwy debut 1959 in "First Impressions," followed by "How to Succeed in Business . . .," "Mame," Brigadoon," "Shenandoah," OB in "Street Scene."

ROSE, CRISTINE. Born Jan. 31, 1951 in Lynwood, Ca. Graduate Stanford U. Debut 1979 OB in "The Miracle Worker," followed by "Don Juan Comes Back from the War," "Hunting Scenes from Bavaria," "Three Acts of Recognition."

ROSE, GEORGE. Born Feb. 19, 1920 in Bicester, Eng. Bdwy debut with Old Vic 1946 in "Henry IV," followed by "Much Ado about Nothing," "A Man for All Seasons," "Hamlet," "Royal Hunt of the Sun," "Walking Happy," "Loot," "My Fair Lady," (CC '68), "Canterbury Tales," "Coco," "Wise Child," "Sleuth," "My Fat Friend," "My Fair Lady," "She Loves Me," "Peter Pan," BAM's "The Play's the Thing," "The Devil's Disciple," and "Julius Caesar," "The Kingfisher," "Pirates of Penzance."

ROSEN, ROBERT. Born Apr. 24, 1954 in NYC. Attended IndU, HB Studio. Bdwy debut 1975 in "Shenandoah," followed by "Marlowe."

ROSENBLATT, MARCELL. Born July 1, in Baltimore, MD. Graduate UNC, Yale. Debut 1979 OB in "Vienna Notes," followed by "Sorrows of Stephen," "The Dybbuk," "Twelfth Night," "Second Avenue Rag," "La Boheme," "Word of Mouth," "Twelve Dreams."

ROSS, ALAN, Born Dec. 1, 1920 in Beverly Hills, Ca. Attended UCLA. Bdwy credits include "Kiss and Tell," "Sweethearts," "Small Wonder," "Dance Me a Song," OB in "Italian Straw Hat."

John Rothman	Dee Etta Rowe	Bo Rucker	Kristin Rudrud	David Sabin	Seret Scott
Joanna Seaton	Brockman Seawell	Debbie Shapiro	Keenan Shimizu	Barbara Sohmers	Count Stoval
George Taylor	Donna Thomason	Jaime Tirelli	Christine Toy	Patrick Tull	Sharon Ullric
Beatrice Winde	Charles White	Mimi Weddell	Bruce Warren	Suzanne Walker	Richard Voigt

Daniel Wirth	Carol Woods	Stephen Wright	Kim Yancey	Peter Yoshida	Karen Ziemba

220

ROSS, JAMIE. Born May 4, 1939 in Markinch, Scot. Attended RADA. Bdwy debut 1962 in "Little Moon of Alban," followed by "Moon Beseiged," "Ari," "Different Times," "Woman of the Year," OB in "Penny Friend," "Oh, Coward!"

ROSS, LARRY. Born Oct. 18, 1945 in Brooklyn, NY. Attended AADA. Bdwy debut 1963 in "How to Succeed . . .," followed by "Fiddler on the Roof," "Frank Merriwell," "Annie."

ROTHMAN, JOHN. Born June 3, 1949 in Baltimore, MD. Graduate Wesleyan U, Yale. Debut 1978 OB in "Rats Nest," followed by "The Impossible H. L. Mencken," "The Buddy System.", "Rosario and the Gypsies," "Italian Straw Hat."

ROUNDS, DAVID. Born Oct. 9, 1930 in Bronxville, NY. Attended Denison U. Bdwy debut 1965 in "Foxy," followed by "Child's Play" for which he received a Theatre World Award, "The Rothschilds," "The Last of Mrs. Lincoln," "Chicago," "Romeo and Juliet," "Morning's at 7," OB in "You Never Can Tell," "Money," "The Real Inspector Hound," "Epic of Buster Friend," "Enter a Free Man," "Metamorphosis in Miniature."

ROWE, DEE ETTA. Born Jan. 29, 1953 in Lewiston, Me. Graduate UHartford. Bdwy debut 1979 in "Most Happy Fella," followed by "Nine."

ROWE, HANSFORD. Born May 12, 1924 in Richmond, Va. Graduate URichmond. Bdwy debut 1968 in "We Bombed in New Haven," followed by "Porgy and Bess," "Nuts," OB in "Curley McDimple," "The Fantasticks," "Last Analysis," "God Says There Is No Peter Ott," "Mourning Becomes Electra," "Bus Stop," "Secret Service," "Boy Meets Girl," "Getting Out," "The Unicorn."

ROY, RENEE. Born Jan. 2, 1935 in Buffalo, NY. Attended Hartford Col. Bdwy debut 1954 in "Ankles Aweigh," followed by "Nature's Way," "By Jupiter," "Zelda," OB in "Company," "Applause."

RUANE, JANINE. Born Dec. 17, 1963 in Philadelphia, PA. Bdwy debut 1977 in "Annie."

RUBINSTEIN, JOHN. Born Dec. 8, 1946 in Los Angeles, CA. Attended UCLA. Bdwy debut 1972 in "Pippin" for which he received a Theatre World Award, followed by "Children of a Lesser God," "Fools."

RUCKER, BO. Born Aug. 17, 1948 in Tampa, Fl. Debut 1978 OB in "Native Son" for which he received a Theatre World Award, followed by "Blues for Mr. Charlie," "Streamers," "Forty Deuce," "Dustoff."

RUDIN, STUART. Born Dec. 16, 1941 in Vancouver, WA. Graduate UWa, EWaStateU. Debut 1974 OB in "Friends," followed by "Great American Stickball League," "Progress."

RUDRUD, KRISTIN. Born May 23, 1955 in Fargo, ND. Graduate Moorhead State U, LAMDA. Debut 1981 OB in "A Midsummer Night's Dream," Bdwy 1981 in "Amadeus."

RUISINGER, THOMAS. Born May 13, 1930 in Omaha, NE. Graduate SMU, Neighborhood Playhouse. Bdwy debut 1959 in "Warm Peninsula," followed by "The Captain and the Kings," "A Shot in the Dark," "Frank Merriwell," "The Importance of Being Earnest," "Snow White," "Manhattan Showboat," "A Stitch in Time," OB in "The Balcony," "Thracian Horses," "Under Milk Wood," "Six Characters in Search of an Author," "Papers," "As to the Meaning of Words," "Damn Yankees" (JB)

RUSKIN, JEANNE. Born Nov. 6 in Saginaw, MI. Graduate NYU. Bdwy debut 1975 in "Equus," OB in "Says I, Says He," "Cassatt," "Inadmissible Evidence," "Hedda Gabler," "Misalliance."

RUTH, RICHARD. Born Oct. 8, 1953 in Fresno, CA. Attended CalStateU. Bdwy debut 1980 in "Blackstone," followed by "The Five O'Clock Girl," OB in "Seesaw."

RYAN, MICHAEL M. Born Mar. 19, 1929 in Wichita, Ks. Attended St. Benedict's Col., Georgetown U. Bdwy debut 1960 in "Advise and Consent," followed by "Complaisant Lover," "Best Friend," OB in "Richard III," "King Lear," "Hedda Gabler," "Barrom Monks," "Portrait of the Artist as a Young Man," "Autumn Garden," "Naomi Court," "Caveat Emptor," "Deli's Fable," "The Price."

RYLAND, JACK. Born July 2, 1935 in Lancaster, Pa. Attended AADA. Bdwy debut 1958 in "The World of Suzie Wong," followed by "A Very Rich Woman," "Henry V," OB in "A Palm Tree in a Rose Garden," "Lysistrata," "The White Rose and the Red," "Old Glory," "Cyrano de Bergerac," "Mourning Becomes Electra," "Beside the Seaside."

SABELLICO, RICHARD. Born June 29, 1951 in NYC. Attended C.W. Post Col. Bdwy debut 1974 in "Gypsy," followed by "Annie," OB in "Gay Divorce," "La Ronde," "Manhattan Breakdown."

SABIN, DAVID. Born Apr. 24, 1937 in Washington, DC. Graduate Catholic U. Debut 1965 OB in "The Fantasticks," followed by "Now Is the Time for All Good Men," "Threepenny Opera," "You Never Can Tell," "Master and Margarita," Bdwy in "The Yearling," "Slapstick Tragedy," "Jimmy Shine," "Gantry," "Ambassador," "Celebration," "Music Is," "The Water Engine," "The Suicide," "Othello."

SACHS, ANN. Born Jan. 23, 1948 in Boston, Ma. Graduate Carnegie Tech. Bdwy debut 1970 in "Wilson in the Promise Land," followed by "Dracula," "Man and Superman," OB in "Tug of War," "Sweetshoppe Miriam," "Festival of American Plays," "Clownmaker."

SACKS, DAVIA. Born July 10 in Flushing, NY. Attended Dade Jr. Col. Debut 1973 OB in "Swiss Family Robinson," followed by "Zorba," Bdwy in "Fiddler on the Roof" (1976), "Evita,"

SADOFF, FRED. Born Oct. 21, 1926 in Brooklyn, NY. Attended Bklyn Col., Neighborhood Playhouse, Actors Studio. Bdwy debut 1949 in "South Pacific," followed by "Wish You Were Here," "Camino Real," OB in "The Collyer Brothers at Home," "Period Piece."

SAFFRAN, CHRISTINA. Born Oct 21, 1958 in Quincy, IL. Attended Webster Col. Bdwy debut 1978 in "A Chorus Line," followed by "A New York Summer," "Music Man," "Sophisticated Ladies."

ST. DAVID, MARTYN. Born Jan. 14 in Southport, NC. Bdwy debut 1981 in "Heartland," OB in "Collective Portraits."

SALISBURY, FRAN. Born Feb 9, 1945 in NYC. Graduate Shaw U., Columbia. Bdwy debut 1972 in "Purlie," followed by "Royal Family," "Reggae," OB in "Prodigal Sister," "The Lion and the Jewel," "Sparrow in Flight," "Helen," "Broadway Soul," "As to the Meaning of Words," "The Scarecrow."

SALOKA, SIOUX. Born June 28, 1952 in St. Paul, Mn. Graduate MacAlester Col., Brandeis U. Debut 1981 OB in "Peep."

SAMUEL, D. PETER. Born Aug. 15, 1958 in Pana, Il. Graduate EastIllU. Bdwy debut 1981 in "The First."

SANAZARO, MARIANNE. Born Nov 9, in St. Louis, MO. Graduate Stephens Col., InU. Debut 1977 OB in "Company," followed by "God Bless You, Mr. Rosewater," Bdwy 1980 in "Annie."

SANCHEZ, JAIME. Born Dec 19, 1938 in Rincon, PR. Attended Actors Studio. Bdwy bow 1957 in "West Side Story," followed by "Oh, Dad, Poor Dad . . .," "Midsummer Night's Dream," "Richard III," OB in "The Toilet" "Conerico Was Here to Stay" for which he received a Theatre World Award, "The Ox Cart," "The Tempest," "Merry Wives of Windsor," "Julius Caesar," "Coriolanus," "He Who Gets Slapped."

SANDY, GARY. Born Dec. 25, 1945 in Dayton, Oh. Attended Wilmington Col., AADA. Debut 1973 OB in "The Children's Mass," followed by "Romeo and Juliet," Bdwy in "Saturday Sunday Monday" (1974), "Pirates of Penzance" (1982).

SAPUTO, PETER J. Born Feb 2, 1939 in Detroit, MI. Graduate EMiU, Purdue U. Debut 1977 OB in "King Oedipus," followed by "Twelfth Night," "Bon Voyage," "Happy Haven," "Sleepwalkers," "Humulus the Mute," "The Freak," Bdwy in "Once in a Lifetime."

SAUNDERS, NICHOLAS. Born June 2, 1914 in Kiev, Russia. Bdwy debut 1942 in "Lady in the Dark" followed by "A New Life," "Highland Fling," "Happily Ever After," "The Magnificent Yankee," "Anastasia," "Take Her, She's Mine," "A Call on Kuprin," "Passion of Josef D.," OB in "An Enemy of the People," "End of All Things Natural," "The Unicorn in Captivity," "After the Rise," "All My Sons," "My Great Dead Sister," "The Investigation," "Past Tense," "Scenes and Revelations," "Zeks."

SAYRE, CLARK. Born Mar. 23, 1960 in Santa Barbara, Ca. Attended UCLA. Bdwy debut 1981 in "Merrilly We Roll Along."

SBARGE, RAPHAEL. Born Feb. 12, 1964 in NYC. Attended HB Studio. Debut 1981 OB in "Henry IV Part I," followed by "The Red Snake," Bdwy in "The Curse of an Aching Heart."

SCARDINO, DON. Born in Feb. 1949 in NYC. Attended CCNY. On Bdwy in "Loves of Cass McGuire," "Johnny No-Trump," "My Daughter, Your Son," "Godspell," "Angel," "King of Hearts," OB in "Shout from the Rooftops," "Rimers of Eldrich," "The Unknown Soldier and His Wife," "Godspell," "Moonchildren," "Kid Champion," "Comedy of Errors," "Secret Service," "Boy Meets Girl," "Scribes," "I'm Getting My Act Together . . . ," "As You Like It," "Holeville," "Sorrows of Stephen," "A Midsummer Night's Dream," "The Recruiting Officer," "Jungle of Cities," "Double Feature," "How I Got That Story."

SCHAUT, ANN LOUISE. Born Nov. 21, 1956 in Minneapolis, MN. Attended UMn. Bdwy debut 1981 in "A Chorus Line."

SCHEINE, RAYNOR. Born Nov. 10 in Emporia, Va. Graduate VaCommonwealthU. Debut 1978 OB in "Curse of the Starving Class," followed by "Blues for Mr. Charlie," "Salt Lake City Skyline," "Mother Courage," "The Lady or the Tiger."

SCHENKKAN, ROBERT. Born Mar. 19, 1953 in Chapel Hill, NC. Graduate UTx, Cornell U. Debut 1978 OB in "The Taming of the Shrew," followed by "Last Days at the Dixie Girl Cafe," "New Jerusalem," "G. R. Point," "The Midnight Visitor," "Key Exchange."

SCHEPS, ERIC. Born Oct. 2, 1958 in Houston, Tx. Attended NTxStateU. Bdwy debut 1981 in "Oh, Brother!"

SCHIMMEL, JOHN. Born Oct. 12, 1948 in Los Angeles, Ca. Graduate Wesleyan U. Bdwy debut 1977 in "The Cherry Orchard," followed by "Runaways," "Pump Boys & Dinettes," OB in "Dispatches," "Conference of the Birds," "Hot Grog," "Cortex," "Good Woman of Setzuan."

SCHNABEL, STEFAN. Born Feb. 2, 1912 in Berlin, Ger. Attended UBonn. Old Vic. Bdwy bow 1937 in "Julius Caesar," followed by "Shoemaker's Holiday," "Glamour Preferred," "Land of Fame," "Cherry Orchard," "Around the World in 80 Days," "Now I Lay Me Down to Sleep," "Idiot's Delight," "Love of Four Colonels," "Plain and Fancy," "Small War on Murray Hill," "A Very Rich Woman," "A Patriot for Me," "Teibele and Her Demon," OB in "Tango," "In the Matter of J. Robert Oppenheimer," "Older People," "Enemies," "Little Black Sheep," "Rosmersholm," "Passion of Dracula," "Biography," "The Firebugs," "Twelve Dreams."

SCHNETZER, STEPHEN. Born June 11, 1948 in Boston, Ma. Graduate UMa. Bdwy debut 1971 in "The Incomparable Max," followed by "Filumena," "A Talent for Murder," OB in "Timon of Athens," "Antony and Cleopatra," "Julius Caesar," "Fallen Angels," "Miss Julie."

SCOTT, GEORGE C. Born Oct. 18, 1927 in Wise, VA. Debut 1957 OB in "Richard III" for which he received a Theatre World Award, followed by "As You Like It," "Children of Darkness," "Desire under the Elms," Bdwy in "Comes a Day," "Andersonville Trial," "The Wall," "General Seegar," "The Little Foxes," "Plaza Suite," "Uncle Vanya," "Death of a Salesman," "Sly Fox," "Tricks of the Trade," "Present Laughter."

SCOTT, MICHAEL. Born Jan, 24, 1954 in Santa Monica, CA. Attended Cal. State U. Debut 1978 (OB and Bdwy) in "The Best Little Whorehouse in Texas," followed by "Happy New Year."

SCOTT SERET. Born Sept. 1, 1949 in Washington, DC. Attended NYU. Debut 1969 OB in "Slave Ship," followed by "Ceremonies in Dark Old Men," "Black Terror," "Dream," "One Last Look," "My Sister, My Sister," "Weep Not for Me," "Meetings," "The Brothers."

SCOTT, SUSAN ELIZABETH. Born Aug. 9 in Detroit, Mi. Graduate UDenver. Debut 1971 OB in "The Drunkard," Bdwy in "Music Is," "On the 20th Century," "Fearless Frank," "1940's Radio Hour."

SEAMAN, PAGE. Born May 20, 1971 in Mt. Kisco, NY. Debut 1979 OB in "The Sound of Music," followed by "The Early Show," "Evil Spirit."

SEAMON, EDWARD. Born Apr. 15, 1937 in San Diego, CA. Attended San Diego State Col. Debut 1971 OB in "The Life and Times of J. Walter Smintheous," followed by "The Contractor," "The Family," "Fishing," "Feedlot," "Cabin 12," "Rear Column," "Devour the Snow," "Buried Child," "Friends," "Extenuating Circumstances," "Confluence," "Richard II," "Great Grandson of Jedediah Kohler," Bdwy in "The Trip Back Down," "Devour the Snow," "The American Clock."

SEATON, JOANNA. Born Mar. 15, 1949 in NYC. Graduate Cornell U. Debut 1975 OB in "Boy Meets Boy," followed by "East of Kansas," "Francis," "Nymph Errant."

SEAWELL, BROCKMAN. Born Jan. 27, 1952 in NYC. Graduate LAMDA, Columbia U. Debut 1977 OB in "As You Like It," followed by "A Man for All Seasons," "The Enchanted."

SECREST, JAMES. Born Nov. 17 in Thomasville, GA. Graduate UNC. Debut 1966 in "Girl in the Freudian Slip," OB in "John Brown's Body," "Trial of the Catonsville Nine," "Private Ear/Public Eye."

SEFF, RICHARD. Born Sept. 23, 1927 in NYC. Attended NYU. Bdwy debut 1951 in "Darkness at Noon," followed by "Herzl," OB in "Big Fish, Little Fish," "Modigliani," "Childe Byron," "Richard II."

SEIDEL, VIRGINIA. Born July 26 in Harvey, Il. Attended Roosevelt U. Bdwy debut 1975 in "Very Good Eddie" for which she received a Theatre World Award, OB in "Hoofers," "Charlotte Sweet."

SELBY, JAMES. Born Aug. 29, 1948 in San Francisco, CA. Graduate Washburn U. Debut 1978 OB in "The Rivals," followed by "Caligula," "L'Ete," "A Prayer for My Daughter," "Amidst the Gladiolas."

SELDES, MARIAN. Born Aug. 23, 1928 in NYC. Attended Neighborhood Playhouse. Bdwy debut 1947 in "Medea," followed by "Crime and Punishment," "That Lady," "Tower Beyond Tragedy," "Ondine," "On High Ground," "Come of Age," "Chalk Garden," "The Milk Train Doesn't Stop Here Anymore," "The Wall," "A Gift of Time," "A Delicate Balance," "Before You Go," "Father's Day," "Equus," "The Merchant," "Deathtrap," OB in "Different," "Ginger Man," "Mercy Street," "Candle in the Wind," "Isadora Duncan Sleeps with the Russian Navy."

SERRA, RAYMOND. Born Aug. 13, 1937 in NYC. Attended Rutgers U., Wagner Col. Debut 1975 OB in "The Shark," followed by "Mamma's Little Angels," "Manny," Bdwy in "The Wheelbarrow Closers," "Marlowe."

SERRANO, CHARLIE. Born Dec. 4, 1952 in Rio Piedras, PR. Attended Brooklyn Col. Debut 1978 OB in "Allegro" followed by "Mama, I Want to Sing," "El Bravo," Bdwy in "Got Tu Go Disco," "Joseph and the Amazing Technicolor Dreamcoat."

SERRECCHIA, MICHAEL. Born Mar. 26, 1951 in Brooklyn, NY. Attended Brockport State U. Teachers Col. Debut 1972 in "The Selling of the President," followed by "Heathen!" "Seesaw," "A Chorus Line," OB in "Lady Audley's Secret."

SETRAKIAN, ED. Born Oct. 1, 1928 in Jenkintown, WV. Graduate Concord Col., NYU. Debut 1966 OB in "Drums in the Night," followed by "Othello," "Coriolanus," "Macbeth," "Hamlet," "Baal," "Old Glory," "Futz," "Hey Rube," "Seduced," "Shout across the River," "American Days," "Sheepskin," Bdwy in "Days in the Trees," "St. Joan," "The Best Little Whorehouse in Texas."

SEVERS, WILLIAM. Born Jan. 8, 1932 in Britton, OK. Attended Pasadena Playhouse, Columbia Col. Bdwy debut 1960 in "Cut of the Axe," OB in "The Moon Is Blue," "Lulu," "Big Maggie," "Mixed Doubles," "The Rivals," "The Beaver Coat," "Twister," "Midnight Mass," "Gas Station."

SEVIER, JACK. Born Apr. 1, 1925 in Chattanooga, Tn. Graduate UChattanooga, UNC. Bdwy debut 1959 in "Destry Rides Again," followed by "My Fair Lady" (1981).

SHALLO, KAREN. Born Sept. 28, 1946 in Philadelphia, Pa. Graduate PaStateU. Debut 1973 OB in "Children of Darkness," followed by "Moliere in spite of Himself," "We Won't Pay!," "The Overcoat," Bdwy 1980 in "Passione."

SHAPIRO, DEBBIE. Born Sept. 29, 1954 in Los Angeles, CA. Graduate LACC. Bdwy debut 1979 in "They're Playing Our Song," followed by "Perfectly Frank," "Blues in the Night," OB in "They Say It's Wonderful," "New Moon in Concert."

SHARKEY, SUSAN. Born Dec. 12 in NYC. Graduate UAZ. Debut 1968 OB in "Guns of Carrar," followed by "Cuba Si," "Playboy of the Western World," "Good Woman of Setzuan," "Enemy of the People," "People Are Living There," "Narrow Road to the Deep North," "Enemies," "The Plough and the Stars," "The Sea," "The Sykovs," "Catsplay," "Ice," "Cubistique," "Frugal Repast," Bdwy 1980 in "The American Clock."

SHAW, MARCIE. Born June 19, 1954 in Franklin Square, NY. Attended UIl. Bdwy debut 1980 in "Pirates of Penzance."

SHEA, JOHN V. Born Apr. 14 in North Conway, NH. Graduate Bates Col., Yale. Debut OB 1974 in "Yentl, the Yeshiva Boy," followed by "Gorky," "Battering Ram," "Safe House," "The Master and Margarita," "Sorrows of Stephen," "American Days," "The Dining Room," Bdwy in "Yentl" (1975) for which he received a Theatre World Award, "Romeo and Juliet."

SHELLEY, CAROLE. Born Aug. 16, 1939 in London, Eng. Bdwy debut 1965 in "The Odd Couple," followed by "Astrakhan Coat," "Loot," "Noel Coward's Sweet Potato," "Hay Fever," "Absurd Person Singular," "The Norman Conquests," "The Elephant Man," OB in "Little Murder," "The Devil's Disciple," "The Play's the Thing," "Double Feature," "Twelve Dreams."

SHELTON, REID. Born Oct. 7, 1924 in Salem, OR. Graduate U. Mich. Bdwy bow 1952 in "Wish You Were Here," followed by "Wonderful Town," "By the Beautiful Sea," "Saint of Bleecker Street," "My Fair Lady," "Oh! What a Lovely War!," "Carousel" (CC), "Canterbury Tales," "Rothschilds," "1600 Pennsylvania Avenue," "Annie," OB in "Phedre," "Butterfly Dream," "Man with a Load of Mischief," "Beggars Opera," "The Contractor," "Cast Aways."

SHELTON, SLOANE. Born Mar. 17, 1934 in Asheville, NC. Attended Berea Col., RADA. Bdwy debut 1967 in "The Imaginary Invalid," followed by "A Touch of the Poet," "Tonight at 8:30," "I Never Sang for My Father," "Sticks and Bones," "The Runner Stumbles," "Shadow Box," "Passione," OB in "Androcles and the Lion," "The Maids," "Basic Training of Pavlo Hummel," "Play and Other Plays," "Julius Caesar," "Chieftains," "Passione," "The Chinese Viewing Pavilion."

SHEPARD, JOAN. Born Jan. 7 in NYC. Graduate RADA. Bdwy debut 1940 in "Romeo and Juliet," followed by "Sunny River," "The Strings, My Lord, Are False," "This Rock," "Foolish Notion," "A Young Man's Fancy," "My Romance," "Member of the Wedding," OB in "Othello," "Plot against the Chase Manhattan Bank," "Philosophy in the Boudoir," "Knitters in the Sun," "School for Wives."

SHEPARD, JOHN. Born Dec. 9, 1952 in Huntington Park, Ca. Graduate UCal/Irvine. Debut 1982 OB in "Scenes from La Vie de Boheme."

SHEPPARD, SUSAN. Born Sept. 21, 1957 in Johannesburg, SAf. Graduate UMi. Bdwy debut 1981 in "Fiddler on the Roof."

SHERWIN, MIMI. Born in NYC. Graduate UMi. Bdwy debut 1980 in "Canterbury Tales," OB in "Street Scene."

SHIMIZU, KEENAN. Born Oct. 22, 1956 in NYC. Graduate HS of Performing Arts. Bdwy 1965 in CC's "South Pacific" and "The King and I," OB in "Rashomon," "The Year of the Dragon," "The Catch," "Peking Man," "Flowers and Household Gods," "Behind Enemy Lines," "Station J."

SHINE, DAVID. Born Sept. 21, 1960 in Dumont, NJ. Graduate NYU, AADA. Bdwy debut 1981 in "Merrily We Roll Along."

SHORT, JOHN. Born July 3, 1956 in Christopher, Il. Graduate Hanover Col. Debut 1981 OB in "Unfettered Letters."

SHORT, SYLVIA. Born Oct. 22, 1927 in Concord, Ma. Attended Smith Col., Old. Vic. Debut 1954 OB in "The Clandestine Marriage," followed by "Golden Apple," "Passion of Gross," "Desire Caught by the Tail," "City Love Story," "Family Reunion," "Beaux Stratagem," "Just a Little Bit Less Than Normal," "Nasty Rumors," "Says I, Says He," "Milk of Paradise," "The Broken Pitcher," Bdwy in "King Lear" (1956), "Hide and Seek."

SHROPSHIRE, NOBLE. Born Mar. 2, 1946 in Cartersville, GA. Graduate LaGrange Col., RADA. Debut 1976 OB in "Hound of the Baskervilles," followed by "The Misanthrope," "The Guardsman," "Oedipus Cycle," "Gilles de Rais," "Leonce and Lena," "King Lear."

SHULL, RICHARD B. Born Feb. 24, 1929 in Elmhurst, NY. Graduate IoStateU. Bdwy debut 1954 in "Black-Eyed Susan," followed by "Wake Up, Darling," "Red Roses for Me," "I Knock at the Door," "Pictures in the Hallway," "Have I Got a Girl for You," "Minnie's Boys," "Goodtime Charley," "Fools," "Oh, Brother!," OB in "Purple Dust," "Journey to the Day," "American Hamburger League," "Frimbo."

SIEGEL, HARVEY. Born Feb. 28, 1945 in NYC. Attended Stella Adler Studio. Debut 1971 OB in "Out of the Death Cart," followed by "The Team," "June Moon," "A Prayer for My Daughter," Bdwy in "Wheelbarrow Closers" (1976).

SIEGLER, BEN. Born Apr. 9, 1958 in Queens, NY. Attended HB Studio. Debut 1980 OB in "Innocent Thoughts, Harmless Intentions," followed by "Threads," "Many Happy Returns," "Snow Orchid," "The Diviners," Bdwy 1981 in "5th of July."

SIFF, IRA. Born Feb. 15, 1946 in NYC. Graduate Cooper Union. Debut 1972 OB in "Joan," followed by "The Faggot," "The Haggadah."

SIGWORTH, NANCY. Born July 13, 1952 in Buffalo, NY. Graduate Hope Col. Debut 1981 OB in "The Scarecrow."

SILLIMAN, MAUREEN. Born Dec. 3 in NYC. Attended HofstraU. Bdwy debut 1975 in "Shenandoah," followed by "I Remember Mama," "Is There Life after High School?," OB in "Umbrellas of Cherbourg," "Two Rooms."

SILVER, JOE. Born Sept. 28, 1922 in Chicago, Il. Attended UIl., AmThWing. Bdwy bow 1942 in "Tobacco Road," followed by "Doughgirls," "Heads or Tails," "Nature's Way," "Gypsy," "Heroine," "Zulu and the Zayda," "You Know I Can't Hear You . . . ," "Lenny," "The Roast," "The World of Sholom Aleichem," OB in "Blood Wedding," "Lamp at Midnight," "Joseph and His Brethern," "Victors," "Shrinking Bride," "Family Pieces," "Cakes with Wine."

SIMMINS, KENNETH. Born July 24, 1951 in Buffalo, NY. Graduate Daemen Col. Debut 1982 OB in "Only Human."

SINGER, MARLA. Born Aug. 2, 1957 in Oklahoma City, Ok. Graduate OKCity U. Debut 1981 OB in "Seesaw."

SISTI, MICHELAN. Born May 27, 1949 in San Juan, PR. Graduate UBuffalo. Debut 1979 OB in "A Midsummer Night's Dream," Bdwy in "Fiddler on the Roof" (1981).

SKAGGS, MARSHA. Born Aug. 23, 1949 in Bedford, Oh. Attended Purdue U., AADA. Bdwy debut 1981 in "They're Playing Our Song," followed by "Einstein and the Polar Bear."

SLATER, CHRISTIAN. Born Aug. 18, 1969 in NYC. Bdwy debut 1980 in "The Music Man," followed by "Copperfield," "Macbeth," OB in "Between Daylight and Boonville."

SMITH, BO. Born Feb. 13, 1952 in Hendersonville, NC. Graduate Northwestern U. LAMDA. Debut 1980 OB in "The Slab Boys," followed by "And I Ain't Finished Yet."

SMITH, COTTER. Born May 29, 1949 in Washington, DC. Graduate Trinity Col. Debut 1980 OB in "The Blood Knot," followed by "Death of a Miner," "A Soldier's Play."

SMITH, JENNIFER. Born Mar. 9, 1956 in Lubbock, Tx. Graduate TxTechU. Debut 1981 OB in "Seesaw," followed by "Suffragette."

SMITH, LOIS. Born Nov. 3, 1930 in Topeka, Ks. Attended UWa. Bdwy debut 1952 in "Time Out for Ginger," followed by "The Young and Beautiful," "Wisteria Trees," "Glass Menagerie," "Orpheus Descending," "Stages," OB in "Sunday Dinner," "Present Tense," "The Iceman Cometh," "Harry Outside," "Hillbilly Women," "Touching Bottom," "Tennessee," "The Articulated Man."

SMITH, LOUISE. Born Feb. 8, 1955 in NYC. Graduate Antioch Col. Debut 1981 OB in "The Haggadah.", followed by "Salt Speaks."

SMITH, SAMMY. Born Mar. 3, 1904 in Brooklyn, NY. Graduate Drake Sch. Bdwy credits include "Buckaroo," "Wish You Were Here," "Plain and Fancy," "Li'l Abner," "How to Succeed in Business . . . ," "Oklahoma!," "The Goodbye People," "Wrong Way Light Bulb," "West Side Story" (1979), "Sugar Babies."

SMITH, SHEILA. Born Apr. 3, 1933 in Conneaut, OH. Attended Kent State U., Cleveland Play House. Bdwy debut 1963 in "Hot Spot," followed by "Mame" for which she received a Theatre World Award, "Follies," "Company," "Sugar," "Five O'Clock Girl," "42nd Street," OB in "Taboo Revue," "Anything Goes," "Best Foot Forward," Sweet Miami," "Fiorello."

SMITROVICH, BILL. Born May 16, 1947 in Bridgeport, CT. Graduate UBridgeport, Smith Col. Bdwy debut 1980 in "The American Clock.", OB in "Zeks."

SMYTHE, MARCUS. Born Mar. 26, 1950 in Berea, Oh. Graduate Otterbein Col., Ohio. Debut 1975 OB in "Tenderloin," followed by "Ten Little Indians," Bdwy in "The Suicide" (1980).

SNOW, NORMAN. Born Mar. 29, 1950 in Little Rock, AR. Juilliard graduate. Debut 1972 OB in "School for Scandal," followed by "Lower Depths," "Hostage," "Timon of Athens," "Cymbeline," "U.S.A.," "Women Beware Women," "One Crack Out," BAM Theatre Co's "A

Winter's Tale," "Johnny on a Spot," "The Wedding," Bdwy in "Three Sisters," "Measure for Measure," "Beggar's Opera," "Next Time I'll Sing to You," "Macbeth.", "Scenes and Revelations."

SOHMERS, BARBARA. Born July 7 in NYC. Attended Antioch Col. Debut 1955 OB in "The Trial," followed by "Spring's Awakening," "Threepenny Opera," Bdwy in "Ned and Jack" (1981).

SOMERS, BRETT. Born July 11, 1927 in New Brunswick, Can. Attended AmThWing, Actors Studio. Bdwy debut 1958 in "Maybe Tuesday," OB in "My Prince My King" (1982).

SOMMER, JOSEF. Born June 26, 1934 in Griefswald, Ger. Graduate Carnegie Tech. Bdwy bow 1970 in "Othello," followed by "Children, Children," "Trial of the Catonsville 9," "Full Circle," "Who's Who in Hell," "Shadow Box," "Spokesong," "The 1940's Radio Show," "Whose Life Is It Anyway?," OB in "Enemies," "Merchant of Venice," "The Dog Ran Away," "Drinks Before Dinner," "Lydie Breeze."

SOPHIEA, CYNTHIA. Born Oct. 26, 1954 in Flint, Mi. Attended UMi. Bdwy debut 1981 in "My Fair Lady," followed by OB in "Lysistrata," "Suffragette."

SOREL, ANITA. Born Oct. 25, in Hollywood, CA. Graduate UUtah, CalState/ Long Beach. Debut 1980 OB in "The Time of the Cuckoo" (ELT) followed by "Bourgeois Gentlemen.", "Hedda Gabler."

SPAISMAN, ZIPORA. Born Jan. 2, 1920 in Lublin, Poland. Debut 1955 OB in "Lonesome Ship," followed by "In My Father's Court," "Thousand and One Nights," "Eleventh Inheritor," "Enchanting Melody, "Fifth Commandment," "Bronx Express," "Melody Lingers On," "Yoshke Muzikant," "Stempenyu," "Generations of Green Fields," "Shop."

SPARER, KATHRYN C. Born Jan. 5, 1956 in NYC. Graduate UChicago. Debut 1982 OB in "Beside the Seaside."

SPINDELL, AHVI. Born June 26, 1954 in Boston, Ma. Attended Ithaca Col., UNH, Juilliard. Bdwy debut 1977 in "Something Old, Something New," OB in "Antony and Cleopatra," "Forty Deuce."

SPIVAK, ALICE. Born Aug. 11, 1935 in Brooklyn, NY. Attended HB Studio. Debut 1954 OB in "Early Primrose," followed by "Of Mice and Men," "Secret Concubine," "Port Royal," "Time for Bed, Take Me to Bed," "House of Blue Leaves," "Deep Six the Briefcase," "Selma."

STANLEY, GORDON. Born Dec. 20, 1951 in Boston, MA. Graduate Brown U., Temple U. Debut 1977 OB in "Lyrical and Satirical," followed by "Allegro," "Elizabeth and Essex," "Two on the Isles," Bdwy in "Onward Victoria" (1980).," Joseph and the Amazing Technicolor Dreamcoat."

STAPLETON, MAUREEN. Born June 21, 1925 in Troy, NY. Attended HB Studio. Bdwy debut 1946 in "Playboy of the Western World," followed by "Antony and Cleopatra," "Detective Story," "Bird Cage," "The Rose Tattoo" for which she received a Theatre World Award, "The Emperor's Clothes," "The Crucible," "Richard III," "The Seagull," "27 Wagons Full of Cotton," "Orpheus Descending," "The Cold Wind and the Warm," "Toys in the Attic," "Glass Menagerie" (1965 & 1975), "Plaza Suite," "Norman, Is That You?" (1981), "Gingerbread Lady," "Country Girl," "Secret Affairs of Mildred Wild," "The Gin Game," "The Little Foxes" (1981).

STARK, MOLLY. Born in NYC. Graduate Hunter Col. Debut 1969 OB in "Sacco-Vanzetti," followed by "Riders to the Sea," "Medea," "One Cent Plain," "Elizabeth and Essex," "Principally Pinter," "Toulouse," "Winds of Change," Bdwy 1973 in "Molly."

STATTEL, ROBERT. Born Nov. 20, 1937 in Floral Park, NY. Graduate Manhattan Col. Debut 1958 OB in "Heloise," followed by "When I Was a Child," "Man and Superman," "The Storm," "Don Carlos," "Taming of the Shrew," "Titus Andronicus," "Henry IV," "Peer Gynt," "Hamlet," "Danton's Death," "Country Wife," "Caucasian Chalk Circle," and "King Lear," "Iphigenia in Aulis," "Ergo," "The Persians," "Blue Boys," "The Minister's Black Veil," "Four Friends," "Two Character Play," "The Merchant of Venice," "Cuchulain," "Oedipus Cycle," "Gilles de Rais," "Woyzeck.", "King Lear," "The Fuehrer Bunker."

STEFAN, MARK. Born Sept. 17, 1972 in NYC. Debut 1981 OB in "Sister Mary Ignatius Explains It All for You," "Actor's Nightmare."

STEIN, JUNE. Born June 13, 1950 in NYC. Debut 1979 OB in "The Runner Stumbles," followed by "Confluence," "Am I Blue."

STEINBERG, ROY. Born Mar. 24, 1951 in NYC. Graduate Tufts U., Yale. Debut 1974 OB in "A Midsummer Night's Dream," followed by "Firebugs," "The Doctor in spite of Himself," "Romeo and Juliet," "After the Rise," "Our Father," "Zeks," Bdwy in "Wings."

STERLING, MARLA. Born Oct. 9, 1949 in Brooklyn, NY. Graduate NYU. Debut 1981 OB in "God, It's Too Late," followed by "Evil Spirit."

STERN, ARLENE. Born March 23 in Boston, Ma. Graduate Northeastern U. Debut 1981 OB in "Final Curtain."

STERNER, STEVE. Born May 5, 1951 in NYC. Attended CCNY. Bdwy debut 1980 in "Clothes for a Summer Hotel." followed by "Oh, Brother!", OB in "Lovesong," "Vagabond Stars."

STERNHAGEN, FRANCES. Born Jan. 13, 1932 in Washington, DC. Vassar graduate, OB in "Admirable Bashful," "Thieves' Carnival," "Country Wife" "Ulysses in Nighttown." "Saintliness of Margery Kemp," "The Room," "A Slight Ache," "Displaced Person," "Playboy of the Western World," "The Prevalence of Mrs. Seal," Bdway in "Great Day in the Morning," "Right Honourable Gentleman," with APA in "Cocktail Party," and "Cock-a-doodle Dandy," "The Sign in Sidney Brustein's Window," "Enemies," (LC), "The Good Doctor," "Equus," "Angel," "On Golden Pond," "The Father.", "Grownups."

STEVENS, FISHER. Born Nov. 27, 1963 in Chicago, Il. Attended NYU. Bdwy debut 1982 in "Torch Song Trilogy."

STEVENS, GARY. Born Dec. 19, 1962 in NYC. Attended Queens Col. Bdwy debut 1971 in "Frank Merriwell," followed by "Merrily We Roll Along."

STEVENS, SUSAN. Born in 1942 in Louisville, KY. Attended Jackson Col., AMDA. Debut 1978 OB in "The Price of Genius," followed by "A Dream Play," "Zeks," "Philistines."

STEVENSEN, SCOTT. Born May 4, 1951 in Salt Lake City, Ut. Bdwy debut 1974 in "Good News" for which he received a Theatre World Award, followed by OB in "2 X 5," "Bea's Place," "The 6 O'Clock Boys."

STEWART, DANIEL. Born June 6, 1957 in Olympia, WA. Attended FLStateU. Debut 1981 OB in "The Miser," followed by "Invitation to a March."

STEWART, SCOT. Born June 3, 1941 in Tylertown, MS. Graduate UMiss. Debut 1975 OB in "New Girl in Town," Bdwy 1979 in "Sugar Babies."

STILLMAN, RICHARD. Born Nov. 24, 1954 in Midland, Mi. Graduate Dartmouth Col. Debut 1979 OB in "Hamlet," followed by "Sea-Dream," Bdwy in "Canterbury Tales" (1980)

STILLMAN, ROBERT. Born Dec. 2, 1954 in NYC. Graduate Princeton U. Debut 1981 OB in "The Haggadah," followed by "Street Scene," "Lola."

STINTON, COLIN. Born Mar. 10, 1947 in Kansas City, MO. Attended Northwestern U. Debut 1978 OB in "The Water Engine" (also Bdwy) for which he received a Theatre World Award followed by "Twelfth Night," "The Beaver Coat.", Bdwy in "The Curse of an Aching Heart."

STITT, DON. Born Jan. 25, 1956 in NYC. Graduate San Francisco State U. Bdwy debut 1982 in "Do Black Patent Leather Shoes Really Reflect Up?"

STOECKLE, ROBERT. Born Sept. 21, 1947 in Port Chester, NY. Graduate Hartt Col. Bdwy debut 1980 in "Canterbury Tales," OB in "110 in the Shade."

STOEGER, FRANK. Born June 14, 1947. Graduate Heidelberg Col. Debut 1981 OB in "Marya," followed by "Raft," "Street Scene."

STOLLER, AMY. Born March 7 in NYC. Attended Mills Col. Debut 1982 OB in "The Sea Anchor."

STONEBURNER, SAM. Born Feb. 24, 1934 in Fairfax, VA. Graduate Georgetown U, AADA. Debut 1960 OB in "Ernest in Love," followed by "Foreplay," "Anyone Can Whistle." Bdwy in "Different Times" (1972), "Bent," "Macbeth" (1981)," "The First."

STOUT, MARY. Born Apr. 8, 1952 in Huntington, WV. Graduate Marshall U. Debut 1980 OB in "Plain and Fancy" followed by "Crisp," Bdwy 1981 in "Copperfield."

STOVALL, COUNT. Born Jan. 15, 1946 in Los Angeles, CA. Graduate UCal. Debut 1973 OB in "He's Got a Jones," followed by "In White America," "Rashomon," "Sidnee Poet Heroical," "A Photo," "Julius Caesar," "Coriolanus," "Spell #7," "The Jail Diary of Albie Sachs," "To Make A Poet Black," "Transcendental Blues," "Edward II," "Children of the Sun," Bdwy in "Inacent Black," "The Philadelphia Story."

STRATTON, RONALD BENNETT. Born Jan. 11, 1942 in Philadelphia, PA. Bdwy debut 1959 in "Kiss Me Kate," followed by "Goldilocks," "Happiest Girl in Town," "Subways are for Sleeping," "Tenderloin," "Kelly," "Her First Roman," "Annie Get Your Gun," "Mame," "Camelot" (1980/1981).

STRAUSS, NATALIE. Born Feb. 29, 1956 in Philadelphia, Pa. Graduate Temple U. Debut 1982 OB in "T.N.T."

STRAUSS, PETER. Born in NYC in 1947. Graduate Northwestern U. Bdwy debut 1981 in "Einstein and the Polar Bear."

STRICKLER, DAN. Born Feb. 4, 1949 in Los Angeles, CA. Graduate CalStateU, Temple U. Debut 1977 OB in "Jules Feiffer's Hold Mel," followed by "Flying Blind," "Coming Attractions.", "Suffragette."

STRIMPELL, STEPHEN. Born Jan. 17, 1937 in NYC. Graduate Columbia U. Bdwy bow 1964 in "The Sunday Man," OB in "School for Scandal," "Henry IV," "Dumbbell People in a Barbell World," "To Be Young, Gifted and Black," "The Disintegration of James Cherry," "The Good Parts."

STRYK, LYDIA. Born Nov. 3, 1958 in DeKalb, IL. Attended London Drama Centre. Debut 1980 OB in "After the Revolution," followed by "Twister."

STUTHMAN, FRED. Born June 27, 1919 in Long Beach, CA. Attended UCa. Debut 1970 OB in "Hamlet," followed by "Uncle Vanya," "Charles Abbott & Son," "She Stoops to Conquer," "The Master Builder," "Taming of the Shrew," "Misalliance," "Merchant of Venice," "Conditions of Agreement," "The Play's the Thing," "Ghosts," "The Father," "Hot 1 Baltimore," "The Cherry Orchard," "The Devil's Disciple," "Bonjour, La, Bonjour," "Misalliance," Bdwy in "Sherlock Holmes" ('75), "Fools."

SULKA, ELAINE. Born in NYC. Graduate Queens Col., Brown U. Debut 1962 OB in "Hop, Signorl," followed by "Brotherhood," "Brothers," "The Last Prostitute," Bdwy in "Passion of Josef D.," "Medea".

SULLIVAN, BRAD. Born Nov. 18, 1931 in Chicago, Il. Graduate UMe. AmThWing. Debut 1961 OB in "Red Roses for Me," followed by "South Pacific," "Hot-House," "Leavin' Cheyenne," Bdwy in "Basic Training of Pavlo Hummel" (1977), "Working."

SULLIVAN, KIM. Born July 21, 1952 in Philadelphia, Pa. Graduate NYU. Debut 1972 OB in "The Black Terror," followed by "Legend of the West," "Deadwood Dick," "Big Apple Messenger," "Dreams Deferred."

SUROVY, NICOLAS. Born June 30, 1944 in Los Angeles, CA. Attended Northwestern U., Neighborhood Playhouse. Debut 1964 OB in "Helen" for which he received a Theatre World Award, followed by "Sisters of Mercy," "Cloud 9," Bdwy in "Merchant," "Crucifer of Blood," "Major Barbara."

SUTTON, DOLORES. Born in NYC; graduate NYU. Bdwy debut 1962 in "Rhinoceros," followed by "General Seeger," OB in "Man with the Golden Arm," "Machinal," "Career," "Brecht on Brecht," "To Be Young, Gifted and Black," "The Web and the Rock," "My Prince My King."

SUTTON, HENRY. Born Aug. 24, 1926 in Baltimore, Md. Graduate Denison, Catholic U. Debut 1956 OB in "The Comedian," followed by "The Rehearsal," "Ticket of Leave Man," "King of the Whole Damn World," "Conflict of Interest," Bdwy in "Promises Promises," "Prisoner of Second Avenue," "Little Me," (1982).

SWIFT, ALLEN. Born Jan. 16, 1924 in NYC. Debut 1961 OB in "Portrait of the Artist," followed by "Month of Sundays," "Where Memories Are Magic," "My Old Friends," "Divine Fire," Bdwy in "The Student Gypsy" (1963), "Checking Out."

SYERS, MARK. Born Oct. 25, 1952 in Trenton, NJ. Graduate Emerson Col. Bdwy debut 1976 in "Pacific Overtures," followed by "Jesus Christ Superstar" (1977), "Evita," "Under Fire."

SZLOSBERG, DIANA. Born Aug. 18, 1957 in NYC. Graduate FlStateU. Debut 1981 OB in "Seesaw."

TARLETON, DIANE. Born Oct. 25, in Baltimore, MD. Graduate UMd. Bdwy debut 1965 in "Anya," followed by "A Joyful Noise," "Elmer Gantry," "Yentl," "Torch Song Trilogy," OB in "A Time for the Gentle People," "Spoon River Anthology," "International Stud," "Too Much Johnson," "To Bury a Cousin," "A Dream Play."

TARLOW, FLORENCE. Born Jan. 19, 1929 in Philadelphia, Pa. Graduate Hunter Col. Bdwy debut 1968 in "Man in the Glass Booth," followed by "Good Woman of Setzuan," "Inner City," "Medea," OB in "Beautiful Day," "Istanbul," "Gorilla Queen," "America Hurrah," "Red Cross," "Promenade," "a Visit," "The Blonde Leading the Blonde."

TABUM, BILL. Born May 6, 1947 in Philadelphia, PA. Graduate Catawba Col. Bdwy debut 1971 in "Man of La Mancha," OB in "Missouri Legend," "Time of the Cuckoo," "Winner Take All?" "Seesaw."

TATUM, MARIANNE. Born Feb. 18, 1951. in Houston, TX. Attended Manhattan School of Music. Graduate 1971 OB in "Ruddigore," followed by "The Sound of Music" (ELT), Bdwy 1980 in "Barnum" for which she received a Theatre World Award.

TAYLOR, ELIZABETH. Born Feb. 27, 1932 in London, Eng. Bdwy debut 1981 in "The Little Foxes," for which she received a Special Theatre World Award.

TAYLOR, GEORGE. Born Sept. 18, 1930 in London, Eng. Attended AADA. Debut 1972 OB in "Hamlet," followed by "Enemies" (LC), "The Contractor," "Scribes," "Says I, Says He," "Teeth 'n' Smiles," "Viaduct," "Translations," "Last of the Knucklemen," Bdwy in "Emperor Henry IV," "The National Health."

TAYLOR, JENNIFER. Born June 15, 1956 in Paris, Fr. Graduate Viterbo Col. Debut 1982 OB in "Teach Me How to Cry."

TEITEL, CAROL. Born Aug. 1, 1929 in NYC. Attended AmTh Wing. Bdwy debut 1957 in "The Country Wife," followed by "The Entertainer," "Hamlet," "Marat/deSade," "A Flea in Her Ear," "Crown Matrimonial," "All Over Town," OB in "Way of the World," "Juana La Loca," "An Evening with Ring Lardner," "Misanthrope," "Shaw Festival," "Country Scandal," "The Bench," "Colombe," "Under Milk Wood," "7 Days of Mourning," "Long Day's Journey into Night," "The Old Ones," "Figures in the Sand," "World of Sholom Aleichem," "Big and Little," "Duet," "Trio," "Every Good Boy Deserves Favor" (LC), "Fallen Angels," "A Stitch in Time," "Faces of Love.", "Keymaker."

TESTA, MARY. Born June 4, 1955 in Philadelphia, PA. Attended URI. Debut 1979 OB in "In Trousers," followed by "Company," Bdwy 1980 in "Barnum."

THACKER, RUSS. Born June 23, 1946 in Washington, DC. Attended Montgomery Col. Bdwy debut 1967 in "Life with Father," followed by "Music! Music!," "Grass Harp," "Heathen," "Home Sweet Homer," "Me Jack You Jill," OB in "Your Own Thing" for which he received a Theatre World Award, "Do Black Patent Leather Shoes Really Reflect Up?," "Dear Oscar," "Once I Saw a Boy Laughing," "Tip-Toes," "Oh, Coward!", "New Moon in Concert."

THOLE, CYNTHIA. Born Sept. 21, 1957 in Silver Spring, Md. Graduate Butler U. Debut 1982 OB in "Nymph Errant."

THOMAS, WILLIAM, JR. Born in Columbus, Oh. Graduate OhStateU. Debut 1972 OB in "Touch," followed by "Natural," "Godspell," "Poor Little Lambs," Bdwy in "Your Arms Too Short to Box with God" (1976).

THOMASON, DONNA. Born Feb. 11, 1954 in MO. Graduate Ct. Col. Bdwy debut 1980 in "Annie."

THOME, DAVID. Born July 24, 1951 in Salt Lake City, UT. Bdwy debut 1971 in "No, No, Nanette," followed by "Different Times," "Good News," "Rodgers and Hart," "A Chorus Line.", "Dancin'," "Dreamgirls."

THOMPSON, EVAN. Born Sept. 3, 1931 in NYC. Graduate UCal. Bdwy bow 1969 in "Jimmy," OB in "Mahagonny," "Treasure Island," "Knitters in the Sun," "Half-Life.", "Fasnacht Day."

THOMPSON, JEFFREY V. Born Mar. 21 1952 in Cleveland, Oh. Graduate OhU. Debut 1976 OB in "Homeboy," followed by "Macbeth," "Season's Reasons," "Helen," "Louis," "Edward II," Bdwy in "Eubie" (1978).

THOMPSON, WEYMAN. Born Dec. 11, 1950 in Detroit, Mi. Graduate Wayne State U, UDetroit. Bdwy debut 1980 in "Clothes for a Summer Hotel," followed by "Dreamgirls."

THORNE, RAYMOND. Born Nov. 27, 1934 in Lackawanna, NY. Graduate UCt. Debut 1966 OB in "Man with a Load of Mischief," followed by "Rose," "Dames at Sea," "Love Course," "Blue Boys," Bdwy 1977 in "Annie."

THRELFALL, DAVID. Born Oct. 12, 1953 in Manchester, Eng. Graduate Polytechnic School of Theatre. Bdwy debut 1981 in "Nicholas Nickleby."

TILLMAN, JUDITH. Born Apr. 25, 1934 in Cleveland, Oh. Graduate Case Western Reserve U. Debut 1963 OB in "The Darker Flower," followed by "Do I Hear a Waltz," "Ten Little Indians."

TIRELLI, JAIME. Born Mar. 4, 1945 in NYC. Attended UMundial, AADA. Debut 1975 OB in "Rubbers," followed by "Yanks 3, Detroit O," "The Sun Always Shines on the Cool," "Body Bags."

TOBIAS, BARBARA. Born Nov. 8, 1954 in Boston, Ma. Graduate UCal/Irvine. Debut 1982 OB in "Nymph Errant."

TOBIE, ELLEN. Born Mar. 26 in Chambersburg, PA. Graduate OhWesleyanU, Wayne State U. Debut 1981 OB in "The Chisholm Trail Went Through Here.", "followed by "Welded."

TOLAYDO, MICHAEL. Born July 23, 1946 in Kenya, Nairobi. Attended Oakland U. Bdwy debut 1970 in "The Cherry Orchard," followed by "The Time of Your Life," "The Robber Bridegroom," "Dirty Linen," "Kingdoms," OB in "Hamlet" (1973), "White Liars."

TOMEI, CONCETTA. Born Dec. 30, 1945 in Kenosha, WI. Graduate UWisc, Goodman School. Debut 1979 OB in "Little Eyolf," followed by "Cloud 9," Bdwy 1979 in "The Elephant Man."

TORN, RIP. Born Feb. 6, 1931 in Temple, Tx. Graduate UTx. Bdwy bow 1956 in "Cat on a Hot Tin Roof," followed by "Sweet Bird of Youth," for which he received a Theatre World Award, "Daughter of Silence," "Strange Interlude," "Blues for Mr. Charlie," "Country Girl," "Glass Menagerie," OB in "Chaparral," "The Cuban Thing," "The Kitchen," "Deer Park," "Dream of a Blacklisted Actor," "Dance of Death," "Macbeth," "Barbary Shore," "Creditors," "Seduced," "The Man and the Fly."

TORRES, ANDY. Born Aug. 10, 1945 in Ponce, PR. Attended AMDA. Bdwy debut 1969 in "Indians," followed by "Purlie," "Don't Bother Me, I Can't Cope," "The Whiz," "Guys and Dolls," "Your Arms Too Short to Box with God," "Reggae," OB in "Billy Noname," "Suddenly the Music Starts," "Louis."

TORRES, LIZ. Born in 1947 in The Bronx, NY. Attended NYU. Debut 1971 OB in "Louis and the Elephant," followed by "She, That One/He and the Other," Bdwy in "The Ritz."

TORRES, MARK. Born May 7, 1955 in Brownsville, TX. Graduate InU, Temple U. Bdwy debut 1980 in "Amadeus."

TOTO, KAREN. Born Mar. 30, 1956 in Philadelphia, Pa. Graduate Temple U. Bdwy debut 1981 in "My Fair Lady."

TOY, CHRISTINE. Born Dec. 26, 1959 in Scarsdale, NY. Graduate Sarah Lawrence Col. Debut 1982 OB in "Oh, Johnny!"

TRUMBO, NANCY. Born Sept. 23, 1945 in Volga, SD. Graduate UCo. Debut 1973 OB in "The Secret Life of Walter Mitty," followed by "Children of Darkness."

TSOUTSOUVAS, SAM. Born Aug. 20, 1948 in Santa Barbara, Ca. Attended UCa., Juilliard. Debut 1969 OB in "Peer Gynt," followed by "Twelfth Night," "Timon of Athens," "Cymbeline," "School for Scandal," "The Hostage," "Women Beware Women," "Lower Depths," "Emigres," Bdwy in "The Three Sisters," "Measure for Measure," "Beggar's Opera," "Scapin," "Dracula."

TUCCI, MARIA. Born June 19, 1941 in Florence, It. Attended Actors Studio. Bdwy debut 1963 in "The Milk Train Doesn't Stop Here Anymore," followed by "The Rose Tattoo," "The Little Foxes," "Cuban Thing," "The Great White Hope," "School for Wives," "Lesson from Aloes," "Kingdoms," OB in "Corruption in the Palace of Justice," "Five Evenings," "Trojan Women," "White Devil," "Horseman Pass By," "Yerma," "Shepherd of Avenue B," "The Gathering."

TUCKER-WHITE, PAMELA. Born Mar. 6, 1955 in Peoria, Il. Graduate UWi, Juilliard. Debut 1981 OB in "How It All Began," followed by "The Dubliners," "The Country Wife."

TULL, PATRICK. Born July 28, 1941 in Sussex, Eng. Attended LAMDA. Bdwy debut 1967 in "The Astrakhan Coat," OB in "Ten Little Indians."

TURETZKY, JOAN. Born Sept. 26. in Brooklyn, NY. Attended Sullivan Co. Com. Col. Debut 1977 OB in "Counsellor-at-Law," followed by "Merton of the Movies,". "Ten Little Indians."

TWOMEY, ANNE. Born June 7, 1951 in Boston, MA. Graduate Temple U. Debut 1975 OB in "Overruled," followed by "The Passion of Dracula," "When We Dead Awaken," Bdwy 1980 in "Nuts" for which she received a Theatre World Award, "To Grandmother's House We Go."

TYRRELL, SUSAN. Born in 1946 in San Francisco, CA. Bdwy debut 1952 in "Time Out for Ginger," OB in "The Knack," "Futz," "A Cry of Players," "The Time of Your Life," "Camino Real," "Father's Day," "A Coupla White Chicks", "Borders."

ULLRICK, SHARON. Born Mar. 19, 1947 in Dallas, Tx. Graduate SMU. Debut 1980 OB in "Vanities," Bdwy 1981 in "Crimes of the Heart."

UNGER, DEBORAH. Born July 2, 1953 in Philadelphia, Pa. Graduate UPittsburg, FlStateU. Debut 1981 OB in "Seesaw."

VALE, MICHAEL. Born June 28, 1922 in Brooklyn, NY. Attended New School. Bdwy debut 1961 in "The Egg," followed by "Cafe Crown," "Last Analysis," "The Impossible Years," "Saturday Sunday Monday," "Unexpected Guests," "California Suite," OB in "Autograph Hound," "Moths," "Now There's the Three of Us," "Tall and Rex," "Kaddish," "42 Seconds from Broadway," "Sunset," "Little Shop of Horrors."

VALENTINE, JAMES. Born Feb. 18, 1933 in Rockford, IL. Attended ULondon, Central Sch. of Drama. Bdwy debut 1958 in "Cloud 7," followed by "Epitaph for George Dillon," "Duel of Angels," "Ross," "Caesar and Cleopatra," "The Importance of Being Earnest," "Camelot" (1980/1981)

VALOR, HENRIETTA. Born Apr. 28 in New Cumberland, PA. Graduate Northwestern U. Bdwy debut 1965 in "Half A Sixpence," followed by "Applause," "Jacques Brel Is Alive," "Annie," OB in "Fashion," "Jacques Brel. . . ,," "A Bistro Car on the CNR," "Vagabond Stars."

VAN NORDEN, PETER. Born Dec. 16, 1950 in NYC. Graduate Colgate U., Neighborhood Playhouse. Debut 1975 OB in "Hamlet," followed by "Henry V," "Measure for Measure," "A Country Scandal," "Hound of the Baskervilles," "Tartuffe," "Antigone," "Bingo," "Taming of the Shrew," "The Balcony," "Shadow of a Gunman," "Jungle of Cities," "Shakespeare's Cabaret," Bdwy in "Romeo and Juliet" (1977), "St. Joan," "Inspector General," "Macbeth," "Little Johnny Jones."

VANNUYS, ED. Born Dec. 28, 1930 in Lebanon, IN. Attended Ind. U. Debut 1969 OB in "No Place to be Somebody," followed by "Conflict of Interest," "The Taming of the Shrew," "God Bless You, Mr. Rosewater," "The Chisholm Trail," "The Unicorn," Bdwy in "Black Terror," "Nuts."

VAN PATTEN, JOYCE. Born Mar. 9 in Kew Gardens, NY. Bdwy bow 1941 in "Popsy," followed by "This Rock, " "Tomorrow the World, " "The Perfect Marriage," "The Wind Is 90," "Desk Set," "A Hole in the Head," "Murder at the Howard Johnson's," "I Ought to Be in Pictures," "Supporting Cast," OB in "Between Two Thieves," "Spoon River Anthology," "The Seagull."

VEAZEY, JEFF. Born Dec. 6 in New Orleans, LA. Bdwy debut 1975 in "Dr. Jazz," followed by "The Grand Tour," "Sugar Babies," OB in "Speakeasy."

VENNEMA, JOHN C. Born Aug. 24, 1948 in Houston, Tx. Graduate Princeton U, LAMDA. Bdwy debut 1976 in "The Royal Family," followed by "The Elephant Man," "Otherwise Engaged," OB in "Loot" (1973), "Statements after an Arrest . . . ," "The Biko Inquest," "No End of Blame."

VENTRISS, JENNIE. Born Aug. 7, 1935 in Chicago, Il. Graduate DePaul U. Debut 1964 OB in "Ludlow Fair," followed by "I Can't Keep Running in Place," Bdwy in "Luv" (1966), "Prisoner of Second Avenue," "Gemini."

VICKERY, JOHN. Born in 1951 in Alameda, Ca. Graduate UCaBerkeley, UCaDavis. Debut 1981 in "Macbeth" (LC), followed by "Ned and Jack," "Eminant Domain," OB in "American Days," "A Call from the East," "Henry IV Part I," "Looking-Glass."

VINOVICH, STEVE. Born Jan. 22, 1945 in Peoria, Il. Graduate UII, UCLA, Juilliard. Debut 1974 OB in "The Robber Bridegroom," followed by "King John," "Father Uxbridge Wants to Marry," "Hard Sell," "Rosa," "Double Feature," Bdwy in "Robber Bridegroom" (1976), "The Magic Show," "The Grand Tour," "Loose Ends."

VIPOND, NEIL. Born Dec. 24, 1929 in Toronto, Can. Bdwy debut 1956 in "Tamburlaine the Great," followed by "Macbeth," OB in "Three Friends," "Sunday Runners," "Hamlet" (ELT), "Routed."

VIRTUE, CHRISTIE. Born Aug. 23 in Berkeley, Ca. Graduate San Diego State U. Debut 1971 OB in "The House of Blue Leaves," followed by "Wonderful Lives," "Lessons," "The Trip Back Down."

VITA, MICHAEL. Born in NYC. Studied at HB Studio. Bdwy debut 1967 in "Sweet Charity," followed by "Golden Rainbow," "Promises, Promises," "Cyrano," "Chicago," "Ballroom," "Charlie and Algernon," OB in "Sensations," "That's Entertainment," "Rocket to the Moon," "Nymph Errant."

VOIGTS, RICHARD. Born Nov. 25, 1934 in Streator, Il. Graduate InU, Columbia U. Debut 1979 OB in "The Constant Wife," followed by "Company," "The Investigation," "Dune Road," "The Collection," "Miracle Man," "As Time Goes By," "Silence," "Station J."

VON DOHLN, CHRISTINE. Born July 1 in Cliffside Park, NJ. Graduate Marquette U, Columbia U. Debut 1977 OB in "The Primary English Class," followed by "Catholic School Girls."

VON SCHERLER, SASHA. Born Dec. 12 in NYC. Bdwy debut 1959 in "Look after Lulu," followed by "Rape of the Belt," "The Good Soup," "Great God Brown," "First Love," "Alfie," "Harold," "Bad Habits," OB in "Admirable Bashful," "The Comedian," "Conversation Piece," "Good King Charles' Golden Days," "Under Milk Wood," "Plays for Bleecker St.," "Ludlow Fair," "Twelfth Night," "Sondra," "Cyrano de Bergerac," "Crimes of Passion," "Henry VI," "Trelawny of the Wells," "Screens," "Soon Jack November," "Pericles," "Kid Champion," "Henry V," "Comanche Cafe," "Museum," "Grand Magic," "The Penultimate Problem of Sherlock Holmes," "Keymaker," "Hunting Scenes from Lower Bavaria."

VON SYDOW, MAX. Born July 10, 1929 in Lund, Sweden. Attended Stockholm Royal Acting Acad. Bdwy debut 1977 in "The Night of the Tribades," followed by "Duet for One" (1981).

VOSBURGH, DAVID. Born Mar. 14, 1938 in Coventry, RI. Attended Boston U. Bdwy debut 1968 in "Maggie Flynn," followed by "1776," "A Little Night Music," "Evita," OB in "Smith."

WALDROP, MARK. Born July 30, 1954 in Washington, DC. Graduate Cincinnati Consv. Debut 1977 OB in "Movie Buff," Bdwy in "The Grand Tour," "Evita."

WALKER, SUZANNE. Born Jan. 17 in Ashtabula, Oh. Attended Butler U. Debut 1971 OB in "Love Me, Love My Children," followed by "Le Bellybutton," Bdwy in "Tricks" (1973), "Molly," "Broadway Follies," "Oh, Brother!"

WALL, BRUCE. Born July 14, 1956 in Bath, Eng. Graduate UToronto, RADA. Debut 1979 OB in "Class Enemy," followed by "The Browning Version."

WALLACE, LEE. Born July 15, 1930 in NYC. Attended NYU. Debut 1966 OB in "Journey of the Fifth Horse," followed by "Saturday Night," "An Evening with Garcia Lorca," "Macbeth," "Booth Is Back in Town," "Awake and Sing," "Shepherd of Avenue B," "Basic Training of Pavlo Hummel," "Curtains," "Elephants," Bdwy in "Secret Affairs of Mildred Wild," "Molly," "Zalmen, or the Madness of God," "Some of My Best Friends."

WANN, JIM Born Aug. 30, 1948 in Chattanooga, Tn. Graduate UNC. Debut 1975 OB in "Diamond Studs," Bdwy 1982 in "Pump Boys & Dinettes."

WARD, JANET. Born Feb. 19 in NYC. Attended Actors Studio, Bdwy debut 1945, in "Dream Girl," followed by "Anne of a Thousand Days," "Detective Story," "King of Friday's Men," "Middle of the Night," "Miss Lonelyhearts," "J. B.," "Cheri," "The Egg," "Impossible Years," "Of Love Remembered," OB in "Chapparal," "The Typists," "The Tiger," "Summertree," "Dream of a Blacklisted Actor," "Cruising Speed 600 MPH," "One Flew over the Cuckoo's Nest," "Love Gotta Come by Saturday Night," "Home Is the Hero," "Love Death Plays," "Olympic Park," "Hillbilly Wives," "Q.E.D."

WARDEN, YVONNE. Born Jan. 16, 1928 in NYC. Attended UCLA, NYU. Debut 1967 OB in "Trials of Brother Jero," followed by "The Strong Breed," "Macbeth," "Waiting for Godot," "Welfare," "Where Have All the Dreamers Gone," "Calalou," "Masque and Dacha."

WARDWELL, JOHN. Born in Rockland, Me. Graduate UMe. Bdwy debut 1967 in "90 Day Mistress," followed by "Nathan Weinstein, Mystic, Conn.," "Fire!," "First Monday in October," "Utter Glory of Morrissey Hall," "Einstein and the Polar Bear," OB in "Single Man at a Party," "In White America," "All the King's Men," "Fireworks," "We Bombed in New Haven," "The Contractor," "The Dog Ran Away," "Richard III," "Good Help Is Hard to Find."

WARE, BARBARA. Born Jan. 12, 1958 in Washington, DC. Graduate NYU. Bdwy debut 1981 in "Lolita."

WARING, TODD. Born Apr. 28, 1955 in Saratoga Springs, NY. Graduate Skidmore Col. Debut 1980 OB in "Journey's End," followed by "Mary Stuart," "Henry IV Part II."

WARREN, BRUCE. Born July 31, 1953 in Ft. Wayne, In. Attended InU, Purdue U. Debut 1981 OB in "Seesaw."

WARREN, DIANE. Born Apr. 6 in Fall River, Ma. Graduate RICol. Debut 1980 OB in "Biography," followed by "Private Ear/Public Eye."

WARREN, JOSEPH. Born June 5, 1916 in Boston, Ma. Graduate UDenver. Bdwy debut 1951 in "Barefoot in Athens," followed by "One Bright Day," "Love of Four Colonels," "Hidden River," "The Advocate," "Philadelphia, Here I Come," "Borstal Boy," "Lincoln Mask," OB in "Brecht on Brecht," "Jonah," "Little Black Sheep," "Black Tuesday," "The Show-Off," "Big Apple Messenger."

WASHINGTON, DENZEL. Born Dec. 28, 1954 in Mt. Vernon, NY. Graduate Fordham U. Debut 1975 OB in "The Emperor Jones," followed by "Othello," "Coriolanus," "Mighty Gents," "Beckett," "Spell #7," "Ceremonies in Dark Old Men," "One Tiger To a Hill," "A Soldier's Play."

WATERS, J. B. Born May 8, 1952 in Lakewood, NJ. Attended AADA. Debut 1981 OB in "King of Hearts."

WATERSTON, SAM. Born Nov. 15, 1940 in Cambridge, MA. Yale graduate. Bdwy bow 1963 in "Oh Dad, Poor Dad," followed by "First One Asleep Whistle," "Halfway Up the Tree," "Indians," "Hay Fever," "Much Ado about Nothing," "Lunch Hour," OB in "As You Like It," "Thistle, in My Bed," "The Knack," "Fitz," "Biscuit," "La Turista," "Posterity for Sale," "Ergo," "Muzeeka," "Red Cross," "Henry IV," "Spitting Image," "I Met a Man," "Brass Butterfly," "Trial of the Catonsville 9," "Cymbeline," "Hamlet," "A Meeting by the River," "The Tempest," "A Doll's House," "Measure for Measure," "Chez Nous," "Waiting for Godot," "Gardenia."

WATSON, LYNN. Born Dec. 19 in Waterloo, Ia. Graduate Ohio U. Debut 1982 OB in "Teach Me How to Cry."

WEAVER, FRITZ. Born Jan. 19, 1926 in Pittsburgh, PA. Graduate UChicago. Bdwy debut 1955 in "Chalk Garden," for which he received a Theatre World Award, followed by "Protective Custody," "Miss Lonelyhearts," "All American," "Lorenzo," "The White House," "Baker Street," "Child's Play," "Absurd Person Singular," OB in "The Way of the World," "White Devil," "Doctor's Dilemma," "Family Reunion," "The Power and the Glory," "The Great God Brown," "Peer Gynt," "Henry IV," "My Fair Lady" (CC), "Lincoln," "The Biko Inquest," "The Price," "Dialogue for Lovers," "A Tale Told."

WEAVER, LYNN. Born May 17 in Paris, Tn. Graduate UTn, Neighborhood Playhouse. Debut 1981 OB in "The Italian Straw Hat."

WEBB, ROBB. Born Jan. 29, 1939 in Whitesburg, Ky. Attended OhStateU. Debut 1976 OB in "Who Killed Richard Cory?," followed by "Chinese Viewing Pavilion," Bdwy in "Sly Fox."

WEBER, FREDRICKA. Born Dec. 22, 1940 in Beardstown, IL. Attended Northwestern U. Bdwy debut 1965 in "Those That Play the Clowns," OB in "Upstairs at the Downstairs," "The Last Sweet Days of Isaac" for which she received a Theatre World Award, "Two."

WEDDELL, MIMI. Born Feb. 15, 1915 in Williston, ND. OB credits include "Woman of No Importance," "Trelawny of the Wells," "Little Eyolf," "A Doll's House," "Hedda Gabler."

WEED, ROBERT. Born Mar, 24, 1971 in New Brunswick, NJ. Debut 1982 OB in "Street Scene."

WEEKS, JAMES RAY. Born Mar. 21, 1942 in Seattle, WA. Graduate UOre., AADA. Debut 1972 in LCR's "Enemies," "Merchant of Venice," "A Streetcar Named Desire," followed by OB's "49 West 87th," "Feedlot," "The Runner Stumbles," "Glorious Morning," "Just the Immediate Family," "The Deserter," "Life and/or Death," "Devour the Snow," "Innocent Thoughts, Harmless Intentions," "The Diviners," "A Tale Told," "Confluence," "Richard II," "Great Grandson of Jedediah Kohler," Bdwy in "My Fat Friend," "We Interrupt this Program," "Devour the Snow."

WEINER, ARN. Born July 19, 1931 in Brooklyn, NY. Attended Pratt, LACC. Bdwy debut 1966 in "Those That Play the Clowns," followed by "Yentl," "The World of Sholom Aleichem," OB in "Come Walk with Me," "Saving Grace," "Some Out, Carlo," "Evenings with Chekhov," "Sunset."

WEISS, JOEL. Born Sept. 21, 1953 in The Bronx, NY. Graduate Lehman Col. Debut 1976 OB in "Speakeasy," followed by "Ofay Watcher," "Sandcastle," "Shooting Gallery," "G. R. Point," "The Miser," "It's Called the Sugar Plum," "King of Hearts."

WELCH, CHARLES C. Born Feb. 2, 1921 in New Britain, Ct. Attended AmThWing. Bdwy debut 1958 in "Cloud 7," followed by "Donnybrook," "Golden Boy," "Little Murders," "Holly Go Lightly," "Darling of the Day," "Dear World," "Follies," "Status Quo," "Shenandoah," OB in "Half-Past Wednesday," "Oh Lady! Lady!," "God Bless You, Mr. Rosewater," "Two."

WELCH, RAQUEL. Born Sept. 5, 1940 in Chicago, Il. Attended San Diego State Col. Bdwy debut 1981 in "Woman of the Year."

WELDON, CHARLES. Born June 1, 1940 in Wetumka, Ok. Bdwy debut 1969 in "Big Time Buck White," followed by "River Niger," OB in "Ride a Black Horse," "Long Time Coming," "Jamimma," "In the Deepest Part of Sleep," "Brownsville Raid," "Great MacDaddy," "The Offering," "Colored People's Time."

WELLS, BEATRICE (formerly B. J.) Born May 4, 1951 in Hartford, Ct. Graduate UCt. Debut 1980 OB in "Fair Play for Eve," followed by "Lysistrata."

WELLS, REBECCA. Born Feb. 3, 1953 in Alexandria, La. Graduate LaStateU. Debut OB 1981 in "Unfettered Letters," followed by "Vatslav."

WETTIG, PATRICIA. Born Dec. 4, in Cincinnati, OH. Graduate Temple U. Debut 1980 OB in "Innocent Thoughts, Harmless Intentions," followed by "The Woolgatherer," "Childe Byron," "A Tale Told," "Threads," "The Dining Room."

WEYENBERG, TRISH. Born Oct. 21, 1949 in Little Chute, Wi. Graduate UWi. Debut 1982 OB in "Lysistrata."

WHITE, CHARLES. Born Aug. 29, 1920 in Perth Amboy, NJ. Graduate Rutgers U, Neighborhood Playhouse. Credits include "Career," "Cloud 7," "Gypsy," "Philadelphia, Here I Come," "Inherit the Wind," "Comes a Day," "Front Page," "Dandelion Wine" (OB), "Kingdoms."

WHITE, JANE. Born Oct. 30, 1922 in NYC. Attended Smith Col. Bdwy debut 1942 in "Strange Fruit," followed by "Climate of Eden," "Take a Giant Step," "Jane Eyre," "Once Upon a Mattress," "The Cuban Thing," OB in "Razzle Dazzle," "Insect Comedy," "The Power and the Glory," "Hop, Signor," "Trojan Women," "Iphigenia in Aulis," "Cymbeline," "Burnt Flowerbed," "Rosmersholm," "Jane White Who?," "Ah, Men," "Lola."

WHITE, JUNE. Born June 10, 1947 in Richmond, Ky. Graduate UDayton, NYU. Debut 1982 OB in "Village Wooing."

WHITE TERRI. Born Jan. 24, 1953 in Palo Alto, CA. Attended USIU. Debut 1976 OB in "The Club," followed by Bdwy in "Barnum" (1980).

WHITTON, MARGARET. (formerly Peggy). Born Nov. 30 in Philadelphia, PA. Debut 1973 OB in "Baba Goya," followed by "Arthur," "The Wager," "Nourish the Beast," "Another Language," "Chinchilla," "Othello," "The Art of Dining," "One Tiger to a Hill," "Henry IV Parts 1 & 2."

WIDDOES, JAMES. Born Nov. 15, 1953 in Pittsburgh, Pa. Attended NYU. Debut 1977 OB in "Wonderful Town," Bdwy 1982 in "Is There Life after High School?" for which he received a Theatre World Award.

WIEST, DIANE. Born Mar. 28, 1948 in Kansas City, MO. Attended UMd. Debut 1976 OB in "Ashes," followed by "Leave It to Beaver Is Dead," "The Art of Dining," for which she received a Theatre World Award, "Bonjour, La, Bonjour," Bdwy in "Frankenstein" (1980), "Othello," "Beyond Therapy."

WILKINSON, KATE. Born Oct. 25 in San Francisco, CA. Attended San Jose State Col. Bdwy debut 1967 in "Little Murders," followed by "Johnny No-Trump," "Watercolor," "Postcards," "Ring Round the Bathtub," "The Last of Mrs. Lincoln," "Man and Superman," "Frankenstein," "The Man Who Came to Dinner," OB in "La Madre," "Earnest in Love," "Story of Mary Surratt," "Bring Me a Warm Body," "Child Buyer," "Rimers of Eldritch," "A Doll's House," "Hedda Gabler," "Real Inspector Hound," "The Contractor," "When the Old Man Died," "The Overcoat," "Villager," "Good Help Is Hard to Find."

WILKOF, LEE. Born June 25, 1957 in Canton, Oh. Graduate UCincinnati. Debut 1977 OB in "Present Tense," followed by "Little Shop of Horrors."

WILLIAMS, CURT. Born Nov. 17, 1935 in Mt. Holly, NJ. Graduate Oberlin Col., UMiami. Debut 1964 OB in "The Fantasticks," followed by "Pinafore," "Mikado," "Night Must Fall," "The Hostage," "Macbeth," "Ice Age," "Colored People's Time," Bdwy 1970 in "Purlie."

WILLIAMS, ELLIS. Born June 28, 1951 in Brunswick, Ga. Graduate Boston U. Debut 1977 OB in "Intimation," followed by "Spell 7," "Mother Courage," Bdwy in "The Basic Training of Pavlo Hummel," "Pirates of Penzance," "Solomon's Child."

WILLIAMSON, NICOL. Born Sept. 14, 1938 in Hamilton, Scot. Bdwy debut 1965 in "Inadmissable Evidence," followed by "Plaza Suite," "Hamlet," "Uncle Vanya," "Macbeth," OB in "Nicol Williamson's Late Show," "Inadmissible Evidence."

WILLIS, ANN. Born Nov. 14 in Providence, RI. Attended AADA. Bdwy debut 1982 in "Candida."

WILLOUGHBY, RONALD. Born June 3, 1937 in Boss, Ms. Graduate Milsaps, Col, North-western U. Debut 1963 OB in "Walk in Darkness," followed by "Little Eyolf," "Antony and Cleopatra," "Balm in Gilead," "Dracula: Sabbat," "The Faggot," "King of the U.S.," "Twelfth Night," "Black People's Party."

WILSON, K. C. Born Aug. 10, 1945 in Miami, Fl. Attended AADA. Debut 1973 OB in "Little Mahogonny," followed by "The Tempest," "Richard III," "Macbeth," "Threepenny Opera," "The Passion of Dracula," "Francis."

WILSON, TREY. Born Jan. 21, 1948 in Houston, Tx. Bdwy debut 1979 in "Peter Pan, " followed by "Tintypes," "The First."

WINDE, BEATRICE. Born Jan. 6 in Chicago, Il. Debut 1966 OB in "In White America," followed by "June Bug Graduates Tonight," "Strike Heaven on the Face," "Divine Comedy," "Crazy Horse," "My Mother, My Father and Me," "Steal Away," Bdwy 1971 in "Ain't Supposed to Die a Natural Death" for which she received a Theatre World Award.

WINKLER, KEVIN. Born Feb. 9, 1954 in Nowata, Ok. Graduate San Diego State U. Debut 1978 OB in "A Midsummer Night's Dream," Bdwy 1981 in "Little Me."

WINTERS, WENDEE. Born Aug. 15 in Chicago, Il. Graduate UCLA. Debut 1982 OB in "Forbidden Broadway."

WIRTH, DANIEL. Born Oct. 3, 1955 in Bay City, Mi. Graduate Central MiU, UCal. Debut 1982 OB in "Twelfth Night," followed by "The Country Wife," "Dubliners."

WISE, WILLIAM. Born May 11 in Chicago, IL. Attended Bradley U., Northern IlU. Debut 1970 OB in "Adaptation/Next," followed by "him," "The Hot l Baltimore," "Just the Immediate Family," "36," "Borders."

WITTER, WILLIAM C. Born Mar. 15, 1950 in Portland, OR. Graduate UWash. Bdwy debut 1980 in "Barnum."

WOHL, DAVID. Born Sept. 22, 1953 in Brooklyn, NY. Debut 1981 OB in "The Buddy System," followed by "Awake and Sing."

WOLF, CATHERINE. Born May 25 in Abington, Pa. Attended Carnegie-Tech, Neighbor-hood Playhouse. Bdwy debut 1976 in "The Innocents," followed by "Otherwise Engaged," OB in "A Difficult Borning," "I Can't Keep Running in Place," "Cloud 9."

WONG, JANET. Born Aug. 30, 1951 in Berkeley, CA. Attended UCal. Bdwy debut 1977 in "A Chorus Line," followed by "Bring Back Birdie," OB in "Oh, Johnny!"

WOOD, JOHN. Born in 1931 in Derbyshire, Eng. Attended Oxford U. Bdwy debut 1967 in "Rosencrantz and Guildenstern Are Dead," followed by "Sherlock Holmes," "Travesties," "Tartuffe," "Deathtrap," "Amadeus."

WOODARD, ALFRE. Born Nov. 8 in Tulsa, Ok. Graduate Boston U. Bdwy debut 1976 in "Me and Bessie," OB in "No So Nice They Named It Twice," "Two by South."

WOODS, CAROL. Born Nov. 13, 1943 in Jamaica, NY. Debut 1980 OB in "One Mo' Time."

WOODS, JAMES. Born Apr. 18, 1947 in Vernal, Ut. Graduate MIT. Bdwy debut 1970 in "Borstal Boy," followed by "Conduct Unbecoming," "Trial of the Catonsville 9," "Moonchil-dren" for which he received a Theatre World Award, "Finishing Touches," OB in "Saved," "Green Julia," "One Act Play Festival," "Gardenia."

WOODS, RICHARD. Born May 9, 1921 in Buffalo, NY. Graduate Ithaca Col. Bdwy in "Beg, Borrow or Steal," "Capt. Brassbound's Conversion," "Sail Away," "Coco," "Last of Mrs. Lincoln," "Gigi," "Sherlock Holmes," "Murder among Friends," "The Royal Family," "Deathtrap," "Man and Superman," "The Man Who Came to Dinner," "The Father," OB in "The Crucible," "Summer and Smoke," "American Gothic," "Four-in-one," "My Heart's in the Highlands," "Eastward in Eden," "The Long Gallery," "The Year Boston Won the Pennant," "In the Matter of J. Robert Oppenheimer" (LC), with APA in "You Can't Take It With You," "War and Peace," "School for Scandal," "Right You Are," "The Wild Duck," "Pantagleize," "Exit the King," "The Cherry Orchard," "Cock-a-doodle Dandy," and "Hamlet," "Crimes and Dreams."

WOODWARD, JOANNE. Born Feb. 27, 1930 in Thomasville, Ga. Attended Neighborhood Playhouse. Bdwy debut 1953 in "Picnic," followed by "The Lovers," "Baby Want a Kiss," "Candida."

WORTH, IRENE. Born June 23, 1916 in Nebraska. Graduate UCLA. Bdwy debut 1943 i "The Two Mrs. Carrolls," followed by "The Cocktail Party," "Mary Stuart," "Toys in th Attic," "King Lear," "Tiny Alice," "Sweet Bird of Youth," "The Cherry Orchard" (LC) "The Lady from Dubuque," "John Gabriel Borkman," OB in "Happy Days," "Letters of Lov and Affection," "The Chalk Garden."

WORTH, PENNY. Born Mar. 2, 1950 in London, Eng. Attended Sorbonne, Paris. Bdw debut 1970 in "Coco," followed by "Irene," "Annie."

WRIGHT, AMY. Born Apr. 15, 1950 in Chicago, IL. Graduate Beloit Col. Debut 1977 O in "The Stronger," followed by "Nightshift," "Hamlet," "Miss Julie," Bdwy in "5th of July (1980).

WRIGHT, MARY CATHERINE. Born Mar. 19, 1948 in San Francisco, CA. Attende CCSF, SFState Col. Bdwy debut 1970 in "Othello," followed by "A History of the America Film," "Tintypes," OB in "East Lynne," "Mimi Lights the Candle," "Marvin's Gardens, "The Tempest," "The Doctor in Spite of Himself," "Love's Labour's Lost," "Pushcart Ped dlers," "Sister Mary Ignatius Explains It All," "Actor's Nightmare."

WRIGHT, MAX. Born Aug. 2, 1943 in Detroit, MI. Attended Wayne State U. Bdwy debu 1968 in "The Great White Hope," followed by "The Cherry Orchard," "Basic Training o Pavlo Hummel," "Stages," "Once in a Lifetime" for which he received a Theatre Worl Award, "The Inspector General," "Richard III," "Lunch Hour," "Henry IV Part 1 & 2"

WRIGHT, STEPHEN. Born July 26 in Chester, SC. Graduate Wofford Col., Neighborhoo Playhouse. Bdwy debut 1977 in "Fiddler on the Roof" followed by 1981 revival.

WYMAN, NICHOLAS. Born May 18, 1950 in Portland, Me. Graduate Harvard U. Bdw debut 1975 in "Very Good Eddie," followed by "Grease," "The Magic Show," "On the 20t Century," "Whoopee!" "My Fair Lady" (1981), OB in "Paris Lights," "When We Dea Awaken."

YACKO, ROBERT. Born Dec. 20, 1953 in Philadelphia, PA. Attended Temple U., Juilliard Debut 1978 OB in "Oh, What a Lovely War," followed by "The Miser," Bdwy in "Fiddle on the Roof" (1981).

YANCEY, KIM. Born Sept. 25, 1959 in NYC. Graduate CCNY. Debut 1978 OB in "Wh Lillie Won't Spin," followed by "Escape to Freedom," "Dacha."

YESCKAS, EMANUEL. Born Mar. 28, 1946 in Mexico. Debut 1981 OB in "Grace."

YODER, JERRY. Born in Columbus, OH. Graduate Ohio State U. Bdwy debut 1973 i "Seesaw," followed by "Goodtime Charley," "Chicago," "Best Little Whorehouse in Texas, OB in "Boys from Syracuse."

YORK, MICHAEL. Born Mar. 27, 1942 in Fulmer, Eng. Attended Oxford U. Bdway debu 1973 in "Outcry," followed by "Bent" (1980), "The Little Prince and the Aviator"(1982.)

YORKE, SALLY. Born Dec. 8, 1953 in Williamsport, PA Graduate PaStateU. Debut 198 OB in "Oh Johnny!"

YOSHIDA, PETER. Born May 28, 1945 in Chicago, IL. Graduate UIll., Princeton U AADA. Debut 1965 OB in "Coriolanus," Followed by "Troilus and Cressida," "Santa Anit '42," "Pursuit of Happiness," "Servant of Two Masters," "The Peking Man," "Monke Music," "Station J."

YOST, JOHN. Born Jan. 30 in NYC. Graduate CCNY. Bdwy debut 1979 in "Evita."

ZACHARY, ALAINA. Born Oct 6, 1946 in Cleveland, OH. Graduate Boston U. Debut 197 OB in "The Proposition," followed by "Secrets," "El Bravo!" Bdwy in "Grease" (1972) "Nine."

ZALKIND, DEBRA. Born Mar. 30, 1953 in NYC. Graduate Juilliard. Appeared with severa dance companies before Bdwy debut 1978 in "The Best Little Whorehouse in Texas."

ZALOOM, PAUL. Born Dec. 14, 1951 in Brooklyn, NY. Graduate Goddard Col. Debut 197 OB in "Fruit of Zaloom," followed by "Zalooming Along," "Zaloominations!"

ZANG, EDWARD. Born Aug. 19, 1934 in NYC. Graduate Boston U. OB in "Good Soldie Schweik," "St. Joan," "Boys in the Band," "The Reliquary of Mr. and Mrs. Potterfield," "Las Analysis," "As You Like It," "More than You Deserve," "Polly," "Threepenny Opera, BAM Co.'s "New York Idea," "The Misanthrope," "Banana Box," "The Penultimate Prob lem of Sherlock Holmes," Bdwy in "Crucifier of Blood," "Amadeus."

ZARISH, JANET. Born Apr. 21, 1954 in Chicago, Il. Graduate Juilliard. Debut 1981 O in "Villager," followed by "Playing With Fire."

ZETTLER, STEPHEN. Born Dec. 21, 1947 in New Jersey. Debut 1981 OB in "The Amazin Casey Stengel," followed by "A Soldier's Play."

ZIEMBA, KAREN. Born Nov. 12, 1957 in St. Joseph, Mi. Graduate UAkron. Debut 198 OB in "Seesaw."

ZIEN, CHIP. Born in 1947 in Milwaukee, WI. Attended UPa, OB in "You're a Good Ma Charlie Brown," followed by "Kadish," "How to Succeed in Business . . ." (ELT), "Dear M G.," "Tuscaloosa's Calling . . .," " Hot l Baltimore," "El Grande de Coca Cola," "Split, "Real Life Funnies," "March of the Falsettos," Bdwy in "All Over Town" (1974), "Th Suicide."

ZIMMERMAN, MARK. Born Apr. 19, 1952 in Harrisburg, PA. Graduate UPa. Debut 197 OB in "Fiorello!," followed by "Silk Stockings," "On a Clear Day You Can See Forever," "11 in the Shade," Bdwy in "Brigadoon" (1981).

ZOBEL, RICHARD. Born June 5, 1952 in West Chester, Pa. Attended Temple U. Debut 1979 OB in "The Taming of the Shrew," followed by "All's Well That Ends Well," "Big Appl Messenger," Bdwy 1980 in "Nuts."

ZOLDESSY, BRIAN. Born Aug. 27, 1953 in The Bronx, NY. Graduate Long Island U Debut 1978 OB in "The Diary of Anne Frank," followed by "House Music," Bdwy 1982 i "The World of Sholom Aleichem."

ZORICH, LOUIS. Born Feb. 12, 1924 in Chicago, IL. Attended Roosevelt U. OB in "Si Characters in Search of an Author," "Crimes and Crimes," "Henry V," "Thracian Horses, "All Women Are One," "Good Soldier Schweik," "Shadow of Heroes," "To Clothe th Naked," "Sunset," "A Memory of Two Mondays," "The Knew What They Wanted," "Th Gathering," "True West," "The Tempest," Bdwy in "Becket," "Moby Dick," "The Od Couple," "Hadrian VII," "Moonchildren," "Fun City," "Goodtime Charley," "Herzl."

OBITUARIES

WILL B. ABLE, 57, eccentric dancer, comic and actor, died of a viral infection Nov. 18, 1981 in St. Louis, Mo., where he was appearing in his "Baggy Pants Revue." He was born in Providence RI, and had appeared on Broadway in "George White's Scandals," "Plain and Fancy," "Midgie Purvis," "All American," "Coco," and OB in "Bella," "9 to 5 to 0," and "Get Thee to Canterbury." He is survived by his widow and daughter.

JACK ALBERTSON, 74, vaudeville, stage, screen and tv performer, died of cancer Nov. 25, 1981 in his home in Hollywood Hills, Ca. Born in Malden, Ma., he appeared in vaudeville as a dancer and straight man before making his Broadway debut in 1941 in "Meet the People," followed by "Strip for Action," "The Lady Says Yes," "Allah Be Praised," "The Red Mill," "The Cradle Will Rock," "Make Mine Manhattan," "High Button Shoes," "Tickets, Please," "Top Banana," "The Subject was Roses" for which he won a Tony, and also an Oscar for the film version, "The Sunshine Boys." Survivors include his wife and daughter.

GLENN ANDERS, 92, Los Angeles-born stage and film actor, died Oct. 26, 1981 in Englewood, NJ. After his 1919 Broadway debut in "Just Around the Corner," he appeared in "Scrambled Wives," "The Ghost Between," "The Demi-Virgin," "Cold Feet," "What's Your Wife Doing?," "Hell-Bent fer Heaven," "So This Is Politics," "Bewitched," "They Knew What They Wanted," "The Constant Nymph," "Murray Hill," "Strange Interlude," "Dynamo," "Hotel Universe," "Farewell to Arms," "In the Meantime," "Midnight," "The Lonely Way," "Another Language," "Love and Babies," "I Was Waiting for You," "False Dreams, Farewell," "Moor Born," "Sleeping Clergyman," "On to Fortune," "If This Be Treason," "There's Wisdom in Women," "Call It a Day," "Masque of Kings," "Three Waltzes," "I Am Different," "Skylark," "Get Away Old Man," "Career Angel," "Soldier's Wife," "Light Up the Sky," "One Bright Day," "The Remarkable Mr. Pennypacker," "Time Remembered," "Bus Stop," "The Visit." No reported survivors.

ELLEN ANDREWS, 65, actress, director and teacher, died May 22, 1982 in NYC. Her career began in "Danton's Death" in 1938, and subsequently she appeared in "The Male Animal," "Holiday," "Drifting Apart," "A Democratic Body," "Too Hot for Maneuvers," "The Mayor of Zalamea," and ELT's "Maedchen in Uniform" and "The Matchmaker." An aunt survives.

ALAN BADEL, 58, stage and film actor, died March 19, 1982 of a heart attack at his home in Chichester, England. His Broadway appearances include "Measure for Measure," "Hamlet" and "The Rehearsal." His widow and daughter survive.

LENNY BAKER, 37, Boston-born actor, died of cancer Apr. 12, 1982 in Hallandale, Fl. In NY he had been seen in "Conerico Was Here to Stay," "Paradise Gardens East," "The Year Boston Won the Pennant," "The Time of Your Life," "Summertree," "Early Morning," "Survival of Joan," "Gallery," "Barbary Shore," "Merry Wives of Windsor," "Pericles," "Secret Service," "Boy Meets Girl," "Henry V," "Measure for Measure," "Freedom of the City" and "I Love My Wife" for which he received a 1977 Tony Award. He is survived by his parents and two brothers.

ROBERT RUSSELL BENNETT, 87, Missouri-born composer, conductor, orchestrator and musical director, died Aug. 18, 1981 in NYC. He was the leading orchestrator of Broadway musicals of his time, having scored about 300, including such hits as "Show Boat," "Oklahoma!," "My Fair Lady," "Rose Marie," "Of Thee I Sing," "Anything Goes," "Carmen Jones," "Annie Get Your Gun," "Kiss Me, Kate," "South Pacific," "The King and I," "The Sound of Music," and "Camelot." He also contributed music and orchestrations to over 30 films, winning an Oscar for "Oklahoma!" He is survived by his widow and a daughter.

RONALD BISHOP, 59, Connecticut-born character actor, died May 21, 1982 in NYC after a brief illness. After his Broadway debut in 1943 in "Othello," his credits include "Julius Caesar," "Playboy of the Western World," "King Lear," "The Visit," "Donogoo," "Man and Superman," "War and Peace," "Judith," "St. Joan," "Honor and Offer," "The Tempest," "Galileo," "Survival of St. Joan," "Total Eclipse," "A Meeting by the River," and "Candida." His mother and sister survive.

SUSAN BLOCH, 42, a public relations agent who specialized in theatre and dance, died May 10, 1982 in Tiburon, Ca., from a kidney disease. Among her many clients were the Lincoln Center Repertory Theater and the Roundabout Theatre. She had also been an instructor at Fordham University. A brother survives.

RUDY BOND, 68, Philadelphia-born stage, screen and tv actor, died of a heart attack March 29, 1982 en route to rehearsals at the Denver Center Theatre. He made his Broadway debut in 1947 in "A Streetcar Named Desire," followed by "The Bird Cage," "Romeo and Juliet," "Glad Tidings," "Golden Boy," 1956 revival of "Streetcar . . .," "Big Man," "Match-Play," "Illya Darling," "Papp," "Night Watch," OB in "O'Daniel," "After the Fall," "Incident at Vichy," "12 Angry Men," "The Birds," "Joan of Lorraine," "Bread," "Armenians," "Dream of a Blacklisted Actor," "From the Memoirs of Pontius Pilate." He is survived by his widow, a daughter, and two sons.

MELVILLE BURKE, 97, St. Louis-born stage, film, tv and radio director, died of kidney failure March 22, 1982 in Honolulu. He had directed more than 40 Broadway productions, including "Her Unborn Child," "Tonight at 12," "Precious," "A Church Mouse," "Adam Had Two Sons," "The Perfect Marriage," "Queer People," "Remember the Day," "Room Service," "Feather in the Breeze," "Love in My Fashion," "Life with Father," "Slightly Married" and "Little A." A son survives.

ALAN CASTNER, 41, Ohio-born actor-dancer, died of a ruptured aneurism Apr. 24, 1982 in Los Angeles, Ca. After his Broadway debut in 1968's "West Side Story," he appeared in "Hello, Dolly!," "George M!," "Foreplay," "Dark of the Moon," "The Boys in the Band," and "The Changing Room." He is survived by his parents, two brothers and two sisters.

HARRY CHAPIN, 38, NYC-born folk-rock composer and performer, was killed July 16, 1981 when the car he was driving was hit from behind by a tractor-trailer. In 1975 he appeared in his own production of "The Night That Made America Famous." This season his "Cotton Patch Gospel" had a successful run. His biggest hit single record was "Taxi" in 1972. Surviving are his widow and five children.

MARY COYLE CHASE, 74, Denver newspaperwoman who became a Pulitzer Prize-winning playwright, died Oct. 20, 1981 after a brief illness in Denver, Col. Her play about the invisible rabbit "Harvey" brought her the Pulitzer Prize. Other efforts were not as successful, including "Now You've Done It," "The Next Half Hour," "Mrs. McThing," "Bernardine" and "Midgie Purvis." Her husband, retired editor, Robert Chase, and three sons survive.

PADDY CHAYEFSKY, 58, playwright and screenwriter, died of cancer Aug. 1, 1981 in NYC. Among his best received plays were "Middle of the Night," "The Tenth Man," "Gideon," "The Passion of Josef D," "The Latent Homosexual." His screenplays brought him three Oscars. His widow and son survive.

HANS CONRIED, 66, Baltimore-born character actor on stage, film and tv, died of a heart attack Jan. 5, 1982 in Burbank, Ca. He made his Broadway debut in 1953 in "Can-Can," followed by "Tall Story," "70 Girls 70," "Irene," and "Something Old Something New." He had appeared in over 100 films. Surviving is his wife of 40 years, 2 sons and 2 daughters.

DULCIE COOPER, 77, Australian-born stage and screen actress, died Sept. 3, 1981 in NYC. Among her many credits are "Topsy and Eva," "The Joker," "Friend Indeed," "Ringside," "Brothers," "Let and Sub-Let," "Singin' the Blues," "Bulls, Bears and Asses," "It Happened Tomorrow," "Tobacco Road," "The New York Idea," "Personal Appearance," and "Angel in the Wings." Two adopted sons survive.

MELVYN DOUGLAS, 80, ne Hesselberg, theatre, film and tv actor, died of pneumonia complicated by a heart ailment on Aug. 4, 1981 in NYC. From Macon, Ga., he came to Broadway in 1928 in "A Free Soul," followed by "Tonight or Never" (starring Helen Gahagan who became his wife until her death in 1980), "Back Here," "Recapture," "No More Ladies," "Mother Lode," "DeLuxe," "Tapestry in Gray," "Two Blind Mice," "The Bird Cage," "The Little Blue Light," "Glad Tidings," "Time Out for Ginger," "Inherit the Wind," "Waltz of the Toreadors," "Juno," "The Gang's All Here," "The Best Man" (that won him a Tony Award), and "Spofford" (his last in 1967). Two performances among his 45 films brought him Academy Awards. He is survived by two sons and a daughter.

PHILIP FAVERSHAM, 75, New York-born stage and film actor, died Apr. 20, 1982 in Vero Beach, Fl. He was the son of actor William Faversham and actress Julie Opp and made his stage debut in "Fly Away Home," subsequently appearing in "Boy Meets Girl," "Chalked Out," "The Hill Between," "Gloriana," "Cue for Passion," "Another Language," "Candida" with Cornelia Otis Skinner. His widow survives.

NEIL FITZGERALD, 90, Irish-born stage, screen and tv actor, died June 15, 1982 in Princeton, N.J. After his NY debut in 1937's "Miles of Heaven," he appeared in "Leave Her to Heaven," "The Wookey," "Plan M," "The Merry Widow," "Without Love," "Ten Little Indians," "You Touched Me!," "The Survivors," "Design for a Stained Glass Window," "High Ground," "To Dorothy, A Son," "Mr. Pickwick," "Abie's Irish Rose," "Tinker's Wedding," "Oscar Wilde," "Monique," "On Baile's Strand," "Death of Chuchulain," "Little Moon of Alban," "Moon in the Yellow River," "Portrait of the Artist as a Young Man," "Barroom Monks," "Roar Like a Dove," "Bridal Night," "Eternal Triangle," "Carricknabauna," "Stephen D," "Hadrian VII," "The Mundy Scheme," "Three Hand Reel," "Murderous Angels," "The Contractor," "All Over." No reported survivors.

JOHN GERSTAD, 57, Boston-born Gjerstad, actor, director, author, producer, died of a heart arrest Dec. 1, 1981 in NYC. After his Broadway debut in 1943's "Othello," he appeared in "Not for Children," "The Male Animal," "The Trial of Lee Harvey Oswald," "Come Summer," "Oklahoma!," "Penny Wars," "Dark of the Moon," "Joy to the World," "Golden Fleecing," "All Over," "All the Girls Came out to Play." He had directed "The Seven Year Itch," "Wayward Saint," "Debut," "Double in Hearts," "Howie." Survivors include his widow, a son and two daughters.

MICHAEL GRANGER, 58, stage, film and tv actor, died of a heart attack Oct. 22, 1981 in NYC. After his 1964 Broadway debut in "Fiddler on the Roof," he appeared in "Whisper in God's Ear," "Danton's Death," "The Country Wife," "The Caucasian Chalk Circle," "The Alchemist," "The East Wind," "A Doll's House" with Liv Ullmann, "Joan of Lorraine" and "Clothes for a Summer Hotel." He had appeared in over 35 motion pictures. No reported survivors.

STANLEY N. GREENE, 70, actor, producer, filmmaker, director, died of cancer July 4, 1981 in his home in New Rochelle, NY. On the NY stage he had performed in "In Abraham's Bosom," "Natural Man," "On Striver's Row," "Another Part of the Forest," "The Big Deal," "The King and the Duke," "Take a Giant Step," "Simply Heavenly," "And the Wind Blows," "The Long Dream," and "Contributions." Surviving are his widow and two sons.

ANN HARDING, 79, nee Anna Gately in San Antonio, Tx., stage and screen actress, died Sept. 1, 1981 after a long illness in her home in Sherman Oaks, Ca. After her 1921 Broadway debut in "Like a King," she appeared in "Tarnish," "Thoroughbreds," "Stolen Fruit," "The Taming of the Shrew," "Schweiger," "The Eskimo," "A Woman Disputed," "The Trial of Mary Dugan" which she played for 437 performances, "Candida" (1937), "General Seeger," "Goodbye My Fancy," and "Abraham Cochrane." She married and divorced actor Harry Bannister and conductor Werner Janssen. A daughter survives.

ROBERT H. HARRIS, 70, NY-born character actor on stage, screen and tv, died Nov. 30, 1981 in Los Angeles, Ca. He appeared with the Yiddish Art Theatre before making his Broadway bow in 1937 in "Many Mansions," followed by "Schoolhouse on the Lot," "Tell My Story," "Any Day Now," "Brooklyn U.S.A.," "Look, Ma, I'm Dancin'," "Richard III," "My Sister Eileen," "Herod and Miriamne," "Somewhere in France," "Foxy," "A Minor Miracle" and "Xmas in Las Vegas." He was probably best known as Jake, Molly's husband, on tv's "The Goldbergs" series. No reported survivors.

RAY HARRISON, 64, St. Louis-born dancer, choreographer and teacher, died July 27, 1981 in Boston after a long illness. On Broadway he had appeared in "Oklahoma!," "Banjo Eyes," "On the Town," "Allegro," "Make Mine Manhattan," "Out of This World," was assistant choreographer for "Kiss Me, Kate," "Out of This World" and "My Darlin' Aida," and choreographed and directed the Off-Broadway hit "Little Mary Sunshine. He subsequently devoted most of his time to teaching. Surviving are his mother, a brother and sister.

VIOLET HEMING, 86, English-born actress, died July 4, 1981 in her NYC home. She made her U. S. debut as Wendy in "Peter Pan" in 1908 and retired in 1945 to marry Judge Bennett Champ Clark. Her Broadway credits include "Sonya," "The Rubicon," "The Rivals," "Lucky One," "But For the Grace of God," "Spring Cleaning," "Trelawny of the 'Wells'," "Chivalry," "The Jest," "Loose Ends," "Mrs. Dane's Defense," "Within the Law," "This Thing Called Love," "Soldiers and Women," "Ladies All," "Divorce Me, Dear," "There's Always Juliet," "All Rights Reserved," "DeLuxe," "Yes, My Darling Daughter," "Summer Night," "Love for Love," "Beverly Hills," "And Be My Love," "Dear Barbarians." Mr. Clark died in 1954. There were no immediate survivors.

ROBERT HERGET, 56, Nebraska-born dancer, choreographer and director, died June 8, 1981 in NYC. After appearing on Broadway in "Allegro," "High Button Shoes," "Lend an Ear" and "Razzle Dazzle," he devoted most of his time to choreographing and directing for television and industrial shows. He choreographed seven productions for Broadway and six Off Broadway. He served for 13 years on the executive board of the Society of Stage Directors and Choreographers. An aunt survives.

STANLEY HOLLOWAY, 91, one of Britain's best-loved actors, died Jan. 30, 1982 in Littlehampton, Sussex, Eng. His NY debut was in 1954 as Bottom in "A Midsummer Night's Dream," but he endeared himself to American audiences with his Alfred Doolittle in "My Fair Lady" on stage and film. He was married twice but left no immediate survivors.

JOHN CECIL HOLM, 76, Philadelphia-born actor, director and playwright, died Oct. 24, 1981 in Westerly, RI. As an actor, he made his NY debut in 1925's "Joan of Arkansas," followed by "A Mighty Man Is He," "The Front Page," "Whirlpool," "Penal Law 2010," "The Up and Up," "Wonder Boy," "Bloodstream," "Dangerous Corner," "Mary of Scotland," "Midgie Purvis," "Gramercy Ghost," "Mr. President," "The Advocate," "Philadelphia, Here I Come" and "Forty Carats." As a playwright he wrote "Three Men on a Horse," "Best Foot Forward," "Banjo Eyes," "Brighten the Corner," "Gramercy Ghost," "Southwest Corner." His wife died in 1959. There were no survivors.

VICTOR JORY, 79, Alaska-born actor on radio, stage, screen and tv, died of a heart attack Feb. 12, 1982 in his apartment in Santa Monica, Ca. His stage appearances include "Lazarus Laughed," "The Two Mrs. Carrolls," "The Perfect Marriage," "Therese," "Henry VIII," "John Gabriel Borkman," "Androcles and the Lion," "Yellow Jack" and "The Devil's Disciple." In recent years he appeared occasionally at the Actors Theatre of Louisville, managed by his son Jon Jory. In addition to his son, a daughter survives.

HERSHY KAY, 62, Philadelphia-born orchestrator and arranger, died of heart failure Dec. 2, 1981 in Danbury, Ct. His Broadway career began with the orchestrations for "On the Town," followed by "Peter Pan," "Sandhog," "Candide," "Livin' the Life," "Juno," "Once upon a Mattress," "The Happiest Girl in the World," "Milk and Honey," "110 in the Shade," "Kelly," "Drat! The Cat!," "I'm Solomon," "Coco," "1600 Pennsylvania Avenue," "On the 20th Century," "Evita," "A Chorus Line" and "Barnum." His widow survives.

PATSY KELLY, 71, Brooklyn-born comedienne on radio, vaudeville, stage, screen and tv, died Sept. 24, 1981 following a stroke in Woodland Hills, Ca. Her Broadway credits include "Harry Delmar's Revels," "Three Cheers," "Sketch Book," "Earl Carroll's Vanities," "The Wonder Bar," "Flying Colors," "Dear Charles," "No, No Nanette" for which she received a Tony Award, and "Irene." She is survived by several nieces and nephews.

TESSA KOSTA, 83, Chicago-born musical star of Broadway, died of a heart attack Aug. 23, 1981 in her NYC home. At the age of 13 George M. Cohan introduced her to Broadway and she became a star in such musicals as "Lassie," "Princess Virtue," "The Chocolate Soldier," "The Beauty Shop," "Chu Chin Chow," "The Royal Vagabond," "Rose of Stamboul," "Princess April," "Princess Ida," "Song of the Flame," "Fioretta," and "The Fortune Teller" after which she retired in 1929. She was married to the late Richard Madden, a theatrical agent. No immediate survivors.

HARVEY LEMBECK, 58, Brooklyn-born character actor, on stage, screen and tv, died of a heart ailment Jan. 5, 1982 in Los Angeles, Ca. His career began with "The Dancing Carrolls," but he reverted to acting in such productions as "Mister Roberts," "Stalag 17, Wedding Breakfast," "Phoenix '55," "South Pacific" and "Oklahoma!" (1958). He was featured in the TV series "You'll Never Get Rich." More recently, in addition to his film work, he had been teaching. He is survived by his widow, a son and a daughter.

LOTTE LENYA, 83, Vienna-born star of German and U.S. stage and films, died of cancer Nov. 27, 1981 in the NYC apartment of a friend. Born Karoline Blamauer, in Austria, she moved to Berlin in 1920 where she met and married Kurt Weill; gaining her first fame in his "Songspiel" and "The Threepenny Opera." They came to New York in 1935, and she subsequently appeared in "The Eternal Road," "Candle in the Wind," "Firebird of Florence," "Barefoot in Athens," "The Threepenny Opera," "Brecht on Brecht," and "Cabaret" for which she received a Tony Award. After Weill's death in 1950, she devoted more time to her film career, and was awarded an Oscar for her performance in "The Roman Spring of Mrs Stone." She was married to editor Robert Davis who died in 1957, and to painter Robert Detweiler who died in 1969. No immediate survivors.

ANITA LOOS, 88, California-born playwright, screenwriter, novelist, died following a heart attack on Aug. 18, 1981 in NYC. Although she wrote other plays, her name is indelibly linked with "Gentlemen Prefer Blondes." She began her career as a child actress but at 13 she began writing and selling some of her work. She was a screenwriter at 19. Her other plays include "The Whole Town's Talking," "The Fall of Eve," "9:15 Revue," "The Social Register," "Happy Birthday," "Gigi," "Cheri," "Gogo Loves You" and "The King's Mare." Her husband, John Emerson, died in 1956. A niece survives.

PAUL LYNDE, 55, Ohio-born character actor and comedian, died of a heart attack Jan. 10, 1982 in his Beverly Hills home. After his Broadway debut in "New Faces of 1952," he appeared in "Bye Bye Birdie." He went to Hollywood to appear in the film version of the latter and became best known as a member of the tv game show "Hollywood Squares" from 1968 to 1981. He had appeared also on several other tv productions. Two sisters survive.

ARCHIBALD MacLEISH, 89, Ilinois-born playwright, poet and statesman, died Apr. 20, 1982 in Boston, Ma. One of his three Pulitzer Prizes was for his play "J.B." in 1959, the other two for his poetry. His widow survives.

ENID MARKEY, 91, Colorado-born stage, screen and tv actress-comedienne died Nov. 15, 1981 of a heart attack in Bay Shore, NY. After a successful career in silent films (she was Tarzan's first Jane), she moved to Broadway with added success in such productions as "Up in Mabel's Room," "The Exciters," "Barnum Was Right," "Something to Brag About," "Find Daddy," "Blond Sinner," "Sisters of the Chorus," "After Such Pleasures," "Good Girl," "Two Bouquets," "Run Sheep Run," "The Man in Possession," "Morning's at Seven," "Beverly Hills," "Ah, Wilderness!," "Pie in the Sky," "Mr. Sycamore," "Sweet Charity," "Last Stop," "Snafu," "Happy Birthday," "Buy Me Blue Ribbons," "Mrs. McThing," "Mrs. Patterson," "Southwest Corner," "Fashion," "The Silver Whistle," "Only in America," "Ballad of the Sad Cafe," "What Did We Do Wrong?" Her husband, George W. Cobb, died in 1948, and there are no survivors.

HUGH MARLOWE, 71, stage, screen, radio and tv actor for over 50 years, died of a heart attack May 2, 1982 in his NYC home. Born Hugh Herbert Hipple in Philadelphia, he began his stage career at the Pasadena Playhouse, Ca., but made his Bdwy debut in 1936 in "Arrest That Woman," followed by "The Millionairess," "Kiss the Boys Goodbye," "Young Couple Wanted," "Flight to the West," "The Land Is Bright," "Lady in the Dark," "Voice of the Turtle," "It Takes Two," "Laura," "Duet for Two Hands," "The Deer Park," "Postcards," "Woman Is My Idea," and the 1974 revival of "All My Sons." He is survived by his second wife and son Hugh, Jr., and two sons Christian and Jeffrey by his first wife, actress K. T. Stevens.

IAN MARTIN, 69, stage, radio and tv actor, died of a heart ailment July 25, 1981 in NYC. Born in Glasgow, Scot., he began his career as a child actor, came to the U.S. in 1928 to attend Harvard U. He then became a radio actor before making his stage debut in "B J" followed by "A Midsummer Night's Dream," "What Every Woman Knows," "All Men Are Alike," "The Devil's Disciple," "Capt. Brassbound's Conversion," "Finian's Rainbow," "Cock-a-Doodle Dandy," "King of Friday's Men," "Victoria Regina," "Spofford," "Lost in the Stars," "The Changing Room." Surviving are his second wife, two sons and two daughters.

JESSIE MATTHEWS, 74, British stage and screen musical comedy star, died of cancer Aug. 20, 1981 in London. She had appeared in New York in "Earl Carroll's Vanities," "Wake Up and Dream," and "Evergreen." Her three marriages ended in divorce. A daughter survives.

FRANK McHUGH, 83, Pennsylvania-born character actor on stage and screen, died Sept. 11, 1981 in Greenwich, Ct., after a short illness. He began his stage career at 11 and toured with many companies before his Bdwy debut in 1925 in "The Fall Guy," followed by "Fog," "Excess Baggage," "Show Girl," "Conflict," "A Funny Thing Happened on the Way to the Forum," and the 1967 revival of "Finian's Rainbow." Surviving are his widow, former actress Dorothy Spencer, a son and a daughter.

ROBERT MONTGOMERY, 77, actor, producer, director on radio, stage, screen and tv, died of cancer Sept. 27, 1981 in NYC. His career began on the stage when he came to NYC from his home in Beacon, NY, and got 3 small parts in William Faversham's "The Mask and the Face." Parts followed in "Dawn," "The Complex," "The Carolinian," "Bad Habits of 1926," "The High Hatters," and "Possession," that won him a Hollywood contract. After his film success, he returned to direct Bdwy productions of "The Big Two," "The Desperate Hours" and "Calculated Risk." From 1950–57, he presided over one of tv's most distinguished dramatic series "Robert Montgomery Presents." He is survived by his second wife, and by his first wife, a son, and a daughter, actress Elizabeth Montgomery.

EDDIE PHILLIPS, 54, Philadelphia-born dancer-comedian, died of cancer, Feb. 28, 1982 in NYC. He had appeared in "Finian's Rainbow," "Love Life," "Miss Liberty," "Kiss Me, Kate," "Guys and Dolls," "Damn Yankees," "Can-Can," "New Girl in Town," "Oh, Kay," "Tenderloin," "Show Boat" and "Molly." Surviving are his widow, a son and a daughter.

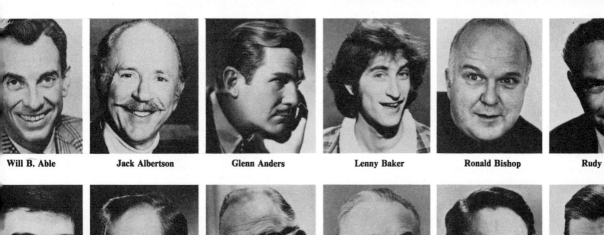

Will B. Able	Jack Albertson	Glenn Anders	Lenny Baker	Ronald Bishop	Rudy Bond

Alan Castner	Hans Conried	Melvyn Douglas	Neil Fitzgerald	John Gerstad	Michael Grang

Ann Harding	Robert H. Harris	Stanley Holloway	John Cecil Holm	Victor Jory	Patsy Kelly

Tessa Kosta	Lotte Lenya	Paul Lynde	Enid Markey	Hugh Marlowe	Ian Martin

Robert Montgomery	Eleanor Powell	Dorothy Raymond	Reta Shaw	Leonard Sillman	Lee Strasber

EDWIN PHILLIPS, 69, Alabama-born actor, died July 26, 1981 in NYC. He made his Broadway debut in 1923 in "Poppy" with W. C. Fields, subsequently appearing in "Brother Rat," "First Crocus," "Three's a Family," "The Farmer's Wife," "Four Walls," "Henry V," "Courage," "Those We Love," "Fly Away Home," "Searching for the Sun," "Me and Juliet," "Sunrise at Campobello." His widow and three daughters survive.

ELEANOR POWELL, 69, Massachusetts-born dancer-actress on stage and screen, died of cancer Feb. 11, 1982 in her Beverly Hills home. Discovered at 12, she made her NY debut at 16 in "The Co-Optimists," subsequently appearing in "Follow Through," "Fine and Dandy," "Music Hall Varieties," "Hot-Cha," "Vanities," "George White's Scandals," "At Home Abroad" and "Crazy Quilt. Hollywood beckoned and she became "Queen of the Taps" in many Hollywood musicals. After her marriage to Glenn Ford (1943) she curtailed her appearances. After their divorce in 1959 she made a short comeback, but retired in 1964. She is survived by her son Peter Ford.

DOROTHY RAYMOND, age unreported, actress, died Oct. 30, 1981 in her native Pittsburgh, Pa. After her 1925 Broadway debut in "The Jazz Singer," she had roles in "Eve's Leaves," "Iphigenia in Aulis," "The Wild Duck," "The Big Blow," "Broken Chain," "Dodsworth," "Woman of Destiny," "Calling All Stars," "Uncle Willie," "Walk in Dark Places," "Compulsion," "The Boy Friend," "Power of Darkness," "The Rose Tattoo" and "Rooms." She was the widow of actor Alfred Webster. A sister and brother survive.

FRED M. SAIDY, 75, co-author of books for Broadway musicals, died May 14, 1982 in Los Angeles, Ca. With E. Y. (Yip) Harburg he collaborated on "Finian's Rainbow," "Flahooley" and "Jamaica." With Sid Herzig, he wrote the book for "Bloomer Girl." Other musicals include "Jollyanna," and "The Happiest Girl in the World." Surviving are his widow, a daughter and two sons.

ROBERT SHAFER, age unreported, Pittsburgh-born actor-singer, died June 19, 1981 at his home in Tenafly, NJ. His Broadway credits include "The Student Prince" (1936), "Rose Marie," "Blossom Time," "My Maryland," "Countess Maritza," "Naughty Marietta," "The Show Is On," "You Said It," "At Home Abroad," "Maytime," "A Wonderful Night," "The Firefly," "Nina Rosa," "Roberta," "Hooray for What!," "Song of Norway," "Allegro," "Damn Yankees." His widow and son survive.

LEON SHAW, Nova Scotia-born actor, age unreported, died of cardiac arrest on June 24, 1981 in NYC. His Broadway credits include "Theatre," "Hamlet," "The Devil's Disciple," "The King and I," "The Boy Friend," "The Living Room," "Around the World in 80 Days," "Canterbury Tales," "Thunder Rock," "The Gambler," "A Girl in My Soup," "No Sex Please, We're British," "Gorey Stories." A brother and sister survive.

RETA SHAW, 69, stage, screen and tv actress, died Jan. 8, 1982 in Encino, Ca. A native of South Paris, Me., she made her Broadway debut in 1947 in "It Takes Two," followed by "Virginia Reel," "Gentlemen Prefer Blondes" (1949), "Picnic," "The Pajama Game," "Annie Get Your Gun." She leaves her husband, actor William Forester, and a daughter.

BURT SHEVELOVE, 66, director and playwright, died Apr. 8, 1982 in his London apartment where he had lived for the past 15 years. Born in Newark, NJ, he began his Broadway career in 1948 when he co-produced, directed and wrote material for the revue "Small Wonder," subsequently directing "Kiss Me, Kate," "Too Much Johnson," "Butter and Egg Man," "Davy Jones's Locker," "Hallelujah Baby!," "The Frogs," "Rockefeller and the Red Indians," "No, No Nanette," and "Happy New Year." His most successful and Tony-winning collaboration was "A Funny Thing Happened on the Way to the Forum." He also won Emmy Awards for some of his many tv productions. His mother and sister survive.

YUKI SHIMODA, 59, stage and screen actor and former dancer, died of cancer May 21, 1982 in Los Angeles, Ca. Born in California, he joined the Chicago Opera Co. ballet before moving to New York. On Broadway he appeare in "Teahouse of the August Moon," "Auntie Mame," and "Pacific Overtures." He appeared in 25 films and numerous tv productions. No reported survivors.

MARIAN SHOCKLEY, age unreported, actress, died Dec. 14, 1981 in Los Angeles, Ca. After her 1936 Broadway debut in "Dear Old Darling," she appeared in "Abie's Irish Rose," "Two Time Mary," "Reno" and "Censored." She was born in Kansas City, Mo., and began her career in Hollywood but moved to New York to star with her late husband, Bud Collyer in the radio dramas "Road of Life" and "The Guiding Light." Surviving are two daughters and a son.

LEONARD SILLMAN, 72, dancer, actor, producer and director, died of cancer, Jan. 22, 1982 in NYC. Born in Detroit, he came to NY and made his debut in 1927 in "Loud Speaker," followed by "Merry-Go-Round," "Fools Rush In," "The Ugly Runts," then produced 13 Broadway editions of "New Faces" revues between 1934 and 1968, launching the careers of many stars. He was also a producer for "If the Shoe Fits," "Happy as Larry," "Mrs. Patterson," "Mask and Gown," "Miss Isobel," "Second String," "The Family Way," "The American Hamburger League" and "Madwoman of Chaillot." A sister survives.

LEE STRASBERG, 80, Polish-born director, film actor, artistic director of the Actors Studio, and "Father of Method Acting in America," died of a heart attack Feb. 17, 1982 in NYC. As a master teacher he guided several generations of actors, and exerted an influence on acting technique in the theatre and films of America. As an actor he had appeared in "Processional," "The Chief Thing," "Garrick Gaieties," "Four Walls," "Red Rust" and "Green Grow the Lilacs," but turned to directing and teaching. In 1974 he returned to acting—in films. He is survived by his second wife and two sons, and two children by his first wife, actress Susan Strasberg, and actor John Strasberg.

TOM TULLY, 85, Colorado-born character actor on stage, screen and tv, died Apr. 27, 1982 after a long illness in Newport Beach, Ca. His Broadway appearances include "Call Me Ziggy," "The White Steed," "The Time of Your Life," "Night Music," "Ah, Wilderness!," "Jason," "The Strings, My Lord, Are False" and "The Sun Field." His widow and several children survive.

HUGH THOMAS, 61, actor, died June 27, 1981 at his home in Wallington, NJ. After his debut in 1943 in "Janie," he appeared in "Chicken Every Sunday," "Earth Journey," "Misalliance," "The Fantasticks," "Twelfth Night," "Hamlet." He had also served on the faculty of the Rutherford (NJ) High School. There are no immediate survivors.

JAY VELIE, 89, former actor and singer whose career covered more than 50 years, died of congestive failure Apr. 22, 1982 at his home in Larchmont, NY. His career began in 1912 in his native Denver, Co., and made his Broadway debut in 1923 in "Little Jessie James," followed by "Round the Town," "Grab Bag," "A la Carte," "Diff'rent," "Pygmalion," "No More Peace," "The Fabulous Invalid," "Counsellor-at-law," "Our Town," "Carousel," "Call Me Madam," "Happy Hunting," "Jennie," "The Sound of Music," "Beyond Desire," "70 Girls 70." A sister survives.

VIRGINIA VESTOFF, 42, stage and screen actress, died of cancer May 2, 1982 in her native NYC. After her 1960 Broadway debut in "From A to Z," she appeared in "Irma La Douce," "Fallout," "The Crystal Heart," "Baker Street," "Ben Bagley's New Cole Porter Revue," "Man with a Load of Mischief," "Love and Let Love," "1776," "Via Galactica," "Nash at 9," "Bocaccio," "Spokesong," "The Boy Friend," "Short-Changed Revue," "Drinks Before Dinner" and "I'm Getting My Act Together." No reported survivors.

GEORGE VOSKOVEC, 76, character actor, director, and playwright, died July 1, 1981 at his home in Pearblossom, Ca. After arriving in the U.S. in 1951 from his native Czechoslovakia, he spent some time at the Cleveland Play House before making his Broadway debut in 1945 in "The Tempest," subsequently appearing in "Happy Journey to Trenton and Camden," "The Lady of Larkspur Lotion," "The Love of Four Colonels," "His and Hers," "The Seagull," "Uncle Vanya," "The Tenth Man," "Big Fish Little Fish," "A Call on Kuprin," "Do You Know the Milky Way?," "Jewish Wife," "Brecht on Brecht," "Caesar and Cleopatra," "Hamlet," "The Physicists," "World of Ray Bradbury," "The Alchemist," "East Wind," "Galileo," "The Other Man," "Oh, Say Can You See L.A.?," "Cabaret," "Penny Wars," "Murderous Angels," "Slow Dance on the Killing Ground," "All Over," "Agamemnon," "Happy Days." His widow and two daughters survive.

HARRY WARREN, 87, composer of more than 300 popular songs, died of kidney failure Sept. 22, 1981 in Los Angeles, Ca. Born in Brooklyn as Salvatore Guaragna, he was largely a self-taught musician, beginning with his father's accordian. In the mid 1920's he began collaborating on hits with Billy Rose who invited him to write songs for shows he was producing: "Sweet and Low," "Crazy Quilt" and "Laugh Parade." All were hits, and Mr. Warren moved to Hollywood to compose for films, his first being "42nd Street" with the late Al Dubin. These songs are now in the Broadway musical of the same name. His final Broadway musical was the 1956 "Shangri-La." In addition to his widow, he leaves a daughter.

Virginia Vestoff

George Voskovec

234

235

238

242

246

248

251

252

254